CALIFORNIA
ROAD ATLAS & DRIVER'S GUIDE

Thomas Bros. Maps ®

TABLE OF CONTENTS

17731 Cowan, Irvine, CA 92714 (714) 863-1984
550 Jackson St., San Francisco, CA 94133 (415) 981-7520
603 West 7th St., Los Angeles, CA 90017 (213) 627-4018

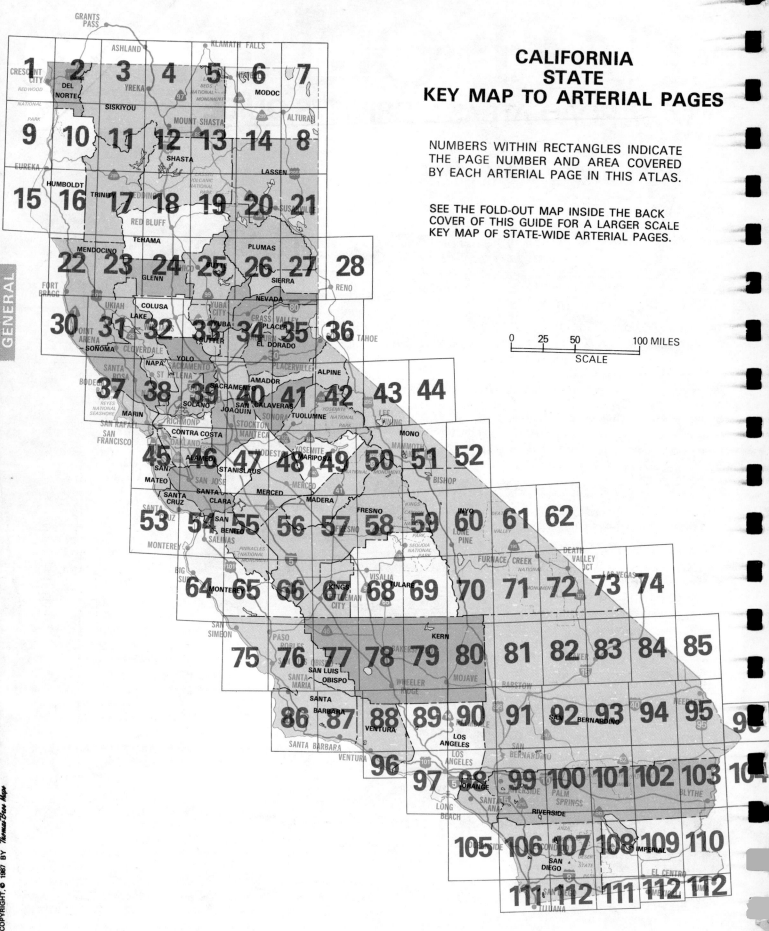

CALIFORNIA STATE KEY MAP TO ARTERIAL PAGES

NUMBERS WITHIN RECTANGLES INDICATE THE PAGE NUMBER AND AREA COVERED BY EACH ARTERIAL PAGE IN THIS ATLAS.

SEE THE FOLD-OUT MAP INSIDE THE BACK COVER OF THIS GUIDE FOR A LARGER SCALE KEY MAP OF STATE-WIDE ARTERIAL PAGES.

SCALE: 0 25 50 100 MILES

LEGEND

EXPLANATION OF MAP SYMBOLS

DETAIL PAGES

ARTERIAL PAGES

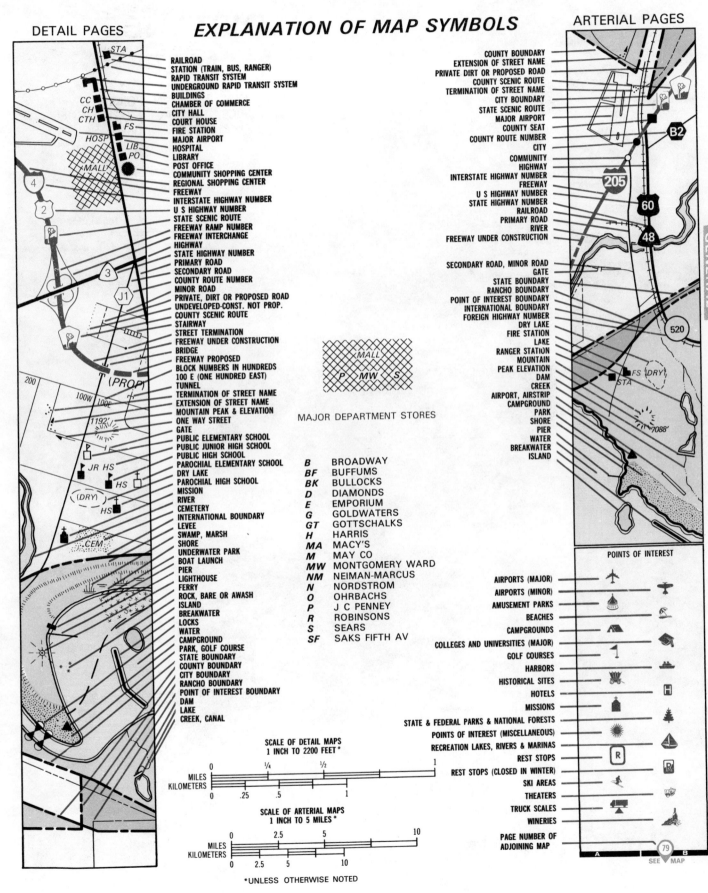

RAILROAD
STATION (TRAIN, BUS, RANGER)
RAPID TRANSIT SYSTEM
UNDERGROUND RAPID TRANSIT SYSTEM
BUILDINGS
CHAMBER OF COMMERCE
CITY HALL
COURT HOUSE
FIRE STATION
MAJOR AIRPORT
HOSPITAL
LIBRARY
POST OFFICE
COMMUNITY SHOPPING CENTER
REGIONAL SHOPPING CENTER
FREEWAY
INTERSTATE HIGHWAY NUMBER
U S HIGHWAY NUMBER
STATE SCENIC ROUTE
FREEWAY RAMP NUMBER
FREEWAY INTERCHANGE
HIGHWAY
STATE HIGHWAY NUMBER
PRIMARY ROAD
SECONDARY ROAD
COUNTY ROUTE NUMBER
MINOR ROAD
PRIVATE, DIRT OR PROPOSED ROAD
UNDEVELOPED-CONST. NOT PROP.
COUNTY SCENIC ROUTE
STAIRWAY
STREET TERMINATION
FREEWAY UNDER CONSTRUCTION
BRIDGE
FREEWAY PROPOSED
BLOCK NUMBERS IN HUNDREDS
100 E (ONE HUNDRED EAST)
TUNNEL
TERMINATION OF STREET NAME
EXTENSION OF STREET NAME
MOUNTAIN PEAK & ELEVATION
ONE WAY STREET
GATE
PUBLIC ELEMENTARY SCHOOL
PUBLIC JUNIOR HIGH SCHOOL
PUBLIC HIGH SCHOOL
PAROCHIAL ELEMENTARY SCHOOL
DRY LAKE
PAROCHIAL HIGH SCHOOL
MISSION
RIVER
CEMETERY
INTERNATIONAL BOUNDARY
LEVEE
SWAMP, MARSH
SHORE
UNDERWATER PARK
BOAT LAUNCH
PIER
LIGHTHOUSE
FERRY
ROCK, BARE OR AWASH
ISLAND
BREAKWATER
LOCKS
WATER
CAMPGROUND
PARK, GOLF COURSE
STATE BOUNDARY
COUNTY BOUNDARY
CITY BOUNDARY
RANCHO BOUNDARY
POINT OF INTEREST BOUNDARY
DAM
LAKE
CREEK, CANAL

COUNTY BOUNDARY
EXTENSION OF STREET NAME
PRIVATE DIRT OR PROPOSED ROAD
COUNTY SCENIC ROUTE
TERMINATION OF STREET NAME
CITY BOUNDARY
STATE SCENIC ROUTE
MAJOR AIRPORT
COUNTY SEAT
COUNTY ROUTE NUMBER
CITY
COMMUNITY
HIGHWAY
INTERSTATE HIGHWAY NUMBER
FREEWAY
U S HIGHWAY NUMBER
STATE HIGHWAY NUMBER
RAILROAD
PRIMARY ROAD
RIVER
FREEWAY UNDER CONSTRUCTION
SECONDARY ROAD, MINOR ROAD
GATE
STATE BOUNDARY
RANCHO BOUNDARY
POINT OF INTEREST BOUNDARY
INTERNATIONAL BOUNDARY
FOREIGN HIGHWAY NUMBER
DRY LAKE
FIRE STATION
LAKE
RANGER STATION
MOUNTAIN
PEAK ELEVATION
DAM
CREEK
AIRPORT, AIRSTRIP
CAMPGROUND
PARK
SHORE
PIER
WATER
BREAKWATER
ISLAND

MALL
P MW S

MAJOR DEPARTMENT STORES

B	BROADWAY
BF	BUFFUMS
BK	BULLOCKS
D	DIAMONDS
E	EMPORIUM
G	GOLDWATERS
GT	GOTTSCHALKS
H	HARRIS
MA	MACY'S
M	MAY CO
MW	MONTGOMERY WARD
NM	NEIMAN-MARCUS
N	NORDSTROM
O	OHRBACHS
P	J C PENNEY
R	ROBINSONS
S	SEARS
SF	SAKS FIFTH AV

SCALE OF DETAIL MAPS
1 INCH TO 2200 FEET *

MILES
KILOMETERS

SCALE OF ARTERIAL MAPS
1 INCH TO 5 MILES *

MILES
KILOMETERS

*UNLESS OTHERWISE NOTED

POINTS OF INTEREST

AIRPORTS (MAJOR)
AIRPORTS (MINOR)
AMUSEMENT PARKS
BEACHES
CAMPGROUNDS
COLLEGES AND UNIVERSITIES (MAJOR)
GOLF COURSES
HARBORS
HISTORICAL SITES
HOTELS
MISSIONS
STATE & FEDERAL PARKS & NATIONAL FORESTS
POINTS OF INTEREST (MISCELLANEOUS)
RECREATION LAKES, RIVERS & MARINAS
REST STOPS
REST STOPS (CLOSED IN WINTER)
SKI AREAS
THEATERS
TRUCK SCALES
WINERIES
PAGE NUMBER OF
ADJOINING MAP

SEE MAP

DISTANCE MAP

DISTANCE BETWEEN POINTS GIVEN IN MILES. MILEAGE DETERMINED BY MOST DIRECT DRIVING ROUTE.

0 25 50 100 MILES
SCALE

MILEAGE CHART

MILEAGE DETERMINED BY MOST DIRECT DRIVING ROUTE

	BAKERSFIELD	CHICO	EUREKA	FRESNO	LAS VEGAS	LONG BEACH	LOS ANGELES	MERCED	MODESTO	OAKLAND	PALM SPRINGS	REDDING	RIVERSIDE	SACRAMENTO	SALINAS	SAN DIEGO	SAN FRANCISCO	SAN JOSE	SAN LUIS OBISPO	SANTA ANA	SANTA BARBARA	SANTA ROSA	SOUTH LAKE TAHOE	STOCKTON	VENTURA
ALTURAS	577	207	292	470	624	705	650	415	374	379	720	142	645	297	471	741	360	392	577	683	737	367	241	342	692
ANAHEIM	138	505	718	245	274	24	30	302	341	443	100	577	42	415	346	86	449	403	235	4	128	485	490	370	102
AUBURN	306	90	321	199	601	441	420	143	106	115	518	175	473	34	207	539	121	151	339	452	444	131	86	70	421
BAKERSFIELD		362	555	107	284	132	113	163	200	285	209	433	177	272	206	232	283	241	114	143	146	340	398	227	115
BARSTOW	129	491	684	236	155	123	131	292	330	414	123	559	78	401	335	180	412	385	264	116	205	469	395	356	174
BENICIA	292	144	287	177	578	429	396	123	84	37	510	187	466	58	106	513	43	49	236	456	341	61	164	74	374
BISHOP	222	360	553	235	284	308	277	223	252	314	308	396	177	265	347	360	335	321	357	301	327	382	176	240	296
BLYTHE	339	705	918	446	208	228	230	501	521	622	129	775	171	616	530	222	619	575	433	202	314	676	686	568	287
BODEGA BAY	404	189	266	249	632	491	451	194	156	74	568	246	527	141	165	594	64	109	294	516	400	23	256	152	431
BURBANK	104	465	659	210	294	31	9	266	304	383	111	536	67	376	304	127	377	334	200	45	93	421	446	330	64
CHICO	362		218	254	620	498	475	198	160	172	575	73	543	89	264	638	180	212	389	509	490	166	170	134	477
CLAREMONT	135	497	691	308	246	47	26	298	336	415	79	568	23	408	336	107	409	366	226	23	118	453	469	360	88
DAVIS	287	83	282	180	582	422	399	134	87	66	499	155	454	15	158	520	74	102	320	433	425	83	127	60	402
DEATH VALLEY	238	530	703	395	213	229	206	393	422	484	306	566	262	435	475	407	505	491	352	324	366	552	346	410	336
EL CENTRO	322	706	872	427	303	219	213	482	520	615	110	775	154	618	536	110	601	561	413	201	308	660	596	554	279
EUREKA	555	218		446	797	683	669	390	353	288	788	149	743	287	381	776	269	323	508	722	614	219	388	332	643
FAIRFIELD	278	132	276	171	561	412	391	118	79	45	489	173	457	43	132	554	55	78	260	423	362	57	150	51	389
FORT BRAGG	460	199	156	353	730	597	551	292	255	180	674	288	629	217	280	669	176	216	401	608	507	119	319	233	534
FRESNO	107	254	446		284	239	220	56	93	178	316	325	272	165	134	339	185	151	140	250	245	233	251	120	222
GRASS VALLEY	329	78	320	222	624	464	443	166	129	138	541	163	496	57	230	562	144	174	362	475	467	154	115	93	444
LAGUNA BEACH	162	528	741	269	288	34	55	324	363	465	115	598	62	437	368	75	471	425	257	19	150	507	511	391	123
LA JOLLA	219	625	763	326	319	90	103	382	419	507	122	667	79	492	428	13	517	449	309	79	203	536	529	450	172
LASSEN NATIONAL PARK	437	102	202	329	695	573	550	273	235	247	650	45	618	164	339	713	255	287	459	584	562	241	199	209	552
LAS VEGAS	284	620	797	284		276	286	446	484	567	276	640	231	567	488	332	568	524	414	269	354	610	466	510	323
LONE PINE	159	420	593	285	224	232	209	283	312	374	277	456	233	325	365	337	395	381	273	245	285	442	236	300	254
LONG BEACH	132	498	683	239	276		24	294	333	417	118	568	60	407	338	103	427	383	218	25	120	477	479	361	93
LOS ANGELES	113	475	669	220	286	24		276	314	393	103	546	56	386	314	119	387	344	204	35	96	431	456	340	66
MAMMOTH LAKES	262	320	513	195	324	348	317	283	212	274	348	356	217	225	307	400	295	281	397	341	367	342	130	200	336
MANTECA	215	147	345	108	499	348	329	54	15	63	425	219	380	44	99	447	73	65	248	382	354	123	144	13	330
MARTINEZ	288	146	290	172	571	424	391	118	79	28	507	191	460	61	101	509	38	47	233	453	338	64	168	70	369
MERCED	163	198	390	56	446	294	276		37	123	368	269	326	109	105	395	130	115	195	305	300	172	194	64	278
MODESTO	200	160	353	93	484	333	314	37		84	410	232	365	72	104	432	92	77	233	344	339	135	156	27	315
MOJAVE	62	424	617	169	229	117	94	225	262	347	162	495	118	334	268	213	345	303	190	130	116	402	351	289	87
MONTEREY	216	278	399	149	504	356	334	115	138	111	433	350	388	190	18	442	122	75	145	367	250	170	272	141	273
NAPA	331	150	255	224	613	463	439	169	130	46	540	191	495	61	145	566	56	88	270	492	363	36	168	69	390
NEEDLES	281	638	821	383	108	269	279	439	476	560	190	729	224	548	481	311	561	517	416	262	352	603	552	508	316
NEVADA CITY	334	83	325	227	629	469	448	171	134	143	546	168	501	62	235	567	149	179	367	480	472	159	110	98	449
NEWPORT BEACH	155	519	735	262	279	21	43	317	366	458	108	592	55	430	361	81	465	418	230	12	141	498	502	382	114
OAKLAND	285	172	288	178	567	417	393	123	84		494	218	449	81	99	520	10	42	224	446	317	60	195	73	344
ONTARIO	141	493	696	247	222	44	37	303	341	420	77	573	21	413	341	125	414	371	232	33	123	458	483	367	103
OXNARD	122	485	650	229	316	85	59	271	322	351	165	555	117	395	252	178	379	329	142	97	38	421	478	349	7
PALMDALE	98	460	653	205	244	81	58	261	298	383	126	531	82	370	304	182	381	339	221	94	116	438	387	325	87
PALM SPRINGS	209	575	788	316	276	118	103	368	410	494		658	56	484	415	135	504	460	306	96	199	554	435	438	172
PALO ALTO	261	213	302	171	544	403	364	135	97	43	480	251	433	120	74	482	33	20	205	426	311	89	223	92	342
PASADENA	109	475	688	216	259	31	7	271	310	394	104	554	52	384	315	134	404	360	210	42	95	454	463	338	68
PLACERVILLE	282	133	331	175	525	416	395	122	83	125	493	205	461	44	177	548	131	127	309	427	429	141	59	55	397
REDDING	433	73	149	325	640	568	546	269	232	218	658		600	161	334	680	218	246	431	579	537	223	249	206	548
RENO	432	104	342	297	444	510	504	241	209	216	510	196	465	132	308	561	223	249	434	503	507	229	61	177	496
RICHMOND	299	163	276	192	581	431	407	137	98	14	508	204	462	74	113	534	24	56	238	460	331	50	181	82	358
RIVERSIDE	177	543	743	272	231	60	56	326	365	449	56	600		439	367	92	463	413	259	43	147	509	379	406	125
SACRAMENTO	272	89	287	165	567	407	386	109	72	81	484	161	439		173	505	87	117	305	418	410	97	107	45	387
SALINAS	206	264	381	134	488	338	314	105	104	99	415	334	367	173		441	101	57	125	349	218	160	251	122	245
SAN BERNARDINO	167	534	714	269	228	63	59	325	362	439	57	595	13	436	360	104	444	401	260	48	154	486	436	389	123
SAN DIEGO	232	638	776	339	332	103	119	395	432	520	135	680	92	505	441		530	462	322	84	216	549	542	493	185
SAN FRANCISCO	283	180	269	185	568	427	387	130	92	10	504	218	463	87	101	530		45	230	452	336	56	192	88	367
SAN JOSE	241	212	323	151	524	383	344	115	77	42	460	246	413	117	57	462	45		185	406	291	96	197	72	322
SAN JUAN CAPISTRANO	163	529	742	270	289	40	55	325	364	466	116	599	63	438	369	66	472	426	258	20	151	508	512	114	124
SAN LUIS OBISPO	114	389	508	140	414	218	204	195	233	224	306	431	259	305	125	322	230	185		238	106	281	382	254	137
SAN MATEO	313	199	288	181	554	413	374	125	86	29	490	237	443	106	84	492	19	30	215	436	321	75	209	78	352
SAN PEDRO	134	496	690	242	285	9	22	298	336	415	126	568	68	408	336	118	409	366	213	37	108	454	478	362	75
SAN RAFAEL	306	167	260	199	588	438	414	144	105	21	515	243	470	83	121	559	18	64	246	470	339	39	181	94	366
SANTA ANA	143	509	722	250	269	25	35	305	344	446	96	579	43	418	349	84	452	406	238		131	488	492	372	104
SANTA BARBARA	146	490	614	245	354	120	96	300	339	317	199	537	147	410	218	216	336	291	106	131		387	490	374	31
SANTA CRUZ	239	230	354	150	524	379	344	116	109	75	456	275	411	146	33	462	74	29	162	390	268	129	229	101	300
SANTA MARIA	145	415	539	171	428	194	170	226	264	255	273	462	221	336	156	290	261	216	31	205	74	312	413	285	103
SANTA ROSA	340	166	219	233	610	477	431	172	135	60	554	223	509	97	160	549	56	96	281	488	387		199	113	414
SAUSALITO	298	183	276	200	583	442	402	145	107	25	519	259	478	99	116	545	15	60	245	467	351	55	207	103	382
SEQUOIA NATIONAL PK	129	343	556	84	408	258	234	139	178	335	235	385	303	252	209	361	272	228	178	269	276	329	335	206	262
SONOMA	331	163	239	224	613	468	439	170	130	46	540	204	495	75	146	584	43	89	271	495	364	20	181	82	391
SONORA	215	189	387	108	498	380	366	52	42	105	420	261	391	86	157	447	115	107	247	357	352	165	139	55	330
SOUTH LAKE TAHOE	398	170	388	251	466	479	456	194	156	195	435	249	379	107	251	542	192	197	382	492	490	199		131	471
STOCKTON	227	134	332	120	510	361	340	64	27	73	438	206	406	45	122	493	88	72	254	372	374	113	131		342
SUSANVILLE	465	105	257	356	599	600	577	299	262	275	677	110	645	191	369	714	252	280	465	613	571	257	133	240	582
UKIAH	402	147	179	295	672	539	493	234	197	135	616	184	571	159	222	611	118	158	343	550	449	62	253	175	476
VALLEJO	310	147	265	203	592	442	418	131	92	25	519	186	474	57	124	545	35	67	249	471	342	46	266	65	370
VENTURA	115	477	643	222	323	93	66	278	315	344	172	548	125	387	245	185	367	322	137	104	31	414	471	342	
YOSEMITE NATIONAL PK	199	263	476	92	435	331	307	83	122	174	408	333	364	172	188	434	184	178	236	342	329	234	133	129	330
YREKA	531	171	205	427	698	657	638	372	335	307	747	98	689	263	423	756	317	346	534	668	630	325	315	297	645
YUBA CITY	313	48	290	206	608	448	427	150	113	122	525	133	480	41	214	546	128	158	346	459	451	201	145	86	428
YUMA	379	742	922	491	299	278	271	545	584	674	169	816	221	655	595	173	655	614	473	260	368	702	646	603	337

CITIES AND COMMUNITIES INDEX

COMMUNITY NAME	CO.	ZIP CODE	PAGE & GRID
A			
ACADEMY	FRCO	93612	57 E2
ACAMPO	SJCO	95226	40 A4
ACTIS	KER	93501	80 A5
ACTON	LACO	93510	89 E4
ADAMS	LAK	95496	31 E4
ADELAIDA	SLO	93446	75 E1
*ADELANTO	SBD	92301	91 A3
ADIN	MOD	96006	14 D3
AERIAL ACRES	KER	93523	80 D5
AETNA SPRINGS	NAPA	94567	32 B5
AFTON	GLE	95920	25 A5
AFTON	SBD	92309	82 D5
AGATE	RCO	91752	99 A2
AGATE BAY	PLA	95711	35 E1
AGOURA	LACO	91301	97 A1
*AGOURA HILLS	LACO	91301	96 E1
AGUA CALIENTE	SDCO	92086	107 C2
AGUA CALIENTE	SON	95476	38 B3
AGUA CALIENTE HOT SPGS	SDCO	92036	107 E4
AGUA DULCE	LACO	91350	89 D4
AGUANGA	RCO	92302	107 A1
AGUEREBERRY POINT	INY	92328	71 D1
AHWAHNEE	MAD	93601	49 C4
AINSWORTH CORNER	SIS		5 C2
*ALAMEDA	ALA	94501	L D5
ALAMO	CC	94507	M A4
ALAMORIO	IMP	92227	109 B4
*ALBANY	ALA	94706	L D4
ALBERHILL	RCO	92303	99 A4
ALBION	MEN	95410	30 B1
ALDERPOINT	HUM	95411	16 D5
ALDER SPRINGS	FRCO	93602	58 A1
ALDER SPRINGS	GLE	95939	23 E3
ALGODONES	BAJA		112 C5
*ALHAMBRA	LACO	91801	R C3
ALLEGHANY	SIE	95910	26 D4
ALLENSWORTH	TUL	93219	68 A4
ALMANOR	PLU	95911	20 B4
ALPAUGH	TUL	93201	67 E4
ALPINE	SDCO	92001	107 B5
ALPINE HEIGHTS	SDCO	92001	107 B5
ALPINE HIGHLANDS	SDCO	92001	107 B5
ALPINE HILLS	SDCO	92001	107 B5
ALPINE HILLS	SMCO	94025	N D3
ALPINE MEADOWS	PLA	95730	35 D2
ALPINE PEAKS	PLA	95730	35 D2
ALTA	PLA	95701	34 E1
ALTADENA	LACO	91001	R C2
ALTA LOMA	SBD	91701	U D2
ALTAMONT	ALA	94550	M D5
ALTAMONT	KLAM		5 C1
ALTA SIERRA	KER	93285	69 C5
ALTAVILLE	CAL	95221	41 B4
ALTA VISTA	INY	93514	51 C3
ALTON	HUM	95540	15 D2
*ALTURAS	MOD	96101	8 A1
ALUM ROCK	SCL	95127	P C3
ALVISO	SCL	95002	P B2
*AMADOR CITY	AMA	95601	40 D2
AMARGOSA VALLEY	NYE		62 E4
AMBLER	TUL	93277	68 B1
AMBOY	SBD	92304	93 E3
AMERICAN HOUSE	PLU	95981	26 C3
*ANAHEIM	ORA	92801	T D2
ANAHEIM HILLS	ORA	92807	T E2
*ANDERSON	SHA	96007	18 C3
ANDERSON SPRINGS	LAK	95461	31 E4
ANDRADE	IMP	92283	112 C5
*ANGELS CAMP	CAL	95222	41 B4
ANGELUS OAKS	SBD	92305	99 E1
ANGWIN	NAPA	94508	38 C1
ANNAPOLIS	SON	95412	30 E5
ANTELOPE	SAC	95842	34 A5
ANTELOPE ACRES	LACO	93534	89 D2
*ANTIOCH	CC	94509	M C3
ANZA	RCO	92306	100 C5
APPLEGATE	PLA	95703	34 D3
APPLE VALLEY	SBD	92307	91 C4
APTOS	SCR	95003	54 B2
ARABIA	RCO	92274	101 B5
ARBUCKLE	COL	95912	32 E3
*ARCADIA	LACO	91006	R C3
*ARCATA	HUM	95521	9 E5
ARCHER	SBD	92319	94 C4
ARCILLA	RCO	91720	99 A3
ARDEN	CLK		74 D3
ARDEN	SAC	95864	40 A1
ARGOS	SBD	92365	93 A2
ARGUS	SBD	93562	71 B5
ARLINGTON	RCO	92503	99 A3
ARMONA	KIN	93202	67 D1
ARNOLD	CAL	95223	41 C3
ARNOLD HEIGHTS	RCO	92508	99 B3
AROMAS	MON	95004	54 C2
ARROWBEAR LAKE	SBD	92308	99 D1
ARROWHEAD SPRINGS	SBD	92404	99 C1
*ARROYO GRANDE	SLO	93420	76 B4
*ARTESIA	LACO	90701	T A1
ARTOIS	GLE	95913	24 D4
*ARVIN	KER	93203	78 E4
ASHFORD JUNCTION	INY	92328	72 C4
ASH HILL	SBD	92304	93 C2
*ASHLAND	JKSN		3 E1
ASPENDELL	INY	93514	51 B5
ASTI	SON	95413	31 C5
*ATASCADERO	SLO	93422	76 A2
*ATHERTON	SMCO	94025	N D2
ATOLIA	SBD	93558	80 E3
*ATWATER	MCO	95301	48 B4
*AUBURN	PLA	95603	34 C3

COMMUNITY NAME	CO.	ZIP CODE	PAGE & GRID
AUBURNDALE	RCO	91760	U E4
*AVALON	LACO	90704	97 E5
AVENAL	KIN	93204	66 E3
AVERY	CAL	95224	41 C3
AVILA BEACH	SLO	93424	76 A4
AVON	CC	94523	38 E4
*AZUSA	LACO	91702	U A1
B			
BABBITT	MIN		44 B1
BADGER	TUL	93603	58 D4
BADWATER	INY	92328	72 A2
BAGDAD	SBD	92304	93 D3
BAKER	SBD	92309	83 B3
*BAKERSFIELD	KER	93301	78 D3
BALBOA	ORA	92661	T C4
BALBOA ISLAND	ORA	92662	T C4
BALCH	SBD	92309	83 B5
BALCH CAMP	FRCO	93657	58 C2
*BALDWIN PARK	LACO	91706	R D3
BALLARAT	INY	93562	71 C3
BALLARD	SB	93441	86 E3
BALLENA	SDCO	92065	107 B4
BALLICO	MCO	95303	48 A3
BANGOR	BUT	95914	25 E5
BANKHEAD SPRINGS	SDCO	92005	111 A4
BANNER	SDCO	92036	107 D4
*BANNING	RCO	92220	100 A3
BANNOCK	SBD		95 B1
BARD	IMP	92222	112 D5
BARDSDALE	VEN	93015	88 D4
BARRETT JUNCTION	SDCO	92017	112 B2
BARSTOW	FRCO	93702	57 B3
*BARSTOW	SBD	92311	91 E1
BARTLETT	INY	93545	60 B5
BARTLETT SPRINGS	LAK	95443	32 A2
BARTON	AMA	92309	41 B2
BASIN	SBD	92309	82 E5
BASSETT	LACO	91746	R D4
BASSETTS	SIE	96125	27 A4
BASS LAKE	MAD	93604	49 E4
BAXTER	PLA	95704	34 E1
BAYSHORE	SMCO	94005	L C5
BAYSIDE	HUM	95524	9 E5
BAYWOOD PARK	SLO	93401	75 E3
BEAR HARBOR	MEN	95489	22 B2
BEAR VALLEY	ALP	95223	41 E2
BEAR VALLEY	MPA	95338	48 E3
BEAR VALLEY	SDCO	92027	106 E3
BEAR VALLEY SPRINGS	KER	93561	79 B4
BEATTY	NYE		62 B2
BEATTY JUNCTION	INYO	92328	61 E4
*BEAUMONT	RCO	92223	99 E3
BECKWOURTH	PLU	96129	27 C2
BEE ROCK	SLO	93928	65 D5
BEL AIRE	MAR	94920	L B4
BEL AIR ESTATES	LACO	90077	Q B4
BELDEN	PLU	95915	26 A1
*BELL	LACO	90201	R B5
BELLA VISTA	KER	93283	79 E1
BELLA VISTA	SHA	96008	18 D2
*BELLFLOWER	LACO	90706	S E1
*BELL GARDENS	LACO	90201	R B5
BELLOTA	SJCO	95236	40 C4
BELL SPRINGS	MEN	95440	22 D1
BEL MARIN KEYS	MAR	94947	L B2
*BELMONT	SMCO	94002	N C2
*BELVEDERE	MAR	94920	L B4
BELVEDERE GARDENS	MAR	94920	L B4
BENBOW	HUM	95440	22 C1
BEND	TEH	96008	18 D4
*BENICIA	SOL	94510	L E3
BEN LOMOND	SCR	95005	N E5
BENTON	MNO	93512	51 C1
BERENDA	MAD	93637	56 E1
*BERKELEY	ALA	94701	L D4
BERRY CREEK	BUT	95916	25 E3
BERRYESSA HIGHLANDS	NAPA	94558	38 D1
BERRYESSA PINES	NAPA	94567	38 C1
BERTELEDA	DN	95531	2 A4
BERTSCH TERRACE	DN	95531	1 E4
BETHANY	SJCO	95376	M E5
BETTERAVIA	SB	93455	86 B1
*BEVERLY HILLS	LACO	90210	Q C3
BIEBER	LAS	96009	14 B3
BIG BAR	AMA	95704	41 A2
BIG BEAR CITY	SBD	92314	92 A5
*BIG BEAR LAKE	SBD	92315	92 A5
BIG BEND	SHA	96011	13 A4
BIG BEND	SON	95476	38 B3
BIG CREEK	FRCO	93605	50 B5
*BIGGS	BUT	95917	25 B5
BIG MEADOW	CAL	95223	41 E2
BIG OAK FLAT	TUO	95305	48 D1
BIG PINE	INY	93513	51 E5
BIG RIVER	SBD	92242	104 A1
BIG SPRINGS	SIS		4 C5
BIG SUR	MON	93920	64 B2
BINGHAMTON	SOL	95625	39 B2
BIOLA	FRCO	93606	57 B3
BIRCH HILL	SDCO	92060	107 A2
BIRCHVILLE	NEV		34 C1
BIRDS LANDING	SOL	94512	39 B4
*BISHOP	INY	93514	51 D4
BITTERWATER	SBT	93930	65 C1
BLACK POINT	MAR	94947	L B2
BLACKWELLS CORNER	KER	93249	77 C1
BLAIRSDEN	PLU	96103	27 A2
BLOCKSBURG	HUM	95414	16 D4
BLOOMINGTON	SBD	92316	99 A2
BLOSSOM	TEH	96080	18 B5
BLOSSOM VALLEY	SDCO	92021	107 A5

COMMUNITY NAME	CO.	ZIP CODE	PAGE & GRID
BLUE DIAMOND	CLK		74 B3
*BLUE LAKE	HUM	95525	10 A5
BLUE LAKES	LAK	95493	31 C2
*BLYTHE	RCO	92225	103 D5
BOCA	NEV	95737	27 E5
BODEGA	SON	94922	37 C3
BODEGA BAY	SON	94923	37 C3
BODFISH	KER	93205	79 C1
BODIE	MNO	93517	43 D3
BOLINAS	MAR	94924	37 E5
BOLSA KNOLLS	MON	93906	54 C3
BOMBAY BEACH	IMP	92257	108 E2
*BONANZA	KLAM		5 E1
BONDS CORNER	IMP	92250	112 C4
BONITA	SDCO	92002	V D4
BONNEFOY	AMA	95642	41 A2
BONSALL	SDCO	92003	106 C2
BOONVILLE	MEN	95415	30 E3
BOOTJACK	MPA	95338	49 B3
BORON	KER	93516	80 E5
BORREGO	SDCO	92004	107 E3
BORREGO SPRINGS	SDCO	92004	107 E2
BOSTONIA	SDCO	92021	V E2
BOULDER CREEK	SCR	95006	N E5
BOULDER OAKS	SDCO	92062	112 D1
BOULEVARD	SDCO	92005	111 A4
BOUSE	LPAZ	92363	104 D3
BOWLES	FRCO	93725	57 C4
BOWMAN	PLA	95707	34 C3
BOYES HOT SPRINGS	SON	95476	38 B3
BOYLE HEIGHTS	LACO	90033	R A4
*BRADBURY	LACO	91010	R E3
BRADLEY	MON	93426	65 E4
BRANSCOMB	MEN	95417	22 D3
BRANT	SBD	92323	84 C5
*BRAWLEY	IMP	92227	109 A4
*BREA	ORA	92621	T D1
BRENDA	LPAZ		104 D4
*BRENTWOOD	CC	94513	M D3
BRENTWOOD	LACO	90049	Q B4
BRICEBURG	MPA	95345	49 B2
BRICELAND	HUM	95440	16 B5
BRIDGE HAVEN	SON	95450	37 C2
BRIDGEPORT	MPA	95306	49 A4
BRIDGEPORT	MNO	93517	43 B3
BRIDGEPORT	NEV	95975	34 B1
BRIDGEVIEW	JOS		2 D1
BRIDGEVILLE	HUM	95526	16 C3
*BRISBANE	SMCO	94005	L C5
BRITE VALLEY	KER	93561	79 C4
BRODERICK	YOL	95605	39 D1
BROOKDALE	SCR	95007	N E5
BROOKINGS	CUR		1 D2
BROOKS	YOL	95606	32 D5
BROOKTRAILS VACATN VLG	MEN	95490	22 E5
BROOKTRAIL VACTN VLG W	MEN	95490	22 E5
BROWNS VALLEY	YUB	95918	33 E1
BROWNSVILLE	YUB	95919	26 A4
BRUCEVILLE	SAC	95683	39 E3
BRUSH CREEK	BUT	95916	25 E3
BRYMAN	SBD	92368	91 B3
BRYN MAWR	SBD	92318	99 C2
BRYTE	YOL	95605	39 D1
BUCKEYE	ED	95634	34 E3
BUCKEYE	SHA	96003	18 B2
BUCKHORN	AMA	95666	41 B2
BUCKHORN SPRINGS	JKSN		4 B2
BUCKMAN SPRINGS	SDCO	92062	112 D1
BUCK MEADOWS	MPA	95321	49 A1
BUCKS BAR	ED	95684	35 A5
BUCKS LAKE	PLU	95971	26 B2
BUELLTON	SB	93427	86 B3
BUENA	SDCO	92083	106 C3
*BUENA PARK	ORA	90620	T B1
BUENA VISTA	AMA	95640	40 D3
BUHACH	MCO	95340	48 B4
BULLHEAD CITY	MOH		85 D4
BUMMERVILLE	CAL	95257	41 B2
BUNTINGVILLE	LAS	96114	21 B4
*BURBANK	LACO	91501	Q E2
BURDELL	MAR	94947	L A1
*BURLINGAME	SMCO	94010	N C1
BURNEY	SHA	96013	13 C5
BURNT RANCH	TRI	95527	10 D5
BURREL	FRCO	93607	57 B5
BURSON	CAL	95225	40 D4
BUTTE CITY	GLE	95920	25 A5
BUTTE MEADOWS	BUT	95921	25 B2
BUTTONWILLOW	KER	93206	78 A3
BYRON	CC	94514	M D4
C			
CABAZON	RCO	92230	100 B3
CABBAGE PATCH	CAL	95223	41 E2
CADENASSO	YOL	95607	32 E5
CADIZ	SBD	92319	94 B4
CADWELL	SON		37 B1
CAIRNS CORNER	TUL	93247	68 C2
CAJON	SBD	92358	91 A5
CAJON PASS	SBD	92397	91 A5
CALABASAS	LACO	91302	97 B1
CALADA	SBD	92309	84 B1
CALAVERITAS	CAL	95249	41 A3
*CALEXICO	IMP	92231	112 B4
CALICO GHOST TOWN	SBD	92398	82 A5
CALIENTE	KER	93518	79 B3
*CALIFORNIA CITY	KER	93505	80 B4
CALIFORNIA HOT SPRINGS	TUL	93207	69 B4
CALIFORNIA VALLEY	SLO	93453	77 B3
CALIMESA	RCO	92320	99 D2
*CALIPATRIA	IMP	92233	109 B3
*CALISTOGA	NAPA	94515	38 A1

COMMUNITY NAME	CO.	ZIP CODE	PAGE & GRID
CALLAHAN	SIS	96014	11 D2
CALNEVA	LAS	96113	21 E5
CALPELLA	MEN	95418	31 B1
CALPINE	SIE	96124	27 B3
CALWA	FRCO	93725	57 C3
*CAMARILLO	VEN	93010	96 C1
CAMBRIA	SLO	93428	75 C2
CAMDEN	FRCO	93656	57 C5
CAMERON CORNERS	SDCO	92006	112 D2
CAMERON PARK	ED	95682	34 C5
CAMINO	ED	95709	35 A4
*CAMPBELL	SCL	95008	P B4
CAMP CONIFER	TUL	93271	59 A5
CAMP CONNELL	CAL	95223	41 D3
CAMP KLAMATH	DN	95548	2 A5
CAMP MEEKER	SON	95419	37 D2
CAMPO	SDCO	92006	112 D2
CAMPO SECO	CAL	95226	40 E3
CAMP SIERRA	FRCO	93634	50 B5
CAMPTONVILLE	YUB	95922	26 B5
CANBY	MOD	96015	14 D1
CANE BRAKE	KER	93255	70 B5
CANOGA PARK	LACO	91303	Q A2
CANTIL	KER	93519	80 C3
CANTUA CREEK	FRCO	93608	56 D5
CANYON CITY	SDCO	92006	112 D2
CANYON CREST HEIGHTS	RCO	92507	99 B2
CANYON DAM	PLU	95923	20 C5
CANYON LAKE	RCO	92380	99 C4
CAPAY	YOL	95607	32 E5
CAPETOWN	HUM	95536	15 C3
CAPISTRANO BEACH	ORA	92624	105 D1
*CAPITOLA	SCR	95010	54 A2
CARBONDALE	AMA	95640	40 C2
CARDIFF-BY-THE-SEA	SDCO	92007	106 B4
CARL INN	TUO	95321	49 C1
CARLOTTA	HUM	95528	16 A2
*CARLSBAD	SDCO	92008	106 B3
*CARMEL	MON	93921	54 A5
CARMEL HIGHLANDS	MON	93921	54 A5
CARMEL VALLEY VILLAGE	MON	93924	54 C5
CARMET	SON	94923	37 C2
CARMICHAEL	SAC	95608	34 A5
CARNELIAN BAY	PLA	95711	36 A1
CARPENTERVILLE	CUR		1 C1
*CARPINTERIA	SB	93013	87 E4
CARQUINEZ HEIGHTS	SOL	94590	38 C4
*CARSON	LACO	90745	S C2
*CARSON CITY	CRSN		36 C2
CARSON HILL	CAL	95222	41 B4
CARTAGO	INY	93549	70 B1
CARUTHERS	FRCO	93609	57 C5
CASA BLANCA	RCO	92504	99 B3
CASA DE ORO	SDCO	92077	V E3
CASITAS SPRINGS	VEN	93001	88 A4
CASMALIA	SB	93429	86 B1
CASPER	MEN	95420	22 B5
CASSEL	SHA	96016	13 D5
CASTAIC	LACO	91310	89 B4
CASTELLA	SHA	96017	12 C3
CASTELLAMMARE	LACO	90290	Q A4
CASTLE CRAG	SHA	96013	12 C3
CASTLE PARK	SDCO	92011	V D5
CASTRO VALLEY	ALA	94546	L E5
CASTROVILLE	MON	95012	54 B3
*CATHEDRAL CITY	RCO	92234	100 D4
CATHEYS VALLEY	MPA	95306	49 A3
CAVE JUNCTION	JOS		2 D1
CAYTON	SHA	96013	13 C4
CAYUCOS	SLO	93430	75 D2
CAZADERO	SON	95421	37 C1
CECILVILLE	SIS	96018	11 B3
CEDAR BROOK	FRCO	93641	58 D3
CEDAR CREST	FRCO	93605	50 C5
CEDAR FLAT	PLA	95711	35 E1
CEDAR GLEN	SBD	92321	91 D5
CEDAR GROVE	ED	95709	35 A4
CEDAR GROVE	FRCO	93641	59 B3
CEDARPINES PARK	SBD	92322	91 B5
CEDAR RIDGE	TUO	95370	41 D4
CEDAR VALLEY	MAD	93644	49 D4
CEDARVILLE	MOD	96104	7 D5
CENTERVILLE	ALA	94536	P A2
CENTERVILLE	DGL		36 C3
CENTERVILLE	FRCO	93654	57 E3
CENTERVILLE	SHA	96001	18 B2
CENTRAL VALLEY	SHA	96019	18 C1
CENTURY CITY	LACO	90067	Q D4
*CERES	STA	95307	7 D3
*CERRITOS	LACO	90701	T B1
CHALFANT	MNO	93514	51 D3
CHALLENGE	YUB	95925	26 B4
CHAMBERS LODGE	PLA	95718	35 E2
CHARLESTON PARK	CLK		74 A2
CHASE	SBD	92364	84 B4
CHATSWORTH	LACO	91311	Q A1
CHAWANAKEE	FRCO	93602	50 A5
CHEMEKETA PARK	SCL	95030	P A4
CHEROKEE	BUT	95965	25 D3
CHEROKEE	NEV	93602	26 C5
CHERRY VALLEY	RCO	92223	99 E2
CHESTER	PLU	96020	20 A4
CHICAGO PARK	NEV	95712	34 C2
*CHICO	BUT	95926	25 B3
CHILCOOT	PLU	96105	27 D2
CHINATOWN	SFCO	94108	142 D2
CHINESE CAMP	TUO	95309	41 B5
*CHINO	SBD	91710	U D3
CHINQUAPIN	MPA	95389	49 D2
CHIQUITA LAKE	ED	95634	35 A3
CHLORIDE CITY	INY	92328	62 A4

***INDICATES INCORPORATED CITY**

COMMUNITY NAME	CO.	ZIP CODE	PAGE & GRID
CHOCTAW VALLEY	KER	93306	78 E2
CHOLAME	SLO	93431	66 D5
*CHOWCHILLA	MAD	93610	48 D5
CHROME	GLE	95963	24 A3
CHUALAR	MON	93925	54 D4
CHUBBUCK	SBD	92319	94 D5
*CHULA VISTA	SDCO	92010	V D4
CIBOLA	LPAZ		110 D2
CIENEGA SPRINGS	LPAZ		104 C1
CIMA	SBD	92323	84 B4
CIRCLE OAKS	NAPA	94599	38 D2
CISCO	PLA	95728	35 B1
CITRUS HEIGHTS	SAC	95610	34 A5
CLAIREMONT	SDCO	92117	V B2
CLARAVILLE	KER	93283	79 D2
*CLAREMONT	LACO	91711	U C2
CLARK	STOR		28 E4
CLARKSBURG	YOL	95612	39 D2
CLARKSVILLE	ED	95682	34 C5
CLAY	SAC	95638	40 B3
*CLAYTON	CC	94517	M B3
CLEAR CREEK	SIS	96039	2 E4
*CLEARLAKE	LAK	95422	32 A3
CLEARLAKE KEYS	LAK	95423	32 A3
CLEARLAKE OAKS	LAK	95423	32 A3
CLEMENTS	SJCO	95227	40 C3
CLEONE	MEN	95437	22 C4
CLIFF HOUSE	TUO	95321	49 B1
CLINTON	AMA	95232	41 A2
CLIPPER GAP	PLA	95703	34 C3
CLIPPER MILLS	BUT	95930	26 A4
CLOVERDALE	SHA	96007	18 B3
*CLOVERDALE	SON	95425	31 C4
*CLOVIS	FRCO	93612	57 D3
CLYDE	CC	94520	M A3
*COACHELLA	RCO	92236	101 B4
*COALINGA	FRCO	93210	66 D3
COALINGA MINERAL SPGS	FRCO	93210	66 B2
COARSEGOLD	MAD	93614	49 C4
COBB	LAK	95426	31 E4
COCKATOO GROVE	SDCO	92010	V E4
CODORA	GLE	95970	25 A5
COFFEE CREEK	TRI	96091	11 E3
COHASSET	BUT	95926	25 C1
COLD SPRINGS	TUO	95370	42 A3
COLES STATION	ED	95684	35 B5
COLEVILLE	MNO	96107	42 D1
*COLFAX	PLA	95713	34 D2
COLLEGE CITY	COL	95931	33 A3
COLLEGEVILLE	SJCO	95206	40 B5
COLLIERVILLE	SJCO	95220	40 B3
COLLINSVILLE	SOL	94585	39 B4
*COLMA	SMCO	94015	L B5
COLOMA	ED	95613	34 D4
*COLTON	SBD	92324	99 B2
COLUMBIA	TUO	95310	41 C4
*COLUSA	COL	95932	32 E2
*COMMERCE	LACO	90040	R B4
COMPTCHE	MEN	95427	30 C1
*COMPTON	LACO	90220	S C1
*CONCORD	CC	94520	M A3
CONFIDENCE	TUO	95370	41 D4
CONSTANTIA	LAS	96019	27 E1
COOKS STATION	AMA	95666	41 C1
COOLIDGE SPRING	IMP		108 C1
COPCO	SIS	96044	4 C2
COPPEROPOLIS	CAL	95228	41 A5
*CORCORAN	KIN	93212	67 E3
CORDELIA	SOL	93063	L E1
*CORNING	TEH	96021	24 D2
*CORONA	RCO	91720	U E4
CORONA DEL MAR	ORA	92625	T C5
*CORONADO	SDCO	92118	V B4
*CORTE MADERA	MAR	94925	L A3
COSO JUNCTION	INY	93542	70 C3
*COSTA MESA	ORA	92626	T C4
COSUMNES	SAC	95683	40 B2
*COTATI	SON	94928	37 E3
COTO DE CAZA	ORA	92678	98 E4
COTTAGE SPRINGS	CAL	95223	41 D2
COTTON CENTER	TUL	93257	68 C3
COTTONWOOD	SHA	96022	18 C3
COULTERVILLE	MPA	95311	48 D2
COURTLAND	SAC	95615	39 D3
COVELO	MEN	95428	23 A3
*COVINA	LACO	91722	U A2
COVINGTON MILL	TRI	96052	11 E5
COWAN HEIGHTS	ORA	92705	98 C4
COW HOLLOW	SFCO	94123	142 A2
COX	RCO	92255	103 C3
COYOTE	SCL	95013	P D4
COYOTE WELLS	IMP	92259	111 C3
COZZENS CORNERS	SON	95441	31 D5
CRAFTON	SBD	92373	99 D2
CRANMORE	SUT	95645	33 B3
CRANNELL	HUM	95530	9 E4
*CRESCENT CITY	DN	95531	1 D4
CRESCENT MILLS	PLU	95934	20 C5
CRESSEY	MCO	95312	48 A4
CREST	SDCO	92021	112 A1
CRESTLINE	SBD	92325	91 C5
CRESTMORE	SBD	92316	99 B2
CRESTON	SLO	93432	76 B2
CRESTVIEW	MNO	93514	50 D1
CROCKETT	CC	94525	L D3
CROMBERG	PLU	96103	27 A2
CROWN POINT	SDCO	92109	V A3
CROWS LANDING	SIS	95313	47 C4
CRUCERO	SBD	92309	83 A5
*CRYSTAL BAY	DGL		36 A1
*CUDAHY	LACO	90201	R B5
CUESTA BY THE SEA	SLO	93402	75 D3
*CULVER CITY	LACO	90230	Q D4
CUMMINGS	MEN	95477	22 D2
CUMMINGS VALLEY	KER	93561	79 B4
CUNNINGHAM	SON	95472	37 E2
*CUPERTINO	SCL	95014	P A3
CURRY VILLAGE	MPA	95389	49 D2
CUTLER	TUL	93615	58 B5
CUTTEN	HUM	95534	15 E1
CUYAMA	SB	93214	87 D1
CUYAMACA	SDCO	92036	107 C4
*CYPRESS	ORA	90630	T B2
D			
DAGGETT	SBD	92327	92 A1
DAIRY	KLAM		5 D1
DAIRYVILLE	TEH	96080	18 D5
DALES	TEH	96080	18 E4
*DALY CITY	SMCO	94014	L B5
DANA	SHA	96036	13 D3
DANA POINT	ORA	92629	105 D1
DANBY	SBD	92332	94 C3
*DANVILLE	CC	94526	M A4
DARDANELLE	TUO	95314	42 B2
DARLINGTONIA	DN	95543	2 A3
DARRAH	MPA	95338	49 C3
DARWIN	INY	93522	70 E2
DATE CITY	IMP	92250	112 C3
DAULTON	MAD	93653	57 B1
DAVENPORT	SCR		53 D2
*DAVIS	YOL	95616	39 C1
DAVIS CREEK	MOD	96108	7 C4
DAVIS DAM	MOH		85 D4
DAWES	SBD	92364	84 A5
DAY	MOD	96056	13 E3
DAYTON	BUT	95926	25 B3
DAYTON	LYON		36 D1
DE BON	SIS	96034	12 C1
DEER PARK	NAPA	94576	38 B1
DEHESA	SDCO	92021	112 A1
*DELANO	KER	93215	68 B5
DEL CERRO	SDCO	92120	V D3
DEL DIOS	SDCO	92025	106 D3
DELEVAN	COL	95988	24 D5
DELFT COLONY	TUL	93619	58 A5
DELHI	MCO	95315	47 E4
DELL	SBD	92371	91 A5
DEL LOMA	TRI	96010	17 A1
*DEL MAR	SDCO	92014	V A1
DEL PASO HEIGHTS	SAC	95838	33 E5
DEL REY	FRCO	93616	57 E4
*DEL REY OAKS	MON	93940	54 B4
DEL RIO WOODS	SON	95448	37 E1
DEL ROSA	SBD	92404	99 C1
DELTA	SHA	96051	12 B4
DEMOCRAT HOT SPRINGS	KER	93301	79 B2
DENAIR	STA	95316	47 E3
DENNY	TRI	95538	10 E5
DENVERTON	SOL	94585	39 A3
DERBY ACRES	KER	93268	77 E3
DE SABLA	BUT	95978	25 C2
DESCANSO	SDCO	92016	107 C5
DESCANSO JUNCTION	SDCO	92016	107 C5
DESERT	SBD	92309	84 C2
DESERT BEACH	RCO	92254	101 D5
*DESERT HOT SPRINGS	RCO	92240	100 D2
DESERT LAKE	KER	93516	80 D5
DESERT SHORES	IMP	92274	108 C1
DESERT VIEW HIGHLAND	LACO	93550	89 E3
DEVILS DEN	KER	93204	67 B5
DEVORE	SBD	92405	99 B1
DIABLO	CC	94528	M B4
DIABLO CASA HOT SPGS	MNO	93546	50 E2
DIAMOND BAR	LACO	91765	U B3
DIAMOND SPRINGS	ED	95619	34 E5
DI GIORGIO	KER	93217	79 A3
DILLON BEACH	MAR	94929	37 D3
DINKEY CREEK	FRCO	93617	58 C1
*DINUBA	TUL	93618	58 A5
DISCOVERY BAY	CC	94514	39 D5
DIXIELAND	IMP	92251	108 D5
*DIXON	SOL	95620	39 B2
DOBBINS	YUB	95935	26 B5
DOG TOWN	CAL	95249	41 B4
DOGTOWN	MPA	95311	48 E2
DOGTOWN	SJCO	95220	40 D3
DORRINGTON	CAL	95223	41 D3
*DORRIS	SIS	96023	5 A2
*DOS PALOS	MCO	93620	56 B2
DOS PALOS Y	MCO	93620	56 A1
DOS RIOS	MEN	95429	23 A3
DOUGLAS CITY	TRI	96024	17 D2
*DOWNEY	LACO	90241	R B5
DOWNIEVILLE	SIE	95936	26 D4
DOYLE	LAS	96019	27 E1
DOYLES CORNER	SHA	96040	13 D5
DOZIER	SOL	94535	39 B3
DRYTOWN	AMA	95699	40 E2
*DUARTE	LACO	91010	R D3
*DUBLIN	ALA	94566	M B5
DUCOR	TUL	93218	68 D4
DULZURA	SDCO	92017	112 B2
DUNCANS MILLS	SON	95430	37 C2
DUNLAP	FRCO	93621	58 C3
DUNLAP	MEN	95490	30 C1
DUNMOVIN	INY	93542	70 C3
DUNN	SBD	92309	82 D5
DUNNIGAN	YOL	95937	33 A4
*DUNSMUIR	SIS	96025	12 B3
DURHAM	BUT	95938	25 B3
DURMID	RCO	92257	108 D1
DUSTIN ACRES	KER	93268	78 A4
DUTCH FLAT	PLA	95714	34 D1
DYER	ESM		52 B2
E			
EADS	SBD	92347	81 C5
EAGLE LAKE RESORT	LAS	96130	20 D2
EAGLE MOUNTAIN	RCO	92241	102 B3
EAGLE ROCK	LACO	90041	R A3
EAGLES NEST	SDCO	92086	107 C2
EAGLEVILLE	MOD	96110	8 D2
EARLIMART	TUL	93219	68 B4
EARP	SBD	92242	104 B1
EAST BAKERSFIELD	KER	93307	78 D3
EAST GUERNEWOOD	SON	95446	37 C1
EAST HIGHLANDS	SBD	92346	99 C1
EAST NICOLAUS	SUT	95622	33 D3
EASTON	FRCO	93706	57 C4
EAST OROSI	TUL	93647	58 B5
*EAST PALO ALTO	SMCO	94303	N E2
EAST QUINCY	PLU	95971	26 D1
EAST SAN DIEGO	SDCO	92105	V C3
EASTSIDE ACRES	MAD	93622	56 C3
EASTSIDE RANCH	MAD	93622	56 C3
ECHO DELL	SDCO	92016	107 C5
ECHO LAKE	ED	95721	35 E4
EDEN GARDENS	SDCO	92075	106 B4
EDEN HOT SPRINGS	RCO	92353	99 D3
EDGEMONT	RCO	92508	99 C3
EDGEWOOD	SIS	96094	12 C1
EDISON	KER	93220	78 E3
EDNA	SLO	93401	76 B4
EDWARDS AIR FORCE BASE	KER	93523	90 C1
EEL ROCK	HUM	95554	16 C4
EHRENBERG	YUMA		103 E5
EL BONITA	SON	95446	37 C1
*EL CAJON	SDCO	92020	V E3
EL CASCO	RCO	92373	99 D2
*EL CENTRO	IMP	92243	109 A5
*EL CERRITO	CC	94530	L C3
ELDERS CORNERS	PLA	95603	34 C3
ELDERWOOD	TUL	93286	58 C5
EL DORADO	ED	95623	34 D5
EL DORADO HILLS	ED	95630	34 C5
ELDRIDGE	SON	95431	38 B3
ELECTRA	AMA	95642	41 A2
EL GRANADA	SMCO	94018	N B2
ELIZABETH LAKE	LACO	93550	89 D3
ELK	MEN	95432	30 C2
ELK CREEK	GLE	95939	24 A4
ELK GROVE	SAC	95624	39 E2
ELK VALLEY	DN	95543	2 C2
ELLWOOD	SB	93117	87 B4
ELMIRA	SOL	95625	39 B2
*EL MONTE	LACO	91731	R D3
*ELMORE	IMP	92227	108 D3
ELM VIEW	FRCO	93725	57 C4
EL NIDO	MCO	95317	56 C1
ELORA	SBD	92364	84 B4
*EL PASO DE ROBLES	SLO	93446	76 A1
EL PORTAL	MPA	95318	49 C2
EL PORVENIR	FRE	93608	56 C5
EL PRADO	SDCO	92104	V B3
*EL SEGUNDO	LACO	90245	Q C5
EL SERENO	LACO	90031	R A3
EL SOBRANTE	CC	94803	L D3
EL TORO	ORA	92630	98 D4
EL TORO MARINE BASE	ORA	92709	98 D4
EL VERANO	SON	95433	L B1
ELVERTA	SAC	95626	33 E5
EMERALD BAY	ED	95733	35 E3
EMERALD BAY	ORA	92651	T D5
*EMERYVILLE	ALA	94608	L C4
EMIGRANT GAP	PLA	95715	35 A1
EMMATON	SAC		M D2
EMPIRE	STA	95319	47 D2
ENCANTO	SDCO	92114	V D4
*ENCINITAS	SDCO	92024	106 B4
ENCINO	LACO	91316	Q B3
ENGINEER SPRINGS	SDCO	92017	112 B2
ENTERPRISE	SHA	96001	18 C2
*ESCALON	SJCO	95320	47 C1
*ESCONDIDO	SDCO	92025	106 D3
ESPARTO	YOL	95627	33 A5
ESSEX	SBD	92332	94 D2
ESTRELLA	SLO	93415	76 B1
ETHEDA SPRINGS	FRCO	93633	58 D4
*ETNA	SIS	96027	11 D1
ETTERSBURG	HUM	95440	16 A5
EUCALYPTUS HILLS	SDCO	92040	V E2
*EUREKA	HUM	95501	15 E1
EUREKA VALLEY	SFCO	94114	45 B2
EVELYN	INY	92384	72 E2
*EXETER	TUL	93221	68 C1
F			
*FAIRFAX	MAR	94930	L A3
*FAIRFIELD	SOL	94533	M A1
FAIRHAVEN	HUM	95564	15 D1
FAIRMEAD	MAD	93610	56 D1
FAIRMONT	LACO	93534	89 C2
FAIR OAKS	SAC	95628	34 A5
FAIR PLAY	ED	95684	41 A1
FAIRVIEW	TUL	93238	69 C4
FALES HOT SPRINGS	MNO	93517	43 A2
FALLBROOK	SDCO	92028	106 C2
FALLEN LEAF	ED	95716	35 E4
FALLON	MAR	94932	37 D3
FALL RIVER MILLS	SHA	96028	13 E4
FAMOSO	KER	93250	78 C1
*FARMERSVILLE	TUL	93223	68 C1
FAWNSKIN	SBD	92333	91 E5
FEATHER FALLS	BUT	95940	26 A4
FELLOWS	KER	93224	77 E4
FELIX	CAL	95228	41 A4
FELTON	SCR	95018	N E5
FENNER	SBD	92332	94 E2
FERN	SHA	96096	19 A1
FERNBROOK	SDCO	92065	107 A4
*FERNDALE	HUM	95536	15 D2
FERRUM	RCO	92257	108 D1
FETTERS HOT SPRINGS	SON	95476	38 B3
FIDDLETOWN	AMA	95629	40 E1
FIELD	SBD	92365	82 C5
FIELDBROOK	HUM	95521	10 A4
FIELDS LANDING	HUM	95537	15 E1
*FILLMORE	VEN	93015	88 D4
FINE GOLD	MAD	93643	49 D5
FINLEY	LAK	95435	31 D3
*FIREBAUGH	FRCO	93622	56 C3
FISH CAMP	MPA	95623	49 D3
FISHEL	SBD	92319	94 D5
FISH ROCK	MEN	95445	30 D4
FISH SPRINGS	INY	93513	59 E1
FIVE CORNERS	LAKE		7 B1
FIVE CORNERS	SJCO	95336	47 C1
FIVE POINTS	FRCO	93624	57 A5
FIVE POINTS	LACO	91732	R D4
FLEETRIDGE	SDCO	92106	V A3
FLETCHER HILLS	SDCO	92020	V D2
FLINN SPRINGS	SDCO	92021	107 A5
FLORIN	SAC	95828	39 E2
FLOURNOY	TEH	96029	24 B2
FLOWING WELLS	RCO	92254	101 C5
FLYNN	SBD	92309	83 E5
*FOLSOM	SAC	95630	34 B5
*FONTANA	SBD	92335	99 B1
FOOTHILL FARMS	SAC	95841	34 A5
FORBESTOWN	BUT	95963	26 A4
FORD CITY	KER	93268	78 A4
FOREST	SIE	95910	26 D4
FORESTA	MPA	95389	49 C2
FOREST FALLS	SBD	92339	100 A2
FOREST GLEN	TRI	96030	17 A3
FORESTHILL	PLA	95631	34 D3
FOREST HOME	AMA	95640	40 C2
FOREST KNOLLS	MAR	94933	38 A5
FOREST LAKE	LAK	95461	32 A4
FOREST RANCH	BUT	95942	25 C2
FOREST SPRINGS	NEV	95945	34 C2
FORESTVILLE	SON	95436	37 D2
FORKS OF SALMON	SIS	96031	11 A2
FORREST PARK	LACO	91350	89 C4
FORT BIDWELL	MOD	96112	7 D3
*FORT BRAGG	MEN	95437	22 C5
FORT DICK	DN	95538	1 D3
FORT IRWIN	SBD	92311	82 B3
*FORT JONES	SIS	96032	3 D5
FORT ORD VILLAGE	MON	93941	54 B4
FORT ROSS	SON	95450	37 B1
FORT SEWARD	HUM	95438	16 D5
*FORTUNA	HUM	95540	15 E2
FOSTER	SDCO	92040	V E1
*FOSTER CITY	SMCO	94404	N D1
FOSTER PARK	VEN	93001	88 A5
FOUNTAIN SPRINGS	TUL	93257	68 E4
*FOUNTAIN VALLEY	ORA	92708	T C3
FOUR CORNERS	SHA	96016	13 C4
FOUTS SPRINGS	COL	95979	24 A5
*FOWLER	FRCO	93625	57 D4
FRANKLIN	SAC	95639	39 E2
FRAZIER PARK	KER	93225	88 D1
FREDA	SBD	92280	103 B2
FREDALBA	SBD	92382	99 D1
FREDERICKSBURG	ALP	96120	36 B4
FREDS PLACE	ED	95720	35 D4
FREEDOM	SCR	95019	54 B2
FREEMAN	KER	93527	80 C1
FREEPORT	SAC	95832	39 E2
FREESTONE	SON	95472	37 D2
*FREMONT	ALA	94536	P A2
FREMONT VALLEY	KER	93519	80 B4
FRENCH CAMP	SJCO	95231	40 B5
FRENCH CORRAL	NEV	95975	34 B1
FRENCH GULCH	SHA	96033	18 A1
FRESH POND	ED	95725	35 B4
FRESHWATER	HUM	95504	16 A1
*FRESNO	FRCO	93706	57 C3
FRIANT	FRCO	93626	57 D2
FROGTOWN	CAL	95222	41 B4
FRUITVALE	KER	93308	78 C3
FRUTO	GLE	95988	24 B4
FULLER ACRES	KER	93307	78 E3
*FULLERTON	ORA	92631	T C1
FULTON	SON	95439	37 E1
FURNACE CREEK INN	INY	92328	62 A5
FURNACE CREEK RANCH	INY	92328	62 A5
G			
GALLINAS	MAR	94903	L B3
*GALT	SAC	95632	40 A3
GANNS	CAL	95223	41 D2
GARBERVILLE	HUM	95440	16 C5
*GARDENA	LACO	90247	S C1
GARDEN FARMS	SLO	93422	76 B2
*GARDEN GROVE	ORA	92640	T C2
GARDEN PARK	ED	95633	34 D4
GARDEN VALLEY	ED	95633	34 D4
GARDNERVILLE	DGL		36 C3
GAREY	SB	93454	86 C1
GARFIELD	KER	93240	79 C1
GARLOCK	KER	93519	80 D3
GARNET	RCO	92258	100 C3
GASQUET	DN	95543	2 A3
GAVIOTA	SB	93017	86 D4
GAZELLE	SIS	96034	4 B5

***INDICATES INCORPORATED CITY**

CITIES AND COMMUNITIES INDEX

COMMUNITY NAME	CO.	ZIP CODE	PAGE & GRID
GENESEE	PLU	95983	26 E1
GENOA	DGL		36 B3
GEORGETOWN	ED	95634	34 E3
GERBER	TEH	96035	24 E1
GEYSERVILLE	SON	95441	31 D5
GIANT FOREST	TUL	93271	59 A4
GIBSONVILLE	SIE	95981	26 D3
GILMAN HOT SPRINGS	RCO	92340	99 E3
*GILROY	SCL	95020	54 D2
GISH	SBD	92371	91 A5
GLAMIS	IMP	92248	109 E4
GLASGOW	SBD	92309	83 D5
GLEN AVON	RCO	92509	99 A2
GLENBROOK	DGL		36 A2
GLENBURN	SHA	96036	13 D4
GLENCOE	CAL	95232	41 B2
*GLENDALE	LACO	91201	Q E3
*GLENDORA	LACO	91740	U A1
GLEN ELLEN	SON	95442	38 B2
GLENHAVEN	LAK	95443	31 E3
GLENN	GLE	95943	25 A4
GLENNVILLE	KER	93226	69 A5
GLEN OAKS	SDCO	92001	107 A5
GLEN VALLEY	RCO	92370	99 B3
GLENVIEW	LAK	95451	31 E4
GLENVIEW	LACO	90290	Q A3
GLENVIEW	SDCO	92021	107 A5
GOFFS	SBD	92332	94 E1
GOLDEN HILLS	KER	93561	79 C4
GOLDEN SHORES	MOH	92363	95 E1
GOLDEN VALLEY	WSH		28 B3
GOLD HILL	ED	95651	34 D4
GOLD HILL	STOR		36 D1
GOLD RUN	PLA	95717	34 D2
GOLD SPRINGS	TUO	93570	41 C4
GOLETA	SB	93017	87 B4
*GONZALES	MON	93926	54 E5
GONZALEZ ORTEGA	BAJA		112 C4
GOOD HOPE	RCO	92370	99 B4
GOODSPRINGS	CLK		74 B4
GOODYEARS BAR	SIE	95944	26 D4
GORDONS WELL	IMP		112 A5
GORMAN	LACO	93534	88 E2
GOSHEN	TUL	93227	68 A1
GOTTVILLE	SIS	96050	3 E3
GOVERNMENT FLAT	TEH	95939	23 D2
GRAEAGLE	PLU	96103	27 A3
GRANADA HILLS	LACO	91344	Q A1
*GRAND TERRACE	SBD	92324	99 B2
GRANGEVILLE	KIN	93230	67 D1
GRANITEVILLE	NEV	95959	26 E5
GRANTVILLE	SDCO	92120	V C3
GRAPEVINE	KER	93301	88 D1
*GRASS VALLEY	NEV	95945	34 C1
GRATON	SON	95444	37 D2
GRAVESBORO	FRCO	93657	58 A3
GRAYSON	STA	95363	47 B3
GRAYS WELL	IMP		112 B5
GREELEY HILL	MPA	95311	48 E1
GREENACRES	KER	93308	78 C3
GREEN ACRES	RCO	92343	99 D4
GREENBRAE	MAR	94904	L B3
GREENFIELD	KER	93309	78 D3
*GREENFIELD	MON	93927	65 B1
GREEN POINT	MAR	94947	L B4
GREEN VALLEY	LACO	91350	89 C3
GREEN VALLEY FALLS	SDCO	92016	107 C5
GREEN VALLEY LAKE	SBD	92341	91 D5
GREENVIEW	SIS	96037	3 D5
GREENVILLE	PLU	95947	20 C5
GREENWOOD	ED	95635	34 D3
GRENADA	SIS	96038	4 B4
*GRIDLEY	BUT	95948	25 C5
GRIMES	COL	95950	33 B2
GRIZZLY FLAT	ED	95636	35 B5
GROMMET	SBD	92280	103 C2
GROSSMONT	SDCO	92041	V D3
GROVELAND	TUO	95321	48 E1
*GROVER CITY	SLO	93433	76 A4
GROVERS HOT SPRINGS	ALP	96120	36 B5
*GUADALUPE	SB	93434	76 B5
GUALALA	MEN	95445	30 D4
GUASTI	SBD	91743	U E2
GUATAY	SDCO	92031	107 C5
GUERNEVILLE	SON	95446	37 C2
GUERNEWOOD PARK	SON	95446	37 C2
GUINDA	YOL	95637	32 D4
*GUSTINE	MCO	95322	47 C5
H			
HACIENDA	SON	95436	37 D1
HACIENDA HEIGHTS	LACO	91745	R E5
HAIGHT-ASHBURY	SFCO	94117	142 A4
*HALF MOON BAY	SMCO	94019	N C2
HALLELUJAH JUNCTION	LAS	96135	27 E2
HALLWOOD	YUB	95901	33 D2
HAMBURG	SIS	96045	3 C4
HAMILTON BRANCH	PLU	96137	20 C4
HAMILTON CITY	GLE	95951	24 E3
HAMMOND	TUL	93271	58 E5
HAMMONTON	YUB	95901	33 E2
HAM'S STATION	AMA	95666	41 C1
*HANFORD	KIN	93230	67 D1
HAPPY CAMP	SIS	96039	3 A4
HARBIN SPRINGS	LAK	95461	32 A4
HARBISON CANYON	SDCO	92021	107 A5
HARBOR	CUR		1 D2
HARBOR CITY	LACO	90710	S C2
HARDWICK	KIN	93230	67 D1
HARMONY	SLO	93435	75 C2
HARMONY GROVE	SDCO	92025	106 D3
HARRIS	HUM	95447	16 D5
HARRISBURG	INY	92328	71 C1
HARRISON PARK	SDCO	92036	107 C4
HARTLEY	SOL	95688	39 A2
HART PARK	KER	93306	78 E2
HARVARD	SBD	92365	82 B5
HASKELL CREEK	SIE	96124	27 B3
HAT CREEK	SHA	96040	13 D5
HATFIELD	SIS	96134	5 D2
HAVILAH	KER	93518	79 C2
*HAWAIIAN GARDENS	LACO	90716	T A2
HAWES	SBD	92347	91 B1
HAWKINSVILLE	SIS	96097	4 A4
*HAWTHORNE	LACO	90250	Q D5
HAWTHORNE	MIN		44 B1
HAYFORK	TRI	96041	17 B2
*HAYWARD	ALA	94544	L E5
HAZEL CREEK	SHA	96017	12 C4
*HEALDSBURG	SON	95448	37 D1
HEBER	IMP	92249	112 A3
HECTOR	SBD	92365	92 D2
HELENA	TRI	96042	17 B1
HELENDALE	SBD	92342	91 B2
HELLS GATE	INY	92328	61 E3
HELM	FRCO	93627	57 A5
HENDERSON	CLK		74 E3
HENDERSON VILLAGE	SJCO		40 A4
*HEMET	RCO	92343	99 E4
HENLEY	KLAM		5 C1
HENLEY	SIS	96044	4 A3
HENLEYVILLE	TEH	96021	24 C1
HERALD	SAC	95638	40 B3
*HERCULES	CC	94547	L C3
HERMIT VALLEY	ALP	95314	42 B1
*HERMOSA BEACH	LACO	90254	S A1
HERNANDEZ	SBT	95043	65 E1
HERNDON	FRCO	93711	57 B3
HESPERIA	SBD	92345	91 B4
HESSEL	SON	95472	37 E3
HICKMAN	STA	95323	47 E2
HIDDEN GLEN	SDCO	92001	112 B1
*HIDDEN HILLS	LACO	91302	97 A1
HIDDEN MEADOWS	SDCO	92026	106 D3
HIDDEN VALLEY LAKE	LAK	95461	32 B4
HIDDEN VALLEY	PLA	95650	34 B4
HIGGINS CORNER	NEV	95603	34 C3
HIGHLAND	SBD	92346	99 C1
HIGHLAND PARK	LACO	90042	R A3
HIGHLANDS HARBOR	LAK	95457	32 A3
HIGHTS CORNER	KER	93308	78 C2
HIGHWAY CITY	FRCO	93705	57 C3
HIGHWAY HIGHLANDS	LACO	91214	Q E2
HILLCREST	SHA	96065	13 B5
HILL HAVEN	MAR	94920	L B4
*HILLSBOROUGH	SMCO	94010	N C1
HILMAR	MCO	95324	47 E4
HILT	SIS	96043	4 A2
HINDA	RCO	92353	99 D2
HINKLEY	SBD	92347	91 C1
HOAGLIN	TRI	95495	16 E5
HOBART MILLS	NEV	95734	27 D5
HOBERGS	LAK	95496	31 E4
HODGE	SBD	92342	91 C2
HODSON	CAL	95228	41 A5
HOLLAND	JOS		2 D1
*HOLLISTER	SBT	95023	54 E3
HOLLOW TREE	MEN	95455	22 B2
HOLLYWOOD	LACO	90028	Q D3
HOLLYWOOD BEACH	VEN	93043	96 A1
HOLLYWOOD-BY-THE-SEA	VEN	93043	96 A1
HOLMES	HUM	95569	16 B3
HOLT	SJCO	95234	39 E5
*HOLTVILLE	IMP	92250	109 B5
HOLY CITY	SCL	95026	P B5
HOME GARDENS	RCO	91720	99 A3
HOMELAND	RCO	92348	99 D4
HOMER	SBD	92332	95 B1
HONBY	LACO	91351	89 C4
HONCUT	BUT	95965	33 D1
HONEYDEW	HUM	95545	15 E4
HOOD	SAC	95639	39 D2
HOOPA	HUM	95546	10 C4
HOPE LANDING	SJCO	95686	39 E3
HOPETON	MCO	95369	48 B3
HOPE VLY FOREST CAMP	ALP	96120	36 B5
HOPLAND	MEN	95449	31 B3
HORNBROOK	SIS	96044	4 B3
HORNITOS	MPA	95325	48 E3
HORSE CREEK	SIS	96045	3 C3
HOT SPRINGS	KLAM		6 A1
HOUGH SPRINGS	LAK	95443	32 A2
HOWLAND FLAT	SIE	95981	26 D3
HUASNA	SLO	93420	76 D4
*HUGHSON	STA	95326	47 E2
HULBURD GROVE	SDCO	92016	107 C5
HULLVILLE	LAK	95469	23 C5
HUME	FRCO	93628	58 E3
HUMPHREYS STATION	FRCO	93612	58 A2
*HUNTINGTON BEACH	ORA	92646	T B4
HUNTINGTON LAKE	FRCO	93634	50 B5
*HUNTINGTON PARK	LACO	90255	R A5
HURLETON	BUT	95962	25 E4
*HURON	FRCO	93234	67 A2
HYAMPOM	TRI	96046	16 E2
HYDESVILLE	HUM	95547	15 E2
I			
IBIS	SBD	92332	95 C1
IDYLLWILD	RCO	92349	100 B4
IDYLWILD	SCL	95030	P B4
IGNACIO	MAR	94947	L B2
IGO	SHA	96047	18 B3
ILLINOIS VALLEY	JOS		2 C2
*IMPERIAL	IMP	92251	109 A5
*IMPERIAL BEACH	SDCO	92032	V B5
IMPERIAL GABLES	IMP	92266	110 A3
INCA	RCO	92255	103 C4
INCLINE	MPA	95318	49 C2
INCLINE VILLAGE	WSH		36 A1
INDEPENDENCE	CAL	95245	41 B2
INDEPENDENCE	INY	93526	60 A3
INDIAN FALLS	PLU	95952	26 C1
INDIAN SPRINGS	SDCO	92035	112 A1
*INDIAN WELLS	RCO	92260	100 E4
*INDIO	RCO	92201	101 A4
*INDUSTRY	LACO	91744	R E4
*INGLEWOOD	LACO	90301	Q D5
INGOT	SHA	96008	18 E1
INSKIP	BUT	95921	25 D1
INVERNESS	MAR	94937	37 D4
INWOOD	SHA	96088	19 A2
INYOKERN	KER	93527	80 D1
*IONE	AMA	95640	40 D2
IOWA HILL	PLA	95713	34 D2
*IRVINE	ORA	92715	T E4
IRVING'S CREST	SDCO	92065	107 A4
IRVINGTON	ALA	94538	P A2
IRWIN	MCO	95380	47 E4
*IRWINDALE	LACO	91706	R E3
ISLA VISTA	SB	93017	87 B4
*ISLETON	SAC	95641	M D2
IVANHOE	TUL	93235	68 B1
IVANPAH	SBD	92364	84 C3
J			
*JACKSON	AMA	95642	40 E2
JACKSON GATE	AMA	95642	40 E2
JACUMBA	SDCO	92034	111 B4
JAMACHA	SDCO	92035	106 E4
JAMESBURG	MON	93924	64 D1
JAMESON	RCO	91720	99 A3
JAMESTOWN	TUO	95327	41 C5
JAMUL	SDCO	92035	112 A1
JANESVILLE	LAS	96114	21 A4
JARBO GAP	BUT	95916	25 D3
JENNER-BY-THE-SEA	SON	95450	37 B2
JENNY LIND	CAL	95252	40 D4
JESMOND DENE	SDCO	92026	106 D3
JIMGREY	SBD	93516	81 A5
JIMTOWN	SON	95959	31 E5
JOHANNESBURG	KER	93528	80 D3
JOHNSONDALE	TUL	93236	69 C4
JOHNSON PARK	SHA	96013	13 C5
JOHNSONS	HUM	95546	10 B2
JOHNSTONVILLE	LAS	96130	21 A3
JOHNSTOWN	SDCO	92021	107 A5
JOHNSVILLE	PLU	95921	26 E3
JOLON	MON	93928	65 B4
JONESVILLE	BUT	95921	19 E5
JOSHUA	SBD	92364	84 B3
JOSHUA TREE	SBD	92252	100 E1
JULIAN	SDCO	92036	107 C3
JUNCTION CITY	TRI	96048	17 C1
JUNE LAKE	MNO	93529	50 D1
JUNE LAKE JUNCTION	MNO	93529	50 D1
JUNIPER HILLS	LACO	93543	90 B4
JUNIPER LAKE RESORT	LAS	96020	20 A3
K			
KAGEL CANYON	LACO	91342	Q D1
KANE SPRING	IMP	92227	108 D3
KARNAK	SUT	95676	33 C4
KAWEAH	TUL	93237	58 E5
KEARNEY PARK	FRCO	93706	57 B3
KEARNY MESA	SDCO		V B2
KEARSARGE	INY	93526	60 A3
KEDDIE	PLU	95952	26 C1
KEELER	INY	93530	60 C5
KEENE	KER	93531	79 B4
KELLOGG	SON	94515	31 E5
KELSEY	ED	95643	34 D4
KELSEYVILLE	LAK	95451	31 D3
KELSO	SBD	92351	83 E5
KENO	KLAM		5 A1
KENSINGTON	CC	94708	L D3
KENSINGTON	SDCO	92116	V C3
KENTFIELD	MAR	94904	L A3
KENTWOOD IN THE PINES	SDCO	92036	107 C4
KENWOOD	SON	95452	38 B2
KEOUGH HOT SPRINGS	INY	93514	51 D4
KERBY	JOS		2 D1
KERCKOFF POWERHOUSE	FRCO	93602	57 E1
KERENS	SBD	92309	83 D5
*KERMAN	FRCO	93630	57 A3
KERN CITY	KER	93309	78 D3
KERNVALE	KER	93240	79 C1
KERNVILLE	KER	93238	69 C5
KESWICK	SHA	96001	18 B2
KETTLEMAN CITY	KIN	93239	67 B3
KEYES	STA	95328	47 D3
KILKARE	ALA	94586	P B1
*KING CITY	MON	93930	65 C2
KING COLE	KLAM		4 D1
KINGS BEACH	PLA	95719	36 A1
*KINGSBURG	FRCO	93631	57 D5
KINGSBURY	DGL		36 B3
KINGS MOUNTAIN PARK	SMCO	94062	N C3
KINGSTON	SBD	92309	73 E5
KINGSVILLE	ED	95623	34 D5
KINGVALE	NEV	95728	35 C1
KINSLEY	MPA	95311	49 A5
KIRKVILLE	SUT	95645	33 B3
KIRKWOOD	ALP	95646	36 A5
KIRKWOOD	TEH	96021	24 D2
KIT CARSON	AMA	95644	35 E5
KLAMATH	DN	95548	2 A5
*KLAMATH FALLS	KLAM		5 B1
KLAMATH GLEN	DN	95548	2 A5
KLAMATH RIVER	SIS	96050	3 D3
KLAU	SLO	93465	75 D1
KLONDIKE	SBD	92304	93 C3
KNEELAND	HUM	95549	16 B1
KNIGHTSEN	CC	94548	M D3
KNIGHTS FERRY	STA	95367	48 A1
KNIGHTS LANDING	YOL	95645	33 C4
KNOB	SHA	96076	17 C3
KNOWLES	MAD	93653	49 B5
KNOWLES CORNER	SON	95472	37 D2
KNOXVILLE	NAPA	95637	32 C4
KONO TAYEE	LAK	95458	31 E3
KORBEL	HUM	95550	10 B5
KORBEL	SON	95446	37 D1
KRAMER	SBD	93516	80 E5
KYBURZ	ED	95720	35 D4
L			
LA BARR MEADOWS	NEV	95945	34 C2
*LA CANADA FLINTRIDGE	LACO	91011	R B2
LA CONCHITA	VEN	93001	87 E5
LA COSTA	SDCO	92008	106 C3
LA CRESCENTA	LACO	91214	R A2
LADERA	SMCO	94025	N D3
*LAFAYETTE	CC	94549	L E4
LA GRANGE	STA	95329	48 C2
*LAGUNA BEACH	ORA	92651	T E5
LAGUNA HILLS	ORA	92653	98 D5
LAGUNITAS	MAR	94938	38 A5
*LA HABRA	ORA	90631	R E5
*LA HABRA HEIGHTS	LACO	90631	R D5
LA HONDA	SMCO	94020	45 D4
LA HONDA PARK	CAL	94020	41 B4
LAIRDS CORNER	TUL	93257	68 B3
LA JOLLA	SDCO	92037	105 G3
LA JOLLA AMAGO	SDCO	92061	107 A2
LAKE ALPINE	ALP	95235	42 A1
LAKE ARROWHEAD	SBD	92352	91 C5
LAKE BERRYESSA ESTATES	NAPA	94567	32 C5
LAKE CITY	MOD	96115	7 D5
LAKE CITY	NEV	95959	26 D5
*LAKE ELSINORE	RCO	92330	99 B4
LAKE FOREST	ORA	92630	98 D4
LAKE FOREST	PLA	95730	35 E2
LAKE HAVASU CITY	MOH		96 B4
LAKEHEAD	SHA	96051	12 C5
LAKE HENSHAW	SDCO	92070	107 B3
LAKE HILLS EST	ED	95630	34 C5
LAKE HUGHES	LACO	93532	89 C3
LAKE ISABELLA	KER	93240	79 C1
LAKE OF THE WOODS	KER	93225	88 C2
*LAKEPORT	LAK	95453	31 D3
LAKESHORE	FRCO	93634	50 C5
LAKESHORE	SHA	96051	12 B5
LAKESIDE	SDCO	92040	V E2
LAKESIDE PARK	LACO	91304	97 B1
LAKE TAMARISK	RCO	92239	102 C4
*LAKEVIEW	LAKE		7 C1
LAKEVIEW	RCO	92353	99 D3
LAKEVIEW	SDCO	92040	107 A5
LAKEVIEW HOT SPRINGS	RCO	92370	99 C3
LAKEVIEW TERRACE	LACO	91340	Q D1
LAKEVILLE	SON	95452	L B1
*LAKEWOOD	LACO	90712	S E2
LA LOMA	STA	95354	47 D2
*LA MESA	SDCO	92041	V D3
*LA MIRADA	LACO	90638	T B1
LA MOINE	SHA	96017	12 C4
LAMONT	KER	93241	78 E3
LANARE	FRCO	93656	57 B5
*LANCASTER	LACO	93534	90 A3
LANDERS	SBD	92284	92 E5
LANGELL VALLEY	KLAM		6 B2
*LA PALMA	ORA	90623	T B2
LA PLAYA	SDCO	92106	V A3
LA PORTE	PLU	95981	26 C3
LA PRESA	SDCO	92077	V E4
*LA PUENTE	LACO	91744	R E4
*LA QUINTA	RCO	92253	100 E4
*LARKSPUR	MAR	94939	L A3
LAS CRUCES	SB	93017	86 D4
LA SIERRA	RCO	92505	99 A3
LAS LOMAS	SON	95728	31 B5
LAS VEGAS	CLK	89114	74 D2
LATHROP	SJCO	95330	47 B1
LATON	FRCO	93242	57 D5
LATROBE	ED	95682	40 C1
LAUGHLIN	CLK		85 D4
LAUREL HEIGHTS	SFCO	94118	141 E3
*LA VERNE	LACO	91750	U B2
LAVIC	SBD	92365	92 E2
*LAWNDALE	LACO	90260	S B1
LAYTONVILLE	MEN	95454	22 D3
LEBEC	KER	93243	88 D1
LEESVILLE	COL	95987	32 B2
LEE VINING	MNO	93541	43 C5
LEGGETT	MEN	95455	22 C2
LE GRAND	MCO	95333	48 D5
LELITER	KER	93527	70 D5
LEMONCOVE	TUL	93244	68 D1
*LEMON GROVE	SDCO	92045	V D3
LEMON VALLEY	WSH	96109	28 B3
*LEMOORE	KIN	93245	67 C1
LENWOOD	SBD	92311	91 D1
LEON	SBD	92392	91 B3
LEONA VALLEY	LACO	93550	89 D3
LEUCADIA	SDCO	92024	106 B3
LEWISTON	TRI	96052	17 D1

*INDICATES INCORPORATED CITY

CITIES AND COMMUNITIES INDEX

COMMUNITY NAME	CO.	ZIP CODE	PAGE & GRID
LIBERTY FARMS	SOL	95647	39 C3
LIDO ISLE	ORA	92663	T C4
LIKELY	MOD	96116	8 B3
LINCOLN	JKSN		4 C2
*LINCOLN	PLA	95648	34 A3
LINCOLN ACRES	SDCO	92050	V D4
LINCOLN VILLAGE	SJCO	95207	40 A5
LINDA	YUB	95961	33 D2
LINDA MAR	SMCO	94044	N B1
LINDA VISTA	SDCO	92111	V B3
LINDCOVE	TUL	93221	68 C1
LINDEN	SJCO	95236	40 C5
*LINDSAY	TUL	93247	68 D2
LINGARD	MCO	95340	48 C5
LITCHFIELD	LAS	96117	21 C3
LITTLE BORREGO	SDCO	92004	108 A3
LITTLE LAKE	INY	93542	70 C4
LITTLE RIVER	MEN	95456	30 B1
LITTLEROCK	LACO	93543	90 B3
LITTLE SHASTA	SIS	96064	4 C4
LITTLE VALLEY	LAS	96053	14 B5
LIVE OAK	SAC	95683	40 C2
*LIVE OAK	SUT	95953	33 C1
LIVE OAK PARK	SDCO	92028	106 C2
LIVE OAK SPRINGS	SDCO	92005	112 E1
*LIVERMORE	ALA	94550	M C5
*LIVINGSTON	MCO	95334	48 A4
LLANADA	SBT	95043	55 D4
LOCH LOMOND	LAK	95426	31 E4
LOCKE	SAC	95649	39 D3
LOCKEFORD	SJCO	95237	40 B4
LOCKWOOD	MON	93932	65 C4
LOCKWOOD VALLEY	VEN	93225	88 C2
LODGE POLE	TUL	93271	59 B4
*LODI	SJCO	95240	40 A4
LODOGA	COL	95979	32 B1
LOGAN HEIGHTS	SDCO	92113	V B4
LOG CABIN	YUB	95922	26 C5
LOG SPRING	TEH	96074	14 E4
LOLETA	HUM	95551	15 E2
*LOMA LINDA	SBD	92354	99 C2
LOMA MAR	SMCO	94021	N C4
LOMA PARK	KER	93306	78 E3
LOMA RICA	YUB	95901	33 E1
LOMA VERDE	MAR	94947	L A2
*LOMITA	LACO	90717	S C2
LOMO	BUT	95942	25 C1
*LOMPOC	SB	93436	86 B3
LONDON	TUL	93631	58 A5
LONE PINE	INY	93545	60 B4
LONG BARN	TUO	95335	41 E4
*LONG BEACH	LACO	90801	S D3
LONGVALE	MEN	95490	22 E4
LONGVIEW	LACO	93553	90 C4
LOOKOUT	MOD	96054	14 B3
*LOOMIS	PLA	95650	34 B4
LOOMIS CORNERS	SHA	96003	18 C2
LORAINE	KER	93518	79 D3
LORELLA	KLAM		6 A1
*LOS ALAMITOS	ORA	90720	T A2
LOS ALAMOS	SB	93440	86 C2
*LOS ALTOS	SCL	94022	N E3
*LOS ALTOS HILLS	SCL	94022	N E3
*LOS ANGELES	LACO	90001	R A4
*LOS BANOS	MCO	93635	55 E1
*LOS GATOS	SCL	95030	P A4
LOS MOLINOS	TEH	96055	24 E1
LOS OLIVOS	SB	93441	86 E3
LOS OSOS	SLO	93401	75 E3
LOS RANCHITOS	MAR	94903	L A3
LOS SERRANOS	SBD	91710	U C3
LOST HILLS	KER	93249	77 D1
LOS TRANCOS WOODS	SMCO	94025	N D3
LOTUS	ED	95651	34 D4
LOVELOCK	BUT	95978	25 D2
LOWER LAKE	LAK	95457	32 A4
*LOYALTON	SIE	96118	27 C3
LUCERNE	LAK	95458	31 D2
LUCERNE VALLEY	SBD	92356	91 E4
LUCIA	MON	93920	64 D3
LUDLOW	SBD	92357	93 B2
LUGO	SBD	92345	91 B4
LUNDY	MNO	93541	43 B4
LUNING	MIN		44 E1
*LYNWOOD	LACO	90262	S D1
LYNWOOD HILLS	SDCO	92010	V D4
LYONSVILLE	TEH	96075	19 C4
LYTTON	SON	95448	31 D5
M			
MACDOEL	SIS	96058	4 E3
MADELINE	LAS	96119	8 B4
*MADERA	MAD	93637	57 A2
MADISON	YOL	95653	33 A5
MAD RIVER	TRI	95552	16 E3
MADRONE	SCL	95037	P D5
MAGALIA	BUT	95954	25 C2
MAGUNDEN	KER	93306	78 E3
MALAGA	FRCO	93725	57 D4
MALIBU BEACH	LACO	90265	97 B2
MALIN	KLAM		5 E2
*MAMMOTH LAKES	MNO	93546	50 D2
MANCHESTER	MEN	95459	30 C3
*MANHATTAN BEACH	LACO	90266	S A1
MANIX	SBD	92365	82 C5
MANKAS CORNER	SOL	94533	L E1
*MANTECA	SJCO	95336	47 B1
MANTON	TEH	96059	19 A3
MANZANITA	SDCO	92005	111 A4
MAPLE CREEK	HUM	95550	16 B1
MARCH FIELD	RCO	92508	99 C3
*MARICOPA	KER	93252	78 A5
*MARINA	MON	93933	54 B4
MARINA	SFCO	94123	142 B1
MARINA DEL REY	LACO	90291	Q B5
MARIN CITY	MAR	94965	L B4
MARINWOOD	MAR	94903	L A3
MARIPOSA	MPA	95338	49 B3
MARIPOSA PINES	MPA	95338	49 B2
MARKLEEVILLE	ALP	96120	36 C5
MARK WEST SPRINGS	SON	95492	37 E1
MARSHALL STATION	FRCO	93651	57 E2
MARTELL	AMA	95654	40 E2
*MARTINEZ	CC	94553	L E3
MARTINS FERRY	HUM	95556	10 C3
MAR VISTA	LACO	90066	Q C4
*MARYSVILLE	YUB	95901	33 D2
MASONIC	MNO	93517	43 C2
MATHER	TUO	95339	42 B5
MAXWELL	COL	95955	32 D1
MAYFAIR	KER	93307	78 E3
*MAYWOOD	LACO	90270	R A4
MCARTHUR	SHA	96056	13 E4
MCCANN	HUM	95569	16 B4
MCCAULEY	MPA	93518	49 C2
MCCLOUD	SIS	96057	12 D2
*MCFARLAND	KER	93250	78 B1
MCKAYS POINT	TUL	93286	68 D1
MCKEE BRIDGE	JKSN		3 C1
MCKINLEYVILLE	HUM	95521	9 E4
MCKITTRICK	KER	93251	77 D3
MCMULLIN	FRCO	93706	57 B4
MEADOW LAKES	FRCO	93602	58 A1
MEADOW VALLEY	PLU	95956	26 B2
MEADOW VISTA	PLA	95722	34 C3
MECCA	RCO	92254	101 C5
MEEKS BAY	ED	95723	35 E2
MEINERS OAKS	VEN	93023	88 A4
MELOLAND	IMP	92243	112 B3
MENDOCINO	MEN	95460	30 B1
MENDOCINO COAST	MEN	95459	30 C3
*MENDOTA	FRCO	93640	56 D3
*MENLO PARK	SMCO	94025	N D2
MENTONE	SBD	92359	99 D2
*MERCED	MCO	95340	48 C4
MERCED FALLS	MCO	95369	48 D3
MERCEY HOT SPRINGS	FRCO	95043	55 E4
MERIDIAN	SUT	95957	33 B2
*MERRILL	KLAM		5 D2
MESA GRANDE	SDCO	92070	107 B3
MESAVILLE	RCO	92255	103 C4
MESQUITE SPRING	INY	92328	61 B2
METTLER	KER	93301	78 E5
MEXICALI	BAJA		112 B4
MEYERS	ED	95731	36 A4
MICHIGAN BLUFF	PLA	95631	35 A2
MIDDLE RIVER	SJCO	95234	39 D5
MIDDLETOWN	LAK	95461	32 A5
MIDLAND	KLAM		5 B1
MIDLAND	RCO	92255	103 B3
MIDPINES	MPA	95345	49 B3
MIDWAY	ALA	94550	M E5
MIDWAY	SHA	96088	19 A2
MIDWAY WELL	IMP		112 E3
MILFORD	LAS	96121	21 C5
*MILLBRAE	SMCO	94030	N C1
MILL CREEK	TEH	96061	19 D4
MILLERS CORNER	MAD	93614	57 C1
MILLIGAN	SBD	92280	94 D5
MILLS ORCHARDS	COL	95955	32 C1
*MILL VALLEY	MAR	94942	L A3
MILLVILLE	SHA	96062	18 D2
MILO	TUL	93265	68 E2
*MILPITAS	SCL	95035	P B3
MILTON	CAL	95230	40 E4
MINA	MIN		44 D2
*MINDEN	DGL		36 C3
MINERAL	TEH	96063	19 C4
MINERAL KING	TUL	93271	59 B5
MINKLER	FRCO	93657	58 A3
MINNEOLA	SBD	92327	92 B1
MINNESOTA	SHA	96001	18 B2
MINTER VILLAGE	KER	93301	78 C2
MIRABEL PARK	SON	95436	37 D2
MIRACLE HOT SPRINGS	KER	93288	79 C1
MIRA LOMA	RCO	91752	98 E2
MIRAMAR	SDCO	92145	V B1
MIRAMAR	SMCO	94019	N B2
MIRA MESA	SDCO	92126	V B1
MIRA MONTE	VEN	93023	88 A4
MIRAMONTE	FRCO	93641	58 C3
MIRANDA	HUM	95553	16 C4
MIRA VISTA	LAK	95461	31 E4
MISSION BEACH	SDCO	92109	V A3
MISSION HIGHLANDS	SON	95476	38 B3
MISSION HILLS	SDCO	92103	V B3
MISSION SAN JOSE	ALA	94538	P B2
MISSION VIEJO	ORA	92675	98 D5
MISSION VILLAGE	SDCO	92123	V C2
MITCHELL MILL	CAL	95255	41 B2
MI-WUK VILLAGE	TUO	95346	41 E4
MOCCASIN	TUO	95347	48 D1
*MODESTO	STA	95350	47 D2
MODJESKA	ORA	92705	98 E4
MOJAVE	KER	93501	80 A5
MOKELUMNE HILL	CAL	95245	41 A3
MONMOUTH	FRCO	93725	57 C4
MONO CAMP	MPA	95338	49 B3
MONO CITY	MNO	93541	43 C4
MONO HOT SPRINGS	FRCO	93642	50 D4
MONO LAKE	MNO	93541	43 C5
MONOLITH	KER	93548	79 D4
MONO VISTA	TUO	95370	41 D4
*MONROVIA	LACO	91016	R D3
MONSON	TUL	93618	58 B5
*MONTAGUE	SIS	96064	4 B4
MONTALVO	VEN	93003	88 B5
MONTARA	SMCO	94037	N B2
*MONTCLAIR	SBD	91763	U C2
*MONTEBELLO	LACO	90640	R C4
MONTECITO	SB	93108	87 D4
MONTE MARIA	MAR	94947	L A2
*MONTEREY	MON	93940	54 B4
MONTEREY HILLS	LACO	90032	R B3
*MONTEREY PARK	LACO	91754	R B4
MONTE RIO	SON	95462	37 C2
MONTESANO	SON	95462	37 C2
*MONTE SERENO	SCL	95030	P A4
MONTEZUMA	SOL	94512	39 B4
MONTGOMERY CREEK	SHA	96065	13 A5
MONTROSE	LACO	91020	Q E2
MOONRIDGE	SBD	92315	92 A5
MOONSTONE	HUM	95570	9 E4
MOORE	SBD	92364	84 D2
*MOORPARK	VEN	93021	88 D5
MOORPARK HOME ACRES	VEN	93021	88 D5
*MORAGA	CC	94556	L E4
MORENA VILLAGE	SDCO	92110	112 D1
MORENO	SDCO	92040	107 A5
*MORENO VALLEY	RCO	92360	99 D3
MORETTIS	SDCO	92070	107 B3
*MORGAN HILL	SCL	95037	P D5
MORMON BAR	MPA	95338	49 B3
MORONGO VALLEY	SBD	92256	100 C2
*MORRO BAY	SLO	93442	75 E3
MOSS BEACH	SMCO	94038	N B2
MOSS LANDING	MON	95036	54 B3
MOUNTAIN CENTER	RCO	92361	100 B4
MOUNTAIN GATE	SHA	96003	18 C1
MOUNTAIN HOME VILLAGE	SBD	92359	99 E1
MOUNTAIN MESA	KER	93240	79 D1
MOUNTAIN RANCH	CAL	95246	41 B3
MOUNTAIN REST	FRCO	93667	58 B1
MOUNTAIN SPRINGS	CLK		74 A3
MOUNTAIN VIEW	RCO	92509	99 A2
*MOUNTAIN VIEW	SCL	94040	N E3
MOUNT AUKUM	ED	95656	40 E1
MOUNT BALDY VILLAGE	SBD	91759	90 E5
MOUNT BULLION	MPA	95338	49 A3
MOUNT HEBRON	SIS	96066	5 A4
MOUNT HELIX	SDCO	92041	V D3
MOUNT HERMON	SCR	95041	P A5
MOUNT LAGUNA	SDCO	92048	107 E5
*MOUNT SHASTA	SIS	96067	12 C2
MOUNT SIGNAL	IMP	92231	112 A4
MT VIEW	JKSN		4 C1
MOUNT WILSON	LACO	91023	R C2
MUGGINSVILLE	SIS	96032	3 C5
MUIR BEACH	MAR	94965	L A4
MURPHYS	CAL	95247	41 C4
MURPHYS RANCH	CAL	95247	41 C4
MURRIETA	RCO	92362	99 C5
MURRIETA HOT SPRINGS	RCO	92362	99 C5
MUSCOY	SBD	92405	99 B1
MYERS FLAT	HUM	95554	16 B4
MYOMA	RCO	92201	101 A4
N			
NAIRN	MCO	95340	48 B4
NANCEVILLE	TUL	93257	68 D3
*NAPA	NAPA	94558	L D1
NAPLES	LACO	90803	S E3
NAPLES	SB	93117	87 A4
NASHVILLE	ED	95675	40 E1
*NATIONAL CITY	SDCO	92050	V C4
NATOMA	SAC	95630	34 B5
NAVARRO	MEN	95463	30 D2
NAVELENCIA	FRCO	93654	58 A4
*NEEDLES	SBD	92363	95 D2
NEENACH	LACO	93534	89 B2
NELSON	BUT	95958	25 B4
NESTOR	SDCO	92154	V C5
*NEVADA CITY	NEV	95959	34 C1
NEW ALMADEN	SCL	95042	P C4
*NEWARK	ALA	94560	P A2
NEW AUBERRY	FRCO	93602	57 E1
NEWBERRY SPRINGS	SBD	92365	92 B2
NEWBURY PARK	VEN	91320	96 D1
NEWCASTLE	PLA	95658	34 C4
NEW CUYAMA	SB	93214	87 C1
NEW DUNN	SBD	92309	82 D5
NEWELL	MOD	96134	5 E3
NEWHALL	LACO	91321	89 C5
NEWHALL RANCH	LACO	91355	89 B4
NEW IDAHO	LAKE		7 B1
NEW IDRIA	SBT	95027	66 A1
*NEWMAN	STA	95360	47 C4
NEW PINE CREEK	MOD	97635	7 C2
*NEWPORT BEACH	ORA	92660	T C4
NEWTOWN	ED	95709	35 A5
NEWVILLE	GLE	95963	24 B3
NEW WASHOE CITY	WSH	95611	36 C1
NICASIO	MAR	94946	37 E4
NICE	LAK	95464	31 D2
NICHOLLS WARM SPRINGS	RCO	92225	103 C5
NICHOLS	CC	94565	39 A4
NICOLAUS	SUT	95659	33 D3
NILAND	IMP	92257	109 B2
NIPINNAWASSEE	MAD	93601	49 C4
NIPOMO	SLO	93444	76 C5
NIPTON	SBD	92364	84 C2
NIXON	WSH	96109	28 E2
NOB HILL	SFCO	94108	142 D2
NOE VALLEY	SFCO	94114	142 A5
*NORCO	RCO	91760	U E4
NORD	BUT	95926	25 A3
NORDEN	NEV	95724	35 C1
NORMAN	GLE	95988	24 D5
NORTH BEACH	SFCO	94133	142 D1
NORTH BLOOMFIELD	NEV	95959	26 D5
NORTH COLUMBIA	NEV	95959	26 C5
NORTH EDWARDS	KER	93523	80 D5
NORTH FORK	MAD	93643	49 E5
NORTH HIGHLANDS	SAC	95660	34 A5
NORTH HOLLYWOOD	LACO	91601	Q C2
NORTH JAMUL	SDCO	92035	112 A1
NORTH LAS VEGAS	CLK		74 D2
NORTH LONG BEACH	LACO	90805	S D2
NORTH RICHMOND	CC	94807	L C3
NORTHRIDGE	LACO	91324	Q B2
NORTH SAN JUAN	NEV	95960	26 B5
NORTH SHORE	RCO	92254	101 D5
NORTHSTAR	PLA	95732	35 E1
NORTHWOOD	SON	95462	37 C2
NORTON AFB	SBD	92409	99 C1
*NORWALK	LACO	90650	T A1
*NOVATO	MAR	94947	L A2
NOYO	MEN	95437	22 C5
NUBIEBER	LAS	96068	14 B3
NUEVO	RCO	92367	99 D3
NYLAND	VEN	93030	88 C5
O			
*OAKDALE	STA	95361	47 D1
OAK GLEN	SBD	92399	99 E2
OAK GROVE VALLEY	SDCO	92086	107 B1
OAKGROVE	TUL	93271	59 A5
OAKHURST	MAD	93644	49 D4
*OAKLAND	ALA	94601	L D4
OAKLEY	CC	94561	M D3
OAK RUN	SHA	96069	18 E1
OAK VIEW	VEN	93022	88 A4
OAKVILLE	NAPA	94562	38 B2
OASIS	RCO	92274	108 B1
OATMAN	MOH		85 E5
OBRIEN	JOS		2 C2
O'BRIEN	SHA	96070	12 C5
OCCIDENTAL	SON	95465	37 C2
OCEAN BEACH	SDCO	92107	V A3
OCEANO	SLO	93445	76 B5
*OCEANSIDE	SDCO	92054	106 B3
OCEAN VIEW	SON	95450	37 C2
OCOTILLO	IMP	92259	111 C3
OCOTILLO WELLS	SDCO	92004	108 B3
OGILBY	IMP	92222	110 B5
OILDALE	KER	93308	78 D2
*OJAI	VEN	93023	88 B4
OLANCHA	INY	93549	70 B1
OLD BOULEVARD	SDCO	92005	111 A4
OLD RIVER	KER	93307	78 C3
OLD STATION	SHA	96071	19 D1
OLD TOWN	LAS	96137	20 C4
OLEMA	MAR	94950	37 E4
OLENE	KLAM		5 C1
OLINDA	ORA	92621	T D1
OLINDA	SHA	96007	18 C3
OLINGHOUSE	WSH		28 E3
OLIVEHURST	YUB	95961	33 D2
OLIVENHAIN	SDCO	92067	106 C4
OLIVE VIEW	LACO	91342	Q C1
OMO RANCH	ED	95661	41 B1
O'NEALS	MAD	93645	57 D1
ONO	SHA	96072	18 A3
*ONTARIO	SBD	91761	U D2
ONYX	KER	93255	69 E5
OPHIR	PLA	95603	34 C4
*ORANGE	ORA	92666	T D2
*ORANGE COVE	FRCO	93646	58 B4
ORANGEVALE	SAC	95662	34 B5
ORCHARD SHORES	LAK	95423	32 A3
ORCUTT	SB	93455	86 C1
ORDBEND	GLE	95943	25 A3
OREGON HOUSE	YUB	95962	26 A5
ORICK	HUM	95555	10 A2
*ORINDA	CC	94563	L E4
ORINDA VILLAGE	CC	94563	45 D1
*ORLAND	GLE	95963	24 D3
ORLEANS	HUM	95556	10 D2
ORO FINO	SIS	96032	3 D5
ORO GRANDE	SBD	92368	91 B3
ORO LOMA	FRCO	93622	56 A2
OROSI	TUL	93647	58 B4
*OROVILLE	BUT	95965	25 C4
ORR SPRINGS	MEN	95482	31 A1
OTAY	SDCO	92011	V C5
OUTINGDALE	ED	95684	34 E5
OWL	RCO	92220	100 A3
*OXNARD	VEN	93030	96 B1
P			
PACHECO	CC	94553	L E3
*PACIFICA	SMCO	94044	N B1
PACIFIC BEACH	SDCO	92109	V A2
*PACIFIC GROVE	MON	93950	54 A4
PACIFIC HEIGHTS	SFCO	94115	142 B2
PACIFIC HOUSE	ED	95725	35 B4
PACIFIC PALISADES	LACO	90272	Q B4
PACOIMA	LACO	91331	Q C1
PAHRUMP	NYE		73 C2
PAICINES	SBT	95043	55 B3
PAINTERSVILLE	SAC	95615	39 D3
PAJARO	MON	95076	54 C2
PALA	SDCO	92059	106 D2
PALA MESA VILLAGE	SDCO	92028	106 D2
PALERMO	BUT	95968	25 D5
PALISADES HIGHLANDS	LACO	90272	Q B4

*INDICATES INCORPORATED CITY

CITIES

CITIES AND COMMUNITIES INDEX

COMMUNITY NAME	CO.	ZIP CODE	PAGE & GRID
PALM CITY	SDCO	92154	V C5
*PALMDALE	LACO	93550	90 A3
PALMDALE EAST	LACO	93550	90 A3
*PALM DESERT	RCO	92260	100 D4
PALMS	LACO	90034	Q C4
*PALM SPRINGS	RCO	92262	100 D3
*PALO ALTO	SCL	94301	N E2
PALO CEDRO	SHA	96073	18 D2
PALOMA	CAL	95252	40 E3
PALOMAR MOUNTAIN	SDCO	92060	107 A2
*PALOS VERDES ESTATES	LACO	90274	S A2
PALO VERDE	IMP	92266	110 C1
PALO VERDE	SDCO	92001	107 B5
PANAMA	KER	93309	78 D3
PANAMINT SPRINGS	INY	93545	71 A1
PANOCHE	SBT	95043	55 D4
PANORAMA CITY	LACO	91402	Q C2
*PARADISE	BUT	95969	25 C3
PARADISE CAY	MAR	94920	38 B5
PARADISE VALLEY	SCL	95037	P D5
PARAISO SPRINGS	MON	93960	64 E1
*PARAMOUNT	LACO	90723	S E1
PARKFIELD	MON	93451	66 C4
PARKER	LPAZ		104 B1
PARK VILLAGE	INY	92328	62 A5
*PARLIER	FRCO	93648	57 E4
*PASADENA	LACO	91101	R B3
PASKENTA	TEH	96074	24 B2
PASO PICACHO	SDCO	92036	107 C4
*PASO ROBLES	SLO	93446	76 A1
PATRICK CREEK	DN	95543	2 B3
*PATTERSON	STA	95363	47 B3
PATTON	SBD	92346	99 C1
PATTON VILLAGE	LAS	96113	21 D5
PAUMA VALLEY	SDCO	92061	106 E2
PAYNES CREEK	TEH	96075	19 B4
PAYNESVILLE	ALP	96120	36 B4
PEANUT	TRI	96041	17 B3
PEARBLOSSOM	LACO	93553	90 C4
PEARDALE	NEV	95945	34 C1
PEARLAND	LACO	93550	90 B3
PEARSONVILLE	INY	93542	70 C5
PEBBLE BEACH	MON	93953	54 A4
PECWAN	HUM	95546	10 B2
PEDLEY	RCO	92509	99 A2
PELICAN CITY	KLAM		5 B1
PENNGROVE	SON	94951	38 A3
PENNINGTON	SUT	95953	33 C1
PENTZ	BUT	95965	25 D3
PEPPERWOOD	HUM	95565	16 A3
PERKINS	SAC	95826	39 E1
*PERRIS	RCO	92370	99 C4
PESCADERO	SMCO	94060	N C4
*PETALUMA	SON	94952	L A1
PETER PAM	TUO	95335	41 E4
PETERS	SJCO	95236	40 C5
PETROLIA	HUM	95558	15 D4
PHILLIPS	ED	95735	35 E4
PHILLIPSVILLE	HUM	95558	16 B5
PHILO	MEN	95466	30 E3
PICACHO	IMP	92222	110 D4
*PICO RIVERA	LACO	90660	R C4
*PIEDMONT	ALA	94611	L D4
PIERCY	MEN	95467	22 C1
PIKE	SIE	95922	26 C5
PILOT HILL	ED	95664	34 C4
PINE COVE	RCO	92349	100 B4
PINECREST	TUO	95364	42 A3
PINEDALE	FRCO	93650	57 C3
PINE FLAT	TUL	93207	69 B4
PINE GROVE	AMA	95665	41 A2
PINE GROVE	LAK	95426	31 E4
PINE GROVE	MEN	95460	30 B1
PINE GROVE	SHA	96003	18 C2
PINE HILLS	SDCO	92036	107 C4
PINEHURST	FRCO	93641	58 D3
PINEHURST	JKSN		4 C1
PINELAND	PLA	95718	35 E2
PINE MEADOW	RCO	92361	100 C5
PINE MOUNTAIN CLUB	KER	93225	88 B1
PINE RIDGE	FRCO	93602	58 B1
PINE VALLEY	SDCO	92062	107 D5
PINNACLE	SBD	93562	81 B1
PINO GRANDE	ED	95634	35 A4
*PINOLE	CC	94564	L C3
PINOLE ESTATES	CC	94564	L D3
PINON PINES	KER	93225	88 C1
PINYON PINES	RCO	92361	100 D5
PIONEER STATION	AMA	95666	41 B2
PIONEERTOWN	SBD	92268	100 D1
PIRU	VEN	93040	88 E4
PISGAH	SBD	92365	92 E2
*PISMO BEACH	SLO	93449	76 B4
*PITTSBURG	CC	94565	M B3
PITTVILLE	SHA	96056	13 E4
PIXLEY	TUL	93256	68 B4
*PLACENTIA	ORA	92670	T D1
*PLACERVILLE	ED	95667	34 E5
PLAINSBURG	MCO	95333	48 D3
PLAINVIEW	TUL	93267	68 C2
PLANADA	MCO	95365	48 D4
PLASSE	AMA	95666	35 E5
PLASTER CITY	IMP	92269	108 D5
PLATINA	SHA	96076	17 D3
PLAYA DEL REY	LACO	90291	97 C2
PLEASANT GROVE	SUT	95668	33 D4
*PLEASANT HILL	CC	94523	L E3
*PLEASANTON	ALA	94566	M C5
PLEASANT VALLEY	ED	95709	35 A5
*PLYMOUTH	AMA	95669	40 D2
*POINT ARENA	MEN	95468	30 C4
POINT LOMA	SDCO	92106	V A3
POINT PLEASANT	SAC	95624	39 D3
POINT REYES STATION	MAR	94956	37 D4
POLLARD FLAT	SHA	96017	12 C4
POLLOCK PINES	ED	95726	35 A4
POMINS	ED	95733	35 E2
POMO	MEN	95469	31 C1
*POMONA	LACO	91766	U C2
POND	KER	93280	68 B5
PONDEROSA	TUL	93208	69 C3
PONDEROSA BASIN	MPA	95338	49 C3
PONDEROSA SKY RANCH	TEH		19 B4
PONDOSA	SIS	96077	13 C3
POPE VALLEY	NAPA	94567	32 C5
POPLAR	TUL	93257	68 C3
PORT COSTA	CC	94569	L D3
PORTER RANCH	LACO	91311	Q A1
*PORTERVILLE	TUL	93257	68 D3
*PORT HUENEME	VEN	93041	96 B1
*PORTOLA	PLU	96122	27 B2
*PORTOLA VALLEY	SMCO	94025	N D3
POSEY	TUL	93260	69 B5
POSTON	LPAZ		104 A2
POSTON 2	LPAZ		104 A3
POTRERO	SDCO	92063	112 C2
POTTER VALLEY	MEN	95469	31 B1
*POWAY	SDCO	92064	V D1
POZO	SLO	93453	76 D3
PRATHER	FRCO	93651	57 E1
PRATTVILLE	PLU	95923	20 B4
PRESIDIO	SFCO	94118	141 D2
PRESIDIO OF SAN FRAN	SFCO	94129	141 D2
PRESTON	SON	95425	31 C4
PRIEST	TUO	95305	48 D1
PRINCETON	COL	95970	25 A5
PRINCETON BY THE SEA	SMCO	94018	N B2
PROBERTA	TEH	96078	24 D1
PROGRESO	BAJA		112 A4
PROJECT CITY	SHA	96079	18 C1
PRUNEDALE	MON	93901	54 C3
PUERTA LA CRUZ	SDCO	92086	107 C2
PULGA	BUT	95965	25 D2
PUMPKIN CENTER	KER	93309	78 D3
Q			
QUAIL VALLEY	RCO	92380	99 C4
QUAKING ASPEN	TUL	93208	69 C3
QUARTZSITE	LPAZ		104 B4
QUINCY	PLU	95971	26 C1
QUINCY JUNCTION	PLU	95971	26 D1
R			
RACKERBY	YUB	95972	25 E5
RAFAEL VILLAGE	MAR	94947	L A2
RAILROAD FLAT	CAL	95248	41 B2
RAINBOW	SDCO	92028	106 D1
RAISIN CITY	FRCO	93652	57 B4
RAMONA	SDCO	92065	107 A4
RAMSEY	LPAZ		104 D4
RANCHITA	SDCO	92066	107 D3
RANCHO BERNARDO	SDCO	92128	106 D4
RANCHO CALIFORNIA	RCO	92390	106 D1
RANCHO CORDOVA	SAC	95670	40 B1
*RANCHO CUCAMONGA	SBD	91730	U D2
*RANCHO MIRAGE	RCO	92270	100 D4
*RANCHO PALOS VERDES	LACO	90274	S B3
RANCHO PENASQUITOS	SDCO	92129	106 D4
RANCHO SAN DIEGO	SDCO	92077	V E3
RANCHO SANTA CLARITA	LACO	91350	89 B4
RANCHO SANTA FE	SDCO	92067	106 C4
RANCHO SANTA MARGARITA	ORA	92688	98 E4
RANCHO TEHAMA	TEH	96021	24 C1
RANDOLF	SIE	96126	27 C4
RANDSBURG	KER	93554	80 D3
RAVENDALE	LAS	96123	8 C5
RAYMOND	MAD	93653	49 B5
RED APPLE	CAL	95224	41 C3
REDBANK	TEH	96080	18 B5
*RED BLUFF	TEH	96080	18 C5
REDCREST	HUM	95569	16 A3
*REDDING	SHA	96001	18 C2
*REDLANDS	SBD	92373	99 C2
RED MOUNTAIN	SBD	93558	80 E3
*REDONDO BEACH	LACO	90277	S A2
REDWAY	HUM	95560	16 B5
*REDWOOD CITY	SMCO	94061	N D2
REDWOOD ESTATES	SCL	95044	P B4
REDWOOD PARK	SMCO	94062	N C2
REDWOOD SHORES	SMCO	94065	N D2
REDWOOD VALLEY	MEN	95470	31 B1
*REEDLEY	FRCO	93654	58 A4
RENO	WSH		28 B4
RENO-STEAD	WSH		28 B3
REPRESA	SAC	95671	34 B5
REQUA	DN	95561	1 E5
RESCUE	ED	95672	34 D5
RESEDA	LACO	91335	Q B2
REWARD	INY	93526	60 B3
RHEEM VALLEY	CC	94570	45 E1
*RIALTO	SBD	92376	99 B1
RICARDO	KER	93519	80 B3
RICE	SBD	92280	103 B2
RICHARDSON SPRINGS	BUT	95978	25 B2
RICH BAR	PLU	95915	26 B1
RICHFIELD	TEH	96083	24 D1
RICHGROVE	TUL	93261	68 C5
*RICHMOND	CC	94801	L C3
RICHMOND	SFCO	94121	141 B4
RICHVALE	BUT	95974	25 C4
*RIDGECREST	KER	93555	80 D1
RIMFOREST	SBD	92378	99 C1
RINCON	SDCO	92082	106 E2
RIO BRAVO	KER	93306	78 E2
*RIO DELL	HUM	95562	15 E3
RIO DELL	SON	95486	37 D2
RIO LINDA	SAC	95673	33 E5
RIO NIDO	SON	95471	37 D1
RIO OSO	SUT	95674	33 D3
*RIO VISTA	SOL	94571	M D2
RIPLEY	RCO	92272	103 D5
*RIPON	SJCO	95366	47 C2
*RIVERBANK	STA	95367	47 D2
RIVERDALE	FRCO	93656	57 B5
RIVER KERN	KER	93238	69 D5
RIVER PINES	AMA	95675	40 E1
*RIVERSIDE	RCO	92501	99 B2
RIVERTON	ED	95725	35 B4
RIVIERA	MOH		85 D4
RIVIERA HEIGHTS	LAK	95443	31 D3
RIVIERA WEST	LAK	95422	31 E3
ROADS END	TUL	93236	69 C4
ROBBINS	SUT	95676	33 C4
ROBINSONS CORNER	BUT	95948	25 C5
ROBLA	SAC	95673	33 E5
ROCKAWAY BEACH	SMCO	94044	N B1
ROCK HAVEN	SDCO	92065	106 E4
*ROCKLIN	PLA	95677	34 B4
ROCKPORT	MEN	95488	22 B3
ROCKVILLE	SOL	94585	38 E3
RODEO	CC	94572	L D3
ROGERS LANDING	MOH		85 D4
*ROHNERT PARK	SON	94928	38 A2
ROHNERVILLE	HUM	95540	15 E2
ROLINDA	FRCO	93705	57 B3
*ROLLING HILLS	LACO	90274	S B3
*ROLLING HILLS ESTATES	LACO	90274	S B2
ROMOLAND	RCO	92380	99 D4
ROSAMOND	KER	93560	90 A1
ROSEDALE	KER	93308	78 C3
*ROSEMEAD	LACO	91770	R C3
ROSEMONT	SDCO	92065	106 E4
*ROSEVILLE	PLA	95678	34 A4
ROSEVILLE	SDCO	92106	V A3
ROSEWOOD	TEH	96022	18 B4
*ROSS	MAR	94957	L A3
ROUGH AND READY	NEV	95975	34 B1
ROUND MOUNTAIN	SHA	96084	13 A5
ROVANA	INY	93514	51 B3
ROWLAND HEIGHTS	LACO	91745	U A3
RUBIDOUX	RCO	92509	99 A2
RUCH	JKSN		3 C1
RUCKER	SCL	95020	P D5
RUMSEY	YOL	95679	32 D4
RUNNING SPRINGS	SBD	92382	99 D1
RUSSIAN HILL	SFCO	94133	142 C2
RUTH	TRI	95526	17 A4
RUTHERFORD	NAPA	94573	38 B2
RYDE	SAC	95680	M E1
S			
SABLON	SBD	92280	103 A1
SABRE CITY	PLA	95660	34 A5
*SACRAMENTO	SAC	95813	39 E1
*SAINT HELENA	NAPA	94574	38 B2
SALIDA	STA	95368	47 C2
*SALINAS	MON	93901	54 C4
SALMON CREEK	SON	94923	37 C2
SALT CREEK LODGE	SHA	96051	12 C5
SALTDALE	KER	93519	80 C3
SALTMARSH	SBD	92280	103 A1
SALTON	RCO	92257	108 D1
SALTON CITY	IMP	92274	108 C2
SALTON SEA BEACH	IMP	92274	108 C1
SALVADOR	NAPA	94558	38 C3
SALTUS	SBD	92304	94 A3
SALYER	TRI	95563	10 D5
SAMOA	HUM	95560	9 D5
SAN ANDREAS	CAL	95249	41 A3
*SAN ANSELMO	MAR	94960	L A3
SAN ARDO	MON	93450	65 D3
SAN BENITO	SBT	95023	55 C5
*SAN BERNARDINO	SBD	92402	99 C1
SANBORN	KER	93501	80 A5
*SAN BRUNO	SMCO	94066	N C1
SAN CARLOS	SDCO	92119	V D2
*SAN CARLOS	SMCO	94070	N D2
*SAN CLEMENTE	ORA	92672	105 D1
SANDBERG	LACO	93532	89 A2
*SAND CITY	MON	93955	54 B4
*SAN DIEGO	SDCO	92101	V B3
SAN DIEGO COUNTRY EST	SDCO	92065	107 B4
*SAN DIMAS	LACO	91773	U B2
SANDS	SBD	92309	83 C5
SANDY	CLK		74 A5
SAN FELIPE	SDCO	92086	107 C3
*SAN FERNANDO	LACO	91341	Q C1
*SAN FRANCISCO	SFCO	94101	L B4
*SAN GABRIEL	LACO	91776	R C3
*SANGER	FRCO	93657	57 E3
SAN GERONIMO	MAR	94963	38 A5
SAN GORGONIO	RCO	92282	100 B3
SAN GREGORIO	SMCO	94074	N C3
*SAN JACINTO	RCO	92383	99 E3
*SAN JOAQUIN	FRCO	93660	56 E4
*SAN JOSE	SCL	95103	P B3
*SAN JUAN BAUTISTA	SBT	95045	54 D3
*SAN JUAN CAPISTRANO	ORA	92675	98 D5
*SAN LEANDRO	ALA	94577	L E5
SAN LORENZO	ALA	94580	L E5
SAN LUCAS	MON	93954	65 D3
*SAN LUIS OBISPO	SLO	93401	76 B3
SAN LUIS REY	SDCO	92068	106 B2
SAN LUIS REY HEIGHTS	SDCO	92028	106 C2
*SAN MARCOS	SDCO	92069	106 D3
SAN MARIN	MAR	94947	L A2
*SAN MARINO	LACO	91108	R C3
SAN MARTIN	SCL	95046	P D5
*SAN MATEO	SMCO	94401	N C1
SAN MIGUEL	SLO	93451	66 A5
SAN ONOFRE	SDCO	92672	105 E1
*SAN PABLO	CC	94806	L C3
SAN PASQUAL	SDCO	92025	106 E3
SAN PEDRO	LACO	90731	S C3
SAN QUENTIN	MAR	94964	L B3
*SAN RAFAEL	MAR	94901	L B3
*SAN RAMON	CC	94583	M B4
SAN SIMEON	SLO	93452	75 B1
*SANTA ANA	ORA	92701	T D3
*SANTA BARBARA	SB	93101	87 C4
*SANTA CLARA	SCL	95050	P B3
*SANTA CRUZ	SCR	95060	53 E2
*SANTA FE SPRINGS	LACO	90670	R C5
SANTA MARGARITA	SLO	93453	76 B3
*SANTA MARIA	SB	93454	86 B1
*SANTA MONICA	LACO	90402	Q B4
*SANTA PAULA	VEN	93060	88 C5
SANTA RITA	ALA	94566	M C5
SANTA RITA	MON	93901	54 C3
SANTA RITA PARK	MER	93660	56 B1
*SANTA ROSA	SON	95401	37 E2
SANTA SUSANA	VEN	93065	89 A5
SANTA SUSANA PARK	VEN	93063	89 A5
SANTA VENETIA	MAR	94903	L B3
SANTA YNEZ	SB	93460	86 E3
SANTA YSABEL	SDCO	92070	107 C3
*SANTEE	SDCO	92071	V D2
SAN YSIDRO	SDCO	92073	V D5
*SARATOGA	SCL	95070	P A4
SATICOY	VEN	93003	88 C5
SATTLEY	SIE	96124	27 C3
SAUGUS	LACO	91350	89 B4
*SAUSALITO	MAR	94965	L B4
SAWYERS BAR	SIS	96027	11 B2
SCALES	SIE	95981	26 C4
SCHELLVILLE	SON	95476	L B1
SCISSORS CROSSING	SDCO	92036	107 D3
SCOTIA	HUM	95565	16 A3
SCOTT BAR	SIS	96085	3 C4
SCOTT DAM	LAK	95469	23 C5
SCOTTS CORNER	ALA	94586	P B1
*SCOTTS VALLEY	SCR	95060	P A5
SCOTTYS CASTLE	INY	92328	61 B1
SCRIPPS MIRAMAR RANCH	SDCO	92131	V C1
SEACLIFF	SFCO	94121	141 C2
SEA CLIFF	VEN	93001	87 E5
*SEAL BEACH	ORA	90740	T A3
SEARCHLIGHT	CLK		85 A2
SEARCHLIGHT JUNCTION	SBD	92332	95 B1
SEARS POINT	SON	94952	L B2
*SEASIDE	MON	93955	54 B4
*SEBASTOPOL	SON	95472	37 E2
SEELEY	IMP	92273	108 E5
SEIAD VALLEY	SIS	96086	3 B3
SEIGLER SPRINGS	LAK	95426	31 E4
*SELMA	FRCO	93662	57 E4
SENECA	PLU	95923	20 C5
SEPULVEDA	LACO	91335	Q B2
SERENE LAKES	PLA	95728	35 C1
SERENO DEL MAR	SON	94923	37 C2
SERRA MESA	SDCO	92123	V C3
SEVEN PINES	INY	93526	59 E3
SHADOW HILLS	LAK	95461	32 A4
SHADY DELL	SDCO	92065	V E1
SHADY GLEN	PLA	95713	34 D2
*SHAFTER	KER	93263	78 B2
SHANDON	SLO	93461	76 D1
SHASTA	SHA	96087	18 B2
SHAVER LAKE HEIGHTS	FRCO	93664	58 B1
SHAVER LAKE POINT	FRCO	93664	50 B5
SHEEP RANCH	CAL	95250	41 B3
SHELL BEACH	SLO	93449	76 B4
SHELL TRACT	SON		39 A5
SHELTER VALLEY RANCHOS	SDCO	92036	107 D4
SHERIDAN	PLA	95681	34 A3
SHERIDAN	SON	95462	37 C2
SHERMAN OAKS	LACO	91403	Q C3
SHINGLE MILL	SON	95480	31 A5
SHINGLE SPRINGS	ED	95682	34 D5
SHINGLETOWN	SHA	96088	19 A3
SHIVELY	HUM	95565	16 B3
SHORE ACRES	CC	94565	39 A4
SHOSHONE	INY	92384	73 A4
SHUMWAY	LAS		21 B1
SIAM	SBD	92319	94 B3
SIERRA BROOKS	SIE	96135	27 D3
SIERRA CITY	SIE	96125	27 A4
*SIERRA MADRE	LACO	91024	R D2
SIERRAVILLE	SIE	96126	27 C4
*SIGNAL HILL	LACO	90806	S D2
SILVERADO CANYON	ORA	92676	98 E4
SILVER CITY	LYON		36 C1
SILVER CITY	TUL	93271	59 B5
SILVER FORK	ED	95728	35 C4
SILVER LAKE	LACO	90039	Q E3
SILVERPEAK	ESM		52 D1
SILVER STRAND	VEN	93030	96 B1
*SIMI VALLEY	VEN	93065	89 A5
SIMMLER	SLO	93453	77 B3
SISQUOC	SB	93454	86 C1
SITES	COL	95979	32 C1
SKAGGS SPRINGS	SON	95448	31 C5
SKIDOO	INY	92328	61 D5
SKYFOREST	SBD	92385	99 C1
SKY LONDA	SMCO	94062	N D3
SKY VALLEY	RCO	92240	100 E3

***INDICATES INCORPORATED CITY**

CITIES AND COMMUNITIES INDEX

COMMUNITY NAME	CO.	ZIP CODE	PAGE & GRID
SLEEPY HOLLOW	MAR	94960	L A3
SLEEPY VALLEY	LACO	91350	89 D4
SLIDE INN	TUO	95335	41 E4
SLOAN	CLK		74 D4
SLOAT	PLU	96127	26 E2
SLOUGHHOUSE	SAC	95683	40 B1
SMARTVILLE	YUB	95977	34 A2
SMITHFLAT	ED	95727	34 E5
SMITH RIVER	DN	95567	1 E3
SMITH STATION	TUO	95321	49 A1
SNELLING	MCO	95369	48 C3
SOBOBA HOT SPRINGS	RCO	92383	99 E3
SODA BAY	LAK	95443	31 D3
SODA SPRINGS	NEV	95728	27 C5
SODA SPRINGS	SON	95728	31 A5
*SOLANA BEACH	SDCO	92075	106 B4
*SOLEDAD	MON	93960	55 A5
SOLEMINT	LACO	91351	89 C4
*SOLVANG	SB	93463	86 E3
SOMERSET	ED	95684	35 A5
SOMES BAR	SIS	95568	10 E2
SOMIS	VEN	93066	88 D5
*SONOMA	SON	95476	L B1
*SONORA	TUO	95370	41 C5
SONORA JUNCTION	MNO	93517	42 E2
SOQUEL	SCR	95073	54 A2
SORRENTO VALLEY	SDCO	92121	V B1
SOULSBYVILLE	TUO	95372	41 D5
SOUSA CORNERS	SON	95401	37 D2
SOUTH BELRIDGE	KER	93251	77 D2
SOUTH DOS PALOS	MCO	93665	56 A2
*SOUTH EL MONTE	LACO	91733	R C4
SOUTH FORK	MAD		49 E5
SOUTH FORK	MPA	95318	49 B2
*SOUTH GATE	LACO	90280	R A5
SOUTH LAGUNA	ORA	92677	T E5
SOUTH LAKE	KER	93283	79 D1
*SOUTH LAKE TAHOE	ED	95705	36 A3
SOUTH OF MARKET	SFCO	94103	143 C4
SOUTH OROVILLE	BUT	95965	25 D4
SOUTH PARK	SON	95404	38 A2
*SOUTH PASADENA	LACO	91030	R B3
*SOUTH SAN FRANCISCO	SMCO	94080	N C1
SOUTH SAN GABRIEL	LACO	91770	R B4
SOUTH TAFT	KER	93268	78 A4
SPANGLER	SBD	93562	81 A2
SPANISH CREEK	PLU	95971	26 D1
SPANISH FLAT WOODLANDS	NAPA	94558	38 D1
SPANISH RANCH	PLU	95956	26 C1
SPARKS	WSH		28 C4
SPAULDING	LAS	96130	20 D1
SPENCEVILLE	NEV	95945	34 B2
SPRECKELS	MON	93962	54 D4
SPRING GARDEN	PLU	95971	26 E2
SPRING TOWN	ALA	94550	M C5
SPRING VALLEY	SDCO	92077	V D3
SPRINGVILLE	TUL	93265	68 E2
SPRINGVILLE	VEN	93010	96 C1
SQUAW VALLEY	FRCO	93646	58 B3
SQUAW VALLEY	PLA	95730	35 D1
SQUIRREL MTN VALLEY	KER	93240	79 D1
STAFFORD	HUM	95565	16 A3
STAGECOACH	LYON		28 E5
STANDARD	TUO	95373	41 D5
STANDISH	LAS	96128	21 B3
STANFIELD HILL	YUB	95918	34 A1
STANFORD	SCL	94305	N D2
STANISLAUS	TUO	95247	41 C4
*STANTON	ORA	90680	T B2
*STATELINE	WSH		36 B3
STAUFFER	VEN	93225	88 C2
STENT	TUO	95347	41 C5
STEVINSON	MCO	95374	47 E4
STEWART	CRSN		36 C2
STEWART-LENNOX	KLAM		5 B1
STEWARTS POINT	SON	95480	30 E5
STINSON BEACH	MAR	94970	L A4
STIRLING CITY	BUT	95978	25 D2
*STOCKTON	SJCO	95201	40 B5
STONYFORD	COL	95979	24 B5
STOVEPIPE WELLS	INY	92328	61 D4
STRATFORD	KIN	93266	67 C2
STRATHMORE	TUL	93267	68 D2
STRAWBERRY	ED	95735	35 D4
STRAWBERRY	TUO	95375	42 A3
STRAWBERRY VALLEY	YUB	95981	26 B4
STRONGHOLD	MOD	96431	5 E3
STUDIO CITY	LACO	91604	Q C3
STYX	RIV	92255	103 C3
SUGAR LOAF	SBD	92386	92 A5
SUGARLOAF VILLAGE	TUL	93260	69 B4
SUGAR PINE	MAD	95389	49 D3
SUGARPINE	TUO	95346	41 D4
*SUISUN CITY	SOL	94585	M A1
SULTANA	TUL	93666	58 B5
SUMMERHOME PARK	SON	95436	37 D2
SUMMERLAND	SB	93067	87 D4
SUMMIT CITY	SHA	96089	18 B1
SUN CITY	RCO	92381	99 C4
SUNLAND	LACO	91040	Q D1
SUNNYBROOK	AMA	95640	40 D2
SUNNYSIDE	SDCO	92002	V D4
SUNNYSLOPE	RCO	93656	99 A2
*SUNNYVALE	SCL	94086	P A3
SUNNY VISTA	SDCO	92010	V D4
SUNOL	ALA	94586	P B1
SUNSET	SFCO	94122	141 B5
SUNSET BEACH	ORA	90742	T A3
SUNSET ESTATES	PLA	95678	33 E4
SUN VALLEY	LACO	91352	Q D2
SUN VALLEY	WSH		28 B4
SURF	SB	93436	86 A3
SURFSIDE	ORA	90743	T A3
*SUSANVILLE	LAS	96130	20 E3
SUTCLIFFE	WSH		28 C1
SUTTER	SUT	95982	33 C2
*SUTTER CREEK	AMA	95685	40 E2
SWANSBORO COUNTRY	ED	95727	35 A4
SWANSEA	INY	93545	60 C5
SWEETBRIER	SHA	96017	12 C3
SWEETLAND	NEV	95959	26 B5
SWEETWATER	LYON		43 C1
SYCAMORE	COL	95957	33 A2
SYLMAR	LACO	91342	Q B1
SYLMAR SQUARE	LACO	91342	Q C1
SYLVIA PARK	LACO	90290	Q A3
T			
*TAFT	KER	93268	78 A4
TAFT HEIGHTS	KER	93268	77 E4
TAHOE CITY	PLA	95730	35 E2
TAHOE PINES	PLA	95718	35 D2
TAHOE VILLAGE	DGL	00025	36 B3
TAHOE VISTA	PLA	95732	36 A1
TAHOMA	PLA	95733	35 E2
TAKILMA	JOS		2 D2
TALENT	JKSN		3 E1
TALMAGE	MEN	95481	31 B2
TAMALPAIS VALLEY	MAR	94941	L A4
TAMARACK	CAL	95223	41 E2
TANCRED	YOL	95606	32 D5
TARZANA	LACO	91356	Q A3
TASSAJARA	CC		46 B1
TASSAJARA HOT SPRGS	MON	93924	64 D2
TAYLORSVILLE	PLU	95983	20 D5
TECATE	BAJA		112 C2
TECATE	SDCO	92080	112 C2
TECOPA	INY	92389	73 A4
TECOPA HOT SPRINGS	INY	92389	73 A4
*TEHACHAPI	KER	93561	79 D4
TEHACHAPI EAST	KER	93561	79 D4
*TEHAMA	TEH	96090	24 D1
TELEGRAPH CITY	CAL	95228	40 E5
TELEGRAPH HILL	SFCO	94133	142 D1
TEMECULA	RCO	92390	106 C1
*TEMPLE CITY	LACO	91780	R C3
TEMPLETON	SLO	93465	76 A2
TENNANT	SIS	96012	5 B5
TERMINOUS	SJCO	95240	39 E4
TERMO	LAS	96132	8 B5
TERRA BELLA	TUL	93270	68 D3
TERRA LINDA	MAR	94903	L A3
THE HIGHLANDS	SMCO	94402	N C2
THE ISTHMUS	LACO	90704	105 D5
THE NARROWS	SDCO	92004	108 A3
THERMAL	RCO	92274	101 B5
THERMALANDS	PLA	95648	34 B3
THE WILLOWS	SDCO	92001	107 B5
THISBE	WSH		28 E4
THOMPSON	LACO	91351	89 C4
THORNE	MIN		44 B1
THORNTON	SJCO	95686	39 E3
*THOUSAND OAKS	VEN	91360	96 E1
THOUSAND PALMS	RCO	92276	100 E3
THREE ARCH BAY	ORA	92677	98 D5
THREE POINT	LACO	93532	89 B2
THREE RIVERS	TUL	93271	58 D5
*TIBURON	MAR	94920	L B4
TIERRA DEL SOL	SDCO	92005	112 E2
TIERRASANTA	SDCO	92124	V C2
TIJUANA	BAJA		111 D2
TIMBER LODGE	MPA	95345	49 B3
TIPTON	TUL	93272	68 B3
TISDALE	SUT	95957	33 B3
TOBIN	PLU	95965	26 A1
TOLLHOUSE	FRCO	93667	58 A2
TOMALES	MAR	94971	37 D3
TOOMY	SBD	92365	92 B1
TOPANGA	LACO	90290	Q A3
TOPANGA PARK	LACO	90290	97 B1
TOPAZ	MNO	96133	36 D5
TOPOCK	MOH		95 E2
*TORRANCE	LACO	90505	S B2
TOWER HOUSE	SHA	96095	18 A2
TOYON	SHA	96019	18 C1
TRABUCO CANYON	ORA	92678	98 E4
*TRACY	SJCO	95376	46 E2
TRAIL PARK	ED	95651	34 E4
TRANQUILLITY	FRCO	93668	56 D4
TRAVER	TUL	93673	57 E5
TRAVIS AIR FORCE BASE	SOL	94535	39 A3
TRES PINOS	SBT	95075	55 A3
*TRINIDAD	HUM	95570	9 E4
TRINITY CENTER	TRI	96091	11 E4
TRIUNFO	VEN	91362	96 E1
TRONA	SBD	93562	71 B5
TROPICO	KER	93560	89 E1
TROWBRIDGE	SUT	95659	33 D3
TROY	PLA	95728	35 B1
TRUCKEE	NEV	95734	27 D5
TUDOR	SUT	95991	33 C3
TUJUNGA	LACO	91042	Q E1
*TULARE	TUL	93274	68 A2
*TULELAKE	SIS	96134	5 D2
TUOLUMNE	TUO	95379	41 D5
TUOLUMNE MEADOWS	TUO	95379	43 A5
TUPMAN	KER	93276	78 B3
*TURLOCK	STA	95380	47 E3
TURTLE ROCK	ORA	92715	98 C4
*TUSTIN	ORA	92680	T E3
TUTTLE	MCO	95340	48 D4
TWAIN	PLU	95984	26 B1
TWAIN HARTE	TUO	95383	41 D4
TWAIN HARTE VALLEY	TUO	95383	41 D4
TWENTYNINE PALMS	SBD	92277	101 B1
TWIN BRIDGES	ED	95735	35 E4
TWIN CITIES	SAC	95632	40 A3
TWIN OAKS	SDCO	92083	106 C3
TWIN PEAKS	SBD	92391	91 C5
TYNDALL LANDING	YOL	95698	33 B4
U			
*UKIAH	MEN	95482	31 B2
ULTRA	TUL	93256	68 D3
*UNION CITY	ALA	94587	P A1
UNIVERSAL CITY	LACO	91608	Q D3
UNIVERSITY CITY	SDCO	92122	V A2
*UPLAND	SBD	91786	U D2
UPPER LAKE	LAK	95485	31 D2
V			
VACATION BEACH	SON	95446	37 C2
*VACAVILLE	SOL	95688	39 A2
VALENCIA	LACO	91355	89 B4
VALERIE	RCO	92274	101 A5
VALINDA	LACO	91744	R E4
VALLECITO	CAL	95251	41 C4
VALLECITO	SDCO	92036	107 E4
*VALLEJO	SOL	94590	L D2
VALLEJO HEIGHTS	SOL	94590	38 D4
VALLEY ACRES	KER	93268	78 A4
VALLEY CENTER	SDCO	92082	106 E2
VALLEY FORD	SON	94972	37 D3
VALLEY HOME	STA	95384	47 D1
VALLEY OF ENCHANTMENT	SBD	92322	91 B5
VALLEY SPRINGS	CAL	95252	40 D3
VALLEY WELLS	INY	92366	71 C4
VAL VERDE	RCO	92370	99 C3
VAL VERDE PARK	LACO	91350	89 A4
VAN NUYS	LACO	91408	Q C2
VENICE	LACO	90291	Q B5
VENTUCOPA	SB	93252	87 E1
VEN-TU PARK	VEN	91320	96 D1
*VENTURA	VEN	93001	88 B5
VERDEMONT	SBD	92407	99 B1
VERDI	WSH		28 A4
VERDI SIERRA PINES	SIE	95737	27 E4
VERDUGO CITY	LACO	91046	Q E2
*VERNON	LACO	90058	R A4
VERONA	SUT	95659	33 D4
VICHY SPRINGS	MEN	95482	31 B2
VICTOR	SJCO	95253	40 B4
VICTORIA	SDCO	92001	107 B5
*VICTORVILLE	SBD	92392	91 C3
VIDAL	SBD	92280	103 E1
VIDAL JUNCTION	SBD	92280	103 D1
VILLA GRANDE	SON	95486	37 C2
*VILLA PARK	ORA	92667	T E2
VINA	TEH	96092	24 E2
VINCENT	LACO	93550	90 A4
VINEBURG	SON	95487	L C1
VINTON	PLU	96135	27 D2
VIOLA	SHA	96088	19 C2
VIRGILIA	PLU	95984	26 B1
*VIRGINIA CITY	STOR		36 D1
VIRGINIA COLONY	VEN	93021	88 E5
*VISALIA	TUL	93277	68 B1
*VISTA	SDCO	92083	106 C3
VISTA VERDE	SMCO	94025	N D3
VOLCANO	AMA	95689	41 A2
VOLCANOVILLE	ED	95634	34 E3
VOLLMERS	SHA	96051	12 B4
VOLTA	MER	93635	55 D1
VORDEN	SAC	95690	M E1
W			
WAHTOKE PARK	FRCO	93654	58 A4
WALKER	MNO	96107	42 E1
WALLACE	ED	95254	40 D3
WALMORT	SAC	95683	40 A2
*WALNUT	LACO	91789	U A3
*WALNUT CREEK	CC	94595	M A4
WALNUT GROVE	SAC	95690	M E1
WALSH LANDING	SON	95450	37 A1
WARM SPRING	LACO	91310	89 B3
WARM SPRINGS	ALA	94538	P B2
WARNER SPRINGS	SDCO	92086	107 C2
*WASCO	KER	93280	78 B1
WASHINGTON	NEV	95986	26 E5
WASHOE	SON	94952	37 E3
WASHOE CITY	WSH		28 B5
*WATERFORD	STA	95386	48 A2
WATERLOO	SJCO	95201	40 B4
*WATSONVILLE	SCR	95076	54 C2
WATTS	LACO	90002	Q E5
WAWONA	MPA	95389	49 D3
WEAVERVILLE	TRI	96093	17 D1
*WEED	SIS	96094	12 C1
WEED PATCH	KER	93307	78 E4
WEIMAR	PLA	95736	34 D3
WEISEL	RCO	91720	99 A3
WEITCHPEC	HUM	95546	10 C3
WELDON	KER	93283	79 D1
WELLSONA	SLO	93446	76 A1
WENDEL	LAS	96136	21 D3
WENTWORTH SPRINGS	ED	95725	35 C3
WEOTT	HUM	95571	16 B4
WEST BRANCH	BUT	95941	25 C1
WEST BUTTE	SUT	95953	33 B2
*WEST COVINA	LACO	91790	U A2
WESTERN ADDITION	SFCO	94115	143 A4
WEST HAVEN	FRCO	93234	67 B2
*WEST HOLLYWOOD	LACO	90069	Q D3
*WESTLAKE VILLAGE	LACO	91361	96 E1
WESTLEY	STA	95387	47 B3
WEST LOS ANGELES	LACO	90025	Q C4
*WESTMINSTER	ORA	92683	T B3
*WESTMORLAND	IMP	92281	109 A4
WEST OF TWIN PEAKS	SFCO	94122	141 D5
WEST PITTSBURG	CC	94565	M B3
WEST POINT	CAL	95255	41 B2
WESTPORT	MEN	95488	22 C4
WEST SACRAMENTO	YOL	95691	39 D1
WEST SIDE	LAKE		7 B1
WESTVILLE	PLA	95631	35 A2
WESTWOOD	LAS	96137	20 C4
WESTWOOD	LACO	90024	97 C4
WEST YERMO	SBD	92327	92 A1
*WHEATLAND	YUB	95692	33 E3
WHEATON SPRINGS	SBD	92364	84 B2
WHEATVILLE	FRCO	93656	57 A5
WHEELER RIDGE	KER	93284	78 D5
WHEELER SPRINGS	VEN	93023	88 A4
WHISKEYTOWN	SHA	96095	18 A2
WHISPERING PINES	LAK	95461	32 A4
WHITE HALL	ED	95725	35 C4
WHITE HORSE	MOD	96054	13 E2
WHITE PINES	CAL	95223	41 C3
WHITE RIVER	TUL	93257	68 E4
WHITETHORN	HUM	95489	22 B1
WHITEWATER	RCO	92282	100 C3
WHITE WOLF	TUO	95389	42 D5
WHITLEY GARDENS	SLO	93436	76 C1
WHITLOW	HUM	95554	16 C4
WHITMORE	SHA	96096	19 A2
*WHITTIER	LACO	90605	R D5
WILBUR SPRINGS	COL	95987	32 C3
WILDOMAR	RCO	92395	99 C5
WILDROSE	INY	93562	71 C2
*WILLIAMS	COL	95987	32 D2
WILLIAMS	JOS		3 A1
*WILLITS	MEN	95490	23 A5
WILLOW CREEK	HUM	95573	10 D5
WILLOW RANCH	MOD	96138	7 C3
*WILLOWS	GLE	95988	24 D4
WILLOW SPRINGS	KER	93550	89 D1
WILMINGTON	LACO	90744	S C2
WILSEYVILLE	CAL	95257	41 B2
WILSONIA	TUL	93633	58 E3
WILTON	SAC	95693	40 B2
WINCHESTER	RCO	92396	99 D4
WINCHUCK	CUR		1 D2
WINDSOR	SON	95492	37 E1
WINTER GARDENS	SDCO	92040	V E2
WINTERHAVEN	IMP	92283	112 C5
*WINTERS	YOL	95694	39 A1
WINTERWARM	SDCO	92028	106 C2
WISHON	MAD	93669	49 E4
WITCH CREEK	SDCO	92065	107 B3
WITTER SPRINGS	LAK	95493	31 D2
WOFFORD HEIGHTS	KER	93285	69 C5
WOLF	NEV	95945	34 B2
WONDER VALLEY	FRCO	93657	58 B3
WOODACRE	MAR	94973	L A3
WOODCREST	RCO	92504	99 B3
WOODFORD	KER	96120	79 B4
WOODFORDS	ALP	96120	36 B4
*WOODLAKE	TUL	93286	58 D5
*WOODLAND	YOL	95695	33 B5
WOODLAND HILLS	LACO	91364	Q A3
*WOODSIDE	SMCO	94062	N D2
WOODSIDE VILLAGE	LACO	91792	R E4
WOODVILLE	TUL	93257	68 C3
WOODY	KER	93287	69 A5
WOOLSEY	SON	95492	37 E2
WORDEN	KLAM		5 B2
WRIGHTS LAKE	ED	95720	35 D4
WRIGHTWOOD	SBD	92397	90 E5
WYANDOTTE	BUT	95965	25 D5
WYNOLA	SDCO	92036	107 C3
Y			
YANKEE HILL	BUT	95969	25 D3
YANKEE JIMS	PLA	95631	34 D3
YERMO	SBD	92398	92 A1
YETTEM	TUL	93670	58 B5
YOLO	YOL	95697	33 B5
*YORBA LINDA	ORA	92686	T E1
YORKVILLE	MEN	95494	31 B4
YOSEMITE FORKS	MAD	93644	49 D4
YOSEMITE VILLAGE	MPA	95389	49 D1
YOUNGSTOWN	SJCO	95220	40 B4
*YOUNTVILLE	NAPA	94599	38 C2
*YREKA	SIS	96097	4 A4
*YUBA CITY	SUT	95991	33 C2
YUCAIPA	SBD	92399	99 D2
YUCCA VALLEY	SBD	92284	100 E1
*YUMA	YUMA		112 D5
Z			
ZAMORA	YOL	95698	33 B4
ZENIA	TRI	95495	16 E4
ZEPHYR COVE	DGL		36 A3

***INDICATES INCORPORATED CITY**

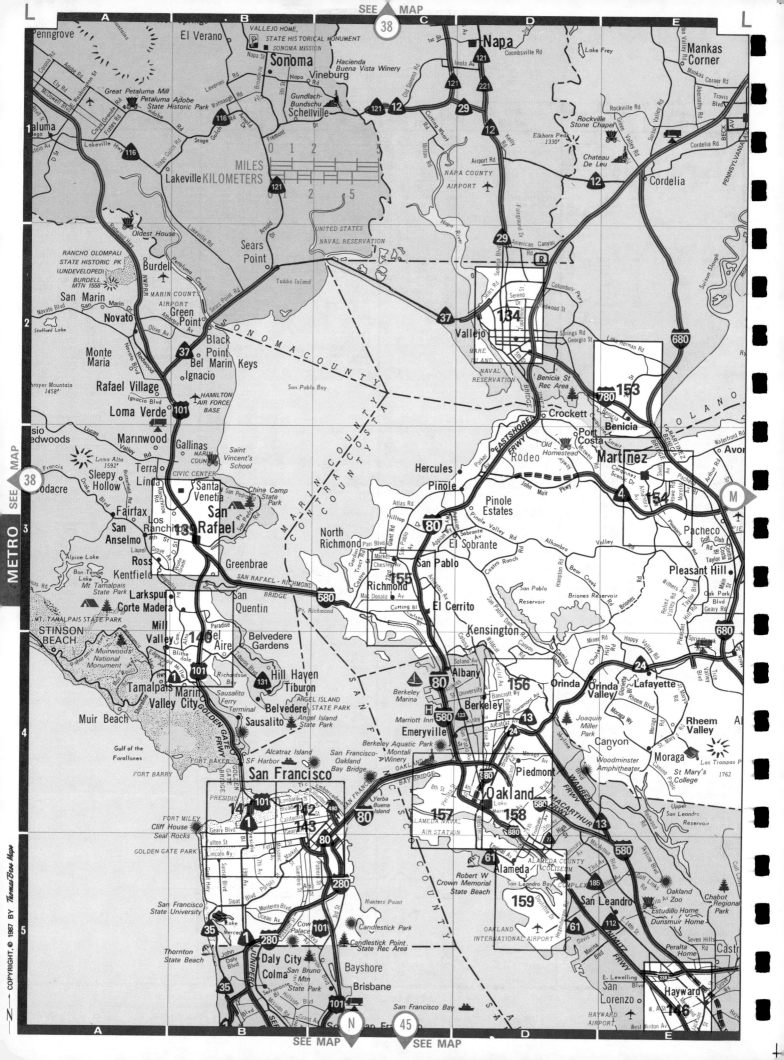

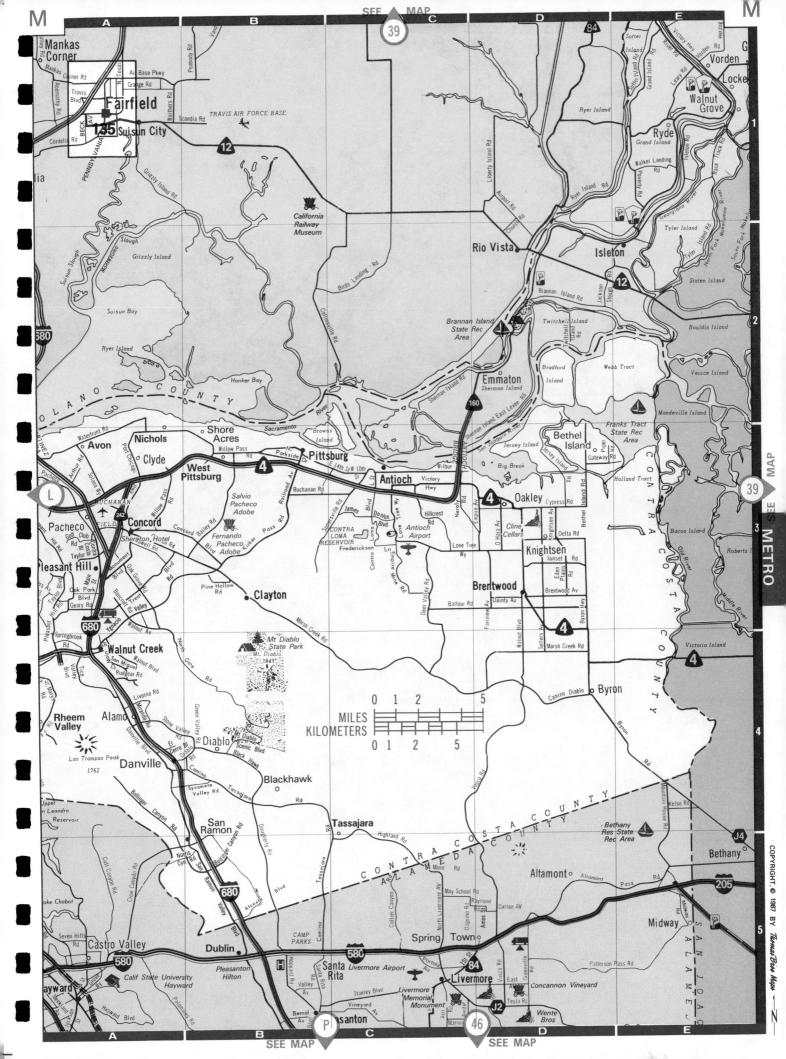

PACIFIC

Pacifica
SHARP PARK BEACH
Rockaway Beach
San Pedro Point
DEVILS SLIDE
Linda Mar
Graywhale Cove State Beach
Montara State Beach
Moss Beach
Montara Mountain
Montara
Moss Beach
AIRPORT
Princeton By The Sea
Pillar Pt.
Miramar
Half Moon Bay
Half Moon Bay State Beach
Higgins Purisima Rd

OCEAN

Obester Winery
Redwood Park
Kings Mtn Park
Sky Londa
San Gregorio State Beach
Pomponio State Beach
San Gregorio
Loma Mar
Pescadero Beach
Pescadero State Beach
Pescadero
North
Butano Cut-Off
Bean Hollow State Beach
Pebble Beach
Lake Lucerne
Bean Hollow Lakes
PIGEON POINT LIGHT HOUSE
Gazos Creek Angling Acess
Ano Nuevo State Reserve
Butano State Park
Big Basin Redwoods State Park
Eagle Rock Lookout 2400'
Boulder Creek
Brookdale
Ben Lomond
Felton
Henry Cowell Redwoods State Park

South San Francisco
San Bruno
Millbrae
San Francisco State Fish and Game Refuge
Hillsborough
San Francisco International Airport
San Francisco Airport Marriott
Hyatt
San Mateo
Burlingame
Sheraton Inn
SAN MATEO BRIDGE
Foster City
BAYSHORE
Belmont
Redwood Shores
Marine World Pkwy
San Carlos
Redwood City
Atherton
Menlo Park
Stanford
Woodside
Searsville Lake
Ladera
Alpine
Felt Lake
Sky Londa
Portola Valley
Los Trancos Woods
Vista Verde
La Honda
Mindego Hill 2127'
Portola State Park
SAN MATEO CO.
STA. CRUZ CO.
Castle Rock State Park
Black Mountain 2750'
Bielawski Moun 3214'

ALAMEDA COUNTY
SAN MATEO COUNTY
San Lorenzo
Hayward
HAYWARD AIRPORT
DUMBARTON BRIDGE
San Francisco Bay Nat'l Wildlife Refuge
E PALO ALTO
PALO ALTO AIRPORT
Palo Alto
Los Altos
FOOTHILL
Mountain View
Los Altos Hills
STEVENS CRK
Stevens Creek Reservoir
Mt. Eden Rd
Saratoga
Congress Springs

JUNIPERO SERRA FRWY
YOUNGER FRWY
CENTRAL EXPWY

METRO

MILES
KILOMETERS
0 1 2 5

COPYRIGHT © 1987 BY Thomas Bros. Maps

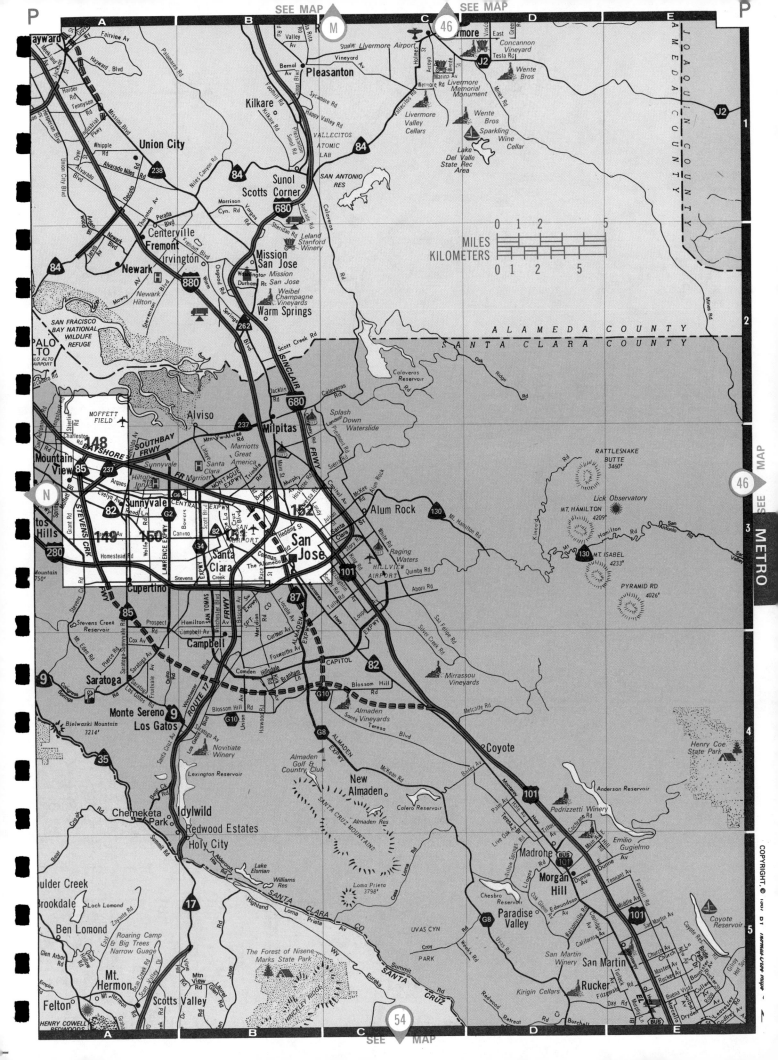

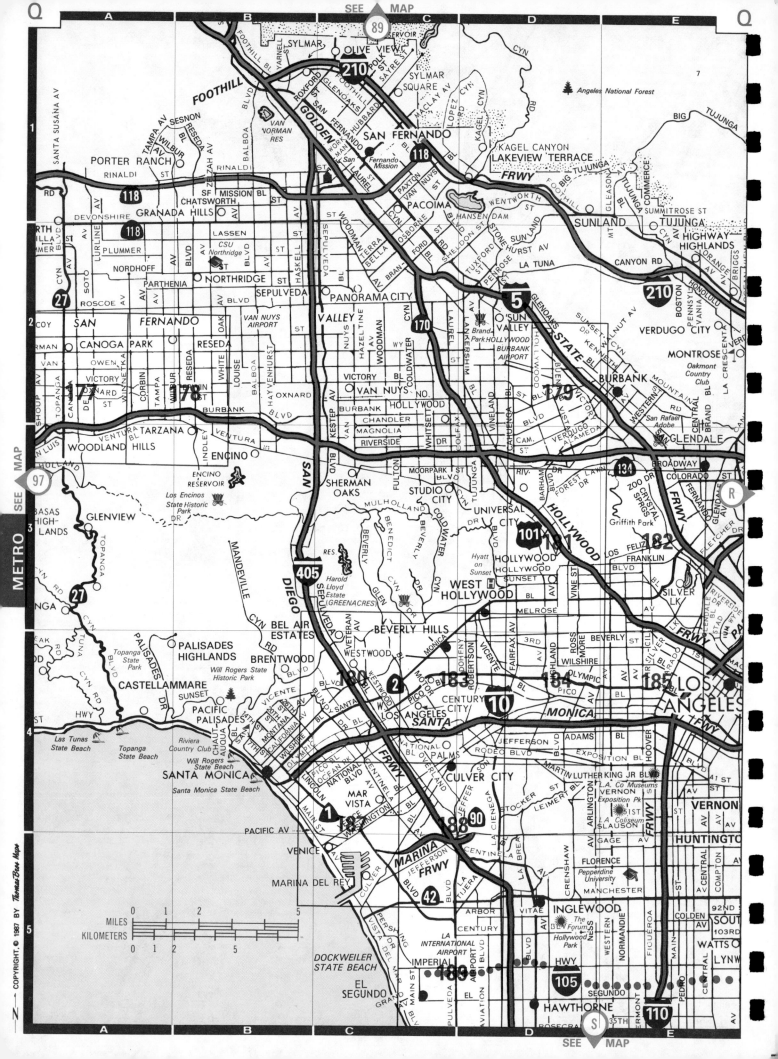

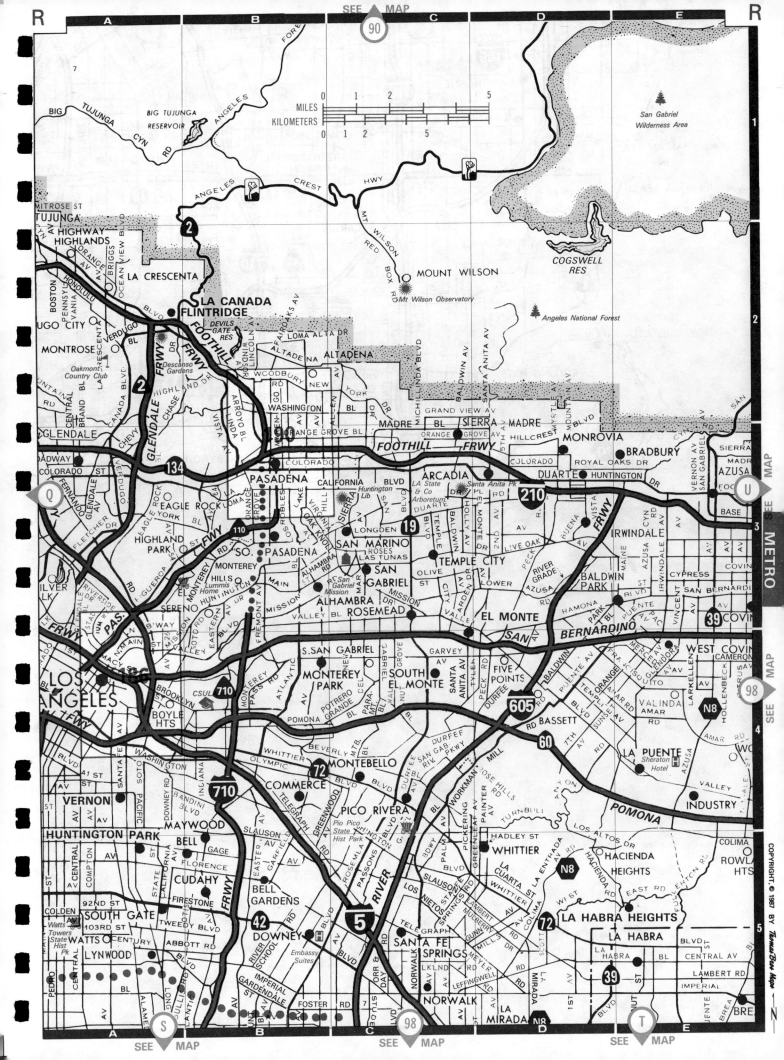

METRO

PACIFIC

OCEAN

EL SEGUNDO
IMPERIAL
SEGUNDO
HAWTHORNE
ROSECRANS
135TH
LAWNDALE BLVD
GARDENA
164TH
182ND
190TH ST
HIGHLAND AV
MANHATTAN
MANHATTAN BEACH
MANHATTAN AV
Hermosa Beach
HERMOSA BEACH
HERMOSA AV
HARBOR DR
Redondo State Beach
REDONDO BEACH
CAMINO REAL

105
110
91 FRWY
213
107
TORRANCE
Torrance Marriott Hotel
CARSON
SEPULVEDA
LOMITA
CRENSHAW
ARLINGTON
NORMANDIE
VERMONT
228TH
220TH ST
223RD ST
FIGUEROA
MAIN
405
SAN DIEGO FRWY
DEL AMO BLVD
Banning Pk HWY
WILMINGTON
ANAHEIM
NEW DOCK ST
SEASIDE
RTE 103
HARBOR
213
110
9TH ST
25TH ST
SAN PEDRO
PASEO DEL MAR
Cabrillo Marine Mus
Royal Palms State Beach
Point Fermin Historic Lighthouse
Cabrillo Beach

PALOS VERDES ESTATES
PALOS VERDES
ROLLING HILLS ESTATES
VIA VAL MONTE
ROLLING HILLS
N7
Wayfarer's Chapel
RANCHO PALOS VERDES
HAWTHORNE
PALOS VERDES DR
COAST
PACIFIC

LYNWOOD
ABBOTT RD
CENTURY
WATTS
COMPTON
REDONDO BEACH
ALONDRA
GARDENA BL
VICTORIA
CSU Dominguez Hills
CARSON
47
710
DEL
DAIRY
SOUTH
AVN. LONG BEACH
LONG BEACH FRWY
SIGNAL HILL
HILL ST
STEARNS
7TH ST
BROADWAY
OCEAN BLVD
LONG BEACH
Long Beach Marina & Marine Stadium
NAPLES
SEAL BEACH
1
103
710
121
ATHERTON
PALO
CSULB
COLORADO ST
2ND ST

PARAMOUNT
GARDENDALE
IMPERIAL
FOSTER
BELLFLOWER
ARTESIA
LAKEWOOD
CENTRALIA
WARDLOW RD
SPRING ST
LOS COYOTES DIAG
STUDEBAKER
19
605
22
SAN GABRIEL FRWY
SAN ANTONIO
PARAMOUNT
GARFIELD
WOODRUFF
BELLFLOWER
CLARK
CHERRY
ORANGE
ATLANTIC
LONG BEACH

MILES 0 1 2 5
KILOMETERS 0 1 2 5

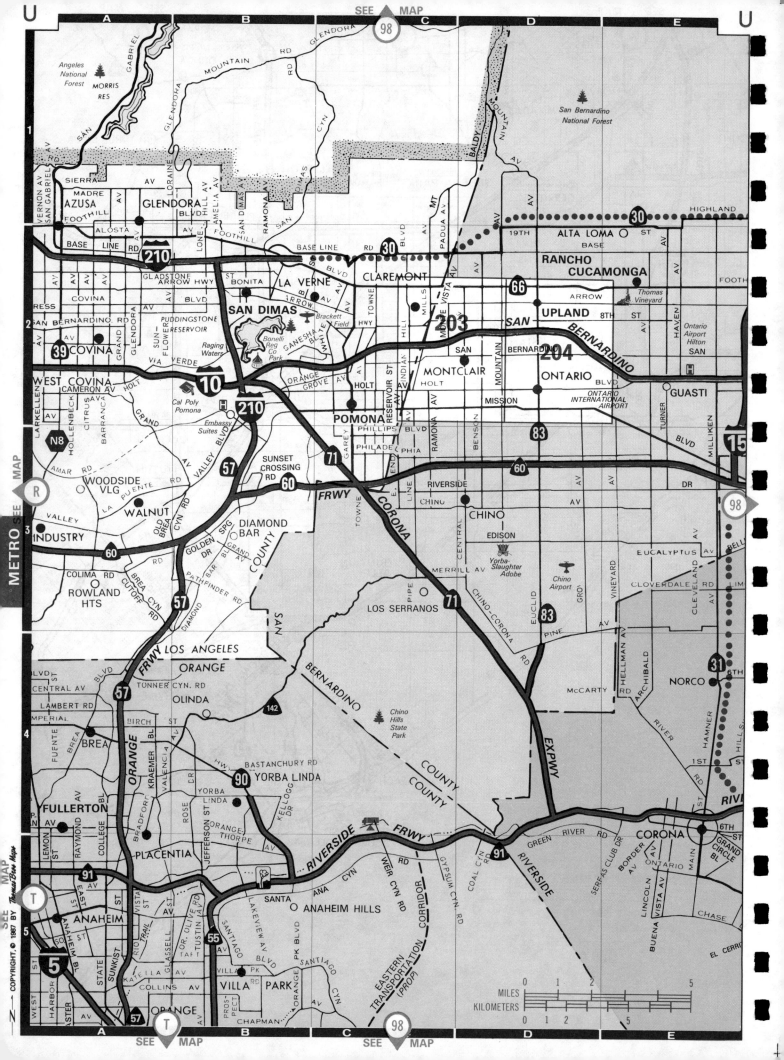

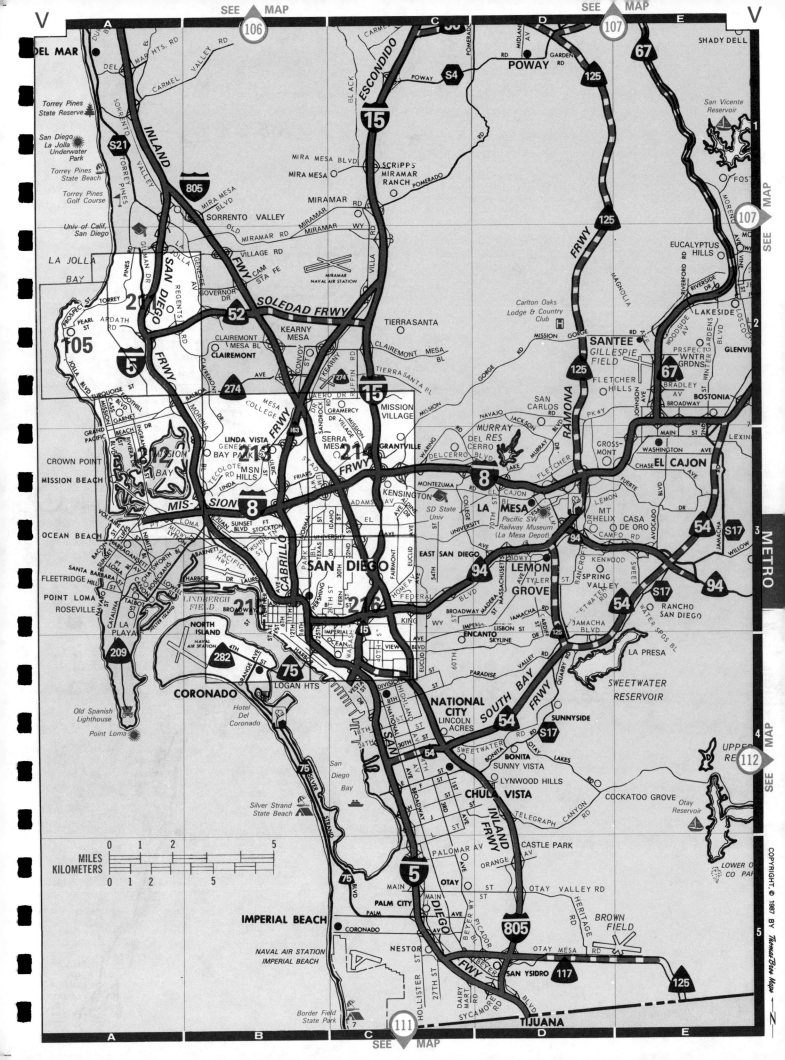

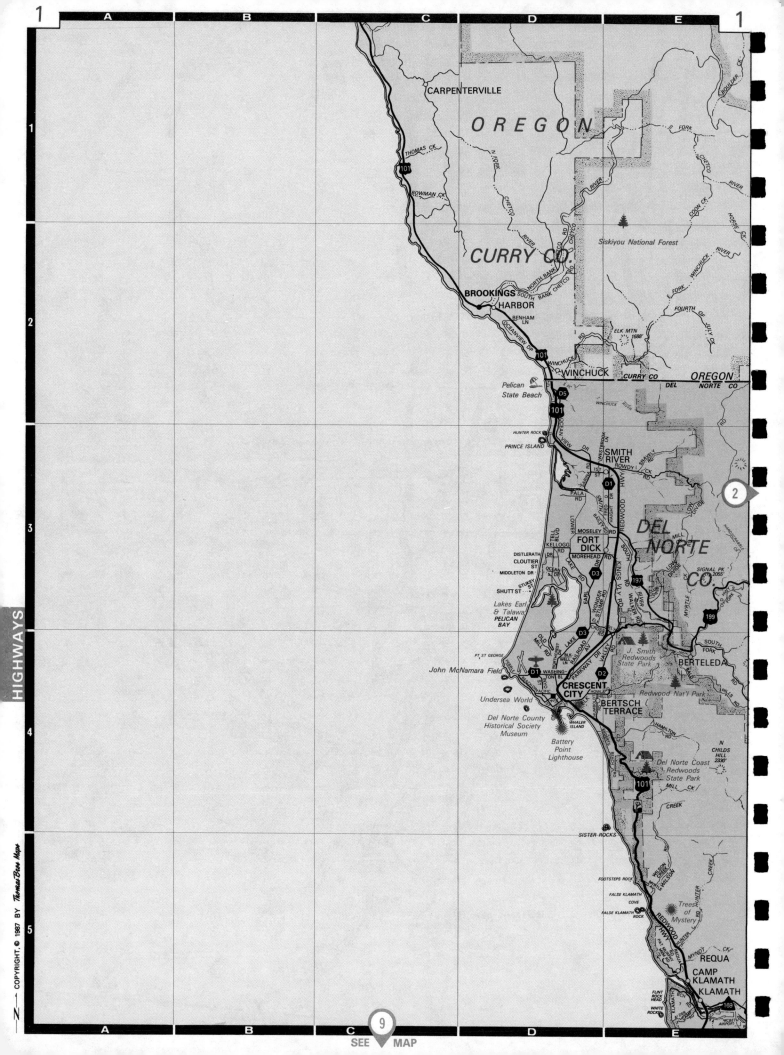

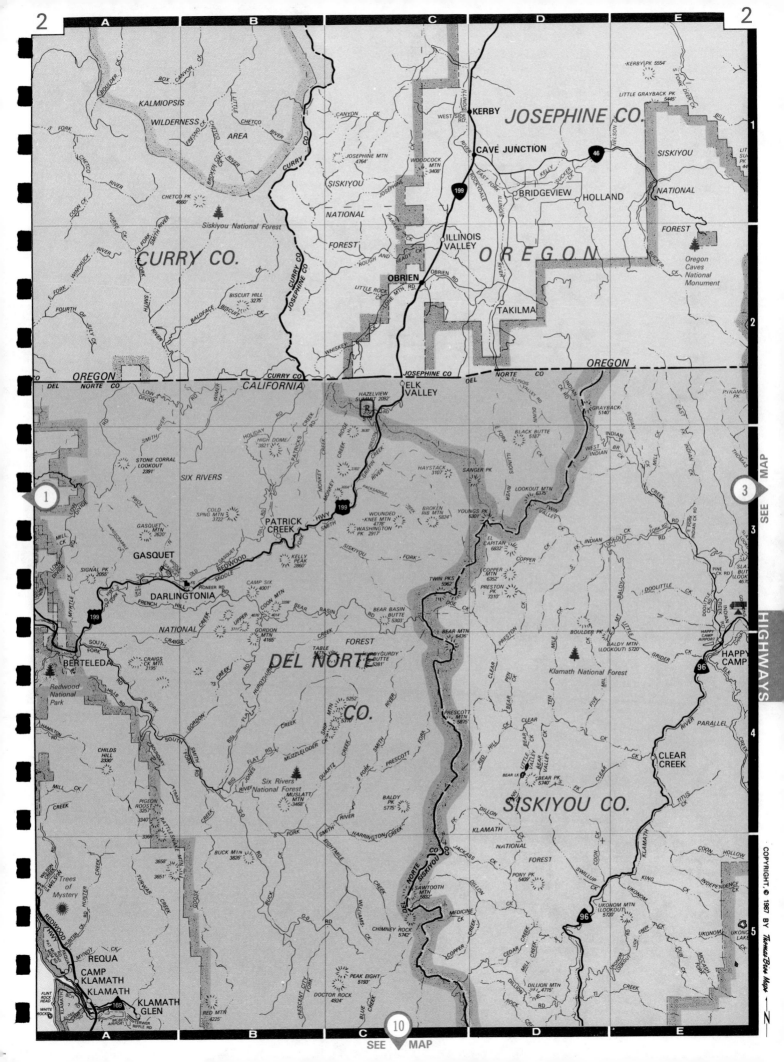

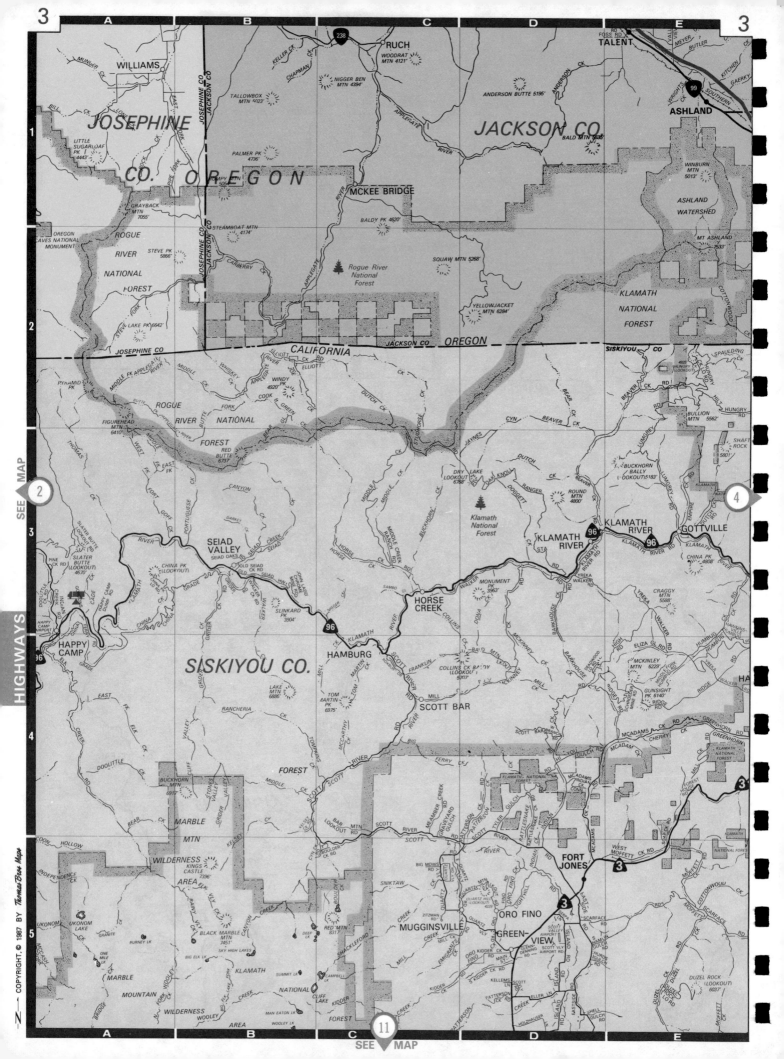

HIGHWAYS

SEE MAP ②

SEE MAP ④

SEE MAP ⑪

SEE MAP ⑪

JOSEPHINE CO. OREGON

JACKSON CO.

WILLIAMS

RUCH

TALENT

ASHLAND

ROGUE RIVER NATIONAL FOREST

MCKEE BRIDGE

ASHLAND WATERSHED

KLAMATH NATIONAL FOREST

CALIFORNIA   JACKSON CO.   OREGON

JOSEPHINE CO

SISKIYOU CO.

ROGUE RIVER NATIONAL FOREST

Klamath National Forest

SEIAD VALLEY

KLAMATH RIVER

KLAMATH RIVER

GOTTVILLE

HAPPY CAMP

HORSE CREEK

HAMBURG

SCOTT BAR

FORT JONES

ORO FINO

MUGGINSVILLE

GREEN-VIEW

MARBLE MTN WILDERNESS AREA

UKONOM LAKE

MARBLE MOUNTAIN WILDERNESS

KLAMATH NATIONAL FOREST

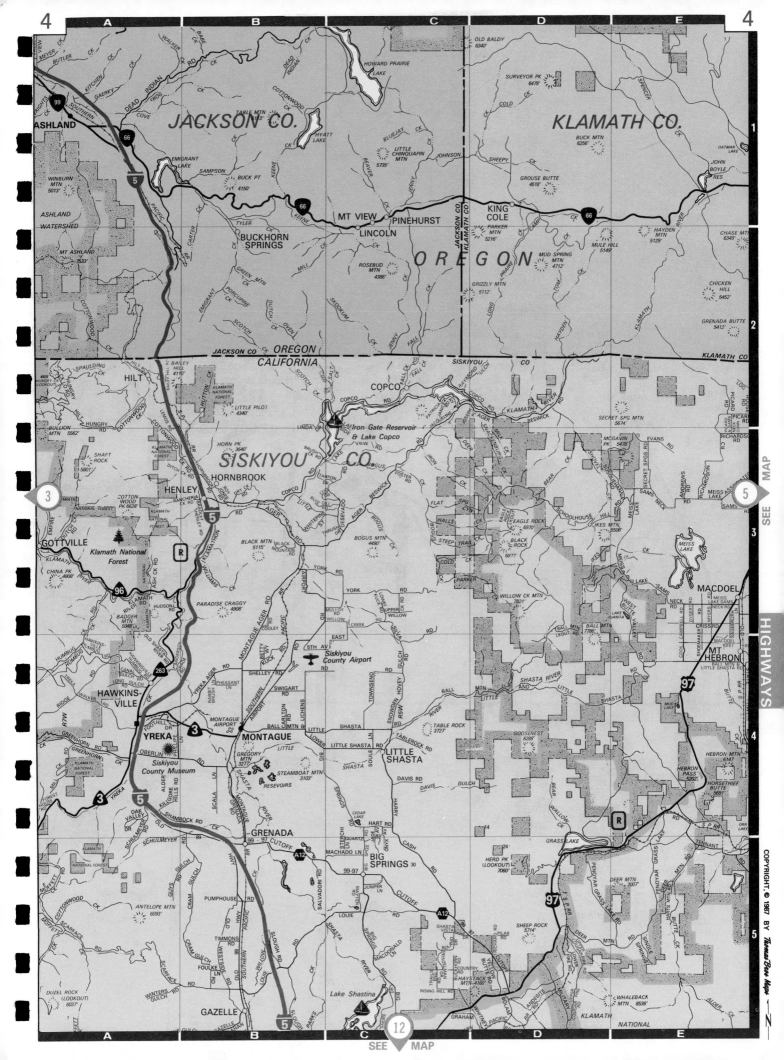

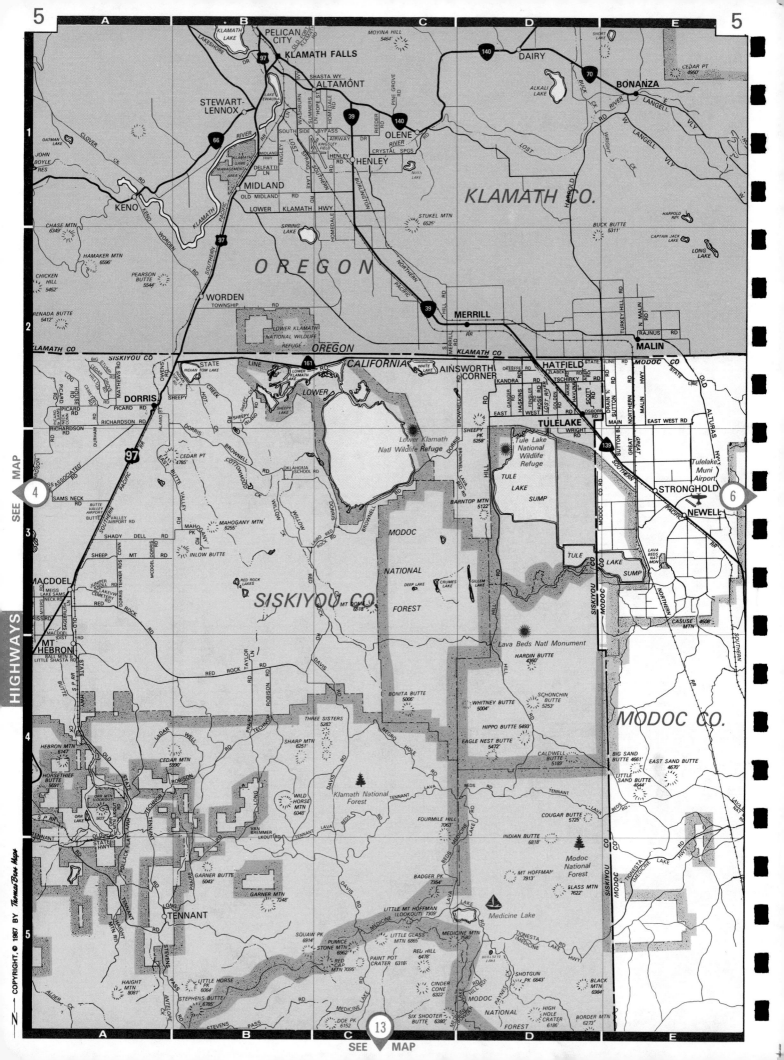

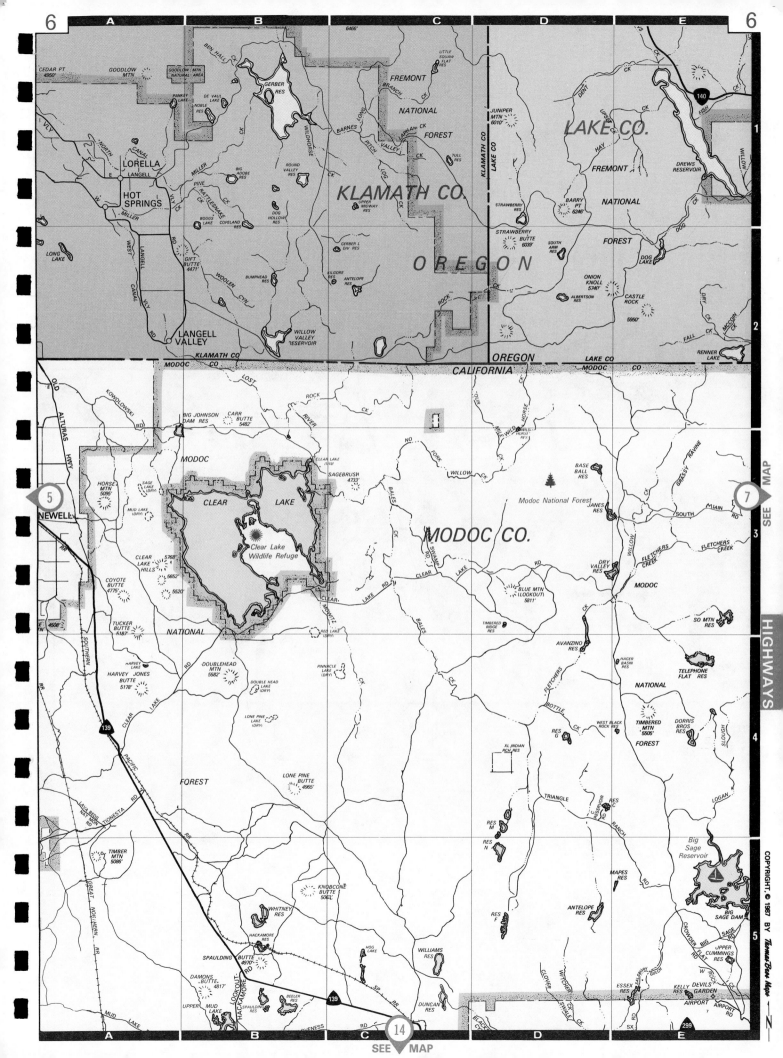

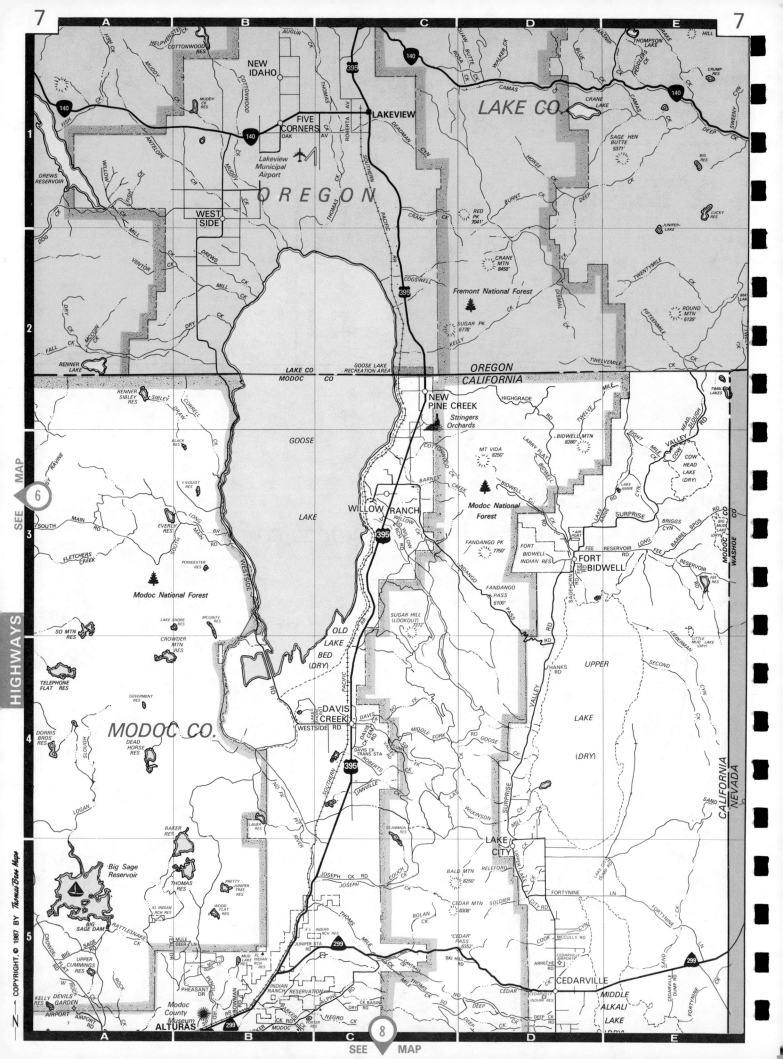

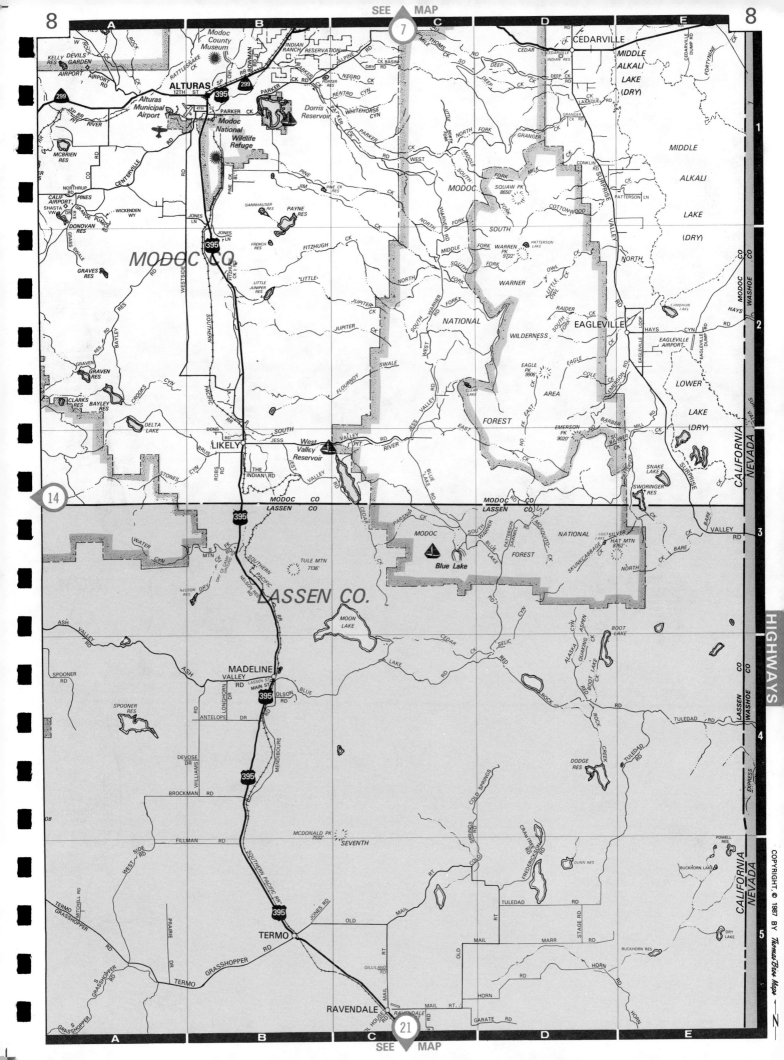

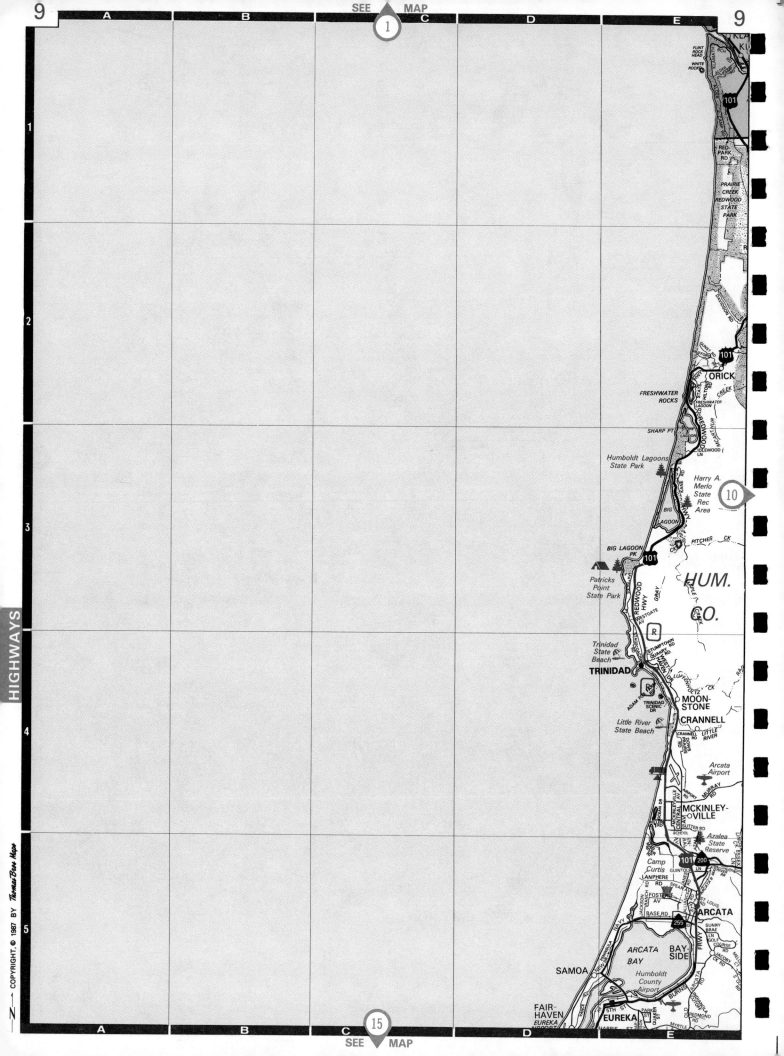

A | B | C | D | E

1

2

3

4

5

FLINT ROCK HEAD
WHITE ROCKS
KLA
KU
101
RED PARK RD

PRAIRIE CREEK REDWOOD STATE PARK

DAVIDSON RD

101
ORICK

FRESHWATER ROCKS

FRESHWATER LAGOON

SHARP PT

Humboldt Lagoons State Park

Harry A. Merlo State Rec Area

10

BIG LAGOON

PITCHER CK

BIG LAGOON PK
101

HUM.
CO.

Patricks Point State Park

REDWOOD HWY

R

Trinidad State Beach
TRINIDAD

MOON-STONE
CRANNELL

Little River State Beach

CRANNELL

LITTLE RIVER

Arcata Airport

MCKINLEY-VILLE

Azalea State Reserve

Camp Curtis
101 200
LANPHERE RD

ARCATA
255

ARCATA BAY
BAY-SIDE

SAMOA

Humboldt County Airport

FAIR-HAVEN
EUREKA

A | B | C | D | E

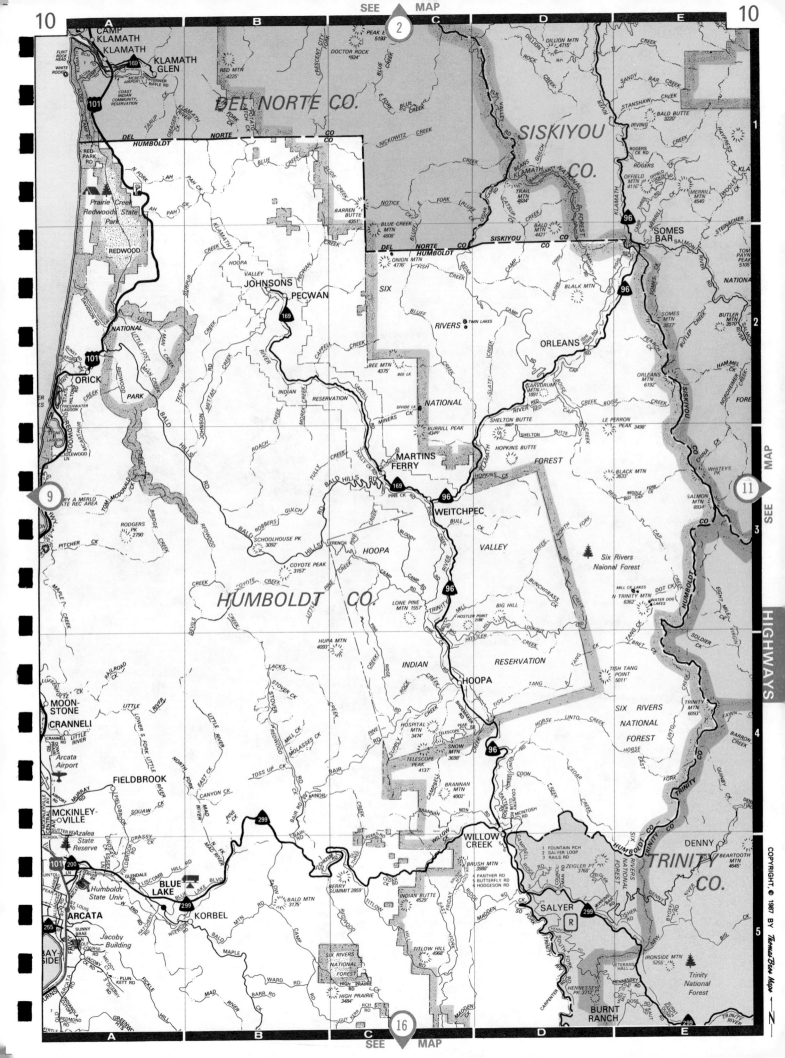

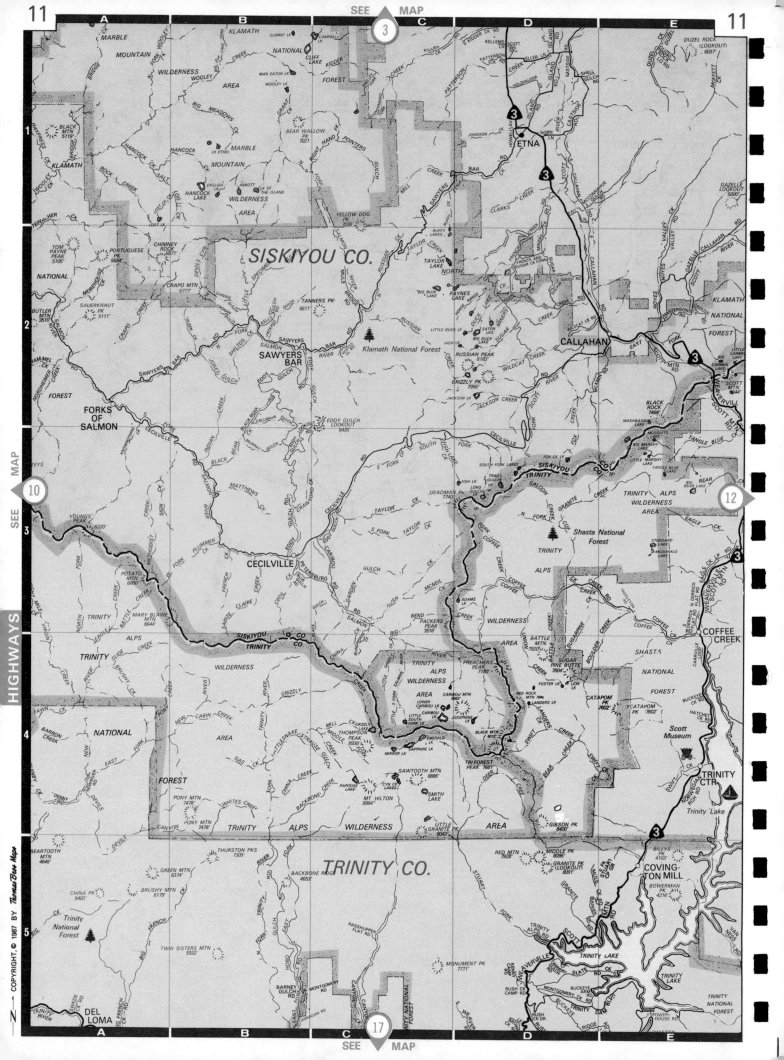

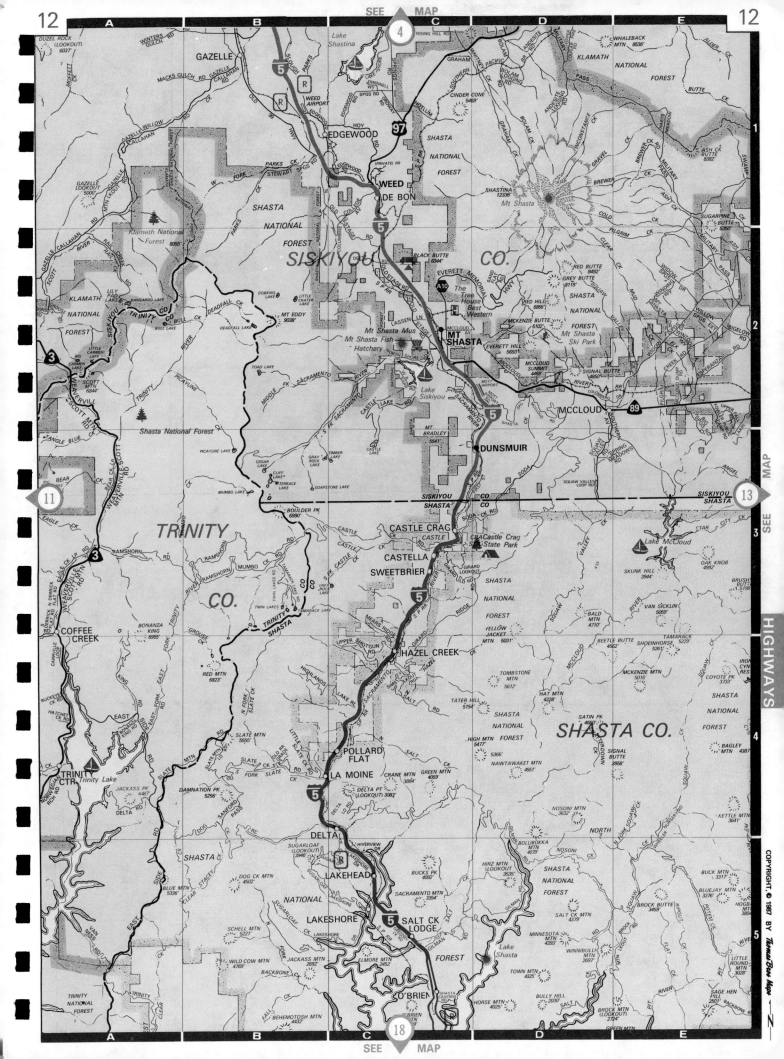

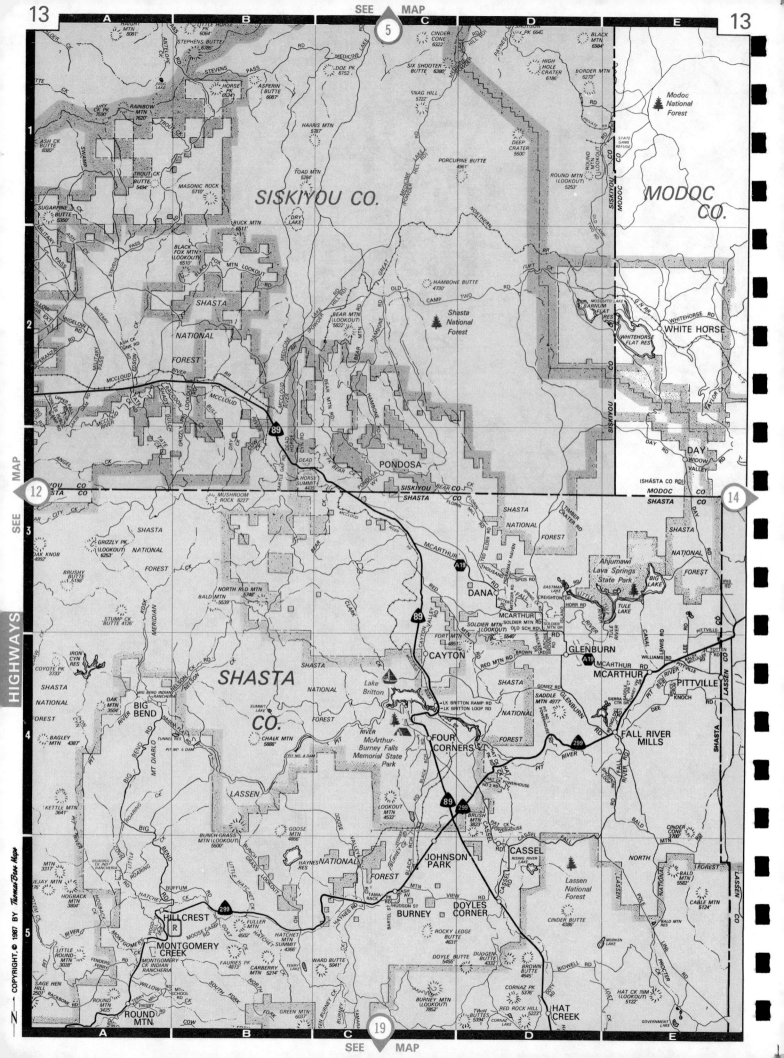

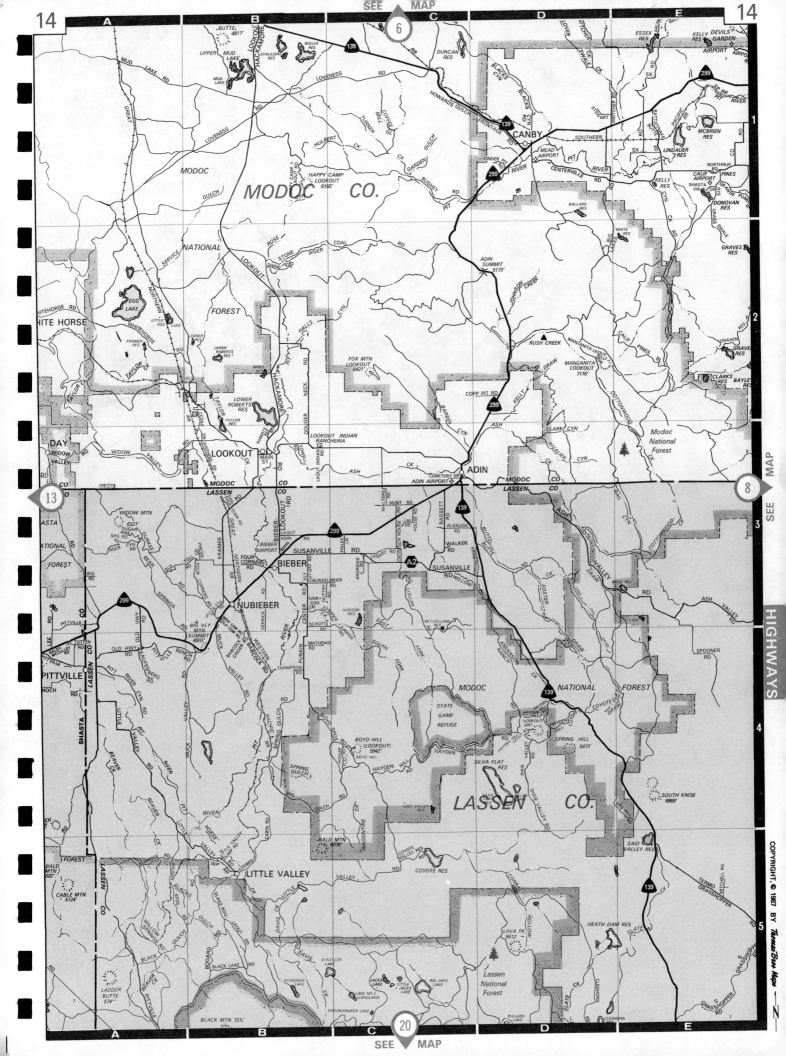

A   B   C   D   E

PACIFIC

OCEAN

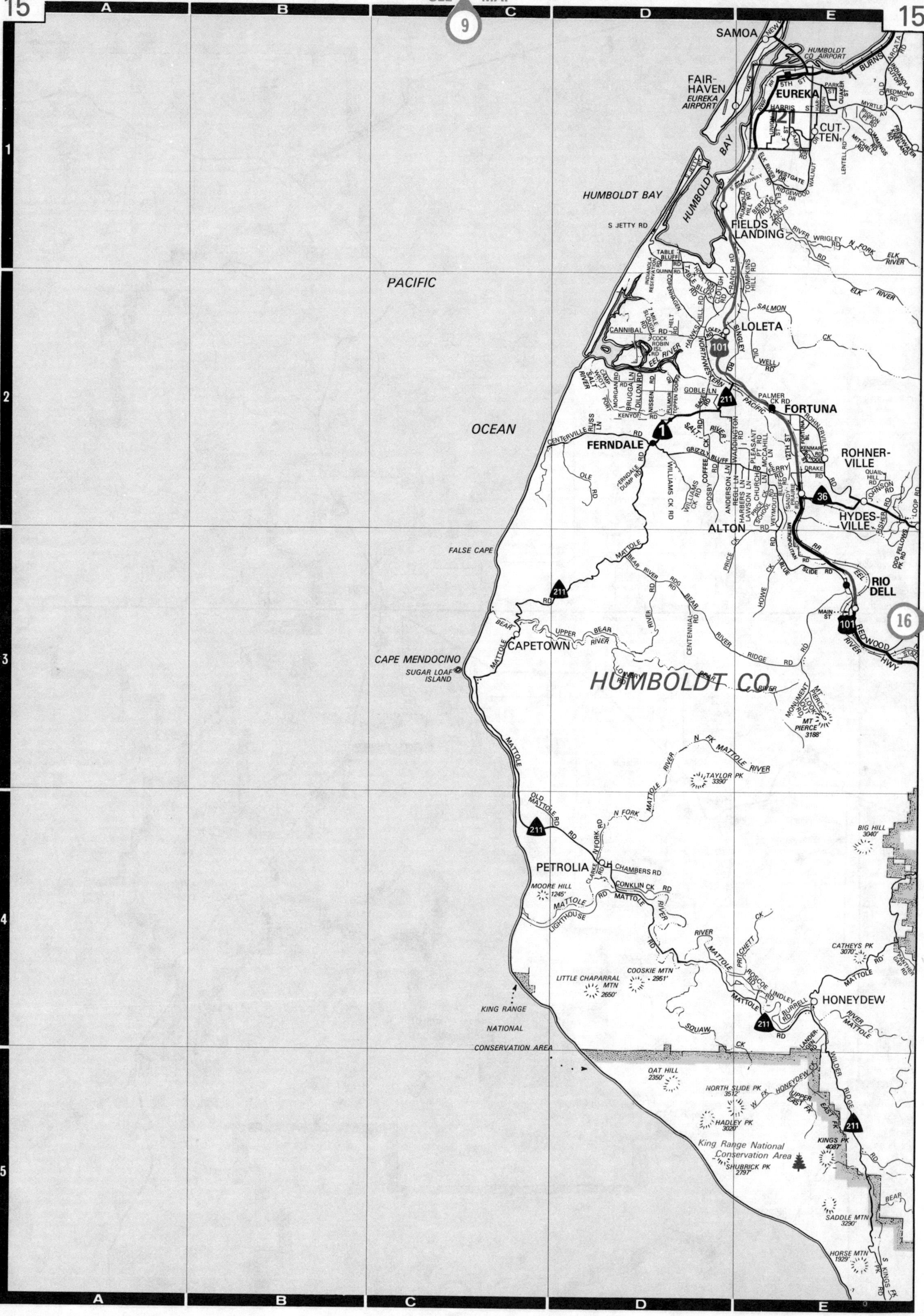

HIGHWAYS

N

COPYRIGHT, © 1987 BY *Thomas Bros Maps*

HUMBOLDT BAY

SAMOA

FAIR-HAVEN
Eureka Airport

EUREKA

CUT-TEN

FIELDS LANDING

S JETTY RD

TABLE BLUFF

LOLETA

101

FORTUNA

211

FERNDALE

1

ROHNER-VILLE

36

ALTON

HYDES-VILLE

FALSE CAPE

211

RIO DELL

101

16

CAPETOWN

CAPE MENDOCINO
SUGAR LOAF ISLAND

HUMBOLDT CO

MT PIERCE 3188'

TAYLOR PK 3390'

MATTOLE RIVER

N FK MATTOLE RIVER

211

OLD MATTOLE RD

PETROLIA

MOORE HILL 1245'

CHAMBERS RD

CONKLIN CK RD

LIGHTHOUSE

BIG HILL 3040'

LITTLE CHAPARRAL MTN 2650'

COOSKIE MTN 2951'

CATHEYS PK 3070'

KING RANGE

NATIONAL

CONSERVATION AREA

HONEYDEW

211

OAT HILL 2350'

NORTH SLIDE PK 3512'

HADLEY PK 3020'

KINGS PK 4087'

211

King Range National Conservation Area

SHUBRICK PK 2797'

SADDLE MTN 3290'

HORSE MTN 1929'

A   B   C   D   E

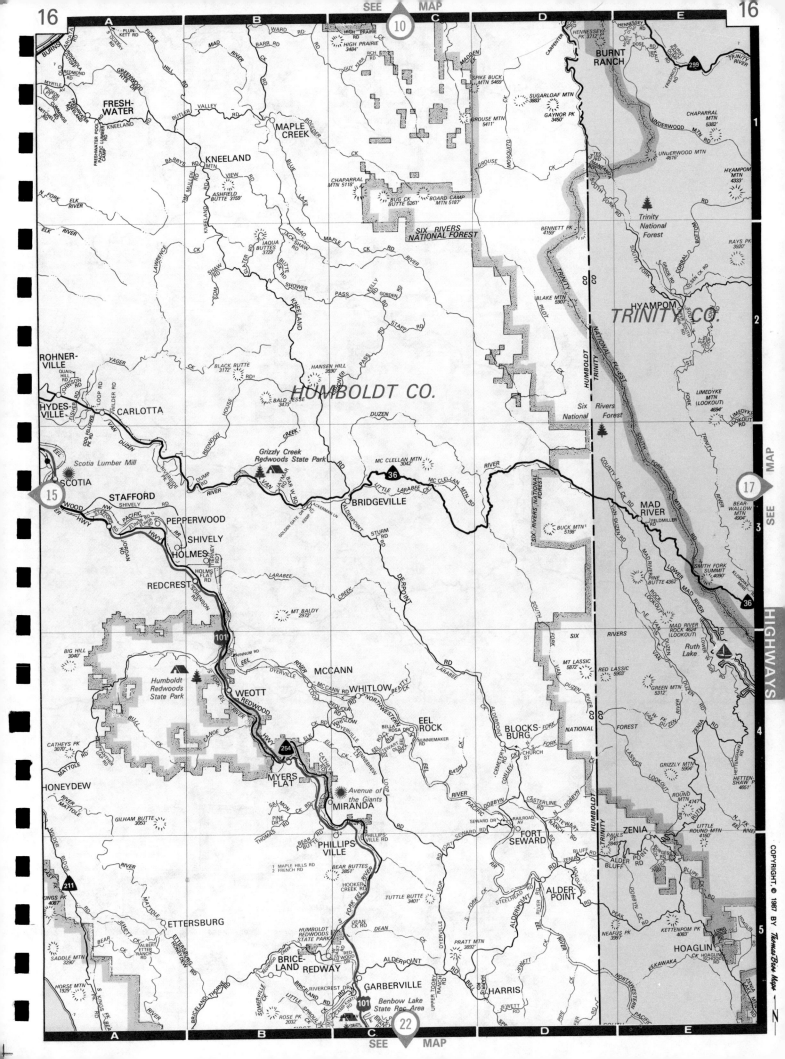

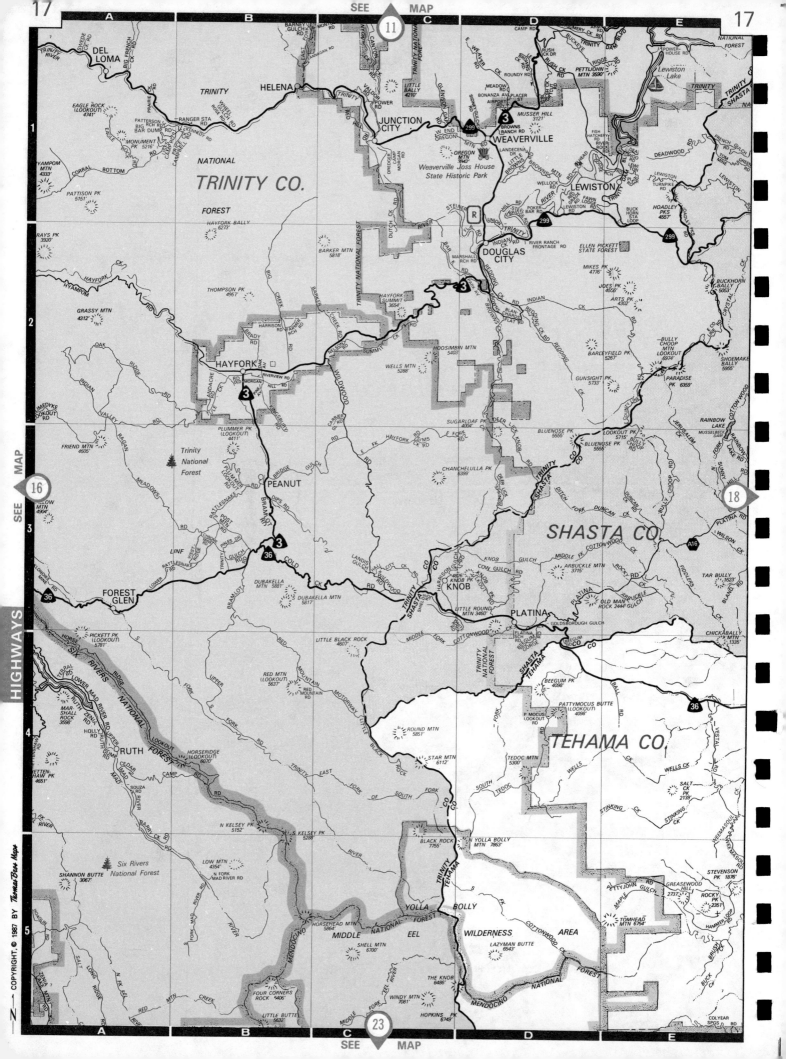

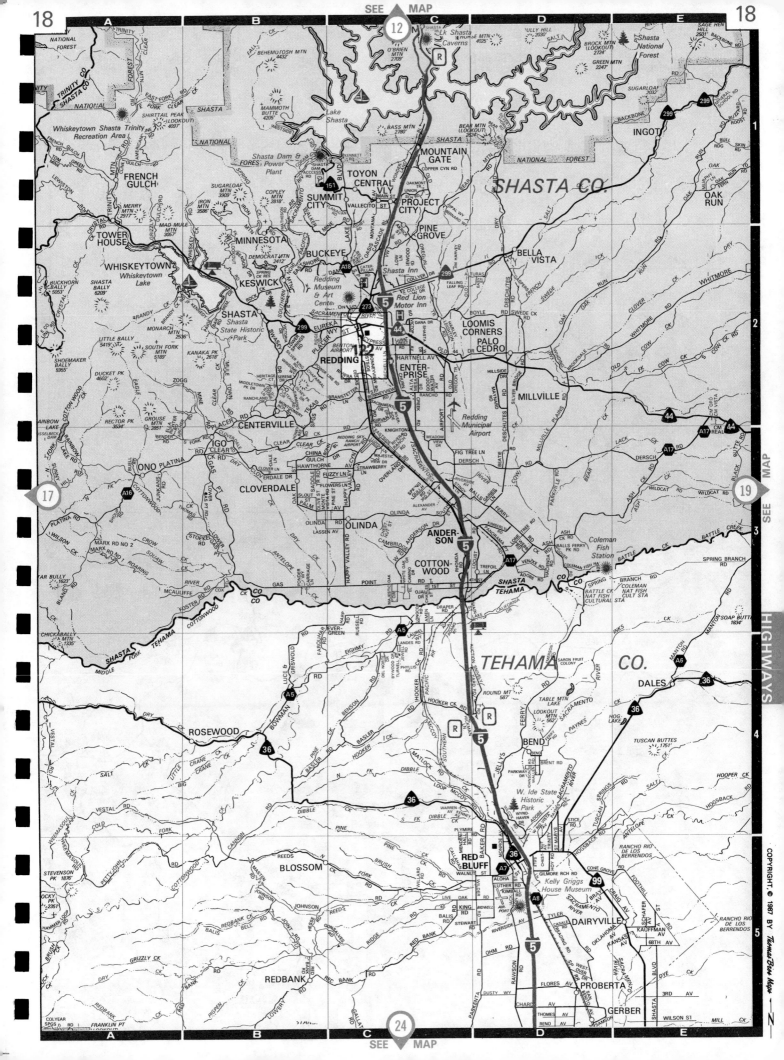

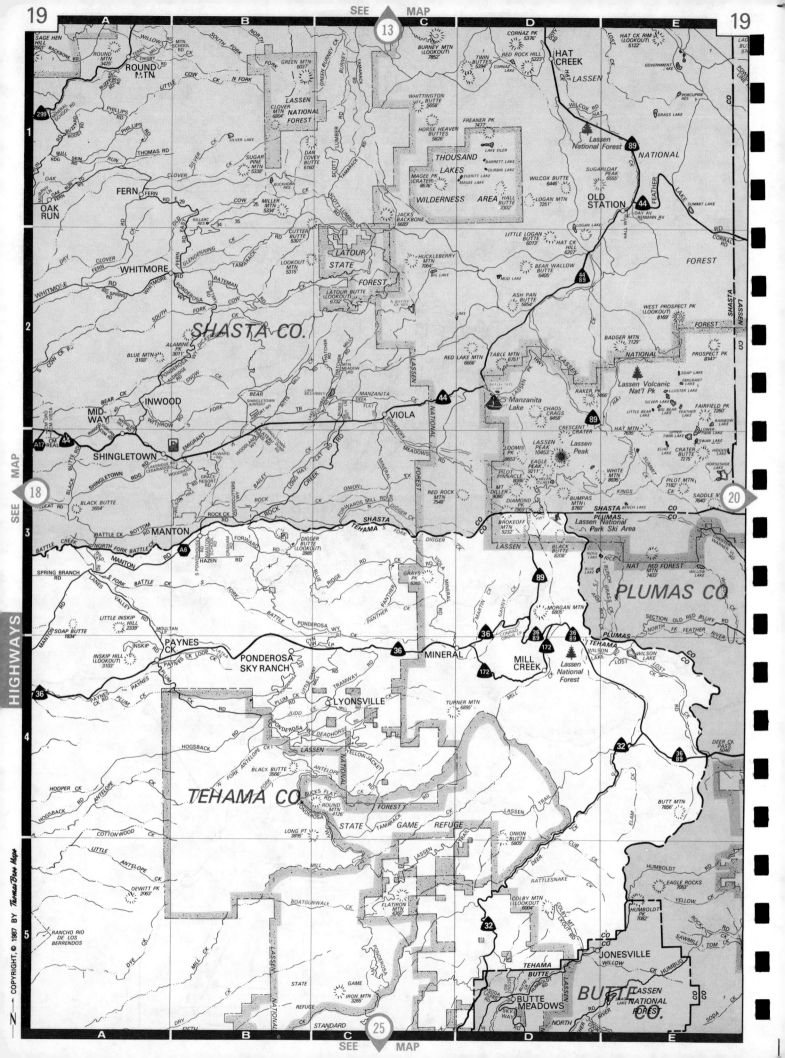

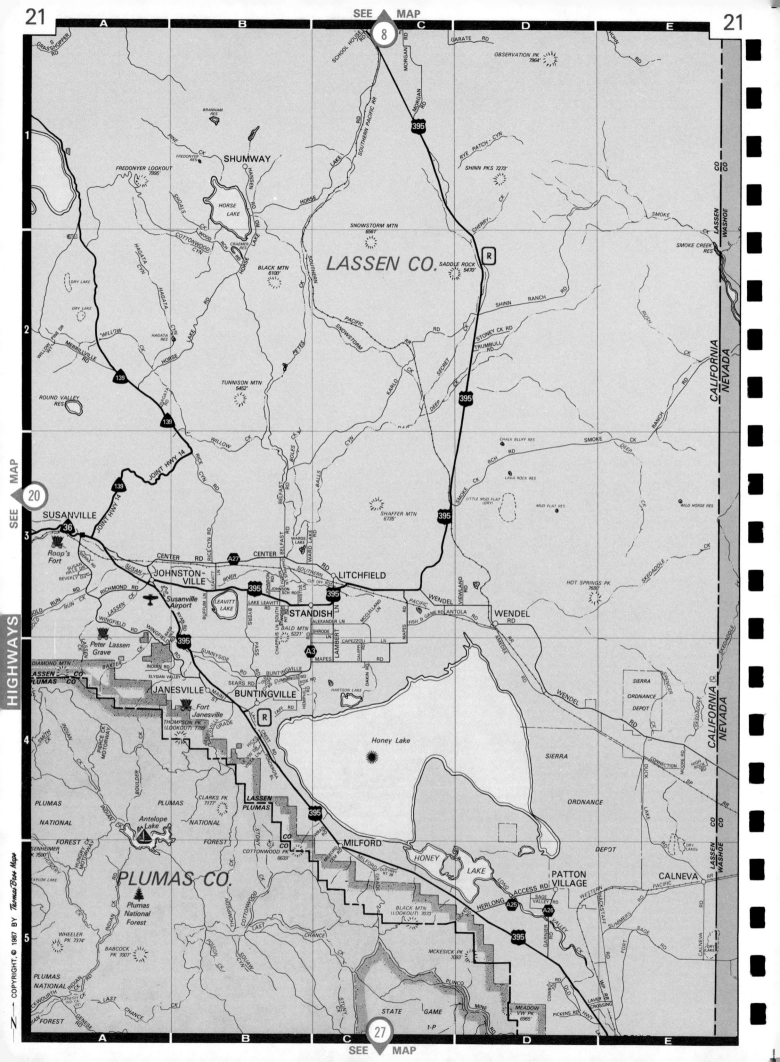

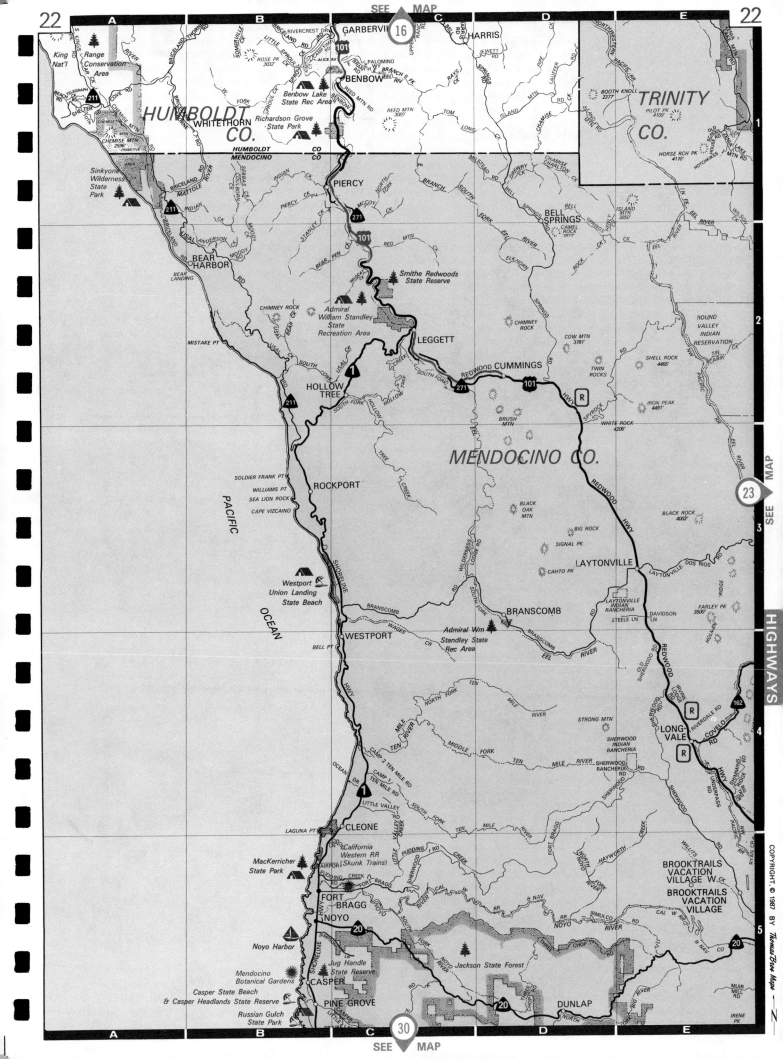

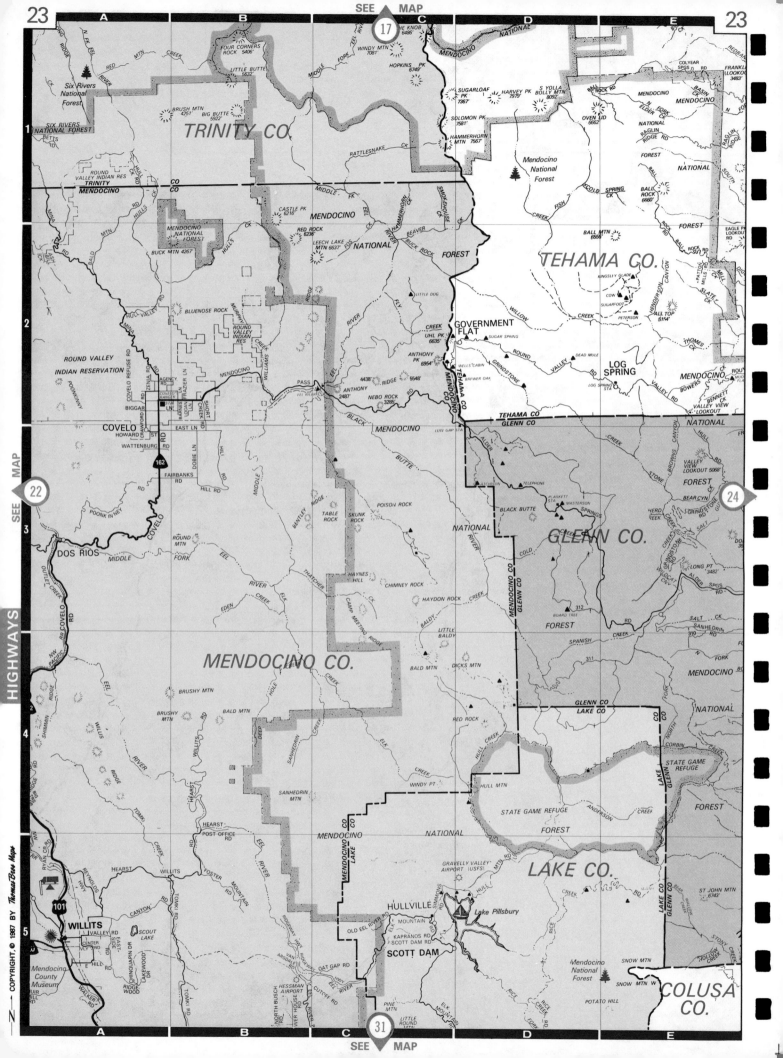

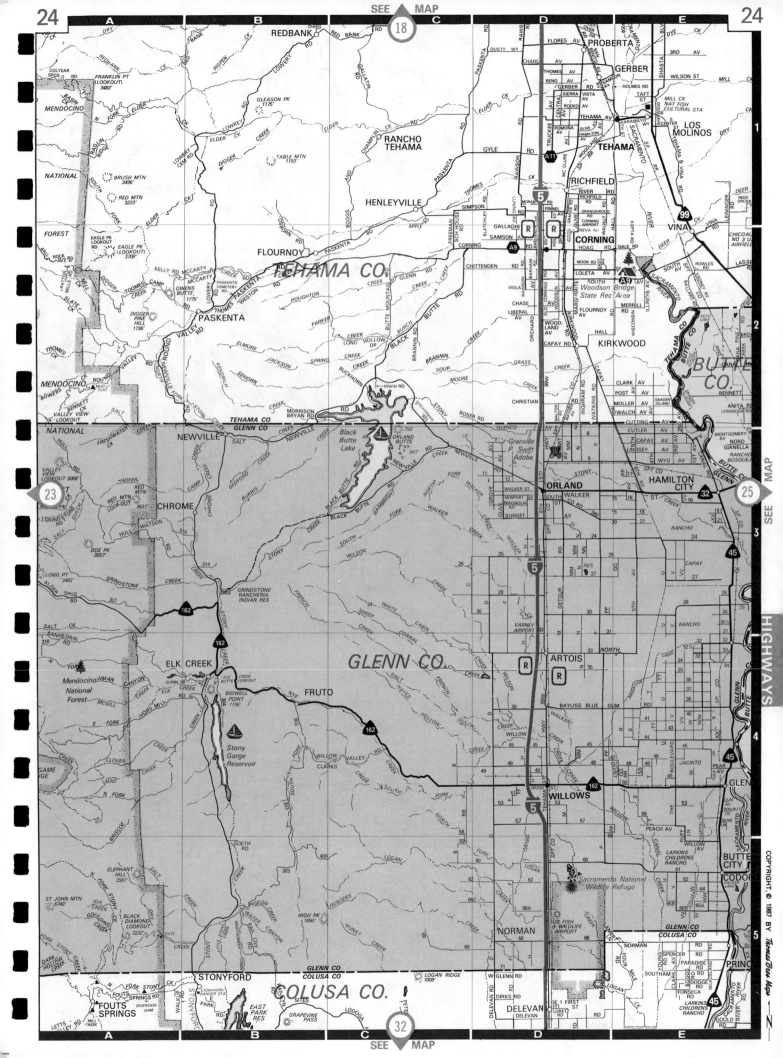

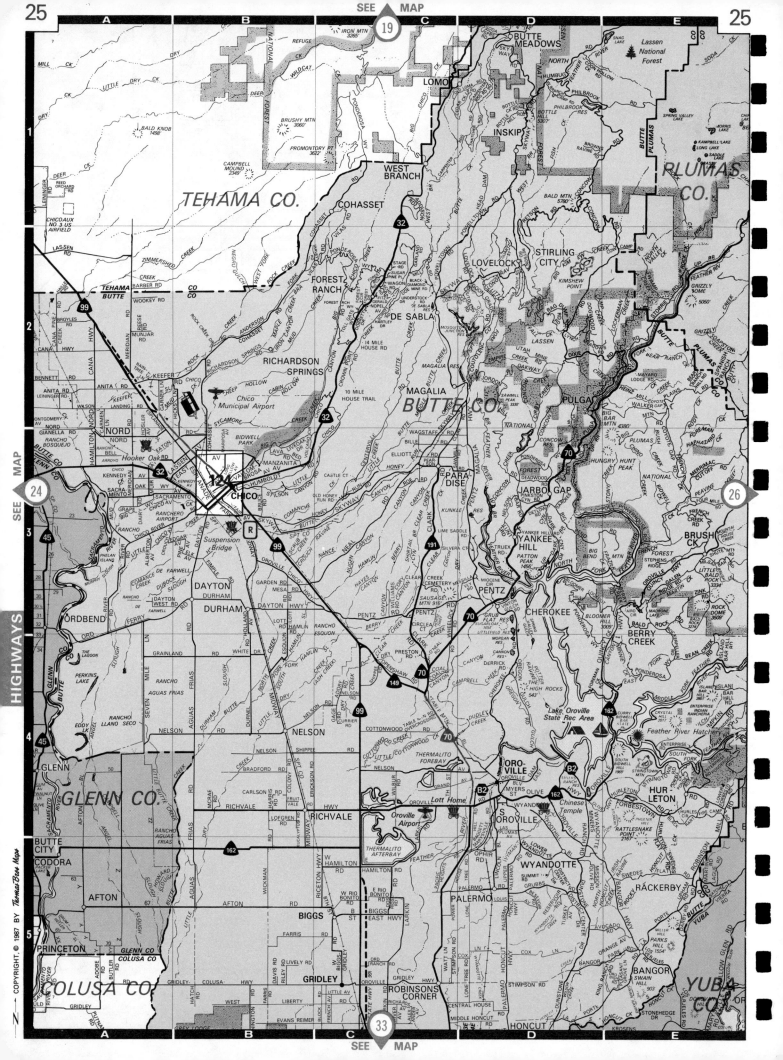

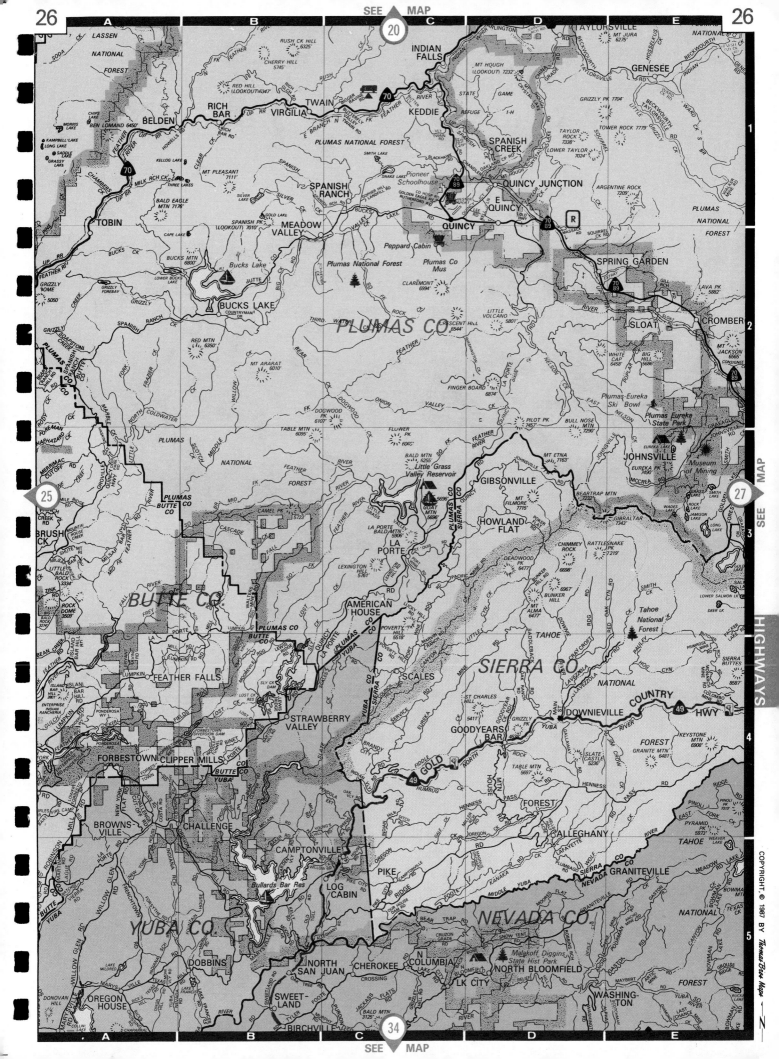

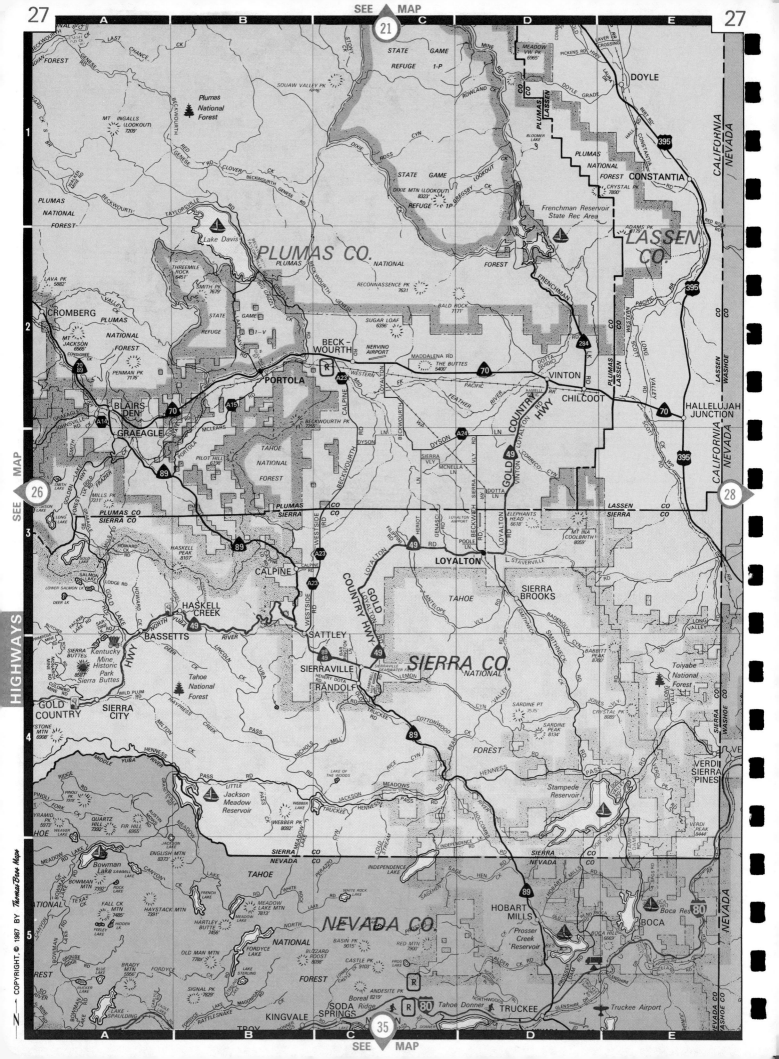

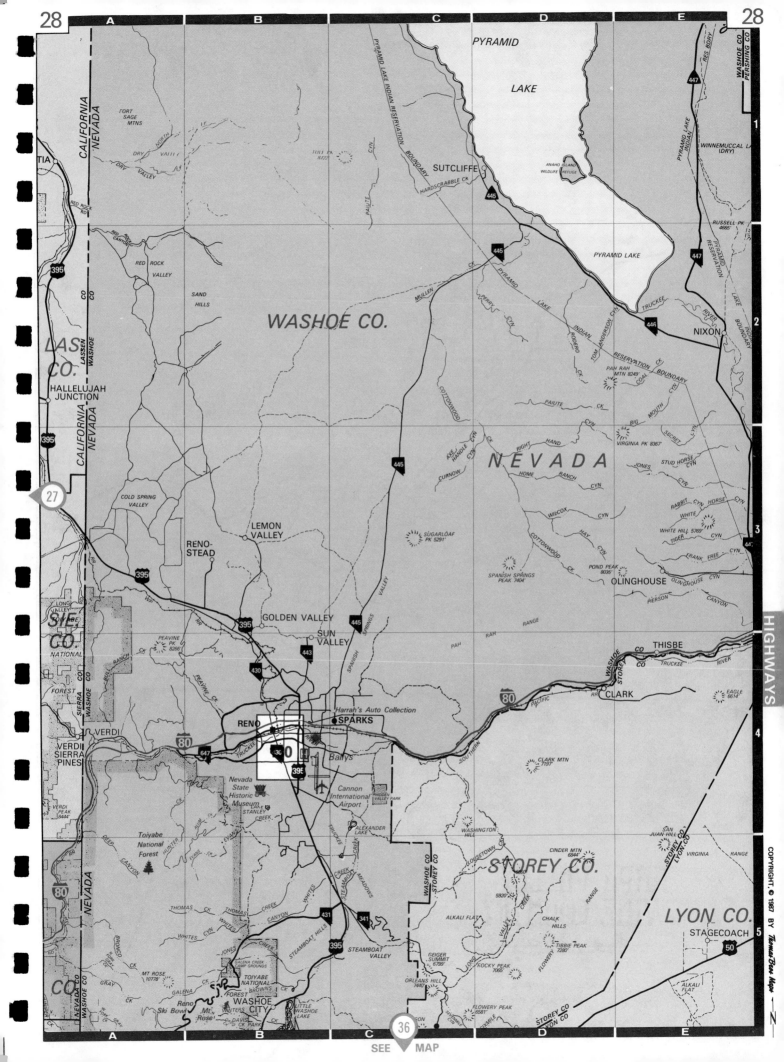

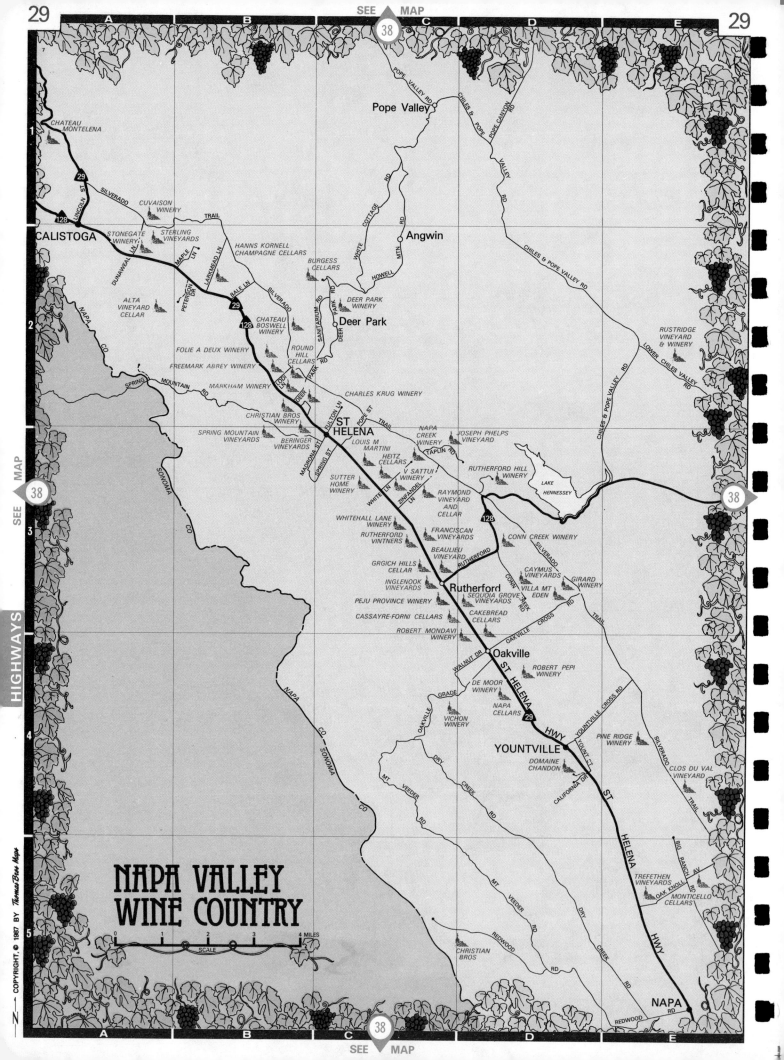

NAPA VALLEY WINE COUNTRY

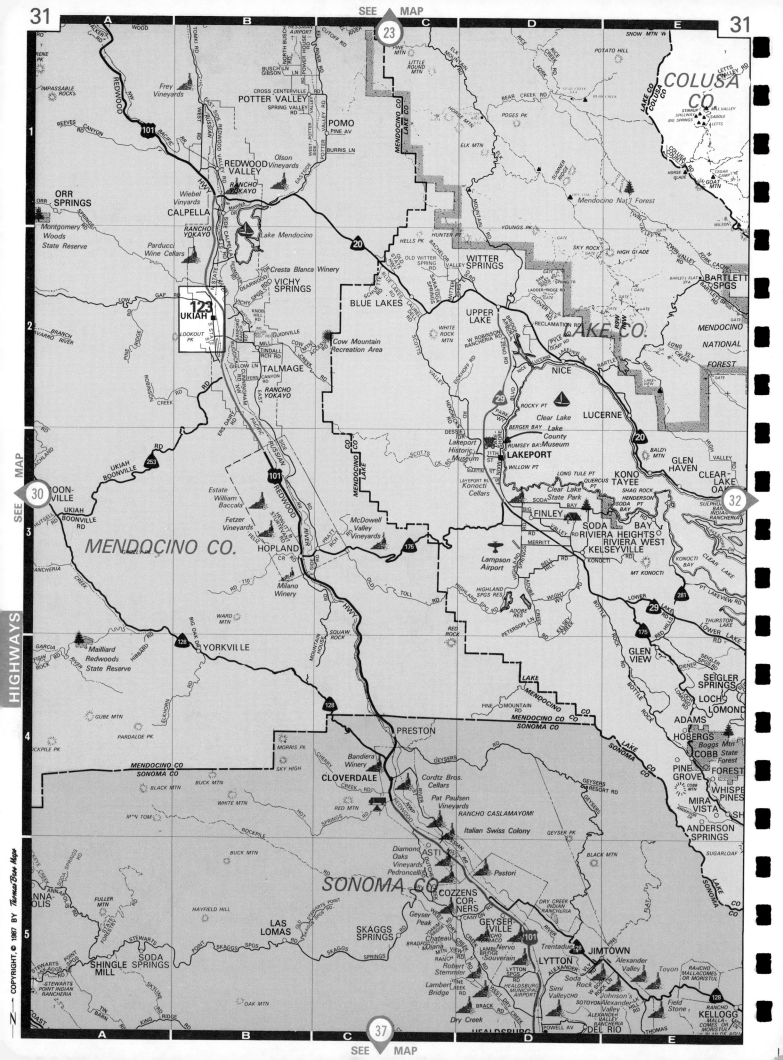

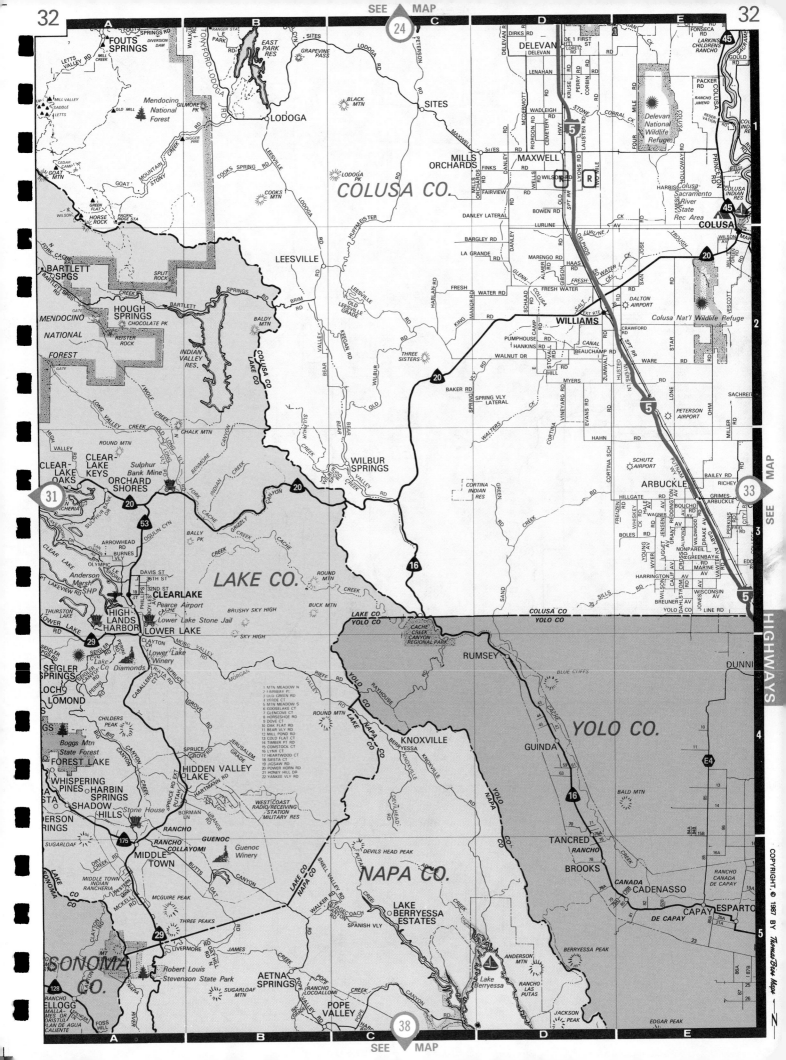

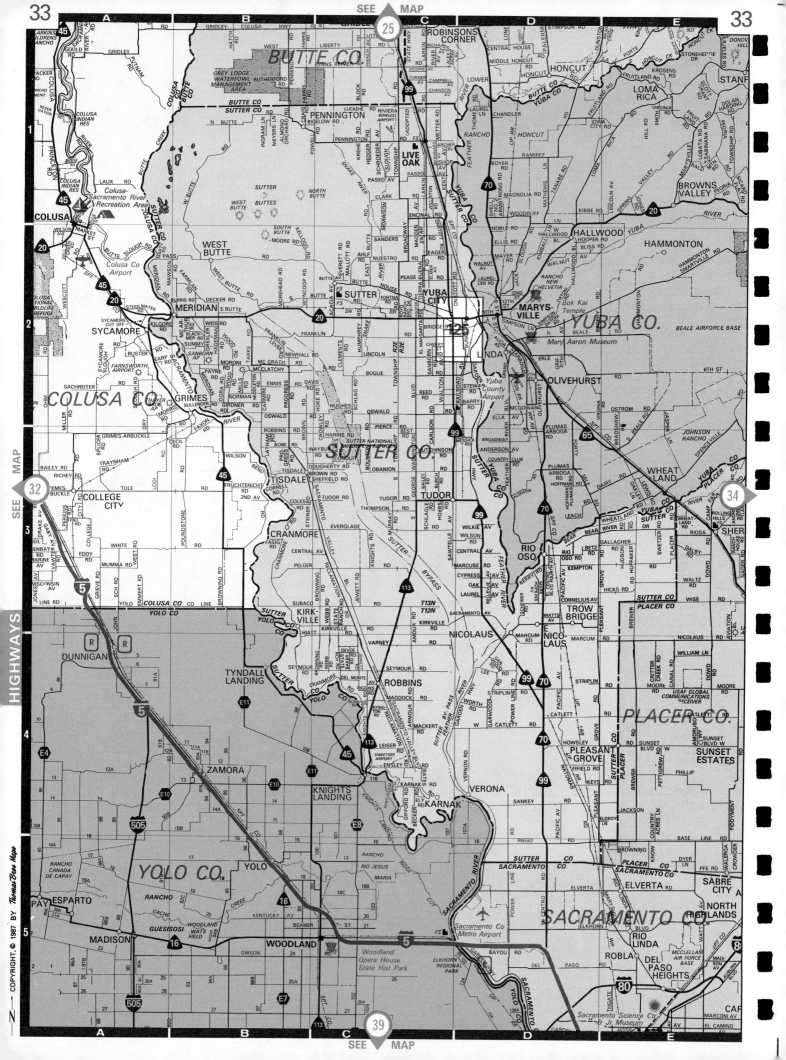

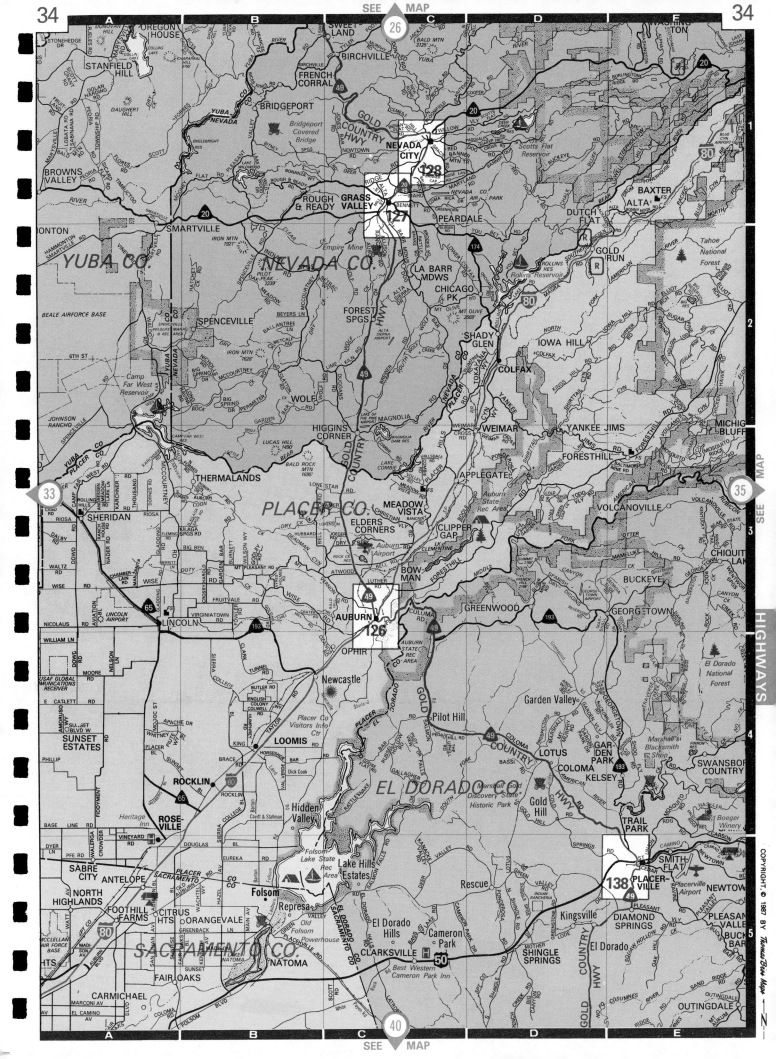

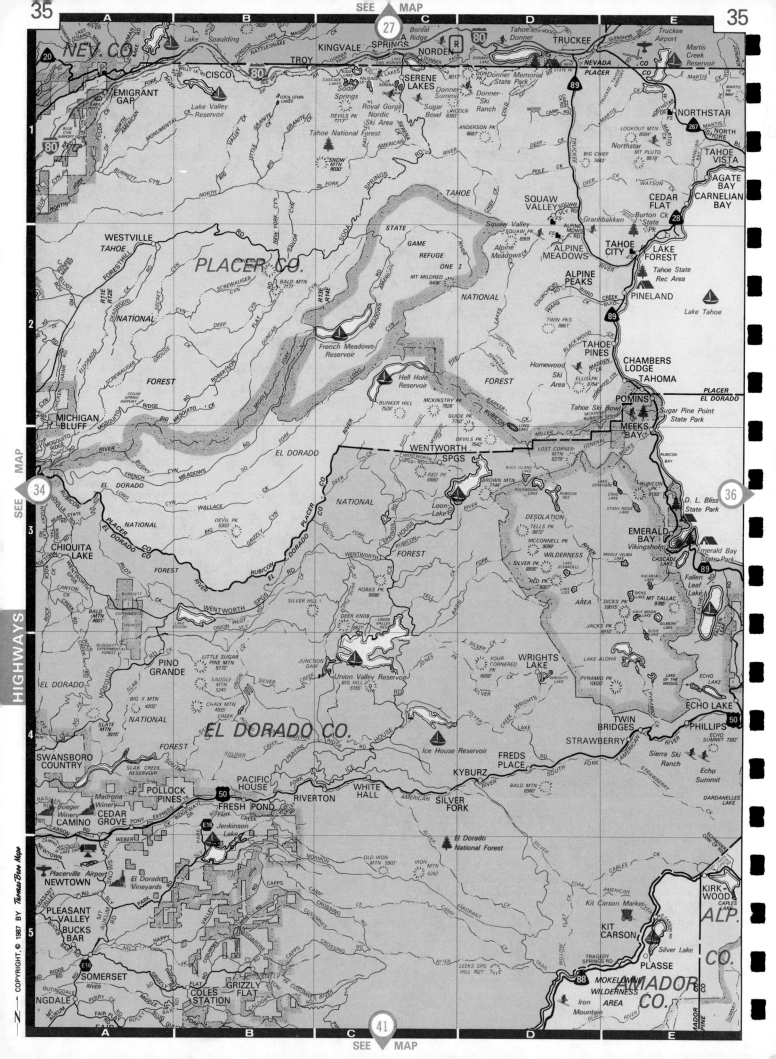

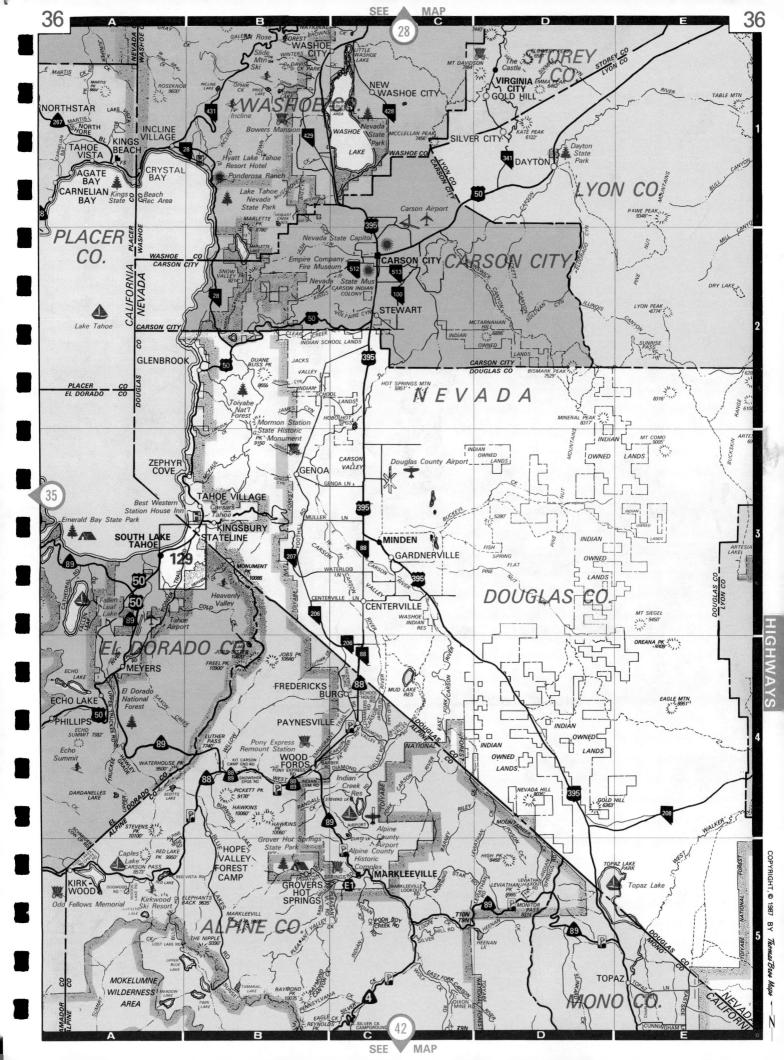

HIGHWAYS

COPYRIGHT, © 1987 BY Thomas Bros. Maps

SONOMA CO.

MARIN CO.

PACIFIC OCEAN

DRAKES BAY

HEALDSBURG

WINDSOR

SANTA ROSA

SEBASTOPOL

COTATI

ROHNERT PARK

DEL RIO WOODS

MARK WEST SPRINGS

KELLOGG

SOUTH PARK

CAZADERO

EL BONITA

RIO NIDO

HACIENDA

GUERNEWOOD PARK
VACATION BEACH

GUERNEVILLE

NORTH WOOD
MONTE RIO

SUMMER HOME PARK

FORESTVILLE

GRATON

JENNER-BY-THE SEA

DUNCANS MILLS

BRIDGE HAVEN

OCEAN VIEW

SERENO DEL MAR

CARMET

OCCIDENTAL

CAMP MEEKER

FREESTONE

KNOWLES CORNER

CUNNINGHAM CADWELL

HESSEL

WASHOE

FORT ROSS

WALSH LANDING

SALMON CREEK

BODEGA BAY

BODEGA

VALLEY FORD

FALLON

DILLON BEACH

TOMALES

PT REYES STATION

INVERNESS

NICASIO

BOLINAS

FOREST KNOLLS

LAGUNITAS

VILLA GRANDE

Point Reyes

Drakes Estero

Bodega Head

Bodega Bay Harbor

Tomales Bay State Park

Point Reyes Beach

Sonoma Coast State Beach

Salt Point State Park

Austin Creek State Rec Area

Armstrong Redwoods State Reserve

Ft Ross State Historic Park

Kruse Rhododendron State Reserve

Windsor Water Works

Healdsburg Municipal Airport

Sotoyome

Simi Valley

Alexander Valley Rancheria

Field Stone

RANCHO KELLOGG MALLA-COMES OR MORISTUL Y PLAN DE AGUA CALIENTE

Stephen Zellerbach

Clos Du Bois

Foppiano

Piper Sonoma Cellars

Rodney Strong

Hop Kiln

Landmark Vineyards

Rancho San Miguel

Korbel Champagne Cellars

J Rochioli Vineyards

Topolos at Russian River

Dehlinger

Sebastopol Indian Rancheria

Graton Rancho Canada de Jonive

Rancho Llano de Santa Rosa

Rancho Cotate

Rancho Estero Americano

Rancho Bodega

Rancho Roblar de la Miseria

Rancho Blucher

Rancho San Antonio

Rancho Nicasio

S.P. Taylor State Park

Golden Gate Nat'l Rec Area

Point Reyes National Seashore

Saint Teresa's Church

Doran Regional Park

Mussel Pt

Goat Rock

Red Hill

Bird Rock

Toms Pt

McClures Beach

Pierce Point

Drakes Estero

Sea Lion Cove

Chimney Rock

Pt Resistance

Millers Pt

Double Pt

Abalone Pt

Kent Lake

FISK MILL COVE

SALT PT GERSTLE COVE

OCEAN COVE Stillwater Cove

TIMBER COVE WINDERMERE PT

FORT ROSS COVE

Tomales Bluff

Dillon Beach

Rancho Nicasio

RANCHO TOMALES

N→

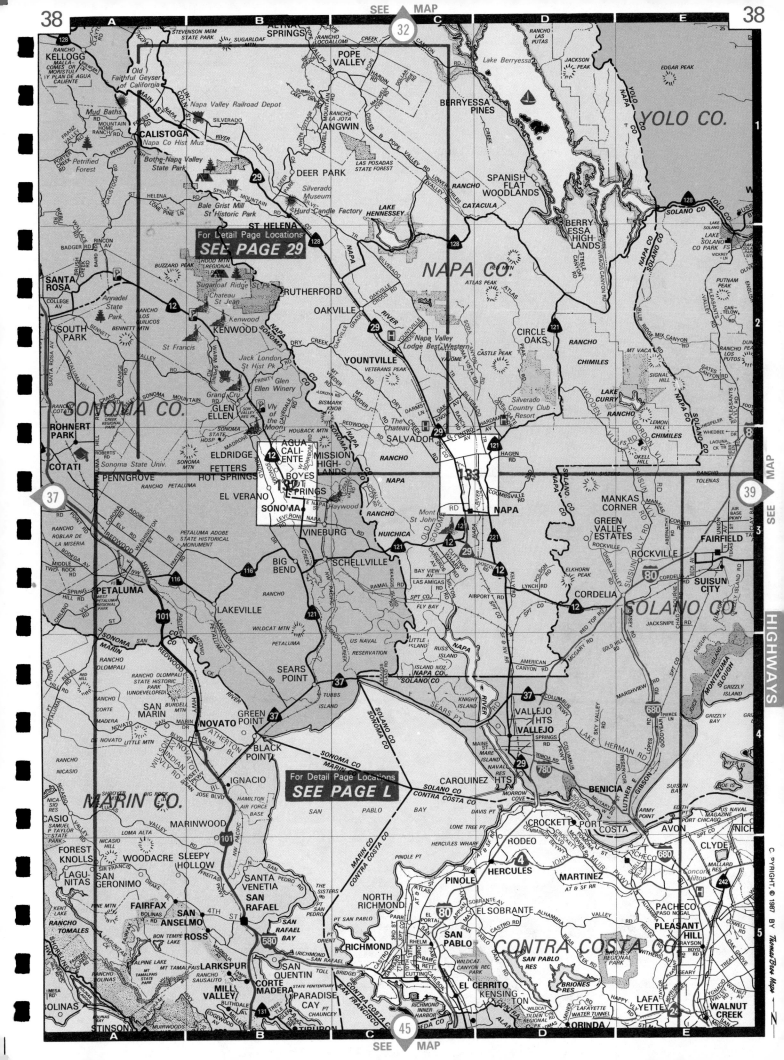

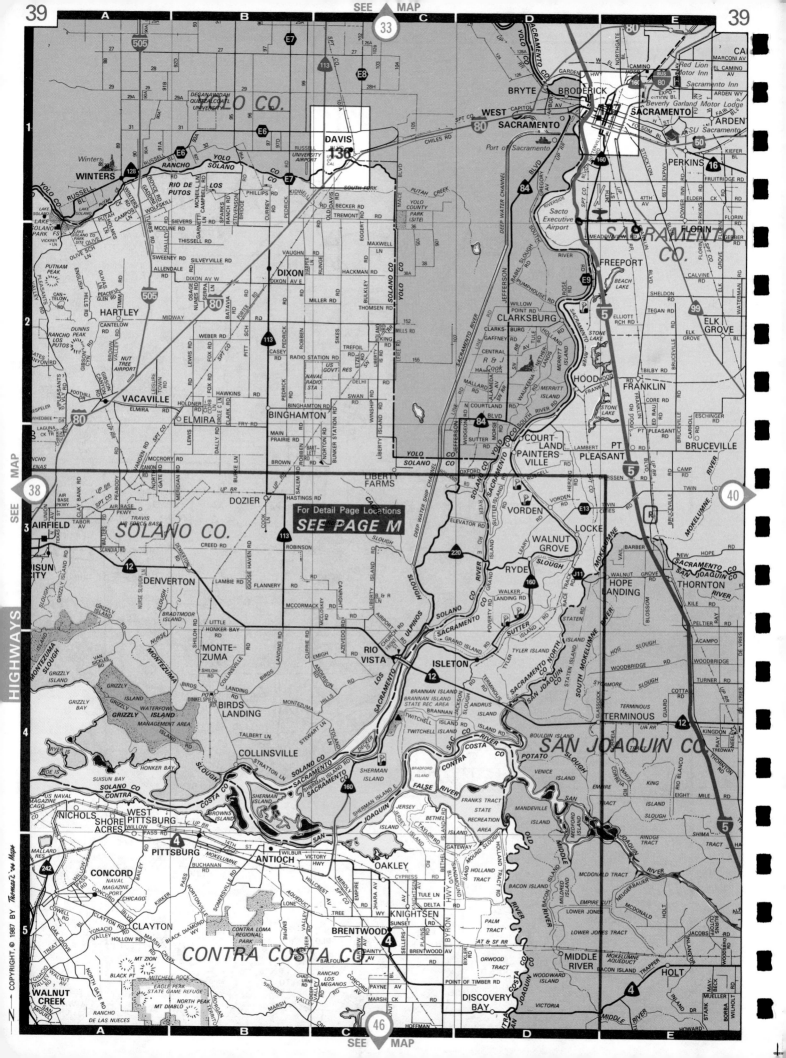

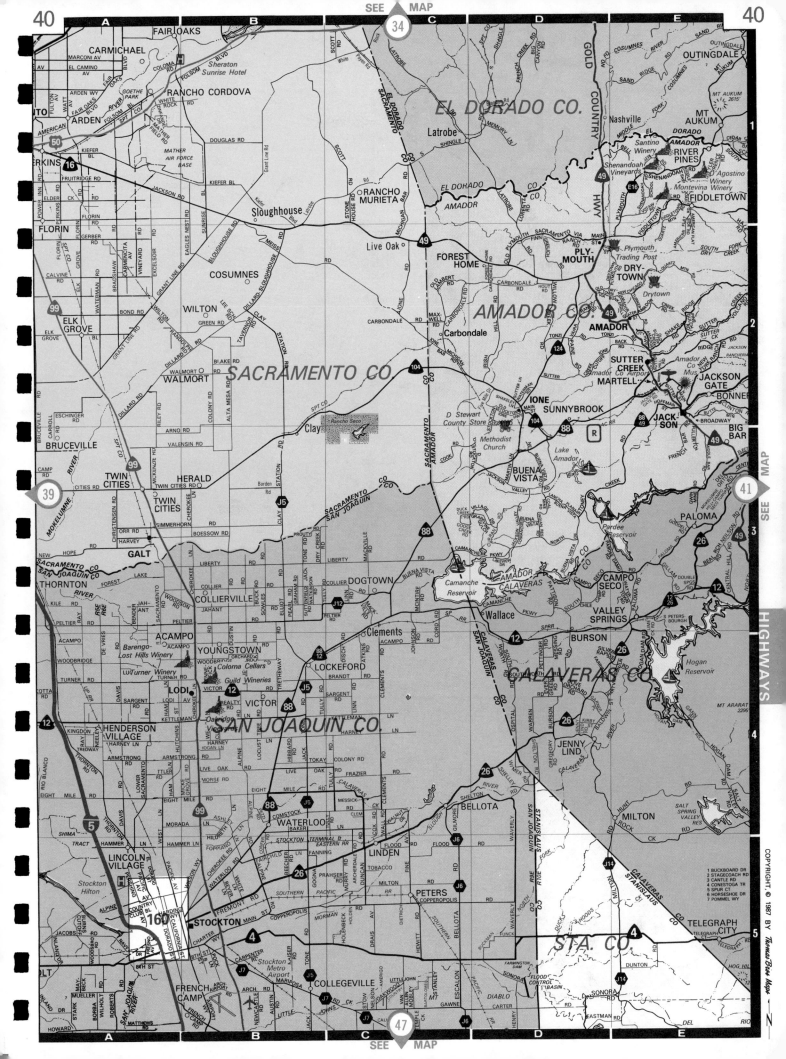

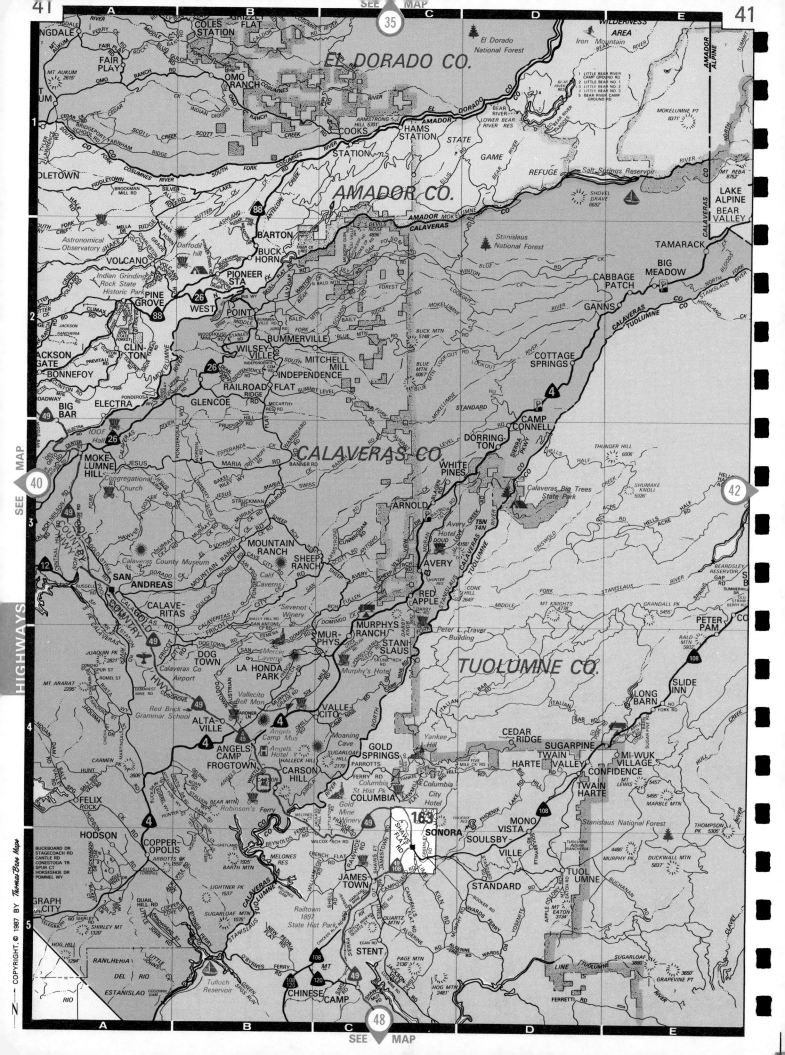

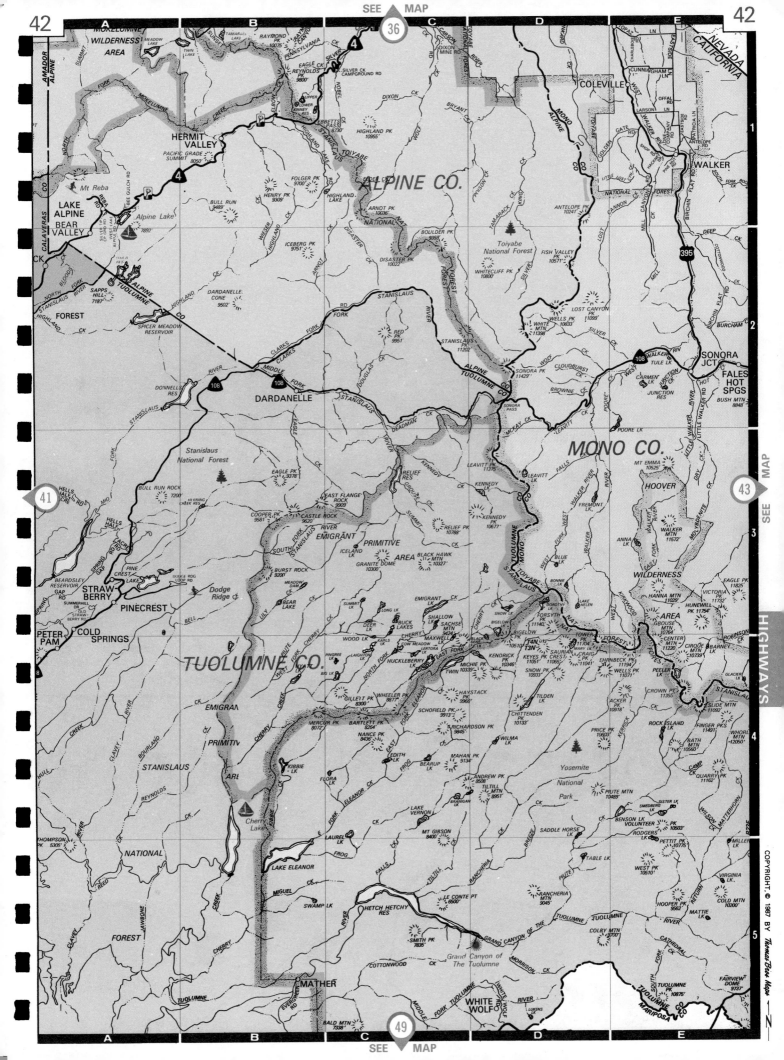

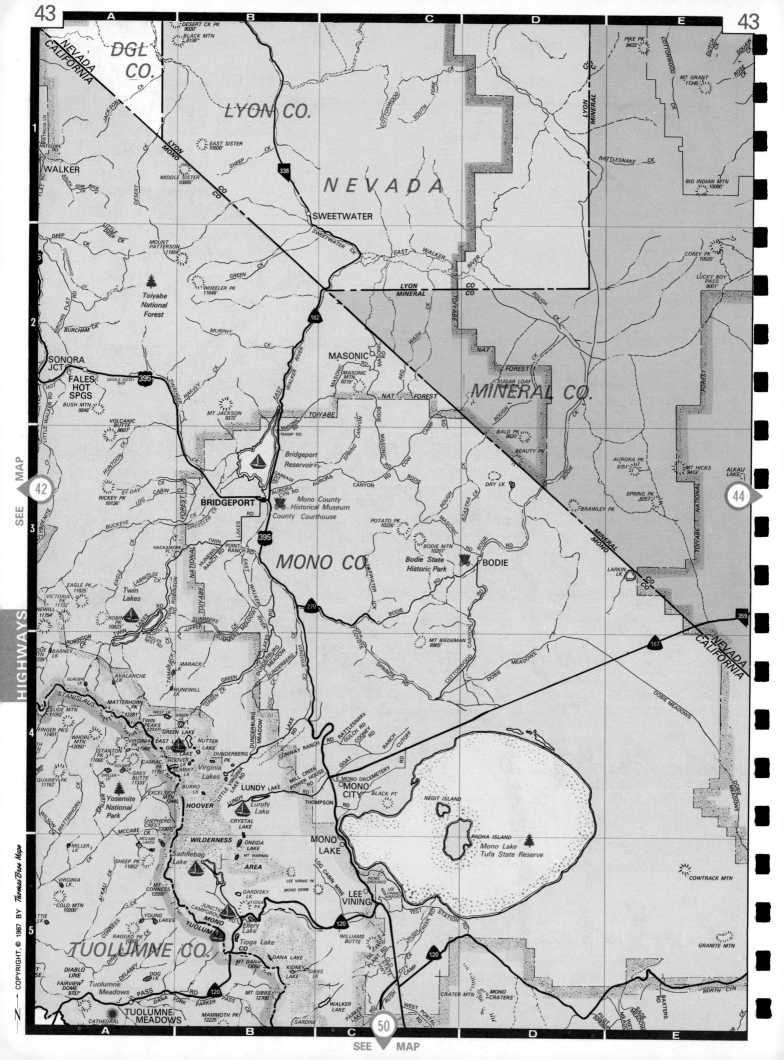

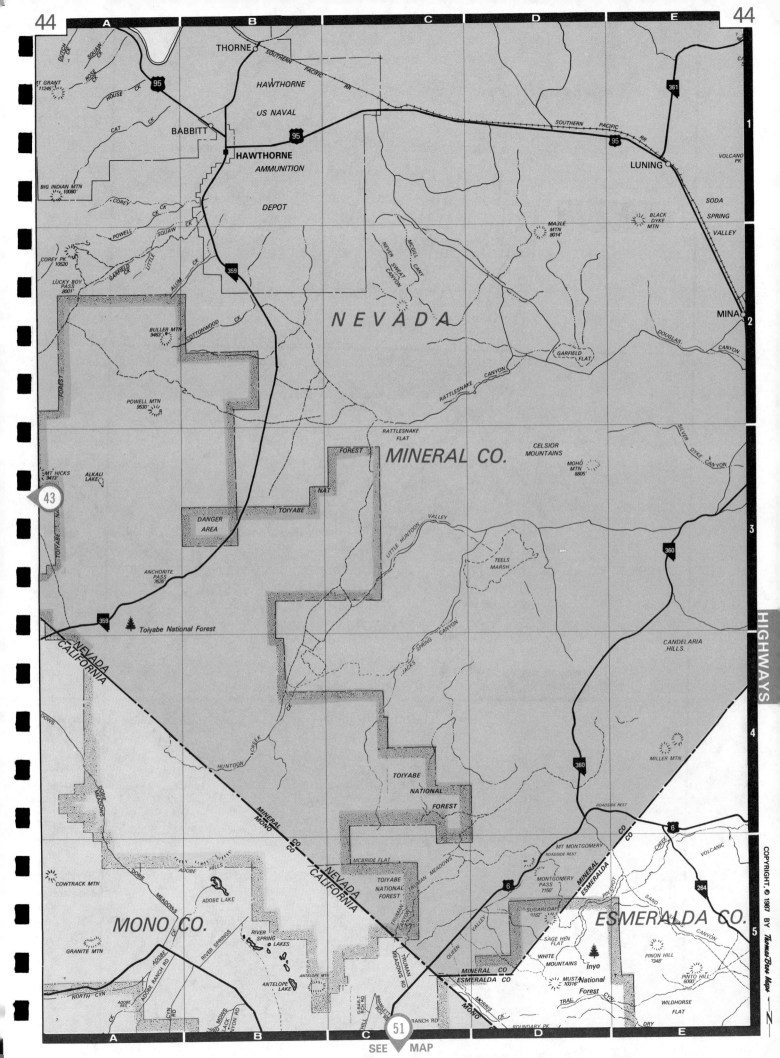

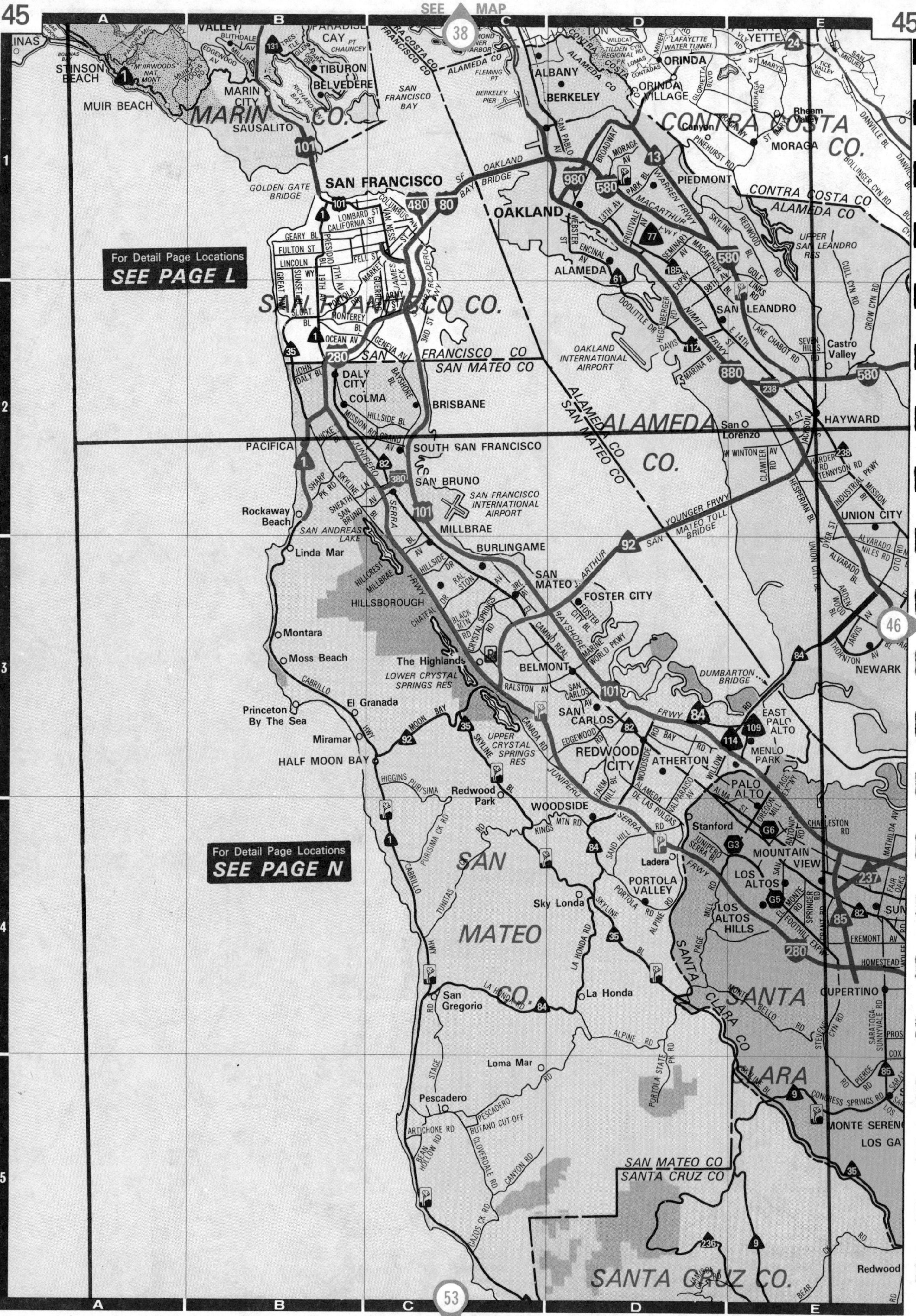

SEE MAP 38

For Detail Page Locations
SEE PAGE L

For Detail Page Locations
SEE PAGE N

HIGHWAYS

STINSON BEACH
MUIR BEACH
MUIR WOODS NAT. MONT.
TIBURON
BELVEDERE
PARADISE CAY
PT CHAUNCEY
VALLEY
BLITHEDALE
MARIN CO.
MARIN CITY
SAUSALITO
GOLDEN GATE BRIDGE
SAN FRANCISCO
SF OAKLAND BAY BRIDGE
LOMBARD ST
CALIFORNIA ST
GEARY BL
FULTON ST
LINCOLN
GREAT HWY
SUNSET WY
19TH AV
PORTOLA DR
MONTEREY BL
SLOAT BL
OCEAN AV
GENEVA AV
MISSION RD
SAN FRANCISCO CO.
SAN MATEO CO
DALY CITY
COLMA
BRISBANE
PACIFICA
SOUTH SAN FRANCISCO
SAN BRUNO
MILLBRAE
SAN FRANCISCO INTERNATIONAL AIRPORT
BURLINGAME
SAN MATEO
FOSTER CITY
HILLSBOROUGH
ROCKAWAY BEACH
SAN ANDREAS LAKE
LINDA MAR
MONTARA
MOSS BEACH
The Highlands
LOWER CRYSTAL SPRINGS RES
BELMONT
RALSTON AV
SAN CARLOS
EL GRANADA
PRINCETON BY THE SEA
MIRAMAR
HALF MOON BAY
UPPER CRYSTAL SPRINGS RES
REDWOOD CITY
ATHERTON
EAST PALO ALTO
MENLO PARK
DUMBARTON BRIDGE
Redwood Park
WOODSIDE
Ladera
PALO ALTO
Stanford
PORTOLA VALLEY
MOUNTAIN VIEW
LOS ALTOS
LOS ALTOS HILLS
SAN MATEO CO.
Sky Londa
SAN GREGORIO
La Honda
CUPERTINO
SANTA CLARA CO.
Loma Mar
Pescadero
PORTOLA STATE PK
MONTE SERENO
LOS GATOS
SAN MATEO CO
SANTA CRUZ CO.
SANTA CRUZ CO.
Redwood

ORINDA
ALBANY
BERKELEY
BERKELEY PIER
OAKLAND
PIEDMONT
MORAGA
CONTRA COSTA CO.
ALAMEDA CO.
CONTRA COSTA CO
ALAMEDA CO
ALAMEDA
SAN LEANDRO
Castro Valley
San Lorenzo
HAYWARD
ALAMEDA CO.
OAKLAND INTERNATIONAL AIRPORT
UNION CITY
NEWARK
SAN MATEO TOLL BRIDGE
LAFAYETTE
Rheem Valley
Canyon
MORAGA
DANVILLE

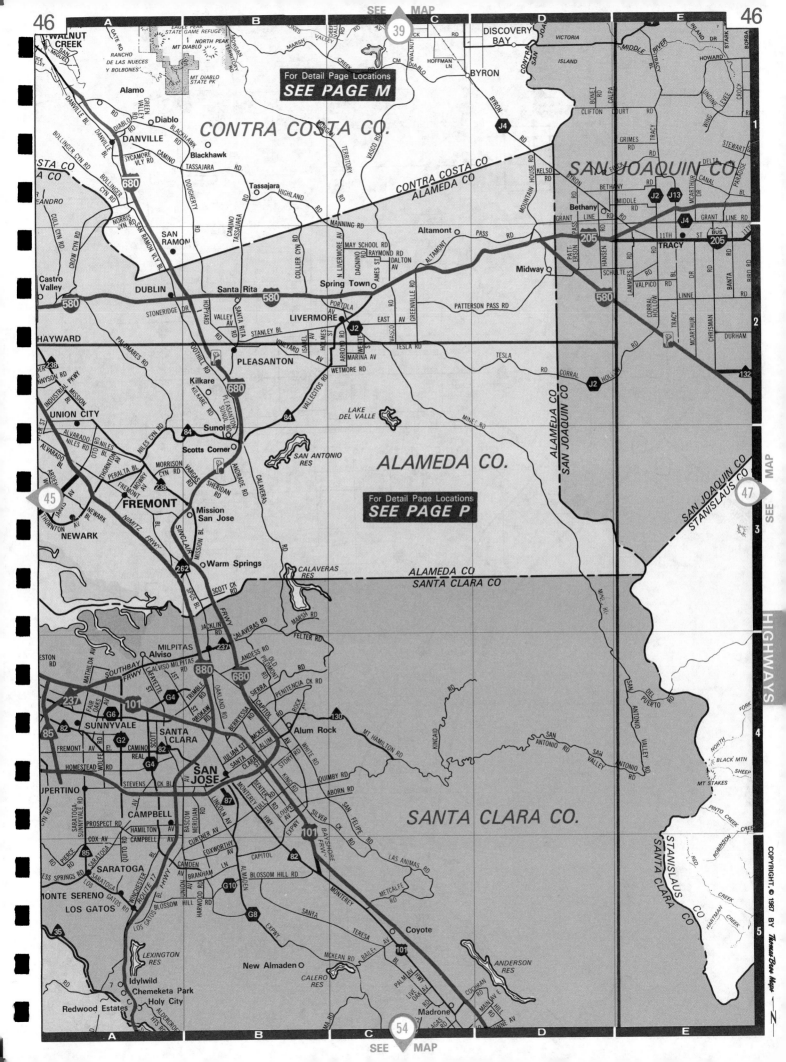

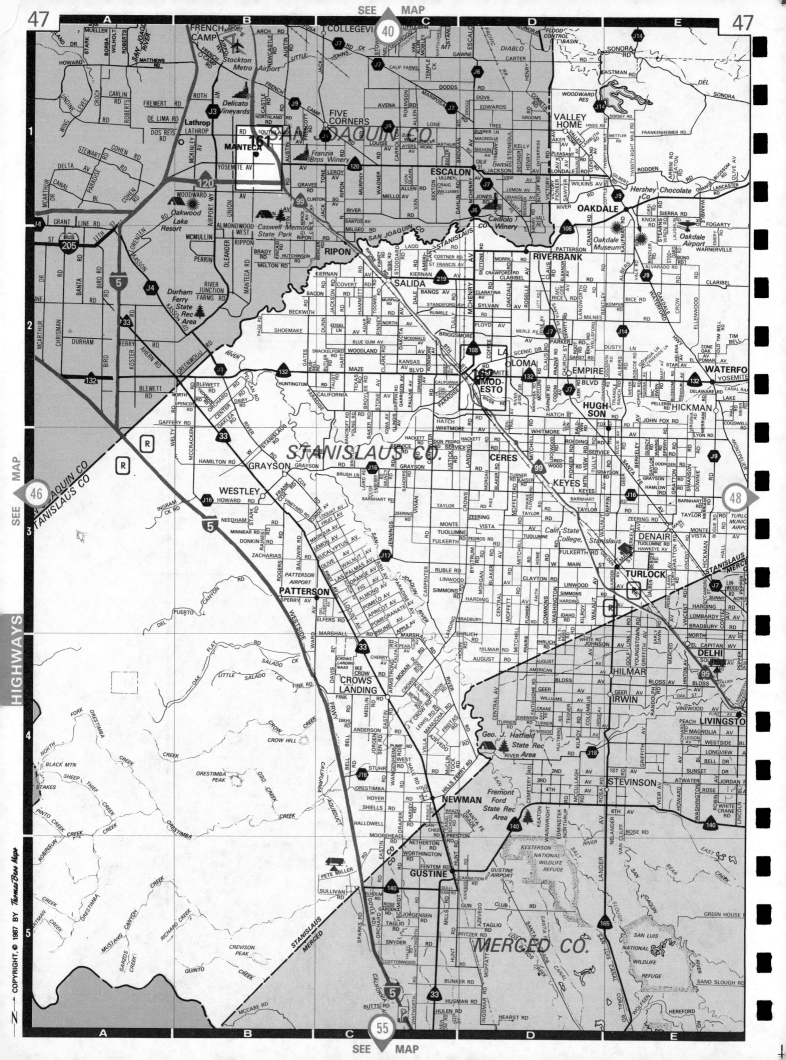

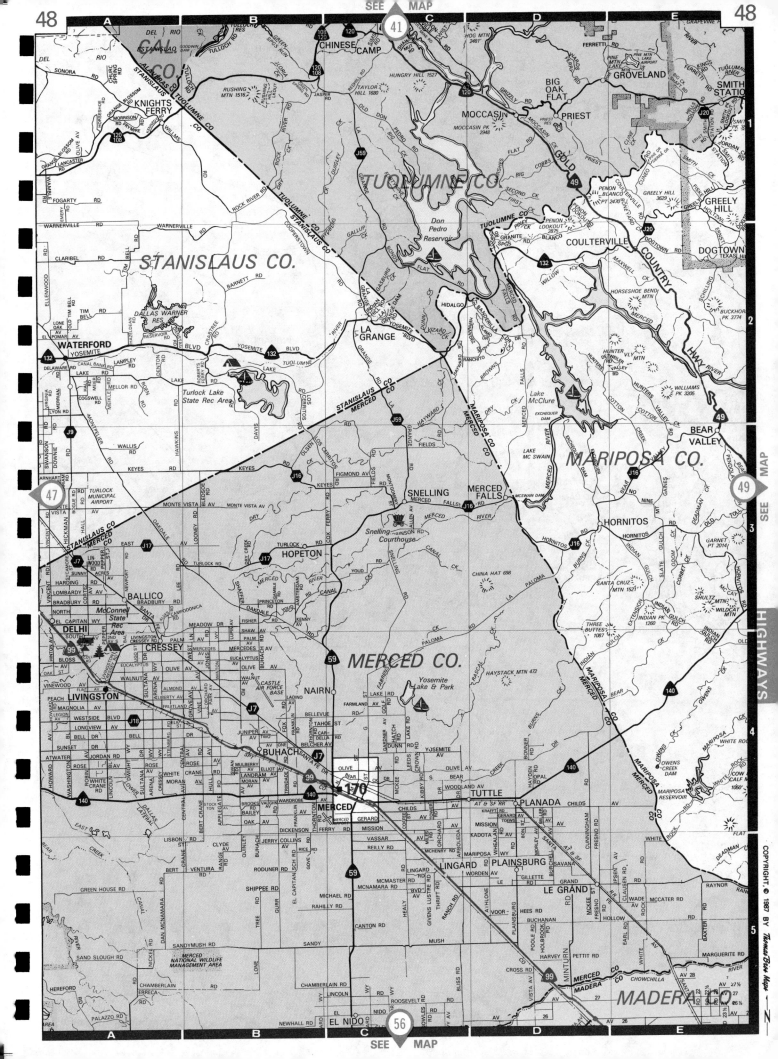

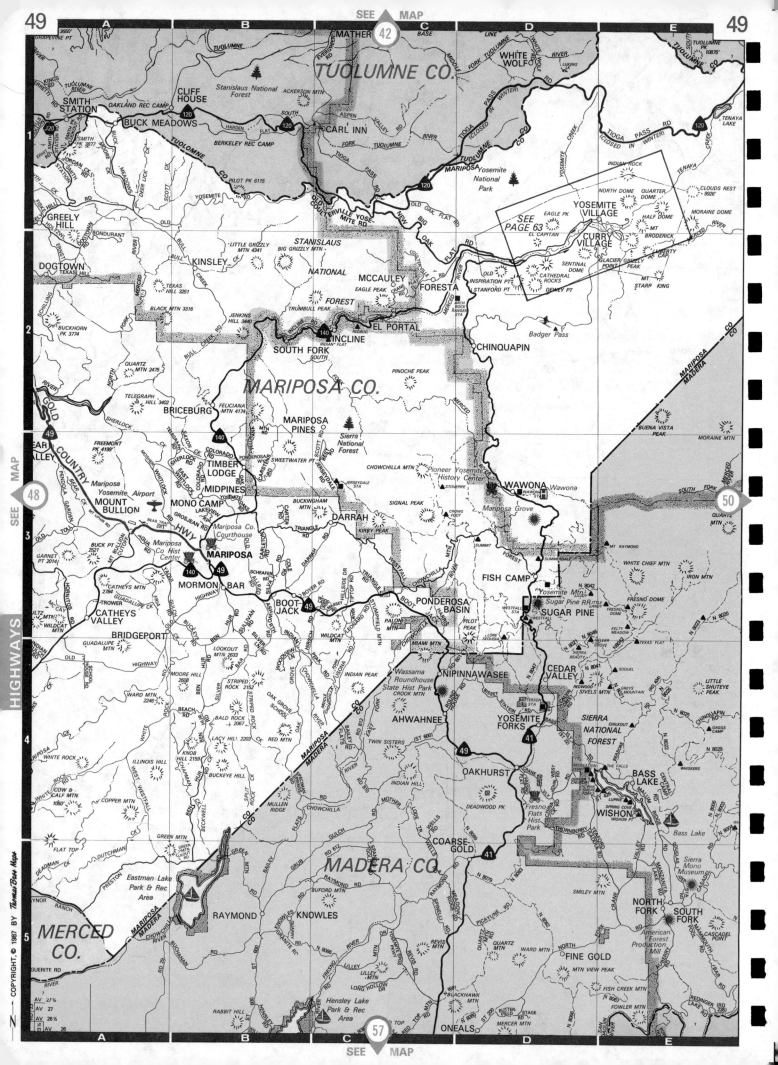

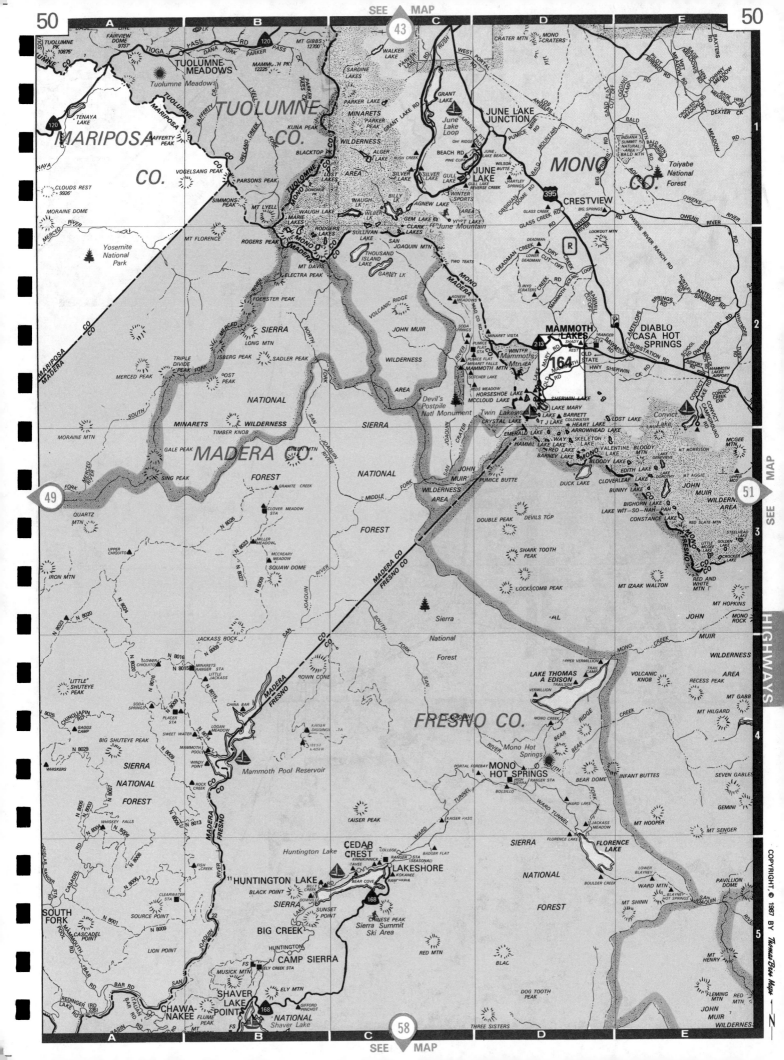

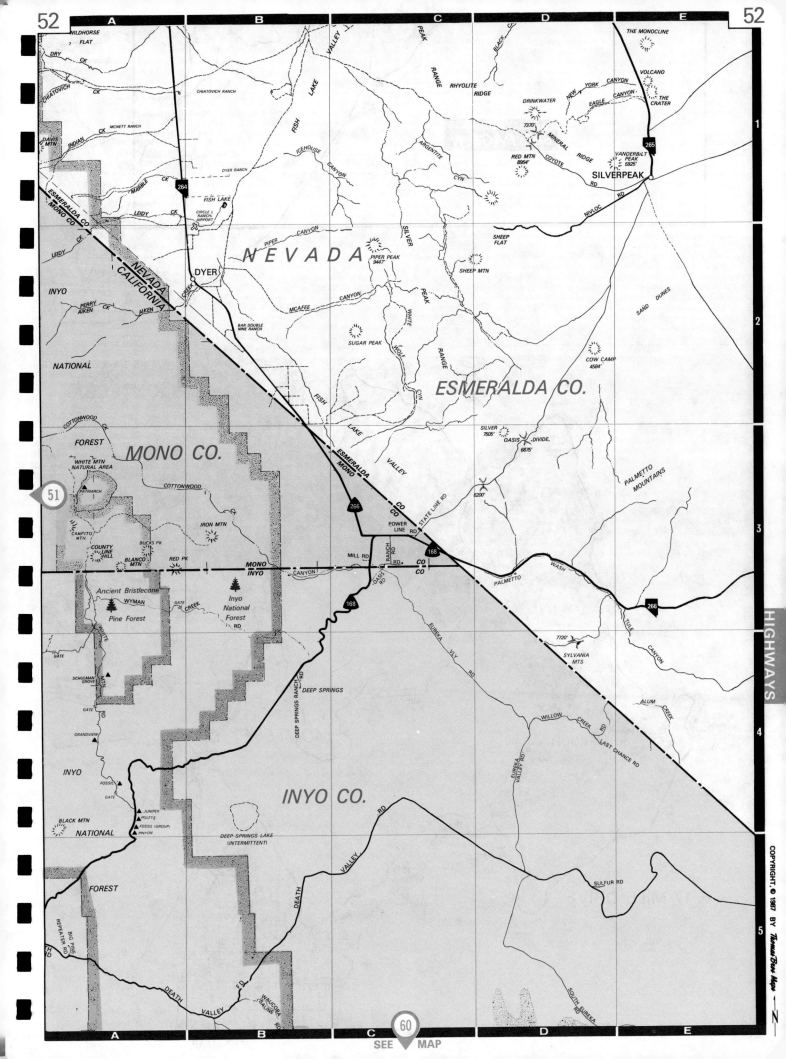

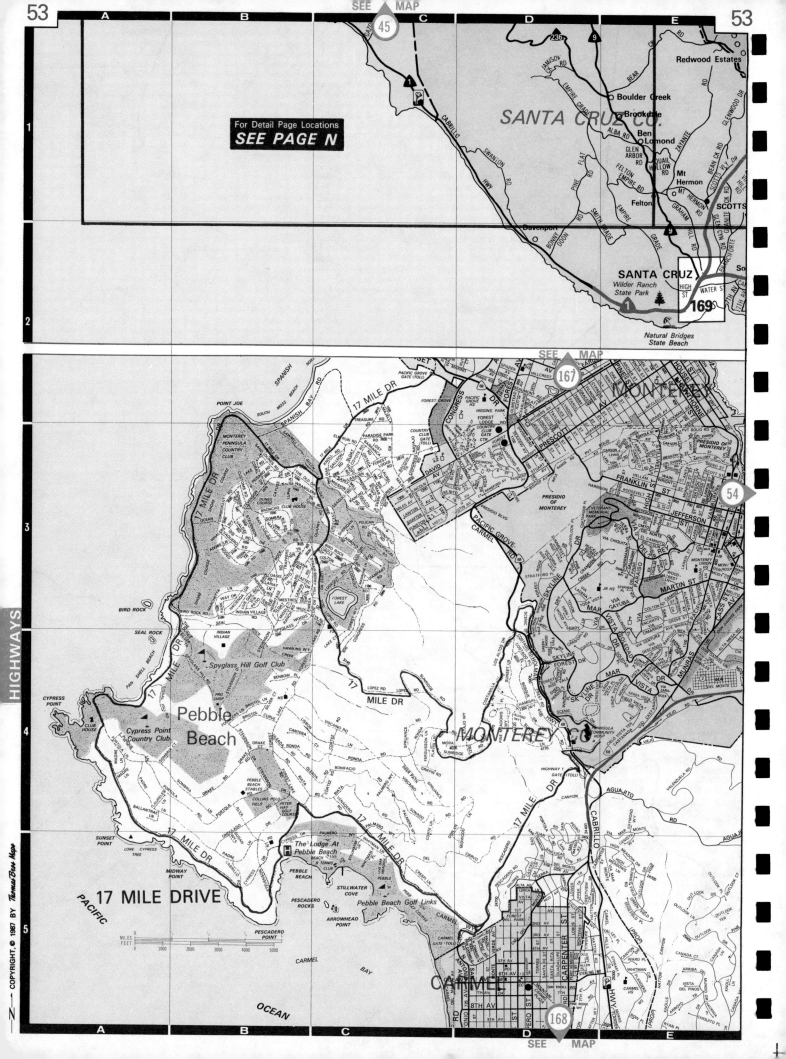

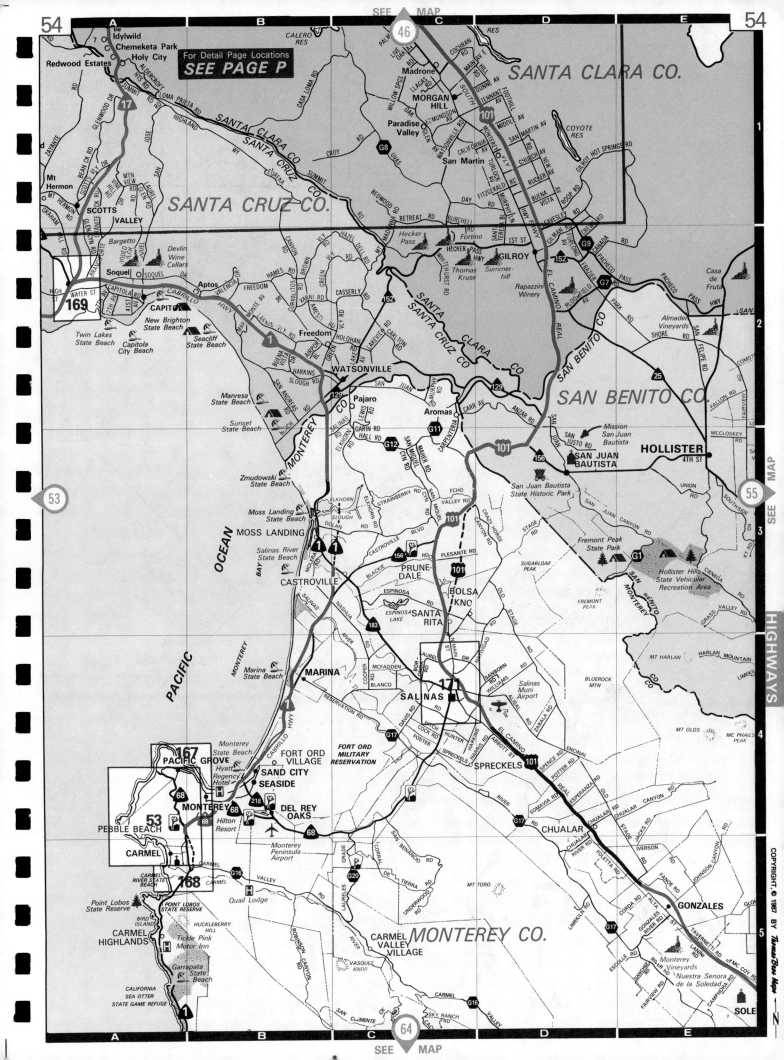

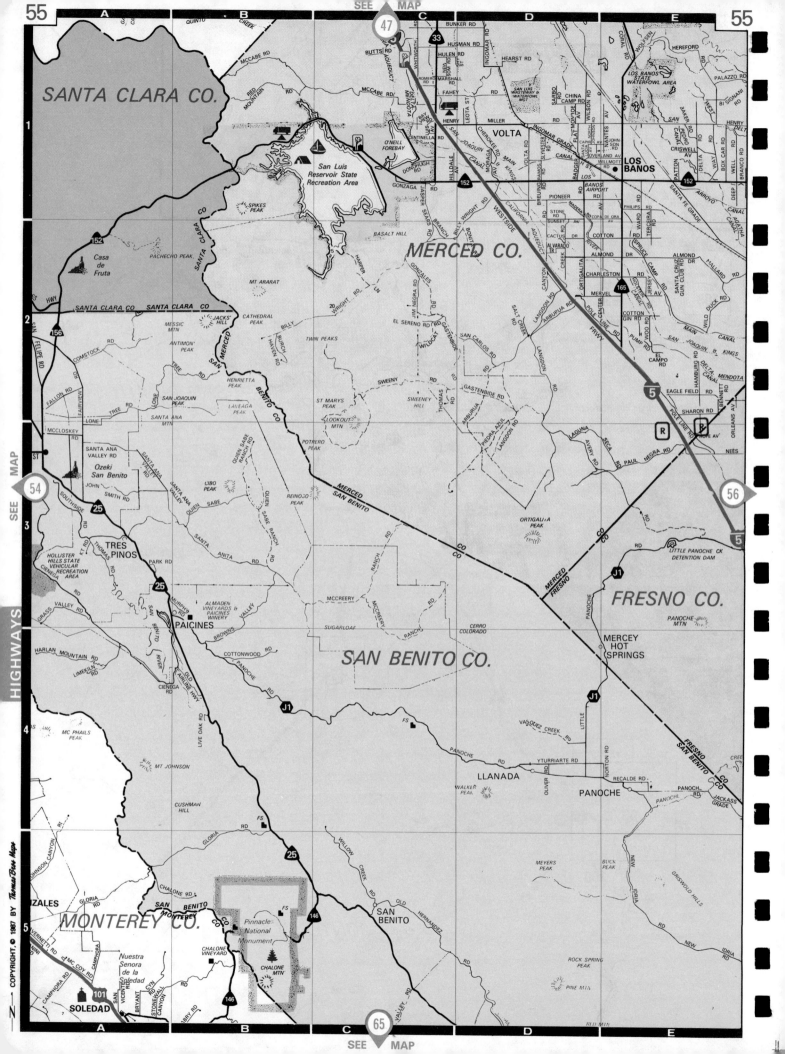

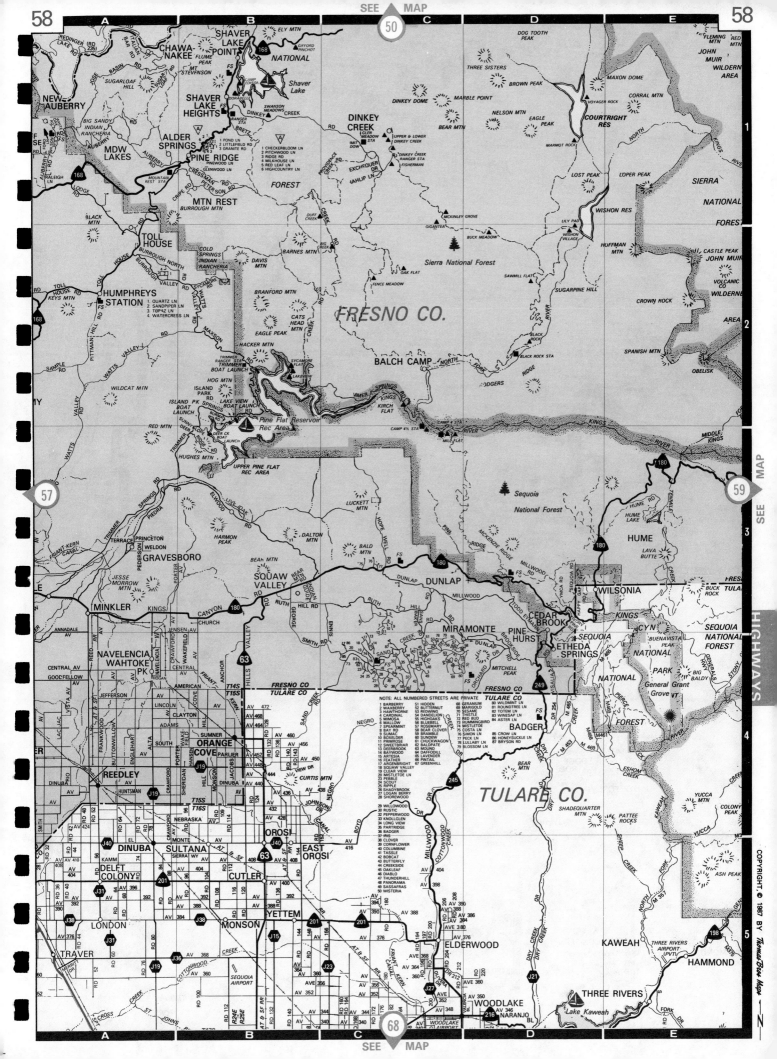

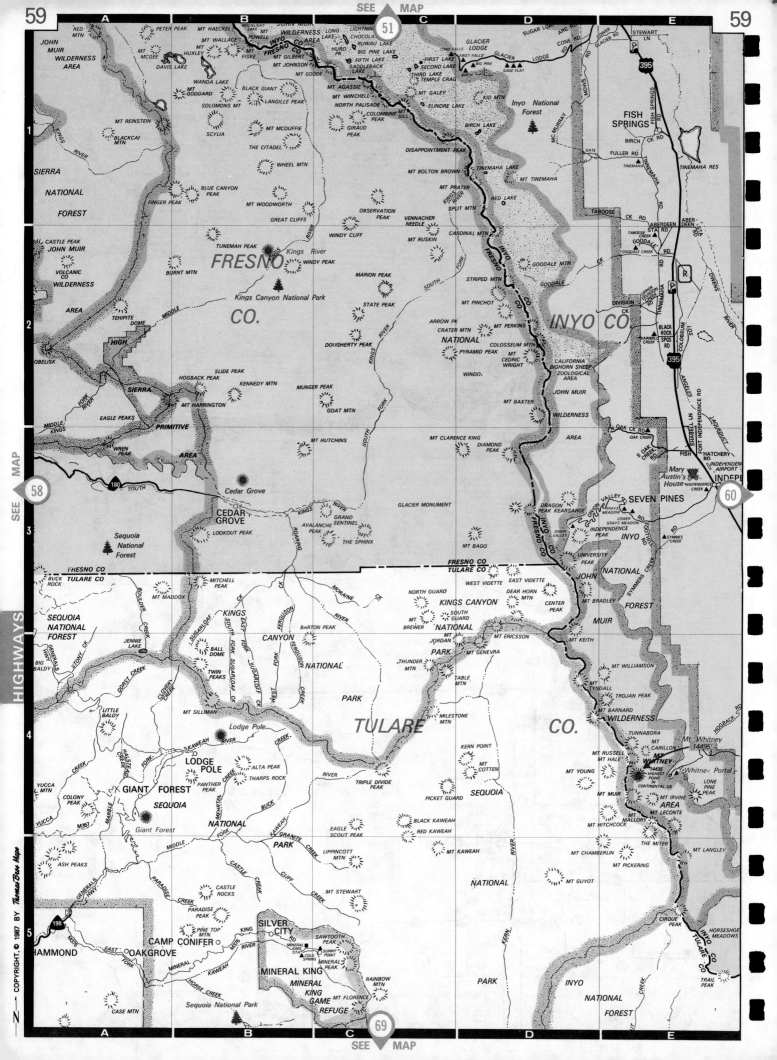

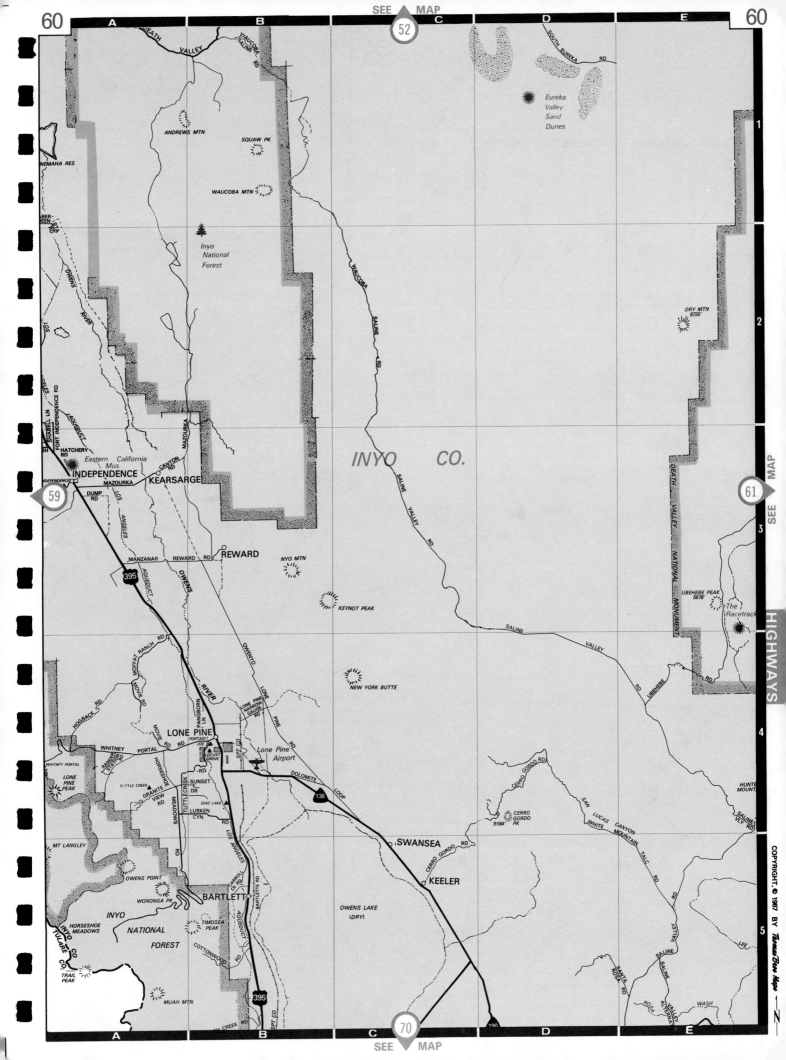

SEE ▼ MAP
52

DEATH VALLEY

YAUCOBA
SALINE RD

South Eureka RD

A   B   C   D   E

1

ANDREWS MTN

SQUAW PK

Eureka
Valley
Sand
Dunes

WAUCOBA MTN

NEMAHA RES

Inyo
National
Forest

WAUCOBA SALINE RD

DRY MTN
8726'

2

OWENS RIVER

SEE
MAP
61

INYO   CO.

HATCHERY RD

Eastern California
Mus

INDEPENDENCE

MAZOURKA

CANYON RD

KEARSARGE

SALINE VALLEY RD

DEATH VALLEY NATIONAL MONUMENT

59

3

DUMP RD

UBEHEBE PEAK
5678'

The
Racetrack

REWARD

MANZANAR REWARD RD

NYO MTN

OWENS

KEYNOT PEAK

SALINE

VALLEY   RD   UBEHEBE

395

MOFFAT RANCH RD

NEW YORK BUTTE

RIVER

OWENYO

LONE PINE

HOGBACK RD

MOVIE RD

LONE PINE NARROW GAUGE RD

LONE PINE RD

4

LONE PINE

PANGBORN LN

PORTAGI I
JOE

LOCUST
GROVE

Lone Pine
Airport

CERRO GORDO RD

HUNTER MOUNT

WHITNEY   PORTAL   RD

RANGER
STATION

HORSESHOE

SUNSET
DR

SPT CO

DOLOMITE

CERRO GORDO RD

SALINE VLY RD

WHITNEY PORTAL

LONE
PINE
PEAK

TUTTLE CREEK

GRANITE
VIEW RD

TUTTLE CREEK

DIAZ LAKE

136

LOOP

CERRO
GORDO
PK
9184'

SAN LUCAS CANYON

WHITE MOUNTAIN TALC RD

MT LANGLEY

MEADOWS

LUBKEN
CYN
RD

LOS ANGELES

SWANSEA

CERRO GORDO RD

5

OWENS POINT

WONONGA PK

BARTLETT

CARROL
CK RD

BARTLETTE RD

AQUEDUCT

KEELER

OWENS LAKE
(DRY)

SALINE VALLEY ALTERNA

LEE

INYO

HORSESHOE
MEADOWS

TIMOSEA
PEAK

NATIONAL

COTTONWOOD RD

SANTA
ROSA RD

ROSA RD

WASH

INYO CO.
TULARE CO.

FOREST

TRAIL
PEAK

MUAH MTN

395

70
SEE ▼ MAP

190

HIGHWAYS

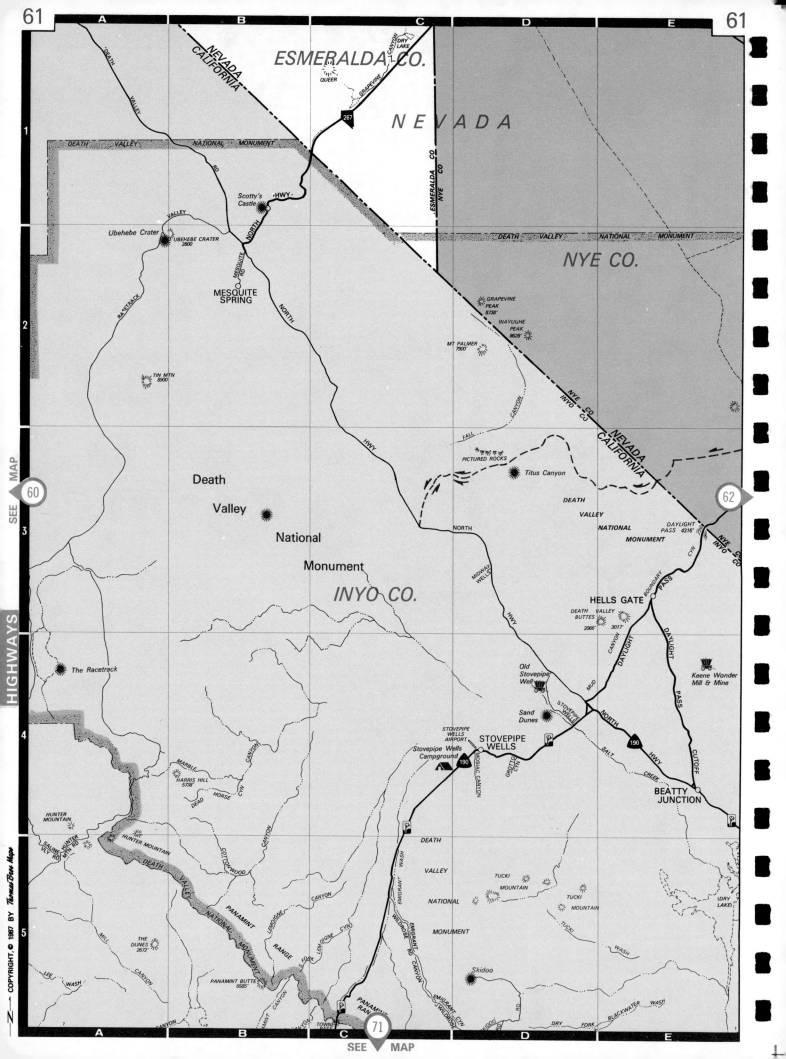

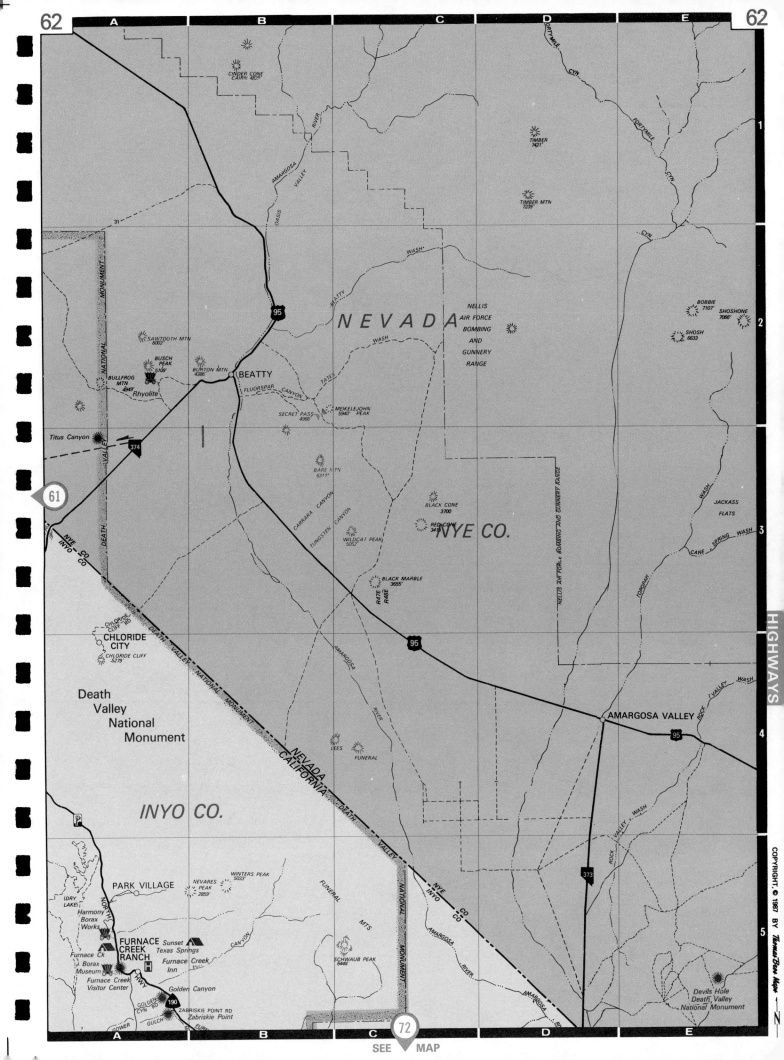

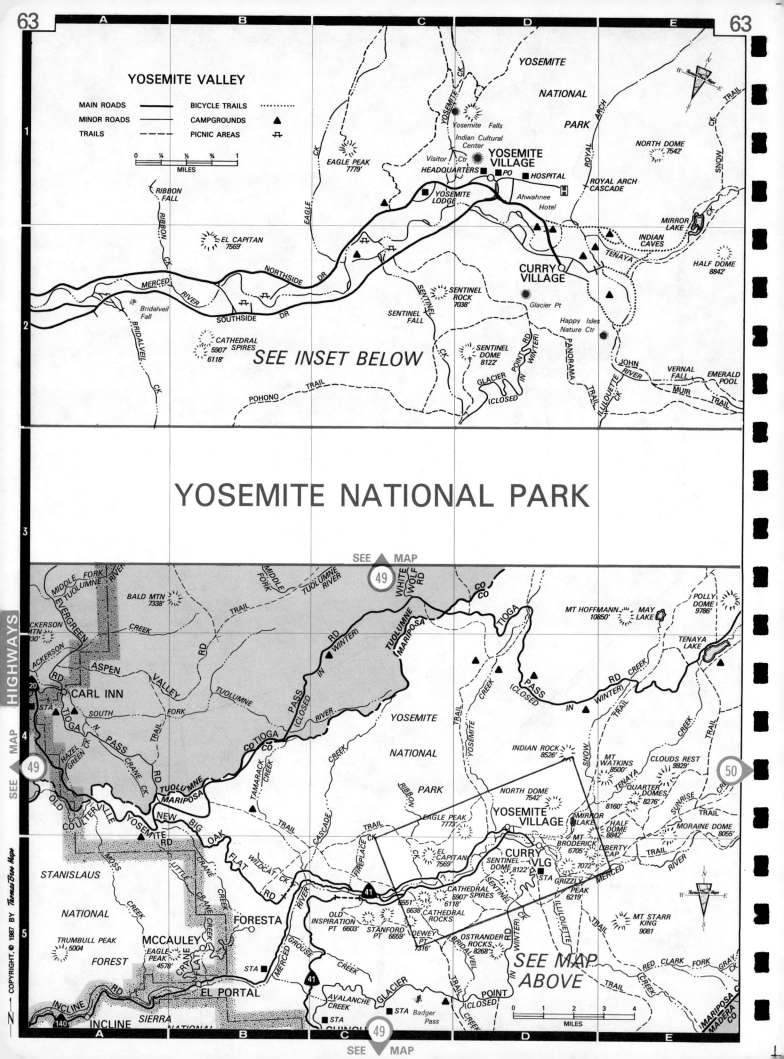

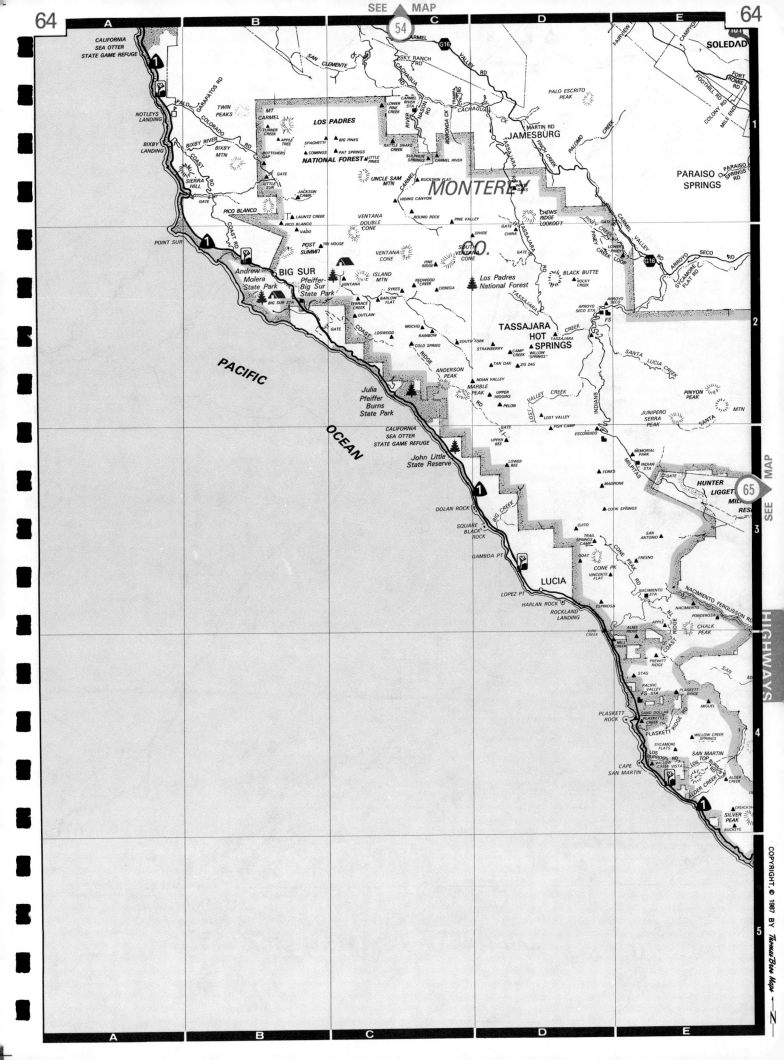

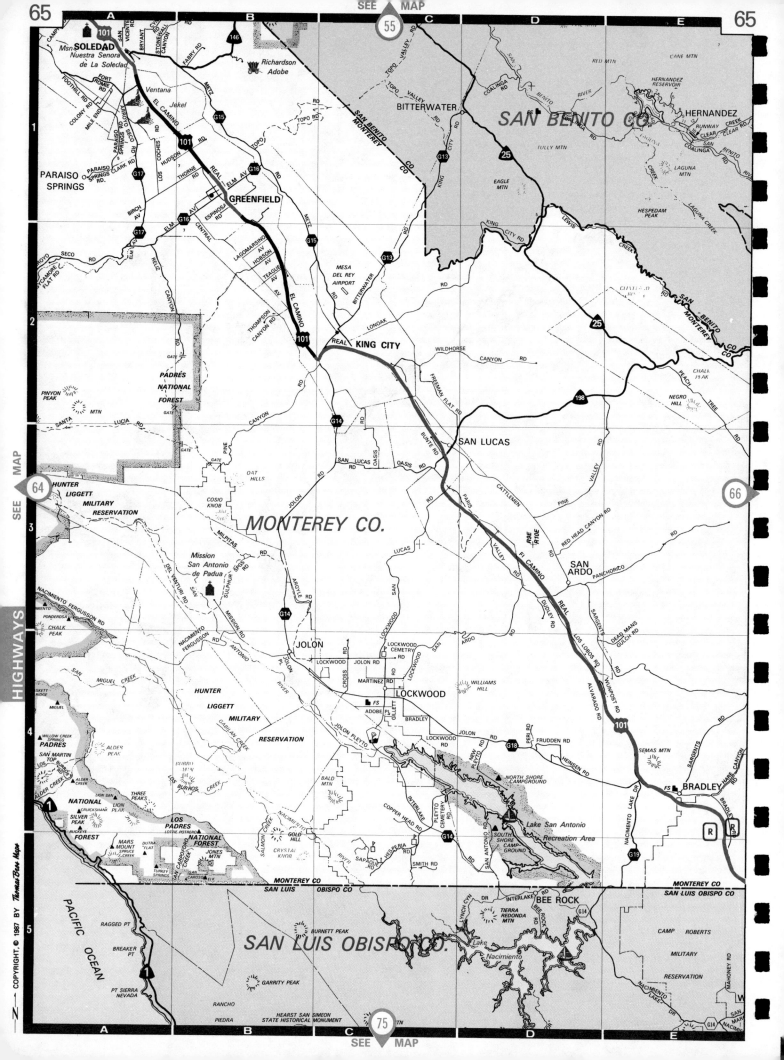

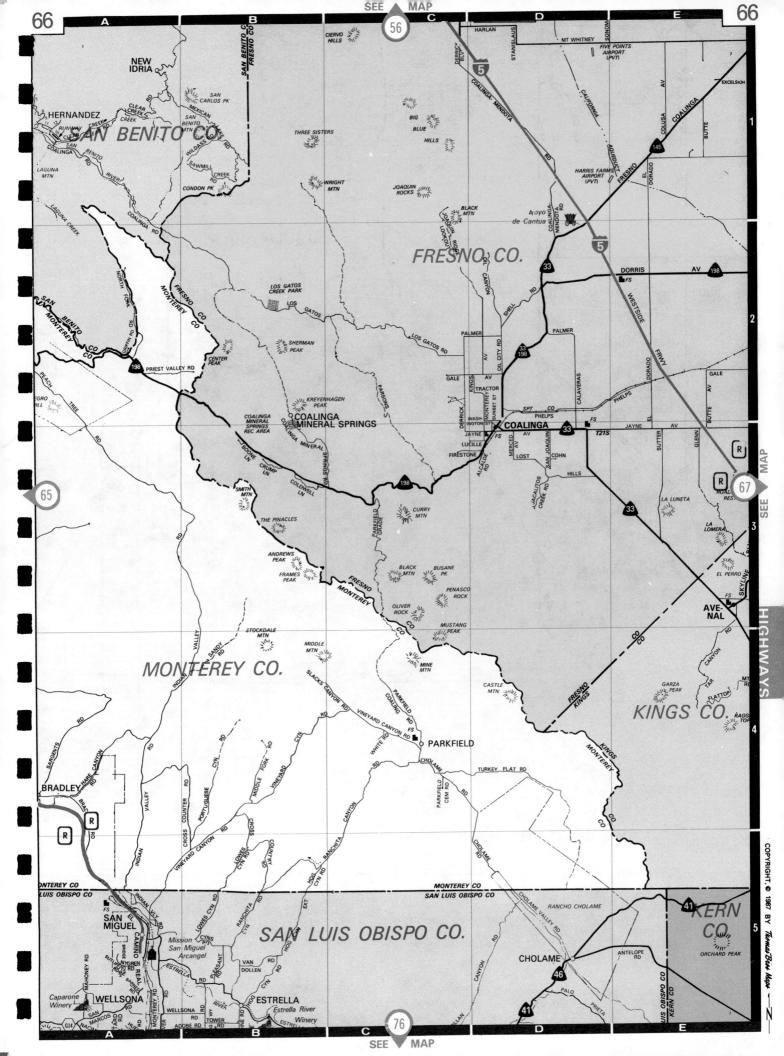

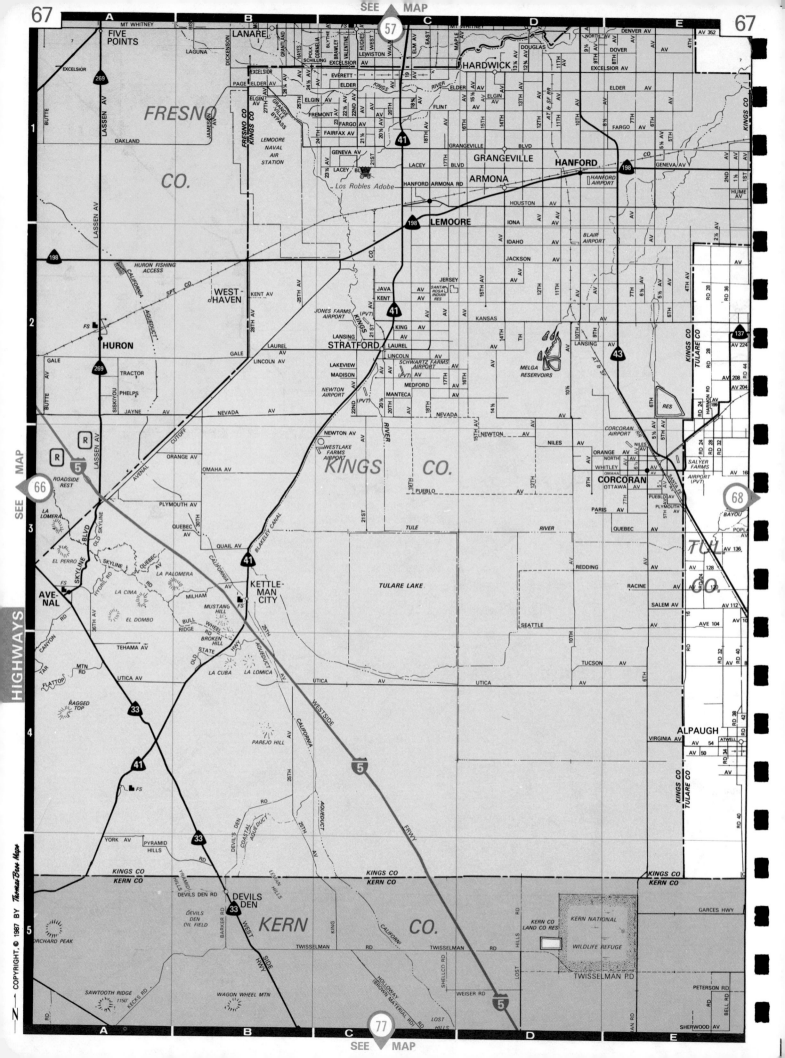

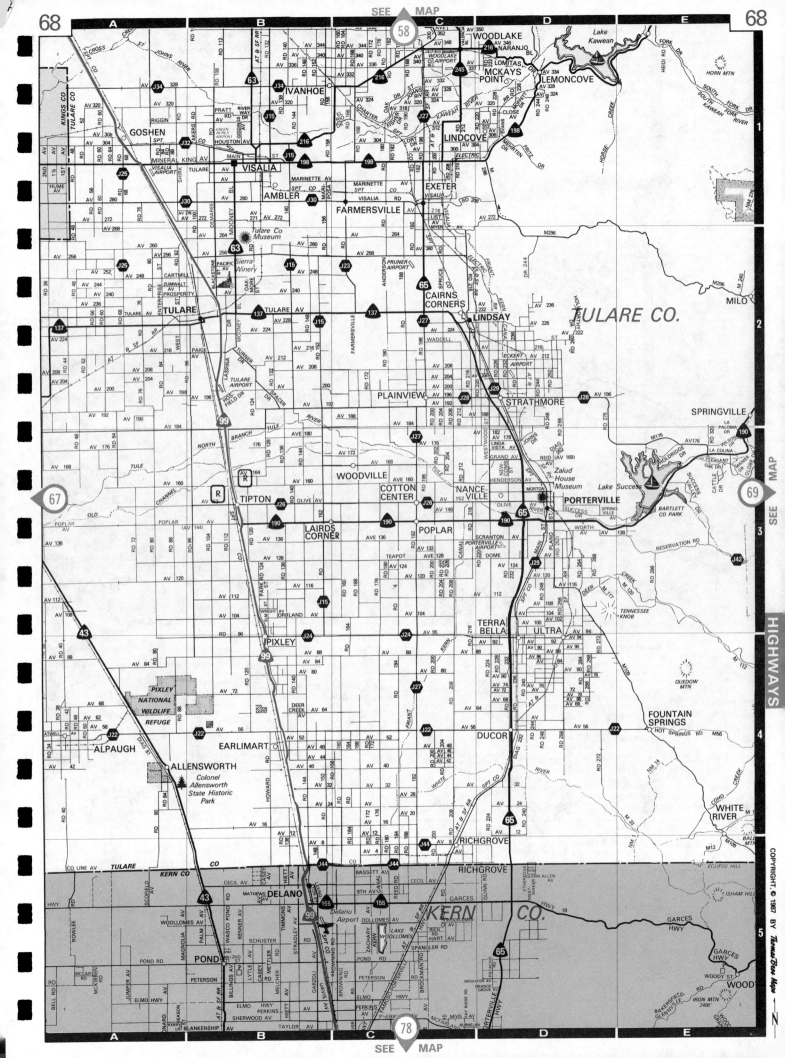

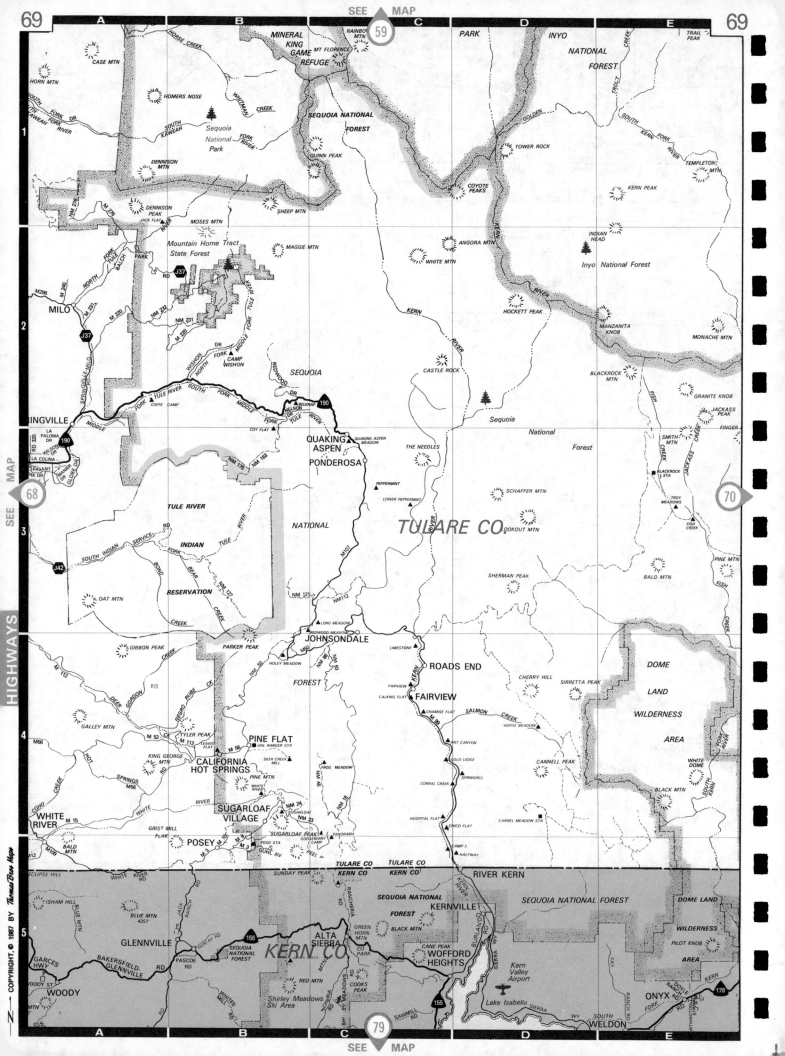

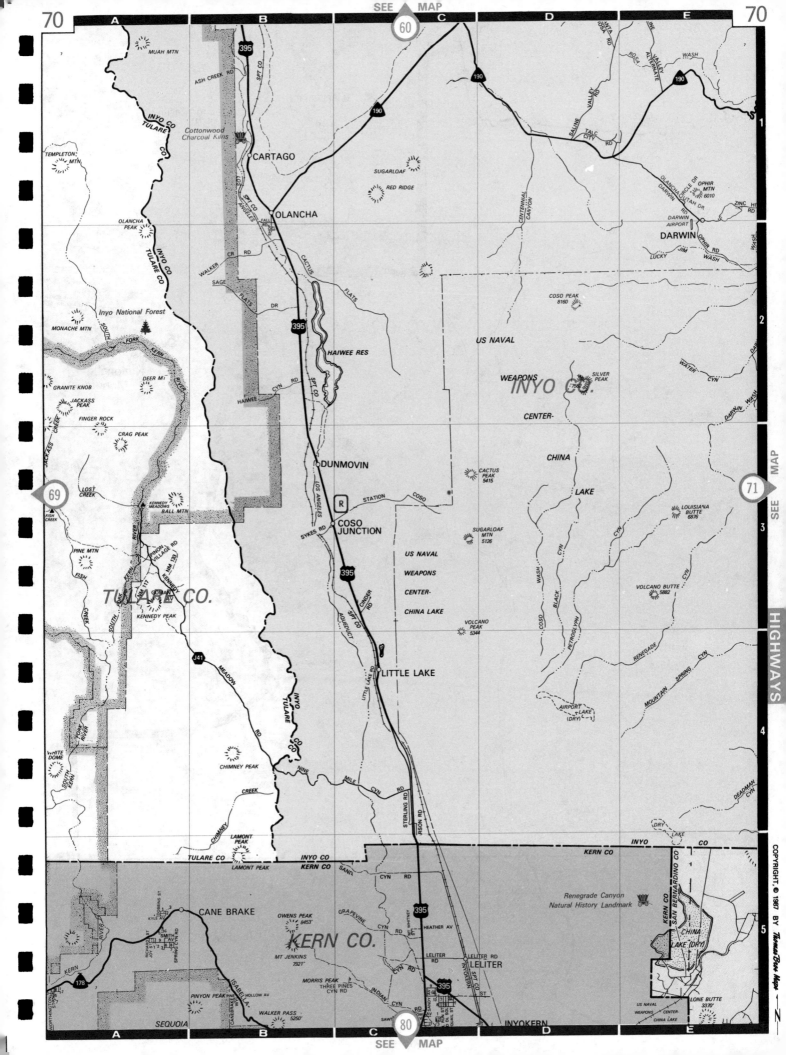

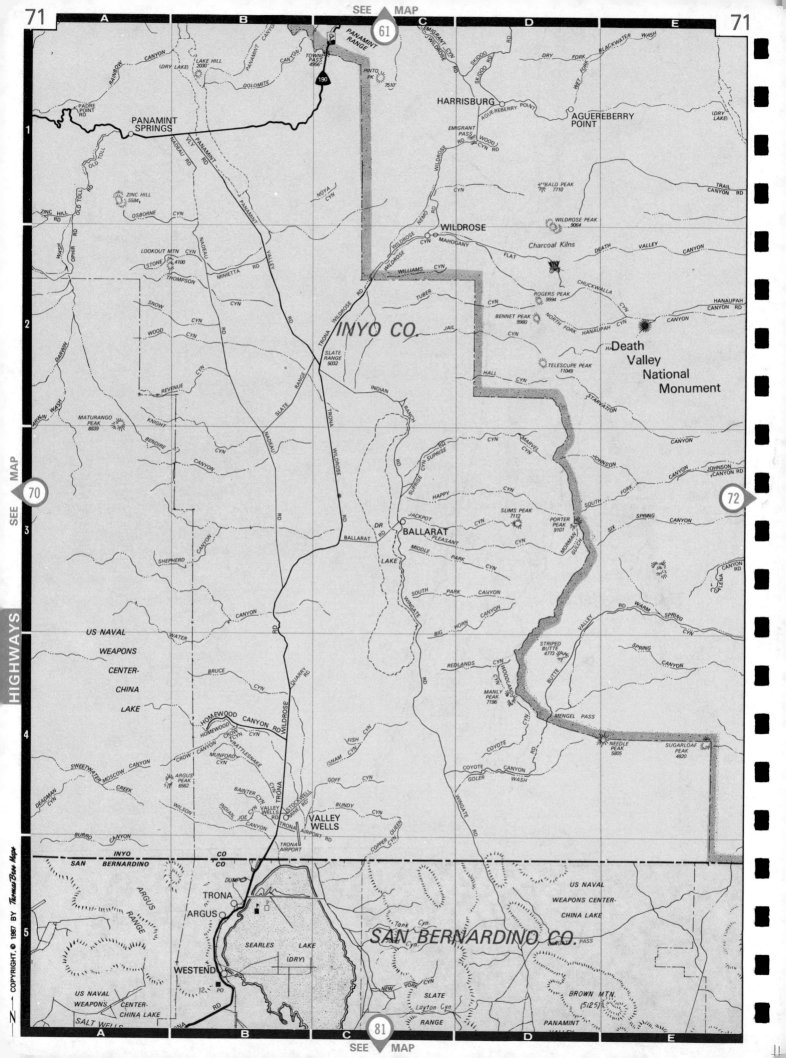

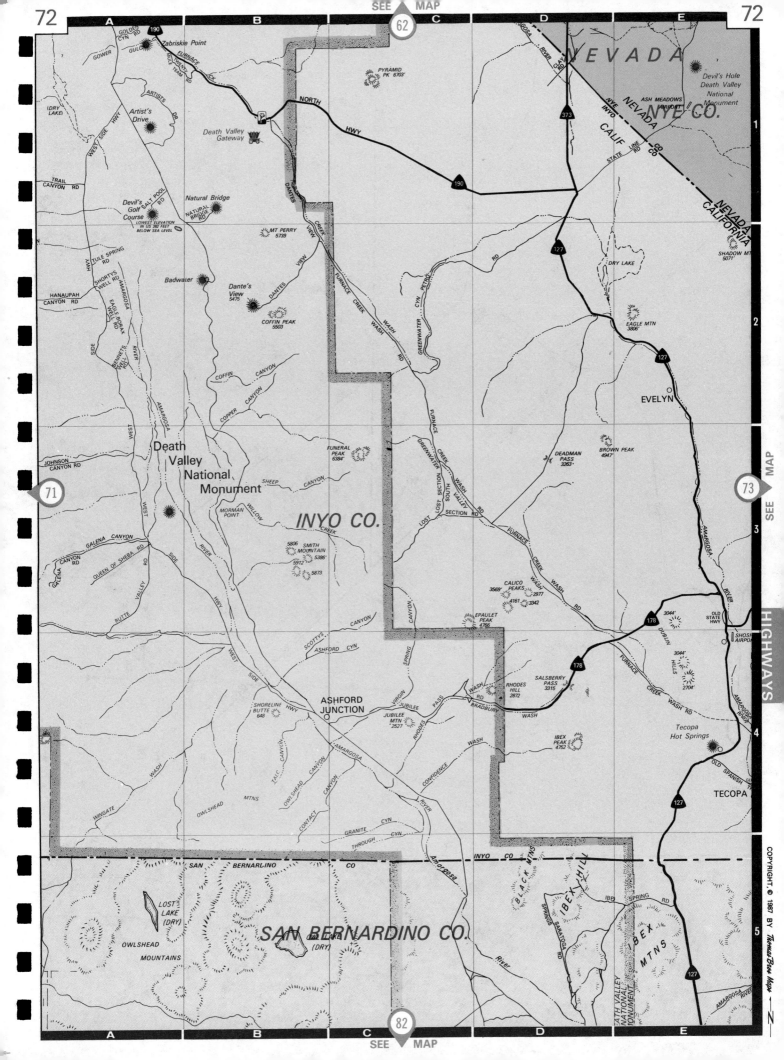

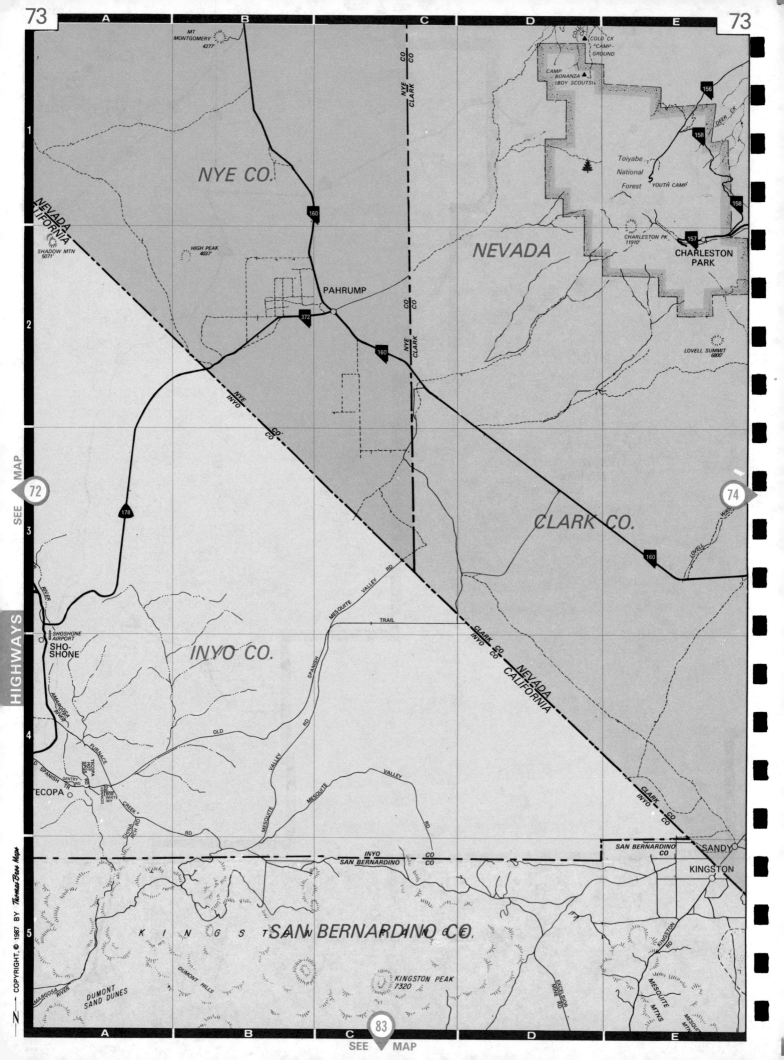

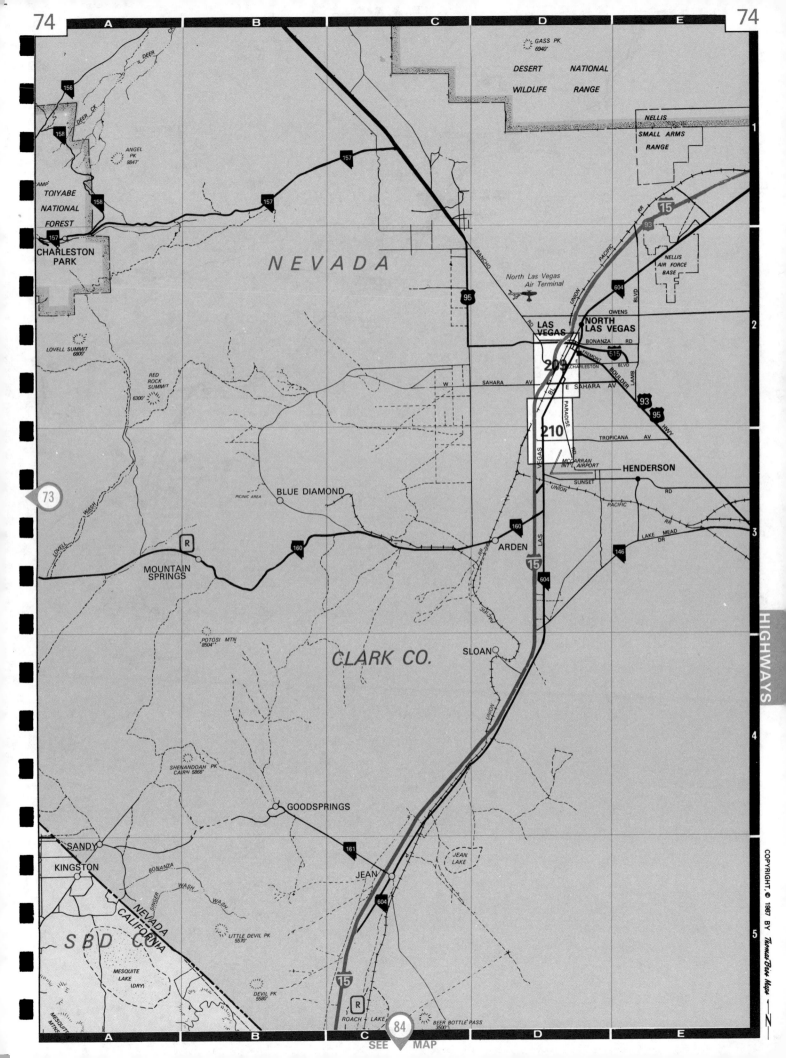

PT SIERRA NEVADA

GARRITY PEAK

RANCHO PIEDRA BLANCA

Hearst San Simeon State Historic Monument

PINE MTN

BLACK OAK MTN ROCKY BUTTE

LIME MTN

NACIMIENTO LAKE DR

G14

CHIMNEY ROCK

ADELAIDA

KLAU

CABRILLO

PT PIEDRAS BLANCAS

SAN SIMEON

San Simeon Inn

Best Western Cavalier Inn

SAN SIMEON PT

SAN SIMEON BAY

RED MTN

SAN SIMEON CK RD

RANCHO SAN SIMEON

CYPRESS MTN

PEACHY CYN

KILER

Wm. Randolph Hearst State Beach

San Simeon State Beach

SIMEON

SAN LUIS OBISPO CO.

PACIFIC

CAMBRIA

SCOTT ROCK

SANTA ROSA

CREEK

BLACK MTN RD

SHADOW CYN RD

Pesenti

Moonstone Inn Motel Mariners Inn

MAIN ST

RANCHO

NORTHERLY BRANCH GREEN VLY RD

VALLEY

46

YORK MTN RD

DOVER CYN RD

York Mountain

OCEAN

Cambria Air Force Sta

GREEN

SANTA ROSA

HARMONY VLY RD

PICACHO

THUNDER CYN RD

COTTONTAIL CK RD

RANCHO

ASUNCION

SAN GREG

HARMONY

RANCHO SAN GERONIMO

VILLA CREEK RD

WHALE ROCK RES

OLD CREEK

SANTA RITA

TORO CREEK RD

PARK RANGE PEAK

CAYUCOS

Cayucos State Beach

MONTECITO RD

RANCHO MORO Y CAYUCOS

LOS

Morro Strand State Beach

Breakers Motel

Atascadero State Beach

DERO

STATE BEACH Morro Rock

MORRO BAY

SAN BERNARDINO

CABRILLO HWY

SAN CK RD

76

Morro Bay Aquarium

STATE PK

HOLLISTER PEAK

SANTA YSABEL RD

CABRILL HWY

Morro Bay State Park

BAYWOOD PARK

7TH ST

RANCHO CANADA DE LOS Y PECHO Y IS

LOS OSOS

CUESTA BY-THE-SEA

LOS OSOS VALLEY RD

Los Osos Oaks State Reserve

CHO VLY RD

Montana De Oro State Park

PREFUMO CYN RD

SEE CYN RD

RANCHO

CANADA DE

SADDLE PEAK

PG&E NUCLEAR POWER PLANT

LOS OSOS

Y PECHO

GREEN PEAK

Y ISLAY

BALD RANCHO

SAN LUIS HILL

PT SAN LUIS

HIGHWAYS

N

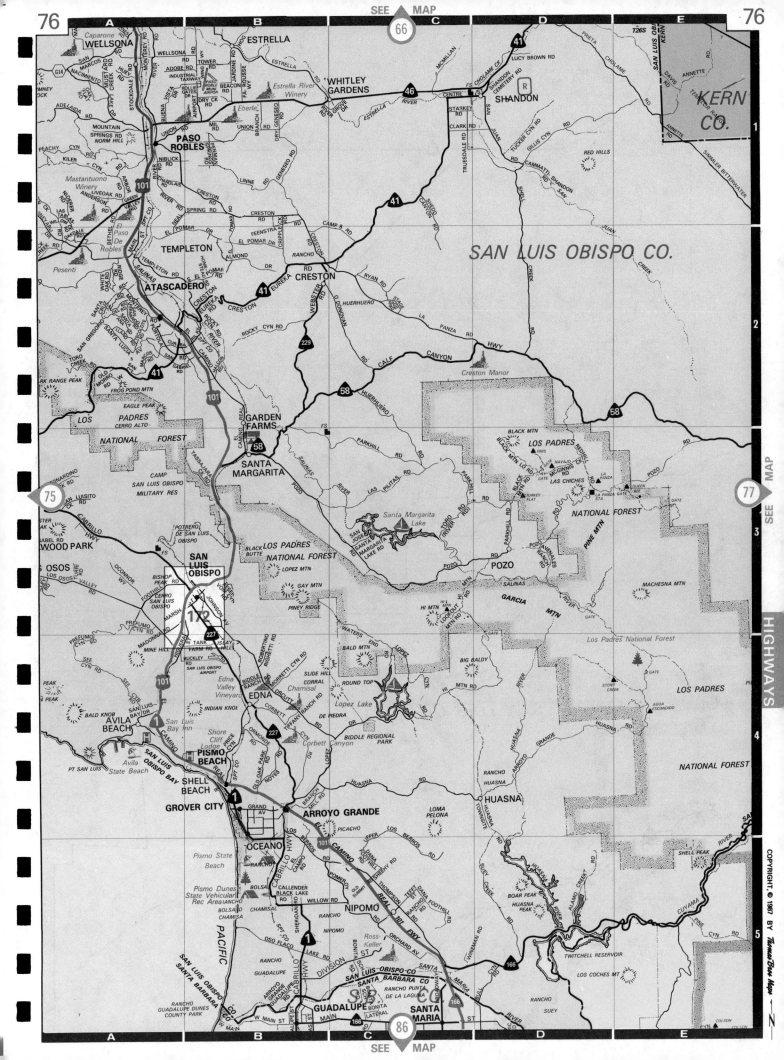

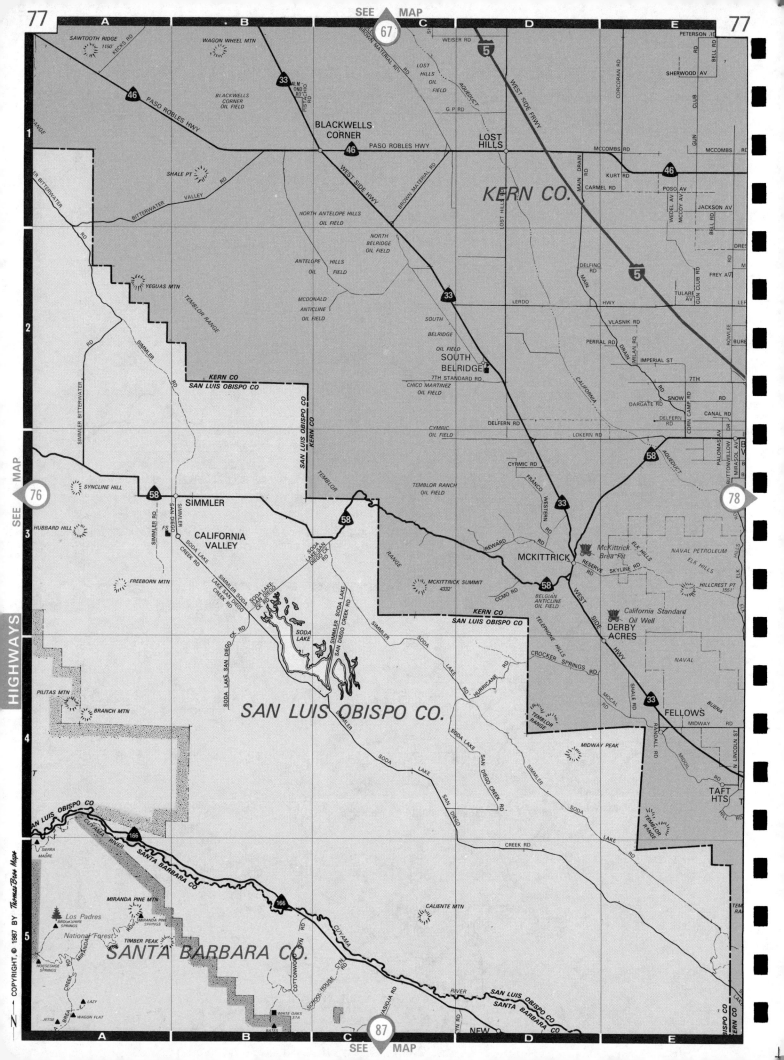

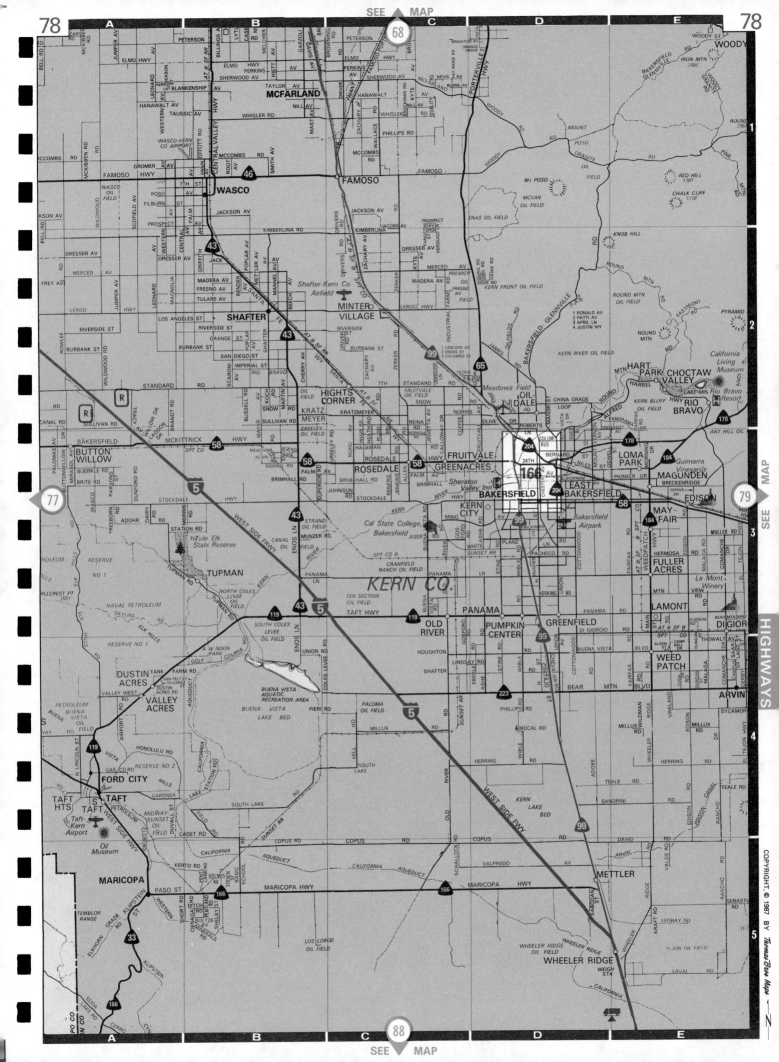

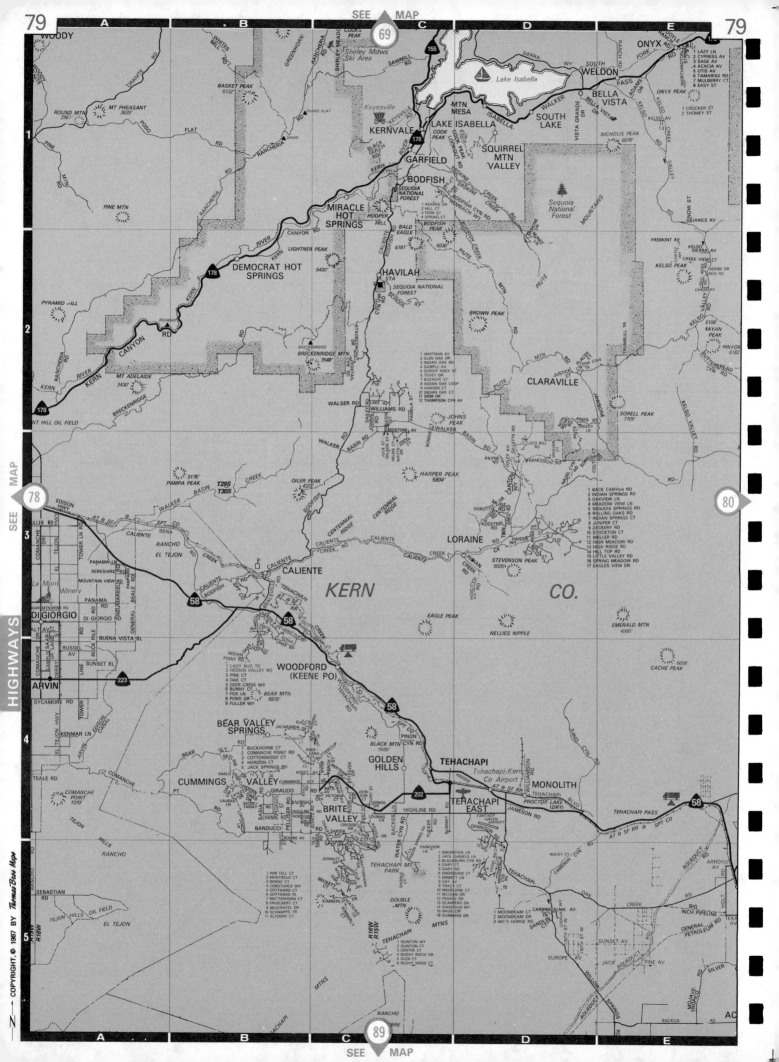

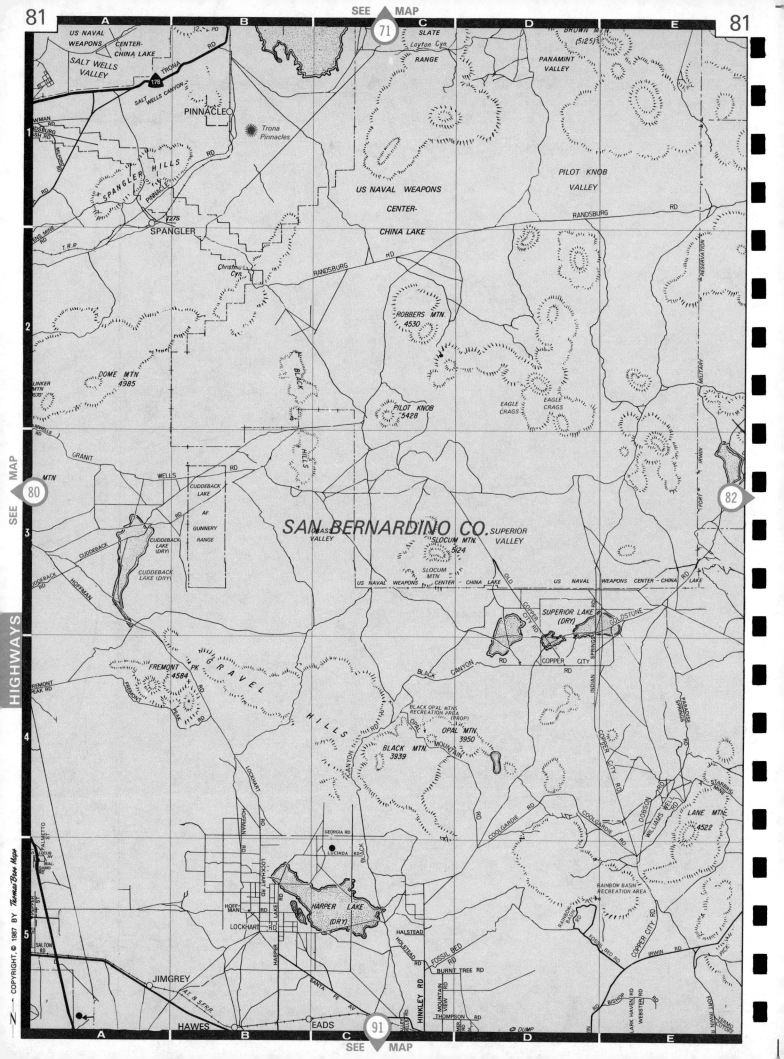

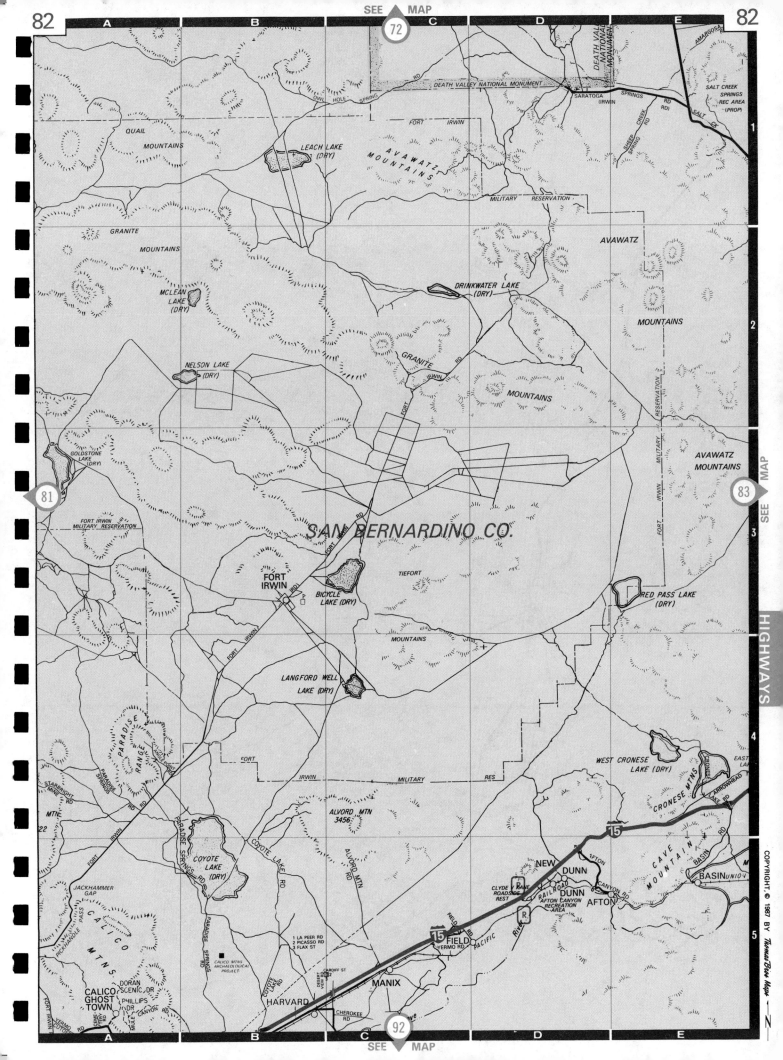

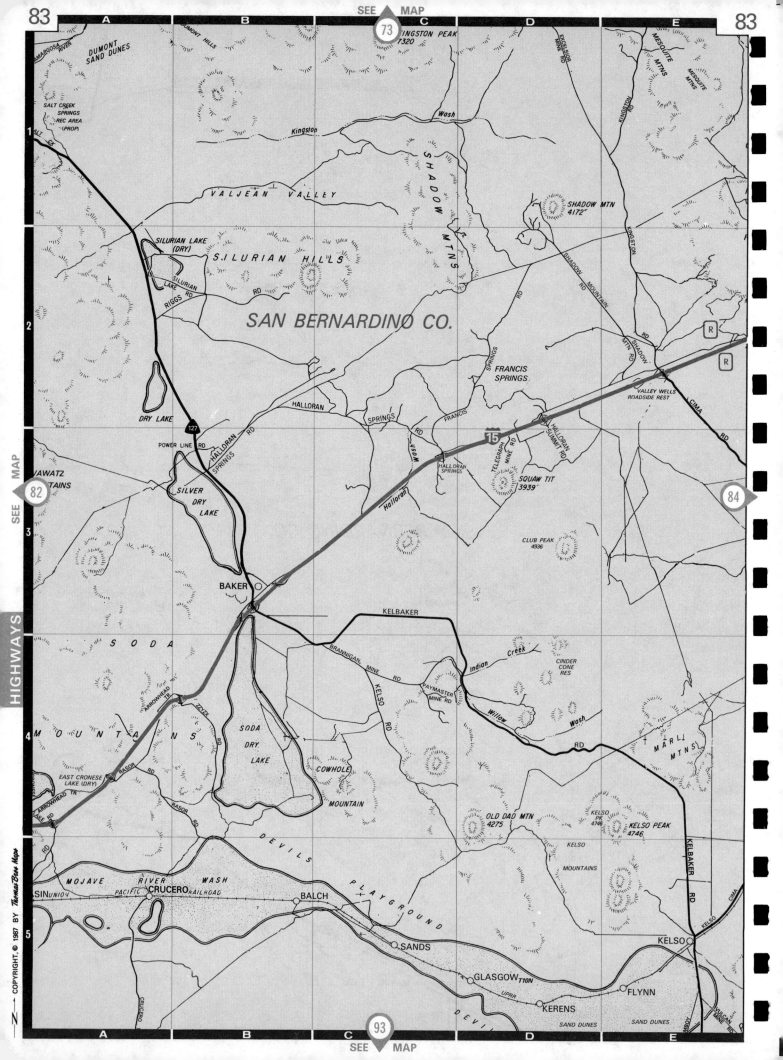

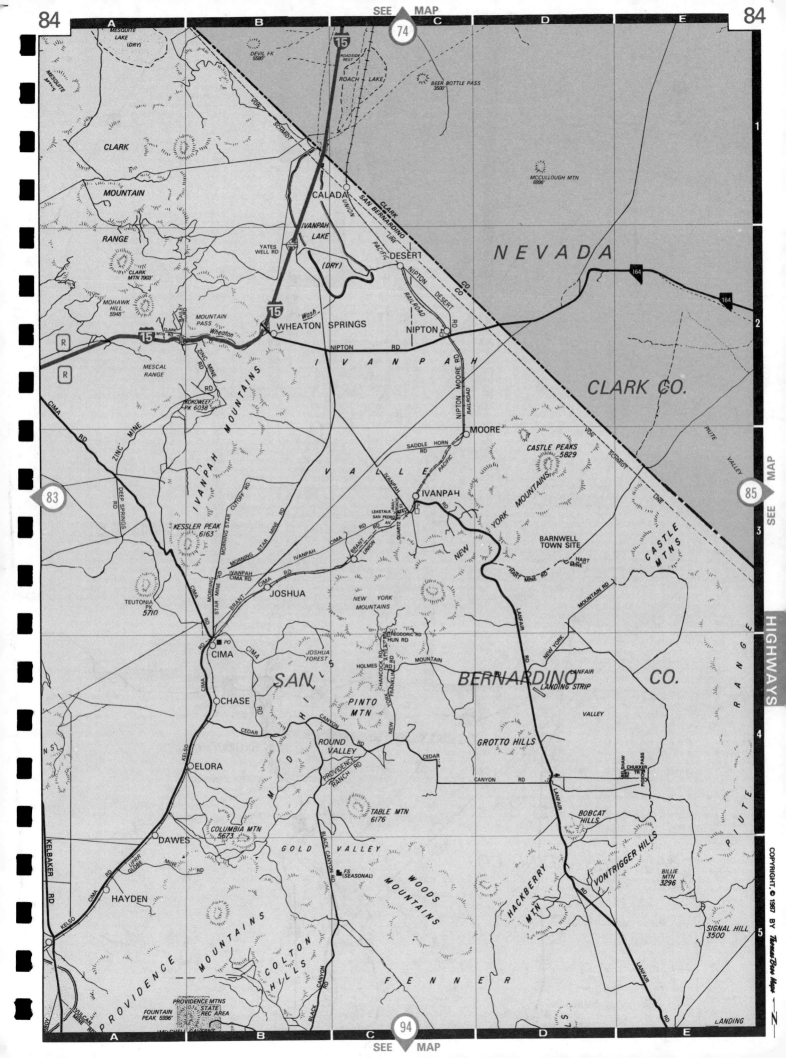

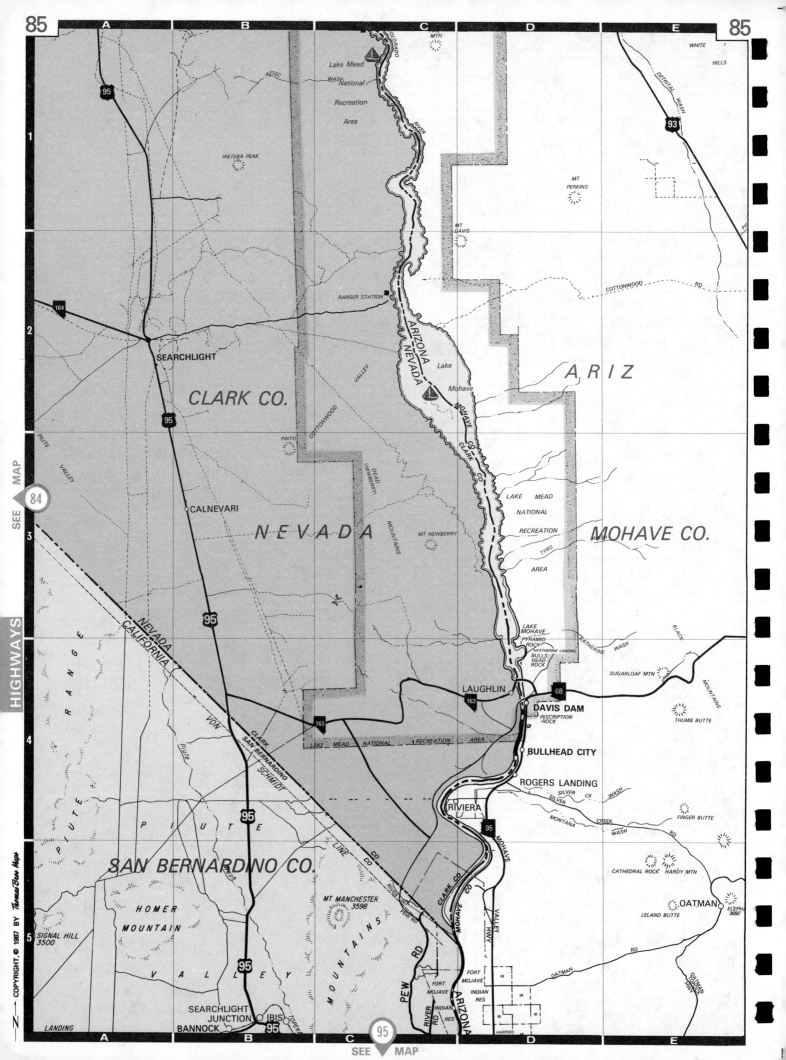

SEE MAP 77

SAN LUIS OBISPO CO
SANTA BARBARA CO

S.L.O. CO.

KERN CO.

WASIOJA RD

RANCHO CUYAMA NO 2
RANCHO

CUYAMA NO 2
CUYAMA
NEW CUYAMA

WASHINGTON ST
JOHNSON ST
CUYAMA ST
WYLIE ST
BELL
SCHAEFFER RD
KIRSCHENMANN RD

166

FOOTHILL RD
PERKINS RD
ALISO RD
FOOTHILL

ALISO PARK RD
ALISO PARK
BRANCH CANYON STA

SCHOOL HOUSE
COTT

WHITE OAKS STA
BATES CANYON

PEAK MTN

MC PHERSON PEAK

HOG PEN SPRING

SAN RAFAEL WILDERNESS

LOS PADRES NATIONAL FOREST

MONTGOMERY POTRERO

WHEAT PEAK

SAN RAFAEL WILDERNESS

BALD MTN

FOX MTN

Los Padres National Forest

166
33

SANTA

SANTA BARBARA CO
VENTURA CO
KERN CO

BALLINGER
BALLINGER CYN
GATE

SANTA BARBARA CYN RD

VENTUCOPA

CUYAMA PEAK
MORRO HILL

LA PANZA AV
EL ROBLAR AV
QUATAL CYN RD

CUYAMA RIVER

VEN. CO.

ZACA LAKE

LOS PADRES NATIONAL FOREST

FIGUEROA MTN
CACHUMA RD
DAVY BROWN
PINO ALTO
FIGUEROA STA
CACHUMA SADDLE STA
CATWAY RD

NIRA
LOST VALLEY

CACHUMA MTN

SAN RAFAEL

SAN RAFAEL MTN

SISQUOC CONDOR SANCTUARY

SAMON PEAK

UPPER TINTA
TINTA

LIZARD HEAD

MINE CAMP
BEAR JUNCTION

RANCHO LA LAGUNA (GUTIERREZ)

MCKINLEY MTN
CACHUMA

FIGUEROA MTN RD

LOS PADRES
WILDERNESS

BIG PINE MTN

MADULCE PEAK

RANCHO

SANTA BARBARA CO.

RANCHO DE CANADA LOS PINOS

BRINKERHOFF AV
LINDA VISTA DR
HAPPY CYN RD
ALISOS AV

LOMA PELONA

CREEK

SEE MAP 86

SEE MAP 88

RANCHO SAN MARCOS

RANCHO TEQUEPIS

LITTLE PINE MTN

HILDRETH PEAK

ARMOUR RANCH RD
Lake Cachuma Recreation Area
CACHUMA
154
CACHUMA CO PK

RANCHO LOMAS LA PURIFICACION

LAKE CACHUMA

LOMA ALTA

NINETEEN OAKS
HIDDEN POTRERO

MONO CREEK

RANCHO LOS PRIETOS Y NAJALAYEGUA

BIG CALIENTE
LOWER CALIENTE

MONTE ARIDO

SANTA YNEZ RIVER
SANTA STAGECOACH RD

SAN MARCOS PASS RD

PARADISE RD

GIBRALTAR RD
REDROCK
CAMUESA RD

CAMUESA

P BAR FLATS
AGUA CALIENTE

OLD MAN MTN

MATILIJA

REFUGIO STA
CAMINO CIELO
SANTA YNEZ PEAK

BROADCAST PEAK
CONDOR PEAK

W CAMINO CIELO
W CAMINO CIELO

KINEVAN RD

154

GIBRALTAR DAM
GIBRALTAR RES

MONO

FORBUSH FLAT
BLUE CANYON

PENDOLA STA

JAMESON LAKE
JUNCAL RD
UPPER SANTA YNEZ RIVER

MURIETTA

NATIONAL FOREST

RANCHO CANADA DEL CORRAL

CALLE LIPIZZANA
CALLE CELESTE
AVD DEL CAPITAN
CALLE QUEBRADA
CALLE REAL

WATER TUNNEL

HIDDEN VLY RD
SAN MARCOS RD

Chumash Painted Caves State Hist Park

LA CUMBRE PEAK
CATHEDRAL PEAK

SANTA YNEZ RIVER

ROMERO CYN
GATE

DIVIDE PEAK

WHITE LEDGE PEAK

Pepper Tree Motor Inn

PATTERSON AV
FAIRVIEW AV

MONTECITO PEAK

NOON PARK

CHISMAHOO MTN

RANCHO LOS DOS PUEBLOS

NAPLES
ELLWOOD
GOLETA
101
SPT
217
SANTA BARBARA
192
144
Clark Bird Refuge
MONTECITO
SYCAMORE
VALLEY RD
192
CARPINTERIA

SNOWBALL MTN

LA GRANADA

El Capitan State Beach
101

Univ of Calif Santa Barbara
HOLLISTER
Sta Barbara Airport

ISLA VISTA

Isla Vista Co Beach Park

Goleta Beach County Park
GOLETA PT

Arroyo Burro Beach County Park

225

NAVAL RES TRAINING CTR
CASTILLO PT
Sheraton Santa Barbara Hotel
Marriott's Santa Barbara Biltmore
SUMMERLAND
101
FRWY
SPT CO
101
150
RANCHO EL RINCON
W CASITAS PASS

224
Carpinteria State Beach

RINCON MTN
RINCON PT
LA CONCHITA
PUNTA GORDA
SEA CLIFF
PITAS PT
VENTURA

SANTA

BARBARA

CHANNEL

PACIFIC

OCEAN

Channel Islands National Park

SAN MIGUEL ISL
SANTA ROSA ISL
SANTA CRUZ ISL
SANTA BARBARA ISL

INSET NOT TO SCALE

HIGHWAYS

N

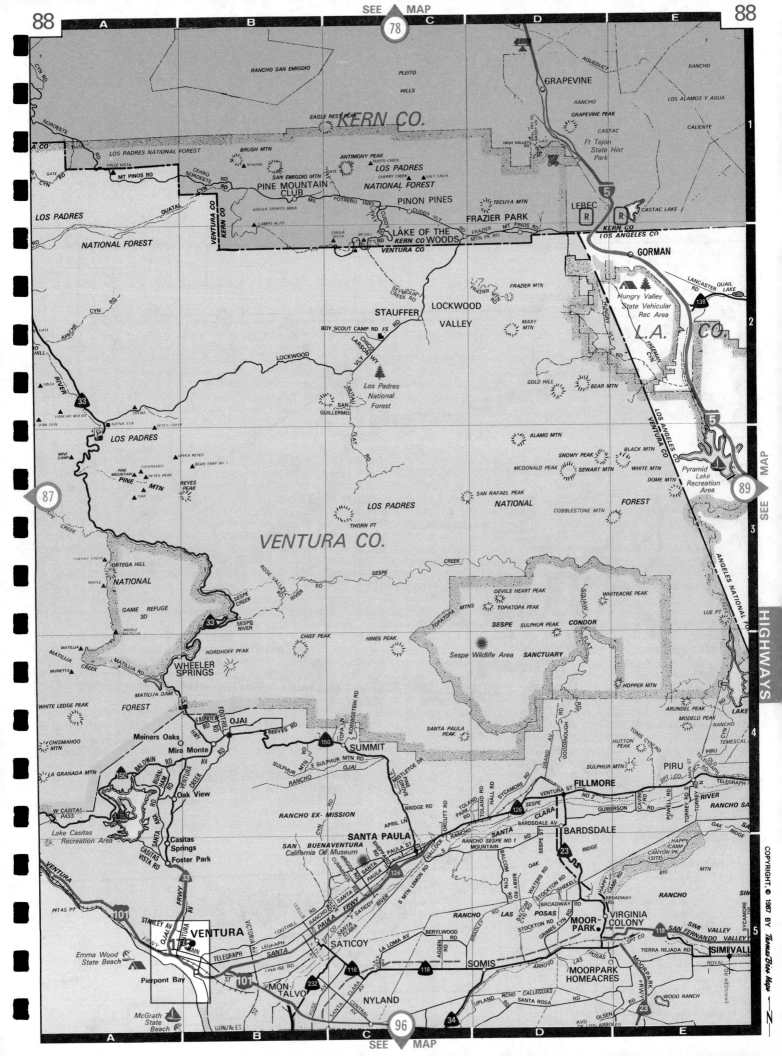

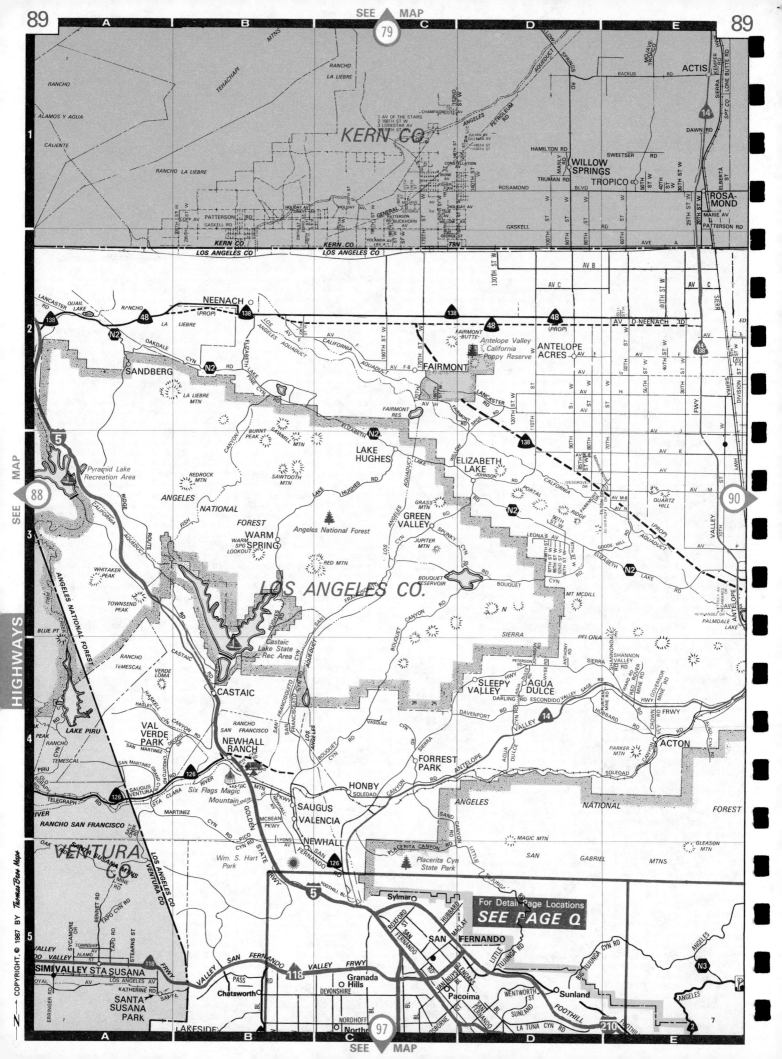

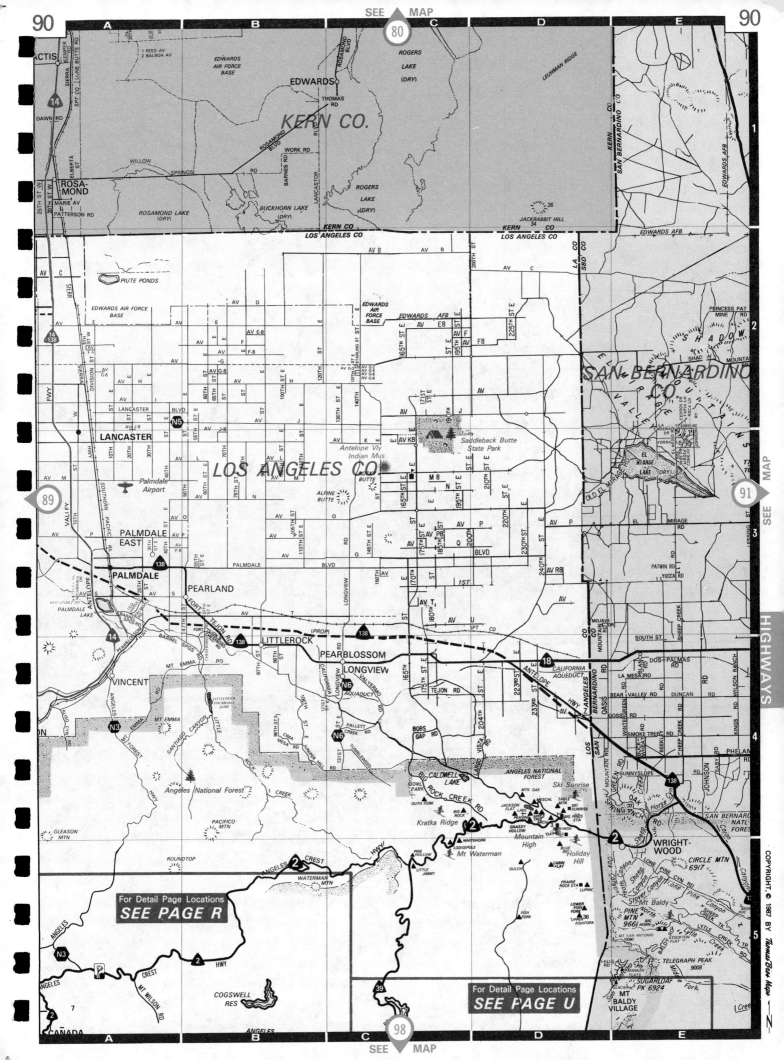

For Detail Page Locations
SEE PAGE R

For Detail Page Locations
SEE PAGE U

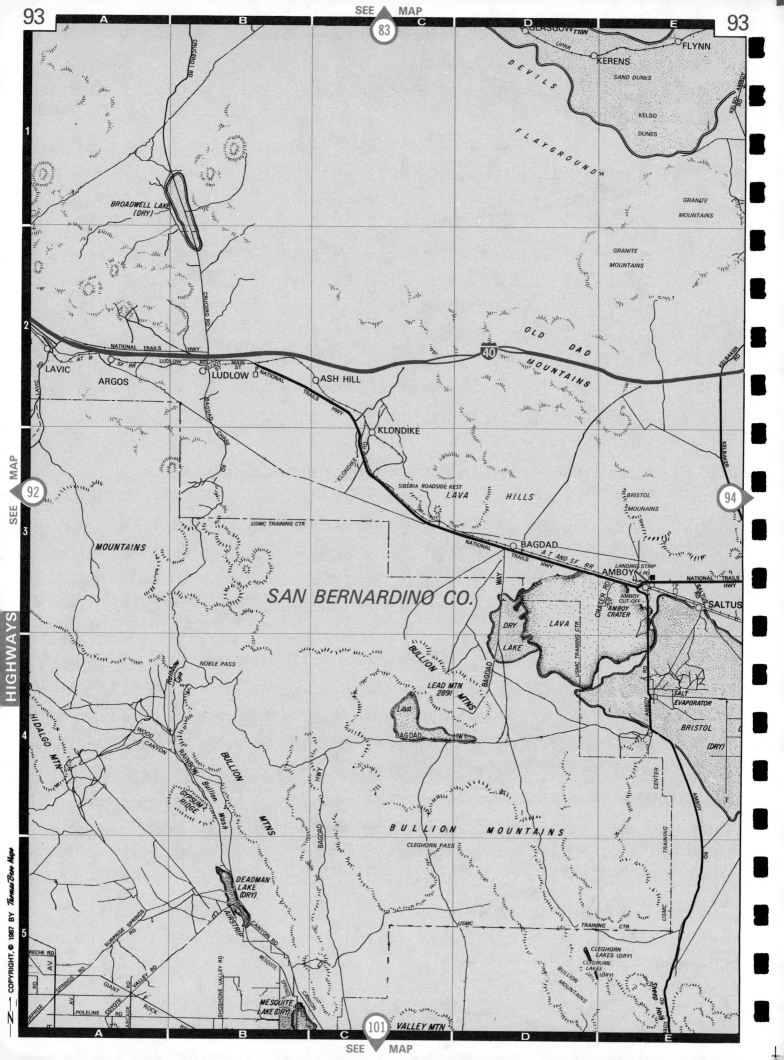

A · B · C · D · E

GLASGOW T10N

DEVILS

FLYNN

KERENS

SAND DUNES

KELSO
DUNES

PLAYGROUND 14

GRANITE
MOUNTAINS

BROADWELL LAKE
(DRY)

GRANITE
MOUNTAINS

1

CRUCERO RD

SEE MAP
92

2

OLD DAD MOUNTAINS

NATIONAL TRAILS HWY

40

LAVIC
AT 8
SF RR
LUDLOW RD
ELLIOT
MAIN
ST
ST
NATIONAL

ARGOS
LUDLOW
NATIONAL
ASH HILL

KELBAKER RD

BAGDAD CHASE RD

KLONDIKE

KLONDIKE RD

3

MOUNTAINS

USMC TRAINING CTR

SIBERIA ROADSIDE REST
LAVA HILLS

BRISTOL
MOUNTAINS

KELBAKER RD

SEE MAP
94

NATIONAL
TRAILS
AT AND SF RR
BAGDAD

HWY
LANDING STRIP
AMBOY P.O.

SAN BERNARDINO CO.

NATIONAL TRAILS HWY

CRATER RD
AMBOY
CUT-OFF
AMBOY
CRATER
SALTUS

WAY
DRY
LAKE
LAVA
USMC TRAINING CTR

AMBOY RD

NOBLE PASS

BULLION

BAGDAD

SALT
EVAPORATOR

RAINBOW CYN

LEAD MTN
2891
MTNS

BRISTOL
(DRY)

4

HIDALGO MTN

WOOD
CANYON

RAINBOW

LAVA
BAGDAD

HWY

BULLION MTNS

Bullion Wash

GYPSUM
RIDGE

CLEGHORN PASS

BULLION   MOUNTAINS

CENTER

AMBOY RD

BAGDAD HWY

TRAINING

5

RECHE RD

SURPRISE SPRINGS RD

DEADMAN LAKE
(DRY)

AIRSTRIP

CANYON RD

USMC

TRAINING CTR

USMC

CLEGHORN LAKES (DRY)
CLEGHORN
LAKES
(DRY)

Sheep Hole

AV
SPRINGS RD
GIANT
COYOTE
RD
VALLEY RD

CASCADE
ROCK
SHOSHONE VALLEY RD
MESQUITE
SPRINGS
CANYON

MESQUITE
LAKE (DRY)

BULLION
MOUNTAINS

SURPRISE
POLELINE
AV
RD

VALLEY MTN

A · B · C · D · E

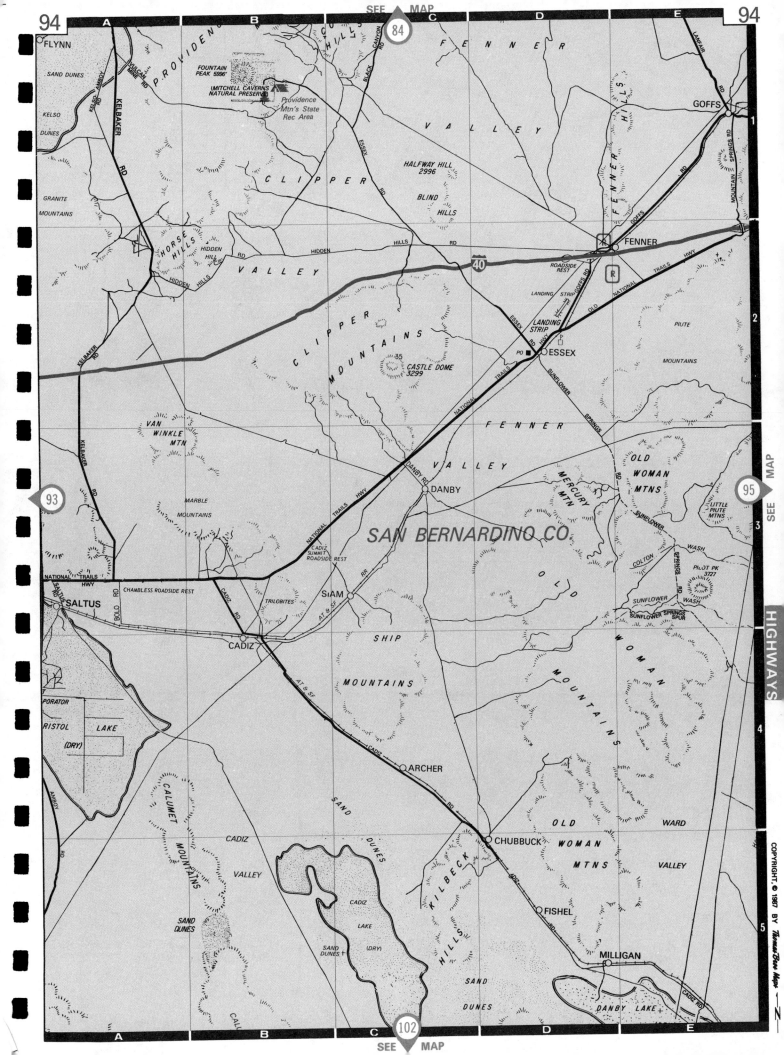

SEE MAP
84

FLYNN

SAND DUNES

KELSO DUNES

GRANITE MOUNTAINS

P. PROVIDENCE

KELSO AMBOY RD

VULCAN MINE RD

KELBAKER RD

FOUNTAIN PEAK 5996'

MITCHELL CAVERNS NATURAL PRESERVE

Providence Mtn's State Rec Area

CO. HILLS

BLACK CANYON RD

FENNER VALLEY

HALFWAY HILL 2996

BLIND HILLS

FENNER HILLS

LANFAIR RD

GOFFS RD

MOUNTAIN SPRINGS RD

GOFFS

HORSE HILLS

HIDDEN HILL

HIDDEN HILLS RD

HIDDEN HILLS RD

ESSEX RD

CLIPPER VALLEY

FENNER

ROADSIDE REST

LANDING STRIP

GOFFS RD

R

NATIONAL TRAILS HWY

OLD

PIUTE MOUNTAINS

KELBAKER RD

CLIPPER MOUNTAINS

85

CASTLE DOME 3299

ESSEX RD

LANDING STRIP

PO ESSEX

NATIONAL TRAILS

SUNFLOWER

VAN WINKLE MTN

FENNER VALLEY

MERCURY MTN

SPRINGS

OLD WOMAN MTNS

93

KELBAKER RD

MARBLE MOUNTAINS

DANBY RD

DANBY

SUNFLOWER RD

LITTLE PIUTE MTNS

SEE MAP 95

SAN BERNARDINO CO.

COLTON

SPRINGS RD

PILOT PK 3727

WASH

NATIONAL TRAILS HWY

CADIZ SUMMIT ROADSIDE REST

RR

SUNFLOWER WASH

SUNFLOWER SPRINGS SPUR

NATIONAL TRAILS HWY

CHAMBLESS ROADSIDE REST

CADIZ RD

TRILOBITES

SIAM

AT & SF

SHIP MOUNTAINS

OLD

HIGHWAYS

SALTUS

SALTUS RD

BOLO RD

CADIZ

AT & SF

CADIZ RD

ARCHER

WOMAN MOUNTAINS

WARD VALLEY

PORATOR

RISTOL LAKE (DRY)

CALUMET MOUNTAINS

CADIZ VALLEY

SAND DUNES

CHUBBUCK

KILBECK HILLS

OLD WOMAN MTNS

AMBOY RD

CADIZ RD

SAND DUNES

CADIZ LAKE (DRY)

FISHEL

COPYRIGHT © 1987 BY Thomas Bros Maps

SAND DUNES

MILLIGAN

CADIZ RD

DANBY LAKE

SEE MAP
102

SEE MAP

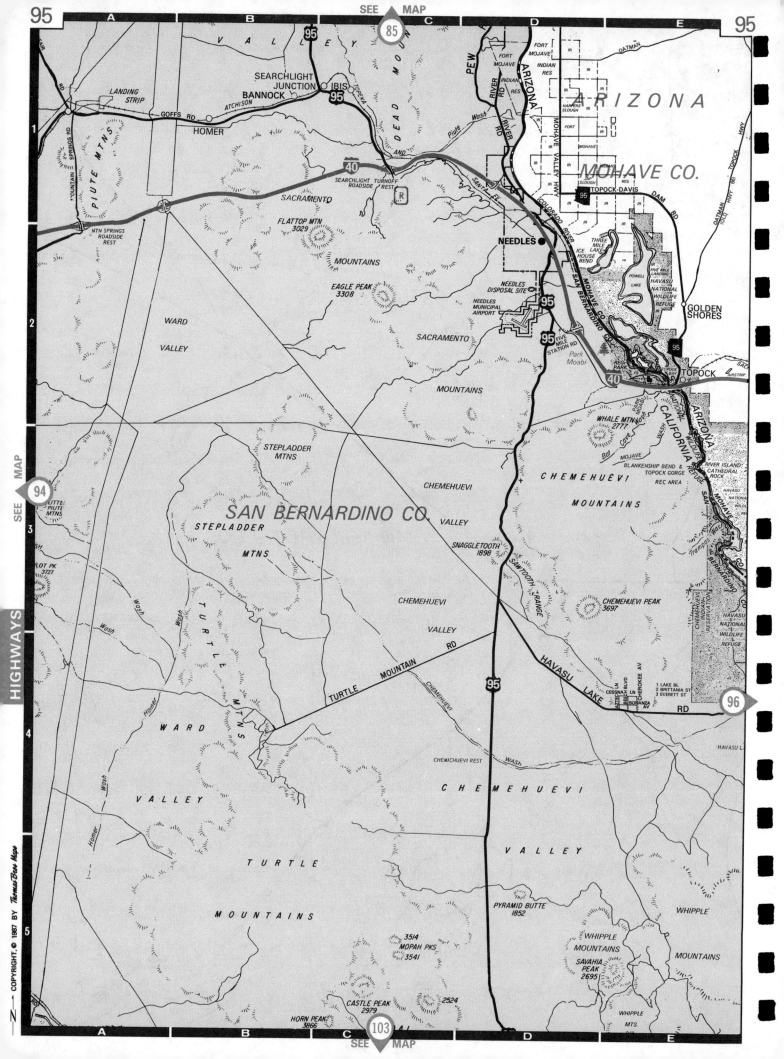

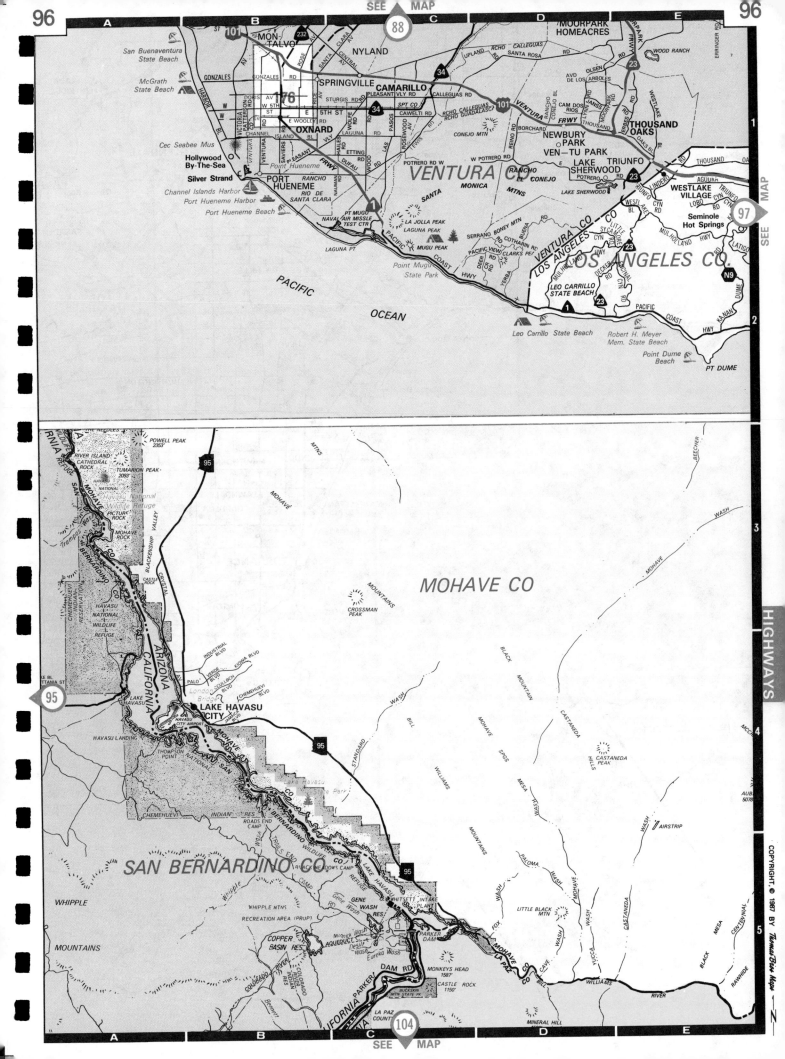

MOORPARK
HOMEACRES

MON-
TALVO
NYLAND
WOOD RANCH

San Buenaventura
State Beach

SPRINGVILLE
CAMARILLO
UPLAND   RCHO   SANTA ROSA

McGrath
State Beach
PLEASANT VLY RD
CALLEGUAS RD
VENTURA
FRWY

OXNARD

STURGIS   RD

RCHO CALLEGUAS
RCHO GUADALASCA

NEWBURY
PARK
VEN—TU PARK

THOUSAND
OAKS

Cec Seabee Mus

Hollywood By-The-Sea

Silver Strand

Channel Islands Harbor
Port Hueneme Harbor
Port Hueneme Beach

PORT
HUENEME

Rancho
Rio de
Santa Clara

VENTURA CO.

SANTA
MONICA

RANCHO
EL
CONEJO

LAKE
SHERWOOD

Lake Sherwood

TRIUNFO

WESTLAKE
VILLAGE

Seminole
Hot Springs

97
SEE MAP

PT MUGU
NAVAL AIR MISSLE
TEST CTR

La Jolla Peak
Laguna Peak

SANTA
MTNS

Serrano Boney MTN

Mugu Peak

LOS ANGELES CO.

LAGUNA PT

Point Mugu
State Park

PACIFIC
COAST
HWY

Pacific View

LEO CARRILLO
STATE BEACH

23

N9

PACIFIC
OCEAN

Leo Carrillo State Beach

Robert H. Meyer
Mem. State Beach

PACIFIC
COAST
HWY

Point Dume
Beach

PT DUME

A   B   C   D   E

THE NEEDLES

POWELL PEAK
2353'

RIVER ISLAND
CATHEDRAL
ROCK

95

MTNS

BEECHER

TUMARION PEAK
2093'

MOHAVE

HAVASU
NATIONAL
Wildlife Refuge

PICTURE
ROCK

MOHAVE
ROCK

BLACKENSHIP VALLEY

MOHAVE
WASH

CHEMEHUEVI
INDIAN
RESERVATION

HAVASU
NATIONAL
WILDLIFE
REFUGE

CASTLE
ROCK

CRYSTAL

MOHAVE CO

MOUNTAINS

CROSSMAN
PEAK

3

BLACK

MOUNTAIN

95

LAKE
BL

INDUSTRIAL   BLVD

PALO   VERDE   BLVD

KIOWA BLVD

CASTANEDA

ARIZONA

CALIFORNIA

Londog
Cull&ch
Bridge

CHEMEHUEVI
BLVD

LAKE
HAVASU

MOHAVE
SPGS

CASTANEDA
HILLS

CASTANEDA
PEAK

95

LAKE HAVASU
CITY

HAVASU
CITY AIRPORT

MESA

WASH

MCCH

4

HAVASU LANDING

MOHAVE

95

STANDARD   WASH

WILLIAMS

AUB
5076

THOMPSON
POINT

NATIONAL   SAN

WASH

AIRSTRIP

CHEMEHUEVI   INDIAN   RES

ROADS END
CAMP

BERNARDINO

WILDLIFE

95

MOUNTAINS

PALOMA

WASH

SAN BERNARDINO CO.

TRAILS END
CAMP

LAKE   HAVASU

REFUGE

WHITSETT INTAKE
PLANT

LITTLE BLACK
MTN

YUCCA

BLACK

5

WHIPPLE

BLACK MEADOWS CAMP

GENE
WASH
RES

WASH

FOX

CENTENNIAL

MOUNTAINS

WHIPPLE MTNS
RECREATION AREA (PRUP)

Gene Wash

GENE
WASH
RES

PARKER
DAM

MOHAVE

CAVE

WASH

RIVER

RAWHIDE

COPPER
BASIN RES

AQUEDUCT

Monica Wash
Desil

Eureka Wash

MONKEYS HEAD
1587'

CASTLE
ROCK 1150'

LA PAZ

MINERAL HILL

COLORADO   RIVER   INDIAN   RES

DAM   RD

BUCKSKIN
MTN STATE PK

LA PAZ COUNTY

PARKER

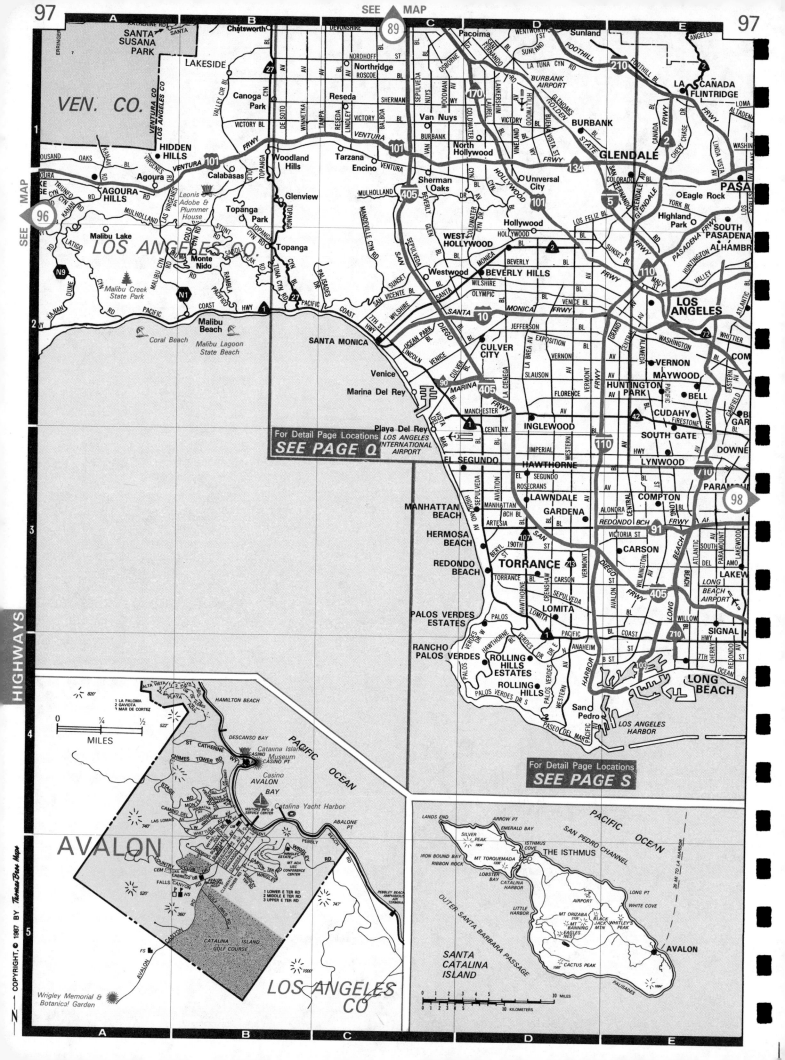

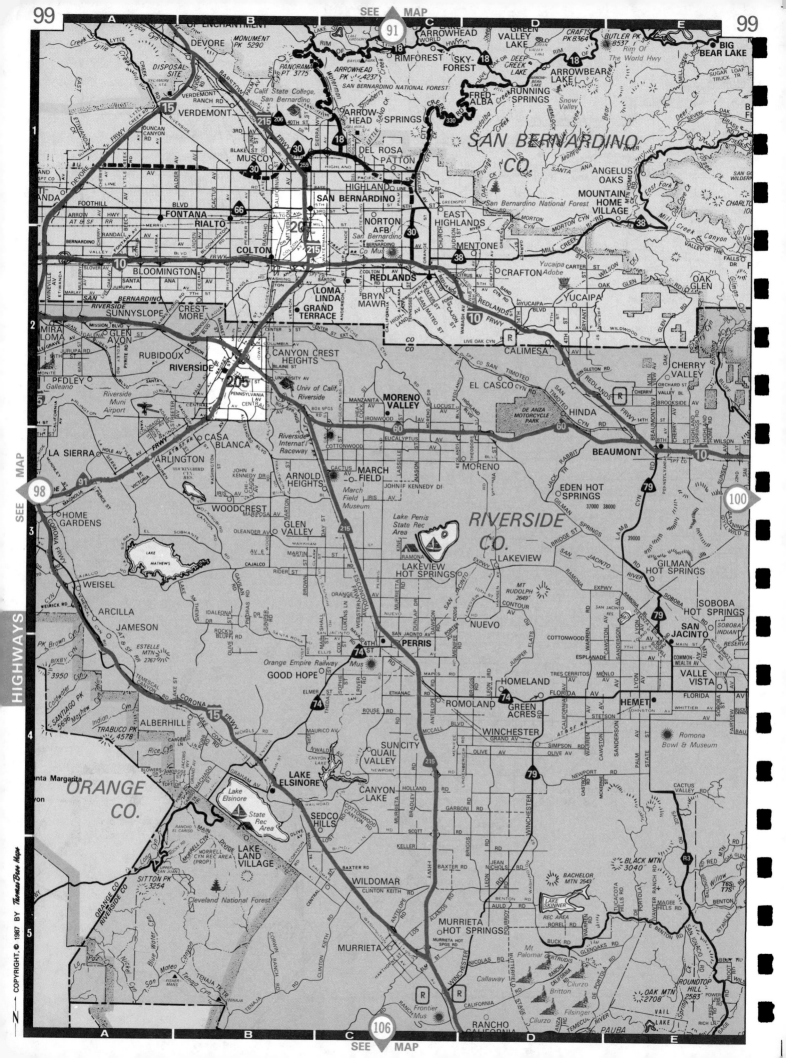

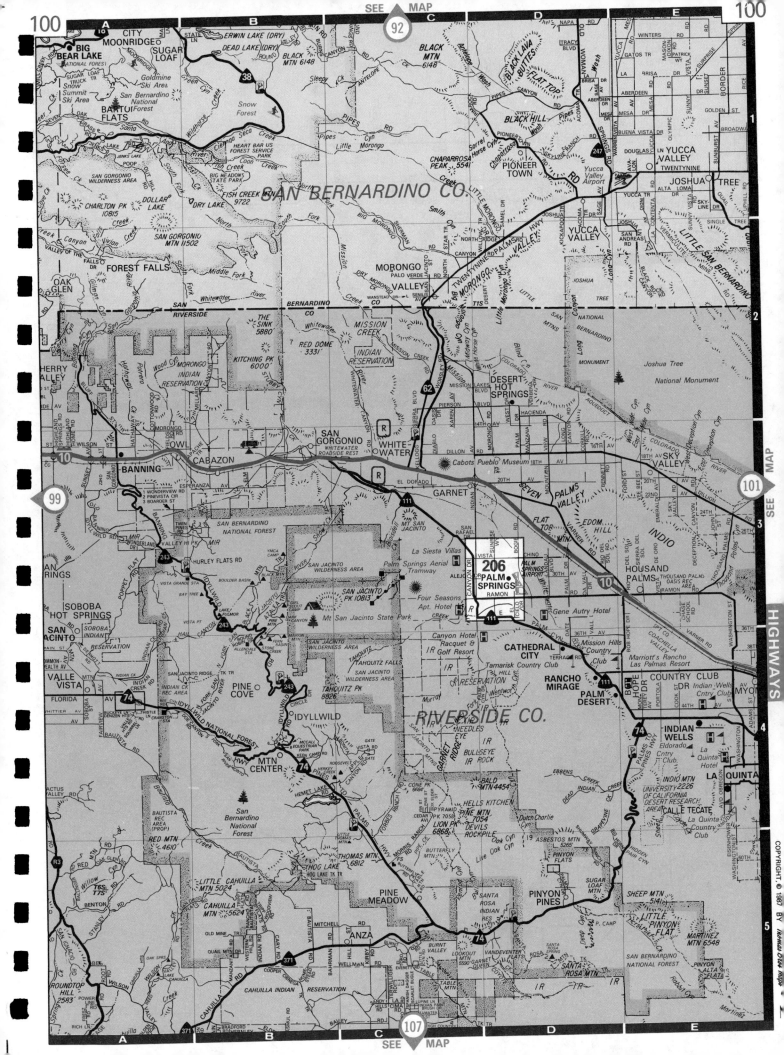

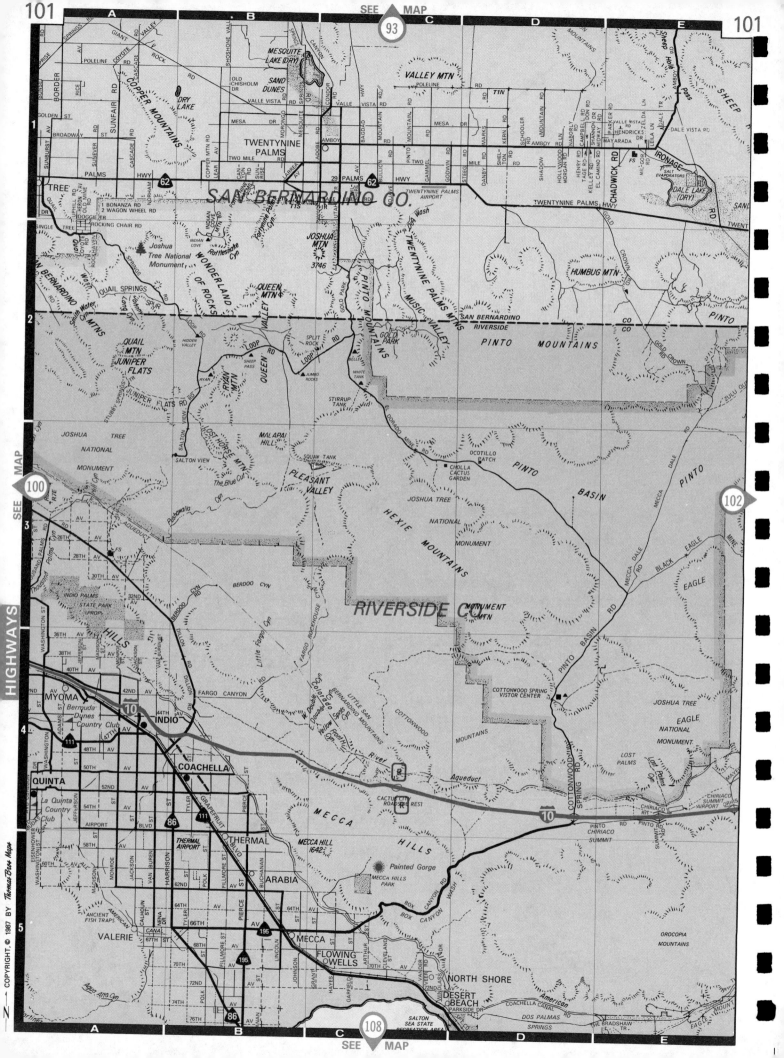

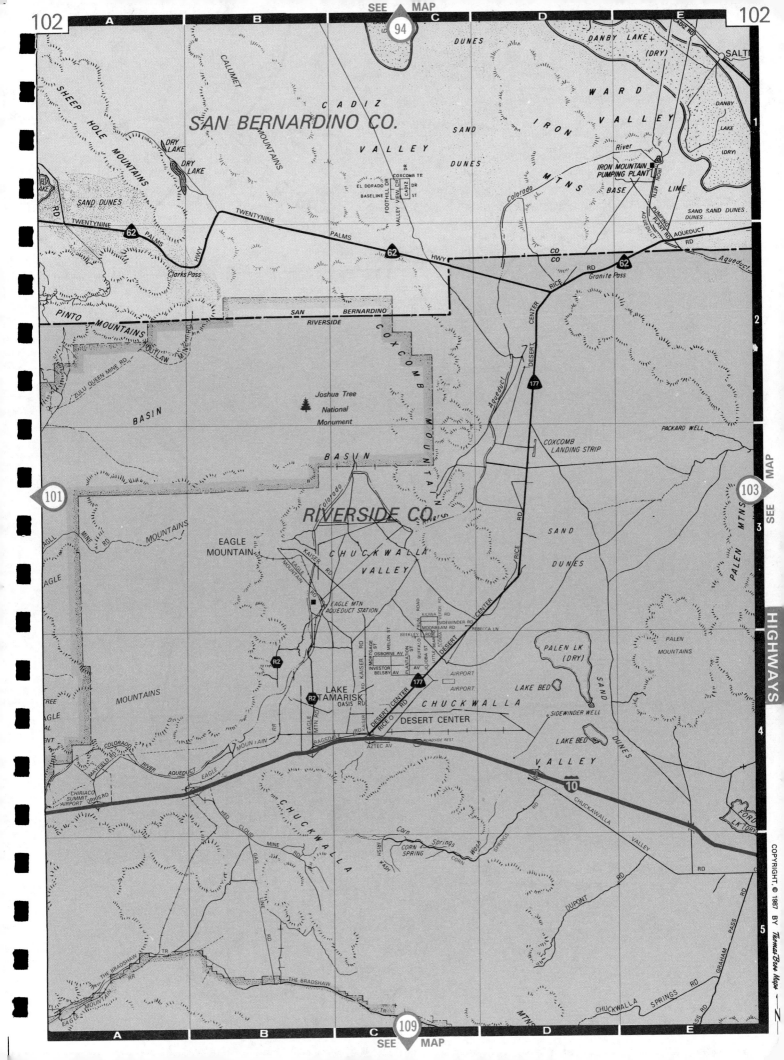

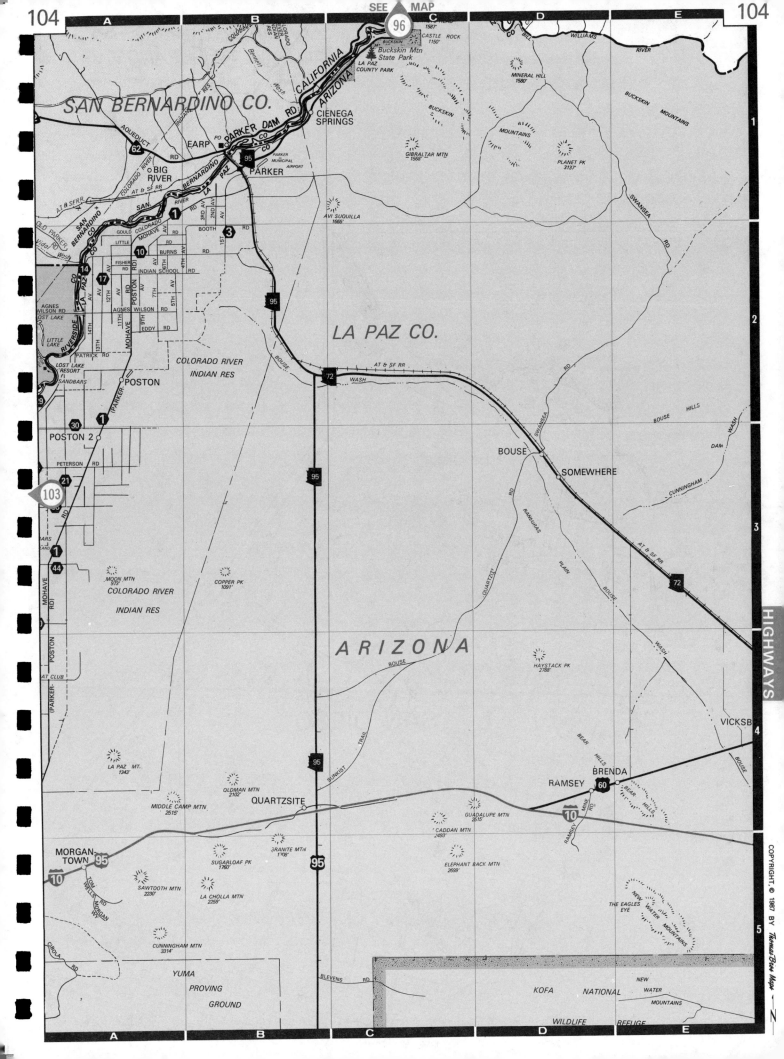

SAN JUAN CAPISTRANO
202
ORANGE CO.
Three Arch Bay
Ritz Carlton Hotel
Dana Point
SAN CLEMENTE
San Clemente State Beach
San Onofre State Park
SAN DIEGO CO.
San Onofre Visitors Ctr.
SAN ONOFRE
San Onofre State Beach
106

LA JOLLA SHORES
ECOLOGICAL STUDY AREA
SAN DIEGO – LA JOLLA UNDERWATER PARK
SPINDRIFT GOLF COURSE
LA JOLLA BAY
ALLIGATOR HEAD
GOLD FISH PT
THE COVE
La Jolla Caves
PT LA JOLLA
ELLEN SCRIPPS PK
Boomer Beach
OCEAN ST
SHELL BEACH
PROSPECT RD
1 UNION PL
Colonial Inn
Wipeout Beach
ELLEN BROWNING SCRIPPS PARK
Hotel La Jolla
COAST BLVD PK
La Jolla
Casa Beach
WHISPERING SANDS
NICHOLSON PT PARK
AL BAHR DR
LUDINGTON PARK
Marine Street Beach
La Jolla County Club
VISTA DE LA PLAYA
MUIRLANDS DR
Windansea Beach
NAUTILUS
NAUTILUS ST
LA JOLLA SCENIC
Playa
PLAYA DEL SUR
KOLMAR ST
ROSEMONT
LA JOLLA STRAND PK
WINAMAR
HERMOSA TER
BIG ROCK REEF
NEWKIRK DR
HAVENHURST
SAN DIEGO
SOLEDAD MTN RD
La Jolla Hermosa Park
Bird Rock
SUN GOLD PT
KATE O. SESSIONS MEMORIAL PARK
CHELSEA
BIRD ROCK
TURQUOISE ST
SAPPHIRE ST
TOURMALINE ST
OPAL ST
LORING ST
BERYL
CHALCEDONY

PACIFIC OCEAN

N

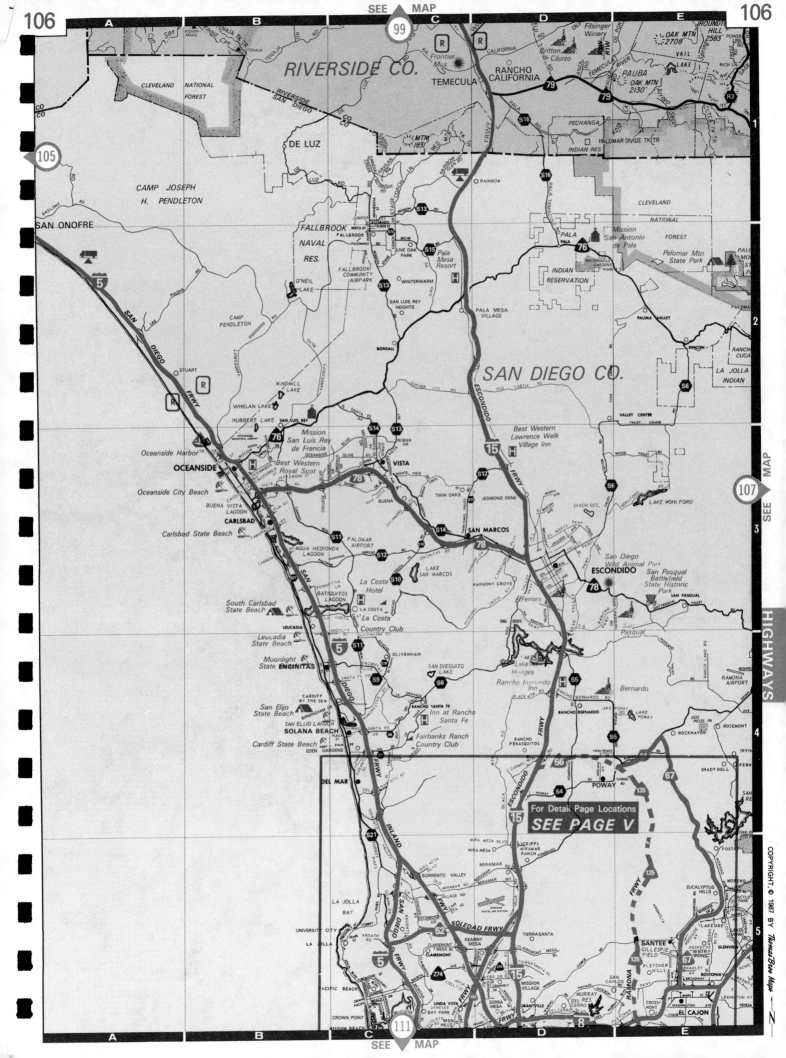

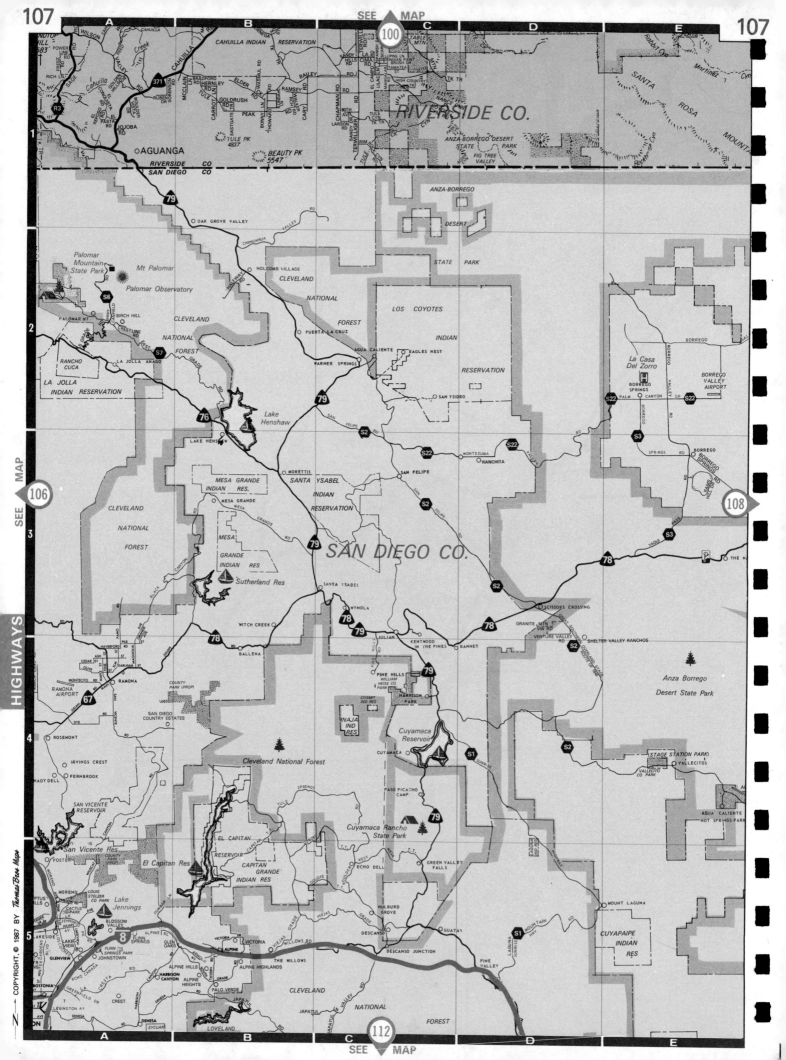

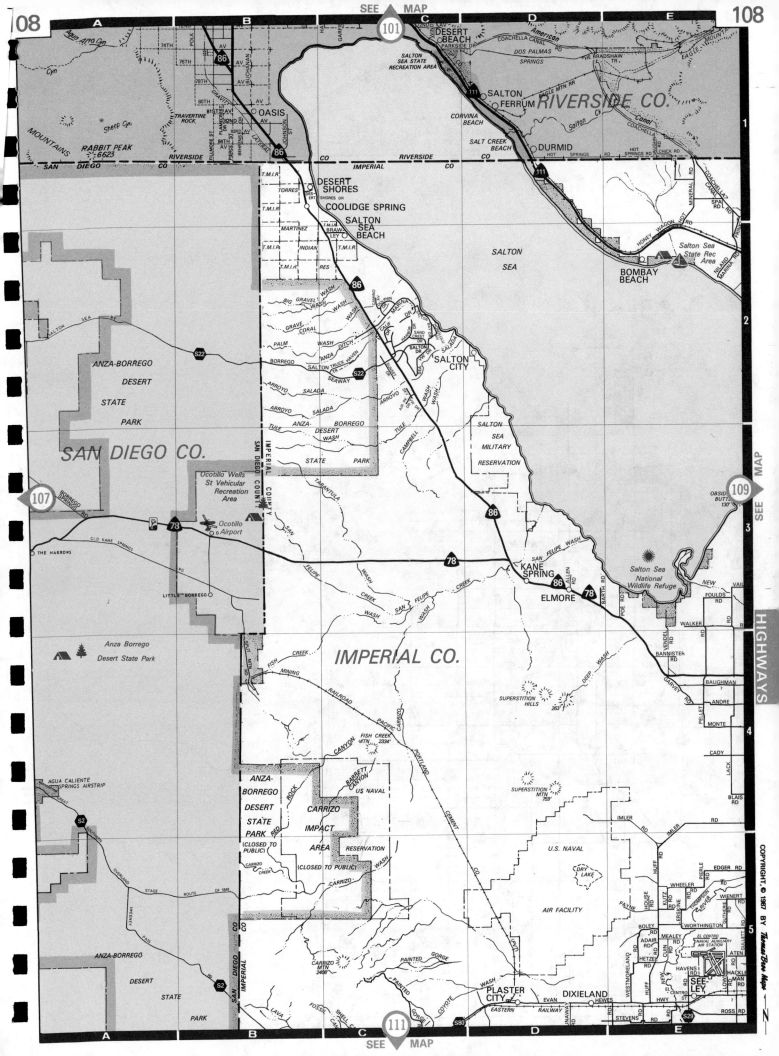

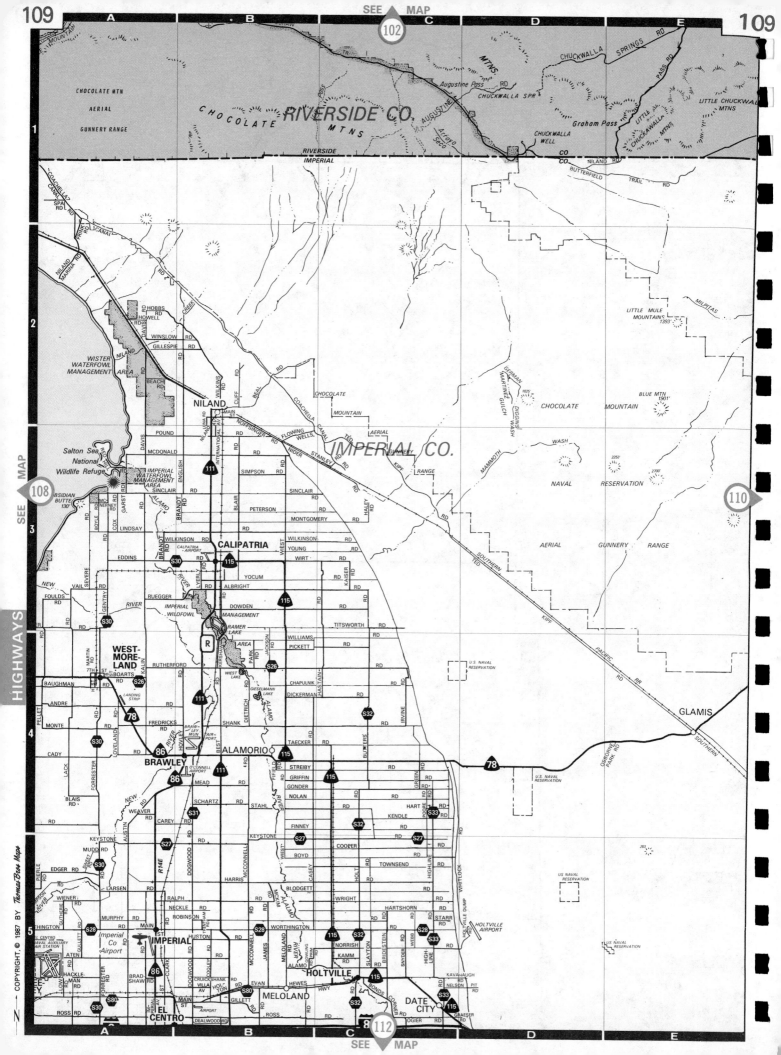

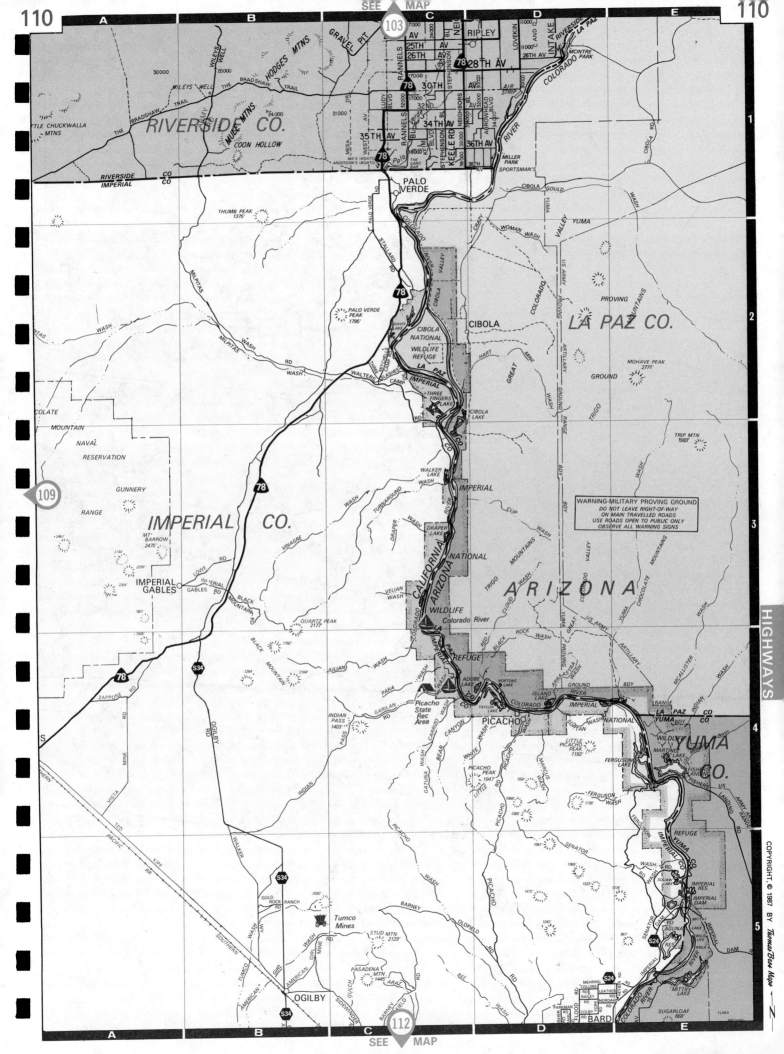

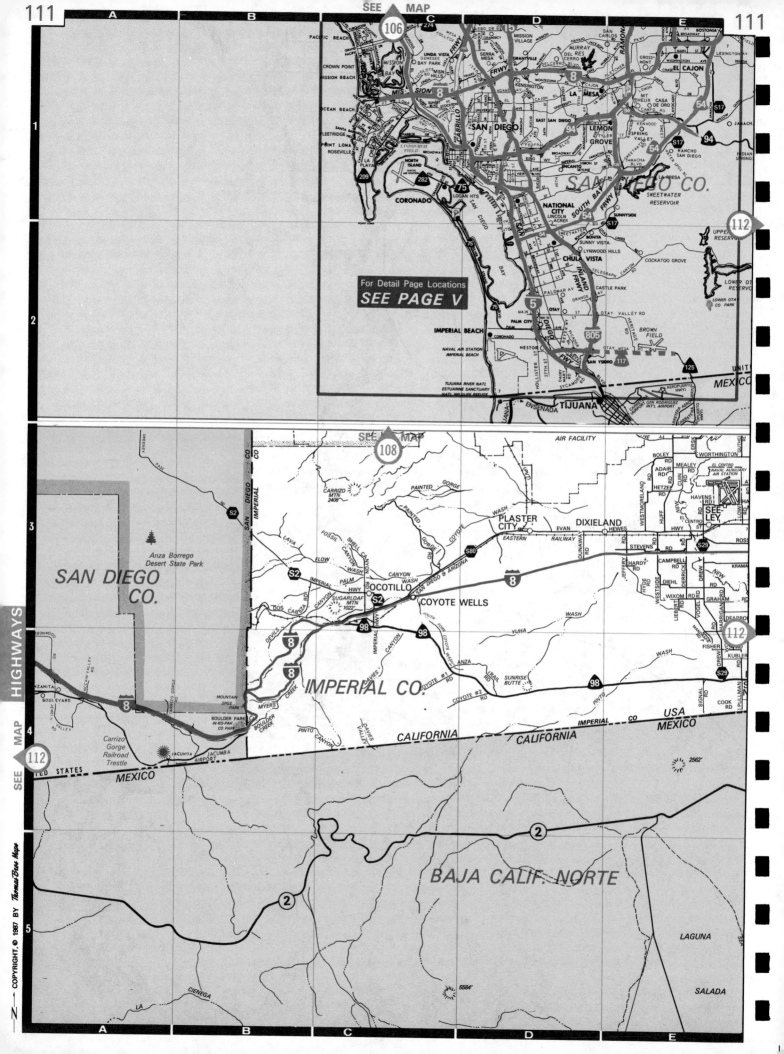

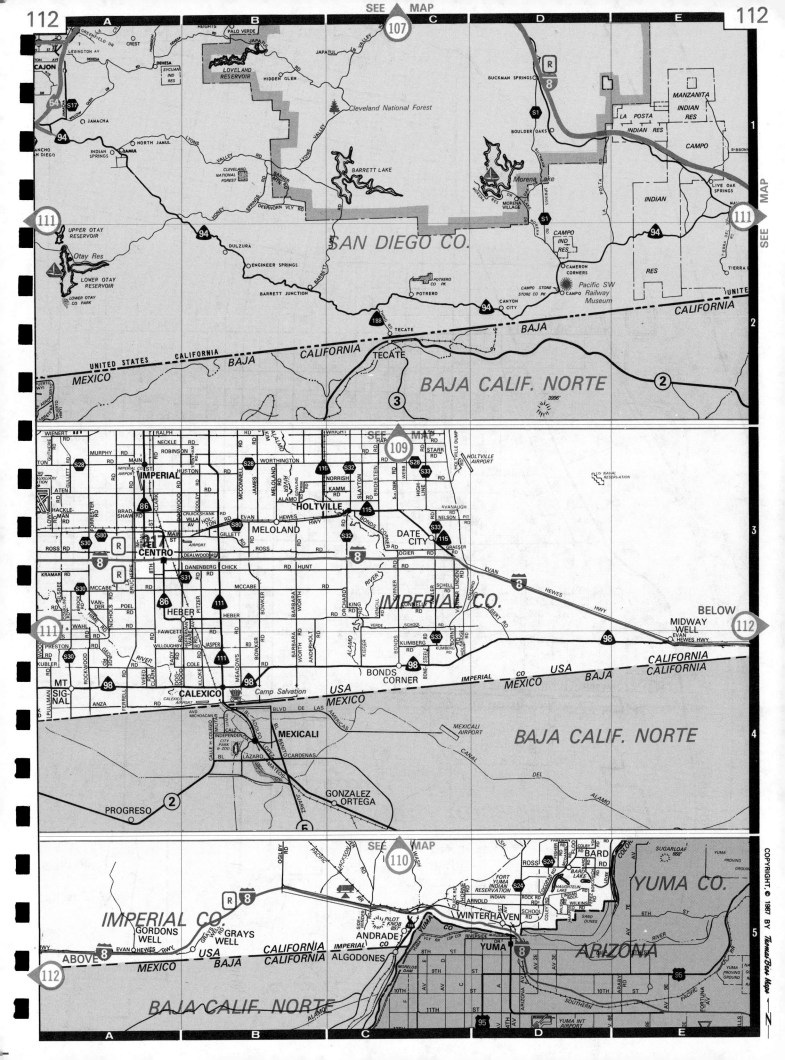

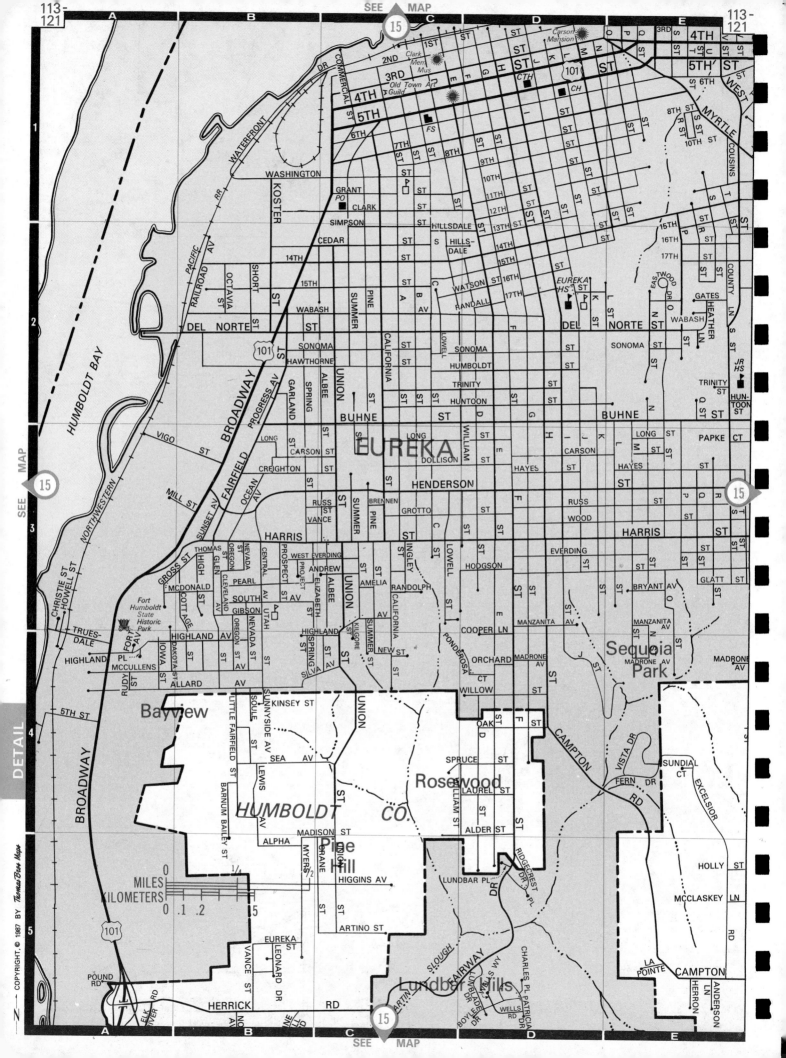

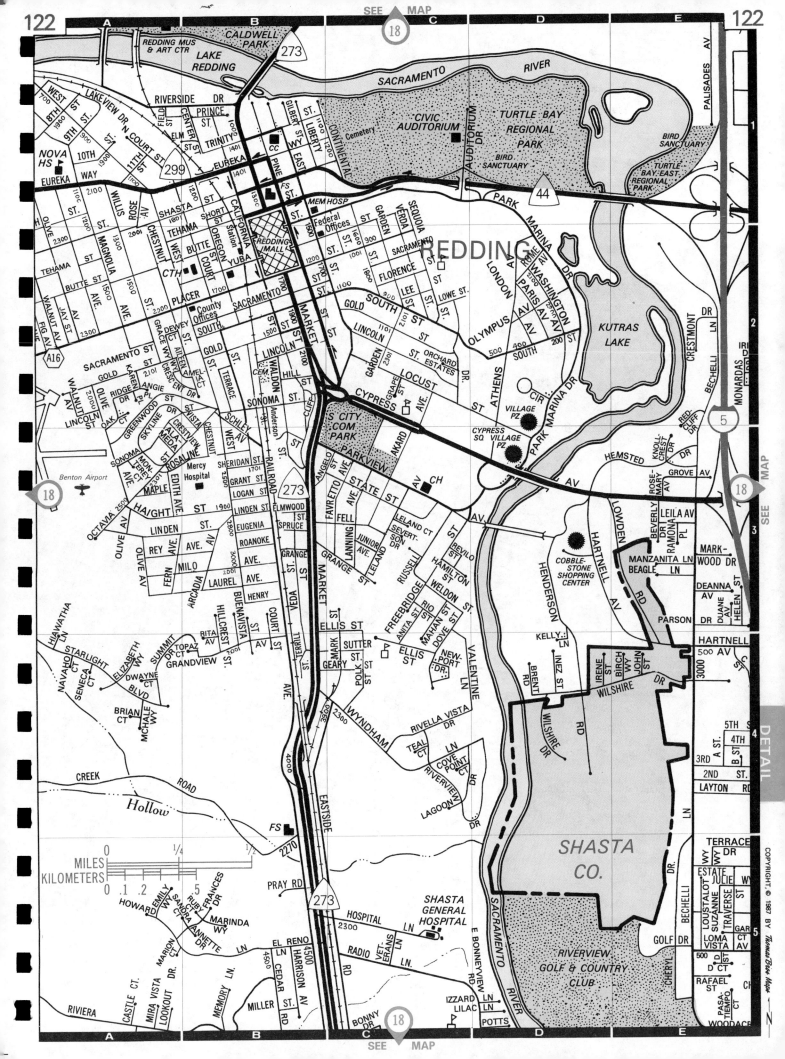

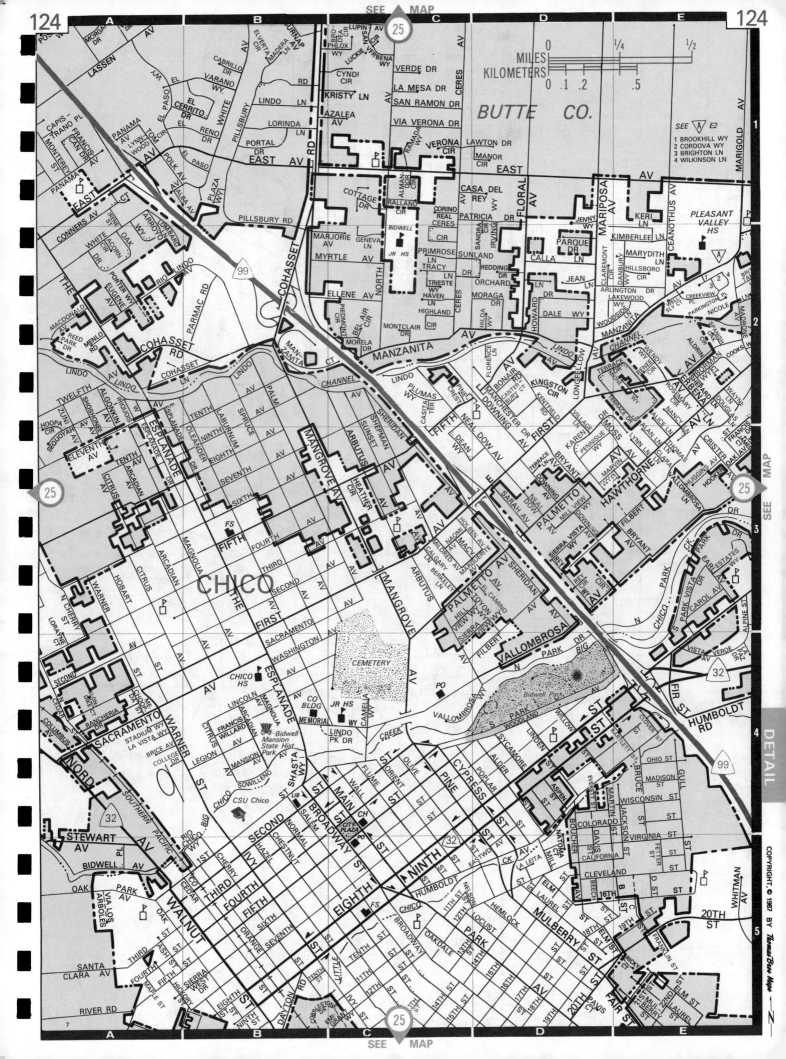

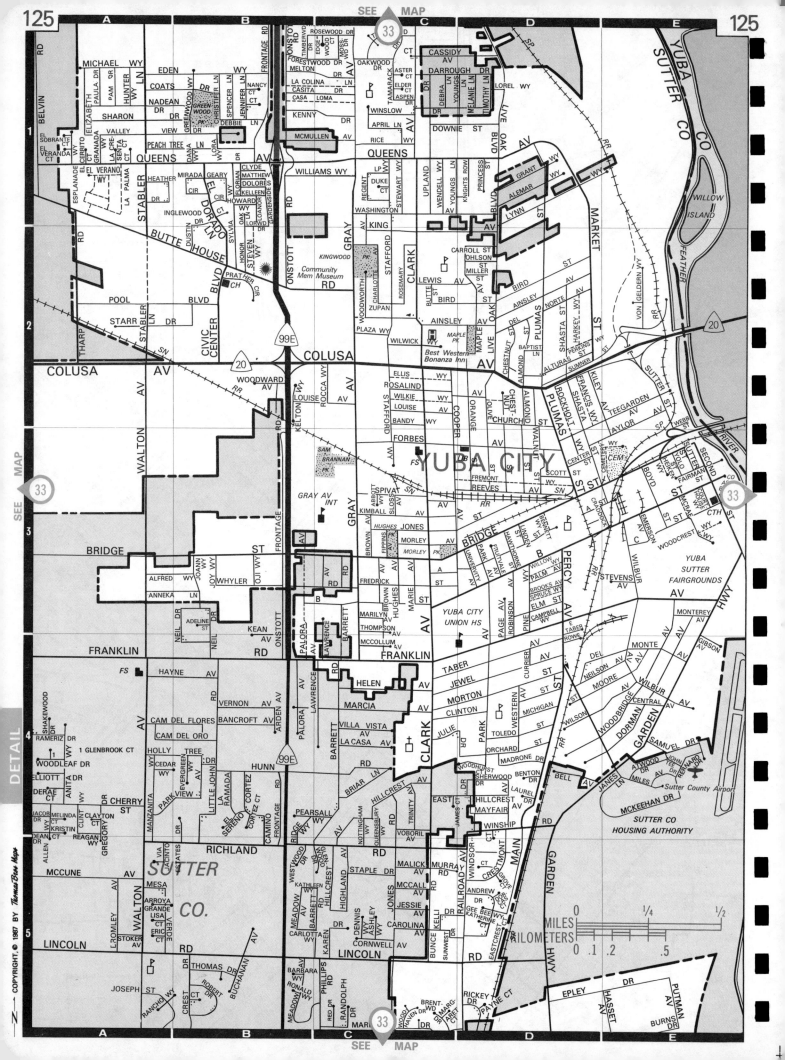

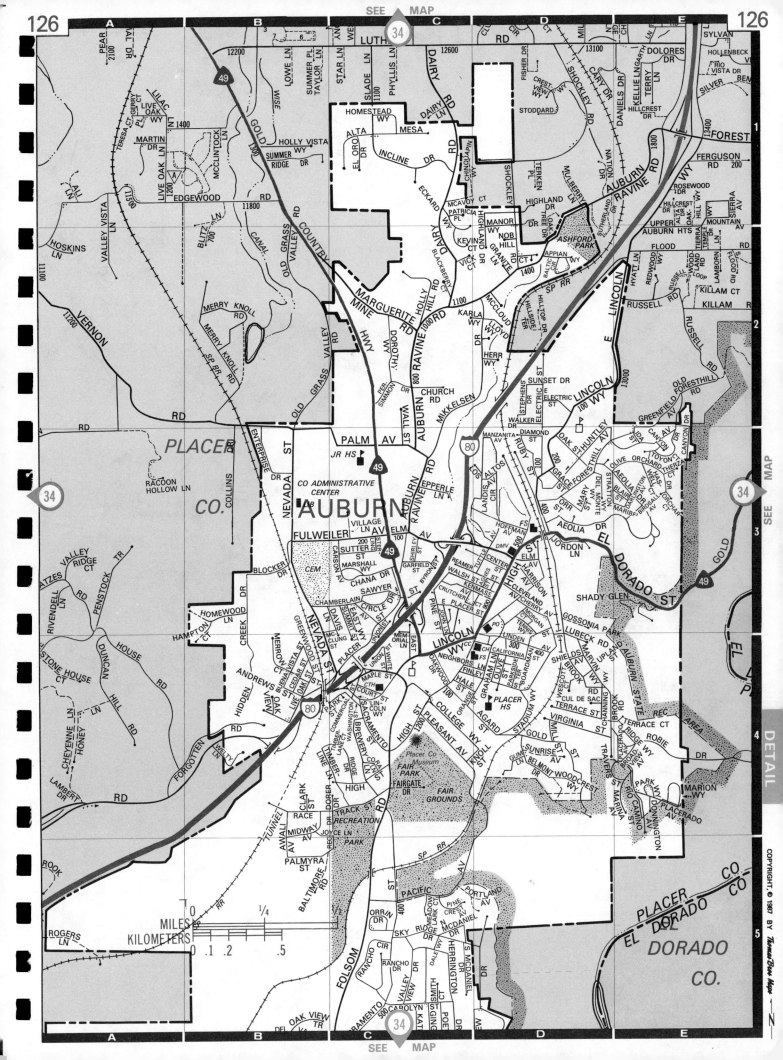

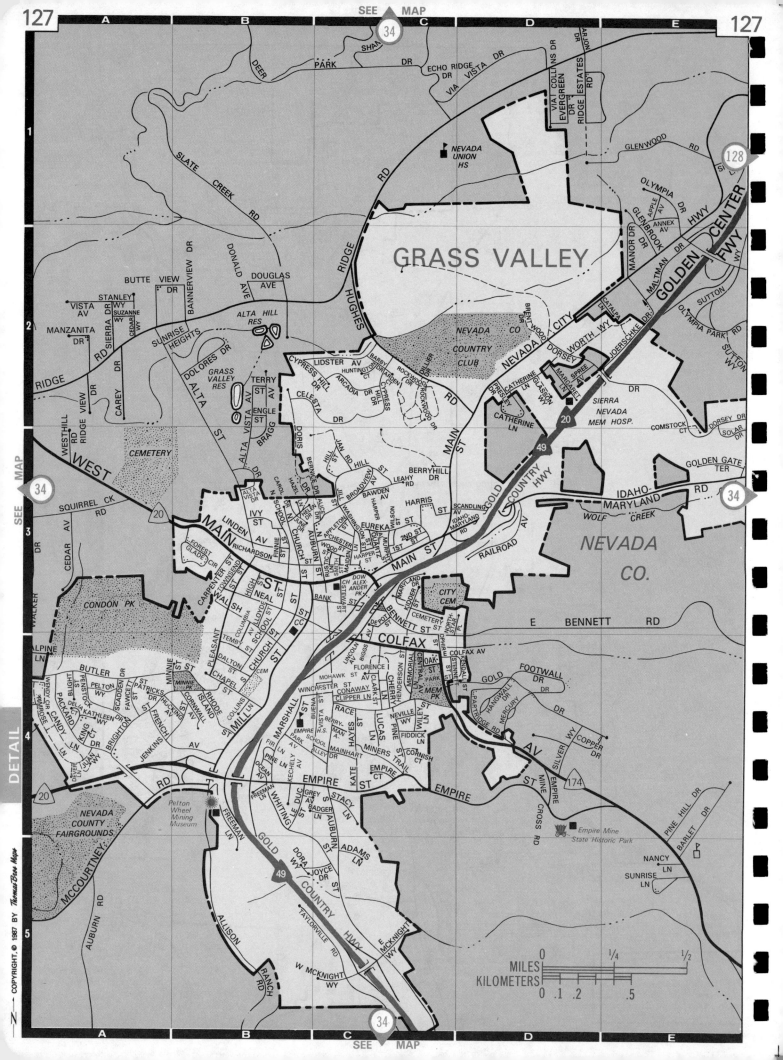

GRASS VALLEY

NEVADA CO.

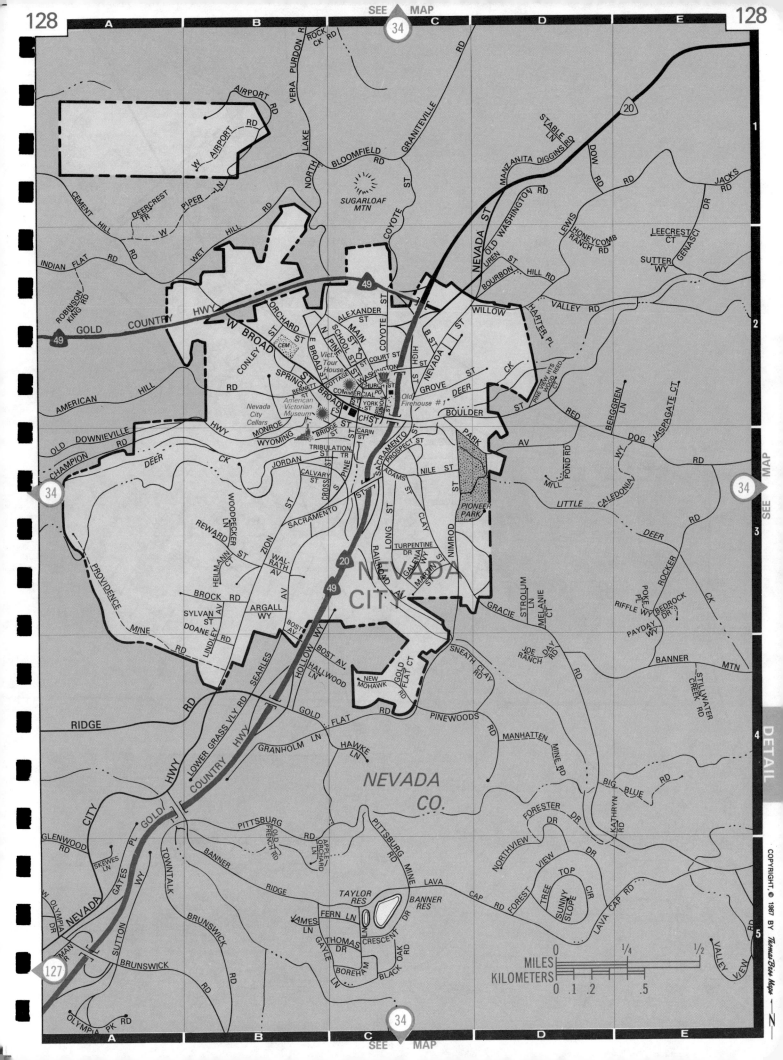

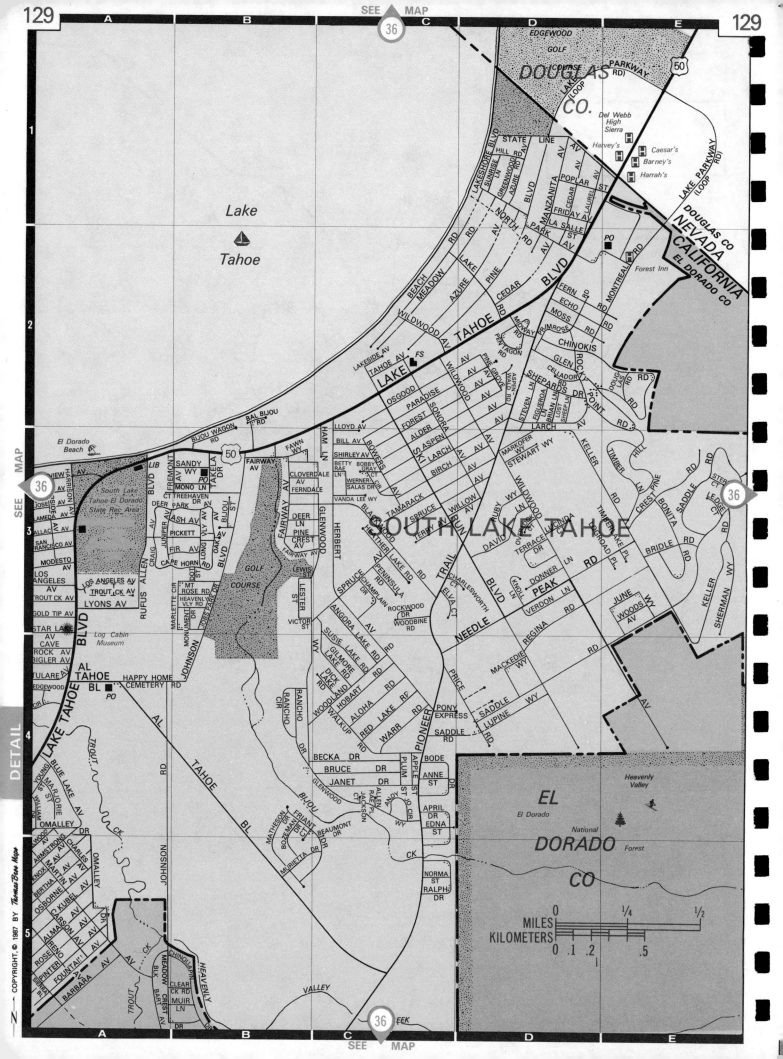

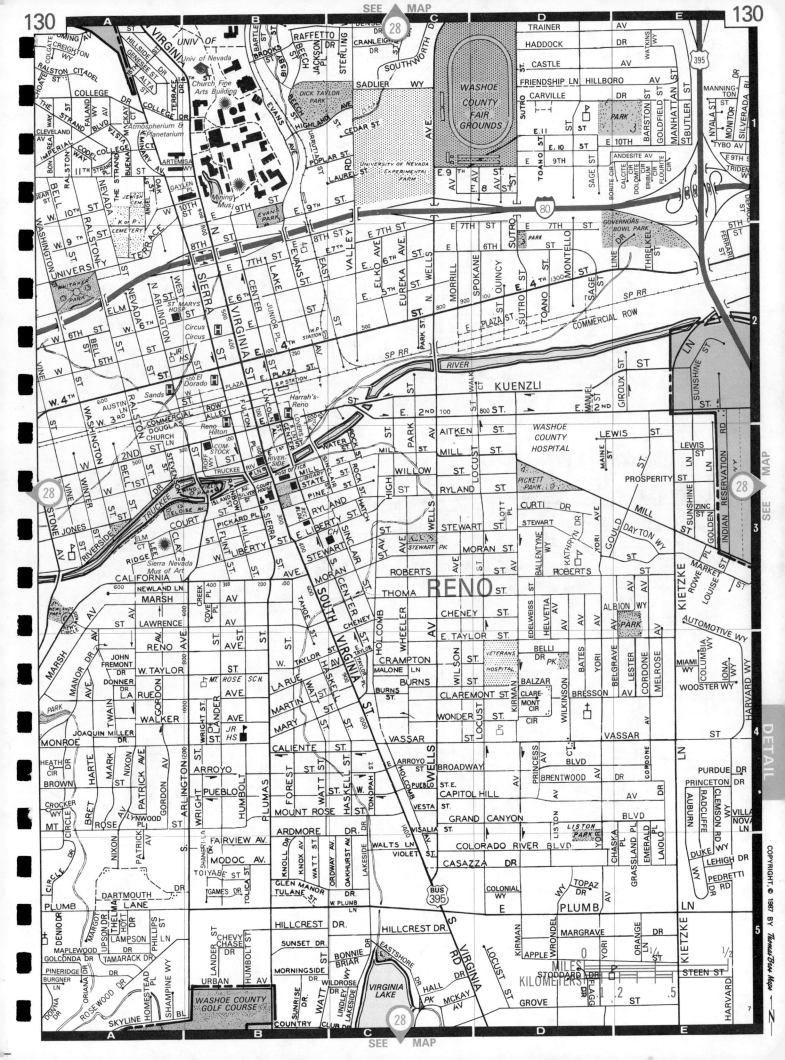

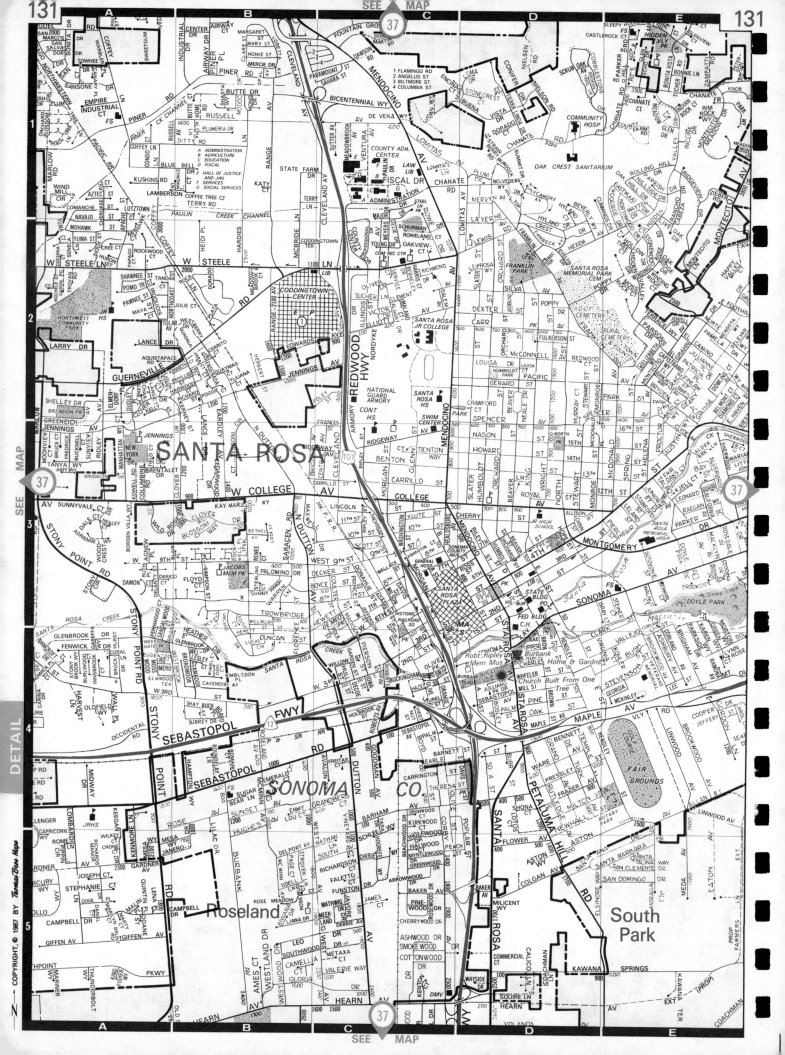

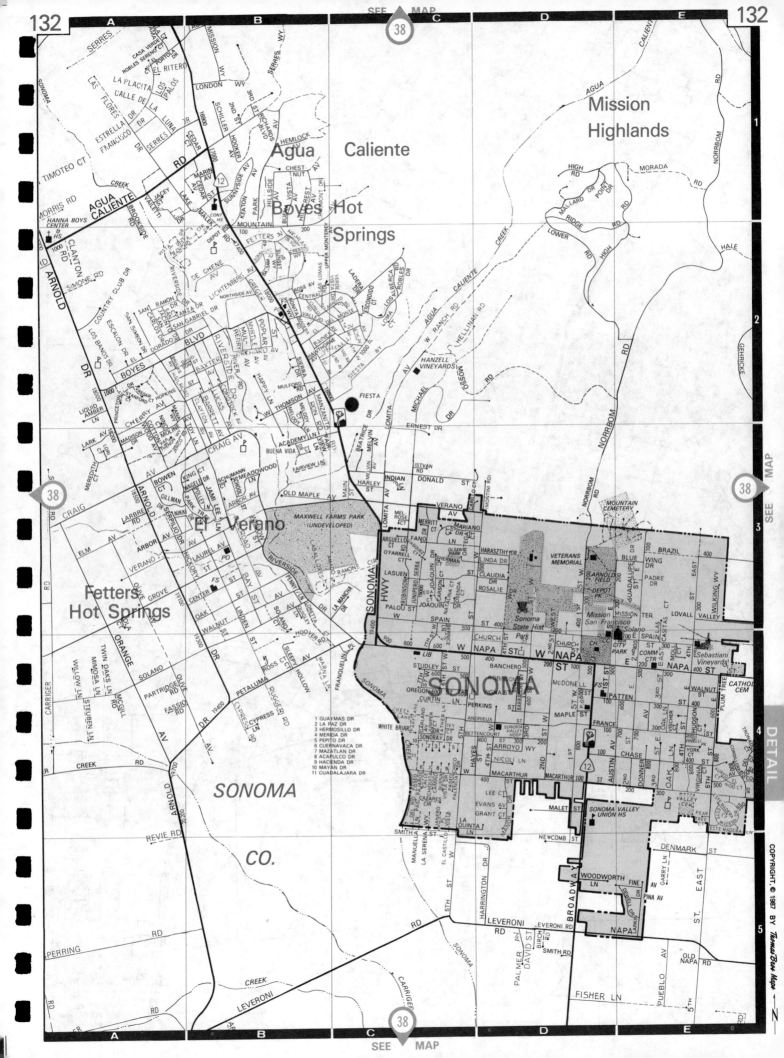

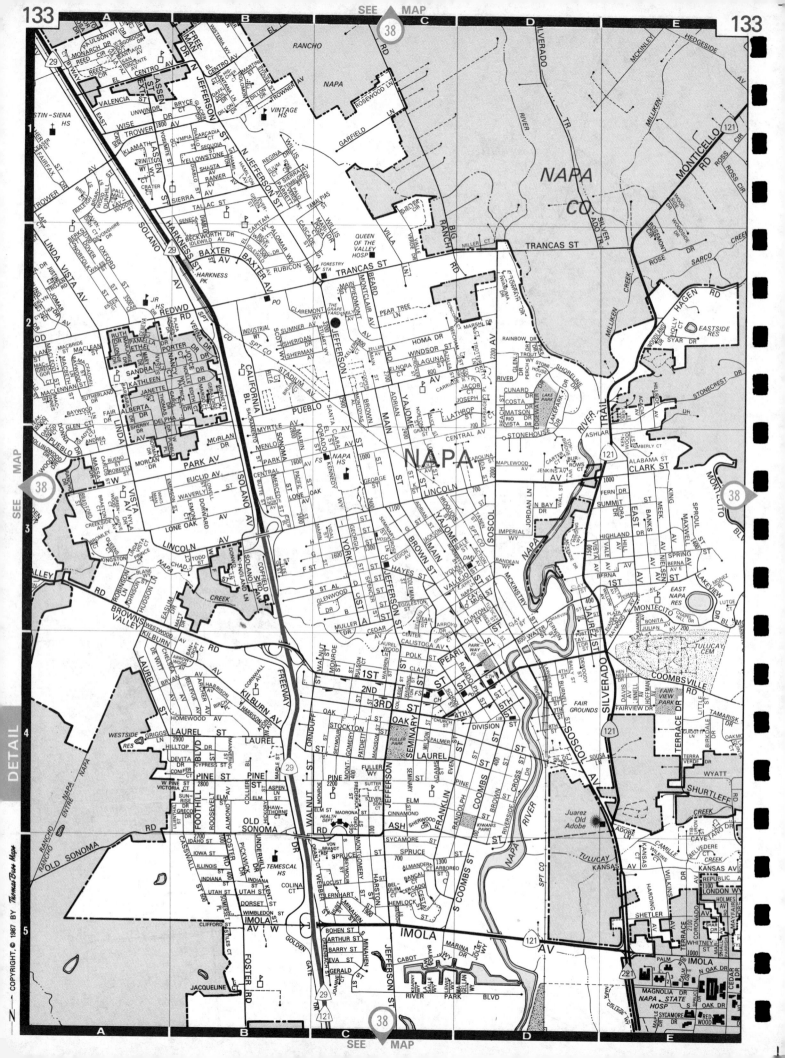

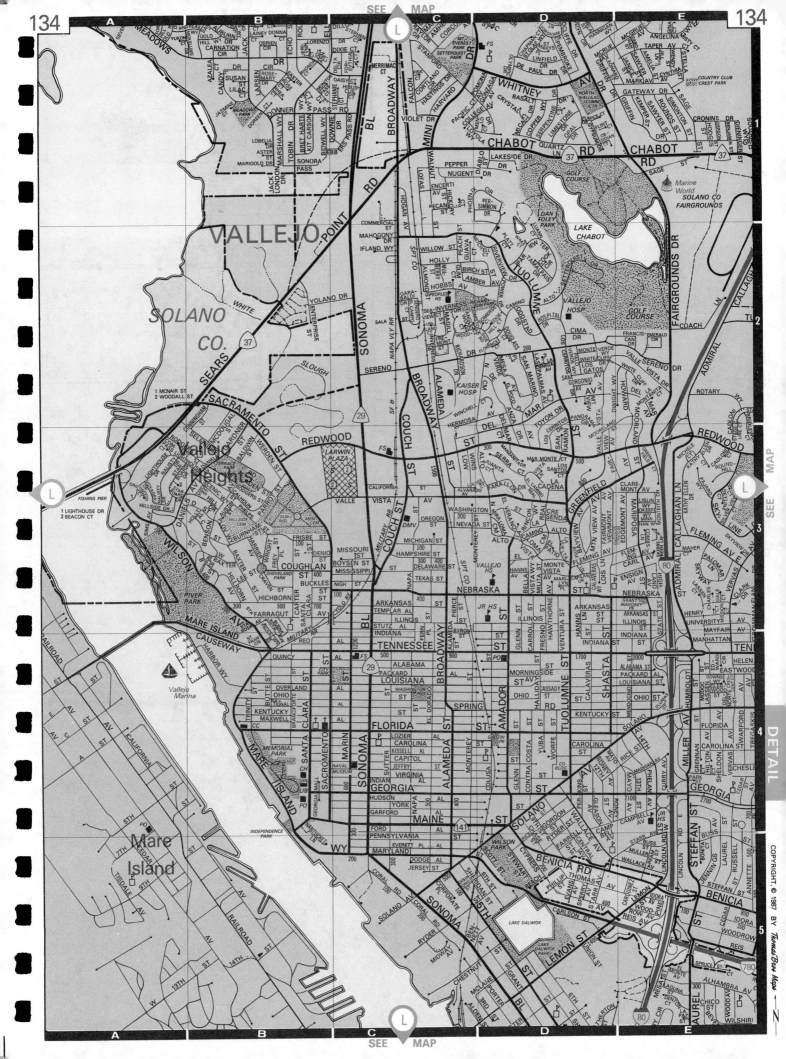

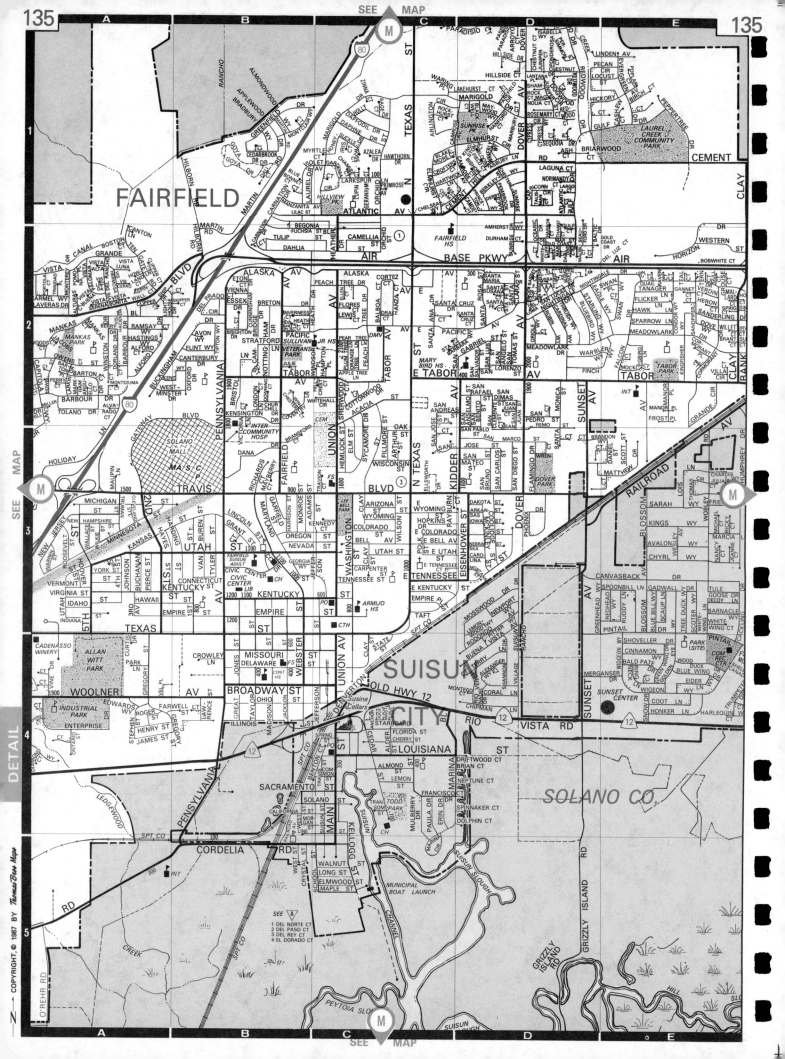

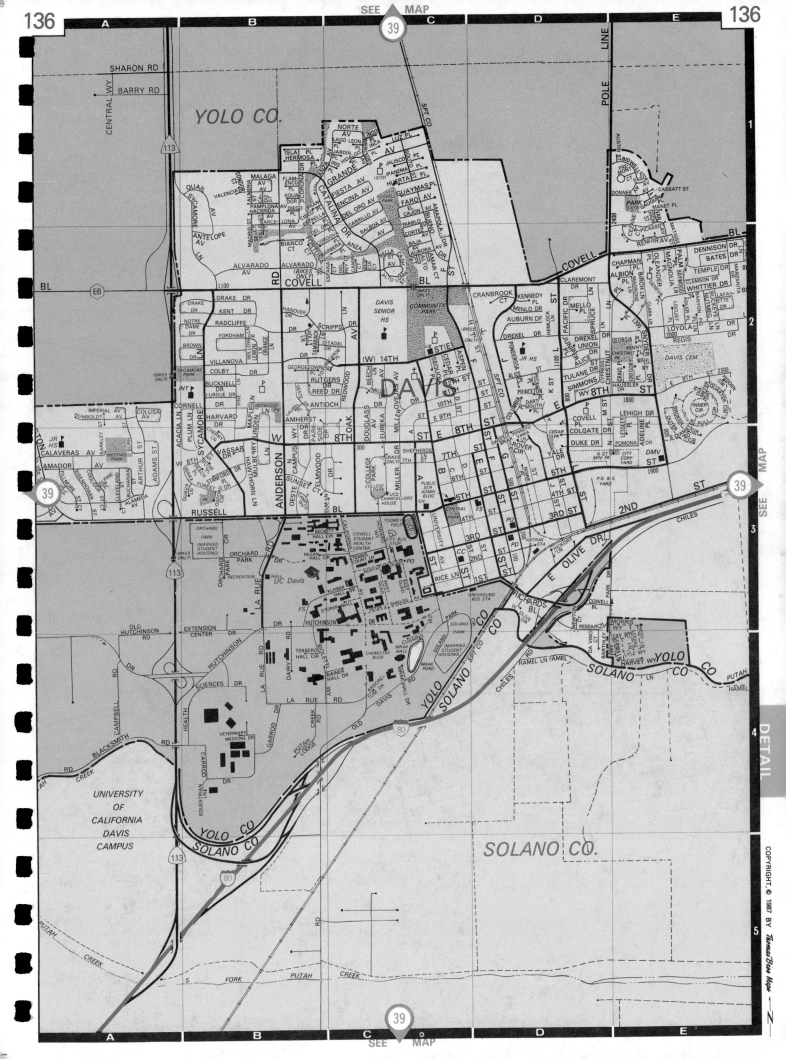

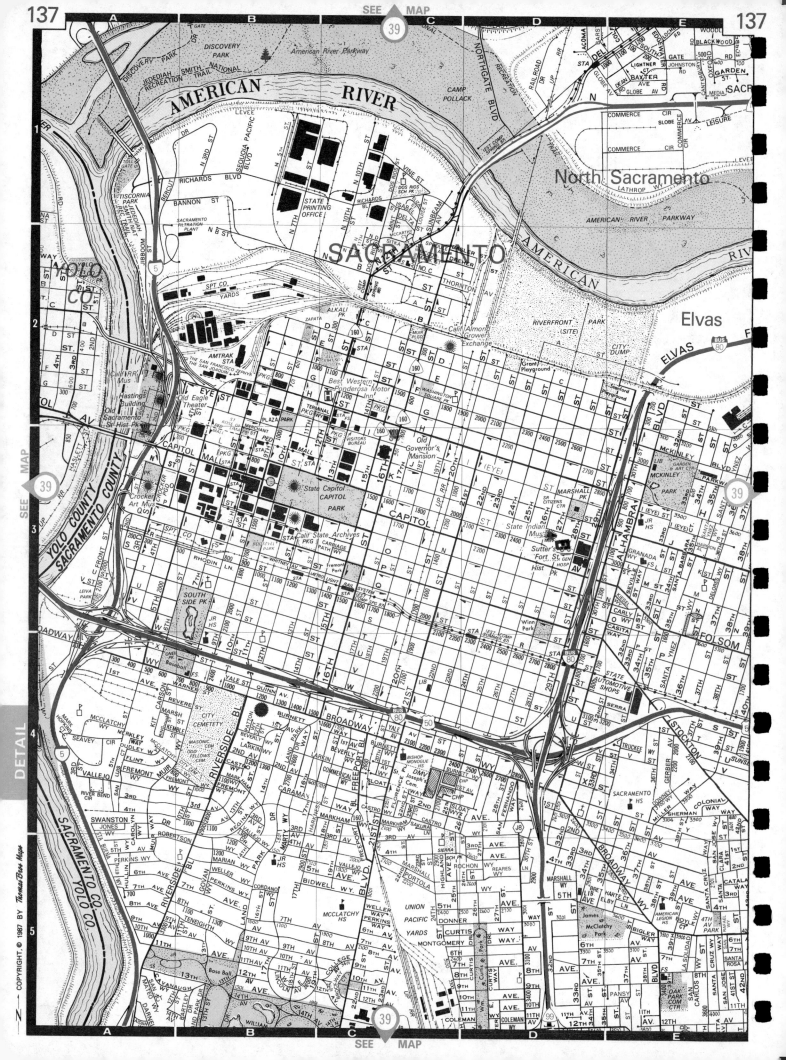

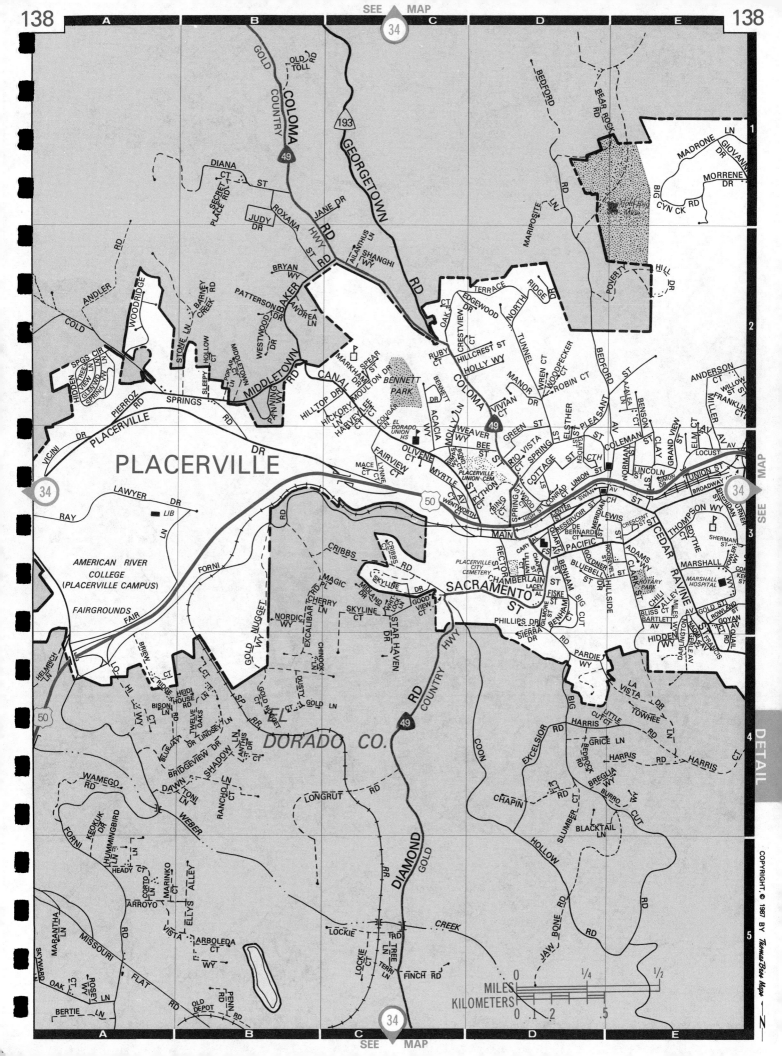

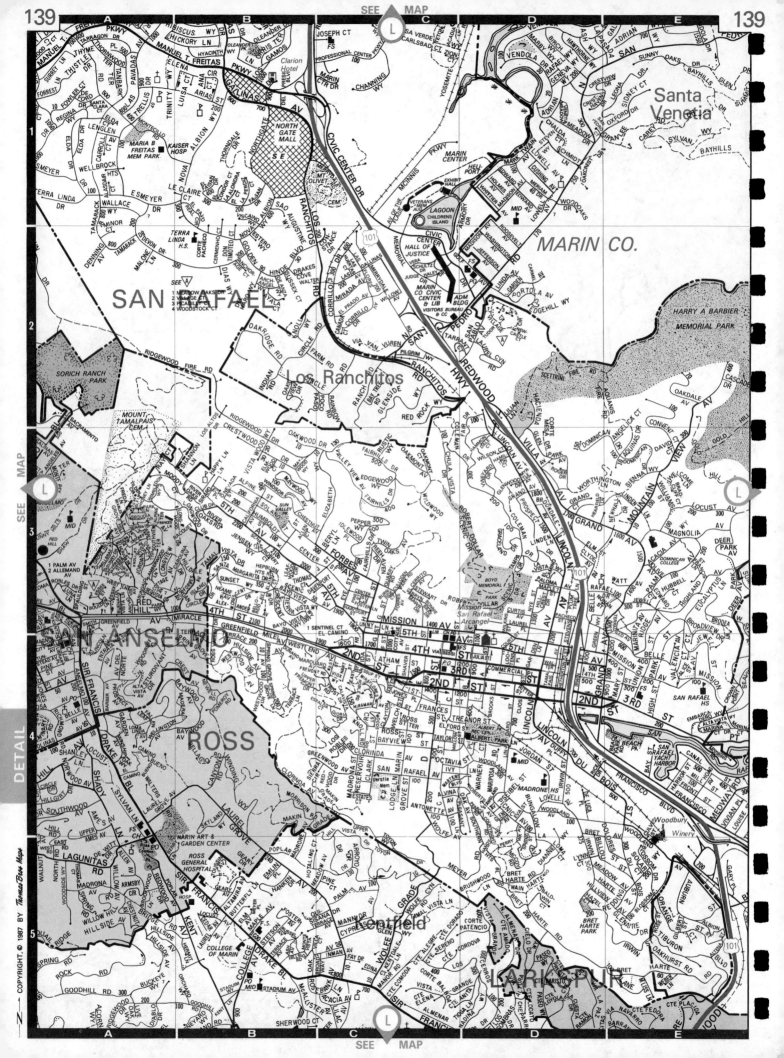

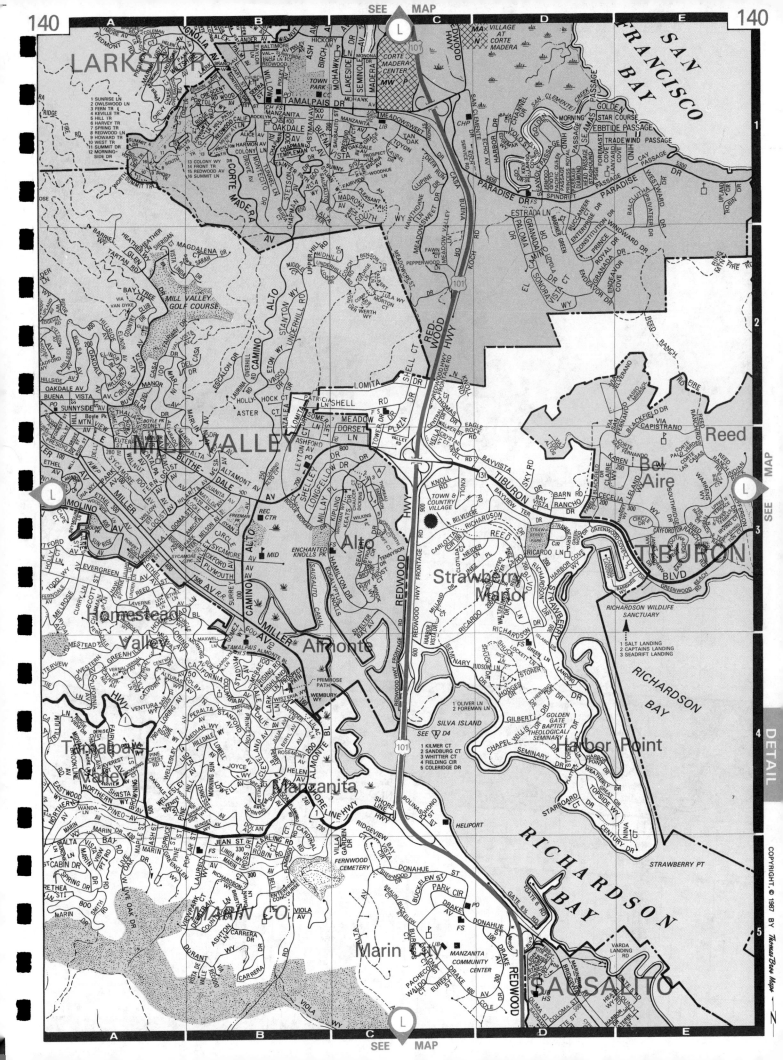

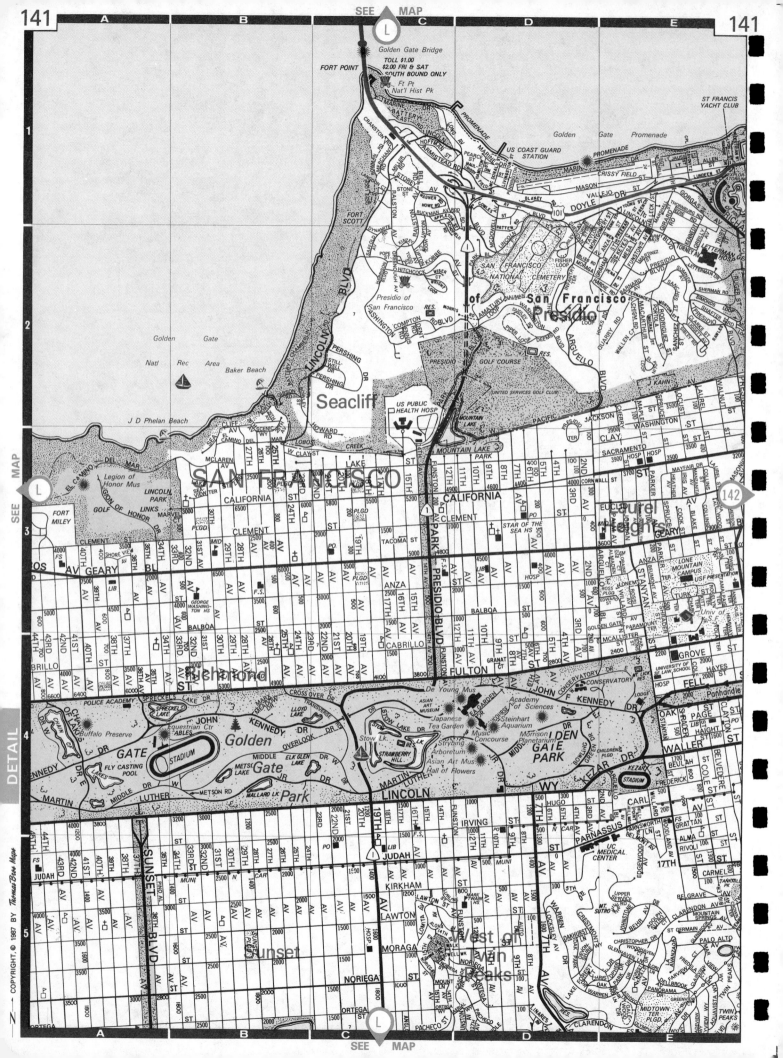

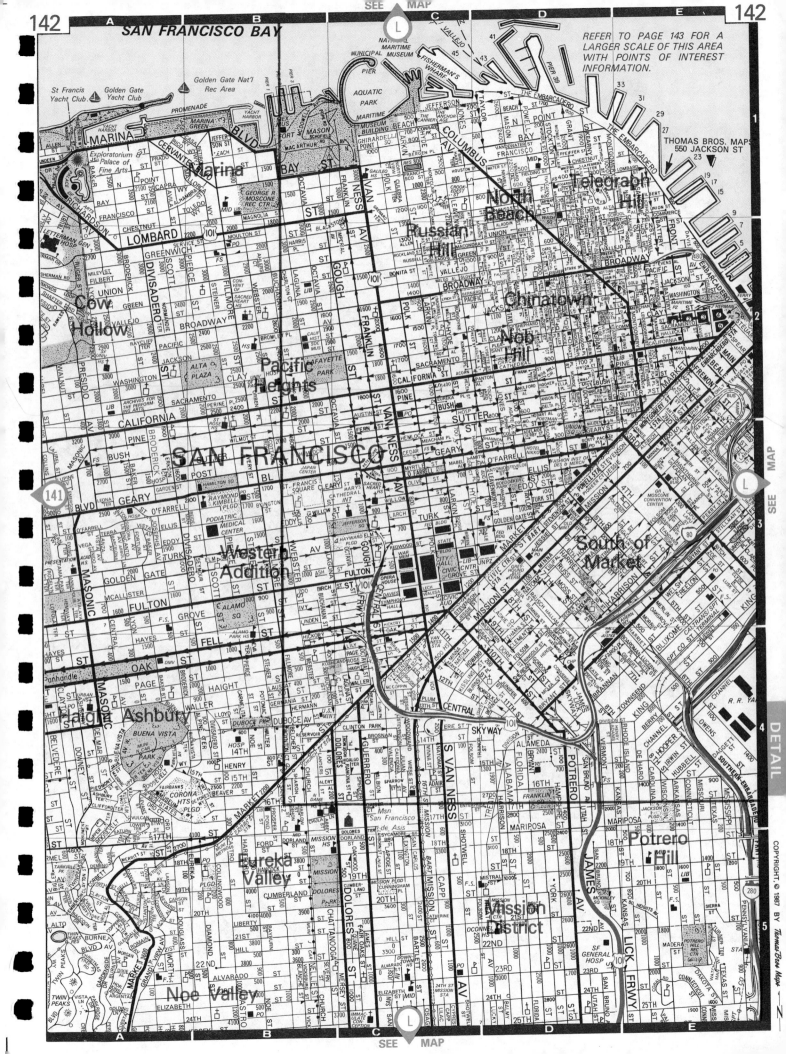

REFER TO PAGE 143 FOR A LARGER SCALE OF THIS AREA WITH POINTS OF INTEREST INFORMATION.

SAN FRANCISCO BAY

THOMAS BROS. MAPS
550 JACKSON ST

SAN FRANCISCO

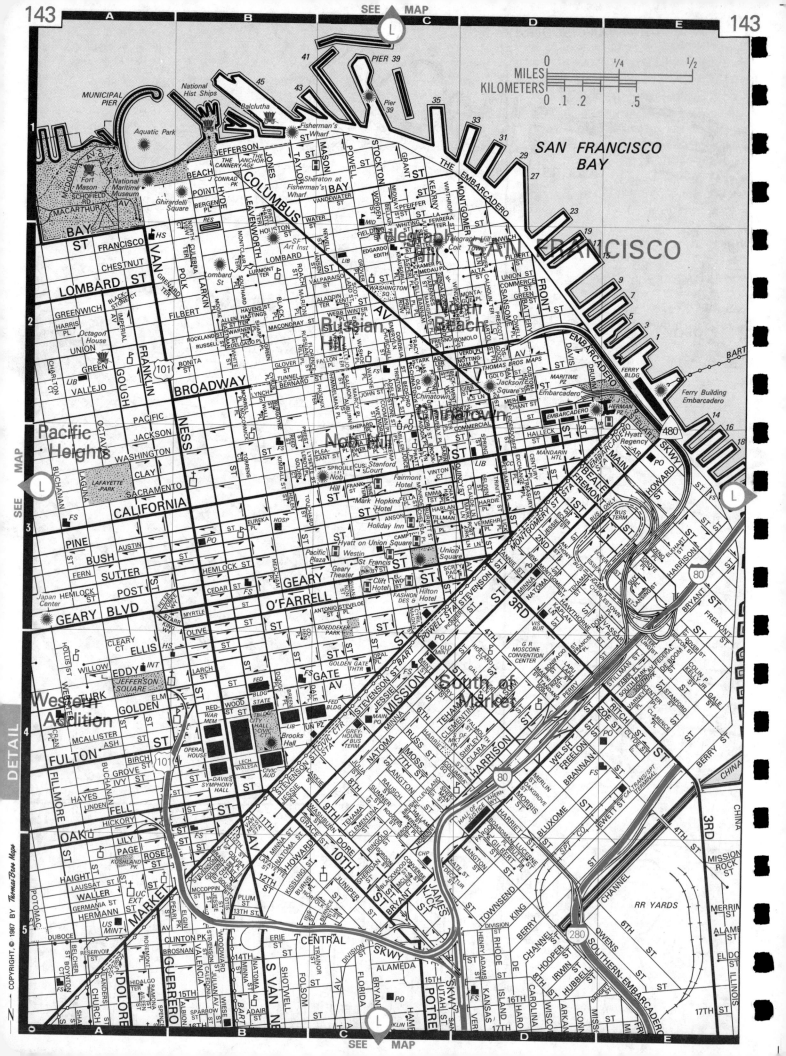

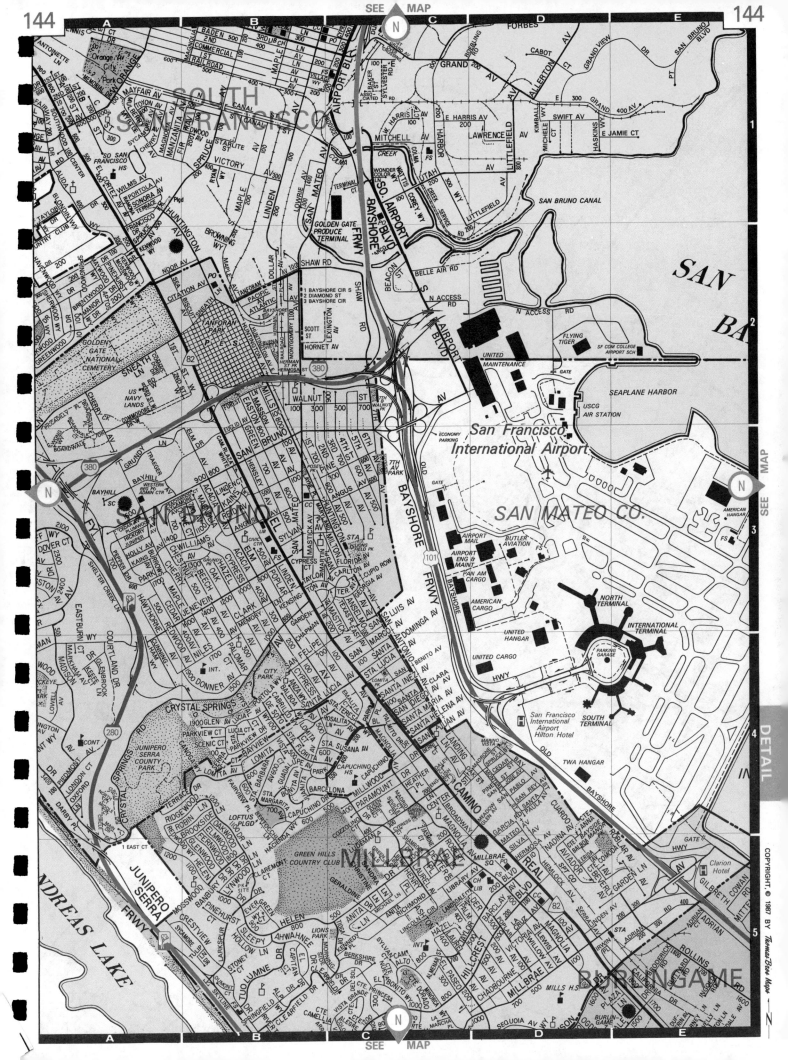

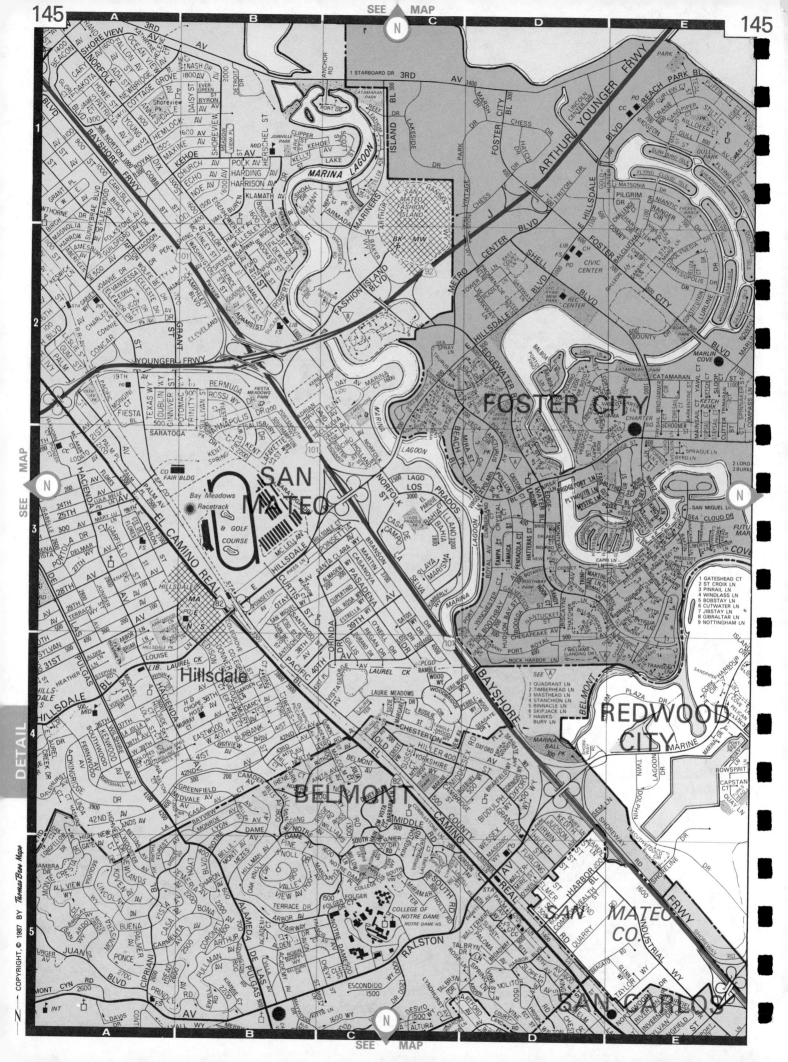

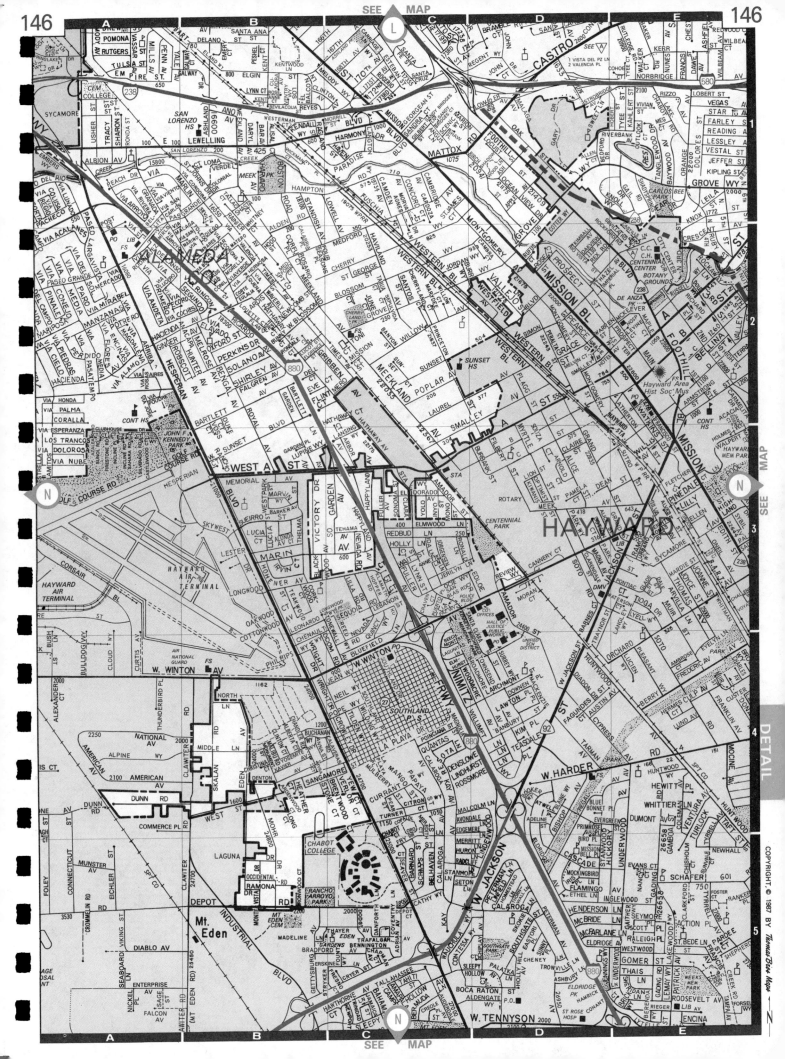

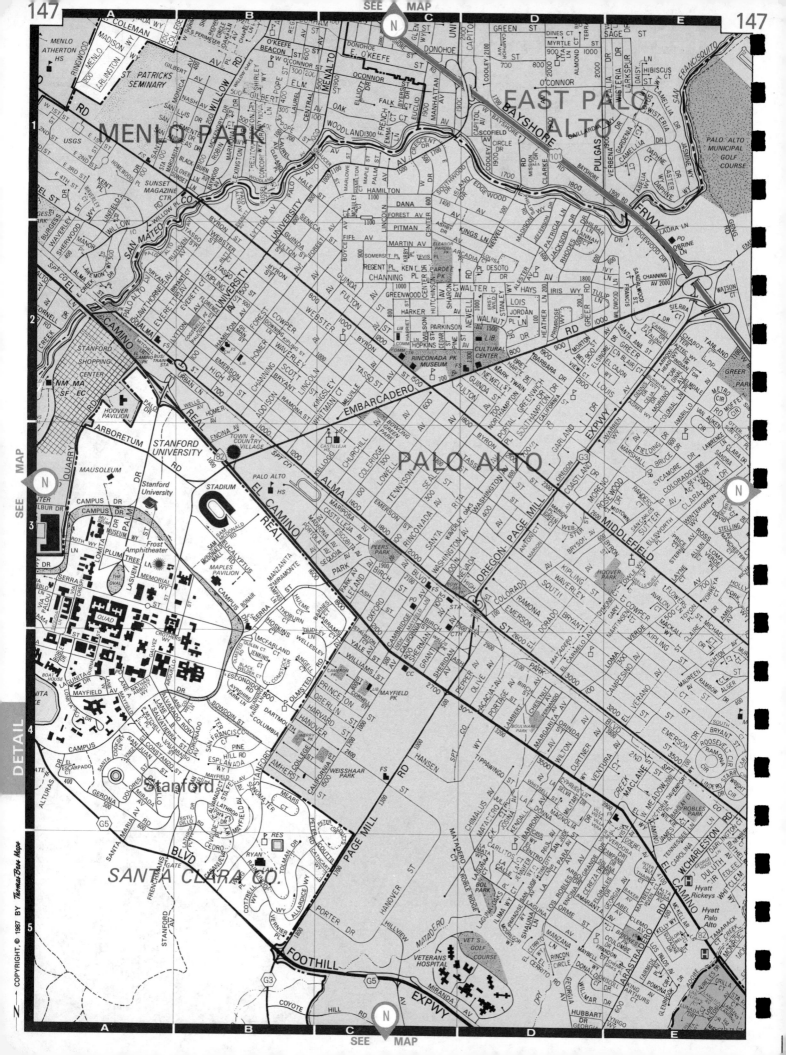

SEE MAP 45

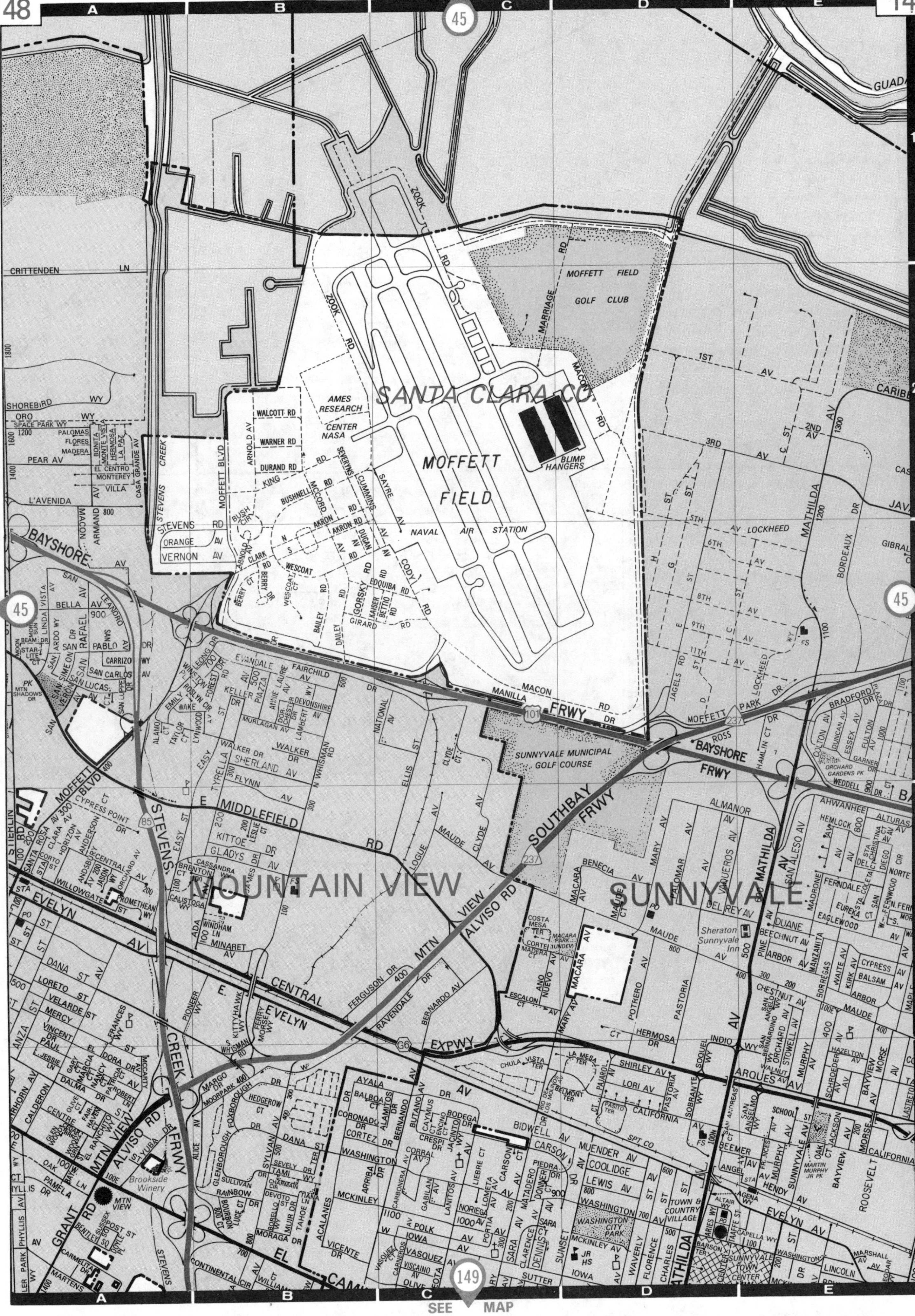

MOFFETT FIELD GOLF CLUB

SANTA CLARA CO.

AMES RESEARCH CENTER NASA

MOFFETT FIELD NAVAL AIR STATION

BLIMP HANGERS

LOCKHEED

MOUNTAIN VIEW

SUNNYVALE

BAYSHORE FRWY

SOUTHBAY FRWY

SUNNYVALE MUNICIPAL GOLF COURSE

Sheraton Sunnyvale Inn

Brookside Winery

101 FRWY

MIDDLEFIELD RD

CENTRAL EXPWY

EVELYN AV

EL CAMINO

GRANT RD

MTN VIEW ALVISO RD

MTN VIEW - ALVISO RD

MATHILDA

MARY AV

MACARA AV

STEVENS CREEK

BAYSHORE AV

DETAIL

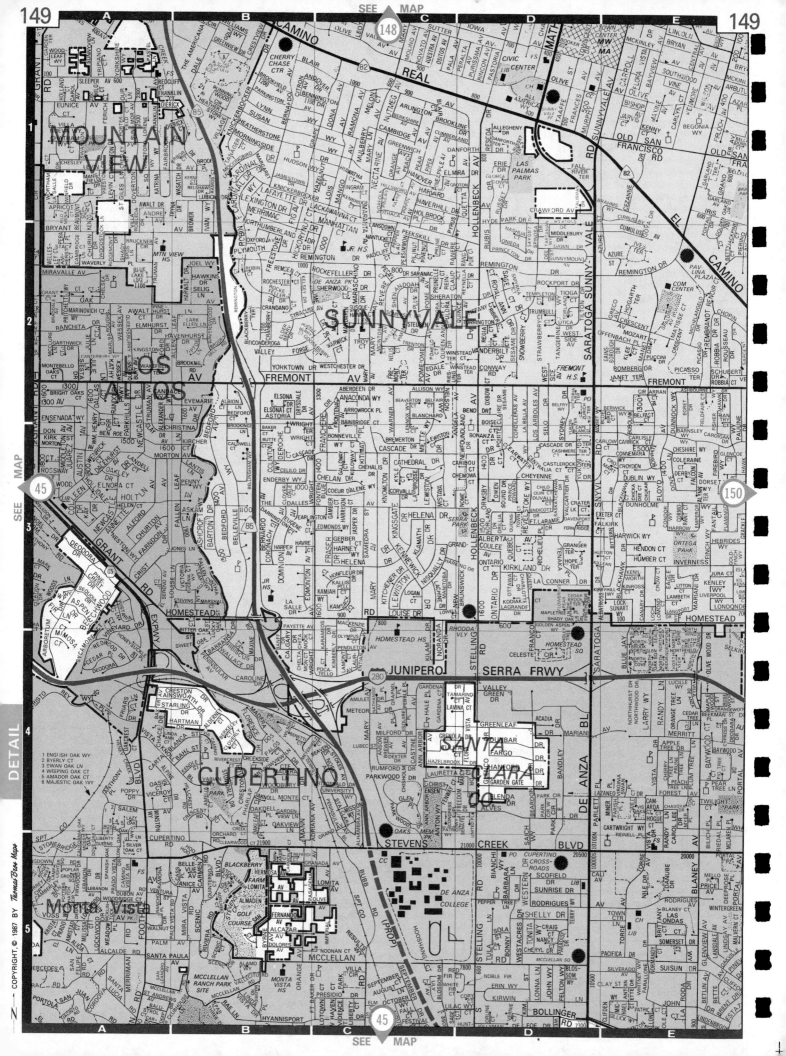

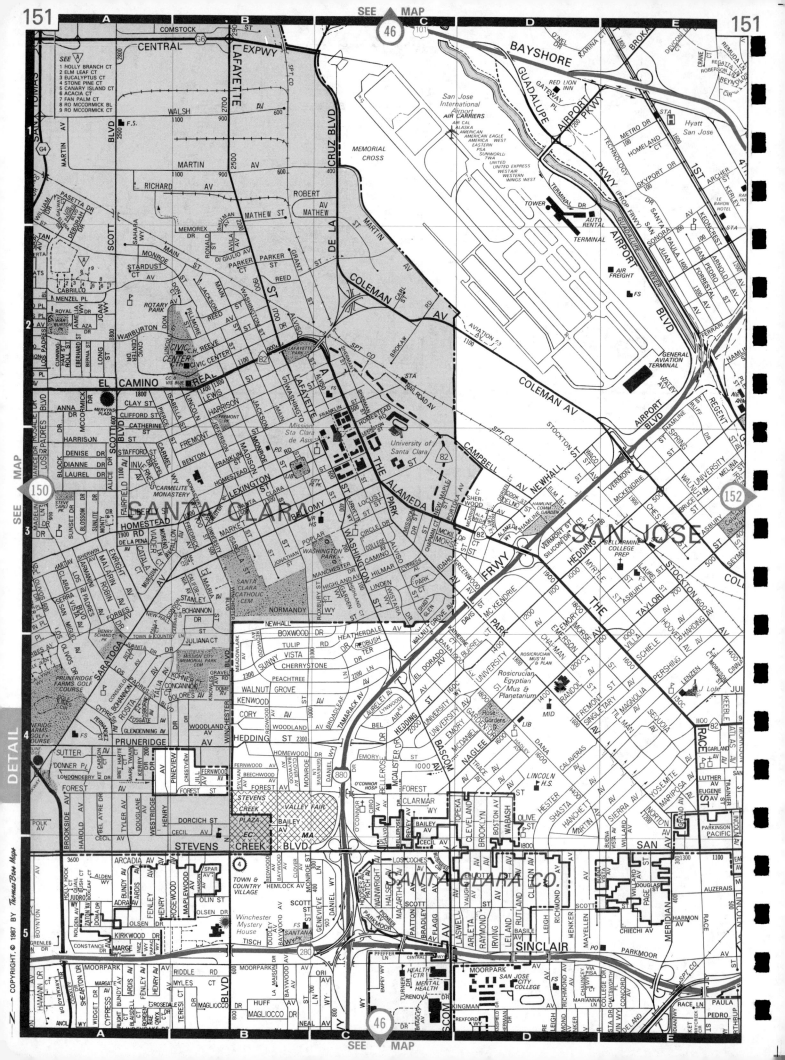

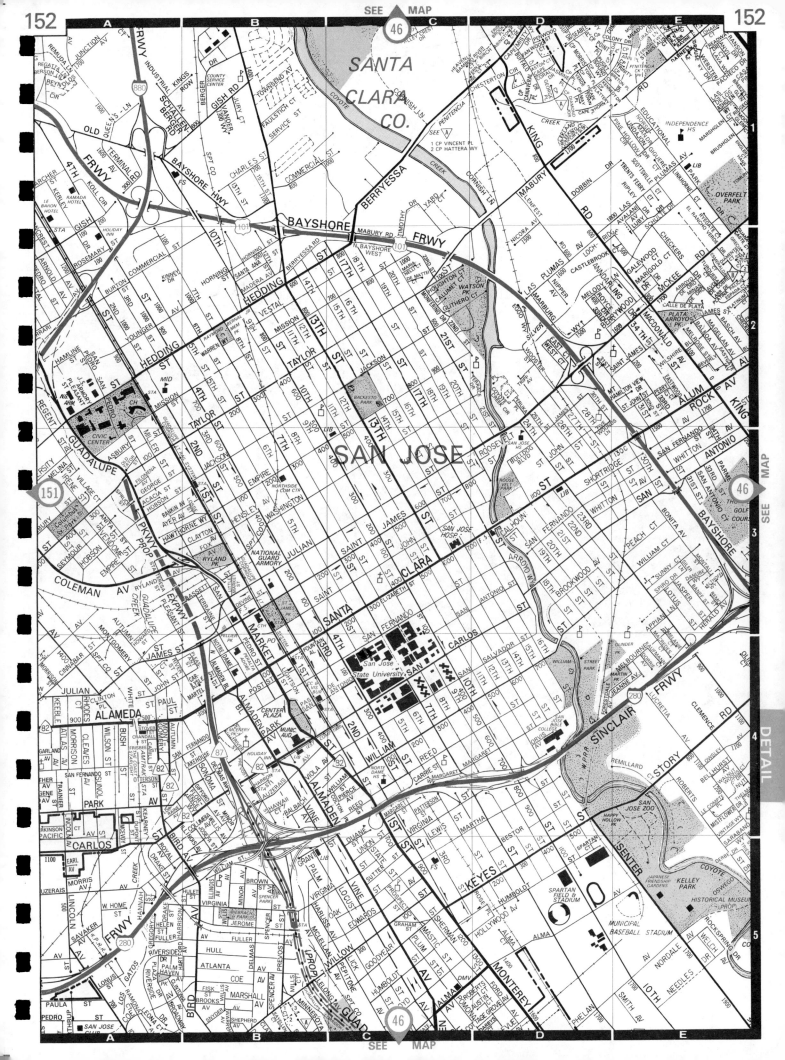

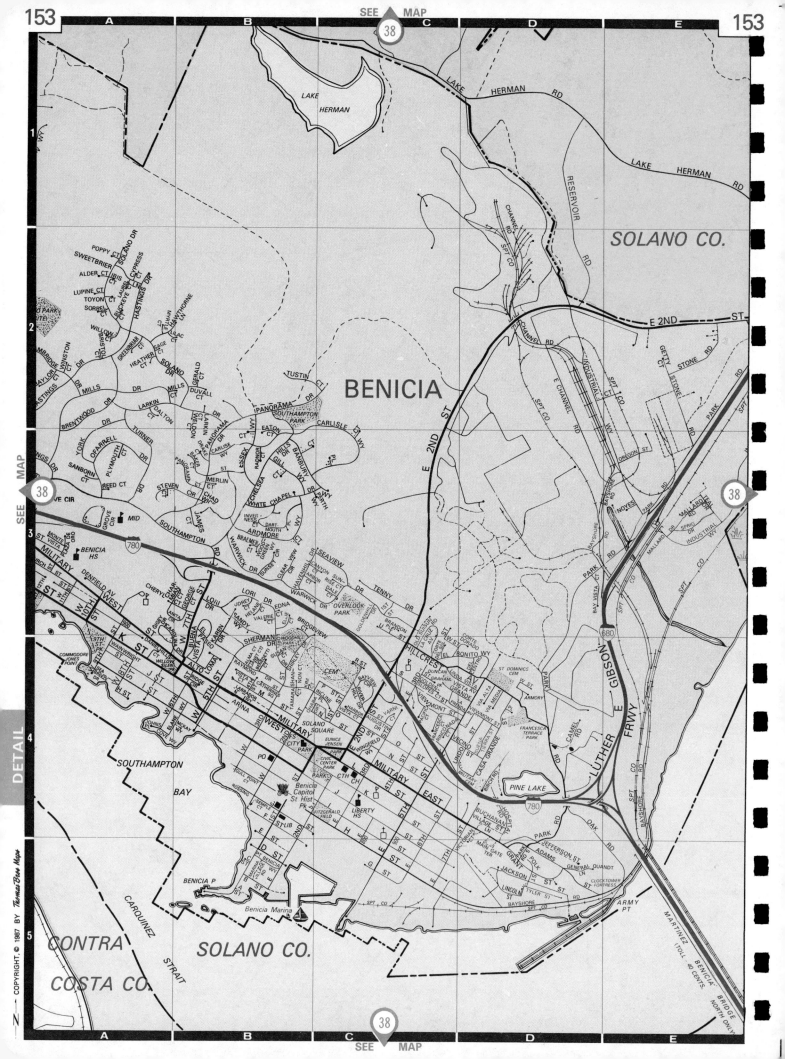

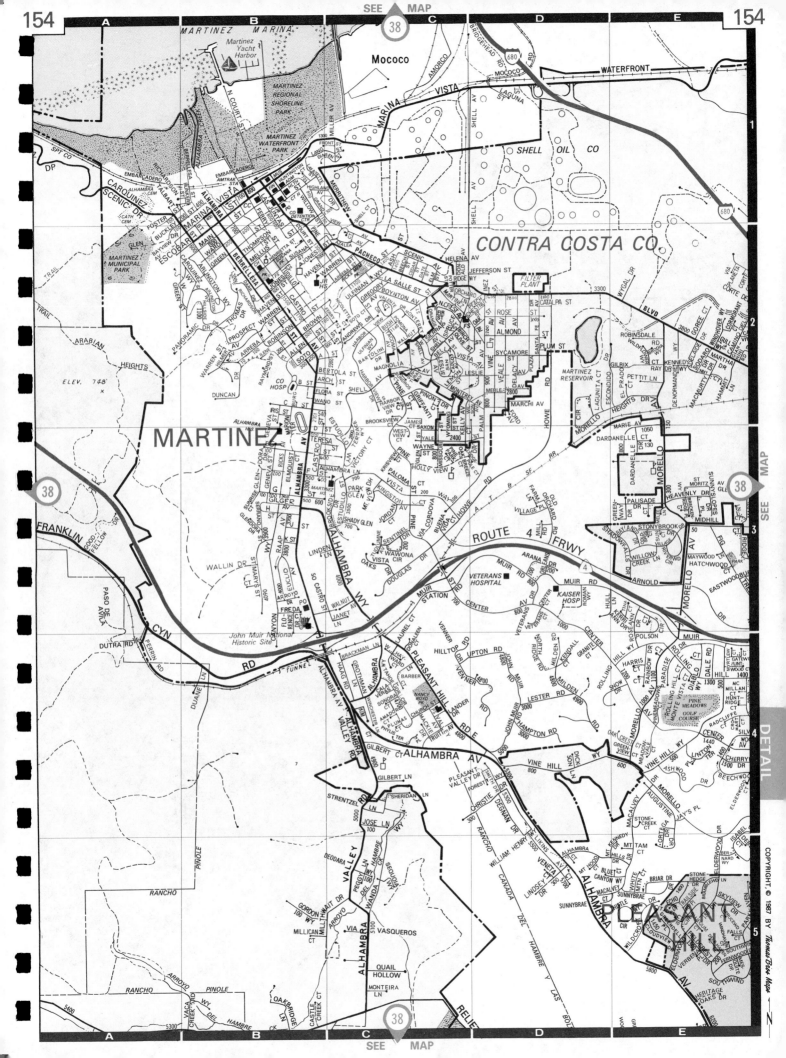

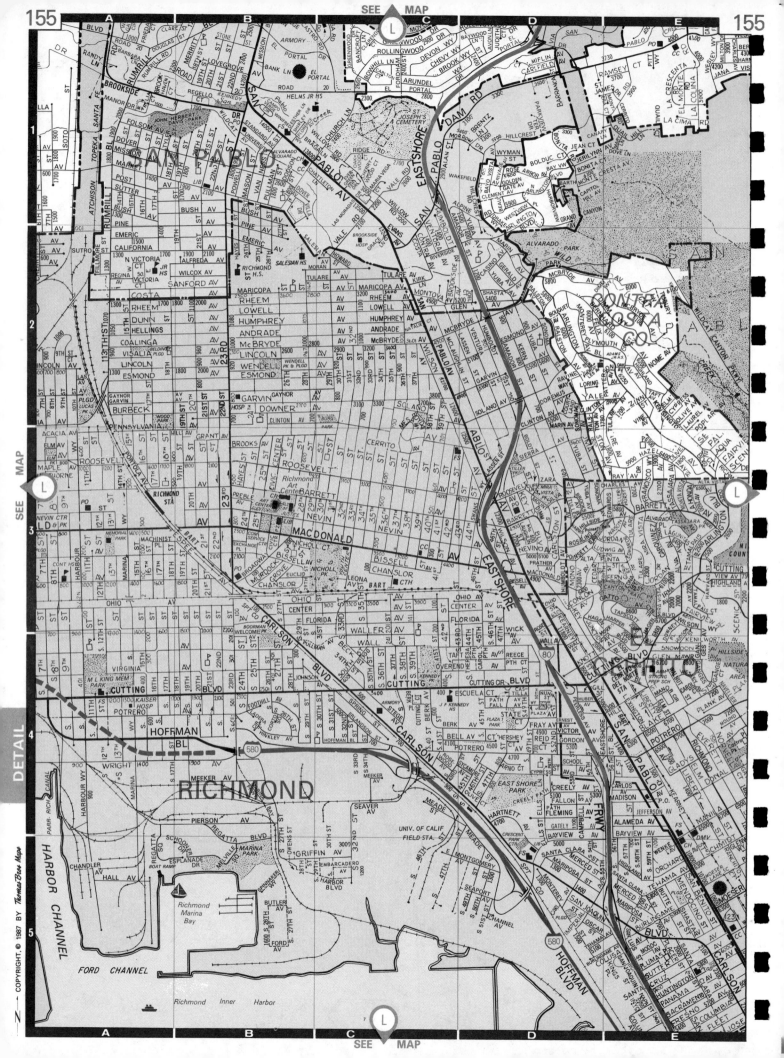

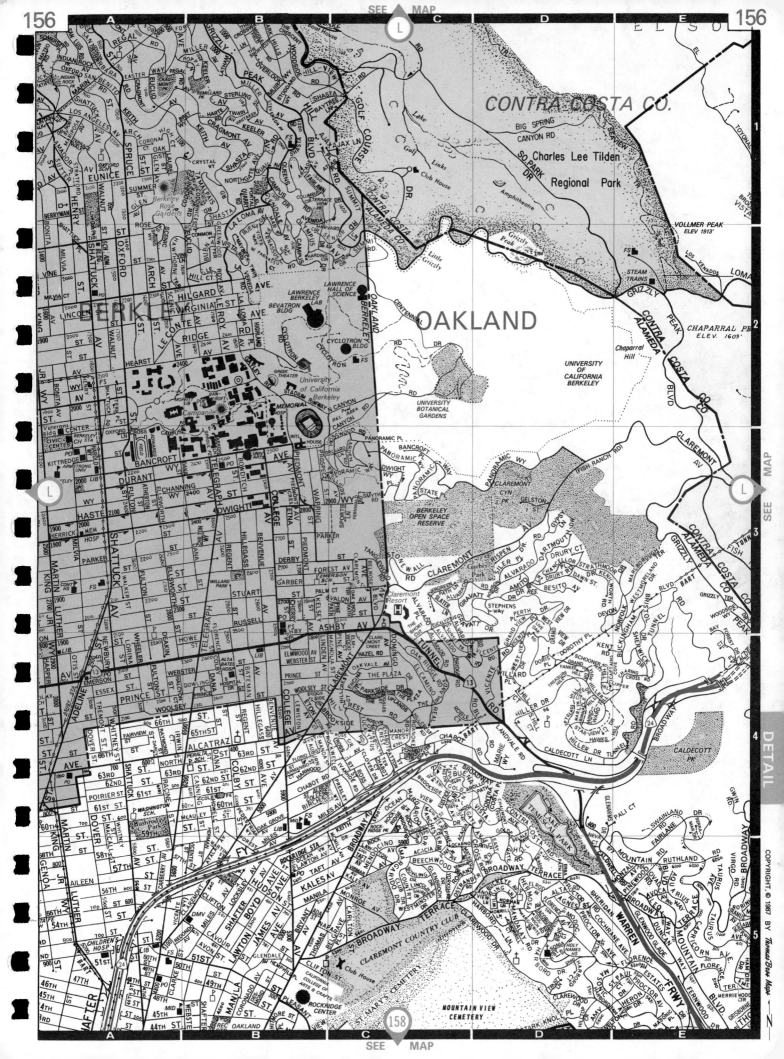

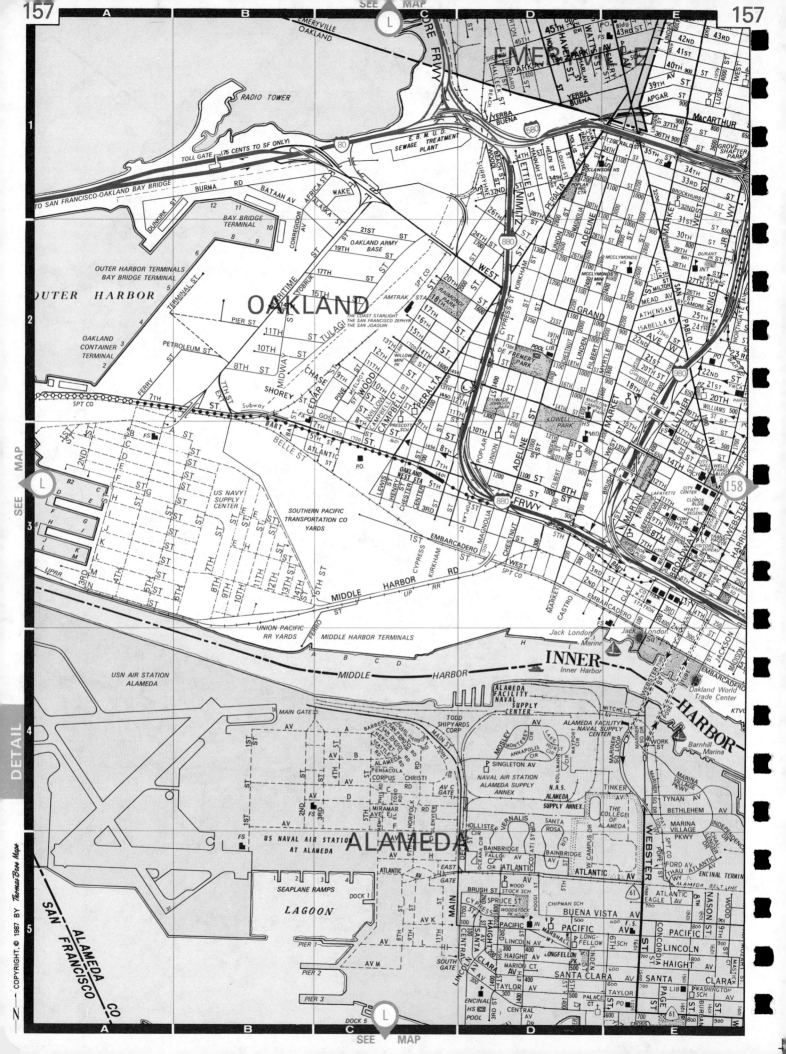

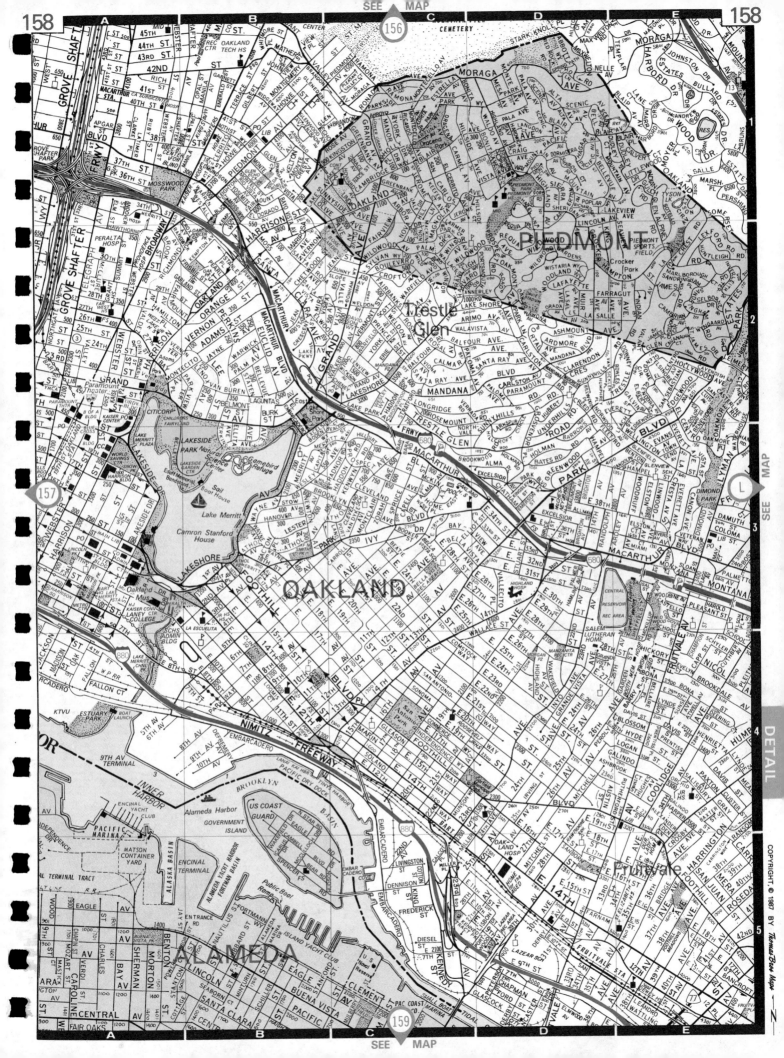

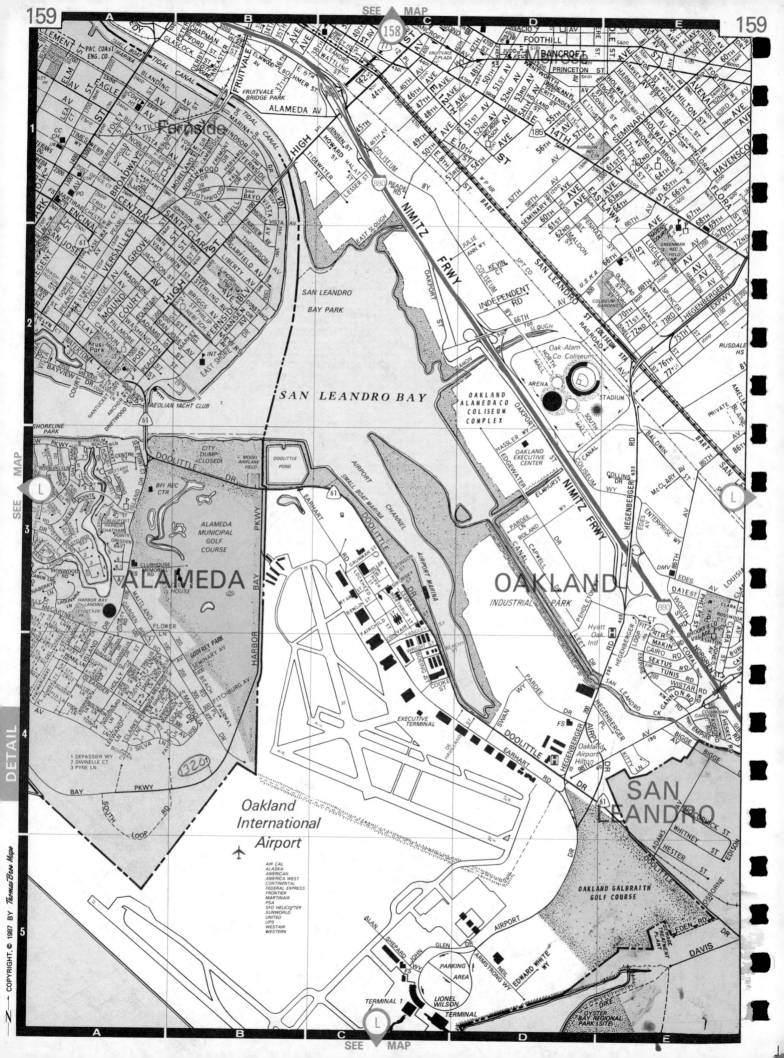

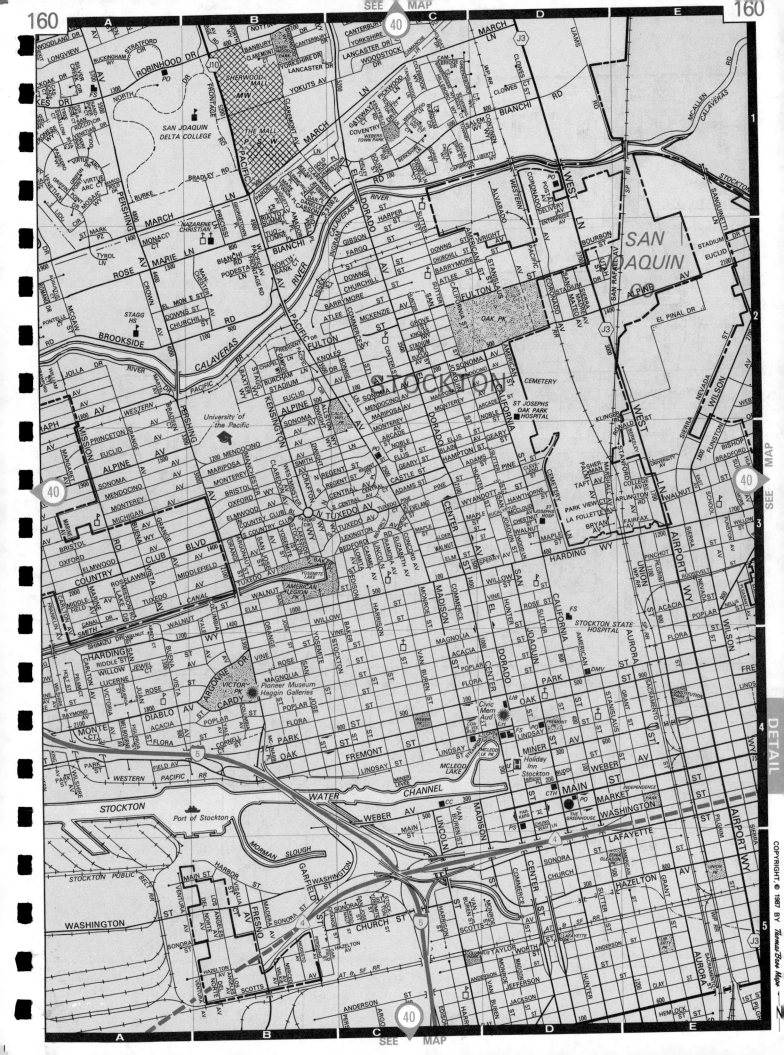

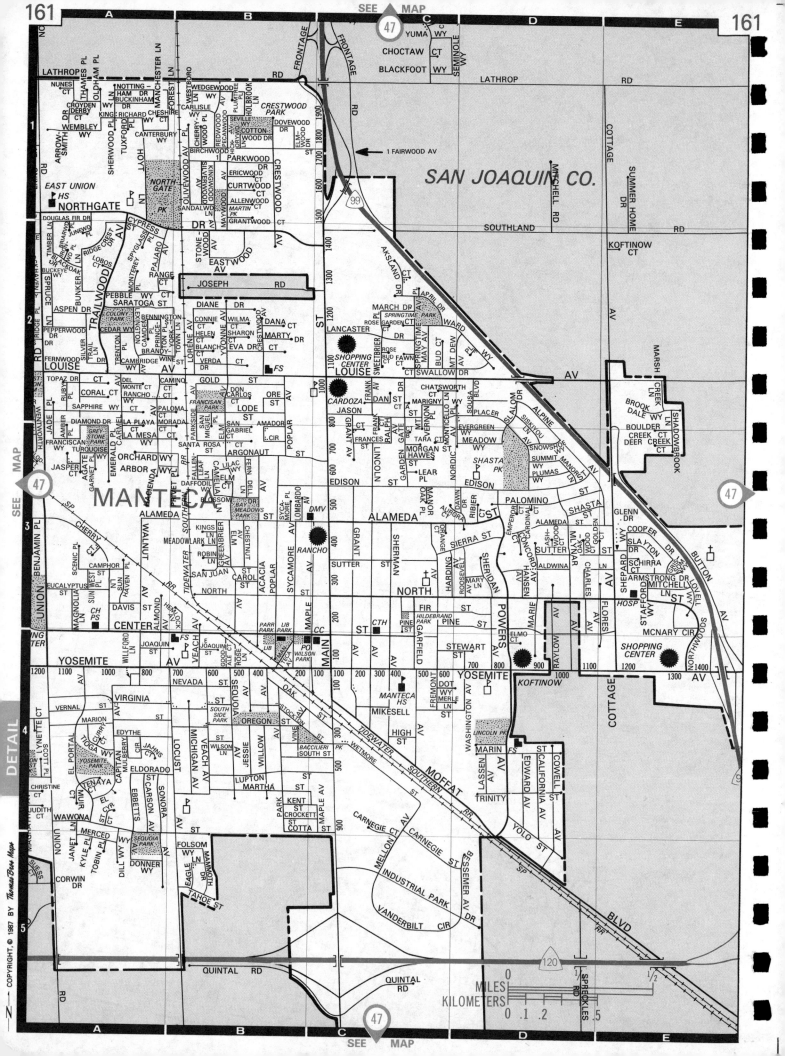

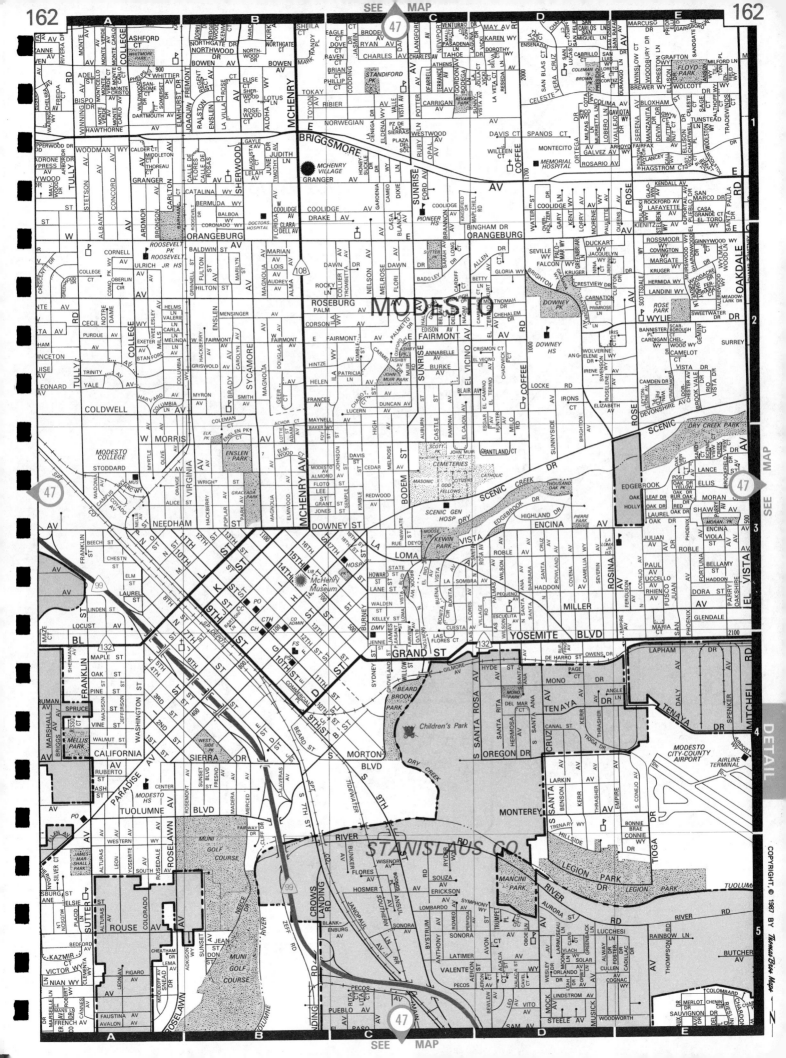

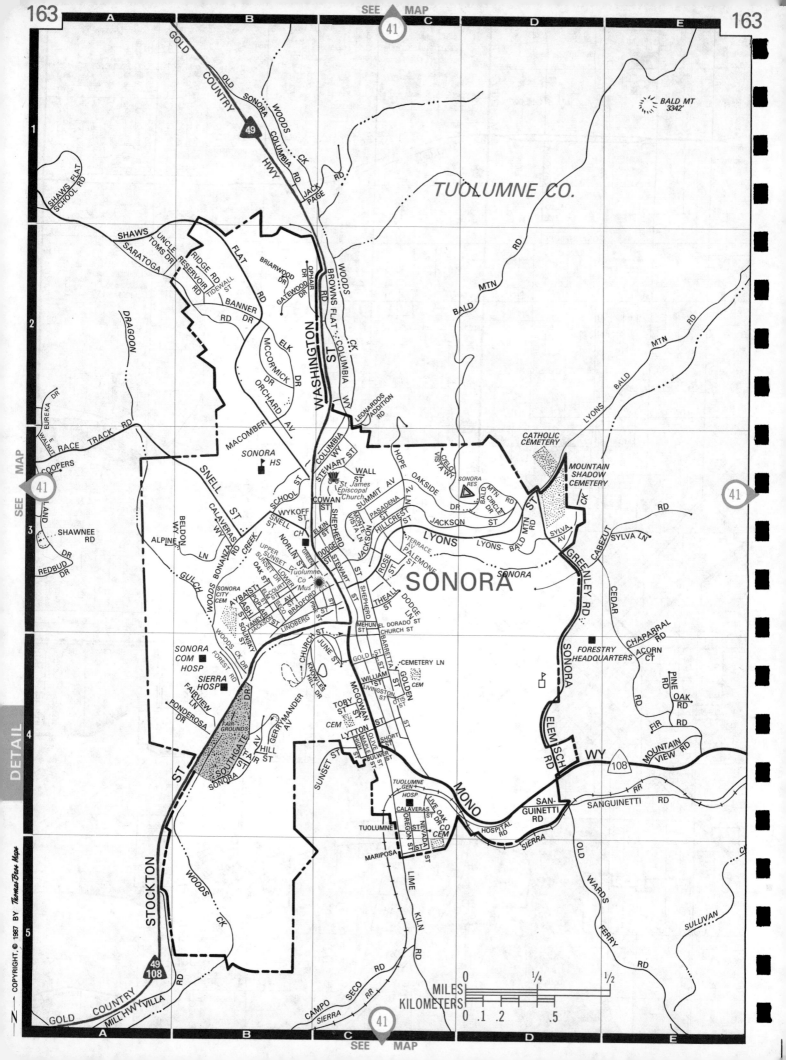

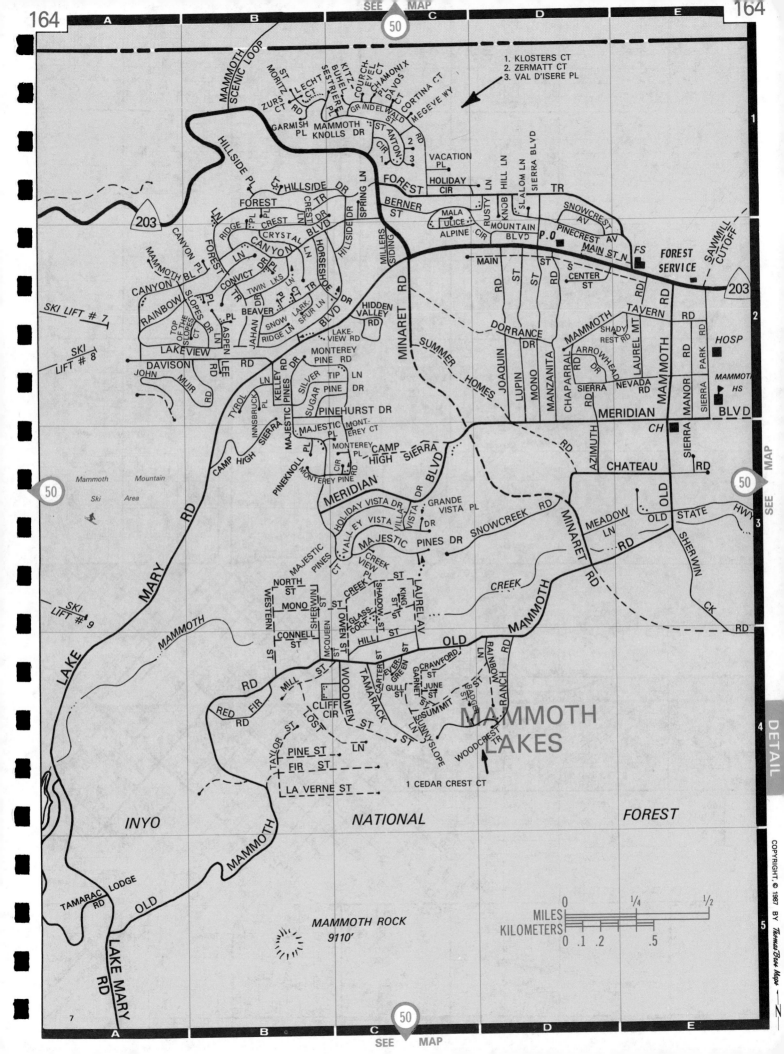

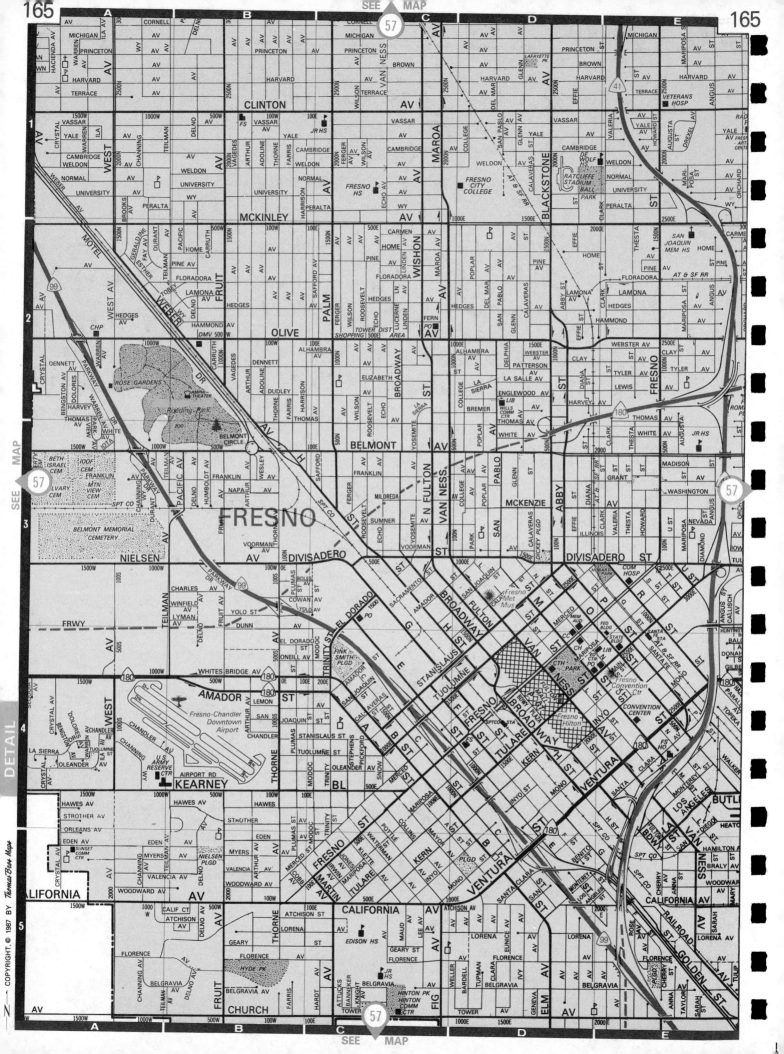

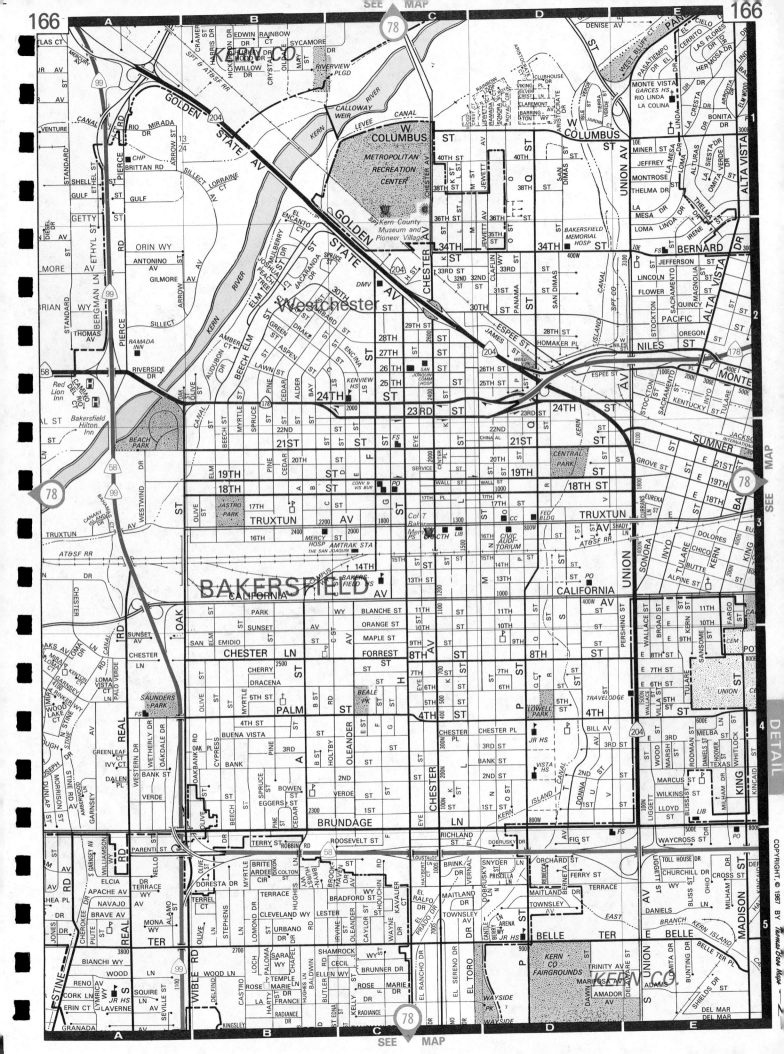

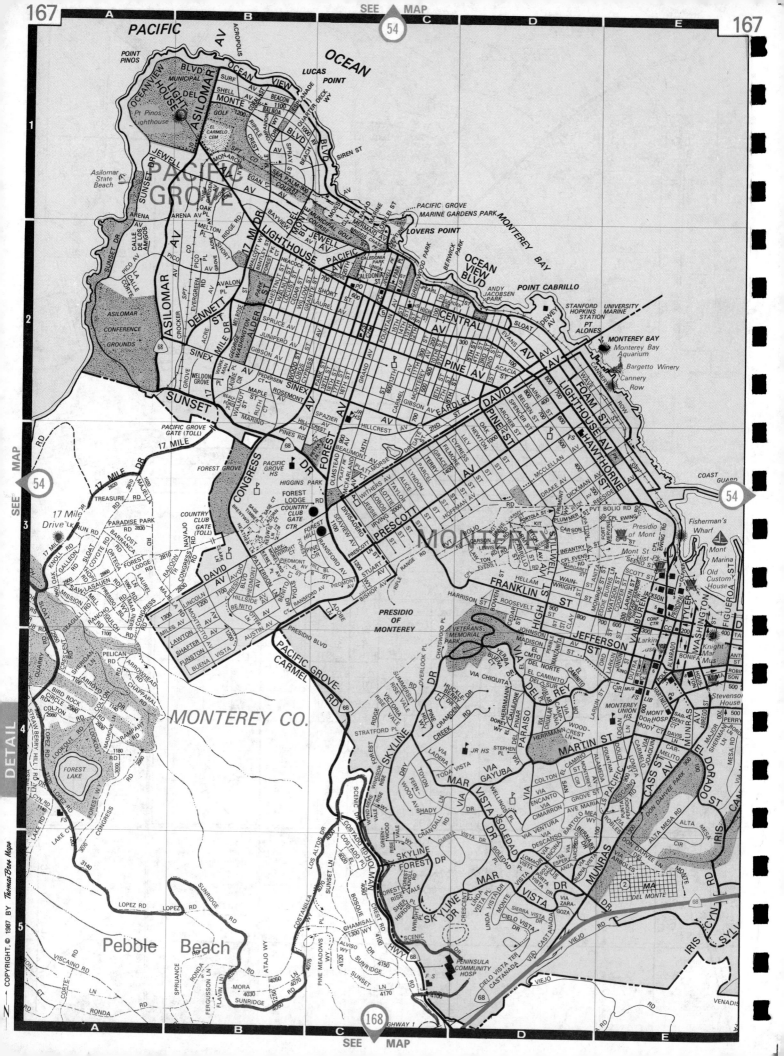

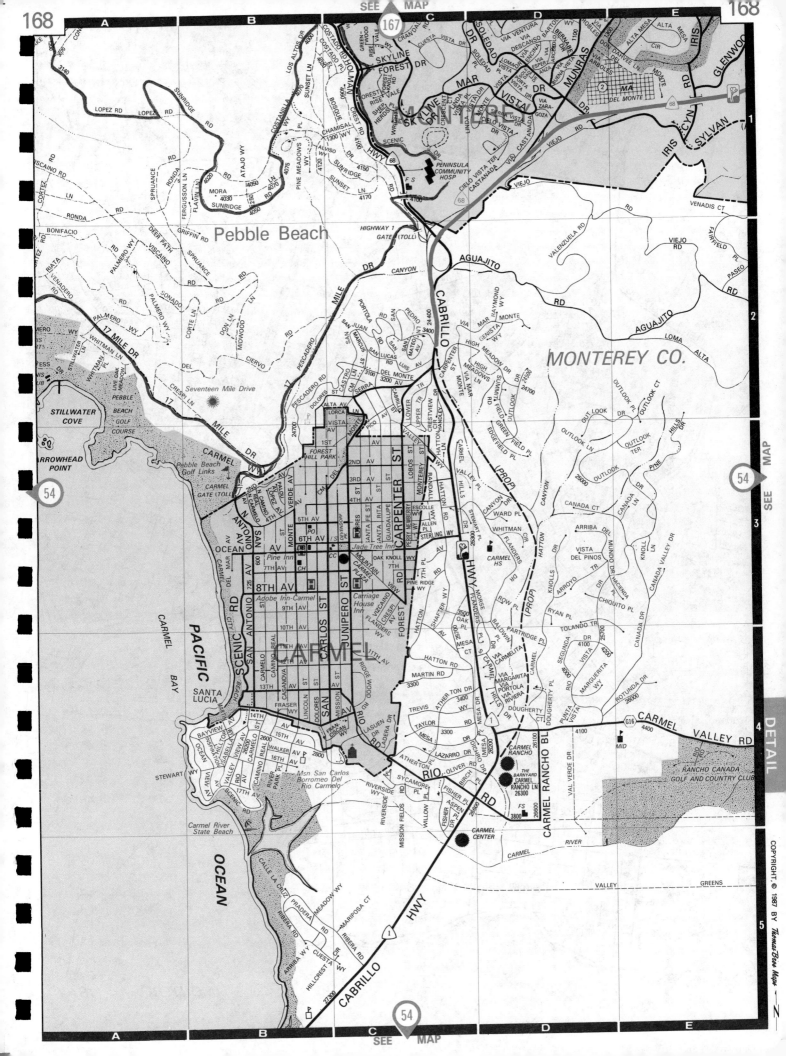

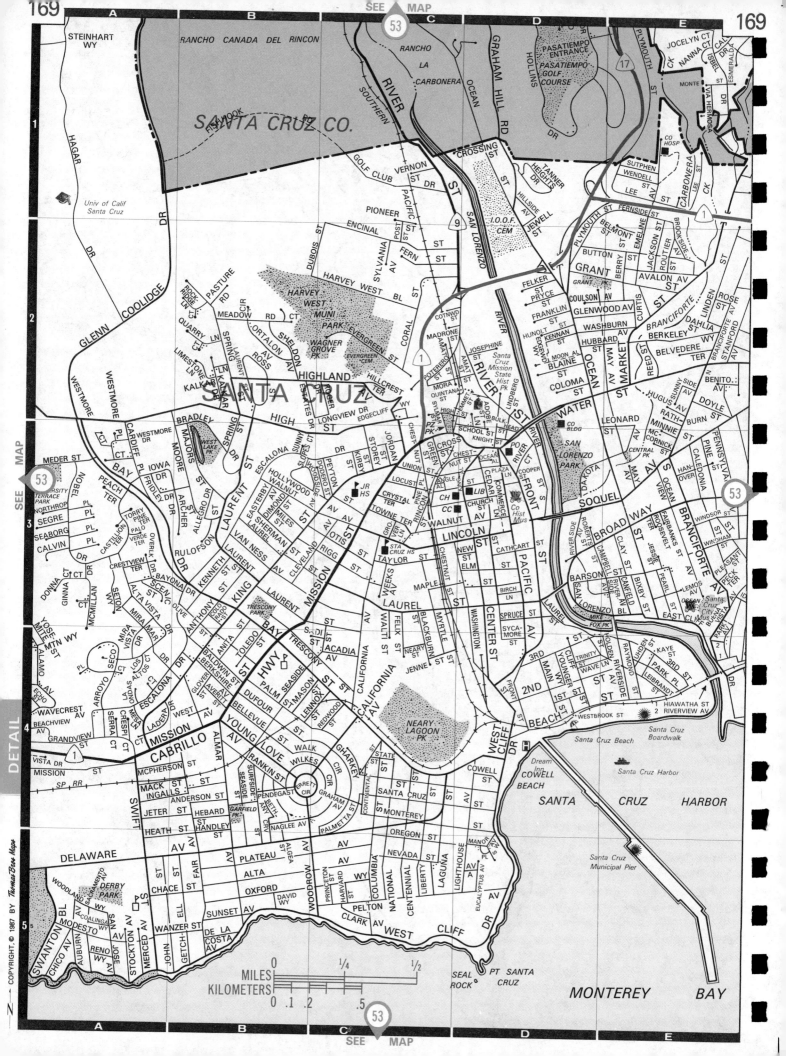

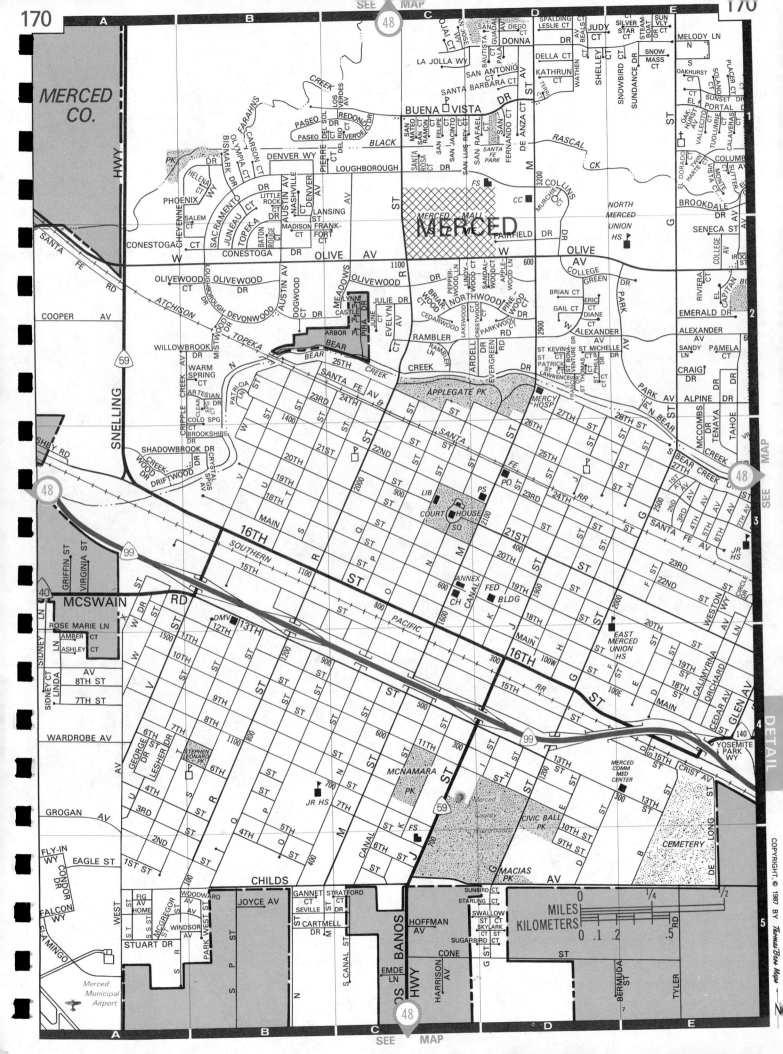

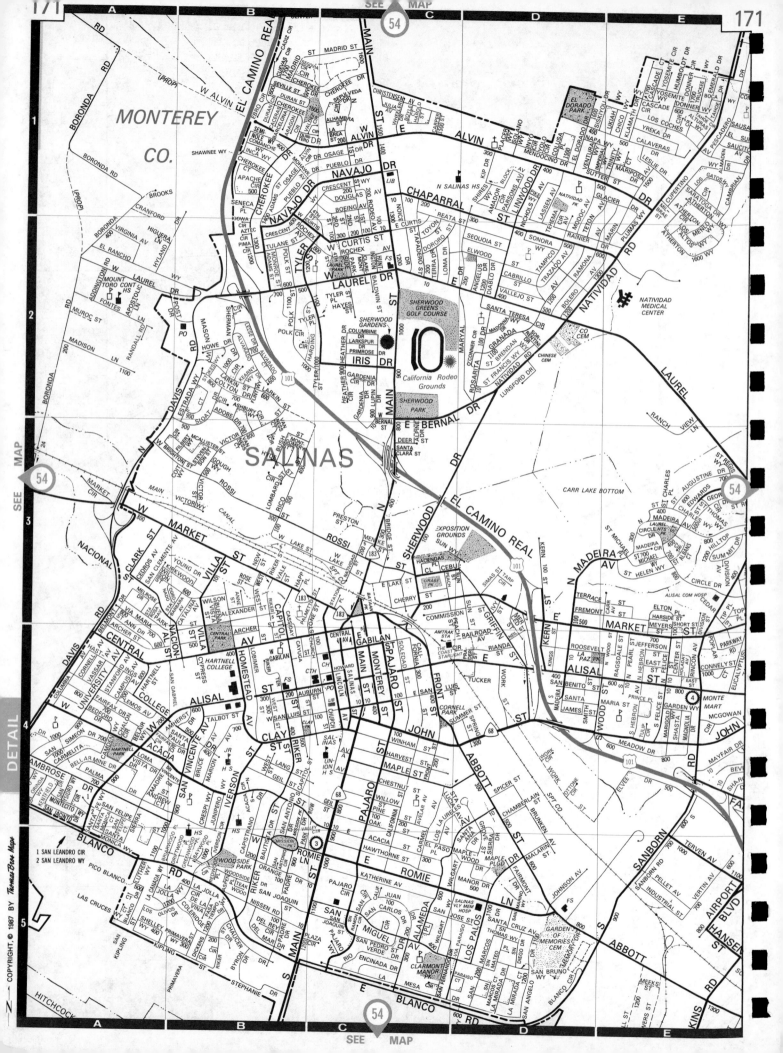

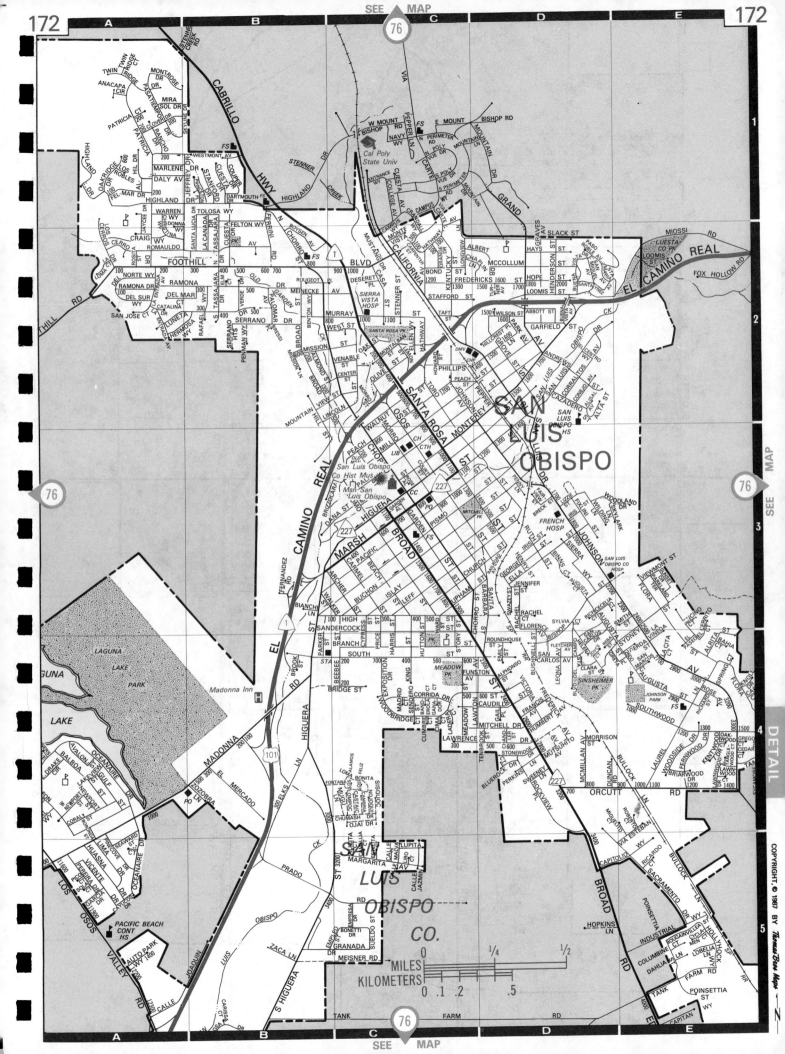

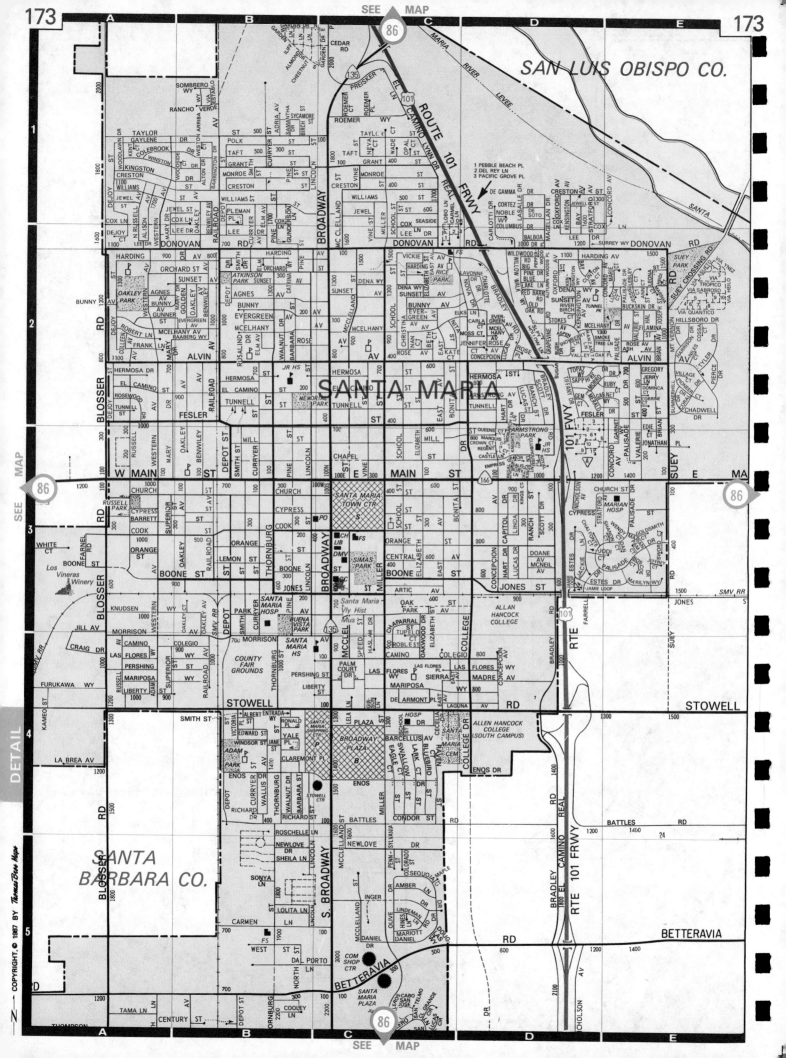

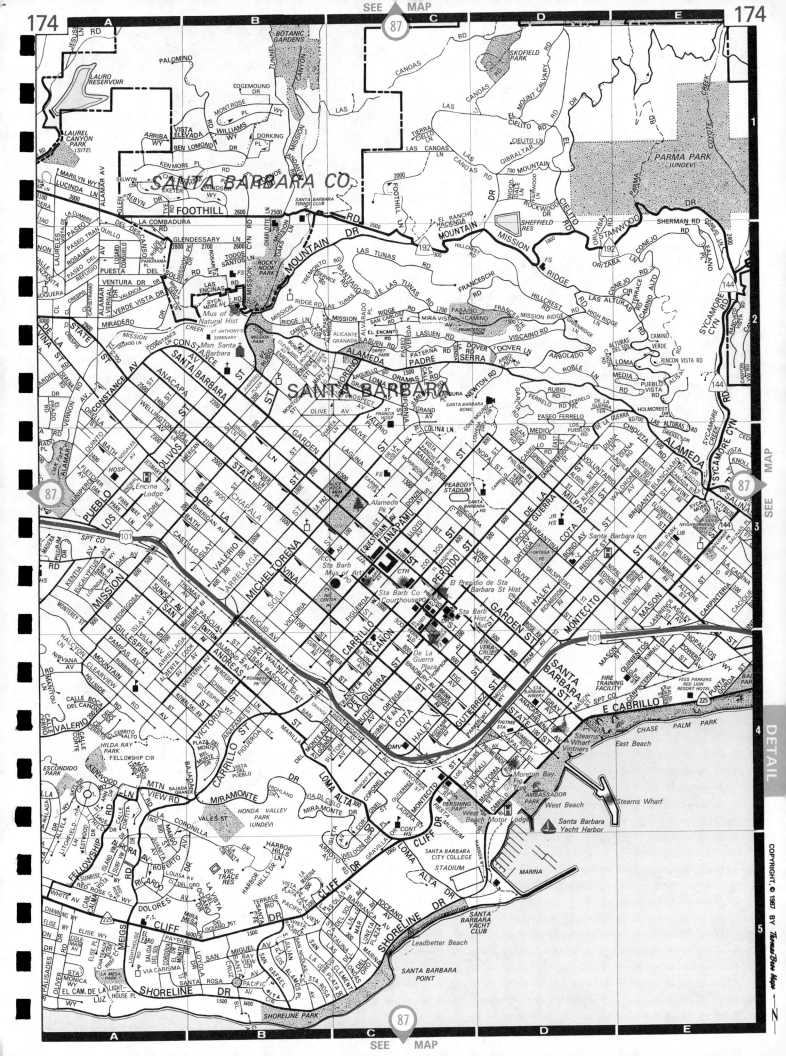

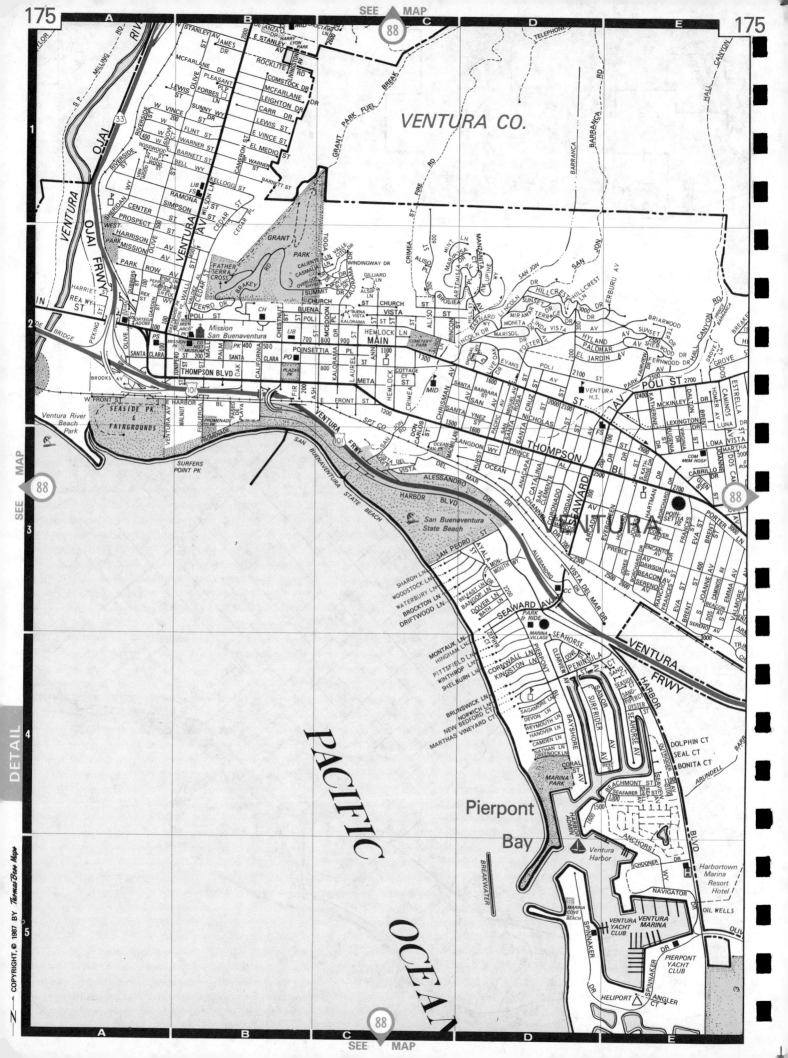

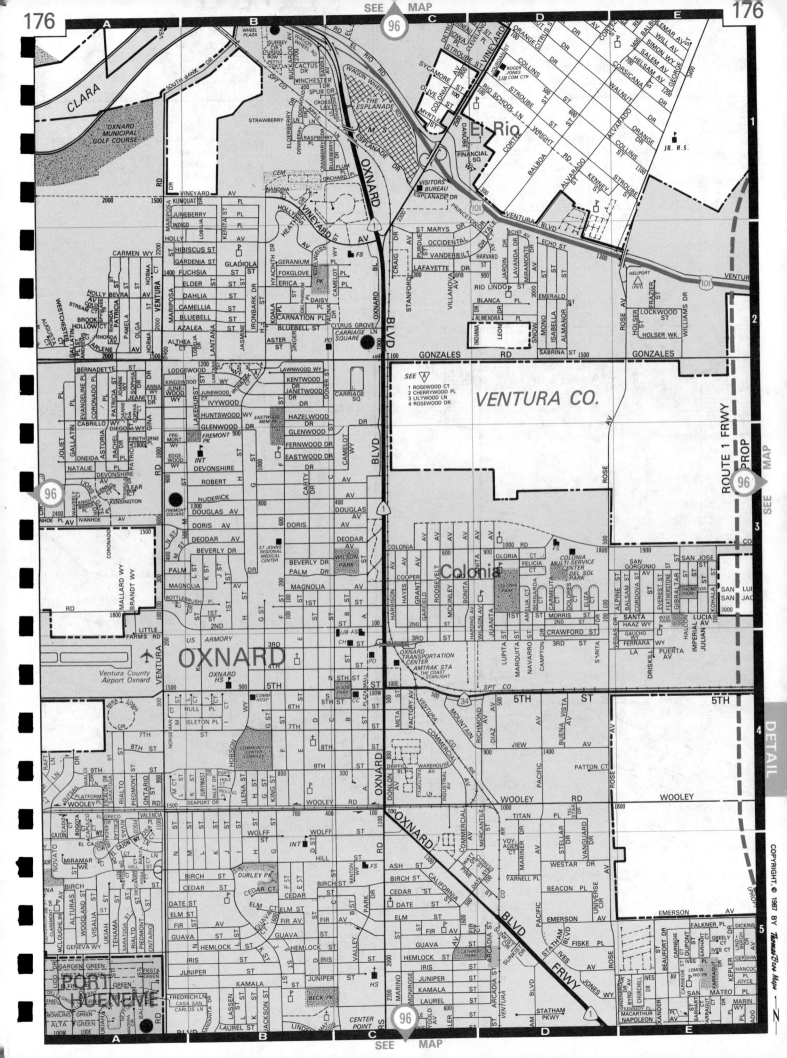

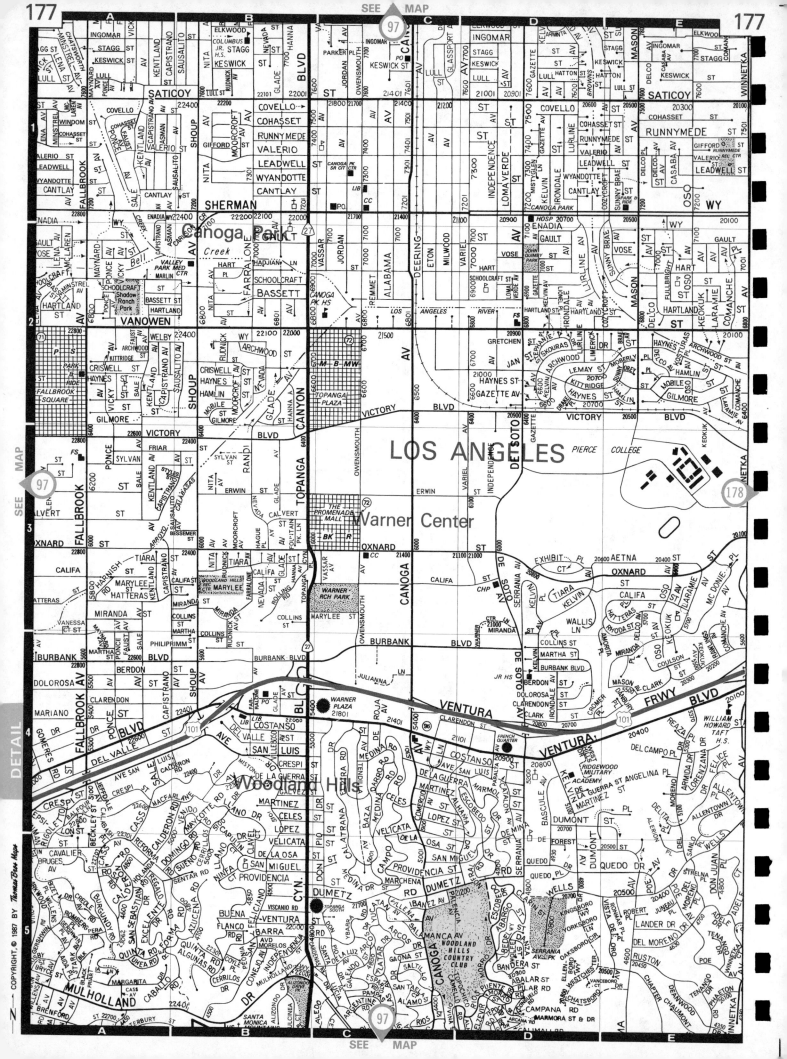

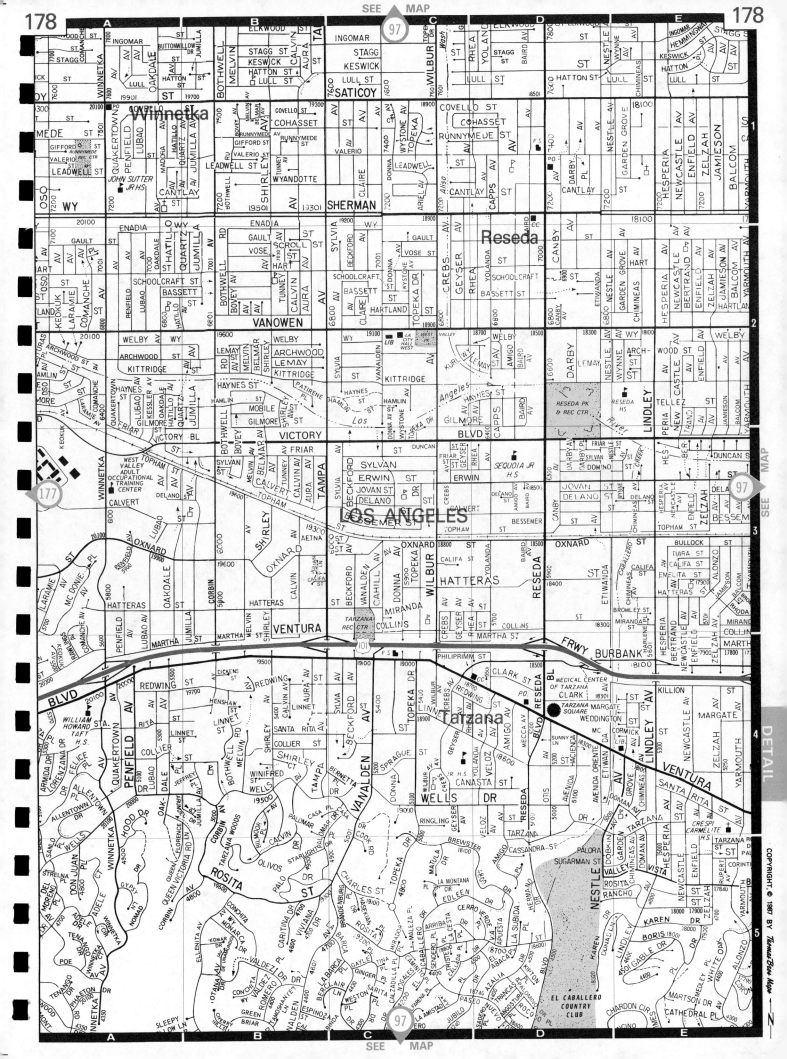

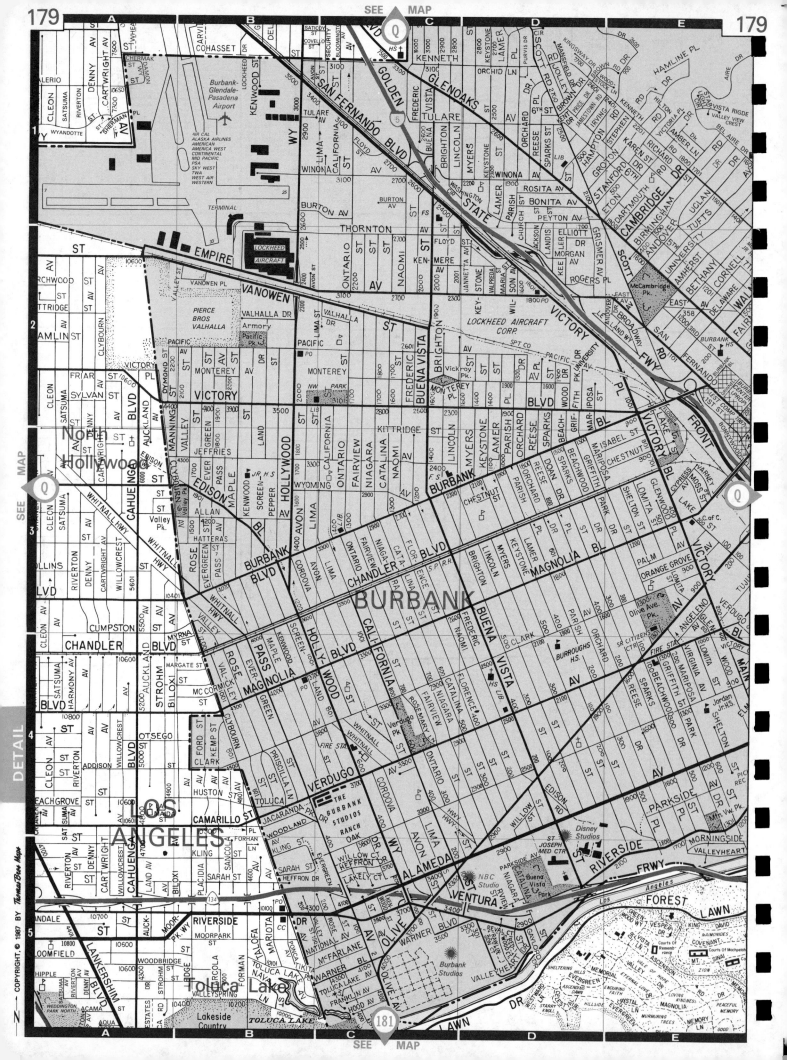

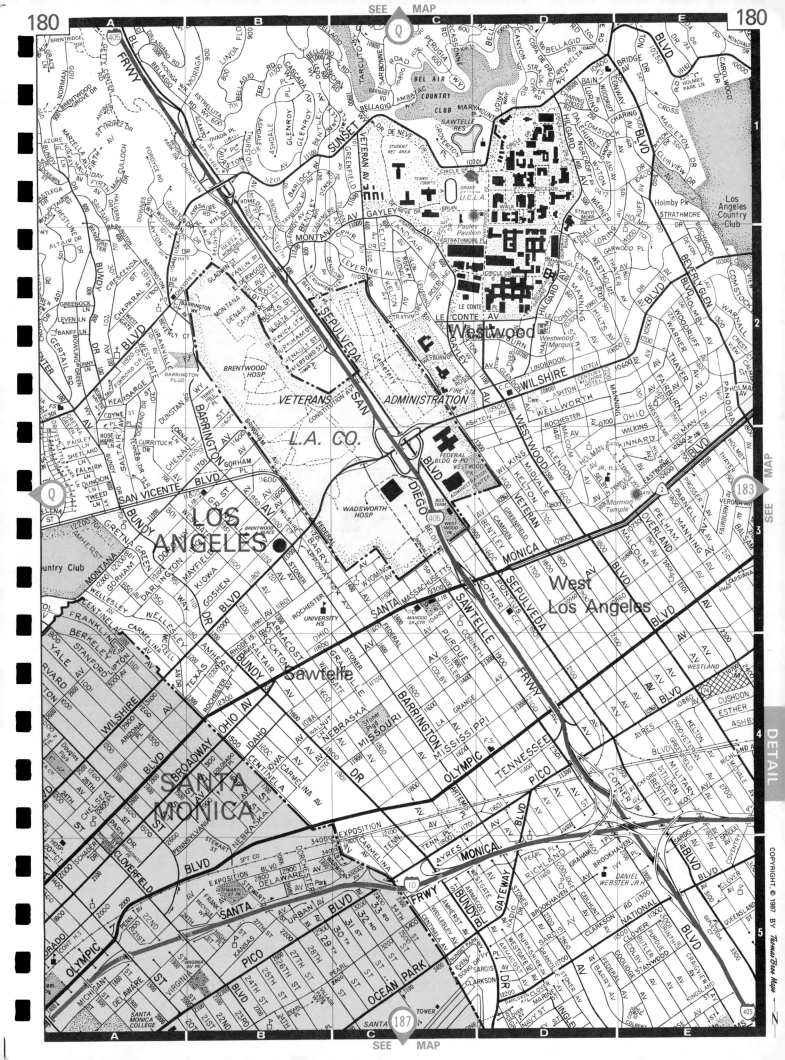

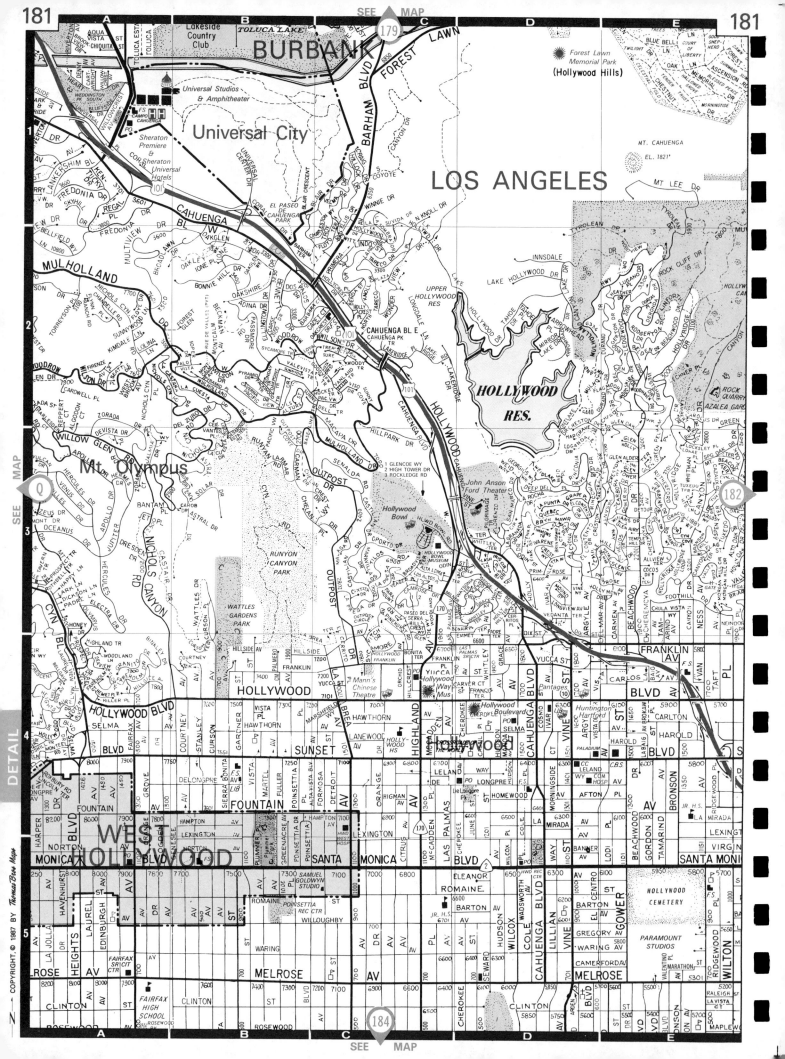

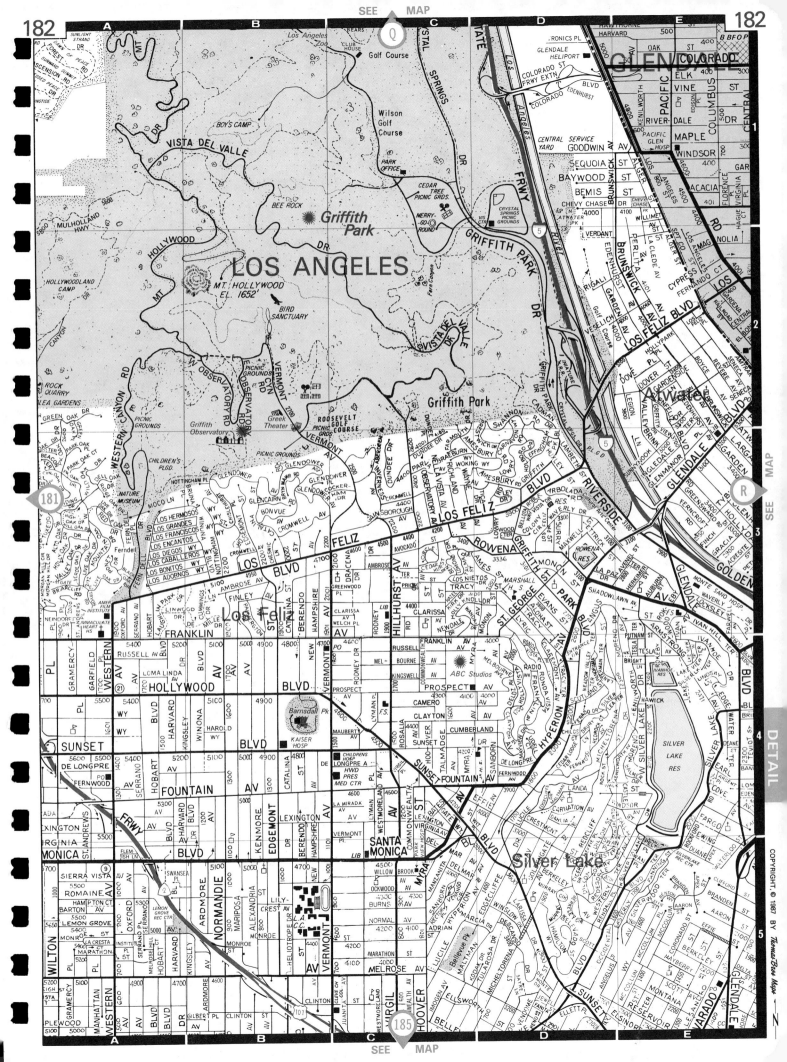

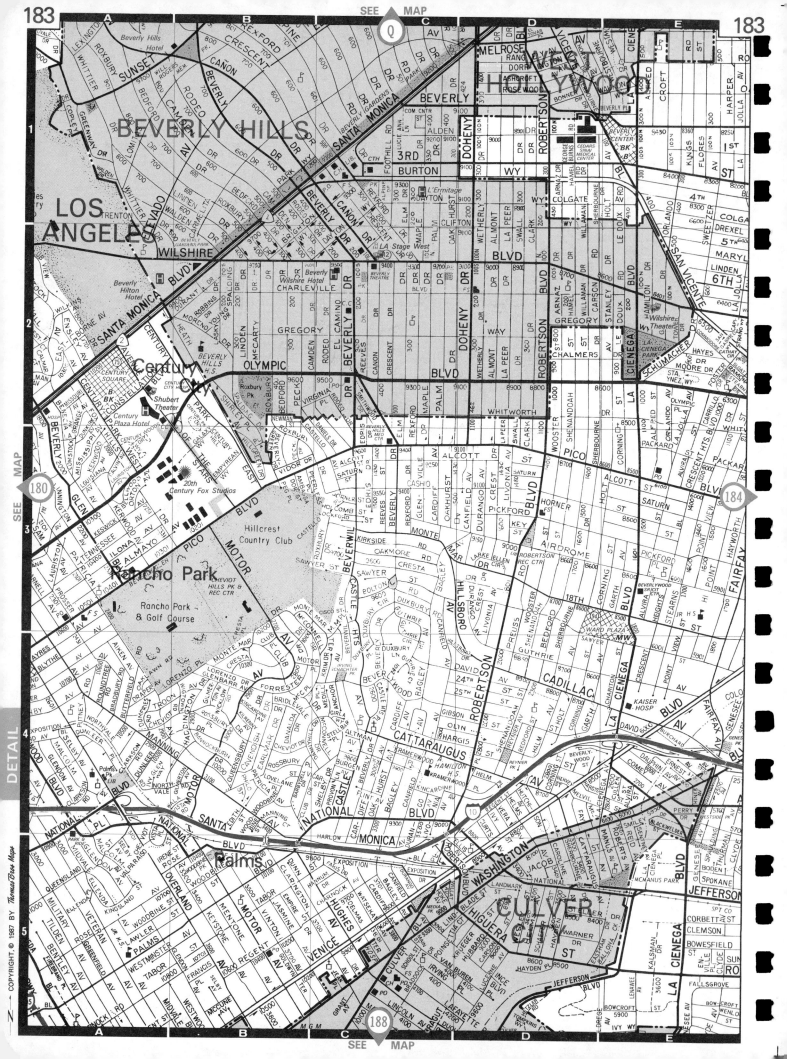

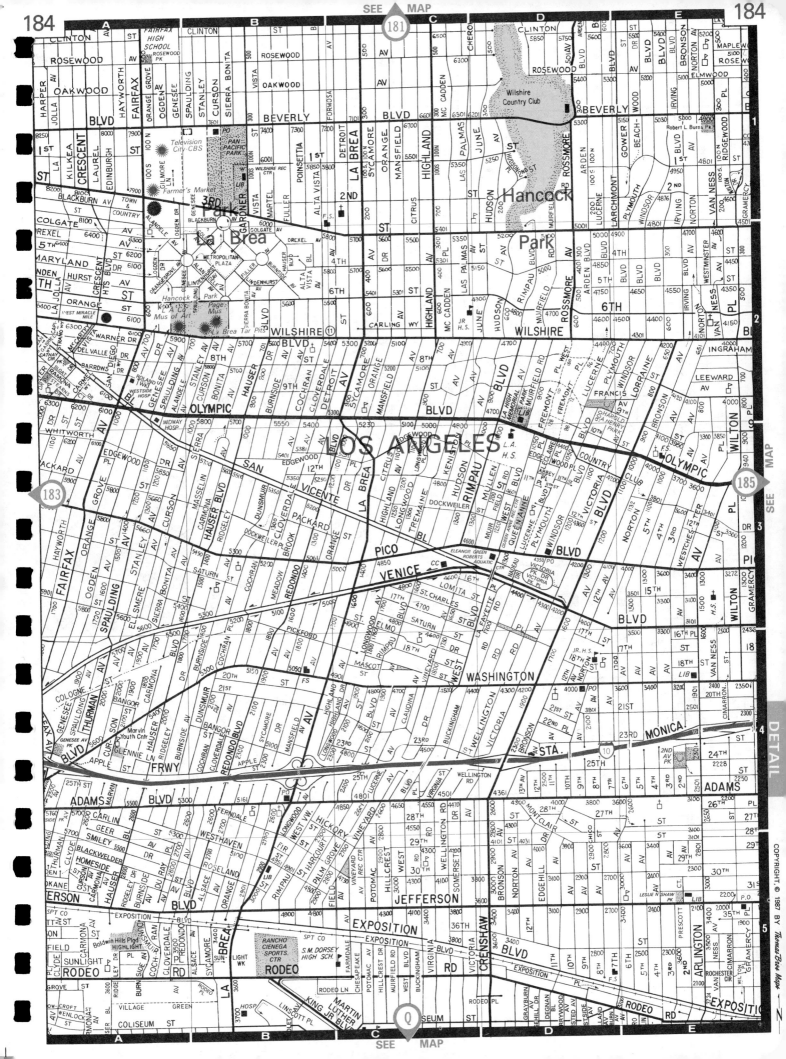

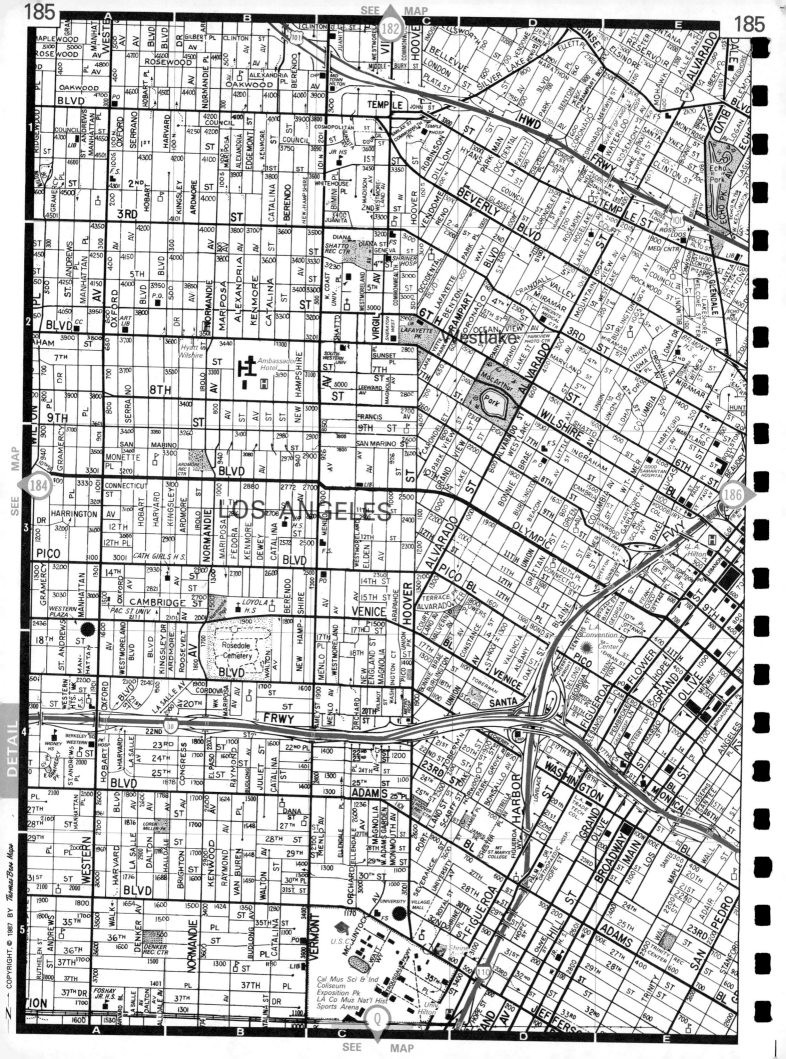

186

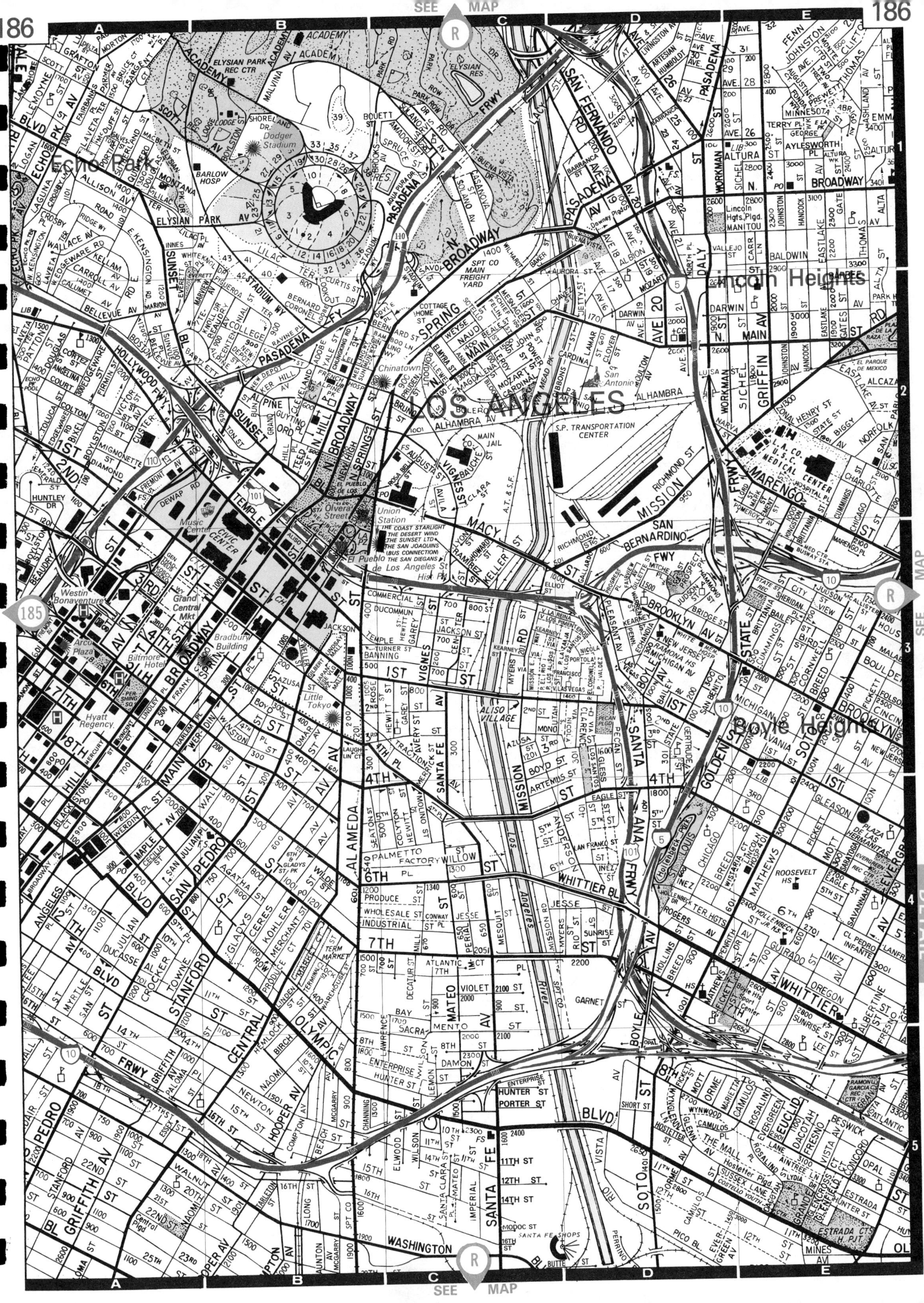
SEE MAP
Echo Park
Elysian Park Rec Ctr
Dodger Stadium
Elysian Res
Barlow Hosp
Lincoln Heights
Lincoln Hgts. Plgd.
SPT CO Main Freight Yard
Chinatown
San Antonio
LOS ANGELES
S.P. Transportation Center
Main Jail
L.A. Co. U.S.C. Medical Center
El Parque de Mexico
Music Center
Civic Center
Olvera Street
Union Station
El Pueblo de Los Angeles St Hist Pk
Westin Bonaventure
Grand Central Mkt
Arco Plaza
Bradbury Building
Biltmore Hotel
Hyatt Regency
Little Tokyo
Aliso Village
Boyle Heights
Hollenbeck Park
Roosevelt HS
Plaza de las Hermanitas
Boyle Hts Sport Center
Hostetler Plgd.
Central Plgd
Santa Fe Shops
Estrada Cts
Ramon Garcia Rec Ctr
Terminal Market
Los Angeles River
Hollywood Fwy
Pasadena Fwy
Golden State Fwy
Santa Ana Frwy
San Bernardino Fwy
Sunset Bl
Broadway
Alameda
Washington
Olympic
Whittier Bl
Mission Rd
Soto St
Brooklyn Av
Pasadena Av
N. Broadway
Temple
Spring
Main
Central
San Pedro
Figueroa
Stadium Wy
Alhambra Av
Macy St
1st St
4th St
6th St
7th St
8th St
Santa Fe
Boyle Av
Griffith Av
Euclid
Marengo
Daly
Workman
Mission
185

COPYRIGHT © 1987 BY Thomas Bros Maps

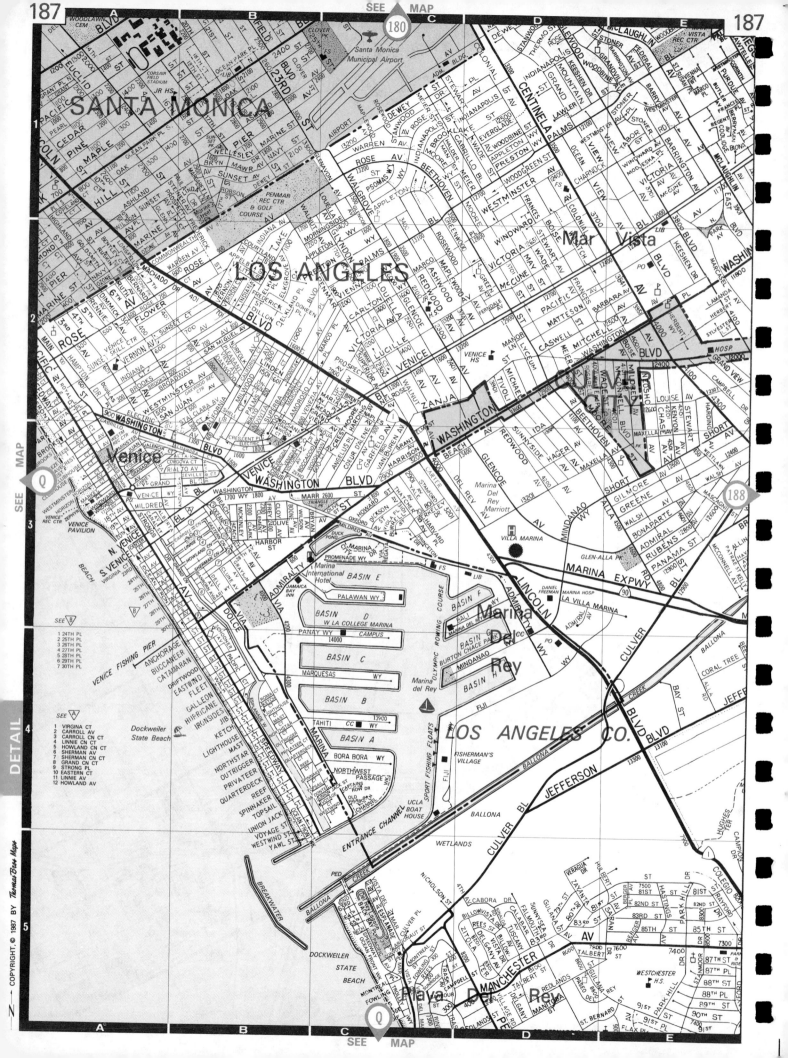

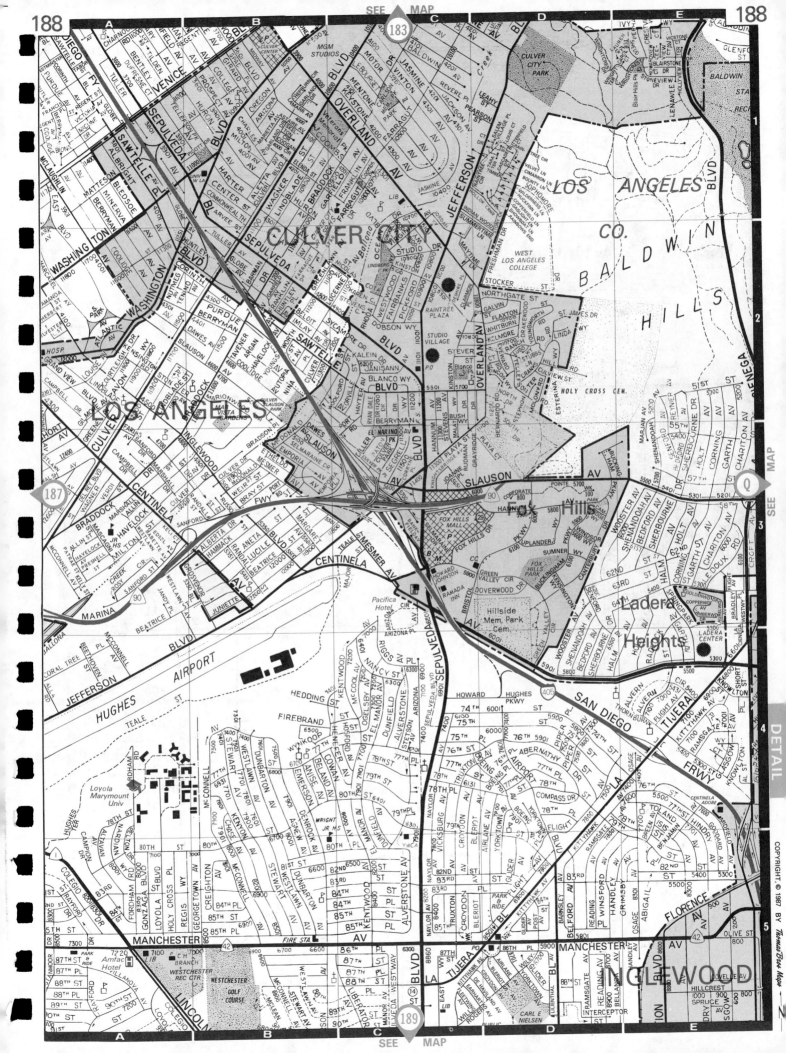

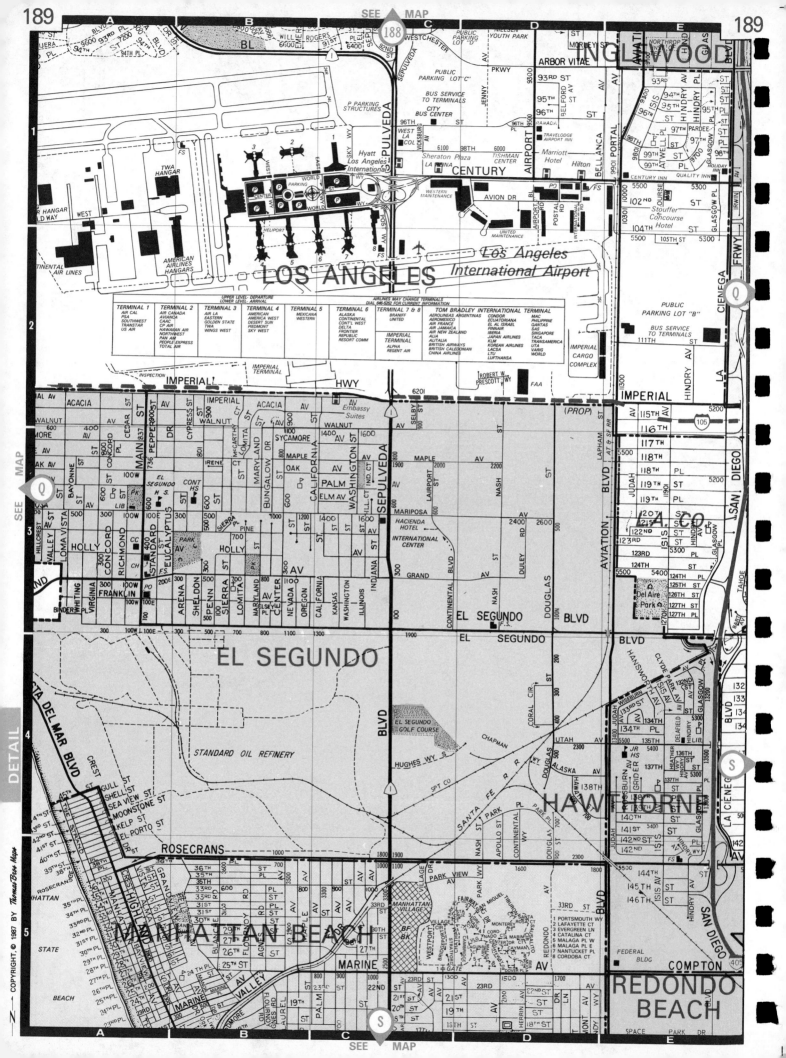

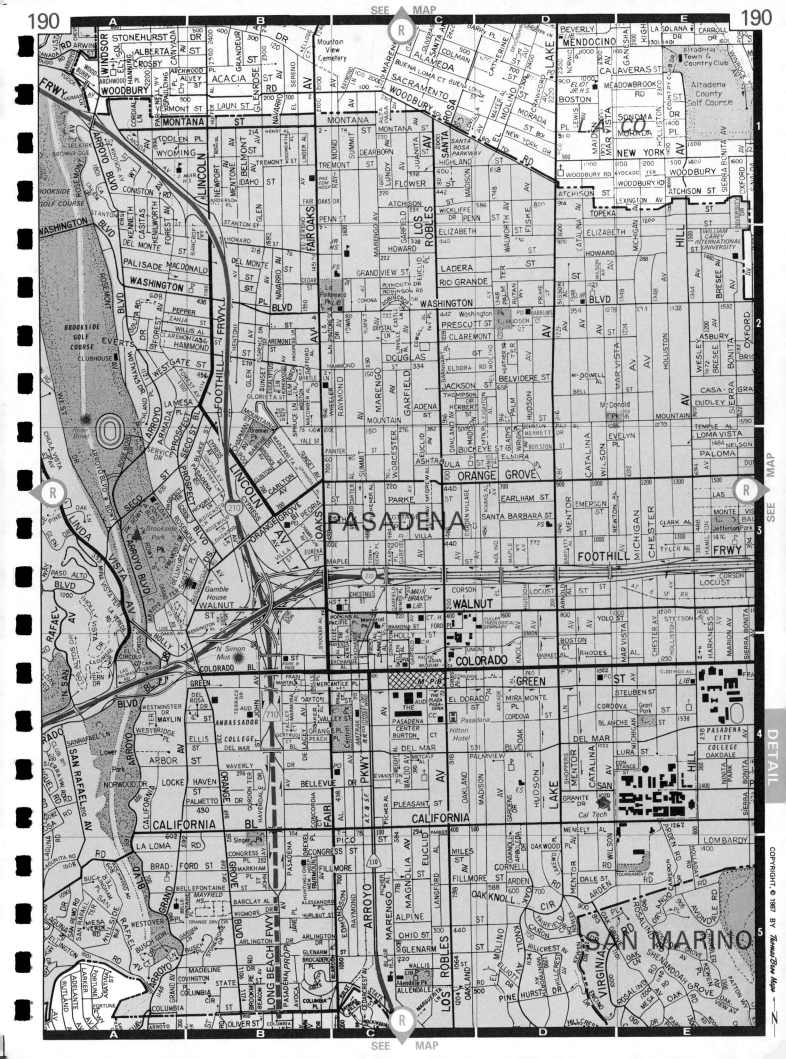

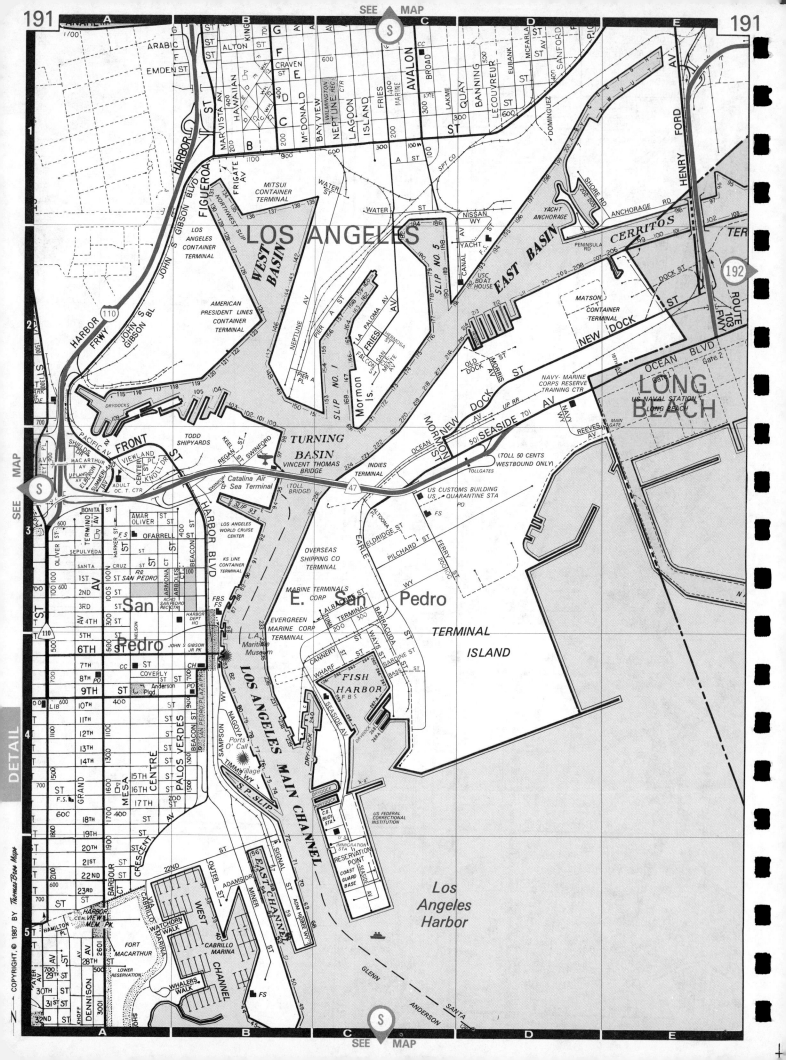

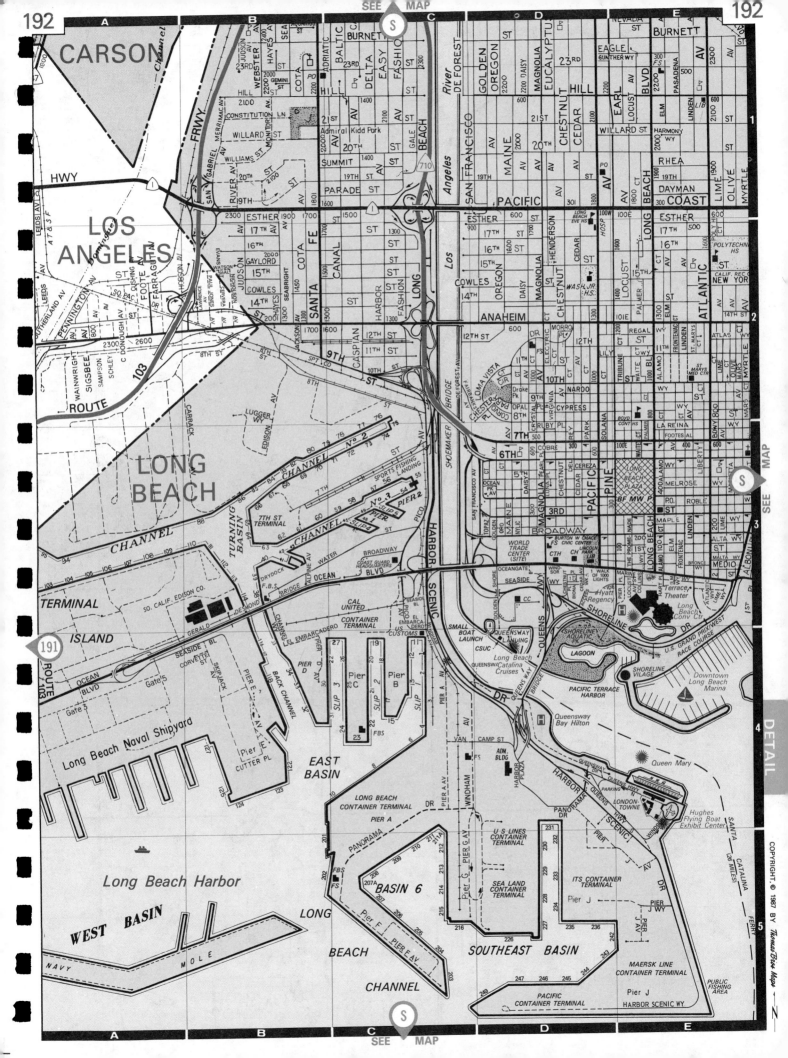

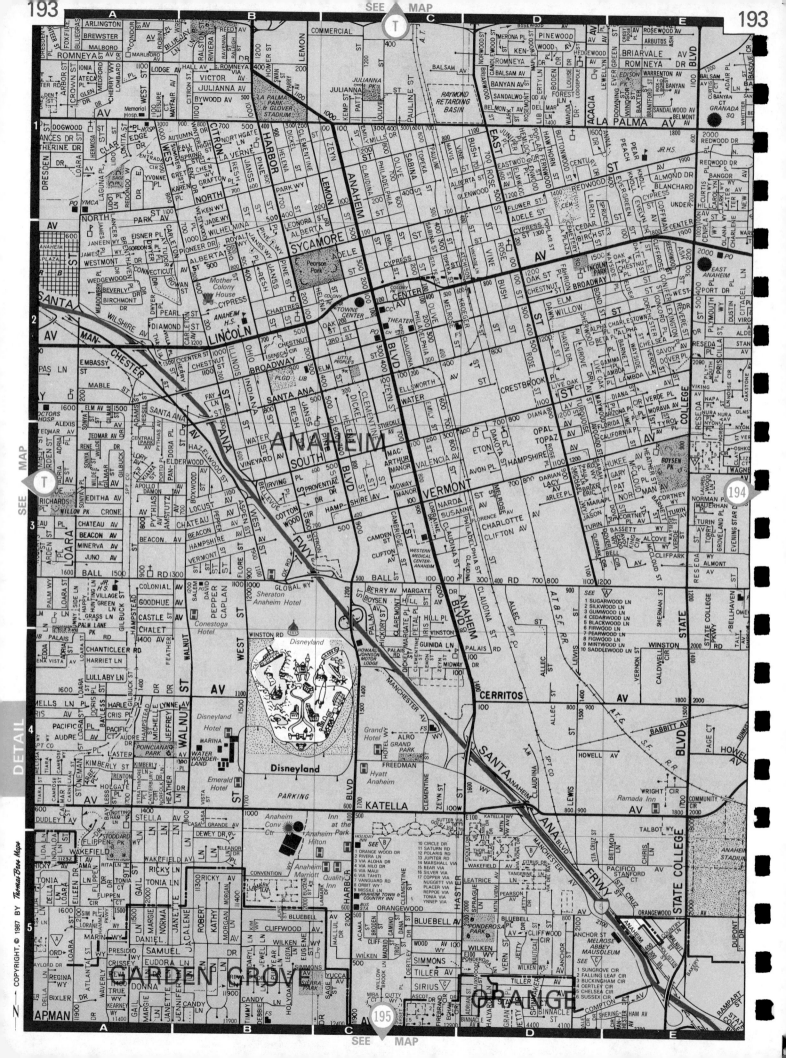

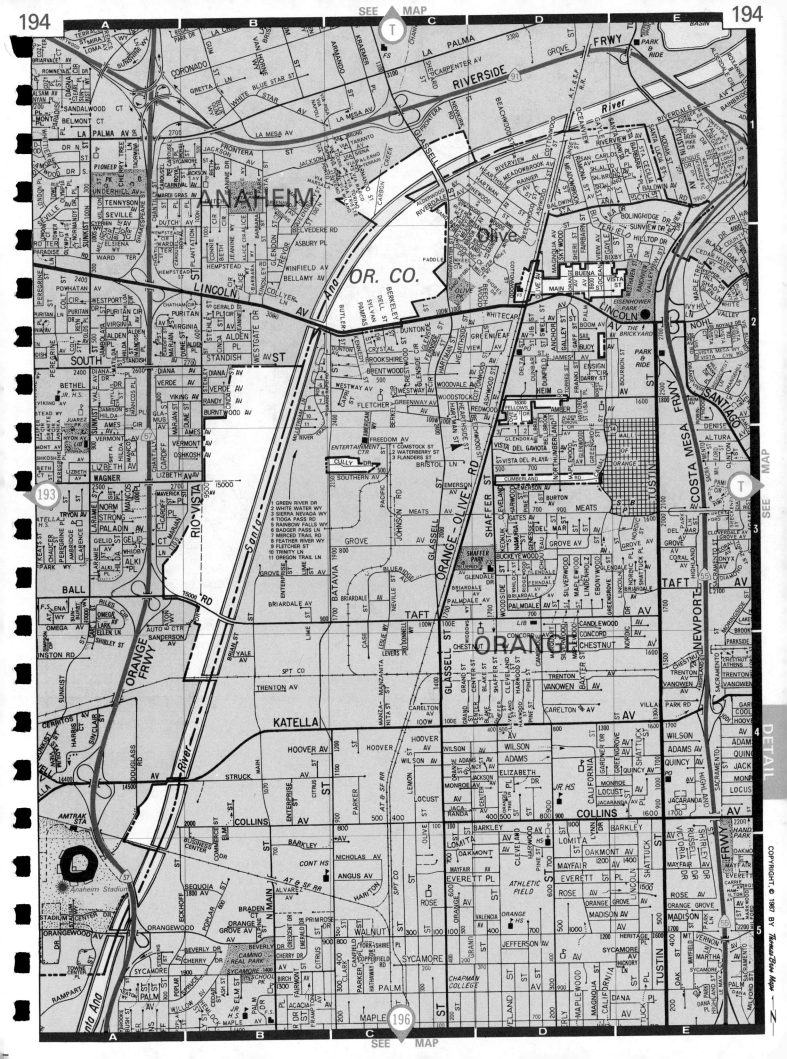

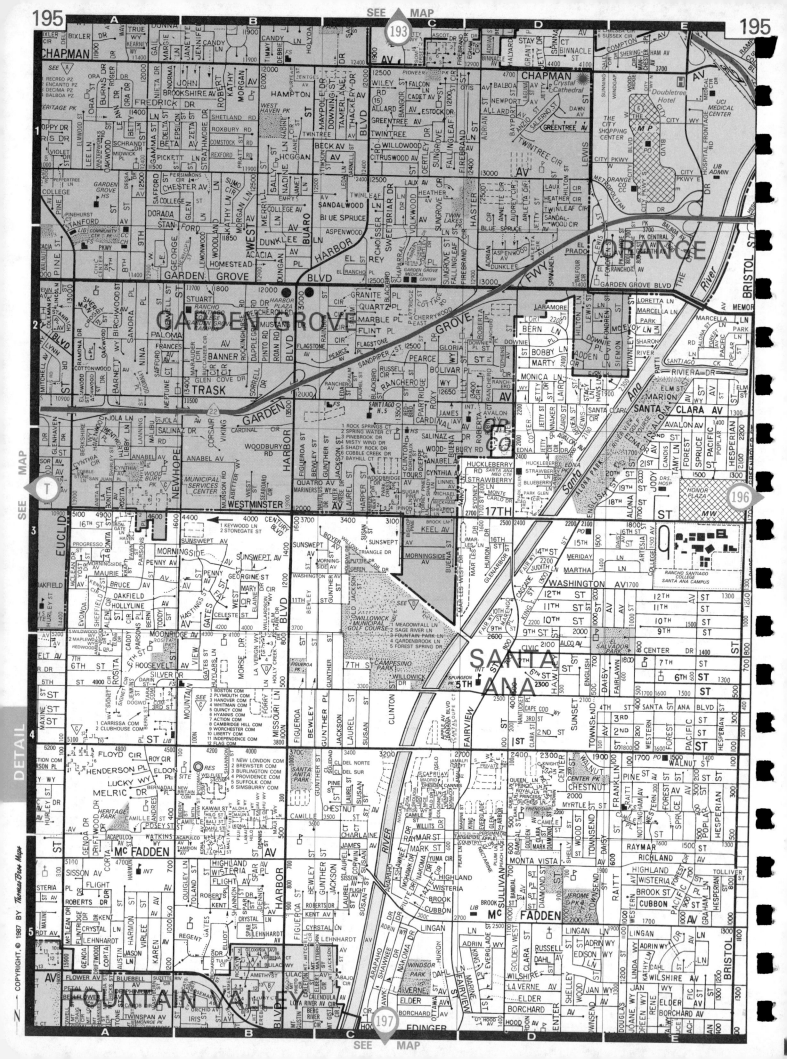

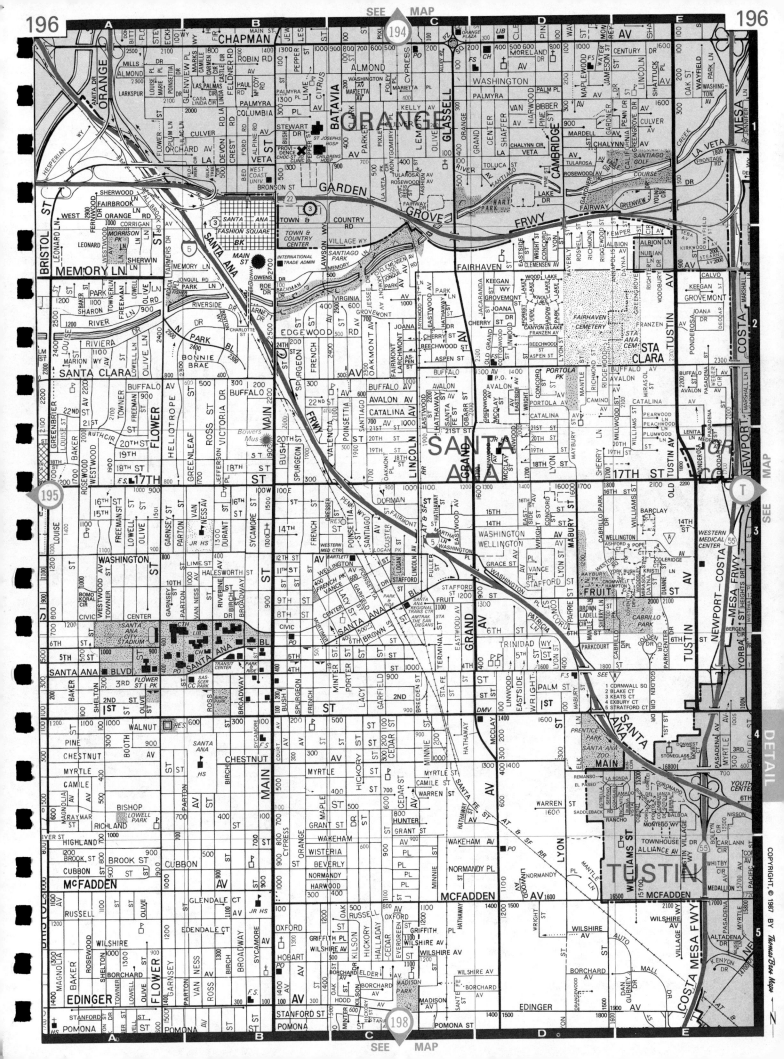

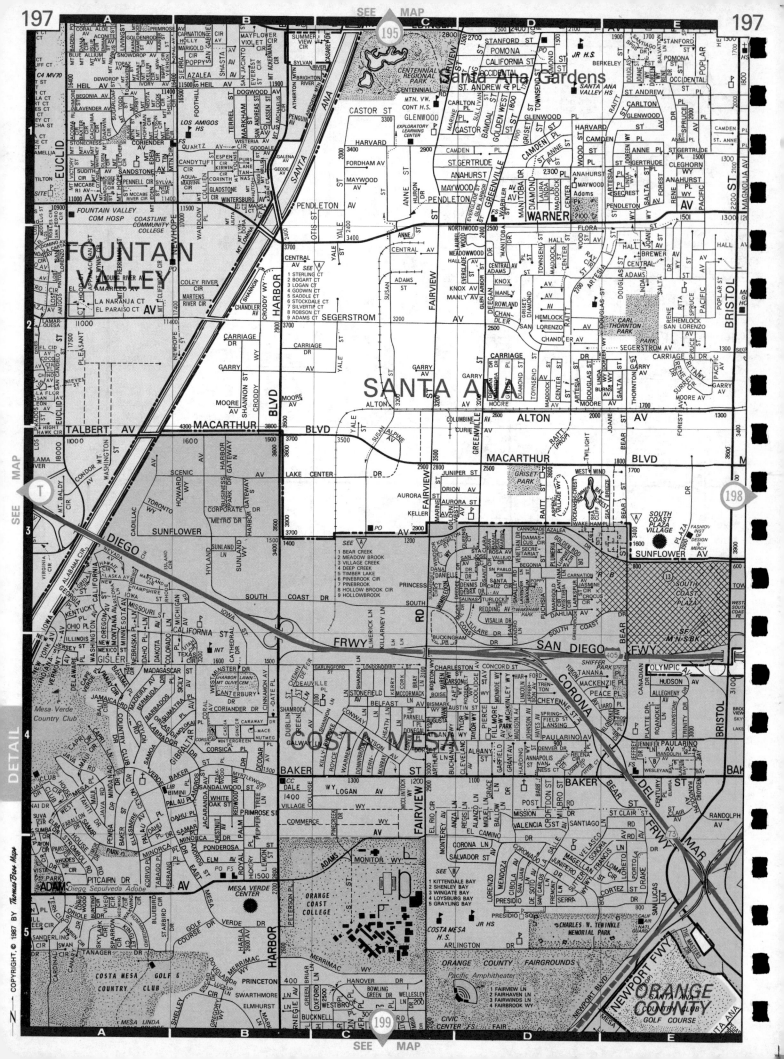

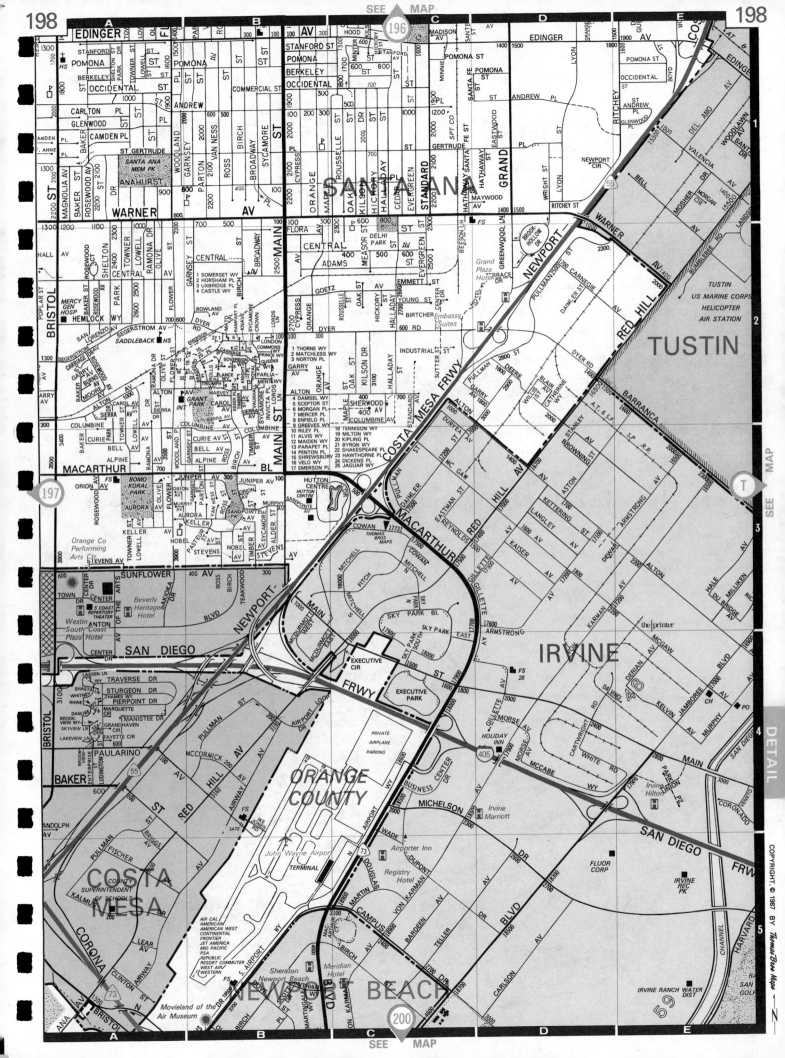

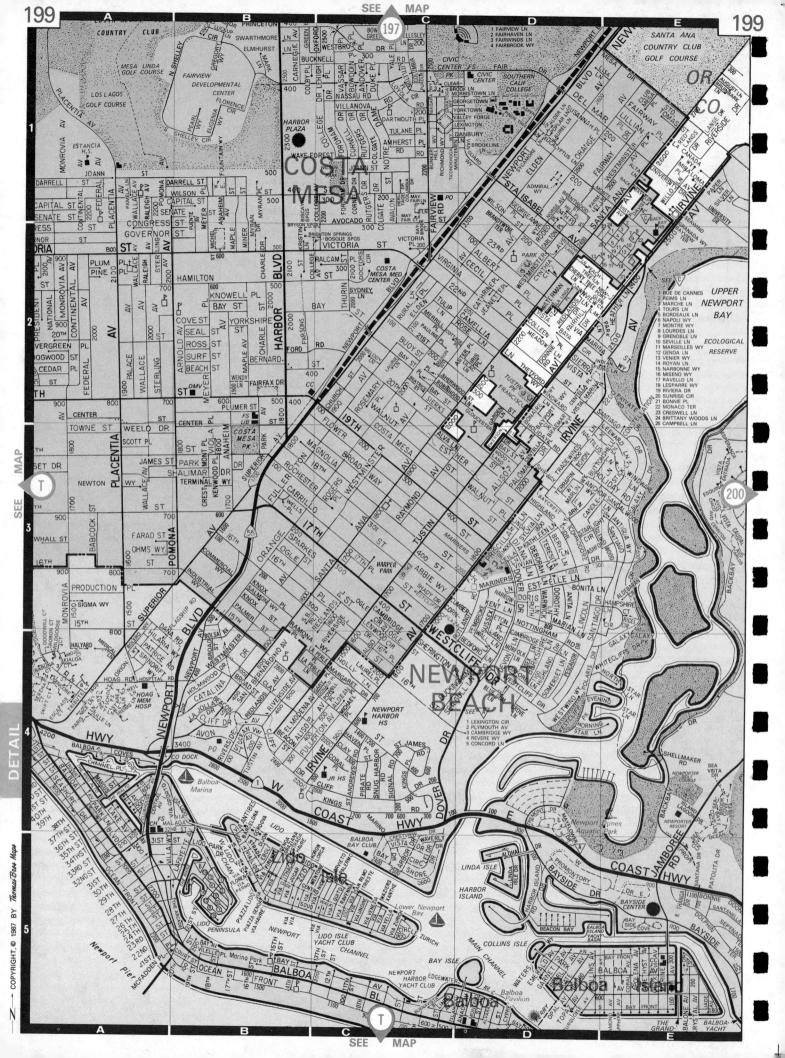

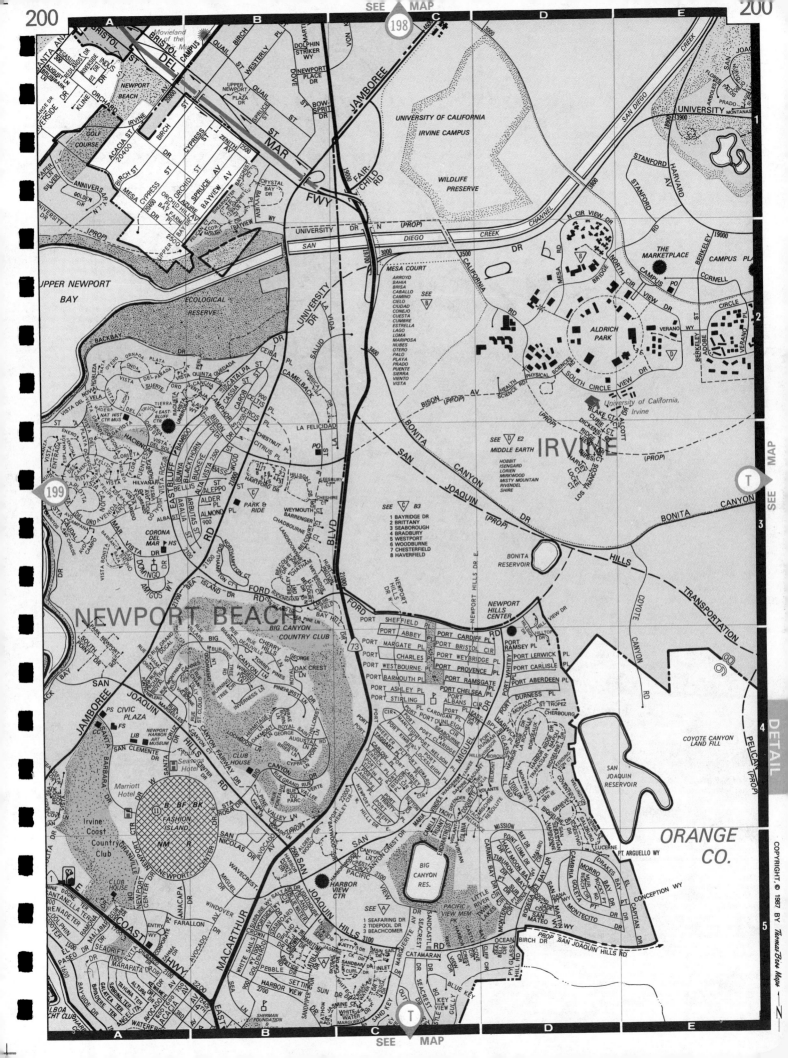

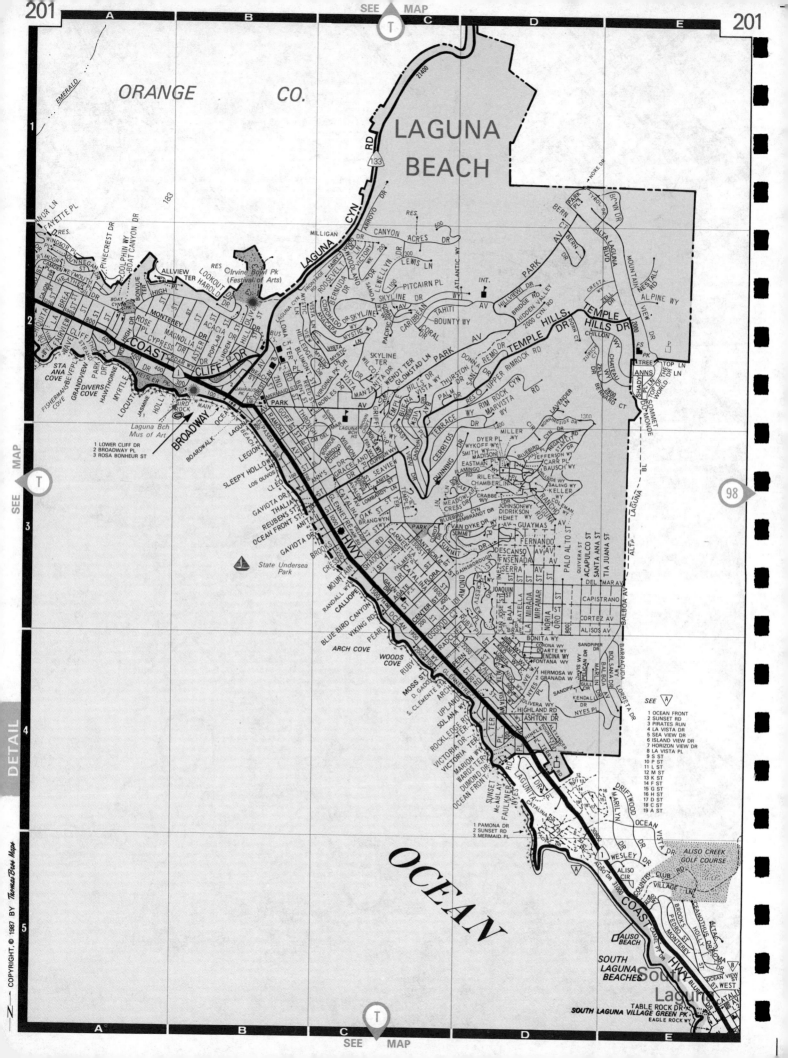

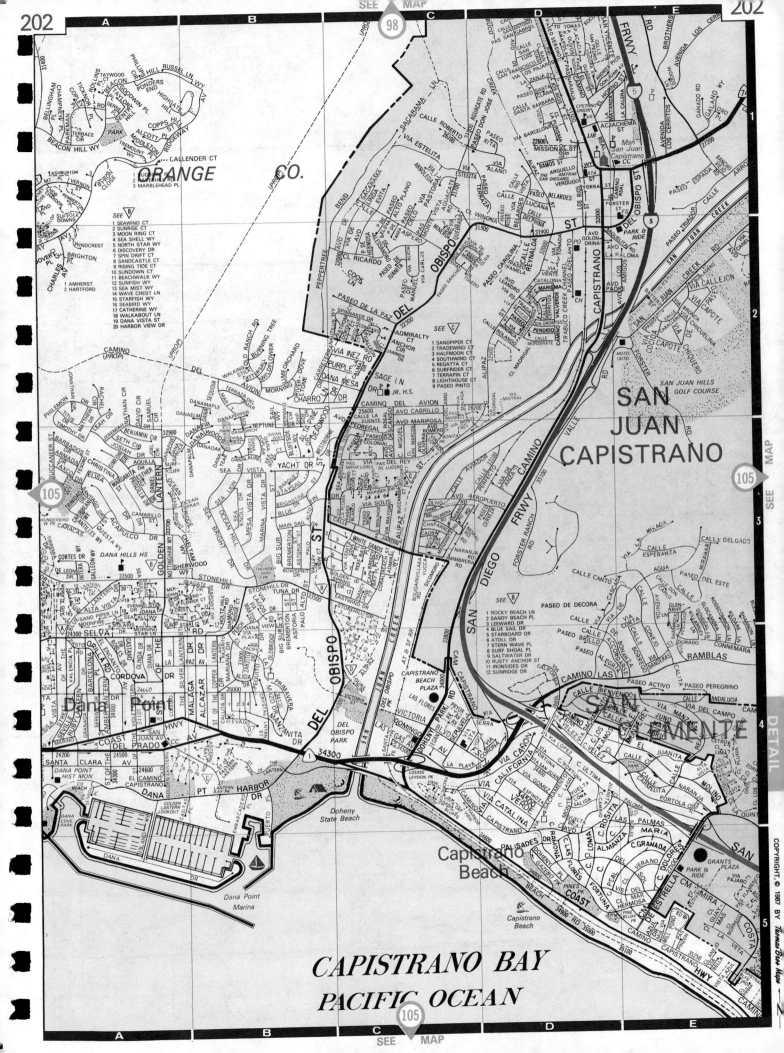

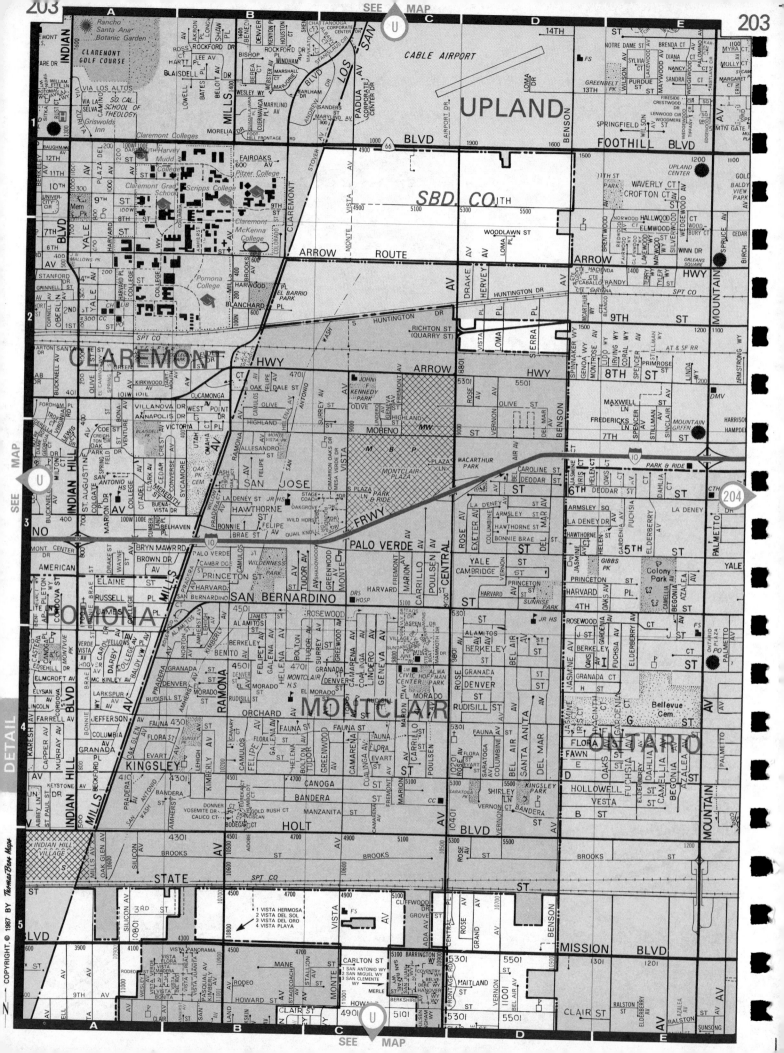

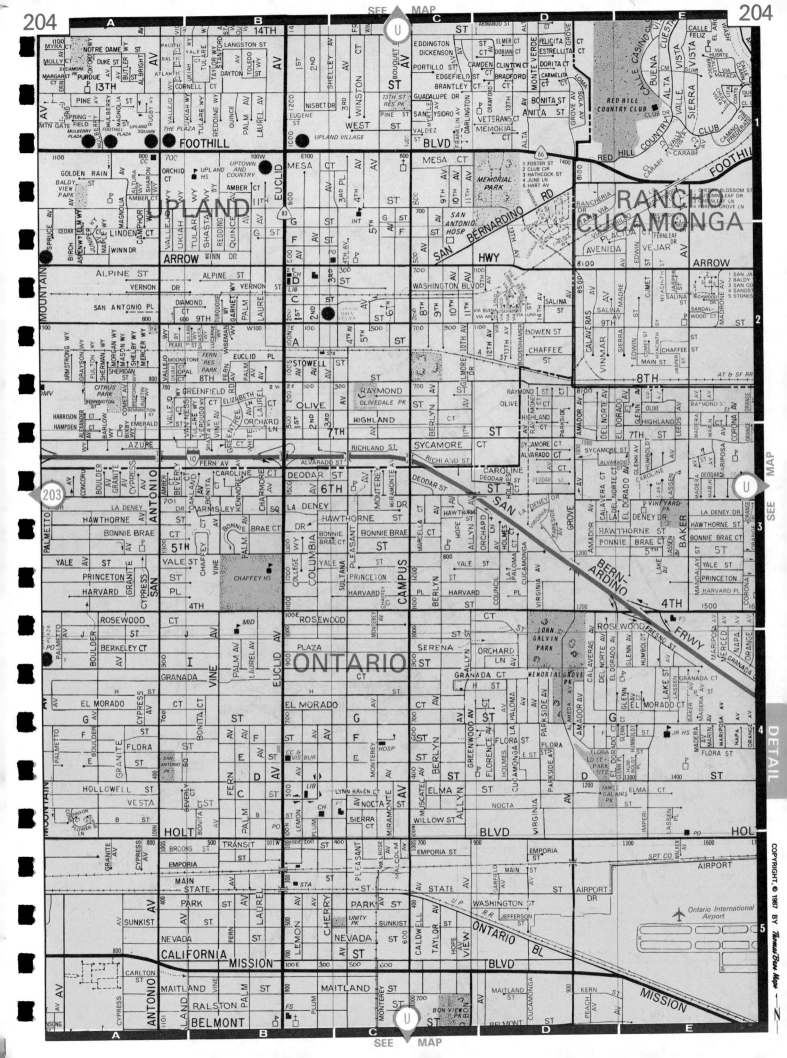

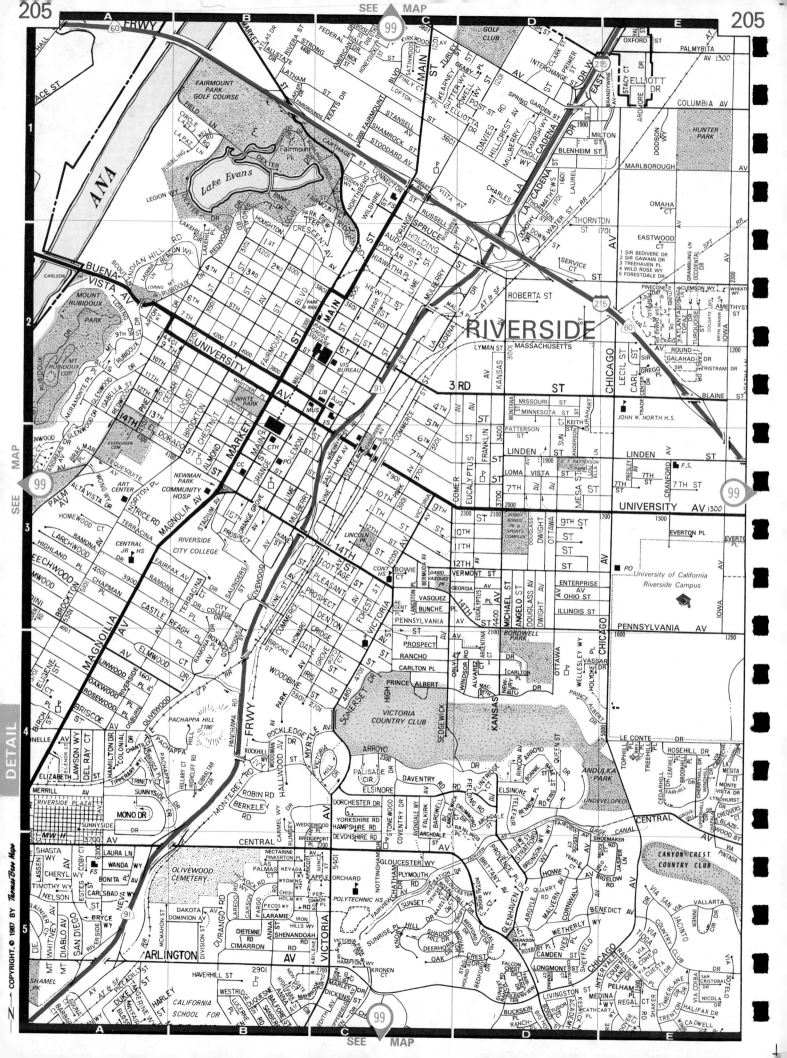

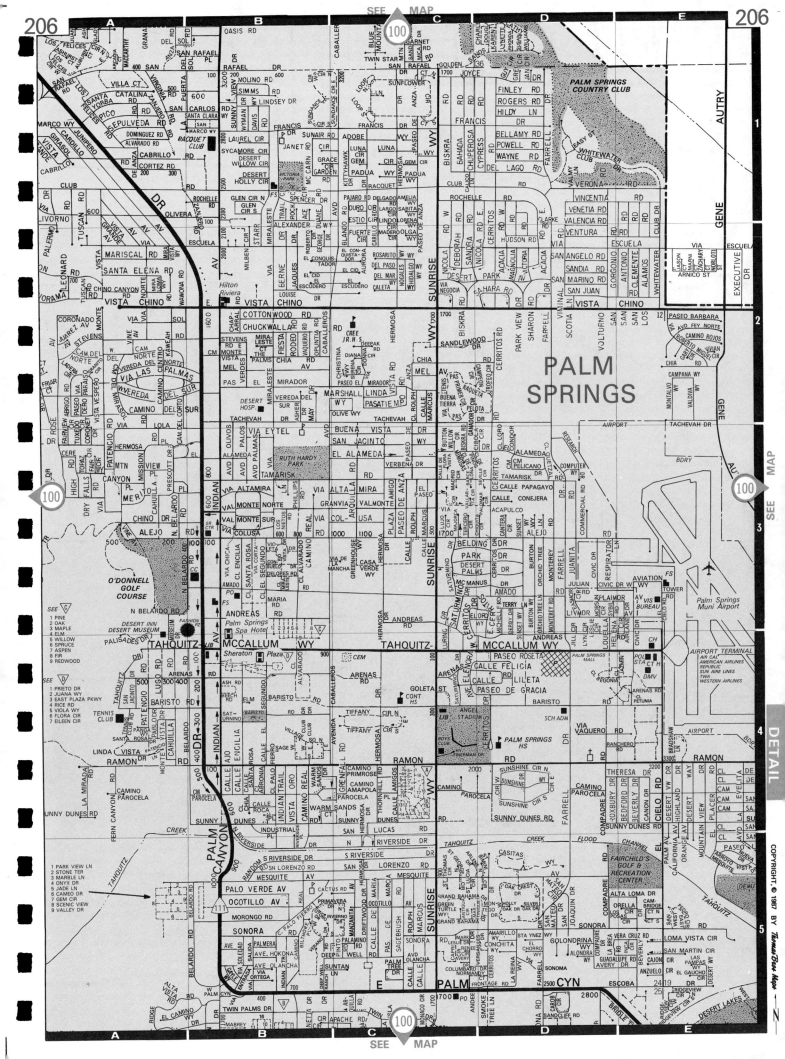

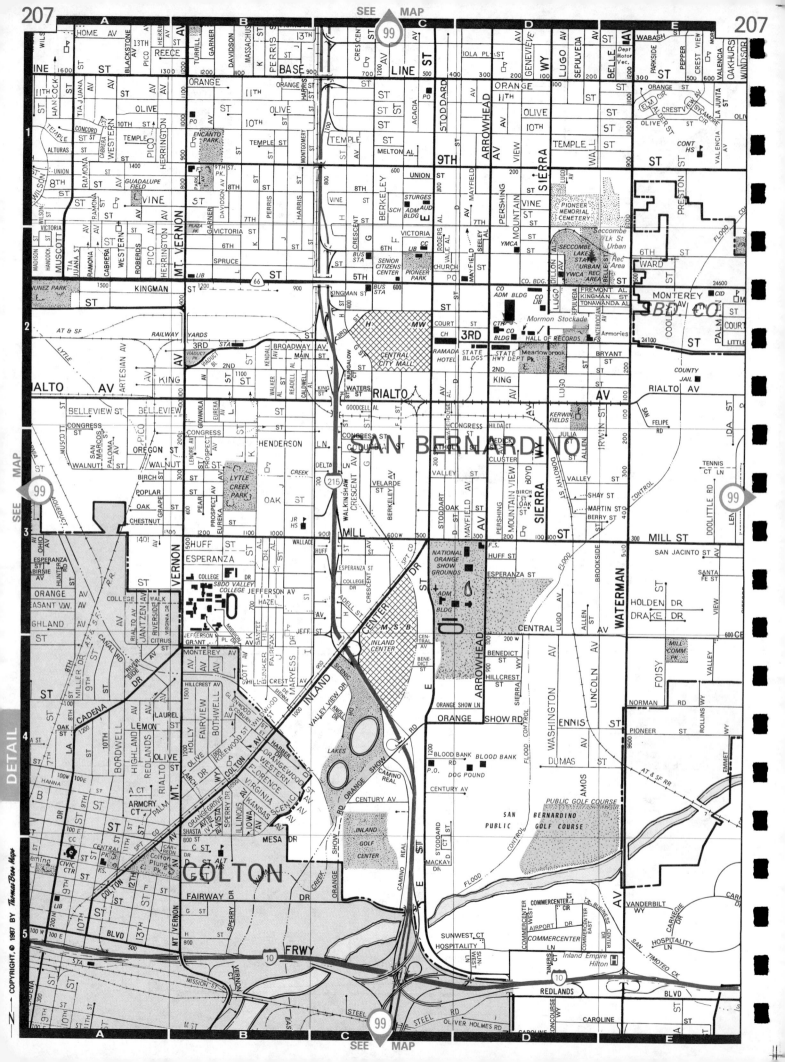

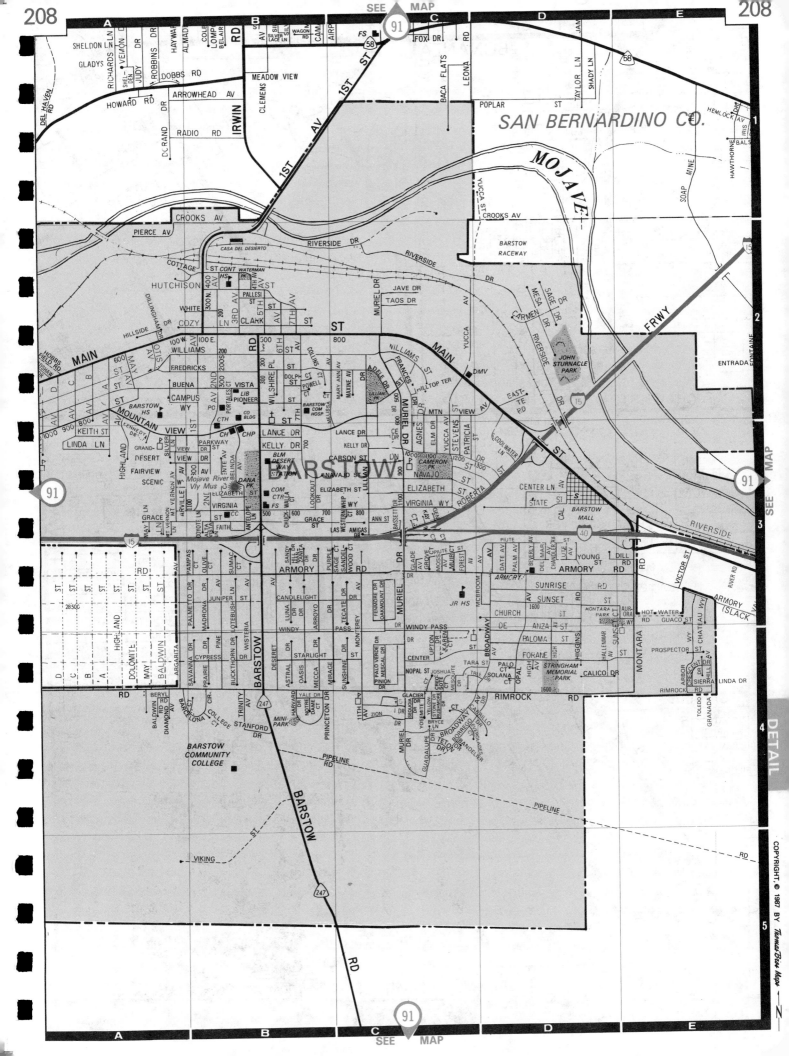

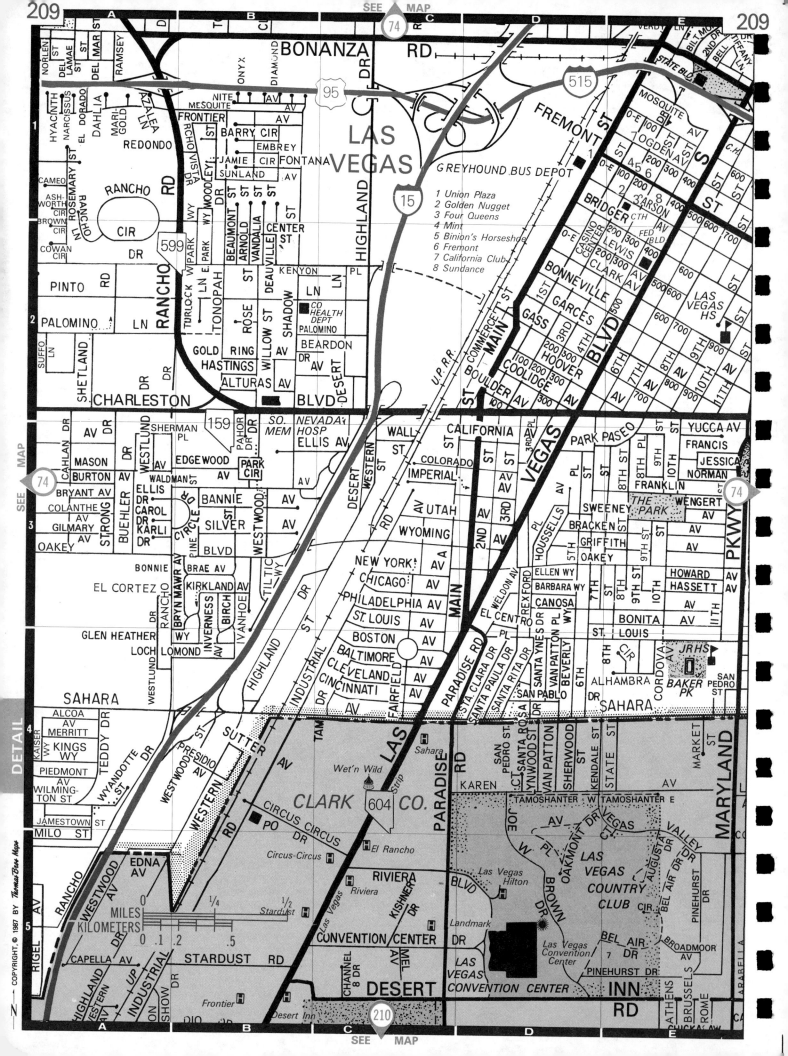

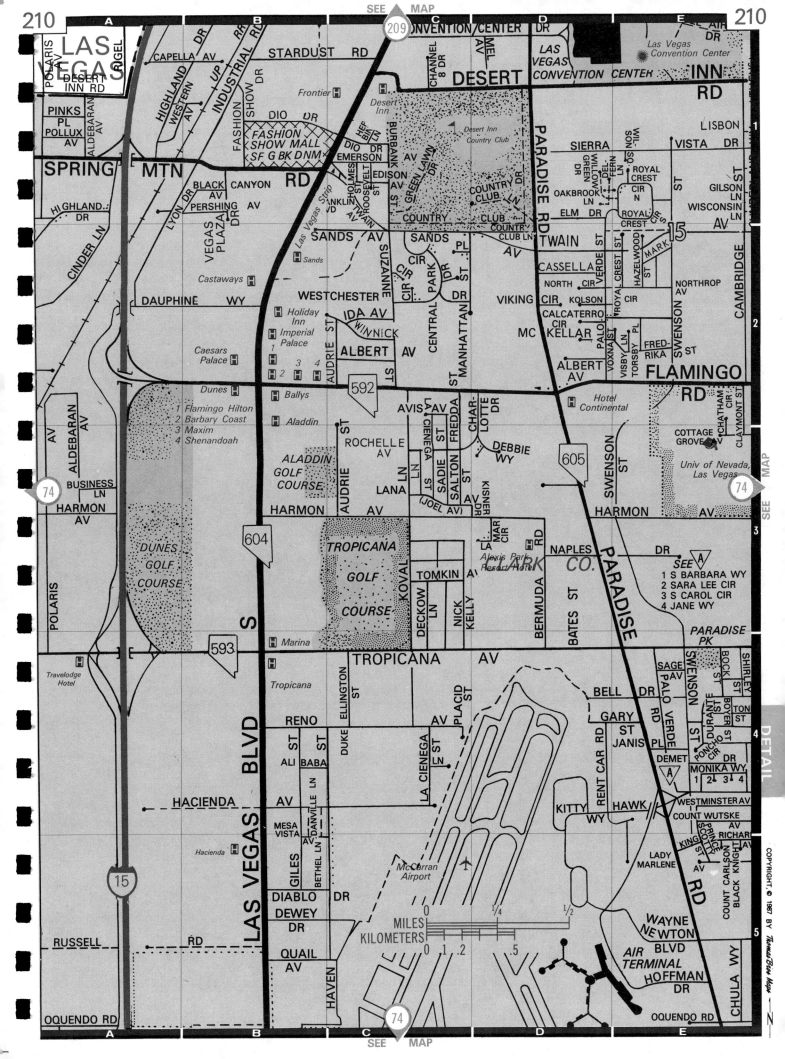

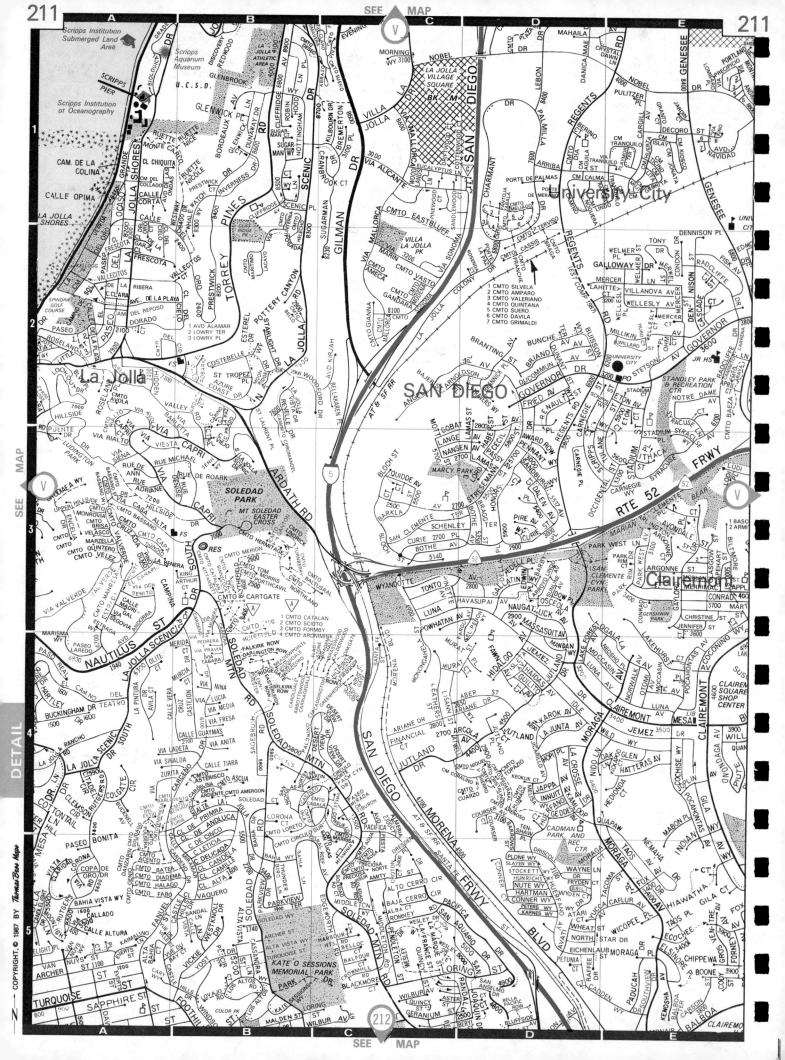

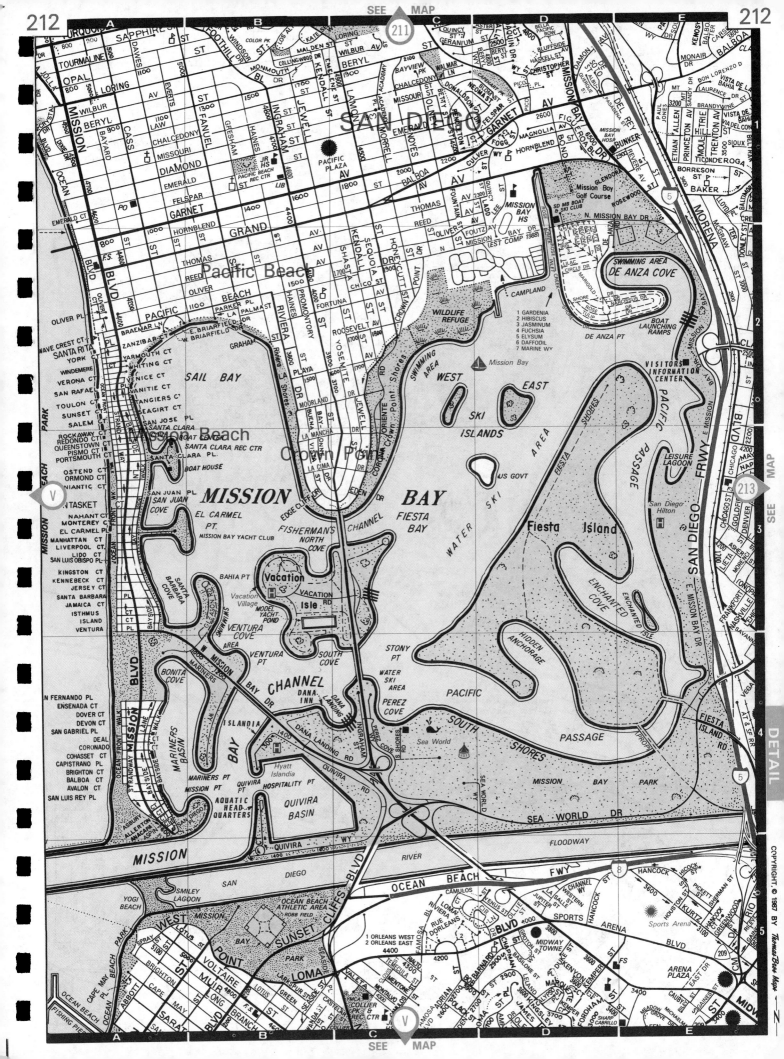

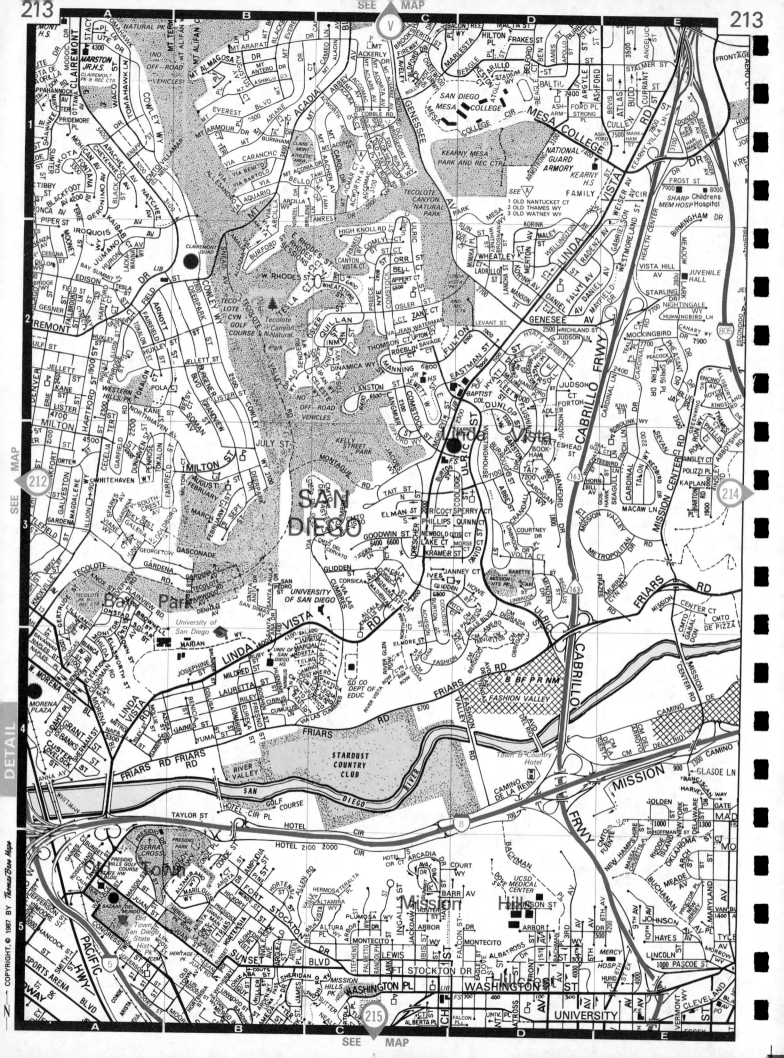

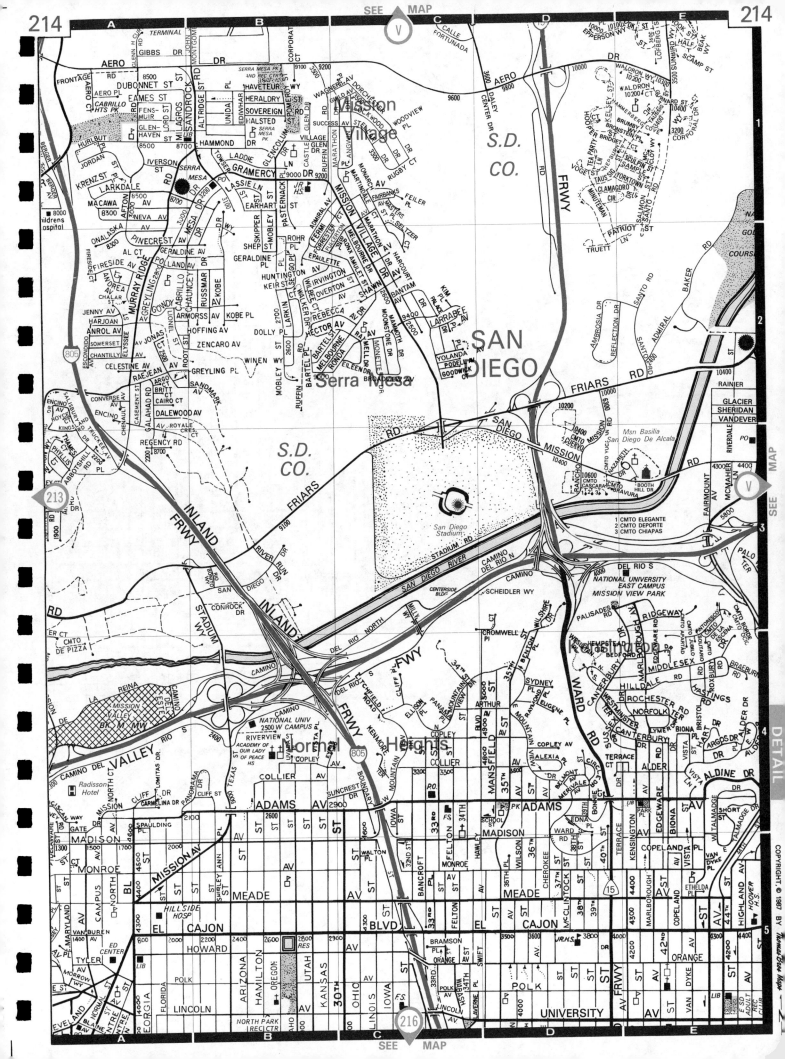

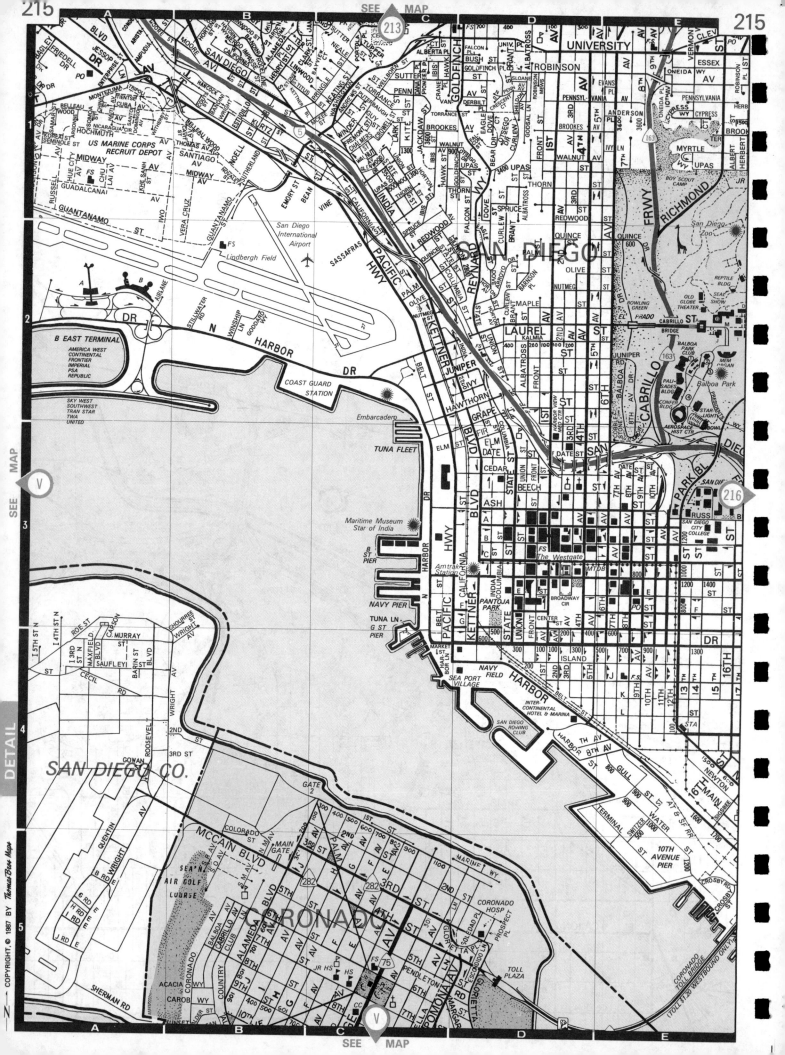

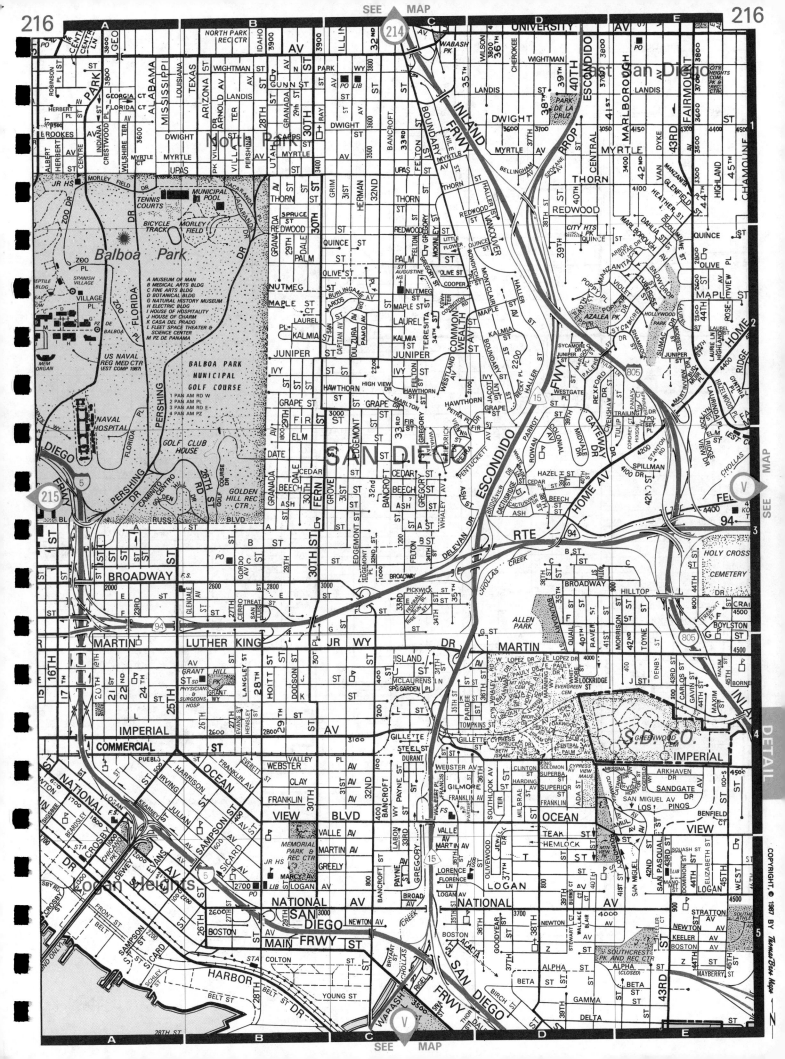

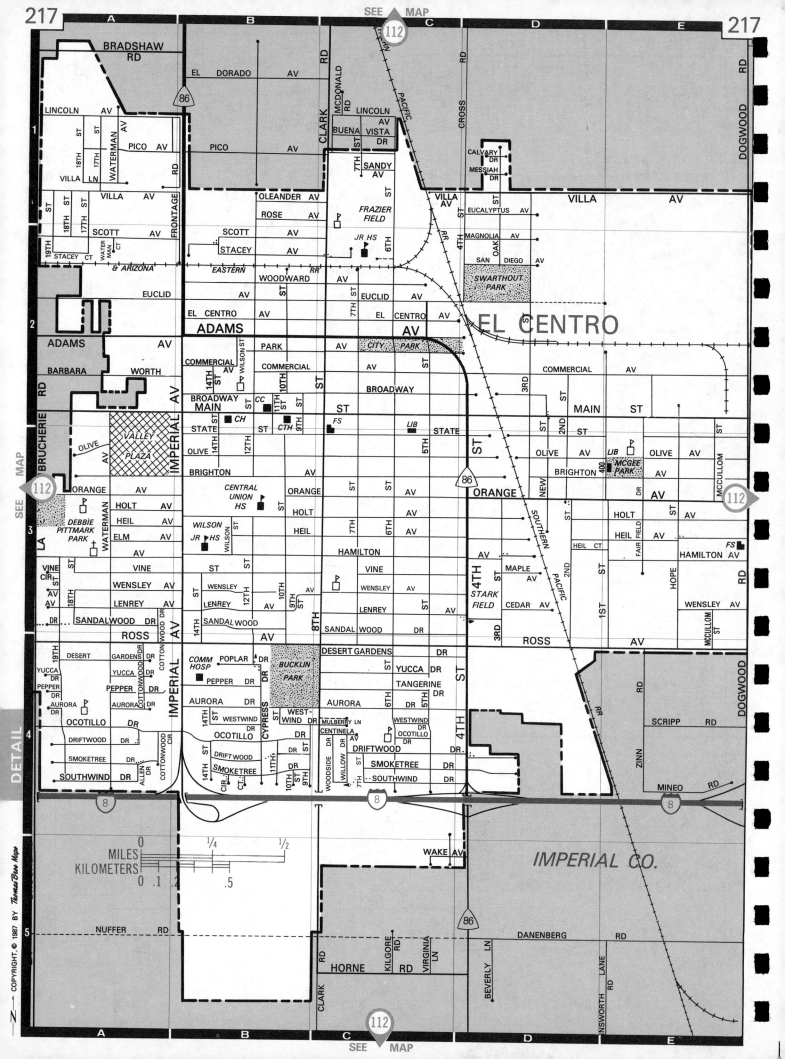

LIST OF ABBREVIATIONS

AL	ALLEY	CR	CRESCENT	KPN	KEY PENINSULA NORTH	RES	RESERVOIR
AR	ARROYO	CRES	CRESCENT	KPS	KEY PENINSULA SOUTH	RIV	RIVER
ARR	ARROYO	CSWY	CAUSEWAY	L	LA	RV	RIVER
AV	AVENUE	CT	COURT	LN	LANE	RO	RANCHO
AVD	AVENIDA	CTE	CORTE	LP	LOOP	S	SOUTH
AVD D LS	AVENIDA DE LOS	CTO	CUT OFF	LS	LAS, LOS	SN	SAN
BCH	BEACH	CTR	CENTER	MDW	MEADOW	SPG	SPRING
BL	BOULEVARD	CV	COVE	MNR	MANOR	SPGS	SPRINGS
BLVD	BOULEVARD	CY	CANYON	MT	MOUNT	SQ	SQUARE
CEM	CEMETERY	CYN	CANYON	MTN	MOUNTAIN	SRA	SIERRA
CIR	CIRCLE	D	DE	MTWY	MOTORWAY	ST	SAINT
CK	CREEK	DL	DEL	MTY	MOTORWAY	ST	STREET
CL	CALLE	DR	DRIVE	N	NORTH	STA	SANTA
CL DL	CALLE DEL	DS	DOS	PAS	PASEO	STA	STATION
CL D LS	CALLE DE LAS	E	EAST	PAS DE	PASEO DE	TER	TERRACE
	CALLE DE LOS	EST	ESTATE	PAS DL	PASEO DEL	THTR	THEATER
CL EL	CALLE EL	EXPWY	EXPRESSWAY	PAS D LS	PASEO DE LAS	TK TR	TRUCK TRAIL
CLJ	CALLEJON	EXT	EXTENSION		PASEO DE LOS	TR	TRAIL
CL LA	CALLE LA	FRWY	FREEWAY	PGD	PLAYGROUND	VIA D	VIA DE
CL LS	CALLE LAS	FRW	FREEWAY	PK	PARK	VIA D LS	VIA DE LAS
	CALLE LOS	FY	FREEWAY	PK	PEAK		VIA DE LOS
CM	CAMINO	GN	GLEN	PKWY	PARKWAY	VIA DL	VIA DEL
CM D	CAMINO DE	GRDS	GROUNDS	PL	PLACE	VIS	VISTA
CM D LA	CAMINO DE LA	GRN	GREEN	PT	POINT	VLG	VILLAGE
CM D LS	CAMINO DE LAS	GRV	GROVE	PY	PARKWAY	VLY	VALLEY
	CAMINO DE LOS	HTS	HEIGHTS	PZ	PLAZA	VW	VIEW
CMTO	CAMINITO	HWY	HIGHWAY	RCH	RANCH	W	WEST
CN	CANAL	HY	HIGHWAY	RCHO	RANCHO	WK	WALK
COM	COMMON	JCT	JUNCTION	RD	ROAD	WY	WAY
				RDG	RIDGE		

INDEX OF CITIES

INDEX OF COUNTIES

STREETS

A

STREET	CO.	PAGE	GRID
A ST	ALA	45	E2
A ST	DVS	136	C3
A ST	DN	1	D4
A ST	H	146	E2
A ST	SBD	92	A1
A ST	SD	215	D3
A ST	TEH	18	E5
A ST W	H	146	B3
ABBOTT DR	KER	80	B3
ABBOTT RD	LACO	R	D5
ABBOTT ST	MON	54	D4
ABBOTT ST	SAL	171	D4
ABBY ST	FRE	165	D3
ABELIA ST	SBD	92	B3
ABELOR RD	INY	51	C4
ABERDEEN DR	SBD	100	E1
ABERDEEN STA RD	INY	59	E1
ABERNATHY RD	SOL	38	E3
ABERNATHY RD	YUB	26	A4
ABLE RD	COL	32	E2
ABORN RD	SCL	46	C4
ABRAM DR	RCO	100	A5
ACACIA AV	ANA	193	D1
ACACIA AV	STA	47	C3
ACACIA AV	SUT	33	C2
ACACIA ST	SAL	171	A4
ACADEMY AV	FRCO	57	E4
ACAMPO RD	SJCO	40	B4
ACARI RD	KER	78	B3
ACKERMAN LN	HUM	16	B3
ACME RD	SUT	33	B3
ACMITE ST	KER	91	E3
ACOMA TR	SBD	100	D1
ADA RD	KER	78	B3
ADAIR RD	IMP	108	E5
ADAIR RD	STA	47	C2
ADAM FOX FRM RD	HUM	9	E4
ADAMS AV	CM	197	C5
ADAMS AV	EC	217	B2
ADAMS AV	FRCO	56	D4
ADAMS AV	FRCO	57	C4
ADAMS AV	FRCO	58	A4
ADAMS AV	ORA	T	C3
ADAMS AV	SD	214	B4
ADAMS AV	SDCO	V	C4
ADAMS AV	SDCO	111	D1
ADAMS BLVD	LA	184	A4
ADAMS BLVD	LA	185	C4
ADAMS BLVD	LACO	Q	B4
ADAMS DR	KER	79	E1
ADAMS RD	TEH	18	C4
ADAMS ST	IMP	109	A5
ADAMS ST	RCO	99	A2
ADAMS ST	RCO	101	A4
ADDISON RD	BUT	25	C1
ADELAIDA RD	SLO	75	E1
ADELAIDA RD	SLO	76	A1
ADELINE ST	B	156	A4
ADELINE ST	O	157	D2
ADELANTO RD	SBD	91	B3
ADML CALLAHN LN	VAL	134	E3
ADOBE DR	KER	79	E2
ADOBE DR	KER	80	A2
ADOBE PL	MON	65	C4
ADOBE RD	BUT	25	C4
ADOBE RD	COL	25	A5
ADOBE RD	KER	78	D4
ADOBE RD	SBD	101	B1
ADOBE RD	SLO	76	A1
ADOBE RD	SHA	18	D3
ADOBE RD	SON	38	A3
ADOBE RD	TEH	18	D4
ADOBE CREEK RD	LAK	31	D3
ADOBE RANCH RD	MNO	44	A5
ADOHR RD	KER	78	A3
ADOLFO LOPEZ BL	BAJA	112	B4
AERO DR	SD	214	A1
AERO DR	SDCO	V	B3
AERO DR	SDCO	111	D1
AEROPUERTO HWY	BAJA	111	E2
AFTON BLVD	GLE	25	A4
AFTON RD	BUT	25	B5
AFTON CANYON RD	SBD	82	D5
AGATE RD	SBD	91	D1
AGER RD	SIS	4	B3
AGER RD	SIS	5	D2
AGER BESWICK RD	SIS	4	C3
AGGEN RD	VEN	88	C5
AGNES WILSON RD	LPAZ	104	A2
AGNES WILSON RD	RCO	103	E2
AGOURA RD	LACO	96	E1
AGUA CALIENT BL	BAJA	111	E3
AGUA CALIENT RD	SB	87	D4
AQUA CALIENT RD	SON	132	A1
AGUA DULCE CYN	LACO	89	D4
AGUA FRIA RD	MPA	49	A3
AGUAJITO RD	MON	53	E4
AGLAJITO RD	MON	168	D2
AGUA MANSA RD	RCO	99	B2
AGUAS FRIAS RD	BUT	25	B4
AGUEREBERRY PT	INY	71	D1
AHERN RD	SJCO	47	A2
AHLF RD	SUT	33	C2
AINSWORTH PL	RCO	107	A1
AIR BASE PKWY	FRFD	135	C2
AIR BASE PKWY	SOL	38	E3
AIR BASE PKWY	SOL	39	A3
AIR BASE RD	SBD	91	B3
AIRD CIR	BUT	25	E3
AIROLA	CAL	41	B4
AIROSA DR	SBD	90	E3
AIROX RD	SB	86	B1
AIR PARK DR	IMP	108	C2
AIRPORT	SJCO	40	B5
AIRPORT BLVD	KER	80	A5
AIRPORT BLVD	LA	188	D5
AIRPORT BLVD	LA	189	D1
AIRPORT BLVD	LACO	Q	B5
AIRPORT BLVD	RCO	101	A4
AIRPORT BLVD	SAL	171	E5
AIRPORT BLVD	SF	144	C1
AIRPORT BLVD	SJ	151	E2
AIRPORT BLVD	SCR	54	B2
AIRPORT BLVD	SON	37	E1
AIRPORT BLVD S	SSF	144	C2
AIRPORT DR	O	159	D5
AIRPORT RD	ALP	36	C4
AIRPORT RD	HUM	9	E4
AIRPORT RD	KER	78	A4
AIRPORT RD	MEN	22	C5
AIRPORT RD	MEN	30	C1
AIRPORT RD	MOD	8	A1
AIRPORT RD	MOD	14	E1
AIRPORT RD	MNO	50	E2
AIRPORT RD	NAPA	38	C3
AIRPORT RD	O	159	D4
AIRPORT RD	SLO	76	B1
AIRPORT RD	SHA	18	C3
AIRPORT RD	SIS	4	B3
AIRPORT RD	SOL	39	C3

STREET	CO.	PAGE	GRID
AIRPORT RD	TRI	17	D1
AIRPORT WY	SJCO	40	B5
AIRPORT WY	SJCO	47	B2
AIRPORT WY	S	160	E3
AIRWAY DR	KLAM	5	C1
AKER AV	STA	47	D1
AKERS RD	TUL	68	B1
AKINS RD	SIS	5	D2
AKRICH ST	SHA	18	C2
ALABAMA ST	SBD	99	C2
ALAMEDA AV	BUR	179	C5
ALAMEDA AV	LACO	Q	B3
ALAMEDA AV	O	159	B1
ALAMEDA AV	SAL	171	C5
ALAMEDA AV	YOL	39	D2
ALAMEDA ST	LA	186	B4
ALAMEDA ST	LACO	97	E2
ALAMEDA ST	LACO	S	D1
ALAMEDA ST	LACO	S	D2
ALAMEDA ST	MAN	161	C3
ALAMEDA ST	VAL	134	C4
ALAMEDA, THE	SJ	151	C2
ALAMEDA, THE	SJ	152	A4
ALAMEDA, THE	SCLR	151	C2
ALAM D LS PULGS	BLMT	145	A4
ALAM D LS PULGS	SM	145	A4
ALAM D LS PULGS	SMCO	45	D4
ALAMEDA PAD SER	STB	174	C2
ALAMITOS AV	LACO	S	D2
ALAMO DR	MPA	48	D2
ALAMO RD	IMP	109	B5
ALAMO ST	LACO	88	E5
ALAMO ST	SIS	5	A2
ALAMO ST	VEN	88	E5
ALAMO ST	VEN	89	A5
ALAMO CREEK RD	SLO	76	D5
ALAMO PINTADO	SB	86	E3
ALBA RD	SCR	53	E1
ALBAUGH RD	LAS	14	C3
ALBERS RD	STA	47	E2
ALBRT ETTER RCH	HUM	16	A5
ALBERTON AV	BUT	25	A3
ALBION LTL RIV	MEN	30	B1
ALBION RIDGE RD	MEN	30	C1
ALBRIGHT RD	IMP	109	B3
ALCALDE RD	FRCO	66	D3
ALCATRAZ AV	O	156	B4
ALDEN ST	KER	78	E4
ALDER AV	SBD	80	E1
ALDER AV	SBD	99	B1
ALDER ST	PAC	167	B2
ALDER CAMP RD	DN	1	E5
ALDER CAMP RD	DN	9	E1
ALDER CAMP RD	DN	10	A1
ALDER CREEK RD	NEV	27	D5
ALDER CK BCH RD	MEN	30	C3
ALDRCRFT HTS RD	SCL	54	A1
ALDERPOINT RD	HUM	16	C3
ALDER PT BLUFF	TRI	16	D5
ALDER SPGS RD	GLE	23	D3
ALDER SPGS RD	GLE	23	E3
ALDER SPGS RD	GLE	24	A3
ALDERPOINT RD	HUM	16	C3
ALDERWOOD DR	SIS	4	A4
ALDINE DR	SD	214	E4
ALDINE DR	SDCO	V	C4
ALDINE DR	SDCO	111	D1
ALDRIDGE RD	SHA	19	A2
ALEJO DR	RCO	100	C3
ALESSANDRO BLVD	RCO	99	B3
ALEXANDER AV	BUT	33	C1
ALEXANDER AV	SHA	18	C3
ALEXANDER LN	LAS	21	C3
ALEXANDR VLY RD	SON	31	D5
ALFALFA AV	STA	47	C4
ALFRD HARRL HWY	KER	78	D2
ALGERINE RD	TUO	41	C5
ALGODON RD	YUB	33	D3
ALGRN WRDS FRRY	TUO	41	C5
ALGOMAN AV	SBD	91	E3
ALHAMBRA	CC	38	E5
ALHAMBRA AV	M	154	B1
ALHAMBRA BLVD	SCTO	137	E3
ALHAMBRA RD	LACO	R	E3
ALHAMBRA WY	M	154	C3
ALHAMBRA VLY RD	CC	38	D5
ALHAMBRA VLY RD	CC	154	C5
ALHAMBRA VLY RD	M	154	C4
ALICE AV	HUM	16	C5
ALICIA AV	YUB	33	D2
ALICIA PKWY	ORA	98	D5
ALISAL RD	MON	54	D4
ALISAL RD	SB	86	E3
ALISAL ST E	SAL	171	D4
ALISAL ST W	SAL	171	B4
ALISO CANYON RD	LACO	89	E4
ALISO CANYON RD	SB	87	C1
ALISO CANYON RD	VEN	88	B5
ALISO PARK RD	SB	87	C1
ALISOS AV	SB	87	A3
ALISOS CYN RD	SB	86	D2
ALLAN RD	AMA	41	A1
ALLEGHANY RD	YUB	26	C5
ALLEN AV	LACO	R	E3
ALLEN AV	LACO	R	A3
ALLEN AV	MCO	48	C3
ALLEN RD	IMP	108	D3
ALLEN RD	KER	78	C3
ALLEN RD	SJCO	47	C1
ALLENDALE RD	SOL	39	A2
ALLERTON AV	SSF	144	D1
ALLIANCE RD	HUM	9	E5
ALLIANCE RD	HUM	10	A5
ALLISON RCH RD	NEV	34	C2
ALLUVIAL AV	FRCO	57	C3
ALMA AV	KER	79	D5
ALMA ST	PA	147	A2
ALMA ST	SJ	152	C5
ALMA ST	SCL	45	D4
ALMADEN AV	SJ	152	B4
ALMADEN BLVD	SJ	152	B4
ALMADEN EXPWY	SCL	46	B5
ALMANOR DR W	PLU	20	B4
ALMER RD	COL	32	D2
ALMOND AV	CLO	32	E3
ALMOND AV	MCO	48	A4
ALMOND AV	STA	47	C3
ALMOND DR	MCO	55	D2
ALMOND DR	MCO	56	A2
ALMOND DR	SLO	76	B2
ALMOND RD	KER	77	B1
ALMND ORCHRD RD	SUT	33	B1
ALMONDWOOD DR	SJCO	47	B2
ALMONTE BLVD	MAR	140	B4
ALOHA ST	TEH	18	D5
ALONA ST	KER	80	A4
ALONDRA	LACO	97	E3
ALONDRA BLVD	LACO	98	A3
ALOSTA AV	LACO	98	C1
ALOSTA AV	LACO	U	D3
ALPHA RD	NEV	26	E5

STREET	CO.	PAGE	GRID
ALPINE AV	FRCO	56	D4
ALPINE AV	SJCO	40	A5
ALPINE AV	S	160	A3
ALPINE BLVD	SDCO	107	A5
ALPINE RD	MOD	7	C5
ALPINE RD	MOD	8	C1
ALPINE RD	SJCO	40	B4
ALPINE RD	SMCO	45	D4
ALPINE MINE RD	ALP	36	A5
ALPS DR	KER	79	C5
ALT CT	RCO	107	C1
ALTA	FRCO	58	A4
ALTA ST	MON	54	E5
ALTA ST	NEV	34	C1
ALTA BONNY NOOK	PLA	34	D1
ALTADENA DR	LACO	98	A1
ALTADENA DR	LACO	R	B2
ALTA SIERRA DR	NEV	34	C2
AL TAHOE BLVD	SLT	129	A4
ALTAIR AV	SDCO	V	C3
ALTAIR AV	SDCO	106	D5
ALTA LOMA DR	SBD	100	E1
ALTA MESA DR	SHA	18	C2
ALTA MESA RD	SAC	40	B2
ALTAMONT PSS RD	ALA	46	C2
ALTA VISTA	AVLN	105	A4
ALTA VISTA	BKD	166	E2
ALTA VISTA DR	KER	78	D3
ALTHEA AV	FRCO	56	A2
ALTON AV	SA	197	D3
ALTUS AV	KER	80	B5
ALUM ROCK AV	SCL	46	B4
ALVARADO BLVD	ALA	45	E3
ALVARADO RD	MON	65	D4
ALVARADO RD	STA	47	E2
ALVARADO ST	LA	185	C3
ALVARADO ST	LACO	Q	C4
ALVARADO ST	SDCO	106	C2
ALVARADO TR	MCO	55	D2
ALVARADO-NILES	ALA	45	E3
ALVES RD	MCO	48	A3
ALVIN AV	SMA	173	B2
ALVIN DR E	SAL	171	D1
ALVIN DR W	SAL	171	C1
ALVISO-MLPTS RD	SCL	46	A4
ALVORD MTN RD	SBD	82	C5
ALWARD RD	SHA	19	B3
AMADOR AV	FRCO	56	D5
AMADOR ST	FRE	165	B4
AMADOR ST	VAL	134	D4
AMADOR CREEK RD	AMA	40	E2
AMAR RD	LACO	98	B2
AMAR RD	LACO	R	C4
AMARGOSA RD	SBD	91	B3
AMARGOSA ST	SBD	92	C2
AMBOY RD	SBD	93	D4
AMBOY RD	SBD	101	C1
AMBOY RD	SBD	101	E1
AMBROSE DR	SAL	171	A4
AMBOY CUTOFF	SBD	93	E3
AMEDEE RD	LAS	21	D4
AMELIA AV	LACO	U	D3
AMEN LN	TEH	18	C3
AMERICAN AV	FRCO	57	A4
AMERICAN AV	FRCO	58	B4
AMERICAN AV	MCO	47	D4
AMERICAN AV	STA	47	C2
AMERICAN CYN RD	NAPA	38	D4
AMERICN FLAT RD	AMA	40	E2
AMRICAN FLT SDE	AMA	40	E1
AMERICN GIRL MN	IMP	110	B5
AMERICN MINE RD	SHA	18	A1
AMERIGO	SJCO	40	C5
AMES ST	ALA	46	C2
AMESTI RD	SCR	54	B2
AMOROSE ST	RCO	99	B4
AMOUR RD	SUT	33	C4
AMSTERDAM RD	MCO	48	B3
ANAHEIM BLVD	ANA	193	C1
ANAHEIM BLVD	ORA	98	C3
ANAHEIM BLVD	ORA	T	C2
ANAHEIM ST	LB	192	D2
ANAHEIM ST	LA	191	A1
ANAHEIM ST	LA	192	D2
ANAHEIM ST	LACO	97	D4
ANAHEIM ST	LACO	S	C2
ANAPAMU ST	STB	174	C3
ANCHO ERIE MINE	NEV	26	E5
ANCHO MINE RD	NEV	26	E5
ANCHOR	FRCO	58	B4
ANDERHOLT RD	IMP	112	B4
ANDERSON DR W	SHA	18	C3
ANDERSON LN	HUM	15	E2
ANDERSON RD	DVS	136	B3
ANDERSON RD	SLO	76	A1
ANDERSON RD	SOL	39	C4
ANDERSON RD	STA	47	C4
ANDERSON RD	TUL	68	C2
ANDERSON ST	SBD	99	C2
ANDERSON CK RD	JKSN	3	D1
ANDERSON GRADE	SIS	4	A4
ANDERSON RCH RD	LAS	14	D4
ANDERSON VLY WY	MEN	30	E3
ANDESITE RD	SIS	4	D5
ANDESITE RD	SIS	12	D1
ANDESITE LOG RD	SIS	12	D1
ANDRADE RD	ALA	46	B3
ANDRE RD	IMP	109	A4
ANDRESSEN RD	PLA	33	E3
ANDREW AV	SB	86	C1
ANDREWS RD	LAS	14	C3
ANDREWS RD	SIS	4	E3
ANGELES CRST HY	LACO	R	D1
ANGELES FRST HY	LACO	90	A4
ANGELES FRST HY	LACO	R	D1
ANITA RD	BUT	25	A2
ANNADALE AV	FRCO	57	B4
ANNADALE AV	FRCO	58	A3
ANNAPOLIS RD	SON	30	E5
ANNAPOLIS RD	SON	31	A5
ANNETTE RD	KER	76	E1
ANNIN AV	KER	78	B1
ANTELOPE DR	LAS	8	B4
ANTELOPE HWY	LACO	90	D4
ANTELOPE RD	MNO	42	E1
ANTELOPE RD	MNO	43	A1
ANTELOPE RD	RCO	99	C4
ANTELOPE RD	SAC	34	A5
ANTELOPE RD	SLO	66	E5
ANTELOPE SPGS	MNO	50	E2
ANTELOPE VLY FY	LACO	89	E2
ANTELOPE VLY RD	SIE	27	C3
ANTHONY RD	LACO	89	D4
ANTOLA RD	LAS	21	C3
ANZA RD	IMP	112	A4
ANZA RD	RCO	106	D1
ANZAR RD	SBT	54	D2
ANZA TRAIL RD	IMP	111	C4
APACHE TR	RCO	100	B3
APACHE CYN RD	VEN	88	A2
APPALOOSA RD	CAL	41	A4

STREET	CO.	PAGE	GRID
APPIAN WY	CC	38	C5
APPLE AV	STA	47	C3
APPLE RD	TEH	24	C2
APPLE CANYON RD	RCO	100	C4
APPLE COLONY RD	TUO	41	D5
APPLEGATE RD	MCO	48	B4
APPLE RANCH RD	TUO	41	E4
APPLE SEED LN	RCO	100	A5
APPLE VALLEY RD	SBD	91	C3
APPLEWHITE	SBD	91	A5
APRICOT AV	STA	47	C3
APRIL LN	VEN	88	C4
AQUEDUCT RD	KER	79	E5
AQUEDUCT RD	KER	80	A5
AQUEDUCT RD	SBD	103	A2
AQUEDUCT RD	SBD	104	A1
ARAMAYO WY	TEH	24	E1
ARASTRADERO RD	PA	147	E5
ARATA LN	SON	37	E1
ARBINI RD	STA	47	E1
ARBOGA RD	YUB	33	D2
ARBOLEDA DR	MCO	48	C5
ARBOR AV	BLMT	145	B5
ARBOR RD	SLO	76	A1
ARBOR WY	MCO	56	C1
ARBORETUM RD	PA	147	A3
ARBOR VITAE ST	ING	189	D1
ARBOR VITAE ST	LA	189	D1
ARBOR VITAE ST	LACO	Q	B5
ARBURUA RD	MCO	55	D2
ARC RD	INY	51	D5
ARCH RD	SJCO	40	B5
ARCH AIRPORT RD	SJCO	40	B5
ARCHER AV	SUT	33	C1
ARCHER RD	SHA	18	B3
ARCHERDALE RD	SJCO	40	C5
ARCHIBALD AV	RCO	98	E3
ARCHIE BROWN RD	SHA	13	D4
ARDATH RD	SD	211	B3
ARDATH RD	SDCO	V	A3
ARDATH RD	SDCO	106	C5
ARDEN DR	LACO	R	B3
ARDEN WY	SAC	40	A1
ARENA WY	MCO	48	A4
ARGO ST	KER	80	D1
ARGONAUT RD	LAK	31	D3
ARGONNE DR	S	160	B4
ARGUELLO BL	SF	141	D2
ARGYLE RD	MON	65	B3
ARLINGTON AV	LA	184	E5
ARLINGTON AV	LACO	Q	C5
ARLINGTON AV	LACO	S	C2
ARLINGTON AV	RIV	205	A5
ARLINGTON AV	RCO	99	A2
ARLINGTON AV S	RENO	130	A5
ARLINGTON RD	PLU	20	D5
ARLINGTON MN RD	RCO	103	B3
ARMORY RD	BARS	208	B3
ARMOUR RD	SUT	33	C4
ARMOUR RANCH RD	SB	86	E3
ARMOUR RANCH RD	SB	87	A3
ARMSTRONG	SJCO	40	A4
ARMSTRONG AV	FRCO	57	D2
ARMSTRONG AV	FRCO	57	D3
ARMSTRONG RD	CAL	41	C3
ARMSTRONG RD	LAS	14	D3
ARMSTRONG RD	RCO	99	A2
ARMSTRONG RD	STA	47	C4
ARMSTRONG RD	YUB	33	D1
ARMSTRNG WDS RD	SON	37	C1
ARMY RD	RCO	110	B1
ARMY ST	SFCO	45	C2
ARNO RD	SAC	40	A3
ARNOLD RD	IMP	112	C5
ARNOLD DR	SON	132	A3
ARNOLD DR	SON	38	B3
ARNOLD WY	SDCO	107	B5
AROSA RD	KER	79	C4
ARQUES AV	SVL	148	E5
ARRECHE RD	MOD	7	D5
ARRELLAGA ST	STB	174	B3
ARROW HWY	CLA	203	C2
ARROW HWY	LACO	98	B1
ARROW HWY	LACO	U	D3
ARROW HWY	MTCL	203	C2
ARROW HWY	ROC	204	A2
ARROW HWY	SBD	98	E1
ARROW HWY	UPL	204	A2
ARROW ROUTE	SBD	203	B2
ARROWHEAD AV	SBDO	207	D4
ARROWHEAD BLVD	RCO	103	D5
ARROWHEAD BLVD	RCO	110	D1
ARROWHEAD RD	LAK	32	A3
ARROWHEAD ST	CAL	41	A5
ARROWHEAD TR	SBD	82	E4
ARROWHEAD TR	SBD	83	A4
ARROWHEAD LK RD	SBD	91	C5
ARROYA AV	MCO	56	A1
ARROYO AV	KER	79	E5
ARROYO AV	KER	80	A5
ARROYO BLVD	LACO	R	D3
ARROYO BLVD	PAS	190	A4
ARROYO PKWY	PAS	190	C5
ARROYO RD	ALA	46	C2
ARROYO RD	SBD	92	A4
ARROYO BURRO RD	SB	87	C4
ARROYO GR GUADL	SLO	76	B5
ARROYO GR GUADL	SLO	86	A1
AROYO GR HUASNA	SLO	76	D4
ARROYO SECO RD	MON	64	E2
ARROYO SECO RD	MON	65	A1
ARTESIA AV	SB	86	B3
ARTESIA BLVD	LACO	97	D3
ARTESIA BLVD	LACO	98	A3
ARTESIA BLVD	LACO	S	B1
ARTESIA FRWY	LACO	98	A3
ARTESIA FRWY	LACO	S	D1
ARTESIA FRWY	LACO	T	A1
ARTHUR	SJCO	47	C1
ARTHUR ST	RCO	101	C5
ARTICHOKE RD	SMCO	45	C5
ARTIC MINE RD	NEV	26	E5
ARTISTS DR	INY	72	A1
ASH AV	SHA	13	C5
ASH AV	STA	47	C3
ASH ST	SD	215	D3
ASH ST	SDCO	107	A4
ASHBY AV	B	156	B3
ASHBY RD	SHA	18	C2
ASH CREEK RD	INY	60	B5
ASH CREEK RD	SHA	18	E3
ASH CREEK RD	SHA	18	D3
ASH CREEK RD	SIS	4	A3
ASH CK SINK RD	SIS	13	A2
ASHE RD	KER	78	D4
ASHLAN AV	FRCO	56	C3
ASHLAN AV	FRCO	57	A5
ASHLEY LN	SJCO	40	B4
ASH VALLEY RD	LAS	14	D3
ASH VALLEY RD	LAS	8	A3
ASHWORTH RD	MPA	49	B3

STREET	CO.	PAGE	GRID
ASILOMAR AV	PAC	167	A2
ASPEN VALLEY RD	TUO	49	C1
ASPEN VALLEY RD	TUO	63	A4
ASSOCIATED RD	SB	86	B1
ASSOCIATED RD	SIS	4	E3
ASSOCIATED RD	SIS	5	A3
ASTER RD	SBD	91	A3
ASTORIA AV	KER	89	C1
ATEN RD	IMP	109	A5
ATHEL ST	KER	80	C1
ATHERTON BLVD	MAR	38	B4
ATHERTON ST	LACO	S	E2
ATHERTON ST	LACO	T	A2
ATHLONE RD	MCO	48	D5
ATKINS RD	SJCO	40	C4
ATLANTIC AV	A	157	D5
ATLANTIC AV	FRFD	135	C1
ATLANTIC AV	LB	192	E2
ATLANTIC AV	LACO	97	E3
ATLANTIC AV	LACO	S	D1
ATLANTIC AV E	FRFD	135	D1
ATLANTIC BLVD	LACO	98	A2
ATLANTIC BLVD	LACO	R	E4
ATLANTIC BLVD	LACO	S	D2
ATLAS	CC	38	C5
ATLAS PEAK RD	NAPA	38	D2
ATTERBERRY CT	KER	79	E2
ATTILA RD	SBD	84	C4
ATWATER	MCO	47	E4
ATWELL AV	TUL	67	E4
ATWELL AV	TUL	68	A4
ATWOOD	PLA	34	C3
AUBERRY RD	FRCO	57	E1
AUBERRY RD	FRCO	58	A1
AUBERRY RD	MAD	49	E5
AUBREY AV	MCO	56	A2
AUBURN BLVD	SAC	34	A5
AUBURN BLVD	SAC	34	A5
AUBURN RD	NEV	34	C2
AUBURN RD	PLA	34	B3
AUBURN FRST HLL	PLA	34	D3
AUBURN RAVNE RD	AUB	126	C3
AUBURN RAVNE RD	PLA	126	C3
AUCTION SNIVELY	TEH	18	D4
AUDUBON DR	FRCO	57	C2
AUGUST AV	MCO	47	D4
AUGUST RD	STA	47	D4
AUGUSTINE RD	RCO	109	C1
AUKLET RD	SBD	92	C1
AULD RD	RCO	99	D5
AURORA CYN RD	MNO	43	B3
AURORA ST	S	160	E5
AUSTIN RD	IMP	109	A5
AUSTIN RD	SJCO	40	B5
AUSTIN RD	SJCO	47	B1
AUSTIN CREEK RD	SON	37	C2
AUSTIN MDWS RD	NEV	27	A4
AUSTRIAN RD	CAL	41	B4
AUTOPSTA TIJ-EN	BAJA	111	D3
AVALON AV	SBD	100	E1
AVALON BLVD	LA	191	C1
AVALON BLVD	LACO	97	E3
AVALON BLVD	LACO	S	C1
AVALON CYN RD	AVLN	105	A5
AVENA	SJCO	47	C1
AVENAL CUTOFF	KIN	67	A3
AVD BERMUDAS	RCO	100	E4
AVD DEL CAPITAN	SB	87	A4
AVD D LS ARBLES	VEN	96	D1
AVD D LS ARBOLS	VEN	88	D5
AVD DL PRESIDNT	ORA	105	E1
AVENIDA DEL SOL	KER	80	C1
AVENIDA ENCINO	RCO	100	D5
AVD LA CUMBRE	RCO	100	D5
AVD LOS FELIZ	RCO	100	D5
AVENIDA OBREGON	RCO	100	E4
AVENUE A	KER	89	E1
AVENUE A	YUMA	112	D5
AVENUE B	LACO	89	D2
AVENUE B	LACO	90	C2
AVENUE C	LACO	89	D2
AVENUE C	LACO	90	D2
AVENUE C	YUMA	112	C5
AVENUE D	LACO	90	B2
AVENUE E	LACO	89	E2
AVENUE E	LACO	90	A2
AVENUE E	RCO	99	B3
AVENUE E	YUMA	112	C5
AVENUE E-8	LACO	90	B2
AVENUE E-8	LACO	90	C2
AVENUE F	LACO	89	B2
AVENUE F	LACO	89	D2
AVENUE F	LACO	90	C2
AVENUE F	SBD	99	D2
AVENUE F-4	LACO	89	E2
AVENUE F-4	LACO	90	A2
AVENUE F-8	LACO	90	D2
AVENUE F-8	LACO	89	C2
AVENUE G	LACO	89	E2
AVENUE G-2	LACO	90	C2
AVENUE G-3	LACO	90	C2
AVENUE G-4	LACO	90	C2
AVENUE G-6	LACO	90	C2
AVENUE G-8	LACO	90	B2
AVENUE H	LACO	89	E2
AVENUE I	LACO	89	E2
AVENUE J	LACO	89	E3
AVENUE J	LACO	90	C2
AVENUE J-8	LACO	90	A2
AVENUE K	LACO	89	E3
AVENUE K	LACO	90	C3
AVENUE K-8	LACO	89	D3
AVENUE L	LACO	89	E3
AVENUE L	LACO	90	B3
AVENUE L	RCO	99	D2
AVENUE M	LACO	89	E3
AVENUE M	LACO	90	B3
AVENUE M-8	LACO	89	E3
AVENUE N	LACO	89	E3
AVENUE N	LACO	90	C3
AVENUE O	LACO	90	A3
AVENUE P	LACO	89	E3
AVENUE P	LACO	90	A3
AVENUE P	LACO	90	D3
AVENUE P-8	LACO	90	A3
AVENUE P-8	LACO	90	C3
AVENUE Q	LACO	90	C3
AVENUE Q	LACO	90	C3
AVENUE R-8	LACO	90	D3
AVENUE S	LACO	89	E3
AVENUE S	LACO	90	A3
AVENUE SAN LUIS	LA	177	B4
AVENUE STANFORD	LACO	89	B4
AVENUE T	LACO	90	B3
AVENUE T	LACO	90	C3
AVENUE TWO	MCO	48	B4
AVENUE U	LACO	90	C3
AVENUE Z	LACO	90	D4
AVENUE ONE	MCO	48	B4
AVENUE 2	TUL	68	D5
AVENUE 4 1/2	MAD	56	E3

STREETS

220
AVENUE 5 — STREET INDEX — BENITO JUAREZ BLVD

STREET	CO.	PAGE	GRID
AVENUE 5	MAD	56	E3
AVENUE 5 1/2	MAD	56	E3
AVENUE 5 1/2	MAD	57	A3
AVENUE 6	MAD	56	E3
AVENUE 6	MAD	57	A3
AVENUE 6 1/2	MAD	57	A3
AVENUE 7 1/2	MAD	56	D3
AVENUE 7 1/2	MAD	56	E3
AVENUE 7 1/2	MAD	57	C3
AVENUE 8	MAD	56	E3
AVENUE 8	MAD	57	A2
AVENUE 8	MAD	57	C2
AVENUE 8	TUL	68	B5
AVENUE 8 1/2	MAD	57	A2
AVENUE 9	MAD	56	E2
AVENUE 9	MAD	57	C2
AVENUE 9 1/2	MAD	56	E2
AVENUE 10	MAD	56	E2
AVENUE 10	MAD	57	B2
AVENUE 10 1/2	MAD	56	E2
AVENUE 10 1/2	MAD	57	A2
AVENUE 11	MAD	56	E2
AVENUE 11	MAD	57	A2
AVENUE 11 1/2	MAD	56	E2
AVENUE 11 1/2	MAD	57	A2
AVENUE 12	MAD	56	E2
AVENUE 12	MAD	57	B2
AVENUE 12	TUL	68	B5
AVENUE 12	TUL	68	C5
AVENUE 12 1/2	MAD	57	B2
AVENUE 13	MAD	56	E2
AVENUE 13 1/2	MAD	56	E2
AVENUE 13 1/2	MAD	57	A2
AVENUE 14	MAD	56	D2
AVENUE 14	MAD	57	C2
AVENUE 14 1/2	MAD	56	E2
AVENUE 14 1/2	MAD	57	A2
AVENUE 14 1/2	MAD	57	C2
AVENUE 15	MAD	56	E2
AVENUE 15 1/2	MAD	56	E2
AVENUE 15 1/2	MAD	57	B2
AVENUE 16	MAD	56	E2
AVENUE 16	TUL	68	B4
AVENUE 16	TUL	68	C4
AVENUE 16 1/2	MAD	56	E2
AVENUE 17	MAD	56	D2
AVENUE 17 1/2	MAD	56	D2
AVENUE 18	MAD	56	D2
AVENUE 18 1/2	MAD	56	D2
AVENUE 19	MAD	56	D1
AVENUE 19 1/2	MAD	56	D1
AVENUE 20	LA	186	D2
AVENUE 20	MAD	56	D1
AVENUE 20 1/2	MAD	56	D1
AVENUE 21	MAD	56	D1
AVENUE 21	MAD	57	A1
AVENUE 21 1/2	MAD	56	D1
AVENUE 22	MAD	56	D1
AVENUE 22 1/2	MAD	56	D1
AVENUE 23 1/2	MAD	56	D1
AVENUE 24	MAD	56	D1
AVENUE 24	TUL	68	B4
AVENUE 24 1/2	MAD	56	E1
AVENUE 25	MAD	56	D1
AVENUE 25 1/2	MAD	56	D1
AVENUE 26	MAD	56	D1
AVENUE 26 1/2	MAD	56	E1
AVENUE 27	MAD	48	D5
AVENUE 27 1/2	MAD	48	E5
AVENUE 28	MAD	48	E5
AVENUE 28	TUL	68	C4
AVENUE 32	TUL	68	B4
AVENUE 40	TUL	68	C4
AVENUE 42	TUL	67	E4
AVENUE 42	TUL	68	C4
AVENUE 42	TUL	68	A4
AVENUE 44	TUL	68	B4
AVENUE 46	TUL	67	E4
AVENUE 46	TUL	68	C4
AVENUE 50	TUL	67	E4
AVENUE 52	TUL	68	B4
AVENUE 52	TUL	68	C4
AVENUE 54	TUL	67	E4
AVENUE 56	TUL	68	B4
AVENUE 58	TUL	68	A4
AVENUE 62	TUL	68	A4
AVENUE 64	TUL	68	D4
AVENUE 66	TUL	68	D4
AVENUE 68	TUL	68	A4
AVENUE 68	TUL	68	D4
AVENUE 70	TUL	68	D4
AVENUE 74	TUL	68	D4
AVENUE 76	TUL	68	D4
AVENUE 78	TUL	68	D4
AVENUE 80	TUL	68	B4
AVENUE 80	TUL	68	C4
AVENUE 84	TUL	68	A4
AVENUE 86	TUL	68	D4
AVENUE 88	TUL	67	E4
AVENUE 88	TUL	68	A4
AVENUE 88	TUL	68	D4
AVENUE 90	TUL	68	D4
AVENUE 92	TUL	68	D4
AVENUE 94	TUL	68	D4
AVENUE 95	TUL	68	C4
AVENUE 96	TUL	68	D4
AVENUE 100	TUL	68	D3
AVENUE 102	TUL	68	D3
AVENUE 104	TUL	67	E3
AVENUE 104	TUL	68	C3
AVENUE 108	TUL	68	A3
AVENUE 108	TUL	68	D3
AVENUE 112	TUL	67	E3
AVENUE 112	TUL	68	D3
AVENUE 116	TUL	68	B3
AVENUE 116	TUL	68	D3
AVENUE 120	TUL	67	E3
AVENUE 120	TUL	68	D3
AVENUE 124	TUL	68	C3
AVENUE 128	TUL	67	E3
AVENUE 128	TUL	68	C3
AVENUE 132	TUL	68	C3
AVENUE 136	TUL	67	E3
AVENUE 136	TUL	68	C3
AVENUE 138	TUL	68	E3
AVENUE 144	TUL	68	A3
AVENUE 152	TUL	68	B3
AVENUE 152	TUL	68	C3
AVENUE 156	TUL	68	D3
AVENUE 160	TUL	68	A3
AVENUE 160	TUL	68	D3
AVENUE 164	TUL	68	B3
AVENUE 168	TUL	68	A3
AVENUE 168	TUL	68	C3
AVENUE 169	TUL	68	D3
AVENUE 172	TUL	68	C3
AVENUE 176	TUL	68	A3
AVENUE 176	TUL	68	C3
AVENUE 178	TUL	68	D3
AVENUE 180	TUL	68	B3
AVENUE 182	TUL	68	D3

STREET	CO.	PAGE	GRID
AVENUE 184	TUL	68	C2
AVENUE 188	TUL	68	D2
AVENUE 190	TUL	68	A2
AVENUE 192	TUL	68	A2
AVENUE 192	TUL	68	B2
AVENUE 196	TUL	68	B2
AVENUE 196	TUL	68	D2
AVENUE 198	TUL	68	A2
AVENUE 199	TUL	67	E2
AVENUE 200	TUL	68	A2
AVENUE 200	TUL	68	C2
AVENUE 204	TUL	67	E2
AVENUE 204	TUL	68	A2
AVENUE 204	TUL	68	C2
AVENUE 204	TUL	68	C4
AVENUE 206	TUL	68	D2
AVENUE 208	TUL	67	E2
AVENUE 208	TUL	68	A2
AVENUE 208	TUL	68	C2
AVENUE 212	TUL	68	B2
AVENUE 212	TUL	68	D2
AVENUE 216	TUL	68	A2
AVENUE 216	TUL	68	D2
AVENUE 222	TUL	68	D2
AVENUE 224	TUL	68	B2
AVENUE 226	TUL	68	D2
AVENUE 228	TUL	68	B2
AVENUE 232	TUL	68	D2
AVENUE 236	TUL	68	A2
AVENUE 236	TUL	68	D2
AVENUE 240	TUL	68	A2
AVENUE 244	TUL	68	A2
AVENUE 248	TUL	68	A2
AVENUE 252	TUL	68	A2
AVENUE 256	TUL	67	E2
AVENUE 260	TUL	68	A2
AVENUE 264	TUL	68	B2
AVENUE 268	TUL	68	A2
AVENUE 271	TUL	68	B1
AVENUE 272	TUL	68	A1
AVENUE 272	TUL	68	D1
AVENUE 276	TUL	68	C1
AVENUE 280	TUL	68	A1
AVENUE 300	TUL	68	C1
AVENUE 304	TUL	68	A1
AVENUE 306	TUL	68	D1
AVENUE 308	TUL	68	A1
AVENUE 312	TUL	68	D1
AVENUE 318	TUL	68	C1
AVENUE 320	TUL	68	A1
AVENUE 320	TUL	68	D1
AVENUE 324	TUL	68	C1
AVENUE 328	TUL	68	A1
AVENUE 328	TUL	68	C1
AVENUE 332	TUL	68	C1
AVENUE 332	TUL	58	C5
AVENUE 334	TUL	58	D5
AVENUE 334	TUL	68	D1
AVENUE 336	TUL	68	B1
AVENUE 336	TUL	58	C5
AVENUE 337	TUL	68	C1
AVENUE 340	TUL	68	B1
AVENUE 340	TUL	58	C5
AVENUE 344	TUL	68	B1
AVENUE 344	TUL	58	C5
AVENUE 346	TUL	68	D1
AVENUE 348	TUL	68	C1
AVENUE 350	TUL	58	D5
AVENUE 352	TUL	57	E5
AVENUE 352	TUL	58	C5
AVENUE 356	TUL	58	B5
AVENUE 356	TUL	58	C5
AVENUE 360	TUL	57	E5
AVENUE 360	TUL	58	C5
AVENUE 364	TUL	58	C5
AVENUE 368	TUL	58	B5
AVENUE 368	TUL	58	C5
AVENUE 376	TUL	57	E5
AVENUE 376	TUL	58	C5
AVENUE 380	TUL	58	C5
AVENUE 384	TUL	58	A5
AVENUE 386	TUL	58	C5
AVENUE 388	TUL	58	C5
AVENUE 390	TUL	57	E5
AVENUE 390	TUL	58	C5
AVENUE 392	TUL	58	A5
AVENUE 394	TUL	58	C5
AVENUE 396	TUL	57	E5
AVENUE 396	TUL	58	A5
AVENUE 398	TUL	58	C5
AVENUE 400	TUL	58	B5
AVENUE 404	TUL	58	B5
AVENUE 404	TUL	58	C5
AVENUE 408	TUL	57	E5
AVENUE 408	TUL	58	B5
AVENUE 410	TUL	57	E5
AVENUE 416	TUL	58	C5
AVENUE 424	TUL	58	A4
AVENUE 428	TUL	58	B4
AVENUE 432	TUL	58	B4
AVENUE 436	TUL	58	B4
AVENUE 438	TUL	58	B4
AVENUE 440	TUL	58	B4
AVENUE 444	TUL	58	B4
AVENUE 448	TUL	58	B4
AVENUE 450	TUL	58	B4
AVENUE 452	TUL	58	B4
AVENUE 456	TUL	58	B4
AVENUE 460	TUL	58	B4
AVENUE 464	TUL	58	B4
AVENUE 468	TUL	58	B4
AVENUE 472	TUL	58	B4
AVERY RD	FRCO	55	E3
AVERY RD	MCO	55	D3
AVERY SHEEP RCH	CAL	41	C3
AVIATION BLVD	ELS	189	E3
AVIATION BLVD	HAW	189	E3
AVIATION BLVD	ING	189	E3
AVIATION BLVD	LA	188	E5
AVIATION BLVD	LA	189	E3
AVIATION BLVD	LACO	97	D3
AVIATION BLVD	LACO	S	B1
AVIATION BLVD	RB	189	E3
AVOCADO BLVD	SDCO	V	D4
AVOCADO BLVD	SDCO	111	E1
AVOCADO RD	BUT	25	E5
AYERS AV	SJCO	47	C1
AYRES HOLMES RD	PLA	34	B3
AZALEA TR	RCO	100	B3
AZEVEDO	MCO	47	D5
AZEVEDO RD	SOL	39	C4
AZEVEDO RD	STA	47	C4
AZTEC AV	RCO	102	C4
AZUSA AV	LACO	98	B2
AZUSA AV	LACO	R	C4
AZUSA CANYON RD	LACO	R	C3
B			
B ST	BUT	25	C5
B ST	DVS	136	C3
B ST	FRE	165	C4
B ST	H	146	E2

STREET	CO.	PAGE	GRID
B ST	IMP	109	A4
B ST	KER	68	B5
B ST	LA	191	B1
B ST	LACO	97	E4
B ST	LACO	98	C2
B ST	LACO	S	C2
B ST	SCTO	137	C2
B ST	SD	215	D3
B ST	SJCO	40	B5
B ST	YUBA	125	D3
B ST	YUB	33	D2
B ST N	SCTO	137	B2
BABCOCK RD	LAS	14	B4
BABCOCK CNDR RD	LAS	14	B4
BABEL SLOUGH RD	YOL	39	D2
BACHELOR VLY RD	LAK	31	C2
BACK BONE RD	NEV	26	D5
BACKBONE RD	SHA	13	A5
BACKBONE RD	SHA	18	E1
BACKES LN	KER	79	C4
BACKUS RD	KER	79	E5
BACON RD	STA	47	B2
BACON ST	SDCO	V	A4
BACON ST	SDCO	111	C1
BACON ISLAND	SJCO	39	E5
BADDAGE RD	RCO	107	B1
BADENOUGH CY RD	SIE	27	D3
BADGER RD	SON	37	E2
BADGER RD	SON	38	A2
BADGER FLAT	MCO	55	D1
BAGDAD HWY	SBD	93	C4
BAGDAD HWY	SBD	101	C1
BAGDAD WY	SBD	93	D4
BAGDAD CHASE RD	SBD	93	B2
BAGGTT MARYSVLL	BUT	25	D5
BAILEY AV	KER	70	A5
BAILEY AV	MCO	48	B4
BAILEY AV	SB	86	B3
BAILEY RD	COL	32	E3
BAILEY RD	CC	39	A5
BAILEY RD	DN	1	E3
BAILEY RD	IMP	110	D5
BAILEY RD	RCO	107	B1
BAILEY RD	SBD	84	A2
BAILEY RD	SCL	46	C5
BAILEY RD	SUT	33	C3
BAILEY FLATS RD	MAD	49	B5
BAILEY HILL RD	SIS	4	A2
BAILY RD	KER	79	B4
BAILY RIDGE RD	CAL	41	C2
BAIN ST	RCO	99	A2
BAIR RD	HUM	10	B4
BAIRD RD	SON	38	A2
BAKER AV	ONT	204	E3
BAKER AV	ORA	T	C3
BAKER AV	ROC	204	E3
BAKER RD	COL	32	C2
BAKER RD	MCO	55	E1
BAKER RD	PLCV	138	B2
BAKER RD	SJCO	40	B4
BAKER RD	STA	47	C3
BAKER RD	TEH	18	D5
BAKER RD	SUT	33	C4
BAKER RD	YUB	26	B5
BAKER ST	CM	197	B4
BAKER ST	CM	198	A4
BAKER CREEK RD	INY	51	D5
BAKER RCH SODA	PLA	34	E2
BAKER RCH SODA	PLA	35	B2
BAKER RILEY WY	CAL	41	B3
BKRSFLD-GLNVLLE	KER	68	E5
BKRSFLD-GLNVLLE	KER	69	A5
BKRSFLD-GLNVLLE	KER	78	D2
BAKRSFLD-MCKITT	KER	78	A3
BALBOA AV	SD	211	E5
BALBOA AV	SD	212	C1
BALBOA AV	SDCO	V	B3
BALBOA AV	SDCO	106	C5
BALBOA BLVD	LACO	97	C1
BALBOA BLVD	NB	199	B5
BALBOA BLVD	ORA	T	C4
BALCH PARK RD	TUL	69	A2
BALCOM CYN RD	VEN	88	D5
BALDERSTON	ED	34	E3
BALD HILL RD	PLA	34	C3
BALD HILLS RD	DN	1	E4
BALD HILLS RD	DN	2	A4
BALD HILLS RD	HUM	10	A2
BALD MOUNTAIN N	CAL	41	C2
BALD MTN RD	CAL	41	B2
BALD MTN RD	HUM	10	B5
BALD MTN RD	MEN	23	A2
BALD MTN RD	MNO	50	D1
BALD MTN RD	MNO	50	E1
BALD MTN RD	SHA	13	E4
BALD MTN RD	YUB	33	E1
BALD MTN LKOUT	SIS	3	D4
BALD MT SPGS RD	MNO	50	E1
BALD ROCK RD	BUT	25	E3
BALDWIN AV	LACO	R	B3
BALDWIN RD	STA	47	B2
BALDWIN RD	STA	47	B3
BALDWIN RD	VEN	88	A4
BALDWIN ST	CAL	40	D4
BALDWIN PARK BL	LACO	R	B4
BALDY RD	SBD	90	E5
BALDY MCCULY RD	SHA	13	E4
BALDY MESA RD	SBD	91	A4
BALE LN	NAPA	29	B2
BALFOUR RD	CC	39	C5
BALIS BELL RD	TEH	18	B5
BALL RD	ANA	193	A3
BALL RD	ANA	194	A3
BALL RD	ORA	98	B3
BALL RD	ORA	T	B2
BALL RD	TEH	17	E4
BALL MT LTL SHA	SIS	4	B3
BALL MT LTL SHA	SIS	5	A4
BALL MTN LKOUT	SIS	4	D3
BALL ROCK RD	TEH	23	E1
BALLANTREE LN	NEV	34	B2
BALLARAT RD	INY	71	C3
BALLARD RD	TEH	24	E2
BALLICO AV	MCO	48	A4
BALLINGER RD	RCO	99	E5
BALLINGR CYN RD	VEN	87	E1
BALLIS RD	TEH	18	C5
BALLS FERRY RD	SHA	18	D3
BALL FERY PK RD	SHA	18	D3
BALSAM RD	SBD	91	B4
BALSAMO RD	SBD	81	A5
BALTIMORE MN RD	PLA	34	E3
BANCROFT AV	O	159	D1
BANCROFT DR	SDCO	V	D4
BANCROFT DR	SDCO	111	E1
BANCROFT RD	STA	47	C3
BANCROFT WY	B	156	A3
BANDERILLA DR	MPA	48	D2
BANDINI BLVD	LACO	R	D4
B & R LN	SOL	39	C3
BANDUCCI RD	KER	79	B4

STREET	CO.	PAGE	GRID
BANGOR AV	KIN	57	E5
BANGOR PARK RD	BUT	25	D5
BANGOR PK CTOFF	BUT	25	E5
BANGS AV	STA	47	C2
BANNER RD	CAL	41	B3
BANNER QUAKR HL	NEV	34	D1
BANNER RDG LAVA	NEV	34	C1
BANNING IDYLLWD	RCO	100	A3
BANNISTER RD	IMP	108	E4
BANTA RD	SJCO	47	E2
BAR RD	MAD	49	E5
BAR RD	MAD	50	A5
BARBARA WRTH RD	IMP	112	B4
BARBER	SJCO	39	E3
BARBER LN	RCO	107	B1
BARBER RD	ALP	36	B4
BARBER RD	TEH	25	A2
BARBER MTN RD	SDCO	112	B1
BARD RD	IMP	110	D5
BARDSDALE AV	VEN	88	D4
BARGLEY RD	COL	32	C2
BARHAM AV	TEH	24	D2
BARHAM BLVD	LA	181	C1
BARHAM BLVD	LACO	Q	B3
BAR K RD	TRI	17	C2
BARKER RD	KER	67	B5
BARKER CREEK RD	TRI	17	B2
BARKER MINE RD	MNO	51	C2
BARKHOUSE CK RD	SIS	3	D3
BARKSHANTY RD	SIS	10	D1
BARLOW LN	INY	51	D4
BAR MTN LOOKOUT	SIS	3	C4
BARNES LN	MEN	23	B2
BARNES RD	KER	90	B1
BARNES RD	SBD	92	D4
BARNES RD	SLO	66	A5
BARNES RD	SLO	76	A1
BARNETT AV	SDCO	V	B4
BARNETT RD	STA	48	B2
BARNEY GULCH RD	TRI	11	B5
BARNHART RD	STA	47	C3
BARNY OLDFLD RD	IMP	110	C5
BARR RD	HUM	10	B5
BARRANCA AV	LACO	U	D4
BARRANCA RD	ORA	98	C4
BARRANCA RD	ORA	T	D3
BARRANCA RD	TUS	198	E2
BARREL SPGS RD	LACO	90	A3
BARREL SPGS RD	MOD	7	E3
BARRETT	CC	38	C5
BARRETT AV	FRCO	57	B5
BARRETT AV	FRCO	57	C5
BARRETT LAKE RD	SDCO	112	B2
BARRINGTON AV	LACO	180	B2
BARRINGTON LN	SIE	27	C4
BARRY RD	SUT	33	D2
BARRYS RD	HUM	16	A1
BARSTOW AV	FRCO	57	B3
BARSTOW AV	FRCO	57	C3
BARSTOW AV	KIN	57	E5
BARSTOW FRWY	SBD	91	A5
BARSTOW FRWY	SBD	99	B1
BARSTOW RD	BARS	208	B3
BARSTOW RD	KER	80	D5
BARSTOW RD	SBD	91	E2
BARSTOW RD	SBD	92	A4
BARTEL ST	SHA	13	C5
BARTELL RD	INY	51	E5
BARTH RD	IMP	108	E3
BARTLE GAP RD	SIS	13	B3
BARTLETT RD	SOL	39	C3
BARTLETTE RD	INY	60	B5
BARTLETT SPG RD	LAK	31	E2
BARTLETT SPG RD	LAK	31	E2
BARTOLOMEI	SJCO	40	C5
BARTOLOMEI	SJCO	47	C1
BARTON	PLA	34	B5
BARTON RD	SBD	99	C2
BARTON ST	RCO	99	B3
BARTON HILL RD	YUB	26	B4
BAR W RD	HUM	16	B3
BASCOM AV	SCL	46	B5
BASCOM AV	SJ	151	C4
BASE LINE AV	SB	86	E3
BASELINE RD	LACO	98	E1
BASE LINE RD	LACO	R	C3
BASE LINE RD	LACO	U	E3
BASE LINE RD	PLA	33	E5
BASELINE RD	SBD	98	E1
BASELINE RD	SBD	101	C1
BASELINE ST	SBDO	207	B1
BASELINE ST	SBD	102	C1
BASIC SCHOOL RD	KER	78	B5
BASILONE RD	SDCO	105	E1
BASIN RD	SBD	82	E5
BASIN ST	KER	79	C2
BASLER RD	TEH	18	B4
BASS	FRCO	56	C3
BASSET RD	LAS	14	C3
BASSETT AV	KER	68	C5
BASS HILL RD	LAS	21	A4
BASS LAKE RD	ED	34	C5
BASS VALLEY RD	MAD	49	D4
BASTANCHURY RD	ORA	T	E1
BATAVIA RD	SOL	39	B2
BATCHELDER RD	SB	86	C2
BATEMAN RD	SHA	19	B2
BATES	SUT	33	C4
BATTL CK BTM RD	SHA	19	A3
BAUGHMAN RD	IMP	108	E4
BAUMBACH AV	KER	79	B4
BAUTISTA RD	RCO	100	A4
BAXTER AV	NAP	133	B2
BAXTER RD	MCO	48	E5
BAXTER RD	RCO	99	C5
BAXTER RD	RCO	99	C5
BAXTERS RD	MNO	43	E5
BAXTERS RD	MNO	50	E1
BAY DR	SC	169	A3
BAY HWY	SON	37	C3
BAY RD	SMCO	45	D3
BAY ST	SF	142	B1
BAY ST	SF	143	A2
BAY ST	SC	169	B4
BAYLEY RES RD	MOD	8	A2
BAYLIS BLUE GUM	GLE	24	D4
BAYOU RD	SAC	33	D5
BAYSHORE BLVD	SMCO	45	C2
BAYSHORE FRWY	BLMT	145	B3
BAYSHORE FRWY	BURL	144	C3
BAYSHORE FRWY	MLBR	144	C3
BAYSHORE FRWY	MVW	148	A3
BAYSHORE FRWY	SJ	151	D1
BAYSHORE FRWY	SJ	152	B1
BAYSHORE FRWY	SM	145	B3
BAYSHORE FRWY	SMCO	45	D3
BAYSHORE FRWY	SMCO	144	C3
BAYSHORE FRWY	SMCO	145	B3
BAYSHORE FRWY	SSF	144	C1
BAYSHORE FRWY	SVL	148	D3
BAYSIDE DR	NB	199	D5

STREET	CO.	PAGE	GRID
BAYSIDE DR	NB	200	A5
BAY VIEW AV	NAPA	38	C3
BAY VIEW RD	MCO	55	C1
BEACH BLVD	ORA	98	B3
BEACH BLVD	ORA	T	B1
BEACH RD	HUM	22	A1
BEACH RD	IMP	109	A2
BEACH RD	MPA	49	B4
BEACH RD	SCR	54	B3
BEACH ST	SF	143	A2
BEACH PARK BL	FCTY	145	D3
BEACON RD	SLO	76	B1
BEACON ST	AVLN	105	B5
BEAL RD	IMP	109	B2
BEALE RD N	YUB	33	D2
BEALE RD S	YUB	33	E3
BEALE ST	SF	143	D4
BEAL RANCH RD	CAL	40	E3
BEAL RANCH RD	CAL	41	A3
BEALEVILLE RD	KER	79	B3
BEAMER ST	YOL	33	B5
BEAN CLIPPER RD	YUB	26	B4
BEAN CREEK RD	BUT	25	E4
BEAN CREEK RD	SCR	54	A1
BEAN HOLLOW RD	SMCO	45	C5
BEAR ST	CM	197	E4
BEAR ST	ORA	T	D3
BEAR BASIN RD	DN	2	B3
BEAR BUTTE RD	HUM	16	B5
BEAR CANYON RD	FRCO	66	B2
BEAR CREEK DR N	MCO	48	C4
BEAR CREEK DR S	MCO	48	C4
BEAR CREEK LOOP	TRI	12	A3
BEAR CREEK RD	CC	38	D5
BEAR CREEK RD	LAK	31	D1
BEAR CREEK RD	SCR	45	E5
BEARD RD	NAP	133	C2
BEAR MTN BLVD	KER	78	D4
BEAR MTN RD	FRCO	58	B3
BEAR MTN RD	SHA	18	C1
BEAR MTN RD	SIS	13	C2
BEAR MTN LKOUT	SHA	18	C1
BEAR MT WINE RD	KER	78	E3
BEAR MT WINE RD	KER	79	A3
BEAR RANCH HILL	BUT	25	E2
BEAR RIVER	AMA	41	D1
BEAR RIVER S	AMA	41	D1
BEAR RIVER DR	SUT	33	D3
BEAR RIV RDG RD	HUM	15	D3
BEAR SPRINGS RD	LAS	14	A3
BEAR TRAP DR	MPA	49	A3
BEAR TRAP RD	NEV	26	C5
BEAR VALLEY	MPA	48	E5
BEAR VLY PKWY	SDCO	106	D4
BEAR VALLEY RD	COL	32	B2
BEAR VALLEY RD	KER	79	B4
BEAR VALLEY RD	SBD	90	E4
BEAR VALLEY RD	SIE	27	D4
BEAR VLY CUTOFF	SBD	91	B4
BEASON ST	KER	78	A1
BEASORE RD	MAD	49	E4
BEATIE RD	SHA	18	D3
BEAUCHAMP RD	COL	32	D2
BEAUMONT AV	RCO	99	E3
BEAUMONT ST	SBD	91	E3
BEAVER CREEK RD	SIS	3	D3
BECHELLI LN	RED	122	E2
BECHELLI LN	SHA	18	C2
BECKER	SUT	33	C4
BECKER RD	SOL	39	C1
BECKET CT	KER	79	C5
BECKWITH RD	SIE	27	D3
BECKWITH RD	STA	47	B2
BECKWRTH CALPNE	PLU	27	C3
BECKWRTH GENESE	PLU	26	E1
BECKWRTH GENESE	PLU	27	B1
BECKWRTH LOYLTN	PLU	27	C3
BCKWRTH TYLRSVL	PLU	26	D1
BCKWRTH TYLRSVL	PLU	27	B2
BEDFORD DR	SBD	92	B1
BEE CANYON RD	RCO	100	A4
BEECH AV	KER	78	B2
BEECH AV	SBD	99	A2
BEECH ST	BKD	166	B2
BEECH ST	SDCO	106	C2
BEECHER RD	SJCO	40	B5
BEE GULCH RD	ALP	42	A1
BEEGUM RD	SHA	17	D4
BEEGUM GORGE RD	SHA	17	D4
BEEKLEY RD	RCO	102	C4
BEEKLEY RD	SBD	90	E4
BEEROCK RD	SLO	65	D5
BEHYMER	FRCO	56	C2
BEHYMER AV	FRCO	57	D2
BELCHER AV	MCO	48	B4
BELFAST RD	LAS	21	B3
BELL	MCO	48	A4
BELL LN	PLU	26	D1
BELL RD	AMA	40	E1
BELL RD	BUT	25	A3
BELL RD	KER	77	E2
BELL RD	KER	78	A2
BELL RD	PLA	34	B3
BELL RD	SB	87	C1
BELL RD	STA	47	C4
BELL ST	SB	86	D2
BELLA ROSA DR	HUM	16	C4
BELLA VISTA DR	KER	79	D1
BELLE TER	KER	166	D5
BELLE GRAVE AV	RCO	99	A2
BELLEVUE AV	SUT	33	D3
BELLEVUE RD	MCO	48	B4
BELLFLOWER BLVD	LACO	98	A3
BELLFLOWER BLVD	LACO	S	E1
BELLFLOWER BLVD	LACO	T	A2
BELLFLOWER ST	SBD	91	B3
BELL HILL RD	LAK	31	D3
BELL MTN RD	SBD	91	C3
BELL SPRINGS RD	HUM	16	C5
BELL SPRINGS RD	MEN	22	D1
BELLVIEW RD	MAD	57	C1
BELMONT AV	FRE	165	C3
BELMONT AV	FRCO	56	C3
BELMONT AV	FRCO	57	C3
BELOMY ST	SCLR	151	B3
BELSBY AV	RCO	102	C4
BELTLINE RD	SHA	18	C2
BENA RD	KER	79	A3
BENBOW DR	HUM	22	C1
BEND	TEH	18	D4
BENDER	SJCO	40	A3
BENDER AV	KER	78	B2
BENDER RD	SHA	18	A3
BENDLER RD	STA	47	E2
BENEDICT CYN DR	LACO	Q	A3
BENHAM LN	CUR	1	D2
BEN HUR RD	MPA	49	B4
BENICIA RD	KIN	57	E5
BENICIA RD	SOL	38	D4
BENICIA RD	VAL	134	D5
BENIT JUAREZ BL	BAJA	112	B4

STREETS

221
BENNER AV
STREET INDEX
BUENA VISTA

STREET	CO.	PAGE & GRID
BENNER AV	KER	68 B5
BENNET RD	LACO	89 A5
BENNET RD	VEN	88 E5
BENNETS WELL RD	INY	72 A2
BENNETT RD	BUT	25 A2
BENNETT RD	MCO	55 E2
BENNETT RD	NEV	34 C1
BENNETT RD	RCO	100 D3
BENNETT VLY RD	SON	38 A2
BENNETT VLY RD	STR	131 D4
BENSON AV	MTCL	203 D3
BENSON AV	ONT	203 D5
BENSON AV	SBD	98 D2
BENSON AV	SBD	203 D3
BENSON AV	UPL	203 D1
BENSON DR	SHA	18 B2
BENSON RD	TEH	18 C4
BENT RD	STA	47 D2
BENTLEY RD	STA	47 D2
BENTON DR	SHA	18 C2
BENTON RD	RCO	99 D5
BENTON RD E	RCO	99 E5
BENTON ST	SCLR	150 C3
BENTON CROSSING	MNO	51 B2
BENTN GBG PT RD	MNO	51 C1
BERDOO CYN RD	RCO	101 B3
BERKELEY AV	STA	47 E3
BERKSHIRE RD	KER	79 A3
BERMUDA DR	SM	145 B2
BERNAL DR E	SAL	171 C3
BERNARD ST	KER	78 D3
BERNARD WY	SHA	18 C1
BERRELLESA ST	M	154 B2
BERRY AV	H	146 E4
BERRY RD	SUT	33 D3
BERRY CREEK RD	BUT	25 E3
BERRYESSA RD	SJ	152 C1
BERRYESSA RD	SCL	46 B4
BERRYSSA KNX RD	NAPA	32 C4
BERT RD	LAS	27 E1
BERTAS RD	HUM	15 E1
BERT CRANE RD	MCO	48 B5
BERTRAM CIR	KER	79 C4
BERYL ST	LACO	97 D3
BERYL ST	LACO	S B1
BERYL ST	SD	105 E5
BERYL ST	SD	212 A1
BERYLWOOD RD	VEN	88 C5
BESSEMR MINE RD	SBD	92 B4
BEST RD	IMP	109 B4
BEST RD	MPA	49 C3
BEST RD	RCO	99 E5
BEST RD	SUT	33 C3
BETHANY RD	SJCO	46 D1
BETHEL AV	FRCO	57 E4
BETHEL RD	SLO	76 A2
BETHEL ISLND RD	CC	39 C5
BETTERAVIA RD	STB	173 C5
BETTERAVIA RD	SB	86 B1
BETTERAVIA RD	SMA	173 C5
BETTS RD	TRI	23 A1
BETTY WY	SIS	4 B4
BETZ RD	SUT	33 D3
BEVERLY	LACO	98 A2
BEVERLY BLVD	BH	183 C1
BEVERLY BLVD	LA	183 C1
BEVERLY BLVD	LA	184 B1
BEVERLY BLVD	LA	185 C1
BEVERLY BLVD	LACO	97 D2
BEVERLY BLVD	LACO	Q C4
BEVERLY BLVD	LACO	183 C1
BEVERLY DR	BH	183 B1
BEVERLY DR	LAS	20 E3
BEVERLY DR	LA	183 B1
BEVERLY DR	LACO	Q A3
BEVERLY GLEN BL	LA	180 E2
BEVERLY GLEN BL	LA	183 A3
BEVERLY GLEN BL	LACO	97 C1
BEVERLY GLEN BL	LACO	Q A3
BEVERWIL DR	BH	183 C3
BEVERWIL DR	LA	183 C3
BEYER BLVD	SDCO	V C5
BEYER BLVD	SDCO	111 D2
BEYER LN	SJCO	40 B5
BEYER WY	SDCO	V C5
BEYER WY	SDCO	111 D2
BEYERS LN	NEV	34 B2
BIANCHI RD	S	160 B2
BIDDLE	SLO	76 B4
BIDWELL RD	SHA	13 D5
BIDWELL CK RD	MOD	7 D3
BIEBER LKOUT RD	LAS	14 B3
BIG BAR DUMP RD	TRI	17 A1
BIG BAR MTN RD	BUT	25 E2
BIG BEN	PLA	34 B3
BIG BEND RD	BUT	25 D3
BIG BEND RD	SHA	13 A4
BIG CANYON	LAK	32 A4
BIG CREEK RD	TRI	17 B2
BIG CREEK RD	PLU	26 B2
BIG CK SHAFT RD	TUO	48 E1
BIG DIPPER	PLA	34 D2
BIGELOW RD	SIS	13 A2
BIGELOW RD	SUT	33 B1
BIG FLAT RD	DN	2 B4
BIG FRCH CK RD	TRI	11 A5
BIGGAR LN	MEN	23 A2
BIGGS EAST HWY	BUT	25 C5
BIG HILL RD	TUO	41 D4
BIG HILL LKOUT	HUM	10 C3
BIG HORN DR	RCO	100 D5
BIG INCH PIPELN	KER	79 E5
BIG INCH PIPELN	KER	80 A5
BIG LAKES RD	MOD	14 D2
BIG MEADOWS RD	SIS	3 C5
BIG OAK DR	MEN	31 B5
BIG PN REPTR RD	INY	51 E5
BIG RANCH RD	NAPA	29 E5
BIG RANCH RD	NAPA	38 C2
BIG RANCH RD	NAPA	133 C2
BIG RESRVOIR RD	PLA	34 E2
BIG ROCK CK RD	LACO	90 C4
BIG SAGE RD	MOD	6 E5
BIG SAGE RD	MOD	7 A5
BIG SANDY RD	MON	66 B4
BIG SPRING DR	NEV	34 B2
BIG SPRING RD	SHA	19 A2
BIG SPRINGS RD	MNO	50 D1
BIG SPRINGS RD	SIS	4 C5
BIG SPRINGS RD	SIS	12 C1
BIG SPRINGS RD	SIS	13 A2
BIG SPGS CUTOFF	PLU	20 B4
BIG STUMP RD	SIS	5 A2
BIG TRAILS DR	MEN	22 E4
BIG TRAILS DR	MEN	23 A4
BIG TREES RD	INY	51 C4
BIG TUJUNGA BL	LACO	Q B1
BIG TUJUNGA CYN	LACO	89 E5
BIG TUJUNGA CYN	LACO	Q C1
BIG VALLEY RD	LAK	31 D3
BILBY RD	SAC	39 E2

STREET	CO.	PAGE & GRID
BILLE RD	BUT	25 C3
BILLIE ST	KER	78 D4
BILLINGS AV	KER	78 B1
BILLINGS LN	RCO	99 B4
BILLY WRIGHT RD	MCO	55 C2
BINET RD	BUT	26 B4
BINGHAMTON RD	SOL	39 B2
BIOLA AV	FRCO	57 B3
BIR RD	INY	51 C4
BIRCH AV	MON	65 A1
BIRCH ST	ORA	98 C3
BIRCH ST	ORA	U D5
BIRCH ST	ORA	T D1
BIRCH CREEK RD	INY	59 E1
BIRCHIM LN	INY	51 C3
BIRCHIN FLAT RD	MNO	42 E2
BIRCHIN FLAT RD	MNO	43 A2
BIRCHVILLE RD	NEV	26 B5
BIRD AV	SJ	152 B5
BIRD RD	SJCO	47 A2
BIRDS LANDNG RD	SOL	39 B4
BIRD SPG CYN RD	KER	80 A1
BIRKHEAD	FRCO	57 C2
BIRMINGHAM DR	SDCO	106 B4
BISCH CT	KER	79 E2
BISHOP AV	FRCO	57 B4
BISHOP AV	FRCO	67 B1
BISHOP AV	SUT	33 C1
BISHOP ST	SNLO	172 D4
BISHOP CK RD E	INY	51 C4
BISHOP CK RD W	INY	51 C4
BISIGNANI RD	MCO	55 E1
BISSET STN RD	MAD	49 D4
BITNEY SPGS RD	NEV	34 B1
BITTERWATER RD	MON	65 C2
BITTRWTR VLY RD	KER	77 A1
BIXBY RD	VEN	88 D5
BIXLER RD	CC	39 D5
BLACK RD	SB	86 B1
BLACK BART RD	BUT	25 E4
BLACK BEAR RD	SIS	11 B2
BLACK BUTTE RD	GLE	24 B3
BLACK BUTTE RD	SHA	19 A3
BLACK BUTTE RD	TEH	24 C2
BLACK CANYON RD	INY	51 E4
BLACK CANYON RD	MNO	44 B5
BLACK CANYON RD	MNO	51 B1
BLACK CANYON RD	SBD	81 C5
BLACK CANYON RD	SBD	84 B5
BLACK CANYON RD	SBD	94 C1
BLACK CANYON RD	SDCO	107 A3
BLACK DIAMND WY	CC	39 B5
BLACK DIAMND MN	BUT	25 C2
BLK EAGLE MN RD	RCO	101 E3
BLACK FOX MTN	SIS	13 B2
BLACK GULCH RD	KER	79 C1
BLACK GULCH RD	LAS	14 A5
BLACK HAWK RD	CC	46 B1
BLACKHAWK RD	PLU	26 C1
BLACK HILLS RD	RCO	100 D4
BLACKIE RD	MON	54 C3
BLACK LAKE RD	LAS	14 B5
BLACKMER RD	SUT	33 B2
BLACKMORE	SJCO	47 C1
BLACK MTN RD	IMP	110 B3
BLACK MTN RD	SDCO	106 D4
BLACK MTN RD	SMCO	45 C3
BLACK MTN RD	SIS	4 B3
BLACK MTN TR	RCO	100 B3
BLACK MTN LO RD	SLO	76 D3
BLACK RANCH RD	SHA	13 C4
BLACK ROCK RD	RCO	103 C5
BLACK ROCK CYN	SBD	100 E2
BLACK RCK MN RD	MNO	51 C2
BLACK ROCK SPGS	INY	59 E2
BLACKS CYN RD	MOD	14 D1
BLACKS RDG LKOT	LAS	14 B5
BLACKSTONE AV	FRE	165 D1
BLACKSTONE ST	TUL	68 B2
BLACKWELL LN	DN	1 D4
BLAGEN RD	CAL	41 C3
BLAINE ST	RCO	99 B2
BLAIR RD	IMP	109 B3
BLAIS RD	IMP	109 A4
BLAKE RD	SAC	40 B2
BLAKE ST	SBD	99 B1
BLAKER RD	STA	47 D3
BLANCHARD FT RD	TRI	17 D2
BLANCO	MON	54 C4
BLANCO RD	MPA	48 D2
BLANCO RD E	MON	171 C5
BLANCO RD E	SAL	171 C5
BLANCO RD W	MON	171 A5
BLANCO RD W	SAL	171 A5
BLAND RD	SHA	17 E3
BLANEY AV	CPTO	149 E5
BLANKENSHIP AV	KER	78 A1
BLANKO RD	SBD	90 E4
BLATCHLEY RD	TEH	24 D2
BLAZING STAR AV	SBD	91 A3
BLEDSOE RD	MCO	48 B3
BLEVENS RD	LPAZ	104 C5
BLEWETT RD	STA	47 B2
BLICKENSTAFF RD	LAS	21 B4
BLISS DR	RCO	107 C1
BLISS RD	MCO	48 C5
BLISS RD	YUB	33 D2
BLITHEDALE AV	MAR	45 B1
BLITHEDALE AV E	MV	140 A3
B L M DUMP RD	LAS	20 E1
BLOCK RD	BUT	25 C5
BLOCK RD	BUT	33 C1
BLODGETT RD	IMP	109 B5
BLOODY CAMP RD	HUM	10 C3
BLOOMR HLL LKOT	BUT	25 D3
BLOOMFIELD AV	LACO	T A1
BLOOMFIELD AV	SCL	54 D2
BLOOMFIELD RD	SON	37 D3
BLOOMFLD GRNTVL	NEV	26 D5
BLOOM'NGTON RD	SBD	99 B2
BLOSS AV	MCO	47 D4
BLOSSER RD	STB	173 A2
BLOSSER RD	SB	86 B1
BLOSSER RD	SMA	173 A4
BLOSSOM	SJCO	39 E3
BLOSSOM AV	MCO	56 A2
BLOSSOM RD	STA	47 E2
BLOSSOM HILL RD	SCL	46 A5
BLOWERS DR	RCO	99 A4
BLUE GILL RD	SIS	4 B3
BLUE GULCH RD	SIS	11 B3
BLUE GUM AV	STA	47 C2
BLUE LAKE BLVD	HUM	10 A5
BLUE LAKE RD	LAS	8 D3
BLUE LAKE RD	MOD	8 C3
BLUE LK MPLE CK	HUM	16 B1
BLUE LAKES RD	ALP	36 B5
BLUE LAKES RD	LAK	31 C2
BLUE MTN RD	CAL	41 C2
BLUE MTN RD	KER	69 A5
BLUE MTN LKT RD	CAL	41 C2

STREET	CO.	PAGE & GRID
BLUE RIDGE RD	SOL	38 E2
BLUE RIDGE RD	TEH	19 B3
BLUE SLIDE RD	HUM	15 E3
BLUFF ST	RCO	100 A2
BLUFF CREEK RD	TRI	16 E5
BLYTHE AV	FRCO	57 C3
BLYTHE AV	FRCO	67 B1
BOARDER ST	RCO	100 A3
BOARTS RD	IMP	109 A4
BOAT HARBOR RD	LAS	20 E2
BOBCAT TR	RCO	100 A5
BOB HOPE DR	RCO	100 E4
BOBS GAP RD	LACO	90 C4
BOB WHITE WY	INY	73 A4
BOCA RD	NEV	27 E5
BOCA SPRINGS RD	NEV	27 E5
BOCA SPGS RD E	NEV	27 E5
BOCKMAN RD	ALA	146 A2
BODEGA AV	SON	38 A3
BODEGA HWY	SON	37 D2
BODEM ST	MDO	162 C3
BODFISH CYN RD	KER	79 D1
BODIE RD	MNO	43 C3
BODIE MASONC RD	MNO	43 C3
BOESSOW RD	SAC	40 B3
BOGARD RD	LAS	14 B5
BOGGS RD	COL	24 E5
BOGGS & CHAMLIN	TEH	24 C2
BOGIE RD	RCO	100 D3
BOGUE RD	STA	47 E3
BOGUE RD	STA	48 A3
BOGUE RD	SUT	33 C2
BOHAN DILLON RD	SON	37 B1
BOHEMIAN HWY	SON	37 C2
BOHN BLVD	SHA	18 C3
BOLAM RD	SIS	4 D5
BOLAM RD	SIS	12 D1
BOLAM LOGGNG RD	SIS	12 D1
BOLES RD	COL	32 E3
BOLEY RD	IMP	108 E5
BOLINGER CYN RD	CC	45 E1
BOLINGER CYN RD	CC	46 A1
BOLO RD	SBD	94 A3
BOLSA AV	ORA	98 B4
BOLSA CHICA RD	ORA	98 B4
BOLSA CHICA RD	ORA	T B3
BON ST	MCO	48 D5
BONANZA AV	TRI	17 D1
BONANZA RD	CLK	74 D2
BONANZA RD	LV	209 B1
BONANZA RD	SBD	101 A1
BONANZA TR	SBD	91 C2
BONANZA WY	NEV	34 B1
BONANZA KING RD	TRI	12 A4
BOND RD	SJCO	40 A2
BOND RD	STA	47 E2
BONDS CORNER RD	IMP	112 C4
BONDS FLAT RD	TUO	48 C2
BONDURANT	MPA	49 A2
BONE STEEL RD	IMP	112 A4
BONETTI RD	SJCO	46 D1
BONITA AV	LACO	98 C1
BONITA AV	LACO	U E3
BONITA RD	MCO	55 D2
BONITA RD	SDCO	V C4
BONITA RD	SDCO	111 D2
BONITA CYN DR	IRV	200 C3
BONITA CYN DR	ORA	98 C4
BONITA CYN DR	ORA	T D4
BONITA LATERAL	SB	76 C5
BONITA LATERAL	SB	86 B1
BONITA SCHL RD	SLO	76 C5
BONITA SCHL RD	SB	76 C5
BONITA SCHL RD	SB	86 B1
BONITA VISTA RD	RCO	100 C5
BONNER RD	MOD	14 D4
BONNEYVIEW RD E	SHA	18 C2
BONNIE CT	KER	79 C3
BONNY LN	RCO	107 B1
BONNY DOON RD	SCR	53 D2
BONNYVIEW RD S	SHA	18 C2
BONVIEW AV	SBD	98 D2
BOOKER RD	TUO	41 D5
BOONE LN	FRCO	66 B3
BOONE ST	SMA	173 A3
BOOTH RD	LPAZ	104 B2
BOOT JACK	MPA	49 C3
BORAX RD	KER	80 D5
BORAX MILL RD	INY	62 A5
BORBA	SJCO	40 A5
BORBA	SJCO	47 A1
BORCHARD	VEN	96 D1
BORDEN RD	SAC	40 B3
BORDEN ST	MAD	57 A2
BORDER AV	RCO	98 E3
BORDER AV	SBD	100 E1
BOREL RD	RCO	99 D5
BORMAN LN	LAK	32 B4
BORNT RD	IMP	112 C4
BORON AV	KER	80 E5
BORREGO SLTN SEA	SDCO	108 A2
BORREGO SPGS RD	SDCO	107 E2
BORREGO VLY RD	SDCO	107 E2
BOSCOVICH RD	IMP	112 D5
BOSTON AV	LACO	Q C2
BOTTINI	TUO	41 E4
BOTTLE CREEK RD	BUT	25 D1
BOTTLE HILL RD	BUT	25 D1
BOTTLE ROCK RD	LAK	31 E4
BOUCHO RD	COL	32 E3
BOULDER AV	SBD	99 C1
BOULDER HWY	CLK	74 D2
BOULDER CK RD	SDCO	107 C5
BOULDER CK RD	SIS	3 C5
BOULEVARD, THE	GLE	24 E4
BL D L AMERICAS	BAJA	112 B4
BOULTON RD	SUT	33 C3
BOUNDARY ST	SD	216 C1
BOUNDARY TR	DN	2 A4
BOUQUET CYN RD	LACO	89 C4
BOUQUET CYN RD	LACO	89 C4
BOUSE QUARTZITE	LPAZ	104 C4
BOW AV	KER	80 C1
BOWEN RD	COL	32 D1
BOWEN RANCH RD	SBD	91 C4
BOWERS AV	SCLR	150 D1
BOWKER RD	IMP	112 B3
BOWKER RD	IMP	112 B4
BOWL PL	SB	86 E3
BOWMAN RD	KER	80 D1
BOWMAN RD	MOD	7 B5
BOWMAN RD	SJCO	47 A1
BOWMAN RD	TEH	18 B4
BOWMAN LAKE RD	NEV	27 A5
BOWMAN LAKE RD	NEV	35 A1
BOX CANYON RD	RCO	101 C5
BOX CAR RD	MCO	55 E1
BOX ELDER ST	RCO	100 C4
BOX SPRINGS BL	RCO	99 B2
BOX SPRINGS RD	RCO	99 C2

STREET	CO.	PAGE & GRID
BOYCE RD	SOL	39 A1
BOYD	CC	38 E5
BOYD DR	TUL	58 C4
BOYD RD	IMP	109 B5
BOYD SPRINGS RD	LAS	14 B4
BOYER RD	MPA	49 C3
BOYER RD	YUB	33 D1
BOYES BLVD	SON	132 A2
BOYLE RD	IMP	109 A3
BOYLE RD	SHA	18 D2
BOYLES AV	LAK	32 A3
BOY SCOUT CP RD	VEN	88 B2
BRACE RD	PLA	34 B4
BRACK RD	SON	31 D5
BRACK RD	SON	37 D1
BRADBURY RD	MCO	47 E3
BRADBURY RD	MCO	48 A3
BRADBURY RD	STA	47 C3
BRADFORD AV	ORA	T D1
BRADFORD RD	BUT	25 B4
BRADFORD RD	RCO	107 B1
BRADLEY AV	SDCO	V D3
BRADLEY AV	SDCO	106 E5
BRADLEY RD	MON	65 E4
BRADLEY RD	RCO	99 C4
BRADLEY RD	VEN	88 C5
BRADLY HENLY RD	SIS	4 B3
BRADLEY LOCK RD	MON	65 C4
BRADSHAW RD	IMP	109 A5
BRADSHAW RD	SAC	40 A2
BRADSHAW RD	YUB	33 E3
BRADSHW TR, THE	RCO	102 A5
BRADSHW TR, THE	RCO	110 B1
BRADY RD	TRI	17 B2
BRAGG RD	RCO	100 A5
BRAMLETT RCH RD	MNO	44 C5
BRAMLOT RD	TRI	17 B3
BRAMLOT RD	TRI	17 B3
BRANCH RD	SLO	76 B1
BRANCH RD E	HUM	22 C1
BRANCH RD W	SIS	3 D4
BRANCH CAMP W	BUT	25 D1
BRANCH MILL RD	SLO	76 B4
BRANCIFORTE DR	SCR	54 A2
BRANCO RD	MCO	55 E1
BRAND BLVD	LACO	Q A1
BRAND BLVD	LACO	Q C3
BRANDON RD	ED	40 D1
BRANDT	IMP	109 A3
BRANDT RD	SJCO	40 C4
BRANDT RD	KER	78 A2
BRANDY CITY RD	SIE	26 C4
BRANDY CREEK RD	SHA	18 A2
BRANFORD ST	LACO	Q A2
BRANHAM LN	SCL	46 B5
BRANNAN ST	SF	143 D5
BRANNAN ISL RD	SAC	39 C4
BRANNAN MTN RD	RD	10 C4
BRANNIGAN MN RD	SBD	83 C4
BRANNIN RD	TEH	24 C2
BRANNON AV	FRCO	56 B2
BRANSCOMB RD	MEN	22 D4
BRANSTETTER LN	SHA	18 C2
BRANT RD	SBD	84 C3
BRANT CIMA RD	SBD	84 B3
BRAWLEY	IMP	108 C2
BRAWLEY AV	FRCO	57 C5
BRAY AV	TEH	18 D5
BRAZO RD	MCO	47 C4
BREA BLVD	ORA	98 C3
BREA BLVD	ORA	R C5
BREA BLVD	ORA	T C1
BREA CANYON RD	LACO	98 C2
BREA CYN CUTOFF	LACO	U D5
BREA CYN CUTOFF	LACO	98 C2
BRECKENRIDGE RD	KER	78 E3
BRECKENRIDGE RD	KER	79 A2
BREEDLOVE RD	ED	34 E3
BRENDA ST	KER	70 A5
BRENT RD	TEH	18 D4
BREUING RD	MCO	55 D1
BRENNAN	SJCO	47 C1
BRENTWOOD AV	CC	39 C5
BRETZ RD	FRCO	58 B1
BREUNER AV	COL	32 E3
BREWER RD	NEV	34 C2
BREWER RD	PLA	33 E4
BREWER CREEK RD	SIS	12 E1
BRICELAND RD	HUM	16 B5
BRICELAND RD	MEN	22 B1
BRICELND THORNE	HUM	16 B5
BRIDESTEIN RD	IMP	109 C5
BRIDGE RD	VEN	88 C4
BRIDGE ST	COL	33 A2
BRIDGE ST	RCO	99 D3
BRIDGE ST	SUT	33 C2
BRIDGE ST	SUT	125 A3
BRIDGE ST	YUBA	125 D3
BRIDGE ARBOR	LAK	31 D2
BRIDGE CK SPGS	LAS	20 C2
BRIDGE GULCH RD	TRI	17 B3
BRIDGPORT SCH RD	ED	41 A1
BRIDGEWAY	MAR	140 D5
BRIGGS AV	LACO	R D2
BRIGGS RD	RCO	99 D4
BRIGGS RD	VEN	88 C5
BRIGGS GRIDLY W	BUT	25 C5
BRIGGSMORE AV	STA	47 C2
BRIGGSMORE AV E	MDO	162 B1
BRIGHTON AV	MDO	162 D2
BRIGHTWOOD	MAD	57 B1
BRIM RD	COL	32 D2
BRIMHALL RD	KER	78 B3
BRINKERHOFF AV	SB	86 E3
BRINKERHOFF AV	SB	87 A3
BRIONES VLY RD	CC	39 B5
BRISTOL RD	VEN	88 B5
BRISTOL ST	CM	197 E4
BRISTOL ST	CM	198 A4
BRISTOL ST	ORA	98 C4
BRISTOL ST	ORA	T D3
BRISTOL ST	ORA	197 E4
BRISTOL ST	SA	195 E5
BRISTOL ST	SA	196 A2
BRISTOL ST	SA	197 E2
BRISTOL ST	SA	198 A2
BRISTOL ST N	NB	200 B1
BRITE RD	KER	78 A3
BRITTO RD	MCO	56 A2
BROAD RD	SLO	172 D5
BROAD ST	NEVC	128 B2
BROAD ST	SNLO	172 C3
BROAD ST W	NEVC	128 B2
BROADWAY	A	157 E3
BROADWAY	ALA	45 D1
BROADWAY	AMA	40 E2
BROADWAY	ANA	193 B2
BROADWAY	EUR	121 A4
BROADWAY	FRE	165 C3
BROADWAY	LB	192 D3
BROADWAY	LA	185 E5

STREET	CO.	PAGE & GRID
BROADWAY	LA	186 A3
BROADWAY	LACO	Q C3
BROADWAY	LACO	S C1
BROADWAY	LACO	S E2
BROADWAY	O	156 C5
BROADWAY	O	158 A2
BROADWAY	SCTO	137 A4
BROADWAY	SBD	92 D5
BROADWAY	SD	215 E3
BROADWAY	SD	216 A3
BROADWAY	SDCO	V D3
BROADWAY	SDCO	V B4
BROADWAY	SDCO	106 E5
BROADWAY	SDCO	106 D3
BROADWAY	SDCO	111 D1
BROADWAY	SDCO	111 D2
BROADWAY	SF	143 A3
BROADWAY	SB	76 C5
BROADWAY	SC	169 E3
BROADWAY	SMA	173 C3
BROADWAY	SMON	180 A4
BROADWAY	SOL	134 C1
BROADWAY	SNMA	132 D5
BROADWAY	SUT	33 C2
BROADWAY	VAL	134 C2
BROADWAY	YUB	33 D3
BROADWAY N	LA	186 C1
BROADWAY N	LACO	R D4
BROADWAY RD	LACO	R A5
BROADWAY RD	VEN	88 D5
BROADWAY ST	FRFD	135 B4
BROADWAY ST	SBD	101 A1
BROADWAY TER	O	156 C5
BROCK RD	IMP	112 A3
BROCKMAN LN	INY	51 D4
BROCKMAN RD	KER	78 C1
BROCKMAN RD	LAS	8 A4
BROCKMAN MLL RD	AMA	41 A1
BROCK MTN LKOUT	SHA	12 E5
BROKAW RD	SJ	151 D1
BROKAW RD	SCL	46 B4
BROKEOFF MDWS	SHA	19 C2
BROOKDALE RD	SHA	18 D2
BROOKHILL RD	MAD	57 C2
BROOKHURST ST	ORA	98 B4
BROOKHURST ST	ORA	T C2
BROOKLYN AV	LA	186 D3
BROOKLYN ST	LACO	R D4
BROOKS RD	MCO	48 B4
BROOKS RD	NEV	34 C2
BROOKS ST	SB	86 D1
BROOKSIDE	FRCO	58 D4
BROOKSIDE AV	RCO	99 E2
BROOKSIDE AV	SBD	99 C2
BROOKSIDE DR	SP	155 A1
BROOKSIDE RD	CAL	41 C2
BROOKSIDE RD	S	160 A2
BROPHY RD	YUB	33 D2
BROWN RD	KER	70 C5
BROWN RD	KER	80 C1
BROWN RD	SB	86 A1
BROWN RD	SHA	13 D4
BROWN RD	SOL	39 B3
BROWN RD	SUT	33 C3
BROWN ST	NAP	133 C3
BROWN ST	RCO	99 B3
BROWNLL LAVA BD	SIS	5 C3
BROWNING	PLA	33 E5
BROWNING RD	COL	33 B3
BROWNING RD	KER	68 C5
BROWNING RD	SUT	33 C3
BROWN MATRL RD	KER	77 C1
BROWNS CREEK RD	TRI	17 D2
BROWNS MTN RD	TRI	17 D1
BROWNS RANCH RD	TRI	17 D1
BROWNS RAVINE	BUT	25 D1
BROWNS VALLEY	SBT	55 B4
BROWNS VLY RD	NAP	133 A3
BROWN VALLEY RD	SOL	39 A2
BROWN VALLEY RD	SCR	54 B2
BROYLE RD	STA	47 C3
BROYLES RD	BUT	25 A2
BROYLES RD	STA	47 C2
BRUCE RD	BUT	25 B3
BRUCE CRUM	SHA	13 E4
BRUCEVILLE RD	SAC	40 A3
BRUCITE ST	KER	91 E3
BRUELLA RD	SJCO	40 B4
BRUGGA LN	HUM	15 D2
BRUNDAGE LN	BKD	166 C5
BRUNDAGE LN	KER	166 C5
BRUNSWICK AV	LA	182 E2
BRUNSWICK RD	NEV	34 C1
BRUS	MOD	8 B3
BRUSH LN	STA	47 C3
BRUSH CREEK RD	SIS	4 B3
BRUSH CREEK RD	SON	37 E2
BRUSH CREEK RD	SON	38 A2
BRUSHY MTN LKOT	HUM	10 C5
BRYAN AV	FRCO	57 B5
BRYANT	FRCO	56 B2
BRYANT ST	SBD	99 D2
BRYANT ST	SF	142 D4
BRYANT ST	SF	143 D5
BRYANT RAVIN RD	BUT	26 A4
BRYANTS CYN RD	MON	55 A5
BRYANTS CYN RD	MON	65 A1
BUARO ST	GGR	195 B2
BUCHANAN RD	CC	39 B5
BUCHANAN RD	MAD	49 B5
BUCHANAN RD	TUO	41 E5
BUCHANAN ST	RCO	101 B5
BUCHANAN HLW RD	MCO	48 D5
BUCK RD	RCO	99 D5
BUCK RD	SJCO	40 B3
BUCKEYE RD	MPA	49 A3
BUCKEYE RD	NEV	34 D1
BUCKEYE ARM RD	TRI	11 D5
BUCKEYE CK RD	SON	31 A5
BUCKEYE CK RD	TRI	11 D5
BUCKEYE CK RD	TRI	12 A4
BUCKEYE CK RD	TRI	17 E1
BUCKEYE RDG RD	TRI	11 D5
BUCKHORN	TEH	24 C2
BUCKHORN AV	KER	89 C1
BUCKHORN RD	SIS	4 C5
BUCKHORN RDG RD	AMA	41 B2
BUCKHORN STA LP	TRI	17 E1
BUCKLEY RD	SLO	76 B4
BUCKMAN FUNCK	SJCO	40 D5
BUCK MEADOWS	MPA	49 A1
BUCKNELL RD	KER	80 D3
BUCKS BAR RD	ED	34 E5
BUCKS FLAT RD	TEH	19 B4
BUCKSKIN RD	CAL	41 A4
BUCKS LAKE RD	PLU	26 C1
BUCKWHEAT RD	SBD	90 E4
BUDDY CT	KER	79 B3
BUELL RD	SHA	18 A3
BUENA CREEK RD	SDCO	106 C3
BUENA VISTA	AMA	40 D3

STREETS

STREET	CO.	PAGE & GRID
BUENA VISTA	LACO	97 D1
BUENA VISTA	SCL	54 D1
BUENA VISTA AV	A	157 D5
BUENA VISTA AV	A	158 B5
BUENA VISTA AV	MV	140 A2
BUENA VISTA AV	RIV	205 A2
BUENA VISTA BL	KER	78 D4
BUENA VISTA BL	KER	79 A4
BUENA VISTA DR	MER	170 C1
BUENA VISTA DR	SBD	100 E1
BUENA VISTA DR	SLO	76 A1
BUENA VISTA DR	SCR	54 B2
BUENA VISTA RD	AMA	40 D3
BUENA VISTA RD	KER	78 C3
BUENA VISTA RD	SBD	91 E4
BUENA VISTA RD	SJCO	40 C3
BUENA VISTA ST	BUR	179 C2
BUENA VISTA ST	LACO	Q B2
BUENA VISTA ST	LACO	R B3
BUENA VISTA ST	VEN	88 D5
BUERER LN	SJCO	47 C1
BUERKLE RD	KER	78 A3
BUFFALO RUN RD	RCO	102 C4
BUFFUM LN	LAS	21 B3
BUFFUM RD	SHA	13 B5
BUHACH RD	MCO	48 B5
BUHNE ST	EUR	121 C2
BULKLEY RD	SOL	39 C2
BULLARD AV	FRCO	56 C3
BULLARD AV	FRCO	57 B3
BULL CANYON RD	SLO	76 D5
BULL CREEK RD	MPA	49 B2
BULLION MTN RD	SBD	101 C1
BULLIS RD	LACO	S D1
BULLRIDGE WHEEL	KIN	67 B4
BULL RUN ST	KER	80 C1
BULL SKIN RIDGE	SHA	19 A1
BULLY CHOOP RD	SHA	17 E3
BULS RD	KER	87 E1
BUMMERVILLE RD	CAL	41 B2
BUNCE RD	SUT	33 D2
BUNCH GRASS LKT	SHA	13 B5
BUNDY DR	LA	180 B4
BUNDY DR	LACO	Q A4
BUNDY CANYON RD	RCO	99 C5
BUNKER RD	MCO	47 C5
BUNKER RD	MCO	55 C1
BUNKER HILL RD	SIE	26 D3
BUNKER STATN RD	SOL	39 C3
BUNNY LN	RCO	100 C5
BUNSELMEIER RD	LAS	14 B3
BUNTE RD	MON	65 C3
BUNTGVLL CUMMGS	LAS	21 B4
BURBANK BLVD	BUR	179 B3
BURBANK BLVD	LA	179 B3
BURBANK BLVD	LACO	97 C1
BURBANK BLVD	LACO	Q A3
BURBANK ST	KER	78 A2
BURCH RD	SUT	33 C3
BURCHELL AV	MCO	48 D5
BURCHELL RD	SCL	54 C1
BURCH HAVEN RD	MCO	55 B2
BURGESS RCH RD	TRI	16 E5
BURKE LN	SOL	39 B3
BURLANDO RD	KER	69 D5
BURLNGTN RDG RD	NEV	34 E1
BURMA RD	NEV	34 C2
BURNES VALLEY	LAK	32 A3
BURNETT	PLA	34 B4
BURNEY ST	MDO	162 C3
BURNHAM RD	VEN	88 A4
BURNS AV	KER	78 C1
BURNS FRWY	HUM	9 E5
BURNS FRWY	HUM	10 A5
BURNS RD	LPAZ	104 A2
BURNS CANYON RD	SBD	100 B1
BURNS CUTOFF	SJCO	40 A5
BURNSIDE LK RD	ALP	36 B4
BURNT RCH DUMP	TRI	10 E5
BURNT TREE RD	SBD	81 C5
BURRELL RD	HUM	15 E4
BURRIS LN	MEN	31 C1
BURRIS RD	SUT	33 B2
BURROUGH N RD	FRCO	58 A2
BURROUGH VLY RD	FRCO	58 A2
BURSON RD	CAL	40 D4
BURTON WY	BH	183 C1
BURTON WY	LA	183 C1
BURTON MESA BL	SB	86 B2
BURWOOD RD	SJCO	47 D2
BUSCH LN	MEN	23 B5
BUSH ST	AMA	40 D2
BUSH ST	SF	142 A3
BUSH ST	SF	143 C4
BUSHARD ST	ORA	T C3
BUSHEY RD	MOD	14 C1
BUSSEL RD	KER	78 B2
BUSTER RD	COL	33 A2
BUTANO CUT-OFF	SMCO	45 C5
BUTCHER RCH RD	SIE	26 E3
BUTLER AV	FRCO	57 C5
BUTLER RD	COL	25 A5
BUTLER RD	STA	47 B2
BUTLER VLY RD	HUM	16 A1
BUTTE AV	FRCO	66 E1
BUTTE AV	SUT	33 C2
BUTTE RD	LAS	14 D3
BUTTE RD E	SUT	33 C2
BUTTE RD N	SUT	33 B1
BUTTE RD S	SUT	33 B2
BUTTE RD W	SUT	33 B1
BUTTE CREEK RD	HUM	16 B2
BUTTE HOUSE RD	SUT	33 C2
BUTTE HOUSE RD	YUBA	125 A2
BUTTEMER RD	SBD	90 E4
BUTTE MTN RD	AMA	40 E2
BUTTE MTN RD	AMA	41 A2
BUTTE MTN RD	TEH	24 C2
BUTTERBREAD CYN	KER	79 E2
BUTTERBREAD CYN	KER	80 A2
BUTTERCUP CT	KER	79 C4
BUTTRFLD STG RD	MAD	49 D5
BUTTRFLD STG RD	MAD	57 D1
BUTTRFLD STG RD	RCO	99 D5
BUTTERFLY PK RD	RCO	100 C5
BTRFLY VLY TWAN	PLU	26 C1
BUTTERMILK RD	INY	51 B4
BUTTERS RD	IMP	109 C4
BUTTE SLOUGH RD	COL	33 A2
BUTTE VALLEY RD	INY	72 A3
BUTTE VLY RD E	SIS	5 A3
BUTTE VLY RD W	SIS	4 E3
BUTTE VLY AIRPT	SIS	5 A3
BUTTONHOOK RD	SB	86 D3
BUTTONWILLOW AV	FRCO	58 A4
BUTTONWILLOW DR	KER	77 E3
BUTTONWILLOW DR	KER	78 A3
BUTTS RD	MCO	47 C5
BUTTS RD	MCO	55 C1
BUTTS CANYON RD	LAK	32 B5
BUZZARD ROOST	SHA	19 A1

STREET	CO.	PAGE & GRID
BVD AV	MCO	48 C5
BYERS PASS RD	LAS	21 B3
BYINGTON RD	SUT	33 C4
BYOFF RD	TRI	10 E5
BYRON HWY	CC	39 D5
BYRON RD	SJCO	46 D1
BYRON RD	CC	46 D1
BYSTRUM RD	STA	47 D3
BYWOOD DR	TEH	18 C4
C		
C ST	KER	68 B5
C ST	SD	215 D3
C ST	YOL	137 A2
CABALLERO CT	LAK	32 A4
CABIN RD	LAS	14 B4
CABRILLO AV	LACO	S C2
CABRILLO BLVD	STB	174 E4
CABRILLO DR	AVLN	105 B5
CABRILLO FRWY	SD	213 D3
CABRILLO FRWY	SD	215 E2
CABRILLO FRWY	SDCO	V B4
CABRILLO HWY	MONT	167 D5
CABRILLO HWY	MONT	168 C2
CABRILLO HWY	MON	53 E5
CABRILLO HWY	MON	54 B4
CABRILLO HWY	MON	168 C2
CABRILLO HWY	SNLO	172 B1
CABRILLO HWY	SLO	75 B1
CABRILLO HWY	SLO	76 B5
CABRILLO HWY	SLO	172 B1
CABRILLO HWY	SMCO	45 B3
CABRILLO HWY	SB	86 B1
CABRILLO HWY	SC	169 A4
CABRILLO HWY	SCR	53 D1
CABRILLO HWY	SCR	54 A2
CACHAGUA RD	MON	54 C5
CACHAGUA RD	MON	64 C1
CACHUMA RD	SB	87 A2
CACTUS AV	RCO	99 C3
CACTUS AV	SBD	99 B1
CACTUS DR	MCO	55 D2
CACTUS FLATS	INY	70 B2
CACTUS VLY RD	RCO	99 E4
CADET RD	KER	78 A4
CADILLAC AV	LA	183 D4
CADIZ DR	SBD	102 C1
CADIZ RD	SBD	94 B3
CADIZ RD	SBD	103 A1
CADY RD	IMP	109 A4
CAHUENGA BLVD	LA	179 A3
CAHUENGA BLVD	LA	181 D5
CAHUENGA BLVD	LACO	Q B3
CAHUENGA BLVD W	LA	181 B2
CAHUILLA RD	RCO	100 B5
CAHUILLA RD	SBD	91 C3
CAHUILLA HTS RD	RCO	100 A5
CAIRO	KIN	57 D5
CAJALCO RD	RCO	99 A3
CAJON BLVD	SBD	91 A5
CAJON ST	SBD	99 C2
CALAVERAS AV	FRCO	56 D4
CALAVERAS AV	FRCO	66 D2
CALAVERAS RD	ALA	46 B3
CALAVERAS RD	SCL	46 B4
CALAVERITAS RD	CAL	41 A3
CALDOR RD	ED	41 B1
CALICO BLVD	SBD	92 A1
CALICO RD	SBD	92 A1
CALIENT-BODF RD	KER	79 B3
CALIENT-BODF RD	KER	79 C2
CALIENTE CK RD	KER	79 C3
CALIFORNIA AV	BKD	166 B3
CALIFORNIA AV	COL	32 E3
CALIFORNIA AV	FRE	165 A5
CALIFORNIA AV	FRCO	56 C3
CALIFORNIA AV	FRCO	57 C3
CALIFORNIA AV	KER	78 D3
CALIFORNIA AV	LACO	R D5
CALIFORNIA AV	MDO	162 A4
CALIFORNIA AV	RENO	130 A3
CALIFORNIA AV	RCO	98 E2
CALIFORNIA AV	RCO	99 D4
CALIFORNIA AV	SCL	54 C1
CALIFORNIA AV	SC	169 C4
CALIFORNIA AV	STA	47 B2
CALIFORNIA BLVD	LACO	R E3
CALIFORNIA BLVD	LACO	R A3
CALIFORNIA BLVD	NAP	133 B2
CALIFORNIA BLVD	PAS	190 A4
CALIFORNIA BLVD	SNLO	172 C2
CALIFORNIA BLVD	SLO	172 C2
CALIFORNIA DR	IMP	108 C2
CALIFORNIA DR	NAPA	29 D4
CALIFORNIA ST	BUR	179 C3
CALIFORNIA ST	EUR	121 C2
CALIFORNIA ST	LACO	98 A1
CALIFORNIA ST	ONT	204 A5
CALIFORNIA ST	SBD	99 B1
CALIFORNIA ST	SDCO	106 B3
CALIFORNIA ST	SF	141 C3
CALIFORNIA ST	SF	142 A3
CALIFORNIA ST	SF	143 B4
CALIFORNIA ST	SFCO	45 B1
CALIFORNIA ST	SJCO	40 A5
CALIFORNIA ST	S	160 D2
CALIF CITY BLVD	KER	80 B4
CALIFRNIA FARMS	SJCO	47 C1
CALIF PINES BL	MOD	14 E2
CALISTOGA RD	SON	38 A1
CALKINS RD	FRCO	57 E1
CALLAHAN RD	TEH	18 C5
CALLAHAN RD E	SIS	11 D1
CALLE DEL SOL	AVLN	105 B5
CALLE ECUESTRE	SB	87 A2
CALLEGUAS RD	VEN	96 C1
CALLE H COLEGIO	BAJA	112 B4
CALLE LIPPIZANA	SB	87 A4
CALLENDR BLK LK	SLO	76 B5
CALLE QUEBRADA	SB	87 A4
CALLE REAL	SB	86 E4
CALLE REAL	SB	87 A4
CALLOWAY DR	KER	78 C3
CALNEVA RD	LAS	21 E5
CALPACK RD	SJCO	46 E1
CALPINE RD	SIE	27 B3
CALPINE LO RD	SIE	27 B3
CALVIN CREST RD	MAD	49 D4
CALVINE RD	SAC	39 E2
CALVINE RD	SAC	40 A2
CALZ	BAJA	112 B4
CALZADA AV	SB	86 E3
CAMANCHE PKWY	CAL	40 D3
CAMANCHE PKWY N	AMA	40 C3
CAMANCHE PKWY S	CAL	40 C3
CAMARES DR	LACO	90 A3
CAMARILLO ST	LA	179 B4
CAMARILLO ST	LACO	Q B3
CAMBRIA AV	FRCO	56 A2
CAMBRIA RD	SBD	91 E4
CAMBRIDGE DR	BUR	179 E2
CAMBRIDGE RD	SHA	18 C3

STREET	CO.	PAGE & GRID
CAMBRIDGE ST	OR	196 D1
CAMBRIDGE ST	SA	196 D1
CAMDEN AV	SCL	46 B5
CAMERON AV	LACO	98 C2
CAMERON AV	LACO	R C4
CAMERON RD	MEN	30 C2
CAMERON CYN RD	KER	79 D5
CAMERON PARK DR	ED	34 C5
CAMINO AV	IMP	108 C2
CAMINO ALTO	MV	140 B3
CM CAPISTRANO	SJC	202 D3
CAMINO CIELO	SB	87 A3
CM DE FLORES	AVLN	105 B4
CM DE LA COSTA	SD	105 A4
CAMINO DL MONTE	AVLN	105 A4
CAMINO DL MONTE	CAR	53 D5
CAMINO DL MONTE	CAR	168 C3
CAMINO DL MONTE	MON	168 C3
CAMINO DIABLO	CC	46 C1
CM DOS RIOS	VEN	96 D1
CM LAS RAMBLAS	SJC	202 D4
CM MIRA COSTA	SCL	202 E5
CAMINO ORO	SHA	19 A2
CAMINO REAL	LACO	S A2
CAMINO REAL	SHA	19 A2
CAMINO SANTA FE	SDCO	106 C5
CM SANTA FE DR	SDCO	V B3
CM TASSAJARA RD	ALA	46 B2
CM TASSAJARA RD	CC	46 A1
CAMINO VISTA	SHA	19 A2
CAMMATTI-SHN RD	SLO	76 D1
CAMP RD	SAC	39 E3
CAMP RD E	COL	32 D2
CAMPBELL	SJCO	47 D1
CAMPBELL AV	BUT	33 C1
CAMPBELL AV	SCL	46 A5
CAMPBELL DR	KER	78 E4
CAMPBELL RD	IMP	111 E3
CAMPBELL RD	SBD	101 D1
CAMPBELL RD	SB	86 C3
CAMPBELL RD	SOL	39 B1
CAMPBL HOT SPGS	SIE	27 C4
CAMPBELL RDG RD	TRI	10 D4
CAMPBLLS FLT RD	TUO	41 C5
CAMP CREEK RD	BUT	25 E2
CAMP CREEK RD	SIS	4 B2
CAMP FAR WST RD	PLA	34 A3
CAMP FAR WST RD	YUB	34 A2
CAMPHORA RD	MON	54 E5
CAMPHORA RD	MON	55 A5
CAMP KIMTU RD	HUM	16 C5
CAMP NINE RD	CAL	41 C4
CAMPO RD	SDCO	V D4
CAMPO RD	SDCO	111 E1
CAMPODONICA RD	MCO	48 A3
CAMPOS LN	SOL	39 A2
CAMP ROCK RD	SBD	92 A1
CAMPO SECO RD	CAL	40 D3
CAMPO SECO RD	TUO	41 C5
CAMP THREE RD	SIS	10 E1
CAMPTON RD	EUR	121 D4
CAMPTON RD	HUM	15 E1
CAMPTONVILLE RD	SIE	26 C5
CAMPUS AV	ONT	204 C3
CAMPUS AV	SBD	98 D1
CAMPUS AV	UPL	204 C3
CAMPUS DR	IRV	198 C5
CAMPUS DR	KER	78 E4
CAMPUS DR	ORA	198 C5
CAMPUS DR	SCL	147 A3
CAMP WEOTT RD	HUM	15 D2
CMP 1 TEN MI RD	MEN	22 C4
CMP 2 TEN MI RD	MEN	22 C4
CAMP 8 RD	SLO	76 C2
CAMUESA RD	SB	87 D3
CANA HWY	BUT	25 A2
CANADA BLVD	LACO	97 E1
CANADA BLVD	LACO	R D3
CANADA RD	SMCO	45 C3
CANADA RD	SCL	54 D2
CANAL AV	FRCO	57 E1
CANAL BLVD	SJCO	46 E1
CANAL BLVD	SJCO	47 A1
CANAL DR	MCO	47 E4
CANAL DR	MCO	48 A4
CANAL RD	GLE	24 E3
CANAL RD	KER	77 E2
CANAL RD	KER	78 A2
CANAL ST	PLCV	138 C3
CANAL BANK RD	STA	47 E2
CANAL BANK RD	STA	48 A2
CANAL GULCH RD	SIS	4 A4
CANAL SCHOOL RD	MCO	47 C4
CANA PINE CREEK	BUT	25 A2
C AND D BLVD	RCO	103 D5
CANFIELD RD	SDCO	107 A2
CANFIELD RD	SON	37 E3
CANNIBAL RD	HUM	15 D2
CANNON RD	SDCO	106 B3
CANNON RD	TEH	18 B5
CANNON ST	SDCO	V A4
CANOGA AV	LA	177 C3
CANON DR	BH	183 B1
CANON RD	SOL	39 A3
CANON ST	SDCO	111 C1
CANON PERDIDO	STB	174 C4
CANRIGHT RD	SOL	39 C3
CANTELOW RD	SOL	38 E2
CANTELOW RD	SOL	39 A2
CANTON RD	MCO	48 C5
CANYON DR	RCO	100 C3
CANYON DR	SBD	82 A5
CANYON RD	INY	52 B3
CANYON RD	MEN	23 A5
CANYON RD	MNO	52 B3
CANYON RD	SBD	93 B5
CANYON RD	SBD	100 C2
CANYON RD	SMCO	45 C5
CANYON RD	SR	139 B4
CANYON RD	SHA	18 C3
CANYON RD	SON	31 D5
CANYON WY	PLA	34 D3
CANYON CREEK RD	MOD	14 E1
CANYON CREEK RD	SIS	3 B5
CANYON CREEK RD	TRI	17 C1
CANYON CREST DR	RCO	99 B2
CANYON VW LOOP	TEH	19 B4
CANYON VIEW RD	SBD	91 D4
CAPAY AV	GLE	24 E3
CAPAY RD	TEH	24 D2
CAPE GLOUCESTER	SBD	91 E2
CAPEZZOLI LN	LAS	21 C4
CAPITAL BLVD	GLE	24 E4
CAPITAN TK TR	SDCO	107 B5
CAPITOL AV	SCTO	137 C3
CAPITOL AV	SCL	46 B4
CAPITOL AV	YOL	137 A2
CAPITOL AV	YOL	39 D1
CAPITOL EXPWY	SCL	46 B5
CAPITOL ST	SAL	171 B3
CAPITOLA RD	SCR	54 A2

STREET	CO.	PAGE & GRID
CAPPELL RD	HUM	10 C2
CAPPS CROSSING	ED	35 B5
CAPRI AV	MCO	55 D1
CARBINE TR	KER	79 D5
CARBON AV	ORA	98 C3
CARBON CYN RD	ORA	U E5
CARBON CYN RD	ORA	T E1
CARBON CYN RD	SBD	98 C3
CARBON CYN RD	SBD	U E5
CARBONDALE RD	AMA	40 C2
CARBONDALE RD	SAC	40 C2
CARDELLA RD	MCO	48 B4
CARDIFF ST	SDCO	V D4
CARDY DR	S	160 B4
CAREY RD	IMP	109 A4
CARGIL LN	RCO	107 C1
CARIBOU RD	SIS	11 C3
CARLETON RD	MPA	49 B3
CARLIN RD	SJCO	46 E1
CARLSBAD BLVD	SDCO	106 B3
CARLSON	CC	38 C5
CARLSON BLVD	R	155 B3
CARLSON RD	BUT	25 B4
CARLSON RD	SUT	33 C3
CARLTON RD	SCR	54 C2
CARLTON RD	SIS	4 B4
CARLUCCI RD	MCO	56 A1
CARLYLE RD	NEV	27 A5
CARMEL RD	KER	77 D1
CARMELLIA AV	FRCO	56 B2
CARMEL MTN RD	SDCO	106 D4
CARMEL RCHO BL	MON	168 D5
CARMEL VLY RD	MON	54 B5
CARMEL VLY RD	MON	64 C1
CARMEL VLY RD	MON	168 E4
CARMEL VLY RD	SDCO	106 C4
CARMEN LN	BUT	25 A3
CARMENCITA AV	SJCO	40 A2
CARMENITA AV	LACO	T A1
CARMIRE RD	SUT	33 B2
CARNATION RD	MCO	47 D5
CARNELIAN BAY	PLA	35 E1
CARNEROS AV	NAPA	38 C3
CARPENTER RD	HUM	10 D5
CARPENTER RD	SJCO	40 B5
CARPENTER RD	STA	47 C3
CARPENTER ST	CAR	53 D5
CARPENTER ST	CAR	168 C3
CARPENTER ST	MON	168 C3
CARPENTERIA	MON	54 C3
CARPINTERIA ST	STB	174 E3
CARPENTER RIDGE	BUT	25 D1
CARR AV	SBT	54 C2
CARRIAGE LN	SHA	18 B3
CARRIER GLCH RD	TRI	17 C3
CARRILLO ST	STB	174 B4
CARRIZO GRGE RD	SDCO	111 A4
CARROLL RD	SAC	40 A3
CARROLL CK RD	INY	60 B5
CARROLTON	SJCO	47 C1
CARROT LN	RCO	107 B1
CARRVILLE LOOP	TRI	11 E4
CARRVILLE LOOP	TRI	12 A4
CARSON RD	ED	34 E5
CARSON ST	LACO	97 D3
CARSON ST	LACO	S B2
CARSTENS RD	MPA	49 B3
CARTER RD	MPA	49 B3
CARTER ST	SBD	99 D2
CARTMILL AV	TUL	68 A2
CARUTHERS AV	FRCO	57 C5
CARVER LN	RCO	99 B4
CASADEL RD	MAD	49 E5
CASADEL RD	MAD	50 A5
CASA DIABLO CTF	MNO	51 B2
CASA DIABLO MN	MNO	51 B2
CASALE RD	TEH	18 D5
CASA LOMA RD	SCL	54 B1
CASCADE BLVD	SHA	18 C2
CASCADE RD	SBD	101 A1
CASCADIAN AV	SBD	91 D3
CASE RD	RCO	99 C4
CASEY AV	KER	68 B5
CASEY AV	SB	86 E3
CASEY RD	IMP	109 B5
CASEY RD	SOL	39 B2
CASITAS VIS RD	VEN	88 A5
CASPR LTL LK RD	MEN	22 C5
CASS ST	MONT	167 E4
CASS ST	MON	53 E3
CASS ST	SDCO	V A3
CASS ST	SDCO	106 C5
CASSEL RD	SHA	13 D5
CASSEL FALL RIV	SHA	13 D4
CASSERLY RD	SCR	54 C2
CASSIDY ST	SDCO	106 B3
CASTAIC RD	LACO	89 B4
CASTAIC CYN RD	LACO	89 B3
CASTERLINE RD	HUM	16 D4
CASTLE CT	BUT	25 D3
CASTLE ST	S	160 C3
CASTLE CREEK RD	SHA	12 C3
CASTLE LAKE RD	SIS	12 C2
CASTRO	CC	38 C5
CASTRO RD	CC	38 D5
CASTRO RD	RCO	99 D4
CASTRO VLY BL	ALA	146 D1
CASTROVILLE BL	MON	54 C3
CATALINA AV	AVLN	105 B5
CATALINA BLVD	SDCO	V A4
CATALINA DR	DVS	136 C1
CAT CANYON RD	SB	86 D2
CATERPILLAR RD	SHA	18 C2
CATFISH BCH RD	PLU	20 B4
CATHEDRAL RD	ED	35 E3
CATHEY RD	HUM	16 B4
CATLETT RD W	SUT	33 D4
CATRINA RD	MCO	56 B1
CATTARAUGUS AV	CUL	183 C4
CATTARAUGUS AV	LA	183 C4
CATTLE DR	TUL	68 E3
CATTLE DRIVE RD	MNO	51 C1
CATTLEMEN RD	MON	65 D3
CATWAY RD	SB	87 A2
CAUGHLIN RD	SBD	91 A3
CAVE CITY RD	CAL	41 B3
CAVEDALE RD	SON	38 B2
CAVIN RD	VEN	88 E4
CAVITT & STLLMN	PLA	34 B4
CAWELTI RD	VEN	96 C1
CAWSTON AV	RCO	99 E4
CAYLEY DR	KER	79 B4
CAYTON VLY RD	SHA	13 C4
CAYUCOS CK RD	SLO	75 D2
CAZADERO HWY	SON	37 C1
CCMO RD	KER	77 D3
CEBADA CYN RD	SB	86 C3
CECIL AV	KER	68 B5
CECIL AV	KER	68 C5
CECIL RD	COL	33 B3
CECILVILLE RD	SIS	11 C3

STREET	CO.	PAGE & GRID
CEDAR AV	FRCO	57 C3
CEDAR AV	FRCO	57 C5
CEDAR AV	RCO	100 C4
CEDAR AV	SBD	99 B2
CEDAR DR	MOD	14 B3
CEDAR ST	SBD	80 E1
CEDAR ST	SDCO	107 A4
CEDAR CAMP RD	HUM	10 C2
CEDAR CAMP RD	SIS	10 C1
CEDAR CAMP RD	TRI	17 A4
CEDAR CANYON RD	SBD	84 B4
CEDAR CREEK RD	ED	40 E1
CEDAR CREEK RD	ED	41 A1
CEDAR CREEK RD	HUM	10 C5
CEDAR CK LP RD	BUT	25 C1
CEDAR GROVE RD	SIS	5 A2
CEDAR RAVINE RD	ED	34 E5
CEDAR RAVINE ST	PLCV	138 E3
CEDARVILLE DUMP	MOD	8 E1
CEDAR WELL	SIS	5 A4
CEDARWOOD CT	SHA	19 A3
CEDROS DR	SBD	90 E2
CEMENT HILL RD	FRFD	135 C1
CEMENT HILL RD	NEV	34 C1
CEMETERY DR	MOD	14 C3
CEMETERY RD	COL	32 D1
CEMETERY RD	HUM	16 D4
CEMETERY RD	MCO	47 D4
CEMETERY RD	MNO	43 C4
CEMETERY RD	SBD	82 A5
CEMETERY RD	SHA	19 B2
CEMETERY RD	SIS	15 A2
CENTENNIAL RD	HUM	15 D3
CENTER AV	MCO	56 B2
CENTER RD	LAS	21 A3
CENTER RD	STA	47 B2
CENTER ST	CAL	41 A3
CENTER ST	MAN	161 A4
CENTER ST	RCO	99 B2
CENTER ST	SBD	99 C2
CENTER ST	SC	169 D3
CENTER ST	S	160 C5
CENTER ST EXT	RCO	99 C2
CENTER ST S	TEH	24 E1
CTR SCH HOUSE	LAS	14 C3
CENTERVILLE LN	DGL	36 B3
CENTERVILLE RD	BUT	25 C3
CENTERVILLE RD	HUM	15 D2
CENTERVILLE RD	MOD	8 A1
CENTERVILLE RD	MOD	14 E1
CENTINELA AV	CUL	187 D1
CENTINELA AV	ING	188 B3
CENTINELA AV	LA	187 D1
CENTINELA AV	LACO	Q A4
CENTINELLA RD	MCO	55 C1
CENTRAL AV	A	158 A5
CENTRAL AV	A	159 A1
CENTRAL AV	FRCO	56 D4
CENTRAL AV	FRCO	57 B4
CENTRAL AV	HUM	9 E4
CENTRAL AV	HUM	10 A4
CENTRAL AV	KER	78 A2
CENTRAL AV	LA	186 B5
CENTRAL AV	LACO	97 E2
CENTRAL AV	LACO	Q C3
CENTRAL AV	LACO	S C1
CENTRAL AV	MCO	47 D4
CENTRAL AV	MON	65 B2
CENTRAL AV	MTCL	203 C3
CENTRAL AV	ORA	R C5
CENTRAL AV	ORA	T C1
CENTRAL AV	PAC	167 C2
CENTRAL AV	RCO	99 B2
CENTRAL AV	RCO	205 B5
CENTRAL AV	SAL	171 A4
CENTRAL AV	SBD	98 D2
CENTRAL AV	RCO	99 B4
CENTRAL AV	SBD	203 C3
CENTRAL AV	SB	86 B3
CENTRAL AV	STA	47 D3
CENTRAL AV	SUT	33 B3
CENTRAL AV	TEH	24 D1
CENTRAL AV	VEN	88 C5
CENTRAL AV	YOL	39 D2
CENTRAL RD	SBD	91 C3
CENTRAL EXPWY	MVW	148 B4
CENTRAL EXPWY	SVL	148 B4
CENTRAL FRWY	SF	143 A5
CENTRAL SKYWAY	SF	142 C4
CENTRAL ST	RCO	99 C5
CENTRAL CAMP RD	MAD	49 E4
CENTRAL HILL RD	CAL	40 E3
CENTRAL HILL RD	CAL	41 A3
CENTRL HOUSE RD	BUT	25 D5
CENTRALIA ST	LACO	S E2
CENTRALIA ST	LACO	T A2
CENTRAL VLY HWY	KER	78 B1
CENTURY BLVD	LA	189 D1
CENTURY BLVD	LACO	97 D2
CENTURY BLVD	LACO	Q B5
CERINI AV	FRCO	57 B5
CERINI AV	FRCO	57 C5
CERRITOS AV	ANA	193 D4
CERRITOS AV	ORA	T B2
CERRO GORDO RD	INY	60 C5
CERRO GORDO RD	INY	60 D4
CERRO NOROESTE	KER	78 A5
CERRO NOROESTE	KER	87 E1
CERVANTES BLVD	SF	142 A1
CHABOT RD	VAL	134 D1
CHADBOURNE RD	CC	39 B5
CHADBOURNE RD	SOL	38 E3
CHADWICK RD	SBD	101 E1
CHAHLIP LN	FRCO	58 C1
CHALET DR	KER	79 C4
CHALFANT RD	MNO	51 D3
CHALFANT LP RD	MNO	51 D3
CHALK BLUFF RD	INY	51 C4
CHALK BLUFF RD	NEV	34 D1
CHALK HILL RD	SON	37 E1
CHALLNGE CTO RD	YUB	26 A4
CHALONE RD	SBT	55 A5
CHAMBERLAIN	PLA	34 A3
CHAMBERLAIN RD	MCO	48 B5
CHAMBERS RD	HUM	15 D4
CHAMBERS WLS RD	SBD	103 E1
CHAMPAGNE AV	KER	89 C1
CHAMPS FLAT RD	LAS	20 C2
CHANAC RD	KER	79 B4
CHANDLER	YUB	33 D1
CHANDLER BLVD	BUR	179 C3
CHANDLER BLVD	LA	179 A4
CHANDLER BLVD	LACO	Q A3
CHANDLER RD	PLU	26 D1
CHANDON AV	BUT	33 C1
CHANNEL ISLD BL	VEN	96 B1
CHAPARAJOS ST	CAL	41 A4
CHAPARRAL DR	SHA	18 B2
CHAPMAN AV	GGR	195 A1
CHAPMAN AV	OR	195 D1
CHAPMAN AV	OR	196 B1

STREETS

STREET	CO.	PAGE	GRID
CHAPMAN AV	ORA	98	C3
CHAPMAN AV	ORA	T	C1
CHAPMAN AV	ORA	T	B2
CHAPMAN DR	CRTM	140	B2
CHAPMAN RD	RCO	107	C1
CHAPPIUS LN N	LAS	21	B4
CHAPPIUS LN S	LAS	21	B4
CHAPULNIK RD	IMP	109	A6
CHARD AV	TEH	18	D5
CHARLEBOIS RD	MNO	42	E1
CHARLES ST	KER	80	D1
CHARLES ST	SHA	18	C3
CHARLESTON BLVD	LV	209	A2
CHARLESTON BL E	CLK	74	D2
CHARLESTON RD	MCO	55	D2
CHARLESTON RD	SCL	45	A4
CHRLSTN RD W	PA	147	E5
CHRLSTN VOLCANO	AMA	41	A4
CHAROLAIS RD	SLO	76	A1
CHARTER WY	SJCO	40	B5
CHARTER OAK DR	TUL	68	C1
CHASE AV	KER	79	C4
CHASE AV	KER	80	A2
CHASE AV	SDCO	V	D3
CHASE AV	SDCO	111	E1
CHASE AV	TEH	24	D2
CHASE DR	RCO	98	E3
CHASE SCHOOL RD	RCO	100	E3
CHATEAU DR	SMCO	45	C3
CHATEAU RD	ML	164	D3
CHATEAU FRESNO	FRCO	57	B4
CHATEAU FRESNO	FRCO	57	B5
CHATSWORTH BLVD	SDCO	V	B3
CHATSWORTH BLVD	SDCO	111	C1
CHECKMATE RD	RCO	100	A5
CHEMEHUEVI BLVD	MOH	96	B4
CHEMISE MTN RD	HUM	22	A1
CHEROKEE LN	SAC	40	B5
CHEROKEE LN	SJCO	40	B3
CHEROKEE RD	BUT	25	D4
CHEROKEE RD	MCO	55	D1
CHEROKEE RD	SBD	82	C5
CHEROKEE RD	SJCO	40	B5
CHERRY AV	FRCO	57	C4
CHERRY AV	FRCO	57	C5
CHERRY AV	KER	78	D2
CHERRY AV	LACO	97	E4
CHERRY AV	LACO	S	C5
CHERRY AV	RCO	99	E3
CHERRY AV	SBD	99	A4
CHERRY AV	STA	47	C4
CHERRY ST	SUT	33	C2
CHERRY CREEK RD	SON	31	C4
CHERRY GLEN RD	SOL	38	E3
CHERRY VLY BLVD	RCO	99	E2
CHERT RD	RCO	107	C1
CHESEBORO RD	LACO	90	B4
CHESTER AV	BKD	166	B4
CHESTER AV	KER	78	D3
CHESTER LN	BKD	166	B4
CHESTR JUNPR LK	PLU	20	B1
CHESTER SKI RD	PLU	20	A4
CHESTR WRNR VLY	PLU	19	E3
CHESTR WRNR VLY	PLU	20	A3
CHESTNUT AV	FRCO	57	C2
CHESTNUT AV	FRCO	57	C5
CHESTNUT AV	SA	196	A4
CHESTNUT AV	TEH	18	D5
CHESTNUT ST	SF	143	A4
CHESTNUT ST	SHA	18	C3
CHESTNUT WY	CAL	41	A4
CHEVALIER RD	KER	78	D4
CHEVY CHASE DR	LACO	97	E1
CHEVY CHASE DR	LACO	R	D3
CHEZEM RD	HUM	10	B5
CHICAGO AV	RIV	205	E4
CHICAGO AV	STA	47	C2
CHICK RD	IMP	112	D5
CHICK RD	RCO	108	E1
CHICKEN HAWK RD	PLA	34	E2
CHICKEN RCH RD	TUO	41	C5
CHICO AV	KIN	57	E5
CHICO CANYON RD	BUT	25	C2
CHICOR LN	SOL	39	B2
CHICO RIVER RD	BUT	25	A3
CHIDAGO LOOP	MNO	51	C2
CHIDAGO CYN RD	MNO	51	B2
CHIHUAHUA VLY	SDCO	107	D3
CHILDS AV	MER	170	B6
CHILDS AV	MCO	48	D2
CHILE CAMP RD	CAL	40	D3
CHILENO VLY RD	SON	37	E3
CHILENO VLY RD	SON	38	A3
CHILES RD	YOL	39	C1
CHILES POPE VLY	NAPA	29	D1
CHILES POPE VLY	NAPA	38	C1
CHILI HILL	PLA	34	B3
CHIMNEY ROCK RD	SLO	75	D1
CHINA CAMP RD	MCO	55	D1
CHINA CREEK RD	MAD	49	D4
CHINA GRADE	SIS	3	A4
CHINA GRADE LP	KER	78	D2
CHINA GRADE RD	PLU	26	D1
CHINA GULCH RD	SHA	18	B1
CHINA LAKE BLVD	KER	80	D1
CHINA PK LO RD	SIS	3	B3
CHINA POINT RD	BUT	25	D2
CHINA RANCH RD	INY	73	A3
CHINO AV	SBD	98	D2
CHINO-CORONA	SBD	98	A5
CHINQUAPIN RD	MAD	49	E4
CHINQUAPIN RD	MAD	50	A1
CHINQUAPIN DR	MEN	23	A5
CHIRIACO RD	RCO	101	E4
CHITTENDEN RD	TEH	24	C2
CHLORIDE RD	SBD	92	B1
CHLORIDE CLF RD	INY	62	A3
CHOLAME RD	MON	66	C4
CHOLAME VLY RD	SLO	66	D5
CHOLLA RD	SBD	91	C4
CHOLLA RD	SBD	92	A5
CHORRO ST N	SNLO	172	A2
CHORRO ST S	SNLO	172	A3
CHOWCHILLA	MAD	56	D3
CHOWCHILLA BLVD	MAD	56	D1
CHOWCHILLA MTN	MPA	49	C5
CHRISMAN RD	SJCO	47	A2
CHRISTENSEN RD	SAC	40	A3
CHRISTIAN RD	TEH	24	C2
CHRISTN VLY RD	PLA	34	C3
CHROME MINE RD	TRI	11	B3
CHUALAR RD	MON	54	D4
CHUALAR CYN RD	MON	54	D4
CHUALAR RIV RD	MON	54	D5
CHUCKAGON DR	CAL	41	A4
CHUCKWALLA RD	SBD	91	D3
CHUCKWL SPGS RD	RCO	102	D2
CHUCKWLA VLY RD	RCO	102	D4
CHUCKWLA VLY RD	RCO	103	E3
CHURCH AV	FRE	165	B5
CHURCH AV	FRCO	57	A3
CHURCH AV	FRCO	57	D3
CHURCH AV	SCL	54	D1
CHURCH LN	HUM	15	E2
CHURCH RD	SOL	39	C4
CHURCH ST	HUM	16	D4
CHURCH ST	SBD	99	C2
CHURCH ST	STA	47	D2
CHURCH ST	S	160	C5
CHURCH HILL RD	CAL	41	A3
CHURCHILL MN RD	INY	51	D3
CHURCH SPGS RD	STA	48	A1
CHURN CREEK RD	SHA	18	C2
CIBOLA RD	LPAZ	103	E5
CIBOLA RD	LPAZ	110	D1
CIENAGA RD	KER	78	A5
CIENEGA RD	SBT	54	A3
CIENEGA RD	SBT	55	A4
CIMA RD	SBD	83	E2
CIMA RD	SBD	84	A2
CIMA MESA RD	LACO	90	B4
CINCHA ST	CAL	41	A4
CINDER RD	INY	70	D3
CINDER PIT RD	MOD	14	D1
CIRCLE DR	INY	70	E1
CIRCLE DR	RCO	100	B4
CIRCLE DR	BUT	25	C3
CIRCLE C LN	SOL	39	B2
CIRCLEA CT	BUT	25	C3
CITRACADO PKWY	SDCO	106	D3
CITRON ST	ANA	193	B1
CITRUS AV	LACO	98	C2
CITRUS AV	LACO	R	C4
CITRUS AV	SBD	99	A2
CITRUS AV	SBD	99	D2
CITRUS AV	SDCO	106	D3
CITRUS AV	SDCO	106	D3
CITY DR, THE	OR	195	E2
CITY CAMP	MNO	43	C5
CITY CREEK RD	SBD	99	C1
CIVIC CENTER DR	SR	139	C1
CIVIC CENTER DR	SA	196	A4
CLAIREMONT DR	SD	214	E4
CLAIREMONT DR	SD	213	A1
CLAIREMONT DR	SDCO	106	C5
CLAIREMONT MESA	SD	211	D4
CLAIREMONT MESA	SDCO	V	B3
CLAIREMONT MESA	SDCO	106	C5
CLAIREMONT MESA	SDCO	106	D5
CLARATINA AV	STA	47	D2
CLAREMONT AV	B	156	C4
CLAREMONT AV	O	156	B5
CLAREMONT BLVD	CLA	203	B2
CLARISSA AV	AVLN	105	A5
CLARK AV	LACO	S	E2
CLARK AV	SB	86	C1
CLARK AV	TEH	24	E2
CLARK AV	YUBA	125	C4
CLARK RD	BUT	25	B3
CLARK RD	BUT	25	C5
CLARK RD	IMP	109	A5
CLARK RD	IMP	112	A4
CLARK RD	MEN	30	D2
CLARK RD	MON	65	A1
CLARK RD	SLO	76	C1
CLARK RD	SOL	39	B2
CLARK RD	STA	47	C2
CLARK RD	SUT	33	C1
CLARK ST	NAP	133	E3
CLARKE RD	HUM	15	D4
CLARK MTN RD	SBD	84	A2
CLARK RANCH RD	MNO	51	C1
CLARKSBURG	YOL	39	D2
CLARKS FORK RD	ALP	42	B2
CLARKSON AV	FRCO	56	D5
CLARKS VLY RD	GLE	24	D2
CLAUS RD	STA	47	D2
CLAUSEN RD	MCO	48	E5
CLAWITER RD	ALA	45	E2
CLAWITER RD	ALA	146	B4
CLAWITER RD	H	146	B4
CLAY RD	INY	72	D1
CLAY ST	SAL	171	B4
CLAY ST	U	123	B3
CLAY BANK RD	SOL	39	A3
CLAY MINE RD	KER	80	C5
CLAY RIVER RD	SBD	91	E1
CLAY STATION RD	SAC	40	B3
CLAYTON AV	FRCO	56	D4
CLAYTON RD	CC	59	A4
CLAYTON RD	NEV	34	A2
CLAYTON RD	SON	38	A5
CLAYTON RD	SON	38	A1
CLAYTON RD	STA	47	D3
CLAYTON CREEK	LAK	32	A4
CLEAR CREEK RD	KER	79	B4
CLEAR CREEK RD	SBT	65	E1
CLEAR CREEK RD	SBT	66	A1
CLEAR CREEK RD	SHA	18	B3
CLEARFIELD DR	MLBR	144	B5
CLEAR LAKE RD	MOD	6	C3
CLEGHORN RD	LAS	14	D5
CLEGHORN CYN RD	SBD	91	B5
CLEM	SJCO	40	C4
CLEMENCEAU AV	FRCO	57	D5
CLEMENTS AV	AVLN	105	A5
CLEMENTS RD	SJCO	40	C4
CLEMENTS RD	SUT	33	C2
CLEVELAND AV	SBD	98	A2
CLEVELAND AV	SD	213	A5
CLEVELAND AV	STA	47	D1
CLEVELAND AV	MCO	56	C1
CLEVELAND ST	RCO	101	D4
CLIFF DR	LAG	201	B4
CLIFF DR	STB	174	A5
CLIFF DR W	SC	169	D4
CLIFF RIDGE RD	MEN	30	C2
CLIFTON CT RD	SJCO	46	D1
CLINE GULCH RD	SHA	18	A1
CLINTON AV	FRE	165	B1
CLINTON AV	FRCO	56	E3
CLINTON AV	FRCO	57	A3
CLINTON AV	KIN	57	E5
CLINTON AV S	SJCO	47	B1
CLINTON RD	AMA	41	A2
CLINTON RD	ED	41	A1
CLINTON RD E	AMA	41	A2
CLINTON RD E	AMA	41	A2
CLINTN KEITH RD	RCO	99	D5
CLIO STATE RD	PLU	26	E1
CLOUGH RD	HUM	15	D2
CLOUTIER ST	DN	1	D3
CLOVER LN	SB	86	E2
CLOVER LN	SB	87	A3
CLOVER LN	SHA	18	B3
CLOVER CREEK RD	KLAM	5	A1
CLOVERDALE DR	SHA	18	B3
CLOVERDALE RD	RCO	98	E2
CLOVERDALE RD	SMCO	45	C5
CLOVERFIELD BL	SMON	180	A5
CLOVERLEAF DR	MAD	57	B2
CLOVER VLY RD	LAK	31	D2
CLOVIS AV	FRCO	57	D5
CLUB DR	DN	1	E3
CLYDE AV	MCO	48	B5
COACHELLA CANAL	RCO	108	D1
COACHLA CNAL RD	IMP	109	D1
COACHLLA CYN RD	RCO	101	D5
COAL RD	RCO	99	B4
COAL CANYON RD	BUT	25	C4
COAL CANYON RD	ORA	98	D3
COALINGA RD	SBT	65	D3
COAL MINE RD	AMA	40	D3
COALNGA MNL SPG	FRCO	66	B3
COAST BLVD S	SD	105	B2
COAST HWY	LAG	201	A2
COAST HWY	ORA	98	A2
COAST HWY	ORA	201	A2
COAST HWY	ORA	202	A5
COAST HWY	SON	30	D5
COAST HWY E	NB	199	B4
COAST HWY E	NB	200	A5
COAST HWY W	NB	199	B4
COAST RD	MON	64	B1
COAST RIDGE TR	MON	64	E4
COCHRAN RD	SCL	54	C1
COCK RBN ISL RD	HUM	15	D2
COCOPAH RD	IMP	112	D5
COD DR	SIS	4	B3
CODONI AV	STA	47	D2
COFFEE RD	KER	78	C2
COFFEE RD	MDO	162	B3
COFFEE ST	STA	47	B3
COFFEE RD	MCO	48	C5
COFFEE CREEK RD	HUM	15	D2
COFFEE CREEK RD	TRI	11	D1
COGSWELL RD	STA	48	A1
COGSWELL RD	SON	37	E3
COHASSET RD	BUT	25	C2
COHASSET RD	C	124	A1
COHEN RD	SJCO	47	A1
COLBY AV	FRCO	66	D3
COLBY MTN LKOUT	TEH	19	D5
COLDEN AV	LACO	Q	C5
COLD CANYON RD	SYB	97	B2
COLD CREEK RD	TRI	17	B3
COLD SPRINGS RD	ED	34	D4
COLD SPRINGS RD	LAS	8	C4
COLDWATR CYN AV	LACO	97	C1
COLDWTR CYN DR	LACO	Q	A2
COLDWELL AV	MDO	162	A2
COLDWELL LN	FRCO	66	B3
COLE RD	IMP	112	B2
COLE GRADE RD	SDCO	106	D2
COLEMAN AV	MP	147	A1
COLEMAN AV	MCO	48	C5
COLEMN FSH HTCH	SHA	4	B1
COLEMN VLY RD	SON	37	D2
COLES RD	SOL	33	B3
COLES LEVEE RD	KER	78	B3
COLFAX	PLA	34	D5
COLFAX AV	LACO	Q	B3
COLFAX AV	NEV	127	C4
COLFAX FRST HLL	PLA	34	C4
COLGATE RD	KER	80	D3
COLIMA RD	LACO	98	D3
COLIN RD	SBD	80	E1
COLLEGE AV	B	156	B3
COLLEGE AV	MAR	139	B5
COLLEGE AV	MDO	162	A2
COLLEGE AV	O	156	B5
COLLEGE AV	SDCO	V	C4
COLLEGE AV	SDCO	111	D1
COLLEGE AV	SON	37	E2
COLLEGE AV	SON	38	A2
COLLEGE AV	STR	131	C5
COLLEGE AV W	STR	131	B3
COLLEGE BLVD	PLA	34	A4
COLLEGE BLVD	SDCO	106	B3
COLLEGE DR	SAL	171	A4
COLLEGE DR	SMA	173	A3
COLLEGE CITY RD	COL	33	A3
COLLEGE HTS BL	KER	80	E1
COLLIER RD	MCO	47	B4
COLLIER RD	MCO	48	A4
COLLIER RD	SJCO	40	B3
COLLIER CYN RD	ALA	46	B2
COLLINS AV	OR	194	D5
COLLINS AV	ORA	T	D2
COLLINS RD	IMP	110	D5
COLLINS RD	INY	51	A4
COLLINSVILLE RD	SOL	39	B4
COLLYER DR	SHA	18	C2
COLOMA RD	ED	34	D4
COLOMA RD	ED	138	A3
COLOMA RD	SAC	40	A1
COLOMA ST	PLCV	138	C2
COLOMBERO DR	SIS	12	D2
COLOMBO MINE RD	SIE	26	E4
COLOMBO MINE RD	SIE	27	A4
COLOMBUS AV	MCO	47	D4
COLONY AV	BUT	25	B4
COLONY RD	MON	64	E1
COLONY RD	MON	65	A1
COLONY RD	SAC	40	B2
COLORADO AV	RCO	99	A3
COLORADO BLVD	LACO	97	E1
COLORADO BLVD	LACO	Q	A1
COLORADO BLVD	LACO	98	A1
COLORADO BLVD	PAS	190	B3
COLORADO RD	FRCO	57	A3
COLORADO RD	MPA	49	B3
COLORADO ST	GLEN	182	E1
COLORADO ST	LACO	S	E2
COLORADO ST	LACO	Q	E2
COLORADO RV RD	RCO	103	D4
COLSEN CYN RD	SB	86	D1
COLT LN	CAL	41	A5
COLTON AV	CLTN	207	B4
COLUMBIA AV	RCO	99	B2
COLUMBIA RD N	KER	80	D4
COLUMBIA RD S	KER	80	D4
COLUMBINE RD	SIS	12	C2
COLUMBUS AV	SF	143	B2
COLUMBUS AV	SFCO	45	C1
COLUMBUS PKWY	SOL	38	D4
COLUMBUS ST	KER	78	D3
COLUSA AV	FRCO	56	E4
COLUSA AV	FRCO	66	E1
COLUSA AV	SUT	125	A2
COLUSA AV	YUBA	125	A2
COLUSA CO RD	COL	31	E1
COLUSA-PRNTN RD	COL	32	E1
COLYEAR SPGS RD	TEH	17	E5
COMAL RD	RCO	99	B4
COMANCHE DR	KER	78	E4
COMANCHE DR	KER	79	A4
COMANCHE PT RD	KER	79	B3
COMBIE RD	NEV	34	C5
COMBIE RD	PLA	34	C3
COMETA RD	SJCO	47	D1
COMM BLVD	SBD	91	C1
COMMERCE AV	LACO	Q	C1
COMMERCIAL ST	SD	216	A4
COMMONS RD	STA	47	D3
COMMONWEALTH	ORA	98	B3
COMMONWEALTH AV	RCO	99	E4
COMPTCHE UKIAH	MEN	30	B1
COMPTON AV	LACO	Q	C5
COMPTON BLVD	LACO	S	B1
COMSTOCK	WSH	130	B3
COMSTOCK RD	SBT	55	A2
COMSTOCK RD	SJCO	40	C4
CONARD RD	LAS	20	B1
CONCHO ST	CAL	41	A4
CONCORD BLVD	CC	59	A5
CONCORD AV	CC	39	C5
CONCOW RD	BUT	25	D1
CONDIT AV	STA	47	B3
CONDOR RD	SBD	92	B1
CONDOR RD	SBD	101	C1
CONDUIT	SUT	33	C3
CONE RD	INY	51	D5
CONE RD 3	LAS	20	B1
CONE GROVE RD	TEH	18	D5
CONEJO AV	FRCO	57	C5
CONEJO AV	FRCO	57	C5
CONEJO DR	SBD	90	B1
CONE PEAK RD	MON	64	E3
CONIFER RD	SJCO	40	D5
CONGRESS AV	MONT	53	B5
CONGRESS AV	PAC	167	B3
CONGRESS ST	SD	213	A4
CONGRESS SPG RD	SCL	45	E5
CONKLIN BLVD	KER	80	C4
CONKLIN RD	MOD	8	D1
CONKLIN CK RD	HUM	15	D4
CONKLING RD	IMP	112	A3
CONN CREEK RD	NAPA	29	D1
CONNECTION	LAS	21	E4
CONNELLY RD	IMP	112	C3
CONRAD GROVE LP	TEH	19	D3
CONSTANCE AV	STB	174	A4
CONSTANTIA RD	LAS	27	E1
CONSTELLATN AV	KER	89	C1
CONSUMNES MINE	ED	35	B5
CONTADAS	CC	38	D5
CONTOUR AV	RCO	99	D3
CONTRA COSTA AV	FRCO	56	D4
CONVENTN CTR DR	CLK	209	A4
CONVICT CPGD RD	MNO	50	E2
CONVICT CK EXP	MNO	51	A2
CONVICT CK EXP	MNO	51	A2
CONVICT LAKE RD	MNO	50	E2
CONVICT LAKE RD	MNO	51	A2
CONVOY ST	SDCO	V	B3
CONVOY ST	SDCO	106	D5
CONWAY RANCH RD	MNO	43	B4
COOK LN	SOL	39	B3
COOK RD	AMA	40	C3
COOK ST	RCO	100	E4
COOK CAMPBLL RD	SIS	3	A3
COOK PEAK LKOUT	KER	79	D1
COOKS CAMP RD	CAL	41	C2
COOKS SPRING RD	LAS	21	C4
COOLEY RD	IMP	109	B5
COOLEY RD	SIS	3	B3
COOLGARDIE RD	SBD	81	B3
COOLIDGE AV	O	158	E2
COOMBSVILLE RD	NAPA	38	D3
COON HOLLOW CK	BUT	25	D1
COOPER LN	IMP	109	C5
COOPER RD	MON	54	C4
COOPER RD	NEV	34	C1
COOPR CIENG T T	RCO	100	B3
COOPERSTOWN RD	STA	48	B2
COPA DE ORA AV	MCO	55	D1
COPCO RD	SIS	4	B3
COPENHAGEN	HUM	15	D2
COPP AV	KER	89	B1
COPPER	FRCO	57	D2
COPPER AV	FRCO	56	A2
COPPER CYN RD	SHA	18	C1
COPPER CITY RD	SBD	81	D4
COPPER COVE DR	CAL	41	A5
COPPER HEAD RD	MON	54	C4
COPPER MTN RD	SBD	101	B1
COPPEROPOLIS	TRI	17	B5
COPPER VISTA WY	SDCO	106	C3
COPP PIT RD	MOD	14	D2
COPUS RD	KER	78	B4
CORAL RD	MCO	47	D4
CORAL RD	MCO	55	D1
CORAM RD	SHA	18	B1
CORBETT CYN RD	SLO	76	B4
CORBIN AV	LA	178	B3
CORBIN RD	COL	32	E1
CORCORAN RD	KER	77	E1
CORD	SJCO	40	D3
CORDA RD	MON	54	C4
CORDELIA RD	SOL	38	E3
CORDELIA RD	SOL	135	B5
CORDELIA RD	SUIS	135	B5
CORE RD	SAC	39	E2
CORKILL RD	RCO	100	D3
CORN CAMP RD	KER	77	D4
CORNELIA AV	FRCO	57	C5
CORNELIUS AV	SUT	33	D3
CORNING RD	TEH	24	C2
CORN SPRINGS RD	RCO	102	C2
CORONA AV	KIN	57	D5
CORONA EXPWY	RCO	98	E3
CORONA EXPWY	SBD	98	D3
CORONA FRWY	RCO	99	A3
CORONA FRWY	SON	38	A3
CORONA D MAR FY	CM	197	D4
CORONA D MAR FY	ORA	98	C4
CORONADO AV	SDCO	V	C4
CORONADO AV	SDCO	111	D2
CORRAL RD	SHA	19	E2
CORRAL RD	SBD	99	A3
CORRL DE TIERRA	MON	54	C5
CORRAL HOLLW RD	SJCO	46	E2
CORRALITOS RD	SCR	54	B2
CORREIA RD	SJCO	39	E4
CORRELL RD	SUT	33	B3
CORTE MADERA AV	CRTM	140	B1
CORTEZ AV	MCO	47	E3
CORTEZ AV	MCO	48	A3
CORTEZ WY	KER	79	E2
CORTEZ WY	KER	79	E2
CORTINA SCH RD	COL	32	D3
CORTINA VNYD RD	COL	32	D3
CORTO RD	SBD	91	D4
CORWIN RD	SBD	91	C3
CORWIN RANCH RD	RCO	99	C3
CORYDON RD	RCO	99	B5
COSGROVE	CAL	41	B4
COSTA RD	MCO	55	C4
COSTNER RD	YUB	33	B4
COTA ST	STB	174	C4
COTHARIN RD	VEN	96	D2
COTTA RD	SJCO	39	E4
COTTAGE AV	MAN	161	E1
COTTAGE AV	SJCO	161	E1
COTTLE RD	STA	47	D1
COTTON RD	MCO	55	C4
COTTON CREEK	MPA	48	D2
COTTON GIN RD	MCO	55	C4
COTTNTAIL CK RD	SLO	75	D2
COTTONWOOD AV	RCO	99	C3
COTTONWOOD AV	RCO	99	D4
COTTONWOOD DR	SBD	92	C1
COTTONWOOD RD	BUT	25	C4
COTTONWOOD RD	INY	60	B5
COTTONWOOD RD	KER	78	D3
COTTONWOOD RD	MCO	47	C5
COTTONWOOD RD	RCO	100	A2
COTTONWOOD RD	SBD	55	B4
COTTONWD CYN RD	MNO	43	C4
COTTONWD CYN RD	RCO	99	C4
COTTONWD CYN RD	SB	77	C3
COTTONWD CK RD	SIS	4	A2
COTTONWD SPG RD	RCO	101	C3
COUCH LN	VAL	134	C3
COUGHLAN ST	VAL	134	B3
COULTERVILLE RD	MPA	49	C2
COUNCIL HILL RD	SIE	26	C1
COUNCILMAN RD	HUM	10	D5
COUNTRY	SJCO	40	C5
COUNTRY RD	SIS	4	B3
COUNTRY CLUB BL	SJCO	40	A5
COUNTRY CLUB BL	SJCO	160	A5
CNTRY CLUB BL	S	160	B3
COUNTRY CLUB DR	RCO	100	D4
COUNTRY CLUB RD	AVLN	105	A5
COUNTRY CLUB RD	HUM	10	D4
COUNTRY CLUB RD	YUB	33	D3
COUNTRYMAN DR	PLU	26	B3
COUNTY RD	INY	51	D5
COUNTY RD	MOD	8	A1
COUNTY RD	MOD	14	E1
COUNTY RD B	GLE	24	C4
COUNTY RD BB	GLE	24	C4
COUNTY RD D	GLE	24	C3
COUNTY RD F	GLE	24	D3
COUNTY RD H	GLE	24	D4
COUNTY RD I	GLE	24	D3
COUNTY RD J	GLE	24	D3
COUNTY RD M	GLE	24	D3
COUNTY RD MM	GLE	24	D3
COUNTY RD N	GLE	24	D3
COUNTY RD NN	GLE	24	D4
COUNTY RD PP	GLE	24	D3
COUNTY RD QQ	GLE	24	D3
COUNTY RD RR	GLE	24	E4
COUNTY RD SS	GLE	24	E4
COUNTY RD T	GLE	24	E4
COUNTY RD TT	GLE	24	E4
COUNTY RD V	GLE	24	E4
COUNTY RD VV	GLE	24	E4
COUNTY RD WW	GLE	24	E4
COUNTY RD XX	GLE	24	E4
COUNTY RD Y	GLE	25	A5
COUNTY RD YY	GLE	25	A5
COUNTY RD Z	GLE	24	E4
COUNTY RD ZZ	GLE	25	A4
COUNTY RD 5	YOL	33	A4
COUNTY RD 7	YOL	33	A4
COUNTY RD 8	YOL	32	E4
COUNTY RD 11	GLE	24	E3
COUNTY RD 11	YOL	32	E4
COUNTY RD 11	YOL	33	A4
COUNTY RD 11A	YOL	32	E4
COUNTY RD 11B	YOL	33	B4
COUNTY RD 12	YOL	33	A4
COUNTY RD 12A	YOL	33	A4
COUNTY RD 13	YOL	33	A4
COUNTY RD 14	YOL	32	E4
COUNTY RD 14A	YOL	33	A4
COUNTY RD 15	GLE	24	E3
COUNTY RD 15B	YOL	32	E4
COUNTY RD 16	YOL	33	A4
COUNTY RD 16A	YOL	33	A4
COUNTY RD 17	YOL	33	A4
COUNTY RD 18	GLE	24	E4
COUNTY RD 18	YOL	33	B4
COUNTY RD 18B	YOL	33	B4
COUNTY RD 18C	YOL	32	E4
COUNTY RD 19	GLE	24	E4
COUNTY RD 19	YOL	33	A4
COUNTY RD 19A	YOL	33	A5
COUNTY RD 20	GLE	24	E4
COUNTY RD 20A	YOL	33	A5
COUNTY RD 21	GLE	24	E3
COUNTY RD 21	YOL	33	A5
COUNTY RD 23	GLE	25	A3
COUNTY RD 24	YOL	33	A5
COUNTY RD 24	YOL	33	D3
COUNTY RD 25	YOL	33	A5
COUNTY RD 25A	YOL	33	A5
COUNTY RD 26	GLE	24	C3

STREET INDEX

STREET	CO.	PAGE & GRID
COUNTY RD 26	YOL	33 A5
COUNTY RD 26A	YOL	33 C5
COUNTY RD 27	GLE	24 D3
COUNTY RD 27	YOL	33 B5
COUNTY RD 28	GLE	24 D3
COUNTY RD 28	YOL	33 A5
COUNTY RD 28H	YOL	39 C1
COUNTY RD 29	GLE	24 E3
COUNTY RD 29	GLE	25 A3
COUNTY RD 29	YOL	39 A1
COUNTY RD 29A	YOL	39 A1
COUNTY RD 30	GLE	24 D3
COUNTY RD 30	GLE	25 A3
COUNTY RD 30	YOL	39 B1
CO RD 30 1/2	GLE	25 A3
COUNTY RD 31	GLE	24 D4
COUNTY RD 31	GLE	25 A3
COUNTY RD 31	YOL	39 A1
COUNTY RD 32	GLE	24 E4
COUNTY RD 32	GLE	25 A4
COUNTY RD 32	YOL	39 B1
CO RD 32 1/2	GLE	24 E4
COUNTY RD 33	GLE	24 D4
COUNTY RD 33	GLE	25 A4
COUNTY RD 34	GLE	24 E4
COUNTY RD 34	GLE	25 A4
COUNTY RD 35	GLE	24 D4
COUNTY RD 36	GLE	24 E4
COUNTY RD 36	YOL	39 C2
COUNTY RD 37	GLE	24 D4
COUNTY RD 38	GLE	24 E4
COUNTY RD 38	YOL	39 C2
COUNTY RD 38A	YOL	39 C2
COUNTY RD 39	GLE	24 D4
COUNTY RD 40	GLE	24 E4
COUNTY RD 41	GLE	24 E4
COUNTY RD 43	GLE	24 E4
COUNTY RD 43	YOL	32 D4
COUNTY RD 44	GLE	24 E4
COUNTY RD 44	YOL	32 D4
COUNTY RD 45	GLE	24 D4
COUNTY RD 45	YOL	32 D4
COUNTY RD 46	GLE	24 E4
COUNTY RD 47	YOL	32 D4
COUNTY RD 48	GLE	24 D4
COUNTY RD 49	GLE	24 D4
COUNTY RD 50	GLE	24 E4
COUNTY RD 50	GLE	25 A4
COUNTY RD 53	GLE	24 E4
COUNTY RD 57	GLE	24 D4
COUNTY RD 58	GLE	24 C4
COUNTY RD 59	GLE	24 D4
COUNTY RD 59	YOL	32 D4
COUNTY RD 60	GLE	24 D5
COUNTY RD 61	GLE	24 E5
COUNTY RD 61	YOL	32 D4
COUNTY RD 62	GLE	24 C5
COUNTY RD 63	GLE	25 A5
COUNTY RD 63	YOL	32 D4
COUNTY RD 64	GLE	24 E5
COUNTY RD 65A	GLE	24 E5
COUNTY RD 65B	GLE	24 E5
COUNTY RD 65C	GLE	24 C5
COUNTY RD 66A	GLE	24 D5
COUNTY RD 66B	GLE	24 E5
COUNTY RD 67	GLE	25 A5
COUNTY RD 68	GLE	24 D5
COUNTY RD 69	GLE	24 C5
COUNTY RD 69	GLE	25 A5
COUNTY RD 70	GLE	25 A5
COUNTY RD 70	YOL	32 D4
COUNTY RD 71	GLE	24 D5
COUNTY RD 71	YOL	32 D4
COUNTY RD 75A	YOL	32 D4
COUNTY RD 76	YOL	32 D5
COUNTY RD 78	YOL	32 D5
COUNTY RD 78A	YOL	32 D5
COUNTY RD 79	YOL	32 E5
COUNTY RD 79A	YOL	32 E5
COUNTY RD 79B	YOL	32 E5
COUNTY RD 80	YOL	32 E5
COUNTY RD 81	YOL	32 E5
COUNTY RD 82	YOL	32 E5
COUNTY RD 82B	YOL	32 E4
COUNTY RD 84A	YOL	32 E4
COUNTY RD 84B	YOL	32 E4
COUNTY RD 85	YOL	32 E5
COUNTY RD 85B	YOL	32 E5
COUNTY RD 86	YOL	32 E4
COUNTY RD 86A	YOL	33 A5
COUNTY RD 87	YOL	33 A5
COUNTY RD 87B	YOL	33 A5
COUNTY RD 88	YOL	33 A4
COUNTY RD 88A	YOL	33 A5
COUNTY RD 88B	YOL	33 A5
COUNTY RD 89	YOL	33 A4
COUNTY RD 90	YOL	39 A1
COUNTY RD 90A	YOL	33 A5
COUNTY RD 91	YOL	33 A5
COUNTY RD 91A	YOL	39 A1
COUNTY RD 91B	YOL	33 A4
COUNTY RD 92	YOL	33 B4
COUNTY RD 92B	YOL	33 A4
COUNTY RD 92C	YOL	33 B5
COUNTY RD 92D	YOL	33 B5
COUNTY RD 92F	YOL	39 B1
COUNTY RD 93	YOL	33 B5
COUNTY RD 93A	YOL	33 B4
COUNTY RD 93B	YOL	33 B4
COUNTY RD 94	YOL	33 B4
COUNTY RD 94A	YOL	33 B5
COUNTY RD 94B	YOL	33 B5
COUNTY RD 95	YOL	33 B4
COUNTY RD 95A	YOL	39 B1
COUNTY RD 96	YOL	33 B5
COUNTY RD 96B	YOL	33 B5
COUNTY RD 97	YOL	33 B5
COUNTY RD 97D	YOL	39 B1
COUNTY RD 98	YOL	33 B5
COUNTY RD 99	YOL	33 B5
COUNTY RD 99E	YOL	33 C5
COUNTY RD 100	YOL	33 C5
COUNTY RD 101	YOL	33 C5
COUNTY RD 101A	YOL	39 C1
COUNTY RD 102	YOL	33 C5
COUNTY RD 102B	YOL	39 C1
COUNTY RD 103	YOL	33 C5
COUNTY RD 104	YOL	39 C1
COUNTY RD 105	YOL	39 C2
COUNTY RD 106	YOL	39 C2
COUNTY RD 107	YOL	33 C5
COUNTY RD 107A	YOL	33 D4
COUNTY RD 108	YOL	33 B4
COUNTY RD 116	YOL	33 C4
COUNTY RD 119	YOL	33 D5
COUNTY RD 122	YOL	33 D5
COUNTY RD 124	YOL	33 D5
COUNTY RD 152	YOL	39 C2
COUNTY RD 155	YOL	39 C2
COUNTY RD 126	YOL	33 D5
COUNTY RD 128A	YOL	39 D1

STREET	CO.	PAGE & GRID
COUNTY RD 200	GLE	24 D3
COUNTY RD 303	GLE	24 B4
COUNTY RD 304	GLE	24 B4
COUNTY RD 307	GLE	24 A3
COUNTY RD 310	GLE	23 E4
COUNTY RD 314	GLE	24 B3
COUNTY RD 315	GLE	24 A3
COUNTY RD 400	GLE	24 B5
COUNTY HOSP RD	PLU	26 C1
COUNTY LINE RD	KER	68 B5
CO LINE RD E	TRI	17 E2
CO LINE RD E	TRI	17 E2
CO LINE CK RD	TRI	16 E3
COURCHEVEL RD	PLA	35 D2
COURSE RD	KER	78 B4
COURT ST	RED	122 B2
COURTLAND RD N	YOL	39 D2
COURTLANDT CT	KER	79 C4
COUTOLENC RD	BUT	25 D2
COVE AV	FRCO	58 B4
COVE RD	SBD	91 E4
COVE RD	SHA	13 A5
COVELL BL	DVS	136 B2
COVELO RD	MEN	23 A3
COVELO RD	MEN	22 E4
COVELO REFUS RD	MEN	23 A2
COVERT RD	STA	47 C2
COVINA BLVD	LACO	R C3
COWBOY CNTRY TR	RCO	107 B1
COWBOY JOE RD	LAS	21 D5
COW CAMP RD	BUT	25 E2
COW CAMP RD	MNO	43 C3
COW CREEK RD S	SHA	18 E2
COW CREEK RD S	SHA	19 A2
COWEL RD	CC	38 E5
COW GULCH RD	SHA	17 D3
COW HAVEN CY RD	KER	80 B1
COW MTN ACCESS	MEN	31 B2
COX AV	SCL	45 E5
COX LN	BUT	25 D5
COX RD	IMP	109 A3
COX RD	SJCO	40 C4
COX RD	SHA	18 B3
COX RD	STA	47 B3
COX ST	RCO	99 C4
COXCOMB TR	SBD	102 C1
COXEY	SBD	91 D4
COX FERRY RD	MCO	48 B3
COYOTE RD	MCO	56 B1
COYOTE RD	SBD	101 A2
COYOTE #1 RD	IMP	111 C4
COYOTE #2 RD	IMP	111 C4
COYOTE CYN RD	INY	71 D4
COYOTE CYN RD	RCO	107 C1
COYOTE GAP RD	BUT	25 E2
COYOTE LAKE RD	SBD	82 B5
COYOTE SPGS RD	MNO	43 C4
COYOTE VLY RD	INY	51 C4
COYOTE VLY RD	SBD	93 A5
COYOTE VLY RES	LAS	14 C5
COZZI AV	MCO	56 A1
CRABTREE RD	LAS	8 D4
CRABTREE RD	STA	48 B2
CRAFTON AV	SBD	99 D2
CRAIG	SJCO	47 C1
CRAIG AV	SON	132 B3
CRAIG AV	TEH	18 E5
CRAIG RD	SUT	33 B1
CRAMER	PLA	34 B3
CRAM GULCH RD	SIS	4 B5
CRANE AV	MCO	47 D4
CRANE RD	STA	47 D2
CRANE CANYON RD	SON	38 A2
CRANE FLAT	MPA	63 B5
CRANE FLAT RD	MPA	49 C2
CRANE VALLEY RD	MAD	49 E5
CRANMORE RD	SUT	33 B3
CRANMORE RD	SUT	33 B4
CRANNELL RD	HUM	9 E4
CRANNELL RD	HUM	10 A4
CRATER RD	SBD	93 E3
CRATER HILL RD	PLA	34 B3
CRAWFORD AV	FRCO	58 A4
CRAWFORD RD	CLO	32 E2
CRAWFORD RD	MEN	23 A2
CRAWFORD RD	STA	47 D2
CRAY CROFT RDG	SIE	26 D4
CRAZY HORSE CYN	MON	54 D3
CREED RD	SOL	39 B3
CREEK RD	MCO	55 D2
CREEK RD	RED	122 A4
CREEK RD	VEN	88 B4
CREEKSIDE CT	KER	79 C4
CREEKSIDE LN	STA	47 E2
CREIGHTON DR	SHA	13 D3
CRENSHAW BLVD	LACO	97 D3
CRENSHAW BLVD	LACO	Q B5
CRENSHAW BLVD	LACO	S B2
CREOLE MINE RD	SBD	92 E4
CRESCENT AV	AVLN	105 B5
CRESCENT AV	ORA	T B2
C RESERVOIR RD	MOD	6 D4
CRESSEY WY	MCO	48 A4
CRESSMAN RD	FRCO	58 B1
CREST DR	RCO	99 B2
CREST RD	LACO	S B2
CRESTLINE RD	SDCO	107 A2
CRESTON RD	SLO	76 B1
CRESTON EUREKA	SLO	76 B2
CRESTN ODONOVAN	SLO	76 C2
CRESTVIEW DR	MNO	51 D2
CRESTVIEW ST	KER	80 C1
CREWS RD	SCL	54 D2
CRIPE RD	FRCO	58 A1
CRIPPEN AV	SBD	91 A3
CRIPPLE CK RD	SLO	76 B2
CRISPIN RD	MEN	30 C3
CRISS RD	SIS	4 E3
CRISS RD	SIS	5 A3
CRISTIANITOS RD	SDCO	105 E1
CRISWELL AV	MCO	55 E1
CROCKER RD	SJCO	46 E1
CROCKER SPGS RD	KER	77 D4
CRONESE LAKE RD	SBD	82 E4
CRONESE LAKE RD	SBD	83 A4
CROOKED MDW RD	MNO	50 E1
CROSBY RD	HUM	15 D2
CROSBY ST	SD	216 A5
CROSBY HAROLD	PLA	34 B3
CROSS RD	COL	32 E2
CROSS RD	MON	65 E4
CROSS CYNS RD	SLO	66 B5
CROSS CTRVILLE	MEN	31 B1
CROSS CNTRY RD	MON	66 B4
CROUCH AV	BUT	25 D3
CROW RD	STA	47 E2
CROW CANYON RD	ALA	45 E2
CROWDER	PLA	33 E5
CROWDER FLAT RD	MOD	6 E5
CROWLEY RD	SUT	33 C3
CROWLEY LAKE DR	MNO	51 A3

STREET	CO.	PAGE & GRID
CROWLEY LAKE PL	MNO	51 A2
CROWLY LK DM RD	MNO	51 B2
CROWN RD	MCO	48 C4
CROWN & PICKLE	SBD	92 D5
CROWN POINT RD	BUT	25 C2
CROWN VLY PKWY	ORA	98 D5
CROWN VALLEY RD	LACO	89 E4
CROWS LANDNG RD	MDO	162 B5
CROWS LANDNG RD	STA	47 C4
CROWS LANDNG RD	STA	162 B5
CROY RD	SCL	54 C1
CRUCERO RD	SBD	83 A5
CRUCERO RD	SBD	93 B1
CRUICKSHANK RD	IMP	112 B3
CRUMP LN	FRCO	66 B3
CRUZON GRADE RD	NEV	26 C5
CRYSTAL AV	MOH	96 A3
CRYSTAL CK RD	SHA	18 A2
CRYSTAL LAKE RD	LACO	U D2
CRYSTAL SPGS AV	SBR	144 A4
CRYSTAL SPGS DR	LA	182 C1
CRYSTAL SPGS DR	LACO	Q C3
CRYSTAL SPGS RD	KLAM	5 C1
CRYSTAL SPGS RD	SMCO	45 C3
CUDA DR	KER	78 E4
CUDDEBACK RD	SBD	80 E3
CUDDEBACK RD	SBD	81 A3
CUDDY VALLEY RD	KER	88 C1
CUDDY VALLEY RD	VEN	88 C2
CUFF RD	IMP	109 B2
CUIN RD	IMP	108 E5
CULL CANYON RD	ALA	45 E2
CULVER BLVD	CUL	183 C5
CULVER BLVD	CUL	188 A3
CULVER BLVD	LA	183 C5
CULVER BLVD	LA	188 A3
CULVER BLVD	LACO	97 C2
CULVER BLVD	LACO	187 D5
CULVER DR	ORA	98 C4
CULVER DR	ORA	T E3
CUMMINGS RD	HUM	15 E1
CUMMINGS RD	VEN	88 B5
CUMMINGS SKYWAY	CC	38 D4
CUMMINGS VLY RD	KER	79 B4
CUNEO RD	MPA	48 E1
CUNNINGHAM LN	MNO	42 E1
CUNNINGHAM RD	CAL	41 C3
CUNNINGHAM RD	MCO	48 D5
CUNNINGHAM RD	MEN	31 B2
CURLEW ST	SD	215 D1
CURRAN RD	AMA	40 D3
CURREY RD	SOL	39 B1
CURRIE RD	SOL	39 C4
CURRIER RD	BUT	25 C4
CURRY AV	SJCO	40 B4
CURTIS ST	SM	145 B3
CURTIS ST W	SAL	171 C2
CURTNER AV	SCL	46 B5
CUSTER AV	FRCO	56 B2
CUSTER AV	SBD	91 E4
CUTCA TRUCK TR	RCO	106 E1
CUTLER AV	GLE	24 E3
CUT OFF RD	LAS	21 C3
CUTOFF RD	MEN	23 C5
CUTTING	CC	38 C5
CUTTING AV	GLE	24 E3
CUTTING BLVD	R	155 A4
CUTTNGS WHRF RD	NAPA	38 C3
CUYAMA ST	SB	87 D1
CYA RD	MPA	49 A3
CYPRESS AV	LACO	R C3
CYPRESS AV	SHA	18 C2
CYPRESS AV	SUT	33 D3
CYPRESS RD	CC	39 C5
CYPRESS RD	MCO	56 A1
CYPRESS RD	SBD	80 E1
CYPRESS ST	C	124 C4
CYPRESS ST	LACO	98 B2
CYPRESS ST	SDCO	112 B1
CYPRESS MTN DR	SLO	75 D1
CYPRUS AV	U	123 B2
CYRMIC RD	KER	77 D3
CYRUS CANYON RD	KER	79 D1
CYRUS CANYON RD	KER	79 D1
D		
D ST	MDO	162 B4
D ST	ONT	203 D4
D ST	SR	139 C4
D ST	SON	38 A3
DAGGETT YERMO	SBD	92 A1
DAGNINO RD	ALA	46 C2
DAHLIN RD	SJCO	47 C2
DAHLSTROM RD	COL	32 E3
DAILEY RD	KER	79 C2
DAINTY AV	CC	39 C5
DAIRY AV	LACO	S D1
DAIRY LN	MCO	56 A1
DAIRY RD	BUT	25 A3
DAIRY RD	KER	78 A3
DAIRY RD	STA	47 B2
DAIRY RD	YUB	33 E3
DAIRY MART RD	SDCO	V C5
DAIRY MART RD	SDCO	111 D2
DAKIN RD	LAS	21 C4
DAKOTA AV	FRCO	57 C3
DAKOTA AV	FRCO	56 E3
DAKOTA AV	STA	47 C2
DALBY	PLA	33 E3
DALE LN	SHA	18 B3
DALE RD	KER	79 B4
DALE RD	STA	47 C2
DALE RD	TEH	24 E2
DALE TR	SBD	101 E1
DALE VISTA RD	SBD	101 E1
DALLY RD	SOL	39 B3
DALTON AV	ALA	46 C2
DALY ST	LA	186 D1
DAMIEN AV	LACO	98 C1
DAMIEN AV	LACO	U E3
DANA DR	SHA	18 C2
DANA FOOTHLL RD	SLO	76 C5
DANBY RD	SBD	101 D1
DANENBERG RD	IMP	112 B3
DANIELS AV	VAL	134 A3
DANLEY LATERAL	COL	32 C1
DANLEY RD	COL	32 D1
DAN MCNAMARA RD	MCO	48 A5
DANTES VIEW	INY	72 B1
DANVILLE BLVD	CC	45 E1
DARBY RD	BUT	25 E5
DARBY RD	CAL	41 C3
DARGATE RD	KER	77 E2
DARK CANYON RD	BUT	25 D3
DARLING RD	LACO	89 D4
DARLING RDG RD	ED	34 E4
DARMS LN	NAPA	38 C2
DARRAH RD	MPA	49 B3
DATE ST	SB	86 C1
DATE PALM DR	RCO	100 D4
DATONI RD	YUB	33 D2
DAUBENBERGER RD	STA	47 E3
DAULTON RD	MAD	56 B1

STREET	CO.	PAGE & GRID
DAULTON RD	MAD	57 B1
DA VALL DR	RCO	100 D3
DAVENPORT RD	LACO	89 D4
DAVEY GLEN RD	SM	145 C4
DAVID AV	MONT	53 C3
DAVID AV	MONT	167 B3
DAVID AV	PAC	167 B3
DAVID RD	KER	78 E5
DAVIDSON	FRCO	56 B2
DAVIDSON RD	HUM	9 E2
DAVIDSON RD	HUM	10 A2
DAVIS AV	FRCO	57 A5
DAVIS AV	FRCO	57 C5
DAVIS AV	KER	78 B1
DAVIS RD	BUT	25 B5
DAVIS RD	IMP	109 A2
DAVIS RD	KER	76 E1
DAVIS RD	MON	54 C4
DAVIS RD	MON	171 A4
DAVIS RD	RCO	99 D3
DAVIS RD	SJCO	40 A4
DAVIS RD	SIS	4 C4
DAVIS RD	SIS	5 B4
DAVIS RD	STA	47 C4
DAVIS RD	STA	48 B3
DAVIS RD	SUT	33 B2
DAVIS ST	ALA	45 D2
DAVIS ST	LAK	32 A3
DAVIS CK CEM RD	MOD	7 C4
DVS CK TRNS STA	MOD	7 C4
DAWN RD	KER	89 E1
DAWN RD	KER	90 A1
DAWSON RD	RCO	99 C3
DAWSON RANCH RD	MNO	51 D2
DAY AV	SHA	19 E1
DAY RD	MOD	13 E3
DAY RD	SCL	54 C1
DAY RD	SHA	13 E3
DAY ST	RCO	99 C3
DAYLIGHT PASS	INY	61 E4
DAYLGHT PS CTOF	INY	61 E3
DAYTON RD	BUT	25 B3
DAYTON WEST RD	BUT	25 B3
DEAD HRS CYN RD	SIS	13 B3
DEAD INDIAN RD	JKSN	4 A1
DEADMAN CK RD	MNO	50 D2
DEAD MANS GULCH	MON	65 E4
DEADWOOD RD	BUT	25 D3
DEADWOOD RD	PLA	35 A2
DEADWOOD RD	TRI	17 E1
DEADWOOD LO RD	SIS	3 D4
DEALWOOD RD	IMP	109 B5
DEAN CREEK RD	HUM	16 C5
DE ANGELIS RD	MCO	47 D4
DE ANZA BLVD	CPTO	149 D4
DE ANZA DR	RCO	99 E3
DEARBORN RD	IMP	111 E3
DEARDORFF RD	CAL	41 B2
DEARWOOD DR	MEN	31 B2
DEATH VALLEY RD	INY	52 B5
DEAVER AV	KER	70 A5
DECPTION CYN RD	RCO	100 E3
DECKER AV	SBD	92 E5
DECKER RD	SUT	33 B2
DECORD DR	LACO	89 A4
DECOTO RD	ALA	45 E3
DEE KNOCH RD	SHA	13 E4
DEEP CREEK RD	MOD	8 D1
DEEP CREEK RD	SBD	91 C5
DEEP SPRINGS RD	SBD	84 A3
DEEP SPGS RANCH	INY	52 B4
DEEP WELL RD	MCO	55 E1
DEER WY	RCO	100 B5
DEER CREEK AV	TUL	68 B5
DEER CREEK RD	SBD	91 C4
DEER CREEK RD	VEN	96 D2
DEER FLAT RD	SHA	19 C2
DEERHORN VLY RD	SDCO	112 B1
DEER LICK KNOB	TRI	17 D2
DEER LICK SPGS	TRI	17 D3
DEER MTN RD	SIS	4 D5
DEER PARK RD	BUT	26 A3
DEER PARK RD	NAPA	29 B2
DEER PARK RD	NAPA	38 B1
DEER SPRING RD	MNO	51 B2
DEER VALLEY	ED	34 C5
DEER VALLEY RD	CC	39 C5
DEER VALLEY RD	CC	46 C1
DEETZ RD	SIS	12 C2
DEFENDER GRADE	AMA	41 B2
DEFRAIN BLVD	RCO	103 D5
DE HARVEY ST	KER	78 D4
DEHESA RD	SDCO	V E3
DEHESA RD	SDCO	107 A5
DE LA CRUZ BL	SCLR	151 C2
DE LA GUERRA ST	STB	174 D3
DEL AMO BLVD	LACO	98 A3
DEL AMO BLVD	LACO	S D1
DE LA VINA ST	STB	174 B3
DELAWARE AV	SC	169 A5
DELAWARE RD	STA	47 E2
DELCERRO BLVD	SDCO	V C3
DELCERRO BLVD	SDCO	111 D1
DEL DIOS HWY	SDCO	106 D4
DELEVAN RD	COL	32 D1
DELFATTI LN	KLAM	5 B1
DELFERN RD	KER	77 D2
DELFIND RD	KER	77 D2
DELHI RD	SOL	39 C2
DELIMA RD	SJCO	47 A1
DEL MAR AV	LACO	R E4
DEL MAR AV	LACO	R A4
DEL MAR AV	VAL	134 D3
DEL MAR BLVD	PAS	190 C4
DEL MAR HTS RD	SDCO	106 C4
DEL MONTE AV	SUT	33 C4
DEL MONTE BLVD	MONT	167 B1
DEL NORTE AV	FRCO	57 A4
DEL NORTE DR	TEH	18 C4
DEL NORTE ST	EUR	121 B2
DEL OBISPO ST	ORA	98 D5
DEL OBISPO ST	ORA	202 B4
DEL OBISPO ST	SJC	202 C2
DEL ORO RD	SBD	91 C4
DEL ORTO RD	CAL	40 E3
DEL ORTO RD	CAL	41 A3
DEL PASO RD	SAC	33 D5
DELPHOS RD	CLO	32 D2
DEL PUERTO AV	STA	47 C3
DEL PUERTO CYN	STA	46 E4
DEL PUERTO CYN	STA	47 A3
DEL REY AV	FRCO	57 E3
DEL REY AV	FRCO	57 E5
DEL ROSA AV	SBD	99 C1
DELTA AV	SJCO	46 E1
DELTA AV	SJCO	47 A1
DELTA RD	CC	39 C5
DELTA RD	MCO	55 E1
DE LUZ RD	SDCO	106 B1
DEMAREE RD	TUL	68 B1
DEMAREST MNE RD	CAL	41 A4

STREET	CO.	PAGE & GRID
DENISE AV	KER	80 A5
DENNETT ST	PAC	167 B2
DENNISON RD	KER	79 D4
DENNY RD	TRI	10 E5
DENNY RD	TRI	11 A4
DENTON RD	MCO	56 A1
DENTON RD	STA	48 A2
DENTN & LEAK RD	MCO	56 B1
DENVER AV	FRCO	56 E4
DENVER AV	KIN	57 E5
DENVERTON RD	SOL	39 B3
DE PORTOLA RD	RCO	99 E5
DEPOT AV	SB	86 C1
DEPOT RD	ALA	146 B5
DEPOT RD	H	146 B5
DEPOT ST	SMA	173 B3
DERBY ST	B	156 B3
DERRICK BLVD	FRCO	66 C2
DERRICK RD	BUT	25 D4
DERRICK RD	IMP	111 E5
DERRICK RD	LAS	14 B3
DERRICK FT RD N	TRI	11 E3
DERRICK FT RD N	TRI	12 A3
DERRICK FT RD S	TRI	12 A3
DERSCH RD	SHA	18 C3
DESCANSO AV	AVLN	105 B5
DESCHUTES RD	SHA	18 D2
DESERT RD	IMP	112 D3
DESERT CTR RICE	RCO	102 C4
DESERT INN RD	CLK	209 C5
DESERT INN RD	CLK	210 C1
DESERT SHORS DR	IMP	108 C1
DESERT VIEW AV	SBD	91 D4
DESERT WILLW TR	SBD	100 D2
DESEVADO RD	SIS	4 C3
DE SOTO AV	LA	177 D3
DE SOTO AV	LACO	177 D4
DESSIE DR	LAK	31 C3
DETLOW RD	BUT	25 D3
DETOUR RD	GLE	24 D3
DETWEILER RD	MPA	48 D2
DEVILS CORRL RD	LAS	20 D3
DEVILS DEN RD	KIN	67 B5
DEVOE RD	SUT	33 C4
DEVONSHIRE BLVD	LACO	97 C1
DEVORE FRWY	SBD	99 A1
DEVORE RD	SBD	99 B1
DEVOSE DR	LAS	8 A4
DE VRIES	SJCO	40 A4
DEWITT RD	STA	47 D2
DE WOLF AV	FRCO	57 D2
DE WOLF AV	FRCO	57 D5
DE WOLF AV	SB	86 B3
DE 1 FIRST ST	COL	32 D1
DIABLO RD	CC	46 A1
DIABLO MINE RD	INY	51 C3
DIABLO MINE RD	MNO	51 C3
DIABLO OASIS DR	RCO	100 C3
DIAGONAL 7	MAD	56 C3
DIAGONAL 11	MAD	56 D1
DIAGONAL 232	TUL	68 D4
DIAGONAL 252	TUL	68 D3
DIAGONAL 254	TUL	68 D3
DIAMOND RD	ED	138 C5
DIAMOND BAR BL	LACO	98 C2
DIAMOND BAR BL	LACO	U D5
DIAMOND MTN RD	PLU	20 E4
DIAMOND VLY RD	ALP	36 C4
DIAZ LN	INY	51 D4
DIAZ ST	KER	80 A4
DICK COOK	PLA	34 B4
DICKERMAN RD	IMP	109 B4
DICKINSON AV	FRCO	57 B4
DICKINSON AV	FRCO	67 B1
DICKNSN FRRY RD	MCO	48 B5
DIDO AV	SBD	92 A3
DIEHL RD	IMP	111 E3
DIEHL RD	STA	47 C4
DIENSTAG RD	STA	48 A2
DIERSSEN RD	SAC	39 E3
DIETRICH	SJCO	40 C5
DIETRICH RD	IMP	109 B4
DIGGER RAVNE RD	PLU	26 C1
DI GIORGIO RD	KER	78 D3
DI GIORGIO RD	KER	79 A3
DILLARD RD	SAC	40 B2
DILLION RD	SIS	10 D1
DILLON RD	HUM	15 D2
DILLON RD	RCO	100 E3
DILLON RD	RCO	100 C3
DILLON BEACH RD	MAR	37 D3
DINKELSPIEL RD	SOL	39 B4
DINKEY CREEK RD	FRCO	58 B1
DINKY AV	KER	89 B1
DINUBA AV	FRCO	56 E4
DINUBA AV	FRCO	57 C4
DINUBA AV	FRCO	58 A4
DIPS RD	TRI	17 B3
DIRKS RD	COL	24 D5
DISCH RD	SJCO	40 C4
DISTELRATH DR	DN	1 D3
DISTRICT CTR DR	BUT	25 D5
DITCH RD	KER	78 A5
DITCH RD	SIE	26 C4
DITCH CREEK RD	SIS	4 A3
DIVISADERO ST	FRE	165 B3
DIVISADERO ST	SF	142 A2
DIVISION ST	LACO	89 E2
DIVISION ST	SDCO	V C4
DIVISION ST	SDCO	111 D1
DIVISION ST	SLO	76 B5
DIVISION CK RD	INY	59 E2
DIXIE RD	BUT	25 D2
DIXIE RD	SBD	91 D1
DXIE CYN RND VY	PLU	20 C5
DIXIE VALLEY RD	LAS	14 D4
DIXON AV E	SOL	39 B2
DIXON AV W	SOL	39 B2
DIXON LN	INY	51 D4
DIXON HILL RD	YUB	26 A5
DIXON MINE RD	ALP	42 C1
DOBBINS ST	KER	70 A5
DOBIE LN	MEN	23 B3
DOBIE MEADOWS	MNO	43 D4
DOBIE MEADOWS	MNO	43 E4
DOBIE MEADOWS	MNO	44 A4
DOBSON RD	SBD	81 E4
DODDS	SJCO	40 C5
DODDS	SJCO	47 C1
DODDS RD	STA	47 C4
DODGE RD	COL	24 E5
DODGE RDG LP RD	TUO	42 A3
DOE MILL RD	BUT	25 C2
DOERKSEN RD	STA	47 E3
DOG BAR RD	NEV	34 C2
DOG CREEK RD	SHA	12 B4
DOGGIE TR	SBD	101 A2
DOGTOWN RD	CAL	41 B4
DOGTOWN RD	MPA	48 E2
DOGTOWN RD	MPA	49 A2
DOG VALLEY RD	SIE	27 E5

STREETS

STREET	CO.	PAGE & GRID
DOGWOOD DR	EC	217 E4
DOGWOOD RD	ALP	36 A5
DOGWOOD RD	IMP	109 A5
DOGWOOD RD	IMP	112 A4
DOHENY DR	BH	183 D2
DOHENY DR	LA	183 D2
DOHENY DR	LACO	Q B4
DOHENY PARK RD	ORA	202 C4
DOLAN RD	MON	54 B3
DOLAN HARDNG RD	YUB	34 A1
DOLLARHIDE RD	NAPA	38 C1
DOLORES ST	SF	142 C5
DOLPHIN AV	KER	80 C1
DOLPHIN DR	IMP	108 C2
DOME AV	TUL	68 D3
DOME ST	SB	86 D1
DOMINION RD	SB	86 C1
DOMINO CT	KER	79 B4
DON RD	SBD	101 D1
DONAHUE RD	SUT	33 C4
DONKIN RD	STA	47 B3
DONNER PASS RD	NEV	27 B5
DONOVAN RD	SMA	173 A2
DON PEDRO RD	STA	47 C3
DONS RD	MOD	8 B2
DOOLITTLE DR	A	159 A3
DOOLITTLE DR	ALA	45 D2
DOOLITTLE DR	O	159 C3
DOOLITTLE CK RD	SIS	2 E3
DOON GRADE	BUT	25 D2
DORA RD	SUT	33 B2
DORA ST	U	123 C3
DORAN SCENIC DR	SBD	82 A5
DORFF LN	HUM	15 D2
DORIS AV	VEN	96 B1
DORNES RD	PLA	34 A3
DORRETT DR	BUT	25 C2
DORRIS AV	FRCO	66 E2
DORRIS BROWNELL	SIS	5 B3
DORRIS TEHNER	SIS	5 A3
DORSEY RD	STA	47 D1
DOS CABEZA RD	IMP	111 B3
DOSE RD	TRI	10 E5
DOS PALMAS RD	SBD	90 E4
DOS REIS RD	SJCO	47 A1
DOS RIOS DR	SBD	90 E3
DOS RIOS LN	STA	47 B3
DOS RIOS RD	BUT	25 C5
DOSTER RD	CAL	41 A3
DOTTA LN	PLU	27 D3
DOTTA GUIDCI RD	PLU	27 D2
DOTY RD	SHA	13 D5
DOUBLE SPGS RD	CAL	40 E3
DOUGHERTY RD	CC	46 B1
DOUGHERTY RD	SUT	33 C3
DOUGLAS	KIN	67 D1
DOUGLAS AV	FRCO	56 C4
DOUGLAS AV	SB	86 B3
DOUGLAS LN	SBD	100 E1
DOUGLAS RD	SAC	40 B1
DOUGLAS ST	ELS	189 D3
DOUGLAS RGR STA	MAD	49 E5
DOVE	SJCO	47 D1
DOVER AV	FRFD	135 D3
DOVER AV	KIN	67 E1
DOVER DR	NB	199 C4
DOVER DR	ORA	T C4
DOVER CANYON RD	SLO	75 E1
DOVER SPG CYN RD	KER	80 A2
DOW BUTTE RD	LAS	20 D1
DOW BUTTE LO RD	LAS	20 D1
DOWD RD	PLA	34 A3
DOWD RD	PLA	33 E4
DOWD CAMP RD	PLA	34 A3
DOWDEN RD	IMP	109 B3
DOWER AV	FRCO	57 B5
DOWER AV	FRCO	57 B3
DOW FLAT RD	LAS	20 D1
DOWNEY AV	LACO	S E1
DOWNEY RD	INY	73 A4
DOWNEY RD	LACO	R D4
DOWNEY ST	MDO	162 B3
DOWNIE RD	STA	47 E3
DOWNIE RD	STA	48 A3
DOWS PRAIRIE RD	HUM	9 E4
DOYLE DR	SF	141 D1
DOYLE GRADE	LAS	27 D1
DOYLE RD	MCO	47 C5
DOYLE RANCH RD	KER	69 E5
DOYLE RANCH RD	KER	79 E1
DRAIN 10 RD	SIS	5 E2
DRAIS AV	SJCO	40 C5
DRAKE AV	COL	32 E3
DRAKE RD	HUM	15 E2
DRAPER RD	STA	47 C4
DRAPER RD	TEH	18 C3
DREDGR CP MORGN	TRI	17 C1
DRESSER AV	KER	78 A2
DREW RD	IMP	111 E3
DREXLER	SUT	33 B2
DRIVE 212	TUL	58 C5
DRIVE 244	TUL	68 D2
DRIVE 254	TUL	58 D4
DRIVER AV	LACO	97 A1
DRIVER RD	KER	68 C5
DRIVER RD	KER	78 C1
DRIVER RD	KER	78 C2
DROBISH RD	BUT	25 E5
DROGE	SJCO	47 C1
DRUM CANYON RD	SB	86 D3
DRUMMOND AV	KER	80 C1
DRY CREEK RD	LAK	32 A5
DRY CREEK RD	MCO	48 B3
DRY CREEK RD	MNO	50 D2
DRY CREEK RD	NAPA	29 C4
DRY CREEK RD	NAPA	38 B2
DRY CREEK RD	PLA	34 C3
DRY CREEK RD	SJCO	40 B3
DRY CREEK RD	SLO	76 B1
DRY CREEK RD	SHA	18 D2
DRY CREEK RD	SIS	4 B3
DRY CREEK RD	SON	31 C5
DRY CREEK RD	TUL	58 D5
DRY CREEK RD W	SON	31 D5
DRY CREEK RD W	SON	37 D1
DRY CK BASIN RD	MOD	8 C1
DRY CK CMP GRND	LAS	8 B3
DRY CREEK CTOFF	MNO	50 D2
DRY GENESEO RD	SLO	76 B1
DRY SLOUGH RD	COL	33 A3
DRYTOWN AMADOR- -VIA BUNKERHILL	AMA	40 E2
DU BOIS ST	SR	139 D4
DUBOIS TK TR	SDCO	107 B5
DUCK CREEK RD	AMA	40 C3
DUCK LAKE RD	LAS	21 E4
DUDLEY RD	MON	65 D3
DUFAU	VEN	96 C1
DUGGANS RD	NEV	34 C2
DUMETZ RD	LA	177 C5
DUMP RD	HUM	16 B3
DUMP RD	INY	60 A3
DUMP RD	LAK	31 D2
DUNAWAY RD	IMP	111 D3
DUNAWEAL LN	NAPA	29 A2
DUNBAR LN	SDCO	107 A5
DUNCAN RD	SBD	90 E4
DUNCAN RD	SJCO	40 C5
DUNCAN ST	KER	78 E4
DUNCAN CYN RD	SBD	99 A1
DUNCAN CREEK RD	SHA	17 E3
DUNDERBURG MDW	MNO	43 B4
DUNE RD	SBD	92 B1
DUNES RD	CLK	210 B2
DUNFORD RD	KER	78 A3
DUNLAP DR	RCO	99 C3
DUNLAP RD	FRCO	58 C3
DUNLAP RD	KER	69 B5
DUNN LN	CAL	41 B5
DUNN RD	MCO	48 C4
DUNN RD	STA	47 B2
DUNNE AV	SCL	P D5
DUNNE AV E	SCL	P D5
DUNSTONE DR	BUT	25 D5
DUNTON RD	STA	40 E5
DUPONT RD	RCO	102 D5
DURANT AV	B	156 A3
DURFEE AV	LACO	R A4
DURHAM RD	SIS	5 A3
DURHAM DAYTN HY	BUT	25 B3
DURHAM FERRY RD	SJCO	47 A2
DURKEE RD	LAS	14 A3
DURNEL RD	BUT	25 B4
DUSTIN RD	SJCO	40 B4
DUSTIN AKERS RD	KER	78 A4
DUSTY LN	STA	47 D2
DUSTY WY	TEH	18 D5
DUSTY MILE RD	SBD	92 D5
DUTCH CREEK RD	SIS	3 E3
DUTCH CREEK RD	TRI	17 C2
DUTCHER CK RD	SON	31 C5
DUTCH MINE RD	TUO	41 C5
DUTTON AV	SON	131 C4
DUTTON AV N	STR	131 B3
DUVALL ST	KER	78 A4
DUZEL CREEK RD	SIS	3 E5
DUZEL CREEK RD	SIS	11 E1
DUZEL RCK LO RD	SIS	3 E5
DUZEL RCK LO RD	SIS	11 E1
DWIGHT WY	MCO	48 A4
DWINNELL WY	SIS	4 C5
DWINNELL WY	SIS	12 C1
DYE RD	SDCO	107 A4
DYER DR	PLU	20 C4
DYER LN	PLA	33 E5
DYER RD	ORA	T D3
DYER ST	ALA	45 E3
DYERVILLE LOOP	HUM	16 B4
DYERVILLE LP RD	HUM	16 A4
DYSERT RD	SIS	4 E3
DYSON LN	PLU	27 C3

E

STREET	CO.	PAGE & GRID
E ST	DVS	136 D3
E ST	EUR	121 C1
E ST	FRE	165 C4
E ST	H	146 E2
E ST	SCTO	137 C2
E ST	SBDO	207 C4
E ST	SBD	99 B2
E ST	SDCO	V C5
E ST	SDCO	111 D2
E ST	YUB	33 D2
EABY RD	SBD	90 E4
EADY RD	IMP	112 A4
EAGER RD	SUT	33 C2
EAGLE AV	FRCO	56 A2
EAGLE BORAX WLL	INY	72 A2
EAGLE CK LP RD	TRI	11 E3
EAGLE CK LP RD	TRI	12 A3
EAGLE FIELD RD	MCO	55 E2
EAGLE LAKE RD	NEV	27 A5
EAGLE MTN RD	RCO	102 B4
EAGLE PK LKOUT	TEH	24 A2
EAGLE ROCK BLVD	LACO	R D3
EAGLE ROCK RD	TRI	17 A1
EAGLE RCK LKOUT	SIS	4 D3
EAGLES NEST RD	MNO	43 A4
EAGLES NEST RD	SAC	40 B2
EAGLEVL DUMP RD	MOD	8 E2
EAGLEVILLE LOOP	MOD	8 E2
EARDLEY AV	PAC	167 C2
EARHART RD	O	159 D4
EARLHAM ST	SDCO	107 A4
EARP RD	COL	33 A2
EAST AV	ALA	46 C2
EAST AV	BUT	25 B3
EAST AV	BUT	124 B1
EAST AV	C	124 A1
EAST AV	FRCO	57 C5
EAST AV	MCO	48 A3
EAST AV	TEH	24 D2
EAST LN	MEN	23 B3
EAST RD	LACO	R C5
EAST ST	ANA	193 D1
EAST ST	AUB	126 C3
EAST ST	ORA	T C2
EAST ST	RED	122 B1
EASTBLUFF DR	NB	200 A3
EAST END AV	SBD	98 D2
EAST END RD	SBD	92 A4
EASTERN AV	LACO	98 A2
EASTERN AV	LACO	R D4
EASTERN AV	LACO	R E5
EAST FORK RD	SHA	18 A1
EAST FORK RD	TRI	11 B5
EAST FORK RD	TRI	17 C3
EAST FORK RD	TRI	12 A4
EAST GRADE RD	SDCO	107 A2
EAST GRADE RD	TRI	16 E2
E FK HAYFORD RD	TRI	17 C3
E FK INDIAN CK	SHA	2 E3
E FK STUART CPG	TRI	11 E5
EASTIN RD	STA	47 C5
EASTMAN RD	STA	40 E5
EASTMAN RD	STA	47 D1
EASTMONT RD	KER	78 E2
EASTSHORE FRWY	ELC	155 D3
EASTSHORE FRWY	R	155 D3
EASTSHORE FRWY	SP	155 D3
EASTSHORE RD	SHA	18 B2
EAST SIDE	PLU	20 D5
EASTSIDE LN	MNO	42 E1
EASTSIDE RD	INY	51 D4
EASTSIDE RD	MEN	23 A5
EAST SIDE RD	MEN	31 B2
EASTSIDE RD	MNO	42 E1
EASTSIDE RD	RED	122 B4
EASTSIDE RD	SHA	18 C2
EASTSIDE RD	SHA	18 C3
EASTSIDE RD	SIS	3 D5
EASTSIDE RD	SIS	11 D1
EAST SIDE RD	TRI	12 A4
E SIDE CALPELLA	MEN	31 B2
E SDE PORTR VLY	MEN	31 B1
E SDE REDWD VLY	MEN	31 B1
EAST WEST RD	SIS	5 D2
EASY ST	KER	79 C4
EASY ST	SHA	18 D2
EATON RD	BUT	25 B3
EATON RD	STA	47 E1
EBERLE RD	KER	78 C4
ECHO PARK AV	LA	185 E1
ECHO PARK AV	LA	186 A1
ECHO VALLEY RD	MON	54 C3
EDDINS RD	IMP	109 A3
EDDY RD	COL	33 A3
EDDY RD	LPAZ	104 A2
EDDY ST	SF	143 B5
EDDY GULCH RD	SIS	11 B2
EDDY GLH LKOUT	SIS	11 B3
EDGAR AV	BUT	25 B3
EDGEMONT ST	LA	182 B5
EDGER RD	IMP	108 E5
EDGEWATER BLVD	FCTY	145 D2
EDGEWOOD AV	MAR	45 B1
EDGEWOOD RD	SMCO	45 D3
EDGEWOOD RD	SIS	12 C1
EDGEWD BIG SPGS	SIS	12 C1
EDINGER AV	ORA	98 B4
EDINGER AV	ORA	T B3
EDINGER AV	SA	196 A5
EDINGER AV	SA	197 C1
EDINGER AV	SA	198 A1
EDINGER ST	FTNV	195 C5
EDINGER ST	SA	195 C5
EDISON AV	SBD	98 D2
EDISON BLVD	BUR	179 B3
EDISON HWY	KER	78 E3
EDISON HWY	KER	79 A3
EDISON RD	KER	78 E3
EDISON ST	SB	86 E3
EDITH AV	TEH	24 D2
EDMINSTER	MCO	47 D4
EDMUNDSON AV	SCL	54 C1
ED POWERS RD	INY	51 C4
ED RAU RD	SAC	39 E2
EDSEL LN	STA	47 C2
EDWARD ST	KER	79 B5
EDWARDS	SJCO	47 D1
EDWARDS ST	ORA	T B3
EEL RIVER RD	MEN	23 B5
EEL RIVER RD	MEN	31 C1
EEL ROCK RD	HUM	16 C4
EGAN RD	TUO	41 C5
EGGERT RD	SOL	39 C2
EHRLICH RD	STA	47 C3
EICKHOFF RD	LAK	31 D2
EIGHMY RD	TEH	18 C4
EIGHTH ST	C	124 C5
EIGHT MILE RD	SJCO	39 E4
EIGHT MILE RD	SJCO	40 A4
EISENHOWER DR	RCO	100 E5
EISENHOWER ST	FRFD	135 D3
ELBERTA ST	KER	89 E1
EL CAJON BLVD	SD	214 A5
EL CAJON BLVD	SDCO	V C4
EL CAJON BLVD	SDCO	111 D1
EL CAMINO AV	SAC	40 A1
EL CAMINO DR	SHA	18 C3
EL CAMINO RD	SBD	101 D1
EL CAMINO CIELO	SB	87 C4
EL CAMINO REAL	BLMT	145 C4
EL CAMINO REAL	BURL	144 B3
EL CAMINO REAL	MP	147 A2
EL CAMINO REAL	MLBR	144 C4
EL CAMINO REAL	MON	54 D4
EL CAMINO REAL	MON	65 A1
EL CAMINO REAL	MON	66 A5
EL CAMINO REAL	MON	171 B1
EL CAMINO REAL	MVW	148 B5
EL CAMINO REAL	ORA	105 E1
EL CAMINO REAL	PA	147 B3
EL CAMINO REAL	SAL	171 D3
EL CAMINO REAL	SBT	54 D2
EL CAMINO REAL	SBR	144 B3
EL CAMINO REAL	SDCO	106 B3
EL CAMINO REAL	SNLO	172 E2
EL CAMINO REAL	SLO	66 A5
EL CAMINO REAL	SLO	76 B2
EL CAMINO REAL	SLO	172 E1
EL CAMINO REAL	SM	145 A3
EL CAMINO REAL	SMCO	45 C3
EL CAMINO REAL	STB	173 D5
EL CAMINO REAL	SB	86 C1
EL CAMINO REAL	SCLR	150 B2
EL CAMINO REAL	SCLR	151 A2
EL CAMINO REAL	SCL	46 A4
EL CAMINO REAL	SCL	54 D2
EL CAMINO REAL	SMA	173 C1
EL CAMINO REAL	SSF	144 B3
EL CAMINO REAL	SVL	150 B2
EL CAMPO RD	MCO	55 E2
EL CAMPO RD	RCO	100 C5
EL CAMPO RD	SLO	76 B5
EL CAPITAN WY	MCO	47 E4
EL CAPITAN WY	MCO	48 A3
EL CAPTN SCH RD	MCO	48 B5
EL CARISO TK TR	RCO	99 B4
EL CENTRO AV	NAPA	38 C3
EL CENTRO BLVD	SUT	33 D3
EL CENTRO RD	SAC	33 D5
EL CENTRO ST	IMP	111 E3
EL CERRITO RD	RCO	98 E3
EL CIELITO RD	STB	174 D1
EL CIELO DR	RCO	100 D3
EL CIELO RD	PMSP	206 E5
EL CONQUISTA RD	RCO	107 A1
ELDER AV	KIN	67 B1
ELDER CREEK RD	RCO	107 B1
ELDER CREEK RD	SAC	40 A1
EL DIABLO RD	SBD	92 E5
EL DORADO AV	FRCO	56 E4
EL DORADO AV	FRCO	66 E2
EL DORADO AV	S	160 C1
EL DORADO DR	RCO	100 C3
EL DORADO DR	SBD	102 C1
EL DORADO ST	AUB	126 B3
EL DORADO ST	FRE	165 C3
EL DORADO ST	MONT	167 E4
EL DORADO ST	SJCO	40 A5
EL DRDO HLLS RD	ED	34 C5
EL DORADO MN RD	RCO	101 C2
ELDRIDGE RD	LAS	14 A5
ELEANOR AV	STA	47 D2
ELEVADO AV	BH	183 A2
ELEVADO RD	SBD	91 B3
ELDER ST	SDCO	106 C2
ELDER CREEK RD	SAC	39 E1
ELECTRA RD	AMA	41 A3
ELEVATOR RD	SOL	39 D3
ELFERS RD	STA	47 B3
ELGIN	MCO	56 B1
ELGIN AV	KIN	67 B1
ELHOLM RD	MCO	47 C5
EL INOR RD N	HUM	16 A3
EL INOR RD S	HUM	16 A3
ELIZA GULCH RD	SIS	3 E4
ELIZABETH LK RD	LACO	89 C3
ELZBTH LK P CYN	LACO	89 B2
ELK	MCO	48 A4
ELK AV	BUT	25 B3
ELK CT	KER	79 B4
ELK CREEK RD	HUM	16 B4
ELK CREEK RD	SIS	3 A4
ELK GROVE BLVD	SAC	39 E2
ELK GROVE BLVD	SAC	40 A2
ELK GRV FLRN RD	SAC	39 E2
ELK GRV FLRN RD	SAC	40 A2
ELK HILLS RD	KER	77 E3
ELK HILLS RD	KER	78 A3
ELKHORN AV	FRCO	56 D5
ELKHORN AV	FRCO	57 D5
ELKHORN BLVD	SAC	33 D5
ELKHORN RD	MEN	31 A4
ELKHORN RD	MON	54 C3
ELKHORN GRAD RD	KER	78 A5
ELKHORN GRADE	FRCO	57 B5
ELK MOUNTAIN RD	LAK	23 C5
ELK MOUNTAIN RD	LAK	31 C1
ELK RIVER RD	HUM	121 A5
ELK RIVER RD	HUM	15 E1
ELK VALLEY RD	DN	1 D4
ELK VALLEY RD	SIS	10 D1
ELK VLY CRSS RD	DN	1 E4
ELLA AV	YUB	33 D2
ELLA RICHTER RD	SHA	18 A3
ELLENA ST	FRCO	57 B5
ELLEN SPGS DR	LAK	32 A4
ELLENWOOD DR	STA	47 E2
ELLENWOOD RD	STA	48 A2
ELLER LN	SIS	3 D5
ELLER LN	SIS	11 D1
ELLIOT	SJCO	40 B3
ELLIOT AV	MCO	48 B4
ELLIOT ST	SBD	93 B2
ELLIOT RCH RD	PLA	34 E2
ELLIOTT RD	BUT	25 C3
ELLIOTT CK RD	SIS	3 E2
ELLIOTT RCH RD	SAC	39 E2
ELLIS AV	RCO	99 C4
ELLIS RD	AMA	41 C1
ELLIS RD	YUB	33 D2
ELLIS ST	SF	143 B5
ELLSWORTH ST	B	156 A3
ELM AV	FRCO	57 C4
ELM AV	MON	65 B1
ELM AV	SBR	144 B3
ELM AV	SDCO	106 B3
ELM ST	BKD	166 B2
ELM ST	RCO	99 C5
ELM ST	SDCO	107 A4
ELM ST	TUL	68 B3
EL MARGARITA RD	SUT	33 C2
EL MEDIO RD	SBD	90 E3
ELMER AV	SUT	33 C2
ELMER ST	RCO	99 B4
ELMIRA RD	SOL	39 A2
EL MIRAGE RD	SBD	90 E3
EL MIRAGE RD	SBD	91 A3
ELMO HWY	KER	78 A1
EL MONTE AV	LACO	R B3
EL MONTE AV	TUL	58 A4
EL MONTE RD	SCL	45 E4
ELNA RD	INY	59 E1
EL NIDO RD	MCO	48 C5
EL NORTE PKWY	SDCO	106 D3
ELORDY LN	SUT	33 E4
EL PASTA RD	RCO	107 A1
EL POMAR AV	STA	47 E2
EL POMAR DR	SLO	76 B2
EL POMAR RD	SLO	76 B2
EL POMAR RO RD	SLO	76 B2
EL PORTAL	CC	38 C5
EL POZO GRADE	SLO	76 D3
EL PRADO	SDCO	V B4
EL RANCHO DR	KER	79 C4
EL REPOSO RD	RCO	107 A1
EL RIO DR	TUL	68 C1
EL ROBLAR	VEN	88 A4
EL ROBLAR ST	SB	87 E1
EL SEGUNDO BLVD	ELS	189 D4
EL SEGUNDO BLVD	LACO	97 D3
EL SEGUNDO BLVD	LACO	Q B5
EL SEGUNDO BLVD	LACO	S C1
EL SERENO RD	MCO	55 C2
EL SOBRANTE RD	RCO	99 B3
EL TEJON HWY	KER	78 E4
EL TEJON HWY	KER	79 A4
EL TORO DR	BKD	166 C5
EL TORO RD	ORA	98 D5
EL TORO RD	ORA	T E4
ELVAS FRWY	SCTO	137 E2
ELVERTA RD	SAC	33 D5
EL VICINO AV	MDO	162 B3
ELWOOD RD	FRCO	58 B3
ELY RD	SUT	33 C4
ELYSIAN VLY RD	LAS	21 A4
EMBARCADRO, THE	SF	143 B2
EMBARCADERO RD	PA	147 C2
EMBRCDRO SKYWAY	SF	143 D3
EMERALD AV	RCO	100 E5
EMERALD AV	STA	47 C2
EMERALD DR	SDCO	106 C3
EMERALD RD	SBD	91 E4
EMERALD RD	STA	47 B2
EMERSON RD	MOD	8 D5
EMERSON RD	TEH	18 D4
EMERY RD	STA	47 E2
EMERY RD	STA	48 D3
EMIGH RD	SOL	39 C4
EMIGRANT RD	PLU	26 D1
EMIGRANT TR	SHA	19 B3
EMMERT RD	COL	33 A3
EMMIGRANT TR	ALP	36 B4
EMPIRE	CC	39 C5
EMPIRE AV	BUR	179 B2
EMPIRE ST	GV	127 B4
EMPIRE ST	NEV	127 C4
EMPIRE CREEK RD	SIS	3 E3
EMPIRE GRADE	SCR	53 D1
EMPIRE MINE RD	CC	39 B5
ENCHNTD FRST RD	RCO	100 A4
ENCINAL	MON	54 D4
ENCINAL AV	ALA	45 D1
ENCINAL RD	SUT	33 C1
ENCINITAS BLVD	SDCO	106 C4
ENCINITAS RD	SDCO	106 C3
END RD W	HUM	10 A5
ENDERTS BCH RD	DN	1 E4
ENGLEHART AV	FRCO	58 A4
ENGLISH RD	IMP	109 A3
ENGLISH COLONY	PLA	34 B4
ENGLISH HILLS	SOL	39 A2
ENNIS RD	FRCO	58 C3
ENNIS RD	SUT	33 B2
ENOS LN	KER	78 B3
ENSLEY RD	SUT	33 C4
ENTERPRISE	SJCO	47 D1
ENTERPRISE RD	BUT	25 E4
ENTERPRISE ST	TUL	68 A2
ERBES RD	VEN	96 E1
EREISTIN DR	SBD	92 D5
ERHIT RD	TUO	48 E1
ERHIT RD	TUO	49 A1
ERICKSON RD	BUT	25 B4
ERLE RD	MCO	48 E5
ERNST	MPA	48 E2
ERNST	MPA	49 A2
ERRECA RD	MCO	48 A5
ERRINGER RD	VEN	88 E5
ERRINGER RD	VEN	89 A5
ERRINGER RD	VEN	97 A1
ERRINGER RD	VEN	96 E1
ERSKINE RD	IMP	108 E5
ERSKINE CK RD	KER	79 D1
ERTESZEK DR	KER	79 C4
ERWIN ST	LA	178 C3
ESCALON BELLOTA	SJCO	40 C5
ESCALON BELLOTA	SJCO	47 C1
ESCHINGER RD	SAC	39 E2
ESCHINGER RD	SAC	40 A2
ESCOBAR ST	M	154 A2
ESCOLLE RD	MON	54 D5
ESCONDIDO AV	SDCO	106 C3
ESCONDIDO FRWY	RCO	99 C3
ESCONDIDO FRWY	SD	216 D3
ESCONDIDO FRWY	SDCO	106 D2
ESCONDIDO RD	LACO	89 D4
ESMERALDA RD	CAL	41 B4
ESPERANZA AV	RCO	100 B3
ESPERANZA RD	MON	54 D4
ESPERANZA RD	SIS	13 A2
ESPINOSA RD	MON	54 C3
ESPINOSA RD	MON	65 B1
ESPLANADE	BUT	25 A2
ESPLANADE AV	RCO	99 D4
ESPLANADE, THE	C	124 B3
ESPOLA RD	SDCO	106 D4
ESQUON RD	BUT	25 B4
ESSEX LN	HUM	10 A5
ESSEX RD	SBD	94 D2
ESTHER AV	MCO	56 B2
ESTRELLA RD	SLO	66 A5
ESTRELLA RD	SLO	76 B1
ETHANAC RD	RCO	99 C4
ETHEREDGE ST	KER	68 D5
ETIWANDA AV	SBD	98 C2
ETTERBG HONEYDW	HUM	16 A5
ETTING RD	VEN	96 C1
ETZEL RD	SOL	39 C2
EUCALYPTUS AV	MCO	48 A4
EUCALYPTUS AV	RCO	99 C3
EUCALYPTUS AV	SBD	98 E2
EUCALYPTUS AV	STA	47 B3
EUCALYPTUS RD	BUT	25 B5
EUCALYPTUS RD	MCO	56 A2
EUCALYPTUS ST	AVLN	105 B5
EUCALYPTUS ST	SB	91 B4
EUCLID AV	ONT	204 B4
EUCLID AV	SBD	98 D2
EUCLID AV	SDCO	V C4
EUCLID AV	SDCO	111 D1
EUCLID AV	SDCO	111 D1
EUCLID AV	SF	141 E3
EUCLID AV	STA	47 E3
EUCLID AV	UPL	204 B1
EUCLID ST	FTNV	197 A3
EUCLID ST	GGR	195 A3
EUCLID ST	ORA	98 B3
EUCLID ST	ORA	T C2
EUCLID ST	SA	195 A5
EUREKA RD	PLA	34 B5
EUREKA RD S	INY	52 D5
EUREKA WY	RED	122 B1
EUREKA WY	SHA	18 C2
EUREKA CYN RD	SCR	54 B1
EUREKA HILL RD	MEN	30 C3
EUREKA MINE RD	SIE	26 C4
EUREKA VLY RD	INY	52 D4
EUROPE AV	KER	79 D5
EVAN HEWES HWY	IMP	111 D3
EVAN HEWES HWY	IMP	112 D3
EVANS	TUL	68 D1
EVANS AV	FRCO	56 B2
EVANS RD	COL	32 D2
EVANS RD	RCO	107 C1
EVANS RD	SIS	4 E3
EVANS REIMER RD	BUT	25 B5
EVELYN AV	MVW	148 B4
EVELYN AV	SVL	148 E5
EVELYN AV	SVL	150 A1
EVERETT AV	KIN	67 C1
EVERETT ST	KER	80 D1
EVERETT MEM HWY	SIS	12 C2
EVERGLADE	SUT	33 C3
EVERGREEN RD	CAL	40 D4
EVERGREEN RD	TEH	18 C4
EVERGREEN RD	TUO	42 B5
EVERGREEN RD	TUO	63 A3
EVERITT RD	SUT	33 C2
EXCELSIOR AV	FRCO	66 E1
EXCELSIOR AV	FRCO	67 C1
EXCELSIOR AV	KIN	67 D1
EXCELSIOR RD	SAC	40 A2
EXCELSIOR MN RD	SBD	73 D5
EXCELSIOR MN RD	SBD	83 D1
EXCELSIOR PT RD	NEV	34 E1
EXCHEQUER	MPA	48 D3
EXCHEQUER DR	FRCO	58 C1
EXCHEQUER DAM	MPA	48 D3
EXP MINE RD	TUO	41 C4
EXPOSITION BLVD	LA	184 C5
EXPOSITION BLVD	LA	185 C5
EXPOSITION BLVD	LACO	97 D2
EXPOSITION BLVD	LACO	Q C4
EXPOSITION BLVD	SAC	39 E1

F

STREET	CO.	PAGE & GRID
F ST	DVS	136 D2
F ST	EUR	121 D3
F ST	FRE	165 D4
F ST	HUM	15 E1
F ST	SBD	99 B1
F ST	SDCO	V C5
F ST	SDCO	111 D2
FABRY RD	MON	55 B5
FAHEY RD	MCO	55 C1
FAIR ST	BUT	25 B3
FAIR ST	BUT	124 E5
FAIRBANKS RD	MEN	23 B3
FAIRCHILD LN	SJCO	40 B5
FAIRFAX	FRCO	56 B3
FAIRFAX AV	KIN	67 C1
FAIRFAX AV	LA	181 A4
FAIRFAX AV	LA	184 A3
FAIRFAX AV	LACO	Q B4
FAIRFAX AV	LACO	181 A4

226
FAIRFAX RD — GAVILAN DR

STREET INDEX

STREET	CO.	PAGE & GRID
FAIRFAX RD	KER	78 E3
FAIRFAX BOLINAS	MAR	38 A5
FAIRFIELD AV	FRFD	135 B3
FAIRFIELD AV	SBD	91 C3
FAIRFIELD ST	EUR	121 B3
FAIRGROUNDS DR	VAL	134 E2
FAIRHAVEN AV	OR	196 C2
FAIRHAVEN AV	ORA	T E2
FAIRHAVEN AV	SA	196 C2
FAIRLANE RD	SBD	92 A4
FAIRMEAD BLVD	MAD	56 E1
FAIRMONT AV	SDCO	V C4
FAIRMONT AV	SDCO	111 D1
FAIRMONT AV E	MDO	162 C2
FAIRMONT RD	LACO	89 C2
FAIRMOUNT AV	SD	214 E5
FAIRMOUNT AV	SD	216 E1
FAIROAKS AV	LACO	R E2
FAIR OAKS AV	LACO	190 B2
FAIR OAKS AV	PAS	190 B4
FAIR OAKS AV	SCL	45 E4
FAIR OAKS AV	SCL	46 A4
FAIR OAKS AV	SVL	149 E1
FAIR OAKS BLVD	SAC	40 A1
FAIR OAKS BLVD	SAC	34 A5
FAIR PLAY RD	ED	41 A1
FAIRVIEW AV	CC	39 C5
FAIRVIEW AV	RCO	100 A4
FAIRVIEW AV	SB	87 B4
FAIRVIEW RD	COL	32 D1
FAIRVIEW RD	CM	199 C1
FAIRVIEW RD	MON	54 E5
FAIRVIEW RD	ORA	98 C4
FAIRVIEW RD	ORA	T C4
FAIRVIEW RD	SBT	54 E2
FAIRVIEW RD	SBT	55 A2
FAIRVIEW RD	SBD	92 C1
FAIRVIEW RD	VEN	88 B4
FAIRWAY DR	CLTN	207 B5
FAIRWAY DR	EUR	121 C5
FAIRWAY DR	LACO	U D4
FAIRWAY PL	SB	86 E3
FAITH HOME RD	MCO	47 D4
FAITH HOME RD	STA	47 D3
FALL RD	INY	70 B2
FALLBROOK AV	LA	177 A4
FALL CREEK RD	SIS	4 C2
FALLEN LEAF RD	ED	35 E3
FALLING LEAF RD	SHA	18 C2
FALLON RD	SBT	54 E2
FALLON RD	SBT	55 A2
FALL RIVER RD	SHA	13 E4
FALLS CYN RD	AVLN	105 A5
FAMOSO HWY	KER	78 A1
FAMOSO-PRTVL HY	KER	78 C1
FANDANGO PSS RD	MOD	7 C3
FANNING	SJCO	40 B5
FANOE RD	MON	54 E5
FARGO AV	KIN	67 C1
FARGO CANYON RD	RCO	101 B4
FARINA ST	RCO	100 A5
FARLEY MINE RD	SBD	91 D3
FARMER RANCH RD	TRI	17 B2
FARMERSVILLE RD	TUL	68 C2
FARM HILL BLVD	SMCO	45 D4
FARMLAN RD	SUT	33 B2
FARMLAND AV	MCO	48 C4
FARNHAM RDG RD	ED	41 A1
FARQUHAR RD	TEH	18 B4
FARRIS DR	CAL	40 D4
FARRIS RD	BUT	25 B5
FARRIS RD	BUT	33 B1
FASIG RD	SUT	33 B3
FAUST RD	STA	47 C2
FAWCETT RD	IMP	112 A5
FAWN LODGE RD	TRI	17 D1
FAXON RD	COL	33 B3
FAY AV	SD	105 B3
FAY LN	SIS	11 D1
FAY RD	MCO	47 D4
FAY RANCH RD	KER	69 E5
FAY RANCH RD	KER	79 E1
FAY RIDGE RD	KER	78 C1
FEATHER LK HWY	LAS	20 A2
FEATHER LK HWY	LAS	20 D3
FEATHER LAKE RD	SHA	19 E1
FEATHER RIV BL	YUB	33 D3
FEDERAL BLVD	SDCO	V C4
FEDERAL BLVD	SDCO	111 D1
FEE RD	MOD	7 D3
FEENSTRA RD	SLO	76 B2
FEE RESRVOIR RD	MOD	7 D3
FELCIANA MTN RD	MPA	49 B3
FELDMILLER RD	TRI	16 E3
FELDSPAR AV	KER	80 D1
FELICITA RD	SDCO	106 D3
FELIZ CREEK RD	MEN	31 B3
FELL ST	SF	141 E4
FELL ST	SF	142 B4
FELL ST	SFCO	45 B1
FELLOWSHIP RD	STB	174 A5
FELTER RD	SCL	46 B4
FELTON EMPRE RD	SCR	53 E1
FENDERS FERRY	SHA	13 A5
FENSLER RD	SIS	5 D2
FENTEM RD	MCO	47 C5
FERGUSON RD	IMP	110 E4
FERN RD	SHA	19 A2
FERN RD E	SHA	19 A1
FERN ST	SD	216 B3
FERN ST	SDCO	V C4
FERN ST	SDCO	111 D1
FERN CANYON DR	MEN	31 B2
FERNDALE DMP RD	HUM	15 D2
FERRELL RD	IMP	112 A4
FERRETTI RD	TUO	41 D5
FERRETTI RD	TUO	48 D1
FERRY RD	TEH	18 D4
FERRY RD E	HUM	15 E2
FESLER ST	SMA	173 B2
FICKLE HILL RD	HUM	10 A5
FIDDLETOWN RD	AMA	40 E2
FIDLTWN QTZ MTN	AMA	40 E1
FIDLTWN SHNDOAH	AMA	40 E1
FIDDLTWN SLV LK	AMA	41 A1
FIDDYMENT	PLA	33 E4
FIELD RD	SBD	82 C5
FIELDBROOK RD	HUM	10 A4
FIELDS RD	MCO	48 C3
FIELDS RD	RCO	100 A3
FIELDS RIDGE RD	BUT	26 B4
FIESTA ISLND RD	SD	212 E4
FIFIELD RD	IMP	109 B4
FIFIELD RD	SUT	33 D4
FIFTH AV	C	124 B3
FIFTH ST	C	124 B5
FIG AV	FRE	165 C5
FIG AV	FRCO	57 C4
FIG AV	FRCO	57 C5
FIG AV	STA	47 C3
FIGMOND AV	MCO	48 C3

STREET	CO.	PAGE & GRID
FIG TREE LN	SHA	18 C3
FIGUEROA ST	LA	185 D5
FIGUEROA ST	LA	191 B1
FIGUEROA ST	LACO	R D3
FIGUEROA ST	LACO	S C2
FIGUEROA ST	MONT	167 E3
FIGUEROA MTN RD	SB	87 B2
FILBURN ST	KER	78 A1
FILIPPINI RD	SIE	27 C3
FILLMAN RD	LAS	8 A4
FILLMORE ST	RCO	101 B5
FILLMORE ST	SF	142 B2
FILLY LN	CAL	41 B5
FIMPLE RD	BUT	25 B3
FINCK RD	SJCO	46 E1
FINE AV	SJCO	40 C5
FINE AV	STA	47 D2
FINK RD	STA	47 C4
FINKS RD	COL	32 D1
FINLEY LN	LAS	14 C3
FINNEL AV	TEH	24 D1
FINNEY RD	IMP	109 B5
FINNEY RD	STA	47 C2
FINNING HILL RD	PLA	34 E2
FIR ST	C	124 E4
FIR ST	RCO	100 C4
FIRE CAMP RD	BUT	25 E4
FIRESTONE	FRCO	66 C3
FIRESTONE BLVD	LACO	97 E2
FIRESTONE BLVD	LACO	R D5
FIRETHORN RD	SBD	92 B3
FIRST AV	C	124 B3
FIRST AV	STA	47 C3
FIRST AV E	C	124 D3
FIRST ST	SIS	12 D3
FISCHER RD	IMP	111 E4
FISH & GAME RD	LAS	21 C3
FISHER AV	KER	89 C1
FISHER DR	TUL	68 C1
FISHER RD	HUM	15 E2
FISHER RD	IMP	110 D5
FISHER RD	LPAZ	104 A2
FISHER RD	MCO	48 B4
FISHER RD	TRI	10 E5
FISHERS LANDING	YUMA	110 E4
FISH HATCHRY RD	INY	59 E3
FISH ROCK RD	MEN	31 A4
FISH ROCK RD	MEN	30 D4
FISH SLOUGH RD	MNO	51 D2
FISH SPRINGS RD	INY	59 E1
FISKE	MPA	48 E1
FISKE	MPA	49 A1
FITCH MTN RD	SON	37 D1
FITZGERALD DR	BUT	25 C2
FITZGERALD RD	SCL	54 D1
FITZHUGH CK RD	MOD	8 B2
FIVE BRIDGES RD	INY	51 D4
FIVE MILE DR	AMA	40 D2
FIVE MILE CK RD	TUO	41 D4
FIVE MI STA RD	SBD	95 D2
FLAMINGO RD	CLK	210 C2
FLANAGAN RD	SHA	18 C1
FLANNERY RD	SOL	39 B3
FLATTOP MTN RD	KIN	67 A4
FLEA VALLEY RD	BUT	25 D2
FLEMING AV E	VAL	134 E3
FLEMING RD	PLA	34 A3
FLETCHER DR	LACO	Q C3
FLETCHER PKWY	SDCO	V D3
FLETCHER PKWY	SDCO	111 E1
FLINT AV	KIN	67 C1
FLINT AV	MCO	47 E4
FLINT AV	MCO	48 A4
FLINT ST	KER	80 C5
FLOOD RD	IMP	110 D5
FLOOD RD	SJCO	40 C5
FLORADALE AV	SB	86 B3
FLORAL AV	C	124 D1
FLORAL AV	FRCO	56 D4
FLORAL AV	FRCO	57 B4
FLORENCE AV	ING	188 E5
FLORENCE AV	LACO	97 D2
FLORENCE AV	LACO	Q C5
FLORES AV	TEH	18 D5
FLORES RD	YUB	34 A1
FLORIDA AV	RCO	99 D4
FLORIDA DR	SD	216 A2
FLORIDA ST	VAL	134 C4
FLORIN RD	SAC	40 A1
FLORIN MILL RD	SHA	13 D3
FLORIN PERKINS	SAC	40 A2
FLOURNOY AV	TEH	24 D2
FLOWER ST	LA	185 E4
FLOWER ST	SA	196 A3
FLOWERS LN	SHA	18 C3
FLOWING WELLS	IMP	109 B3
FLOYD AV	FRCO	57 B3
FLOYD AV	STA	47 D2
FLYNN RD	INY	51 D4
FLYNN CREEK RD	MEN	30 D2
FOAM ST	MONT	167 D2
FOAM ST	MON	53 E2
FOGARTY RD	STA	47 E1
FOGARTY RD	STA	48 A1
FOGG RD	SAC	39 E2
FOLETTA RD	MON	54 D5
FOLEY AV	KER	79 D3
FOLSOM AV	FRCO	56 B2
FOLSOM BLVD	SAC	34 B5
FOLSOM BLVD	SAC	39 E1
FOLSOM BLVD	SAC	40 A1
FOLSOM BLVD	SCTO	137 E4
FONSECA RD	COL	24 E5
FONTANA AV	SBD	99 A2
FOOLISH PLSR RD	RCO	107 A1
FOOTE RD	SIE	26 C5
FOOTHILL AV	O	159 D1
FOOTHILL BLVD	ALA	146 D1
FOOTHILL BLVD	BUT	25 D4
FOOTHILL BLVD	CLA	203 C1
FOOTHILL BLVD	CPTO	149 A5
FOOTHILL BLVD	H	146 E2
FOOTHILL BLVD	LACO	89 C5
FOOTHILL BLVD	LACO	89 E5
FOOTHILL BLVD	LACO	98 B1
FOOTHILL BLVD	LACO	98 C1
FOOTHILL BLVD	LACO	Q A1
FOOTHILL BLVD	LACO	R C3
FOOTHILL BLVD	NAP	133 B4
FOOTHILL BLVD	O	158 B3
FOOTHILL BLVD	ORA	T E2
FOOTHILL BLVD	ROC	204 B1
FOOTHILL BLVD	SBD	99 A1
FOOTHILL BLVD	SD	105 D5
FOOTHILL BLVD	SD	212 B1
FOOTHILL BLVD	SDCO	V A3
FOOTHILL BLVD	SDCO	106 C5
FOOTHILL BLVD	SNLO	172 A2
FOOTHILL BLVD	UPL	203 C1
FOOTHILL BLVD	UPL	204 B1
FOOTHILL DR	SBD	102 C1

STREET	CO.	PAGE & GRID
FOOTHILL DR	SIS	4 A4
FOOTHILL DR	SOL	39 A2
FOOTHILL EXPWY	PA	147 C5
FOOTHILL EXPWY	SCL	45 E4
FOOTHILL EXPWY	SCCO	149 A4
FOOTHILL FRWY	LACO	97 D1
FOOTHILL FRWY	LACO	98 A1
FOOTHILL FRWY	LACO	R D2
FOOTHILL FRWY	LACO	R A3
FOOTHILL FRWY	PAS	190 B2
FOOTHILL RD	ALA	46 B2
FOOTHILL RD	DGL	36 B3
FOOTHILL RD	INY	59 E3
FOOTHILL RD	MNO	51 C1
FOOTHILL RD	MON	64 E1
FOOTHILL RD	MON	65 A1
FOOTHILL RD	SBD	91 D4
FOOTHILL RD	SBD	92 A4
FOOTHILL RD	SLO	76 A3
FOOTHILL RD	STB	174 B1
FOOTHILL RD	SB	87 D1
FOOTHILL RD	SB	174 B1
FOOTHILL RD	SCL	54 D1
FOOTHILL RD	TEH	18 E5
FOOTHILL RD	VEN	88 B4
FOOTHILL RD	VEN	88 B5
FOPPIANO LN	SJCO	40 B5
FORBES N	PLA	34 B3
FORBES S	PLA	34 A3
FORBES AV	SR	139 C3
FORBES RANCH RD	RCO	100 C4
FORBESTOWN RD	BUT	25 B3
FORBESTOWN RD	BUT	26 A4
FRBSTOWN RES RD	BUT	26 A4
FORD RD	NB	200 B3
FORD ST	RCO	100 E3
FORD ST	SBD	99 C2
FORDYCE LAKE RD	NEV	27 B5
FOREMAN CIR RD	BUT	25 D4
FOREST	MPA	49 D3
FOREST AV	MONT	53 D2
FOREST AV	PAC	167 C3
FOREST BLVD	KER	80 B4
FOREST CIR	BUT	25 C2
FOREST DR	BUT	25 E2
FOREST RD	CAR	168 C4
FOREST TR	ML	164 B1
FOREST HOME BL	SBD	99 E2
FORST HM CRBNDL	AMA	40 D2
FOREST HOUSE	SIS	3 E4
FOREST LAKE	SJCO	40 A3
FOREST LAWN DR	LA	179 E5
FOREST LAWN DR	LA	181 C1
FOREST LAWN DR	LACO	Q B3
FOREST RANCH RD	BUT	25 C2
FOREST RANCH WY	BUT	25 C2
FORGAY RD	PLU	20 D5
FORREST ST	BKD	166 C4
FORRESTER RD	IMP	109 A4
FORSYTHE RD	YUB	26 A5
FT BRAGG SHERWD	MEN	22 C5
FT CADY RD	SBD	92 C1
FORT INDEPNDNCE	INY	59 E3
FORTNA RD	SUT	33 C2
FORT ROMIE RD	MON	64 E1
FORT ROMIE RD	MON	65 A1
FORT ROSS RD	SON	37 B1
FORT SAGE RD	LAS	21 E5
FORT SEWARD RD	HUM	16 C5
FORT STOCKTN DR	SD	213 B5
FORT STOCKTN DR	SDCO	V B4
FORT STOCKTN DR	SDCO	111 C1
FORT TEJON RD	LACO	90 B3
FT TEJON CHSBRO	LACO	90 B3
FORTUNA BLVD	HUM	15 E2
FORTY MILE RD	YUB	33 D3
FORTYNINE LN	MOD	7 D5
FORTYNINE PALMS	SBD	101 B1
FORWARD RD	TEH	19 B3
FORWARD ST	SD	105 B5
FORWARDS MILL	SHA	19 C2
FOSS RD	JKSN	3 D1
FOSS HILL	SON	32 A5
FOSSIL BED RD	SBD	81 C5
FOSTER	MON	54 C4
FOSTER RD	LACO	R E5
FOSTER RD	LACO	S E1
FOSTER RD	LACO	T A1
FOSTER RD	NAP	133 B5
FOSTER RD	SHA	18 B3
FOSTER RD	SIS	4 C3
FOSTER CITY BL	FCTY	145 D2
FOSTER CITY BL	SMCO	45 D3
FOSTER MTN RD	MEN	23 B5
FOULDS RD	IMP	108 E3
FOULKE LN	SIS	4 B5
FOUNTAIN AV	LA	182 A4
FOUNTN HOUSE RD	YUB	26 B5
FOUR CORNERS RD	LAS	14 B3
FOUR MILE RD	COL	24 E5
FOUR MILE RD	COL	32 E1
FOUR MIL RDG RD	BUT	25 E3
FOURTEENTH ST	EUR	121 B2
FOURTH AV	SUT	33 D3
FOURTH ST	C	124 B3
FOUSSAT RD	SDCO	106 B3
FOUTS SPRGS RD	COL	24 A5
FOWLER AV	FRCO	57 D2
FOWLER AV	FRCO	57 D5
FOWLER RD	PLA	34 A3
FOWLER PBLC CMP	SIS	13 A2
FOX RD	LAS	21 B4
FOX RD	MCO	48 B4
FOX RD	STA	47 D2
FOX RD	SOL	39 B2
FOXEN CANYON RD	SB	86 D1
FOXWORTHY AV	SCL	46 B5
FRAGUERO RD	TUO	41 C5
FRANCESCHI RD	KER	79 D3
FRANCISCO ST	SF	143 A3
FRANCISQUITO AV	LACO	R C4
FRANCISQITO CYN	LACO	89 C3
FRANCIS SPGS RD	SBD	83 C2
FRANCO WSTRN RD	KER	77 D3
FRANK AV	KER	70 A5
FRANK COX RD	STA	47 B3
FRANKENHEIMR RD	STA	47 E1
FRANKLIN AV	LA	181 E4
FRANKLIN AV	LA	182 A4
FRANKLIN AV	LACO	Q C3
FRANKLIN AV	YUBA	125 C4
FRANKLIN BLVD	SAC	39 E2
FRANKLIN BLVD	SCTO	137 D5
FRANKLIN RD	MCO	48 B4
FRANKLIN RD	SBD	84 C4
FRANKLIN RD	SUT	33 B2
FRANKLIN RD	SUT	125 A4
FRANKLIN ST	MDO	162 A4
FRANKLIN ST	MONT	167 D3
FRANKLIN ST	MON	53 E3
FRANKLIN ST	SF	143 A4

STREET	CO.	PAGE & GRID
FRANKLIN CYN RD	M	154 A3
FRANKLIN LEVEE	SUT	33 B2
FRANK SNATRA DR	RCO	100 D4
FRANKWOOD AV	FRCO	58 A4
FRANZ VALLEY RD	SON	38 A1
FRANZ VLY SCHL	SON	38 A1
FRASER RD	KER	78 C3
FRATES RD	SON	38 A3
FRAZIER LN	MEN	23 B2
FRAZIER RD	FRCO	57 E1
FRAZIER RD	SJCO	40 C4
FRAZIER MTN RD	VEN	88 C2
FRAZR MTN PK RD	KER	88 C2
FRAZIER PK RD	SCL	54 D2
FRAZINE RD	STA	47 D2
FREDERICK AV	SJCO	47 B2
FREDERICK ST	RCO	99 C3
FREDERICKSBURG	ALP	36 C4
FREDERICKSON RD	LAS	8 D5
FRED HAIGHT DR	DN	1 E3
FREDRICKS RD	IMP	109 A4
FREEBORN RD	KER	78 A3
FREEDOM BLVD	SCR	54 B2
FREEMAN FLAT RD	MON	65 C2
FREEMN SCH HSE	TEH	24 C2
FREEPORT BLVD	SCTO	137 C5
FREITAS PKWY	MAR	38 B5
FREITAS RD	STA	47 C4
FREMONT AV	KER	79 E2
FREMONT AV	KIN	67 B1
FREMONT AV	LSAL	149 B2
FREMONT AV	LACO	R E4
FREMONT AV	SCL	45 E4
FREMONT AV	SVL	149 B2
FREMONT BLVD	ALA	46 A3
FREMONT RD	SBD	92 C1
FREMONT RD	SJCO	40 B5
FREMONT ST	CLK	74 D2
FREMONT ST	LV	209 D1
FREMONT ST	SBD	99 D2
FREMONT ST	SF	143 D4
FREMONT ST	S	160 C4
FREMONT PEAK RD	SBD	81 A4
FRENCH AV	BUT	33 C1
FRENCH RD	HUM	16 B5
FRENCH&SUGAR CK	SIS	11 D2
FRENCH BAR RD	AMA	40 E3
FRENCH CAMP RD	HUM	10 C3
FRENCH CAMP RD	SJCO	40 B5
FRENCH CAMP RD	SJCO	47 B1
FRENCH CREEK RD	BUT	25 E3
FRENCH CREEK RD	ED	40 D1
FRENCH CREEK RD	SIS	11 D2
FRENCH FLAT RD	TUO	41 B5
FRENCH GULCH RD	CAL	41 B4
FRENCH GULCH RD	SHA	18 A1
FRENCH HILL RD	DN	2 A3
FRENCHMAN LK RD	PLU	27 D2
FRENCHTOWN RD	YUB	26 A5
FRENZEN RD	COL	32 E3
FRESH WATER RD	COL	32 C2
FRESHWTR KNEELD	HUM	15 E1
FRESHWTR LGN RD	HUM	9 E3
FRESHWATER POOL	HUM	16 A1
FRESNO AV	KER	78 B2
FRESNO AV	KER	78 C2
FRESNO AV	SJCO	40 A5
FRESNO AV	SJCO	160 B5
FRESNO AV	S	160 B5
FRESNO RD	MCO	48 D5
FRESNO ST	FRE	165 E2
FRESNO ST	FRCO	57 C3
FRESNO-COALINGA	FRCO	66 E1
FRESNO FLAT RD	MAD	49 D4
FRESZ RD	RCO	106 E1
FREWERT RD	SJCO	47 A1
FREY AV	KER	77 E2
FREY AV	KER	78 A2
FREY RANCH RD	BUT	26 B3
FRIANT RD	FRCO	57 C2
FRIANT RD	MAD	57 D2
FRIARS RD	SD	213 A4
FRIARS RD	SD	214 D2
FRIARS RD	SDCO	V B3
FRIARS RD	SDCO	111 D1
FRIARS RD	SDCO	214 B3
FRICOT CITY RD	CAL	41 B4
FRIDAY RIDGE RD	HUM	10 C5
FRIEDRICH RD	TRI	10 E5
FRIEDRICH RD	TRI	16 E1
FRIEL RD	CLO	33 A3
FRINK RD	IMP	109 A2
FRISBY RD	SHA	19 A1
FRITZ DR	TUL	68 D1
FRONT ST	DN	1 D4
FRONT ST	LA	191 A3
FRONT ST	SAL	171 C4
FRONT ST	SF	143 D3
FRONT ST	SC	169 D3
FRONT ST	SOL	39 C4
FRONTAGE RD	CAL	40 E3
FRONTAGE RD	CAL	41 A3
FRONTIER RD	SBD	91 C2
FRUCHTENICHT RD	COL	33 B3
FRUDDEN RD	MON	65 D4
FRUIT AV	FRE	165 B2
FRUIT AV	FRCO	57 C4
FRUIT AV	FRCO	57 C5
FRUIT AV	STA	47 B3
FRUIT ST	SA	196 D3
FRUITLAND AV	MCO	48 A4
FRUITLAND AV	YUB	33 D1
FRUITRIDGE RD	SAC	39 E1
FRUITRIDGE RD	SAC	40 A1
FRUITVALE AV	ALA	45 D1
FRUITVALE AV	KER	78 D3
FRUITVALE AV	O	158 E4
FRUITVALE AV	O	159 B1
FRUITVALE RD	BUT	25 B4
FRUITVALE RD	PLA	34 B3
FRY RD	SOL	39 B3
FRYMIRE RD	STA	48 A1
FUENTE ST	ORA	T C1
FUENTE DR	SDCO	V D3
FUERTE DR	SDCO	111 E1
FUGLER RD	SB	86 C1
FULKERTH RD	STA	47 C3
FULLEN RD	CAL	41 C3
FULLER LN	AMA	40 E3
FULLER RD	INY	59 E1
FULLERTON RD	LACO	98 B2
FULLERTON RD	LACO	R C5
FULLERTON RD	ORA	U D5
FULMOR RD	HUM	15 D2
FULMOR TOPPEN	HUM	15 D2
FULTON AV	SAC	40 A1
FULTON LN	NAPA	29 C2
FULTON RD	SON	37 E2
FULTON ST	B	156 A3
FULTON ST	SF	141 D4
FULTON ST	SF	142 A3

STREET	CO.	PAGE & GRID
FULTON ST	SF	143 A5
FULTON ST	SFCO	45 B1
FULTON ST	S	160 B2
FULTON ST N	FRE	165 C3
FULWEILER AV	AUB	126 B3
FURLONG AV	SCL	54 D2
FURNACE CK RD	SBD	91 E4
FURNC CK WSH RD	INY	72 C2
FURNC CK WSH RD	INY	73 A4
FUZZY LN	SHA	18 C3
G		
G ST	DVS	136 D3
G ST	FRE	165 C4
G ST	HUM	9 E5
G ST	HUM	10 A5
G ST	MER	170 D4
G ST	MCO	48 C4
G ST	MCO	48 C4
G ST	MDO	162 B4
G ST	SCTO	137 C2
GABY AV	COL	32 E3
GADDINI	SOL	39 A1
GAFFERY RD	STA	47 A3
GAFFEY ST	LA	191 A5
GAFFEY ST	LACO	S C3
GAFFNEY RD	YOL	39 D2
GAGE AV	LACO	Q C5
GAGE RD	BUT	25 C4
GAINES LN	SHA	18 D3
GALE AV	FRCO	66 C2
GALE RD	SBD	91 E2
GALENA ST	RCO	99 A2
GALENA CYN RD	INY	72 A3
GALEPPI RD	LAS	21 C4
GALLAGHER AV	TEH	24 D2
GALLAGHER RD	SUT	33 E3
GALLATIN RD	LAS	20 E2
GALLATIN RD	TEH	18 C5
GALLAWAY RD	SIE	26 D4
GALLINAS AV	SR	139 B1
GALLOPADE TR	SBD	80 E1
GALVEZ AV	FRCO	56 B2
GAMBLE RD	MCO	48 B3
GAMMEL RD	SBD	101 C1
GANESHA BLVD	LACO	98 C2
GANESHA BLVD	LACO	U E3
GANGER RD	SIS	5 D2
GANN RD	CAL	40 E4
GAP FOLSOM RD	CAL	41 C2
GARAPATOS RD	MON	64 B1
GARATE RD	LAS	8 C5
GARBAGE DUMP RD	LAS	14 B3
GARBAGE PIT RD	MNO	43 B3
GARBAGE PIT RD	MNO	50 D1
GARBONI RD	RCO	99 D4
GARCES HWY	KER	67 E5
GARCES HWY	KER	68 C5
GARCES HWY	KER	69 A5
GARCIA RIVER RD	MEN	30 C3
GARDEN HWY	SAC	39 D1
GARDEN HWY	SUT	33 D2
GARDEN HWY	SUT	125 D5
GARDEN HWY	YUBA	125 E4
GARDEN RD	SDCO	106 E4
GARDEN ST	STB	174 B3
GARDENA BLVD	LACO	S C1
GARDEN BAR	PLA	34 B3
GARDEN BAR RD	NEV	34 B3
GARDENDALE ST	LACO	R E5
GARDENDALE ST	LACO	S E1
GARDEN GROVE BL	GGR	195 A2
GARDEN GROVE BL	OR	195 D2
GARDEN GROVE BL	ORA	98 B4
GARDEN GROVE BL	ORA	T C2
GARDEN GROVE FY	GGR	195 B2
GARDEN GROVE FY	OR	195 B2
GARDEN GROVE FY	OR	196 C1
GARDEN GROVE FY	ORA	98 B4
GARDEN GROVE FY	ORA	T C2
GARDEN VLY RD	ED	34 D4
GARDEN VLY RD	YUB	26 B5
GARDINER FRY RD	TEH	24 E2
GARDNER AV	MCO	48 C4
GARDNER LN	CAL	41 B4
GARDNER ST	LA	184 B1
GARDNER ST	VAL	134 B3
GARDNER FLD RD	KER	78 A4
GAREY AV	LACO	98 D2
GAREY AV	LACO	U E4
GAREY AV	SB	86 C1
GARFIELD AV	FRCO	57 B3
GARFIELD AV	FRCO	57 B5
GARFIELD AV	LACO	98 A2
GARFIELD AV	LACO	R E5
GARFIELD AV	LACO	S D1
GARFIELD AV	ORA	98 B4
GARFIELD AV	ORA	T B3
GARFIELD AV	SAC	34 A5
GARFIELD ST	RCO	101 C5
GARIN RD	MON	54 C2
GARLAND RD	BUT	25 C2
GARLOCK RD	KER	80 D2
GARNER LN	BUT	25 B2
GARNER PL	CAL	40 D4
GARNER RD	STA	47 D2
GARNET AV	SD	212 A1
GARNET AV	SDCO	V A3
GARNET AV	SDCO	106 C5
GARNET ST	SBD	99 D2
GARNETT LN	SOL	39 B2
GARNIER RD	LAS	21 D5
GARRARD	CC	38 C5
GARRET	PLA	34 D2
GARRETT DR	RCO	100 A5
GARRISON AV	STA	47 C2
GARST RD	IMP	109 A3
GARST RD	STA	47 D2
GARVEY AV	LACO	98 A2
GARVEY AV	LACO	R A4
GARVEY RD	IMP	108 E4
GARWOOD RD	SUT	33 D4
GARZOLI AV	KER	78 B1
GAS COMPANY RD	KER	78 A4
GASKELL RD	KER	89 B2
GASKELL RD	KER	89 D1
GAS LINE RD	RCO	102 B5
GASPERS RD	SHA	18 D2
GAS POINT RD	SHA	18 B3
GAS POINT RD	SHA	18 B3
GASQUET FLAT RD	DN	2 A3
GASTENBIDE RD	MCO	55 C2
GASTON RD	NEV	26 E5
GATES RD	STA	47 B2
GATES RD	TRI	16 D1
GATES CANYON RD	SOL	38 E2
GATES CANYON RD	SOL	39 A2
GATEWAY	CC	39 D5
GATEWAY BLVD	LA	180 D5
GATEWAY BLVD	KER	80 E1
GATOS TR	SBD	100 E1
GAVILAN DR	RCO	99 B3

STREETS

227
GAVIOTA
STREET INDEX
HARPER LAKE RD

STREET	CO.	PAGE & GRID	
GAVIOTA	AVLN	105	A4
GAVIOTA BCH RD	SB	86	D4
GAVIOTA STA RD	SB	86	D4
GAVILAN RD	SDCO	106	C1
GAWNE CARTER RD	SJCO	40	C5
GAWNE CARTER RD	SJCO	47	C1
GAZELLE CALLAHN	SIS	4	B5
GAZELLE CALLAHN	SIS	11	E2
GAZELLE CALLAHN	SIS	12	A1
GAZELLE MTN LKT	SIS	12	A1
GAZOS CREEK RD	SMCO	45	C5
G-BAR-T RCH RD	MNO	44	C5
G-BAR-T RCH RD	MNO	51	C1
GEARY BLVD	SF	141	A3
GEARY BLVD	SF	142	A3
GEARY BLVD	SFCO	45	B1
GEARY RD	CC	38	E5
GEARY ST	SF	143	A4
GEER AV	MCO	47	D4
GEER RD	STA	47	E3
GELDING RD	CAL	41	B4
GENASCI RD	SIE	27	C3
GENE AUTRY TR	PMSP	206	E2
GENERL BEALE RD	KER	79	A3
GENRL PETROLEUM	KER	79	E5
GENRL PETROLEUM	KER	80	A5
GENRL PETROLEUM	KER	89	C1
GENERALS HWY	TUL	58	E3
GENERALS HWY	TUL	59	A5
GENESEE AV	SD	211	E1
GENESEE AV	SD	213	C1
GENESEE AV	SDCO	V	B3
GENESEE AV	SDCO	106	C5
GENESEE INDN CK	PLU	26	E1
GENESEO RD	SLO	76	B1
GENEVA AV	KIN	67	C1
GENOA LN	DGL	36	B3
GENTRY RD	IMP	109	A3
GENTRY RD	INY	72	E4
GENTRY RD	INY	73	A4
GEORGE RD	IMP	112	A4
GEORGE SMITH RD	FRCO	58	B3
GEORGETOWN	ED	34	E3
GEORGETOWN RD	ED	34	E4
GEORGETOWN RD	PLCV	138	C1
GEO WSHNTN BL S	SUT	33	C3
GEORGIA LN	STA	47	E2
GEORGIA RD	SBD	81	C5
GEORGIA ST	VAL	134	C4
GEORGIA SLID RD	ED	34	D3
GEPHART RD	KER	80	D5
GERARD AV	MCO	48	C4
GERBER RD	SAC	40	A2
GERBER RD	TEH	18	D5
GERKIN RD	INY	51	D4
GERRIE LN	RCO	107	C1
GETTYSBURG AV	FRCO	56	C3
GETTYSBURG AV	FRCO	57	A3
GEYSERS RD	SON	31	D4
GEYSRS RESRT RD	SON	31	D4
GHOST TOWN RD	SBD	92	A1
GIANT ROCK RD	SBD	92	E5
GIANT ROCK RD	SBD	93	A5
GIBRALTAR RD	SB	87	C3
GIBSON LN	MEN	23	B5
GIBSON RD	COL	32	D2
GIBSON RD	YOL	33	B5
GIBSON CYN RD	SOL	39	A2
GIDDINGS AV	TUL	68	B1
GIELOW LN	MEN	31	B2
GIFFORD RD	SUT	33	C4
GILBERT RD	STA	47	D1
GILLAM RD	CAL	40	E3
GILLESPIE RD	IMP	109	A2
GILLESPIE ST	STB	174	A4
GILLETT RD	IMP	109	B5
GILLETT RD	MON	65	C4
GILLETTE RD	KER	79	D3
GILLETTE RD	MCO	48	D5
GILLILAND RD	LAS	8	C5
GILLIS CYN RD	SLO	76	D1
GILLMAN AV	KER	89	D1
GILL RANCH RD	PLU	26	E2
GILL STA COSO	INY	70	C3
GILMAN DR	SD	211	C2
GILMAN DR	SDCO	V	A3
GILMAN DR	SDCO	106	C5
GILMAN RD	SCL	54	D2
GILMAN RD	SHA	12	D4
GILMAN SPGS RD	RCO	99	D3
GILMORE	SJCO	40	C4
GILMOR RANCH RD	TEH	18	D5
GILROY HT SP RD	SCL	54	D1
GIRARD AV	SD	105	B3
GIRARD LO RD	SHA	12	C3
GIRARD LOOKOUT	SHA	12	C3
GIRARD RIDGE RD	SHA	12	C4
GIRAUDO RD	KER	79	B4
GIRD RD	SDCO	106	C2
GIRDNER RD	SUT	33	B2
GIRVAN RD	SHA	18	C2
GISH ST	SJ	152	A2
GIVENS LUSTR RD	MCO	48	C5
GLACIER LODG RD	INY	51	D5
GLACIER PT RD	MPA	63	C5
GLADDING RD	PLA	34	A3
GLADSTONE ST	LACO	U	D3
GLASSCOCK RD	SJCO	39	E4
GLASSELL ST	OR	194	C4
GLASSELL ST	OR	196	C1
GLASSELL ST	ORA	98	C3
GLASSELL ST	ORA	T	D2
GLASS FLOW RD	MNO	50	D1
GLEASON RD	SBD	92	D5
GLEN AV	MER	170	E4
GLEN RD	SB	87	B4
GLEN ALPINE RD	ED	35	E4
GLEN ANNIE RD	SB	87	B4
GLEN ARBOR RD	SCR	53	E1
GLENBURN RD	SHA	13	D4
GLEN CANYON RD	SCR	54	A1
GLENCO AV	GLE	24	D3
GLENDALE AV	LACO	97	E1
GLENDALE AV	LACO	Q	C3
GLENDALE BLVD	LA	182	E3
GLENDALE BLVD	LA	185	E2
GLENDALE BLVD	LACO	Q	C4
GLENDALE DR	HUM	10	A5
GLENDALE FRWY	LACO	R	D3
GLENDORA AV	LACO	98	B2
GLENDORA AV	LACO	U	D3
GLENDORA MTN RD	LACO	98	C1
GLENDORA MTN RD	LACO	U	D2
GLENISON GAP RD	TRI	17	C1
GLENN AV	FRCO	66	E3
GLENN DR	GLE	24	A4
GLENN RD	TEH	24	C2
GLENN RD W	COL	24	D5
GLENN-ALLEN AV	KER	68	D5
GLENN COOLDG DR	SC	169	A2
GLENN COOLDG DR	SCR	169	A2
GLENNDENNING RD	SIS	3	D5
GLENOAKS BLVD	BUR	179	C1
GLENOAKS BLVD	LA	179	C1
GLENOAKS BLVD	LACO	89	D5
GLENOAKS BLVD	LACO	97	D1
GLENOAKS BLVD	LACO	Q	A1
GLENOAKS RD	RCO	99	D5
GLENSHIRE DR	NEV	27	D5
GLENWOOD DR	SCR	54	A1
GLENWOOD LN	FRCO	58	B1
GLOBE DR	TUL	69	A3
GLOBE MINE RD	SBD	84	A5
GLORIA RD	MON	54	E5
GLORIA RD	MON	55	A5
GLORIETTA BLVD	CC	45	D1
G-O RD	DN	2	B4
GOAT MTN RD	COL	32	A1
GOBBI ST	U	123	C4
GOBLE LN	HUM	15	D2
GODDELL RD	CAL	40	E3
GODFREY RCH RD	SLO	75	E1
GODLEY	PLA	34	B3
GODWIN RD	SBD	101	C1
GOETZ RD	RCO	99	C4
GOFFS RD	SBD	94	D2
GOFFS RD	SBD	95	A1
GOGNA	SJCO	40	B5
GOLD CROWN RD	RCO	101	E2
GOLD CROWN RD	SBD	101	E1
GOLDEN AV	SBD	99	C1
GOLDEN RD	SIS	5	D2
GOLDEN ST	SBD	100	E1
GOLDEN CYN RD	INY	72	A1
GOLDEN CTR FRWY	GV	127	E2
GOLDEN CTR FRWY	NEV	127	E2
GOLDEN EAGLE AV	PLU	26	C1
GOLDEN GATE AV	SF	142	A3
GOLDEN GATE AV	SF	143	A5
GOLDEN GATE DR	HUM	16	B3
GOLDEN GATE RD	MNO	42	D1
GOLDN LK FOREST	PLU	26	E3
GOLDENROD AV	FRCO	57	A4
GOLDEN SPG DR	LACO	U	D4
GOLDEN STATE AV	BKD	166	C2
GOLDEN STATE BL	FRCO	57	E5
GOLDEN STATE BL	STA	47	D3
GOLDEN STATE DR	MAD	57	A2
GOLDEN STATE FY	BUR	179	C1
GOLDEN STATE FY	LA	179	C1
GOLDEN STATE FY	LA	182	D1
GOLDEN STATE FY	LA	186	D3
GOLDEN STATE FY	LACO	89	B4
GOLDEN STATE FY	LACO	97	D1
GOLDEN STATE FY	LACO	Q	A1
GOLDN TROUT CRS	BUT	26	B4
GOLDENWEST AV	ORA	98	B4
GOLDEN WEST ST	ORA	T	B3
GOLD HILL	ED	34	D4
GOLDHILL RD	PLA	34	B3
GOLD HILL RD	SOL	38	D4
GOLD LAKE RD	PLU	27	A3
GOLD LAKE RD	SIE	27	A3
GOLD PARK	SBD	101	C2
GOLD RCK RCH RD	IMP	110	B5
GOLD RUN RD	LAS	20	E4
GOLDRUSH RD	RCO	107	B1
GOLDSBOROUGH GL	SHA	17	D3
GOLD STONE LN	SHA	18	B2
GOLDSTONE RD	SBD	81	E3
GOLD STRIKE RD	CAL	41	A3
GOLER RD	KER	80	E2
GOLF RD	MCO	48	C4
GOLF COURSE RD	HUM	10	A5
GOLF LINK RD	AVLN	105	B5
GOLF LINK RD	MCO	47	E4
GOLF LINKS RD	ALA	45	E2
GOMAN AV	TUL	70	A3
GOMER AV	KER	78	A1
GOMEZ RD	SHA	13	D4
GONDER RD	IMP	109	B4
GONSALVES RD	TEH	18	C5
GONZAGA RD	MCO	55	C1
GONZALES RD	MCO	55	C2
GONZALES RD	VEN	88	B5
GONZALES RD	VEN	96	B1
GONZALES RIV RD	MON	54	E5
GOODALE RD	INY	59	E2
GOODE HILL RD	LACO	89	E3
GOODENOUGH RD	VEN	88	D4
GOODFELLOW AV	FRCO	57	E4
GOODWATER AV	SHA	18	C2
GOODWIN DR	SBD	91	A4
GOODWIN RD	STA	47	D2
GOODYEAR RD	SOL	38	E4
GOODYEAR CK RD	SIE	26	D4
GOOLSBY RCH RD	MNO	51	C1
GOOSE CREEK RD	AMA	40	C3
GOOSE HAVEN RD	SOL	39	B3
GOOSE RANCH RD	TRI	17	D1
GOOSE VALLEY RD	SHA	13	C4
GOPHER CYN RD	SDCO	106	C2
GOPHR HLL LNDFL	PLU	26	C1
GORDEN RD	HUM	16	C2
GORDONS FRRY RD	SIS	3	A3
GORDON VLY RD	NAPA	38	E2
GORDON VLY RD	SOL	38	E2
GORGE RD	INY	51	C3
GORMAN RANCH	PLA	34	E3
GOSFORD RD	KER	78	C3
GOSS RD	SBD	90	E4
GOUDIE TRUCK TR	SDCO	107	C5
GOUGER NECK RD	MOD	14	B3
GOUGH ST	SF	142	C2
GOUGH ST	SF	143	A4
GOULD AV	LACO	S	B1
GOULD RD	COL	25	A5
GOULD RD	LPAZ	104	A2
GOVE RD	MCO	48	B5
GOVER RD	SHA	18	D3
GOVERNOR DR	SD	211	D2
GOVERNOR DR	SDCO	V	B3
GOVERNOR DR	SDCO	106	C5
GOVERNOR MN RD	LACO	89	E4
GOWER ST	LA	181	E5
GOWLING RD	IMP	109	B5
G P RD	KER	77	C1
GRACE RESORT RD	SHA	19	B3
GRACIE RD	NEV	34	C1
GRACIOSA RD	SB	86	C2
GRAEAGLE RD	SIE	26	E3
GRAEAGLE RD	SIE	27	A3
GRAEAGL JHNSVLL	PLU	26	E2
GRAESER RD	IMP	112	C3
GRAHAM	SIS	12	C1
GRAHAM AV	RCO	99	B4
GRAHAM RD	FRCO	57	A4
GRAHAM RD	IMP	111	E3
GRAHAM RD	SJCO	40	B3
GRAHAM RD	TEH	19	B3
GRAHAM HILL RD	SC	169	D1
GRAHAM HILL RD	SCR	54	A1
GRAHAM HILL RD	SCR	169	D1
GRAHAM PASS RD	RCO	109	E1
GRAINLAND RD	BUT	25	A4
GRAMERCY DR	SD	214	B1
GRAMERCY DR	SDCO	V	C3
GRAMERCY DR	SDCO	111	D1
GRANADA AV	SAL	171	D2
GRAND AV	BUT	25	C4
GRAND AV	ELS	189	A3
GRAND AV	LA	185	D4
GRAND AV	LACO	97	E2
GRAND AV	LACO	98	C2
GRAND AV	LACO	Q	A5
GRAND AV	LACO	U	D4
GRAND AV	LACO	S	A1
GRAND AV	O	158	A2
GRAND AV	ORA	98	C4
GRAND AV	ORA	T	D3
GRAND AV	PAS	190	A5
GRAND AV	P	158	C1
GRAND AV	RCO	99	D4
GRAND AV	RCO	99	B4
GRAND AV	RCO	99	E4
GRAND AV	SA	196	D4
GRAND AV	SA	198	D1
GRAND AV	SD	212	B2
GRAND AV	SDCO	V	A3
GRAND AV	SNLO	172	D1
GRAND AV	SLO	76	B4
GRAND AV	SMCO	45	C2
GRAND AV	SR	139	D3
GRAND AV	SB	86	E3
GRAND AV	TUL	68	D3
GRAND AV	VEN	88	D4
GRAND AV	YUB	33	D2
GRAND AV E	SSF	144	C1
GRAND AV W	O	157	D2
GRAND ST	MDO	162	C4
GRAND CIRCLE BL	RCO	98	E3
GRANDE AV	DVS	136	C1
GRANDE PUMICE	MOD	8	A1
GRANDE PUMICE	MOD	14	E1
GRAND ISLAND RD	SAC	39	D4
GRANDON RD	RCO	107	C1
GRAND VIEW AV	LACO	R	A3
GRANDVILLE RD	MCO	56	B2
GRANGE RD	LAK	32	B4
GRANGE AV	PLA	34	B4
GRANGE RD	SON	38	A2
GRANGE RD	TEH	24	D2
GRANGER CK RD	MOD	8	D1
GRANGEVILLE BL	KIN	67	C1
GRANGEVLLE BYPS	KIN	67	B1
GRANITE RD	KER	78	D1
GRANITE RD	KER	79	A1
GRANITE RD	MAD	49	B5
GRANITE RD	SBD	92	A4
GRANITE CK RD	SCR	54	A2
GRNIT MTN VW RD	SDCO	107	D3
GRANITE PARK RD	TRI	11	D5
GRANITE SPGS RD	MPA	48	D2
GRANITE VIEW RD	INY	60	A4
GRANITEVILLE RD	NEV	27	A4
GRANIT WELLS RD	SBD	81	A3
GRANT AV	ALCO	146	A2
GRANT AV	COL	32	E3
GRANT AV	SF	143	C2
GRANT RD	LSAL	149	A3
GRANT RD	MCO	56	C1
GRANT RD	MVW	148	A5
GRANT RD	SCL	45	E4
GRANT ST	RCO	101	C5
GRANT ST	SM	145	A2
GRANT ST	SMA	173	B1
GRANT LAKE RD	MNO	50	C1
GRANTLAND AV	FRCO	57	B2
GRANTLAND AV	FRCO	67	B1
GRANT LINE RD	SAC	40	A2
GRANT LINE RD	SJCO	47	A2
GRAPE WY	BUT	25	A3
GRAPEFRUIT BLVD	RCO	101	B4
GRAPEVNE CYN RD	KER	70	C5
GRAPEVNE CYN RD	SBD	91	D5
GRAPEVINE GULCH	AMA	40	D3
GRAPP LN	RCO	107	C1
GRASS RD	SBD	100	A1
GRASSHOPPR RD S	LAS	8	A5
GRASSHOPPR RD S	LAS	14	E5
GRASSHOPPER FLT	TRI	11	C5
GRASS VALLEY RD	SBT	54	E3
GRASS VALLEY RD	SBT	55	A3
GRATON RD	SON	37	D2
GRATTON RD	STA	47	E3
GRAVEL PIT RD	RCO	103	C5
GRAVEN RES RD	MOD	8	A2
GRAVEN RES RD	MOD	14	E2
GRAVES RD	SJCO	47	B1
GRAVEYARD GULCH	SIS	3	C5
GRAY AV	YUBA	125	C2
GRAYSON	CC	38	E5
GRAYSON RD	STA	47	B3
GREAT CIR DR	KER	80	B4
GREAT HWY	SFCO	45	B2
GREAT NORTHERN	MOD	5	E3
GREAT SO OVRLND	SDCO	108	A5
GREELEY RD	KER	78	C3
GREELY HILL RD	MPA	48	E1
GREELY HILL RD	MPA	49	A1
GREEN RD	COL	32	D3
GREEN RD	IMP	109	C4
GREEN RD	SAC	40	B2
GREEN RD	SBD	90	D4
GREENBACK LN	SAC	34	B5
GREENBAY RD	COL	32	E3
GREENFIELD AV	VAL	134	D3
GREENFIELD DR	SDCO	V	E3
GREENFIELD DR	SDCO	107	A5
GREEN HILL RD	SON	37	D2
GREENHORN RD	NEV	34	C1
GREENHORN RD	SIS	4	A4
GREEN HOUSE RD	MCO	47	E5
GREEN HOUSE RD	MCO	48	A5
GREEN LAKES RD	MNO	43	B4
GREENLEAF AV	LACO	R	B5
GREENLEY RD	TUO	41	C5
GREENLEY RD	TUO	163	D3
GREEN MTN RD	MAD	49	B5
GREEN MTN LKOUT	MPA	49	B5
GREEN RIVER RD	RCO	98	D3
GREENSPOT RD	SBD	99	C1
GREENSPOT RD	SBD	99	D2
GREEN SPRING RD	TUO	48	B1
GREENSTONE	ED	34	D5
GREENTREE BLVD	SBD	91	B4
GREEN VALLEY RD	CC	46	A1
GREEN VALLEY RD	ED	34	D5
GREEN VALLEY RD	SCR	54	B2
GREEN VALLEY RD	SOL	38	D3
GREEN VALLEY RD	SON	37	D2
GREENVILLE RD	ALA	46	C2
GREENVILLE ST	ORA	T	C3
GREENVILLE ST	SA	197	D3
GRNVLL RND VLY	PLU	20	C5
GREENVLL WLF CK	PLU	20	C5
GREENWALD AV	RCO	99	B4
GREENWOOD AV	FRCO	57	E4
GREENWOOD AV	LACO	R	E5
GREENWOOD AV	LACO	R	A5
GREENWOOD RD	ED	34	D4
GREENWOOD RD	SJCO	47	A2
GREENWD HTS DR	HUM	10	A5
GREEN, W S RD	COL	32	E2
GREGORY AV	YOL	39	D1
GREGORY RD	CAL	40	D4
GREGORY CK RD	SHA	12	C5
GREILICH RD	AMA	40	D2
GRIDER RD	SIS	3	B3
GRIDER CREEK RD	SIS	3	B4
GRIDLEY RD	COL	25	B5
GRIDLEY-COLUSA	BUT	25	B5
GRIEVE RD	COL	33	A3
GRIFFIN AV	LA	186	E2
GRIFFIN RD	IMP	109	B4
GRIFFIN RD	STA	47	C2
GRIFFIN ST	SAL	171	D3
GRIFFITH AV	KER	78	B2
GRIFFITH AV	MCO	47	E4
GRIFFITH AV	YUB	33	D2
GRIFFITH PK BL	LA	182	D3
GRIFFITH PK DR	LA	182	D2
GRIFFITH PK DR	LACO	Q	C3
GRIMES AV	STA	47	C2
GRIMES RD	SJCO	46	E1
GRIMES-ARBKL RD	CLU	33	A3
GRIMES CYN RD	VEN	88	D5
GRIMSEL DR	KER	79	C5
GRINDSTONE RD	GLE	23	E3
GRINDSTONE RD	GLE	24	A3
GRIZZLY RD	PLU	27	B2
GRIZZLY RD	TUO	48	D1
GRIZZLY BLUF RD	HUM	15	D2
GRIZZLY GLCH RD	SHA	18	A2
GRIZLY HLL RD N	NEV	26	C5
GRIZZLY ISLD RD	SOL	38	E3
GRIZZLY ISLD RD	SOL	39	A3
GRIZZLY ISLD RD	SOL	135	D5
GRIZZLY PEAK BL	B	156	B1
GRIZZLY PEAK BL	CC	156	E2
GRIZZLY PEAK BL	O	156	B1
GRZZLY PK LKOUT	SIS	13	B3
GROOMS	SJCO	47	D1
GROSJEAN	MPA	49	B3
GROTTO CANYON	INY	61	D4
GROUSE CREEK RD	SIS	11	E2
GROUSE RIDGE RD	NEV	27	A5
GROVE AV	GLE	24	D3
GROVE AV	MCO	48	B4
GROVE AV	ONT	204	D3
GROVE AV	ROC	204	D3
GROVE AV	SBD	98	E2
GROVE AV	U	123	B3
GROVE RD	SUT	33	D3
GROVE ST	SON	132	A3
GROVE WY	ALCO	146	D2
GROVE SHFTR FWY	O	156	B5
GROVE SHFTR FWY	O	157	E3
GROVE SHFTR FWY	O	158	A2
GRUB GULCH RD	MAD	49	B5
GRUBBS RD	BUT	25	D5
GSCHWEND RD	MEN	30	D2
GUADALUPE PKWY	SJ	151	D1
GUADALUPE PKWY	SJ	152	A3
GUADALUPE ST	SB	86	A1
GUALALA LOOKOUT	MEN	30	D4
GUALALA RDG RD	MEN	30	D4
GUERNEVILLE HWY	SON	37	C1
GUERNEVILLE RD	STR	131	A2
GUERNEVILLE RD	SON	37	E2
GUERRERO ST	SF	142	C4
GUERRERO ST	SFCO	45	C2
GUIBERSON RD	VEN	88	D4
GUIDIVILLE RES	MEN	31	B2
GUINTOLI LN	HUM	9	E5
GUINTOLI LN	HUM	10	A5
GULCH RD	TRI	17	B3
GULLETT RD	IMP	109	A5
GULLEY VIEW DR	RCO	107	C1
GULLING ST N	PLU	27	B2
GULLING ST S	PLU	27	B2
GUM AV	GLE	25	A4
GUN CLUB RD	KER	77	E2
GUN CLUB RD	MCO	47	D5
GUNN AV	LACO	R	B5
GUNST RD	HUM	9	E2
GUNST RD	HUM	10	A2
GURR RD	MCO	48	B5
GUTHERIE RD	IMP	108	E5
GUTIERREZ ST	STB	174	C4
GUTTRY RD	LAS	14	B3
GUY KERR RCH RD	HUM	10	C5
GUYS GULCH RD	SIS	4	A5
GWIN MINE RD	CAL	40	E3
GYLE RD	TEH	24	D1
GYPSUM CYN RD	ORA	98	D3
H			
H ST	BKD	166	C4
H ST	BEN	153	C5
H ST	EUR	121	D1
H ST	FRE	165	B3
H ST	IMP	109	A4
H ST	KER	78	D3
H ST	MCO	55	D1
H ST	MDO	162	B3
H ST	SCTO	137	B2
H ST	SAC	39	E1
H ST	SBD	91	D1
H ST	SDCO	V	C5
H ST	SDCO	106	B4
H ST	SDCO	111	D2
H ST	SR	139	C3
H ST	SB	86	B3
HAAS RD	COL	32	D2
HACIENDA AV	RCO	100	D2
HACIENDA AV	SM	145	A3
HACIENDA BLVD	LACO	98	B2
HACIENDA BLVD	LACO	R	B5
HACIENDA BLVD	KER	80	B4
HACIENDA RD	SHA	18	D3
HACKAMORE PL	MNO	43	A3
HACKETT RD	STA	47	C3
HACKLEMAN RD	IMP	109	A5
HACKMAN RD	SOL	39	C2
HACKNEY DR	MNO	42	E1
HACKSTAFF RD	LAS	21	E5
HAGATA RD	LAS	21	A2
HAGEMAN RD	KER	78	C3
HAGEMAN RD	SUT	33	B2
HAGEN RD	NAPA	38	D3
HAGEN RD	NAPA	133	E2
HAGEN FLAT RD	SHA	13	A4
HAHN RD	COL	32	D3
HAIGHT MTN RD	SIS	5	A5
HAILES RD	VEN	96	C1
HAILLE RD	TEH	25	A2
HALE AV	COL	32	E3
HALE RD	AMA	41	A2
HALEY RD	IMP	109	C3
HALEY RD	MCO	47	C5
HALEY ST	STB	174	C4
HALF MOON BY RD	SMCO	45	C3
HALFWAY RD	SDCO	107	B2
HALL AV	SJCO	47	D1
HALL RD	LAS	27	E1
HALL RD	MON	54	C3
HALL RD	SON	37	E2
HALL RD	STA	47	E3
HALL RD	STA	48	A2
HALL RD	TEH	24	D2
HALL RD	VEN	88	D4
HALL WY	SHA	19	E2
HALL CITY CK RD	TRI	17	C3
HALLEY RD	SOL	39	A2
HALLOCK	VEN	88	C5
HALLORAN SPG RD	SBD	83	B3
HALLORAN SUMMIT	SBD	83	D2
HALLOWELL RD	STA	47	C4
HALLS FLAT RD	LAS	20	A2
HALLS GRADE RD	RCO	100	B3
HALLWOOD BLVD	YUB	33	D2
HALLWOOD BLVD W	YUB	33	D2
HALSTEAD	SBD	81	C5
HAM LN	SJCO	40	A4
HAMBONE RD	SIS	13	C2
HAMBURG RD	MCO	55	E2
HAMES RD	SCR	54	B2
HAMILTON	YOL	39	D2
HAMILTON AV	ORA	T	B4
HAMILTON AV	SCL	46	A5
HAMILTON AV	TEH	24	D1
HAMILTON RD	DN	1	E4
HAMILTON RD	KER	89	D1
HAMILTON RD	STA	47	B3
HAMILTON RD E	BUT	25	C5
HAMILTON RD W	BUT	25	C5
HAMLTN NORD CNA	BUT	25	A3
HAMILTN VICTORA	ORA	98	B4
HAMLIN RD	BUT	25	C3
HAMLIN GULCH RD	SIS	3	E5
HAMLOW RD	STA	47	E3
HAMMER LN	SJCO	40	A5
HAMMER LOOP RD	TEH	18	A5
HAMMETT RD	STA	47	C2
HAMMIL RD	MNO	51	D2
HAMMONTON RD	YUB	33	E2
HAMMNTN SMRTVLL	YUB	33	E2
HAMNER AV	RCO	98	E3
HANAUPAH CYN RD	INY	72	A2
HANAWALT AV	KER	78	A1
HANCOCK RD	SBD	84	C4
HANEY VIEW DR	SHA	13	E4
HANFORD ARMONA	KIN	67	C1
HANKINS RD	COL	32	D2
HANKS RD	MOD	7	D4
HANSEN	FRCO	58	B4
HANSEN AV	RCO	99	D3
HANSEN RD	LAS	21	B1
HANSEN RD	SJCO	46	D2
HANSEN ST	SAL	171	E5
HAPGOOD RD	SB	86	C3
HAPPY TR	SBD	92	D5
HAPPY CAMP LKOT	MOD	14	B1
HAPPY CAMP RD	VEN	88	D5
HAPPY CAMP DUMP	SIS	3	A3
HAPPY CANYON RD	SB	87	A3
HAPPY GAP RD	TUL	58	D3
HAPPY VALLEY RD	CC	45	D1
HAPPY VALLEY RD	ED	35	A5
HAPPY VALLEY RD	SHA	18	C3
HARBERS LN	HUM	15	E2
HARBISON RD	COL	32	E1
HARBISON CYN RD	SDCO	107	A5
HARBOR	YOL	39	D1
HARBOR BLVD	ANA	193	B1
HARBOR BLVD	CM	197	B5
HARBOR BLVD	CM	199	B2
HARBOR BLVD	FTNV	195	B5
HARBOR BLVD	FTNV	197	B2
HARBOR BLVD	GGR	195	B3
HARBOR BLVD	LA	191	B3
HARBOR BLVD	LACO	S	C3
HARBOR BLVD	ORA	98	B3
HARBOR BLVD	ORA	T	C2
HARBOR BLVD	SA	195	B5
HARBOR BLVD	SA	197	B2
HARBOR BLVD	VENT	175	E4
HARBOR BLVD	VEN	96	B1
HARBOR DR	IMP	108	C2
HARBOR DR	SD	215	D4
HARBOR DR	SD	216	B5
HARBOR DR	SDCO	V	B4
HARBOR DR N	SD	215	B2
HARBOR FRWY	LA	185	D4
HARBOR FRWY	LA	191	A2
HARBOR FRWY	LACO	97	D4
HARBOR FRWY	LACO	S	C2
HARBOR WY	R	155	A3
HARBOR SCNIC DR	LB	192	C3
HARDEN FLAT	TUO	49	B1
HARDER RD	ALA	45	E2
HARDER RD W	H	146	D4
HARDIN RD	NAPA	32	C5
HARDIN RD	NAPA	38	C1
HARDING AV	STA	47	D3
HARDING RD	MCO	47	E3
HARDING RD	MCO	48	A3
HARDING WY	SJCO	40	A5
HARDING WY	S	160	A4
HARDMAN AV	NAPA	38	C2
HARDRK DAVIS RD	SBD	91	B3
HARDY RD	IMP	111	E3
HARE CANYON RD	MON	65	E4
HARE CANYON RD	MON	66	A4
HARKINS	MON	54	C4
HARKINS RD	SAL	171	E5
HARKINS SLGH RD	SCR	54	B2
HARKNESS DR	PLU	20	A3
HARKNESS ST	NAP	133	A2
HARLAN AV	FRCO	66	D1
HARLAN AV	FRCO	57	C5
HARLAN RD	COL	32	C2
HARLAN MTN RD	SBT	54	E4
HARLAN MTN RD	SBT	55	A4
HARLEY LEIGHTON	SHA	18	C2
HARMON RD	MCO	56	B1
HARMON RD	TUL	67	E2
HARMONY GRVE RD	SDCO	106	C3
HARMONY VLY RD	SLO	75	C2
HARNEY	SJCO	40	A4
HARP RD	TEH	18	C3
HARPER LN	MCO	55	C2
HARPER LN	SOL	39	B2
HARPER RD	IMP	112	D5
HARPER LAKE RD	SBD	81	B5

COPYRIGHT, © 1987 BY Thomas Bros Maps

STREETS

HARPOLD RD

228

INDEPENDENCIA MATEOS

STREET INDEX

STREET	CO.	PAGE & GRID
HARPOLD RD	KLAM	5 D1
HARRIGAN RD	IMP	111 E3
HARRINGTON AV	COL	32 E3
HARRIS	MPA	49 C3
HARRIS RD	BUT	25 B4
HARRIS RD	HUM	16 D5
HARRIS RD	IMP	109 B5
HARRIS RD	MON	54 C4
HARRIS RD	SUT	33 C3
HARRIS ST	EUR	121 B3
HARRIS ST	HUM	9 E5
HARRIS ST	HUM	15 E1
HARRISON AV	HUM	9 E5
HARRISON AV	HUM	15 E1
HARRISON RD	TRI	17 B2
HARRISON ST	O	158 B2
HARRISON ST	RCO	101 B5
HARRISON ST	SF	143 D5
HARRISN GLCH RD	SHA	17 C3
HARRIS RANCH RD	MNO	51 D2
HARROD RD	SBD	92 A4
HARROLD RD	SJCO	47 D1
HARRY CASH RD	SIS	4 C4
HART AV	KER	68 C5
HART RD	IMP	109 C4
HART RD	SIS	4 C4
HART RD	STA	47 C2
HART FLAT RD	KER	79 B3
HARTLEY DR	BUT	25 C2
HARTMANN RD	LAK	32 B4
HART MINE RD	SBD	84 D3
HARTNELL	RED	122 E4
HARTNELL AV	SHA	18 C2
HART OAKS DR	KER	79 B3
HARTSHORN RD	IMP	109 C5
HARTS MEADOW	SIS	12 E1
HARTS MTN RD	SIS	4 E5
HARTVICKSON LN	CAL	40 E4
HARVARD AV	IRV	200 E1
HARVARD AV	ORA	T E3
HARVARD RD	SBD	92 C1
HARVARD MINE RD	TUO	41 C5
HARVEY RD	BUT	25 C2
HARVEY RD	SAC	40 A3
HARVEY RD	STA	47 C4
HARVEY RD 1	LAS	20 C1
HARVEY RD 2	LAS	20 C1
HARVEY RD 4	LAS	20 C1
HARVY MTN LO RD	LAS	20 C1
HARVY PETTIT RD	MCO	48 D5
HARVY VLY RD	LAS	20 C1
HARWOOD RD	SCL	46 B5
HASKELL AV	LACO	Q A2
HASKINS RD	SIS	5 D2
HASKINS VALLEY	BUT	26 A3
HASLEY CYN RD	LACO	89 A4
HASSLER RD	ED	34 E4
HASTAIN RD	IMP	109 B4
HASTE ST	B	156 A3
HASTER ST	ANA	193 D5
HASTER ST	ANA	195 C1
HASTER ST	ORA	T C2
HATCHET CK RD	TRI	11 E4
HAT CREEK PK RD	SHA	13 D4
HAT CK PWRHOUSE	SHA	13 D4
HAT CK PWRHS #2	SHA	13 D4
HATCH RD	BUT	25 B5
HATCH RD	MCO	48 C4
HATCH RD	STA	47 C2
HATCHET CK RD	NEV	34 B2
HATCHET CK RD	TRI	12 A4
HATHAWAY ST	RCO	100 B3
HAUSER BLVD	LA	184 B3
HAUSER BR RD	SON	37 A1
HAVASU LAKE RD	SBD	95 D4
HAVEN AV	SBD	98 E2
HAVEN RD	SBD	80 E5
HAVENS RD	IMP	108 E5
HAVERFORD RD	SDCO	107 A4
HAVLINA ST	SIS	5 D2
HAWEE CANYON RD	INY	70 B2
HAWKEYE AV	STA	47 E3
HAWKINS RD	SOL	39 B2
HAWKINS RD	STA	48 A3
HAWKINS BAR RD	TRI	10 D5
HAWKNSVLLE HMBG	SIS	3 E4
HAWKNSVLLE HMBG	SIS	4 A4
HAWKS HILL RD	HUM	15 D2
HAWLEY GRADE	ED	36 A4
HAWTHORNE AV	C	124 D3
HAWTHORNE AV	SHA	18 B3
HAWTHORNE BLVD	LACO	97 D3
HAWTHORNE BLVD	LACO	S B2
HAWTHORNE ST	MONT	167 D3
HAWTHORNE ST	RCO	99 C5
HAWVER RD	CAL	41 A3
HAYDEN RD	MCO	48 D4
HAYDEN HILL RD	LAS	14 C4
HAYDN HLL CTOFF	LAS	14 D4
HAYDN HLL LKOUT	LAS	14 D4
HAYES AV	FRCO	57 B3
HAYES AV	FRCO	57 B5
HAYES ST	NAP	133 C3
HAYES ST	RCO	101 C5
HAYNES RD	SBD	91 E3
HAYNES RD	SHA	13 C5
HAYS CANYON RD	MOD	8 E2
HAYWARD RD	MCO	48 C2
HAZEL AV	SAC	34 B5
HAZELDEAN RD	STA	48 A2
HAZEL DELL RD	SCR	54 C2
HAZEL VALLEY RD	ED	35 B4
HAZELTINE AV	LACO	Q A2
HAZELTON AV	S	160 E5
HAZEN RD	TEH	19 B3
HEACOCK ST	RCO	99 C2
HEAD DAM RD	BUT	25 D1
HEALDSBURG AV	SON	37 E2
HEALY RD	MCO	48 C5
HEARST RD	MCO	47 D5
HEARST RD	MCO	55 D1
HEARST POST OFC	MEN	23 B4
HEARST WLLTS RD	MEN	23 A5
HEATH RD	KER	78 C3
HEATHER AV	KER	70 C5
HEATHER AV	MAD	57 B1
HEATHER DR	FRFD	135 C2
HEBER RD	IMP	112 B3
HECKER PASS HWY	SCL	54 C2
HECTOR RD	SBD	92 D2
HEDDING ST	SJ	151 C4
HEDDING ST	SJ	152 B2
HEDGER RD	SUT	33 C1
HEFFERNAN AV	IMP	112 A4
HEGAN LN	BUT	25 B3
HEGENBRGR EXPWY	ALA	45 D2
HEGENBRGR EXPWY	O	159 E2
HEGENBERGER RD	ALA	45 D2
HEGENBURGER RD	O	159 E3
HEIDI RD	TUL	68 E1
HEINSEN RD	MON	65 D4

STREET	CO.	PAGE & GRID
HEINZELMAN DR	SIS	4 C5
HEISKELL DR	MAD	57 B1
HEITT AV	KER	68 B5
HELEN DR	MLBR	144 B5
HELENA AV	STA	47 E2
HELENDALE RD	SBD	91 B2
HELLMAN AV	RCO	98 E2
HELLS HALF ACRE	SIE	26 D4
HELLS HALF ACRE	TUO	41 D3
HELLS HALF ACRE	TUO	42 A3
HELLS HOLLOW RD	TUO	48 E1
HELMS CT	KER	79 C3
HEMET LAKE RD	RCO	100 B4
HEMPHILL RD	LAS	21 B4
HENDERSON AV	TUL	68 D3
HENDERSON RD	FRCO	57 B4
HENDERSON RD	FRCO	57 C4
HENDERSON RD	RED	122 D3
HENDERSON ST	EUR	121 C3
HENDRICKS DR	SBD	101 E1
HENDRICKS RD	LAK	31 C2
HENLEY RD	KLAM	5 C1
HENNESSEY RD	HUM	10 D5
HENNESSEY RD	TRI	10 E5
HENNESS PASS RD	SIE	26 D4
HENNESS PASS RD	SIE	27 A4
HENRY RD	SBD	101 D1
HENRY RD	SJCO	40 D5
HENRY RD	SJCO	47 D1
HENRY ST	B	156 A1
HENRY DOTA RD	SIE	27 C4
HENRY FORD AV	LA	191 E1
HENRY FORD AV	LB	191 E2
HENRY MILLER AV	MCO	56 A1
HENRY MILLER RD	MCO	55 C1
HENSLEY RD	MAD	57 B1
HEREFORD RD	MCO	47 E5
HEREFORD RD	MCO	48 A5
HEREFORD RD	MCO	55 E1
HEREFORD RD	SBD	92 B1
HERIOT LN	PLU	27 C3
HERIOT LN	SIE	27 C3
HERITAGE CT	SHA	18 B2
HERITAGE RD	SDCO	V D5
HERITAGE RD	SDCO	111 E2
HERLONG ACCESS	LAS	21 D5
HERMOSA AV	LACO	S A1
HERMOSA RD	KER	78 E3
HERMOSA RD	VEN	88 B4
HERNANDEZ DR	LACO	90 A3
HERNANDEZ DR	MPA	48 C2
HERNDON AV	FRCO	56 B3
HERNDON AV	FRCO	57 C3
HERNLEY RD	RCO	107 B1
HERON AV	SBD	101 A1
HERRICK RD	HUM	121 B5
HERRING RD	KER	78 C4
HERZOG RD	SAC	39 D3
HESPELER RD	SOL	38 E2
HESPERIA RD	MON	65 C5
HESPERIA RD	SBD	91 B4
HESPERIAN BLVD	ALA	45 E2
HESPERIAN BLVD	ALCO	146 A2
HESPERIAN BLVD	H	146 A2
HESSE RD	TEH	18 B5
HETTENSHAW RD	TRI	16 E4
HETZEL RD	IMP	108 E5
HEWES AV	ORA	98 C4
HEWES AV	ORA	T E2
HEWITT	SJCO	40 C5
HEWLTT STURTVNT	MEN	31 B3
HEYSER RD	IMP	110 D5
HIALEAH WY	RCO	100 C5
HIATT RD	SUT	33 B4
HIAWATHA AV	AVLN	105 A4
HIBBARD RD	MEN	31 A4
HIBBARD RD	SJCO	40 B4
HICKEY BLVD	SMCO	45 B2
HICKMAN LN	TEH	18 C4
HICKMAN RD	STA	47 E3
HICKMAN RD	STA	48 A3
HICKS	LAS	21 B4
HICKS LN	BUT	25 B2
HICKS RD	SUT	33 E3
HIDALGO ST	MPA	48 C2
HIDDEN HILLS RD	SBD	94 A2
HIDDEN OAKS DR	KER	79 B4
HIDDEN VLY RD	SB	87 B4
HIDEAWAY HAVEN	SHA	13 D3
HIEROGLYPH RD	MNO	51 C2
HIETT AV	KER	78 B1
HIGDON RD	CAL	41 B2
HIGGINS AV	BUT	33 C1
HIGGNS PURSM RD	SMCO	45 C3
HIGH RD	SBD	91 D4
HIGH RD	SIS	3 E4
HIGH ST	A	159 A2
HIGH ST	AUB	126 D3
HIGH ST	MONT	167 D3
HIGH ST	MON	53 E3
HIGH ST	O	159 B1
HIGH ST	SC	169 B3
HIGH ST	SCR	53 E2
HIGHGRADE RD	MOD	7 E2
HIGHLAND AV	FRCO	57 D2
HIGHLAND AV	LA	181 C4
HIGHLAND AV	LA	184 C1
HIGHLAND AV	LACO	97 D3
HIGHLAND AV	LACO	Q B4
HIGHLAND AV	LACO	S A1
HIGHLAND AV	MB	189 A5
HIGHLAND AV	SBD	98 E1
HIGHLAND AV	SBD	99 C2
HIGHLAND AV	SDCO	V C4
HIGHLAND AV	SDCO	111 D1
HIGHLAND AV	U	123 B3
HIGHLAND BLVD	RCO	99 D2
HIGHLAND DR	CLK	209 A5
HIGHLAND DR	LACO	R D2
HIGHLAND DR	SNLO	172 B2
HIGHLAND RD	CC	46 B1
HIGHLAND WY	SCR	54 B1
HIGHLND HOME RD	RCO	99 E3
HIGHLAND LK RD	ALP	42 B1
HIGHLAND SPG RD	LAK	31 D3
HIGHLND SPGS RD	RCO	99 E3
HIGHLAND VLY RD	SDCO	106 E4
HIGHLANDS LK RD	SHA	12 B4
HIGHLINE RD	IMP	109 C5
HIGHLINE RD	KER	79 B4
HIGHLINE RD	KER	79 C4
HIGH PRAIRIE RD	HUM	10 C5
HIGHRIDGE RD	LACO	S B3
HIGH ROCK RD	LAS	21 E4
HIGH SCHOOL RD	SON	37 D2
HIGH VALLEY RD	KER	88 D1
HIGH VALLEY RD	LAK	31 E2
HIGH VALLEY RD	LAK	31 E3
HIGH VALLEY RD	LAK	32 A3
HY TO THE STARS	SDCO	107 A2
HIGUERA ST	SLO	76 A4

STREET	CO.	PAGE & GRID
HIGUERA ST	SNLO	172 B4
HIGUERA ST S	SNLO	172 B5
HILDRETH LN	SJCO	40 B4
HILDRETH RD	MAD	57 D1
HILL	FRCO	58 B4
HILL AV	PAS	190 E2
HILL RD	COL	32 D2
HILL RD	CC	38 E5
HILL RD	KER	78 C4
HILL RD	KLAM	5 C2
HILL RD	MEN	23 B3
HILL RD	SCL	54 D1
HILL RD	SIS	5 D3
HILL RD	YUB	33 E1
HILL RD E	MEN	23 A5
HILL ST	AVLN	105 B4
HILL ST	LA	185 D5
HILL ST	LA	186 A3
HILL ST	LACO	S D2
HILL ST	ML	164 C4
HILL ST	SDCO	V A4
HILL ST	SDCO	106 B3
HILL ST	SDCO	111 C1
HILLCREST AV	BEN	153 C4
HILLCREST AV	CC	39 C5
HILLCREST BLVD	LACO	R B3
HILLCREST BLVD	MLBR	144 D5
HILLCREST BLVD	SMCO	45 B3
HILLCREST ST	KER	80 E1
HILLDALE AV	MCO	55 C1
HILLDALE AV	MCO	86 E1
HILLER RD	HUM	9 E4
HILLER ST	BLMT	145 C4
HILLGATE RD	COL	32 E3
HILLHURST AV	LA	182 C3
HILLMAN AV	BLMT	145 B4
HILLSBORO AV	LA	183 D5
HILLSDALE AV	SCL	P B4
HILLSDALE BL E	FCTY	145 D2
HILLSDALE BL E	SM	145 B3
HILLSDALE BL W	SM	145 A4
HILLS FERRY RD	MCO	47 C4
HILLSIDE AV	RCO	98 E3
HILLSIDE BLVD	SMCO	45 B2
HILLSIDE DR	MPA	49 C3
HILLSIDE DR	SMCO	45 C3
HILLSIDE DR	SHA	18 D2
HILL SIDE STA	LAS	14 B3
HILLSIDE VIS RD	RCO	107 C1
HILLS VALLEY RD	FRCO	58 B4
HILLTOP	SHA	18 C2
HILLTOP RD	SIS	5 A2
HILL VIEW TK TR	SBD	91 C2
HILMAR RD	STA	47 D4
HILT RD	SIS	4 A2
HILT HUNGRY RD	SIS	4 A2
HILTON PACK STA	MNO	51 A3
HILTONS RD	HUM	9 E2
HILTONS RD	HUM	10 A2
HIME RD	IMP	112 A3
HI MOUNTAIN RD	SLO	76 C3
HINDS RD	STA	47 D1
HINKLEY RD	SBD	81 C5
HINTON AV	MCO	47 E4
HIRSCH RD	MPA	49 B4
HIRSCHDALE RD	NEV	27 E5
HITCHCOCK RD	MON	54 C4
HI YOU GULCH RD	SIS	3 D4
HOADLEY PKS RD	SHA	17 E1
HOAG RD	TEH	24 D2
HOAGLAND RD	HUM	16 D5
HOAGLIN RD	TRI	16 D5
HOAGLIN SCH RD	TRI	16 E5
HOBART AV	FRCO	56 B2
HOBART MILLS RD	NEV	27 D5
HOBBS RD	IMP	109 A2
HOBBS RD	SUT	33 C3
HOBO GULCH RD	TRI	11 B5
HOBSON AV	MON	65 B2
HOBSON WY	RCO	103 C5
HOFFMAN BLVD	R	155 A4
HOFFMAN LN	CC	39 C5
HOFFMAN RD	SBD	80 E3
HOFFMAN RD	SBD	81 A3
HOFFMAN RD	YUB	33 D3
HOFFMAN ST	AMA	40 E2
HFMN PLUMAS RD	YUB	33 D3
HOGAN	FRCO	58 A4
HOGAN LN	SJCO	40 B4
HOGAN DAM RD	CAL	40 E4
HOGAN DAM RD	CAL	40 E4
HOGBACK RD	INY	60 A4
HOG CANYON RD	KER	79 D3
HOG CANYON RD	SLO	76 B1
HOG CANYON EXT	SLO	66 B5
HOGIN RD	STA	47 C4
HOG LAKE TK TR	RCO	100 B5
HOGSBACK RD	TEH	18 D5
HOGSBACK RD	TEH	19 B4
HOKE RD	SUT	33 C2
HOLBROOK RD	MCO	48 D5
HOLCOMB CK RD	SBD	91 E5
HOLCOMB VLY RD	SBD	91 E5
HOLCOMBS RD	SIE	27 D4
HOLDEN	SJCO	40 C5
HOLDNER RD	SOL	39 B2
HOLDRIDGE DR	TUL	68 E3
HOLDRIDGE RD	IMP	112 C3
HOLE AV	RCO	99 A3
HOLENBECK	SJCO	40 C5
HOLIDAY AV	KER	89 C1
HOLIDAY RD	DN	2 B3
HOLLAND	YOL	39 D2
HOLLAND AV	BUT	25 B3
HOLLAND RD	RCO	99 C4
HOLLAND RD	SOL	39 C3
HOLLND TRACT RD	CC	39 D5
HOLLENBECK AV	LACO	R C4
HOLLENBECK AV	SVL	149 D2
HOLLISTER AV	SB	87 B4
HOLLISTER ST	SDCO	V C5
HOLLISTER ST	SDCO	111 D2
HOLLOW LN	SHA	18 C2
HOLLOW RD	CC	39 A5
HOLLOWAY RD	COL	32 E1
HOLLOWAY RD	KER	77 C1
HOLLOW LOG RD	PLA	34 E2
HOLLY AV	LACO	R B3
HOLLY RD	SBD	91 A3
HOLLY RD	TRI	17 A2
HOLLYWOOD BLVD	LA	181 A4
HOLLYWOOD BLVD	LA	182 A4
HOLLYWOOD BLVD	LACO	97 D2
HOLLYWOOD BLVD	LACO	Q B3
HOLLYWOOD FRWY	LA	181 B2
HOLLYWOOD FRWY	LA	185 D1
HOLLYWOOD FRWY	LA	186 A2
HOLLYWOOD FRWY	LACO	97 D1
HOLLYWOOD FRWY	LACO	Q B3
HOLLYWOOD LN	SBD	101 D1
HOLLYWOOD WY	BUR	179 B3

STREET	CO.	PAGE & GRID
HOLLYWOOD WY	LA	179 B3
HOLLYWOOD WY	LACO	97 D1
HOLLYWOOD WY	LACO	Q B2
HOLMAN HWY	MONT	167 C5
HOLMAN HWY	MON	53 D4
HOLMAN HWY	MON	168 C1
HOLMES AV	KER	78 B5
HOLMES LN	SOL	39 A2
HOLMES RD	SBD	84 C4
HOLMES RD	TEH	24 E1
HOLMES ST	ALA	46 C2
HOLMS FLAT RD	HUM	16 B3
HOLOHAN RD	SCR	54 C2
HOLSTEAD RD	SBD	81 C5
HOLT	SJCO	39 E5
HOLT AV	LACO	U D4
HOLT BLVD	MTCL	203 B5
HOLT BLVD	ONT	203 B5
HOLT BLVD	ONT	204 A5
HOLT BLVD	POM	203 B5
HOLT BLVD	SBD	98 D2
HOLT RD	IMP	109 C5
HOLT RD	KER	79 E5
HOLT RD	KER	80 A5
HOLTON RD	IMP	109 B5
HOLTVLE DUMP RD	IMP	109 C5
HOLTZWL	MPA	48 E2
HOLTZWL	MPA	49 A2
HOLWORTHY DR	TUL	68 D2
HOLZHAUSER LN	SIS	11 D1
HOME AV	SD	216 D3
HOME AV	SDCO	V C4
HOME AV	SDCO	111 D1
HOMEDALE RD	KLAM	5 C1
HOMES RD	SBD	91 E4
HOMESTEAD AV	SAL	171 B4
HOMESTEAD RD	SLO	76 B2
HOMESTEAD RD	SCL	45 E4
HOMESTEAD RD	SCLR	150 C3
HOMESTEAD RD	SCLR	151 A3
HOMESTEAD RD	SVL	150 C3
HOMEWOOD CYN RD	INY	71 B4
HONDA RD	SB	86 B3
HONEY BEE RD	SHA	18 B3
HONEY RUN RD	BUT	25 C3
HONEY SPGS RD	SDCO	112 B1
HONEY WAGON RD	IMP	108 E2
HONOLULU AV	IMP	108 C2
HONOLULU AV	LACO	Q C2
HONOLULU RD	KER	78 A4
HOOD FRANKLN RD	SAC	39 E2
HOOKER CREEK RD	HUM	16 C5
HOOKER CREEK RD	TEH	18 C4
HOOKTON RD	HUM	15 D1
HOOPER RD	SUT	33 C2
HOOPER RD	YUB	33 D2
HOOVER RD	MCO	56 C1
HOOVER ST	LA	185 C3
HOOVER ST	LACO	Q C4
HOOVER FLAT RD	LAS	14 C4
HOPE ST	KLAM	5 C1
HOPE ST	LA	185 E4
HOPLAND ST	SBD	91 B3
HOPPER RD	STA	47 E2
HOPYARD RD	ALA	46 B2
HORIZON RD	SBD	91 B3
HORIZON ST	SBD	91 C4
HORN LN	SIS	11 D1
HORN RD	LAS	8 C5
HORNBROOK RD	SIS	4 B3
HORNITOS RD	MPA	48 D3
HORR RD	SHA	13 D3
HORSE CANYON RD	KER	80 B1
HORSE CREEK RD	SIS	3 C3
HORSE LAKE RD	LAS	21 C1
HORSE LINTO RD	HUM	10 D4
HORSE RDG LKOUT	TRI	17 A4
HORSESHOE RD	STA	47 E1
HORSESHOE RD	STA	48 A1
HORSESHOE BR RD	PLA	34 B4
HORSESHOE HL RD	MAR	37 E5
HORSESHOE MDWS	INY	60 A4
HORTON CREEK RD	INY	51 C4
HOSFIELD DR	TUL	68 B2
HOSKING RD	KER	78 D3
HOSLER AV	BUT	25 A3
HOSPITAL LN	RED	122 C5
HOTCHKISS RD	TRI	22 E1
HOT CK RANCH RD	MNO	50 E2
HOT CK RANCH RD	MNO	51 A2
HOTLUM	SIS	12 C1
HOT SPRINGS RD	ALP	36 B5
HOT SPRINGS RD	RCO	108 D1
HOT SPRINGS RD	TUL	68 E4
HOT SPRINGS RD	TUL	69 A4
HOUGHTON AV	TEH	24 D2
HOUGHTON RD	KER	78 C4
HOUSE RD	IMP	108 E5
HOUSE RD	LAS	14 C3
HOUSTON AV	KIN	67 D1
HOUSTON AV	TUL	68 B1
HOUT RD	AMA	40 D2
HOVLEY RD	IMP	109 A4
HOWARD	SJCO	47 A1
HOWARD AV	FRCO	57 A5
HOWARD AV	FRCO	57 A3
HOWARD AV	MCO	47 E4
HOWARD AV	MCO	48 A4
HOWARD AV	SD	214 A5
HOWARD RD	MCO	47 E4
HOWARD RD	RCO	107 B1
HOWARD RD	STA	47 B5
HOWARD RD	TUL	68 B4
HOWARD ST	MEN	23 A3
HOWARD CREEK RD	SIE	27 A3
HOWARD MTHWS RD	SJCO	40 A5
HOWRDS GLCH FTG	MOD	14 C1
HOWE CREEK RD	HUM	15 E3
HOWELL AV	KER	80 C1
HOWELL AV	SIS	11 D1
HOWELL RD	IMP	109 A2
HOWELL MTN RD	NAPA	29 C2
HOWELL MTN RD	NAPA	38 B1
HOWELLS RD	PLU	26 B1
HOWLAND HILL RD	DN	1 D4
HOWSLEY RD	SUT	33 D4
HOY RD	SIS	12 C1
HOY RD	TEH	18 D5
HOYER RD	STA	47 C4
HUASNA RD	SLO	76 C4
HUASNA TOWNSITE	SLO	76 D4
HUB CT	CAL	41 A5
HUBBARD	PLA	34 B3
HUBBARD RD	LACO	89 E4
HUBBARD ST	LACO	89 C5
HUBBARD ST	LACO	Q A1
HUDSON AV	FRCO	56 B2
HUDSON RD	CAL	41 A5
HUDSON RD	MON	65 A1
HUDSON RD	SIS	4 A3
HUDSON RD	SUT	33 E3

STREET	CO.	PAGE & GRID
HUDSON ST	SHA	13 C5
HUERHUERO L PNZ	SLO	76 C2
HUEY RD	SLO	76 A1
HUFF RD	IMP	108 E5
HUFF RD	SBD	91 E3
HUFF ST	RCO	107 C1
HUFFAKER RD	SUT	33 E3
HUFFMEISTER RD	COL	32 C2
HUFFORD RD	HUM	9 E2
HUFFORD RD	HUM	10 A2
HUGHES AV	CUL	183 C5
HUGHES AV	FRCO	57 C4
HUGHES AV	FRCO	67 C1
HUGHES AV	LA	183 C5
HUGHES LN	KER	78 D3
HUGHES RD	GV	127 C2
HUGHES RD	NEV	127 C2
HUGHES RD	SUT	33 C2
HULEN RD	MCO	47 C5
HULEN RD	MCO	55 C1
HULL AV	MCO	48 B4
HULL RD	GLE	24 A3
HULL CREEK RD	TRI	23 A1
HULL MTN RD	LAK	23 D5
HULL VALLEY RD	MEN	23 A2
HULTBERG RD	MCO	47 D4
HULTBERG RD	STA	47 D3
HUMBOLDT AV	FRCO	56 E3
HUMBOLDT AV	FRCO	57 A3
HUMBOLDT RD	BUT	19 D5
HUMBOLDT RD	BUT	25 B3
HUMBOLDT RD	C	124 E4
HUMBOLDT RD	DN	1 E4
HUMBOLDT RD	PLU	19 E5
HUMBOLDT RD	PLU	20 A5
HUMBLDT HILL RD	HUM	15 E1
HUMBUG RD	PLU	19 E5
HUMBUG RD	PLU	20 A5
HUMBUG CREEK RD	SIS	4 A4
HUMBUG HUMBOLDT	PLU	20 B4
HUME AV	KIN	67 E1
HUME RD	FRCO	58 E3
HUMPHREY CIR	PLU	20 D5
HUMPHREY RD	SUT	33 C2
HUN RD	SBD	84 C4
HUNEWILL RCH RD	MNO	43 B3
HUNGRY CK MTRWY	PLU	20 E5
HUNGRY CK LO RD	SIS	4 A2
HUNGRY VLY RD	VEN	88 D2
HUNT RD	CAL	40 E4
HUNT RD	CAL	41 A4
HUNT RD	IMP	112 B3
HUNT RD	LAS	14 C3
HUNT RD	MCO	47 C5
HUNTER	MON	54 C4
HUNTER BLVD	RCO	103 D4
HUNTER ST	CAL	41 A5
HUNTER CREEK RD	DN	1 E5
HUNTER CREEK RD	DN	2 A5
HUNTER MTN RD	INY	61 A4
HUNTERS VLY RD	MPA	48 E2
HUNTINGTON AV	SBR	144 C3
HUNTINGTON DR	LACO	97 E2
HUNTINGTON DR	LACO	R D3
HUNTINGTON RD	MAD	57 C2
HUNTINGTON RD	STA	47 B2
HUTCHINS ST	SJCO	40 A4
HUTCHINSON RD	SJCO	47 B2
HUTCHINSON RD	SUT	33 C3
HUNTLEY MINE RD	MNO	50 E2
HUNTSMAN AV	FRCO	56 E4
HUNTSMAN AV	FRCO	57 C4
HUNTSMAN AV	FRCO	58 A4
HUPP COUTOLENC	BUT	25 D2
HURDS GULCH RD	SIS	3 D5
HURLES CIR	BUT	25 E4
HURLETON RD	BUT	25 E4
HURLTN SWDS FLT	BUT	25 E4
HURLEY FLATS RD	RCO	100 B3
HURRICANE RD	SLO	77 D4
HUSMAN RD	MCO	47 C5
HUSMAN RD	MCO	55 C1
HUSTED RD	COL	32 E2
HUSTON RD	IMP	109 B5
HUTCHINS	MCO	56 B1
HUTSELL RD	MEN	30 E3
HYAMPOM RD	TRI	17 A2
HYDE RD	IMP	111 E3
HYDE ST	FRCO	57 B5
HYDRIL RD	KIN	67 A3
HYPERION AV	LA	182 D4
I		
I AV	SBD	91 C4
I ST	BEN	153 A4
I ST	EUR	121 D1
I ST	MDO	162 B3
IBEX SPRING RD	SBD	72 D5
ICE HOUSE RD	ED	35 C3
ICE HOUSE RD	ED	35 C4
ICELAND RD	NEV	27 E5
IDAHO AV	KIN	67 D2
IDAHO RD	STA	47 D3
IDAHO ST	SDCO	V B4
IDAHO ST	SDCO	111 D1
IDAHO-MARYLAND	NEV	34 C1
IDAHO-MARYLD RD	GV	127 D3
IDAHO-MARYLD RD	NEV	127 D3
IDALEONA DR	RCO	99 B3
IDLEWOOD LN	HUM	9 E3
IDLEWOOD LN	HUM	10 A3
IKE CROW RD	STA	47 C4
ILLINOIS AV	STA	47 C2
ILLINOIS AV	TEH	24 E2
ILLINOIS VLY RD	DN	2 D2
IMLER RD	IMP	108 E4
IMOLA AV	NAP	133 C5
IMOLA AV W	NAP	133 B5
IMPERIAL AV	EC	217 B4
IMPERIAL AV	IMP	109 A5
IMPERIAL AV	SD	216 A4
IMPERIAL AV	SDCO	V B4
IMPERIAL AV	SDCO	111 D1
IMPERIAL HWY	IMP	111 B3
IMPERIAL HWY	LA	189 B2
IMPERIAL HWY	LACO	97 D3
IMPERIAL HWY	LACO	98 B3
IMPERIAL HWY	LACO	Q A5
IMPERIAL HWY	LACO	R C5
IMPERIAL HWY	LACO	S A1
IMPERIAL HWY	ORA	R C5
IMPERIAL HWY	ORA	T C1
IMPERIAL ST	KER	77 E2
IMPERIAL ST	KER	78 B2
IMPERIAL DAM RD	IMP	110 E5
IMPERL GABLS RD	IMP	110 B3
INCLINE RD	MPA	49 B2
INCLINE RD	MPA	63 A5
INDEPENDENCE RD	CAL	41 B2
INDPNDCE CEM RD	CAL	41 B2
INDEPNDNC LK RD	SIE	27 C5
INDEPNDNCIA MAT	BAJA	112 B4

STREETS

STREETS

STREET	CO.	PAGE & GRID		STREET	CO.	PAGE & GRID		STREET	CO.	PAGE & GRID		STREET	CO.	PAGE & GRID		STREET	CO.	PAGE & GRID
INDIA ST	SD	215 C1		ISLAND RD	SIS	3 D5		JEAN BLANC RD	INY	51 D3		JORDAN RD	MCO	48 A4		KELSO RD	KER	79 E1
INDIAN AV	PMSP	206 B4		ISLAND RD	SIS	11 D1		JEANESE	TUO	41 C5		JORDAN CREEK RD	MPA	48 E1		KELSO RD	SBD	83 E1
INDIAN AV	RCO	100 C3		ISLAND BAR HILL	BUT	25 E4		JEAN NICHOLS RD	RCO	99 D5		JORDAN CREEK RD	MPA	49 A1		KELSO AMBOY RD	SBD	93 E1
INDIAN RD	LAS	21 A4		ISLAND MTN RD	HUM	22 D1		JEFF ST	KER	80 C1		JORDAN HILL RD	BUT	25 D2		KELSO AMBOY RD	SBD	94 A1
INDIANA AV	MCO	56 B1		ISLAND MTN RD	TRI	22 D1		JEFFERSON AV	FRCO	56 E4		JORGENSEN RD	MCO	47 C5		KELSO CIMA RD	SBD	83 E5
INDIANA AV	STA	47 E2		ISLAND PARK RD	FRCO	58 B2		JEFFERSON AV	FRCO	57 C4		JORGENSEN RD	STA	47 C4		KELSO CIMA RD	SBD	84 A4
INDIANA ST	LACO	R D4		ISPEN AV	MCO	48 E5		JEFFERSON AV	FRCO	58 A4		JOSE BASIN RD	FRCO	50 A5		KELSO CK VLY RD	KER	79 E1
INDIANA RCH RD	YUB	26 A5		ITALIAN BAR RD	FRCO	50 A5		JEFFERSON AV	RCO	99 C5		JOSE BASIN RD	MAD	58 A1		KELSO VALLEY RD	KER	79 E2
INDIANA SCH RD	YUB	26 A5		ITALIAN BAR RD	TUO	41 C4		JEFFERSON BLVD	CUL	183 D5		JOSEPH PL	SIS	4 C2		KELSO VALLEY RD	KER	80 A2
INDIAN CYN RD	KER	70 C5		IVANHOE RD	SBD	91 E4		JEFFERSON BLVD	CUL	188 C1		JOSEPH CREEK RD	MOD	7 C5		KEMP CT	HUM	16 B3
INDIAN CYN RD	KER	80 C1		IVANPAH RD	SBD	84 C3		JEFFERSON BLVD	LA	183 D5		JOSHUA BLVD	KER	80 C5		KEMPER RD	KER	80 A5
INDIAN CEM RD	ALP	36 B4		IVANPAH CIMA RD	SBD	84 B3		JEFFERSON BLVD	LA	185 A5		JOSHUA DR	SBD	100 D2		KEMPER RD	STA	47 D2
INDIAN COVE CIR	SBD	101 B2		IVERSON LN	LAS	14 B3		JEFFERSON BLVD	LACO	97 D2		JOSHUA LN	SBD	100 E2		KEMPTON RD	SUT	33 D3
INDIAN CV E RD	SBD	101 B2		IVERSON RD	MEN	30 D4		JEFFERSON BLVD	LACO	Q D4		JOSHUA RD	SBD	91 C3		KENDALL RD	KER	80 D1
INDIAN CV W RD	SBD	101 B2		IVERSON RD	MON	54 E5		JEFFERSON BLVD	LACO	187 D4		JOSHUA RD	SBD	91 D4		KENDALL DR	SBD	99 B1
INDIAN CV MT RD	SBD	101 B2		IVERSON ST	SAL	171 A4		JEFFERSON BLVD	LACO	188 A4		JOSHUA WY	KER	79 D5		KENDLE RD	IMP	109 C4
INDIAN CREEK RD	ALP	36 C5		IVESGROVE RD	LACO	89 D3		JEFFERSON BLVD	YOL	137 D2		JOSHUA TREE RD	SBD	92 C5		KENMAR LN	KER	79 A4
INDIAN CREEK RD	KER	79 D3		IVORY MILL RD	GLE	24 A4		JEFFERSON ST	MONT	167 D4		JOY RD	SON	37 C2		KENMAR RD	HUM	15 C2
INDIAN CREEK RD	MNO	51 D2		IVY AV	MCO	56 C1		JEFFERSON ST	NAP	133 C4		JOY ST	KER	70 A5		KENNEBRAW LN	HUM	16 C4
INDIAN CREEK RD	PLU	20 E5		J ST	DVS	136 D2		JEFFERSON ST	ORA	T D1		J T CROW RD	STA	47 C4		KENNEDY AV	BUT	25 A3
INDIAN CREEK RD	RCO	100 A5		J ST	MDO	162 B3		JEFFERSON ST	RCO	101 A4		JUAN ST	SD	213 A5		KENNEDY RD	STA	48 A1
INDIAN CREEK RD	SIS	2 D2		J ST	MER	170 C5		JEFFERSON ST	SDCO	106 B3		JUAN ST	SDCO	V B4		KENNEDY RD	TRI	17 B1
INDIAN CREEK RD	SIS	3 D4		J ST	SCTO	137 E3		JEFFERSON ST	SF	143 A2		JUAN DIEGO-				KENNEDY MEADOW	TUL	70 A3
INDIAN CREEK RD	TRI	17 D2		J ST	SDCO	V D2		JEFFERSON ST N	NAP	133 B1		-FLATS RD	RCO	100 A5		KENNEDY MEM DR	SHA	18 B2
INDIAN DIGGINS RD	ED	41 B1		J ST	SDCO	111 D2		JEFFERY RD	IMP	111 C5		JUBILEE PASS RD	INY	72 C4		KENNEFICK RD	SJCO	40 B4
INDIAN FLAT RD	NEV	34 C1		JACALITOS CK RD	FRCO	66 D3		JEFFERY RD	ORA	98 C4		JUDSON ST	SBD	99 C2		KENNETH AV	SAC	34 B5
INDIAN GUIDE	FRCO	58 B3		JACARANDA DR	KER	79 B4		JEFFERY RCH RD	MNO	51 D2		JULIAN AV	KER	89 D1		KENNETH RD	LACO	Q C3
INDIAN GULCH RD	MPA	48 E3		JACK AV	KER	78 B2		JEFFREY RD	ORA	T E3		JULIAN AV	SDCO	V E3		KENNETT RD	SHA	18 C1
INDIAN GULCH RD	MPA	49 A4		JACKASS FLTS RD	NEV	26 C5		JELLYS FERRY RD	TEH	18 D4		JULIAN RD	SDCO	107 A5		KENNEY AV	TEH	18 C4
INDIAN GLCH EXT	MPA	48 D4		JACKASS FLTS RD	NEV	34 C1		JENEVEIN AV	SBR	144 B3		JULIAN ST	SCL	46 B4		KENNY AV	MCO	48 B4
INDIAN HILL BL	CLA	203 A3		JACKASS GRADE	SBT	55 E4		JENKINS RD	KER	78 D3		JULIAN ST	SJ	152 B4		KENNY CAMP RD	TRI	11 D5
INDIAN HILL BL	LACO	98 D2		JACKASS GRADE	SBT	56 A4		JENKS LAKE RD	SBD	100 A1		JULIE ST	KER	79 C3		KENO WORDEN RD	KLAM	5 A1
INDIAN HILL BL	POM	203 A5		JACKASS HILL RD	TUO	41 C5		JENNINGS RD	STA	47 C3		JUMAR CT	RCO	107 B1		KENT AV	KIN	67 B2
INDIAN HILL RD	RCO	100 C5		JACK CREEK RD	SLO	75 E2		JENNINGS PK RD	SDCO	V C2		JUMPER AV	KER	78 A2		KENT AV	KIN	67 C2
INDIAN HILL RD	SIE	26 C4		JACK CREEK RD	SLO	76 A2		JENNY LIND RD	CAL	40 D4		JUNCAL RD	SB	87 D4		KENT AV	MAR	139 B5
INDIAN HILL RD	STA	48 C2		JACKLIN RD	SCL	46 B4		JENSEN AV	COL	32 E3		JUNE ST	SBD	99 B1		KENT AV	SUT	33 C1
INDIANOLA AV	FRCO	57 E4		JACK PINE AV	KER	79 E5		JENSEN AV	FRCO	56 C4		JUNE LK BCH RD	MNO	50 C1		KENTUCKY AV	YOL	33 B5
INDIANOLA CTOFF	HUM	9 A5		JACK RABBIT TR	RCO	99 D3		JENSEN AV	FRCO	57 A3		JUNIPER AV	MCO	48 B4		KENTUCKY ST	FRFD	135 B3
INDIANOLA CTOFF	HUM	10 A5		JACK RANCH RD	KER	69 B5		JENSEN RD	SLO	75 E1		JUNIPER LN	SIS	4 C5		KENWOOD	SDCO	111 A1
INDIANOLA RESRV	HUM	15 E2		JACK RANCH RD	KER	80 D1		JERROLD AV	FRCO	56 B2		JUNIPER RD	RCO	99 B3		KENWOOD DR	SDCO	V D4
INDIAN OLE RD	LAS	20 C4		JACKS RD	MON	54 E5		JERRY COLLNS AV	MCO	48 B5		JUNIPER ST	SDCO	106 C2		KEOUGH HOT SPGS	INY	51 D5
INDIAN PAINT DR	RCO	100 C5		JACK SHAW RD	HUM	16 B2		JERSEY	MCO	55 E2		JUNIPER FLTS RD	RCO	99 D4		KERN RD	SBD	101 D1
INDIAN PASS RD	IMP	110 B4		JACK SLOUGH RD	YUB	33 D2		JERSEY AV	KIN	67 C2		JUNIPER FLTS RD	RCO	101 A2		KERN ST	SAL	171 C4
INDIAN PEAK RD	MPA	49 B3		JACKSNIPE RD	SOL	38 E3		JERSEYDALE RD	MPA	49 C3		JUNIPER HILL RD	LACO	90 D3		KERN CANYON RD	KER	79 A2
INDIAN POINT RD	KER	79 B4		JACKSON	PLA	33 E4		JERSEY ISLAND	CC	39 C4		JUNIPER KNOLL	SIS	5 A3		KERN RIV CYN RD	KER	79 B2
INDIAN RANCH RD	INY	71 C2		JACKSON AV	KER	77 E1		JERUSALEM GRADE	LAK	32 B4		JUNIPER LAKE RD	LAS	20 A3		KERTO RD	KER	78 A5
INDIAN RES RD	AMA	40 D3		JACKSON AV	KER	78 B1		JESS VALLEY RD	MOD	8 B4		JUNIPERO SRA BL	SCL	45 C4		KERSHAW RD	IMP	109 A3
INDIAN ROCK RD	IMP	112 D5		JACKSON AV	KIN	67 D2		JESUS MARIA RD	CAL	41 A3		JUNIPERO SRA FY	CPTO	149 C4		KESTER AV	LACO	Q A3
INDIANS RD	MON	64 D2		JACKSON AV	SJCO	47 D1		JETTY RD S	HUM	15 D1		JUNIPERO SRA FY	CPTO	150 A4		KESWICK DAM RD	SHA	18 B2
INDIAN SCHOL RD	LPAZ	104 A2		JACKSON DR	SDCO	V D5		JEWELL AV	PAC	167 A1		JUNIPERO SRA FY	MLBR	144 A5		KETTLEMAN LN	SJCO	40 B4
INDIAN SRVCE RD	TUL	69 A3		JACKSON DR	SDCO	106 D5		JEWELL RD	TEH	18 C4		JUNIPERO SRA FY	SJ	150 A5		KETTNER BLVD	SD	215 D4
INDIAN SPGS RD	ALP	36 D5		JACKSON DR	IMP	109 B4		JEWELL VLY RD	SDCO	111 A4		JUNIPERO SRA FY	SMCO	45 C4		KETTNER BLVD	SDCO	V B4
INDIAN SPGS RD	NEV	34 B2		JACKSON RD	SAC	40 A1		JEWETT RD	HUM	16 D5		JUNIPERO SRA FY	SCL	149 C4		KEYES RD	MCO	48 B3
INDIAN SPGS RD	SBD	81 D4		JACKSON RD	SBD	91 D3		JEWETT RD	SUT	33 C3		JUNIPER STA RD	MOD	7 B5		KEYES RD	STA	47 D3
INDIAN TOM LAKE	SIS	5 B2		JACKSON RD	STA	47 C2		JEWETTA AV	KER	78 C3		JURS RD	CAL	41 B2		KEYES RD	STA	48 A3
INDIAN VLY RD	MAR	38 A4		JACKSON ST	ALA	45 E2		J HELT RD	HUM	15 D2		JURUPA AV	RCO	99 A2		KEYES ST	SJ	152 D5
INDIAN VLY RD	MON	56 A5		JACKSON ST	RCO	99 A3		JIM DAY RD	SHA	13 E4		JURUPA AV	SBD	99 A2		KEYS RD	SUT	33 D4
INDIAN VLY RD	SIE	26 C4		JACKSON ST	RCO	101 A4		JIM HARVEY RD	SHA	18 C2		JURUPA RD	RCO	99 A2		KEYSTONE RD	IMP	109 A5
INDIAN VLY RD	SLO	66 A5		JACKSON ST	SF	143 D3		JIM NEGRA RD	MCO	55 D2		JUSTICE CT	KER	79 D2		KEYSVILLE RD	KER	79 C1
INDIAN VLY RD	TRI	17 A2		JACKSON ST	H	146 D4		JOAQUIN RD	ML	162 B5		JUSTICE RD	TRI	16 E5		KEZAR DR	SF	141 B4
INDIAN WELLS RD	KER	80 D1		JACKSON ST W	H	146 D4		JOAQUIN RDG LKT	FRCO	66 C2		JUTLAND DR	SIS	21 C4		KIBBE RD	YUB	33 D1
INDIO AV	SBDO	100 E1		JACKSON GATE RD	AMA	40 D2		JOEGER	PLA	34 C3		J W BARR	SIS	12 C2		KIDDER CREEK RD	SIS	3 C5
INDUSTRIAL BLVD	MOH	96 B4		JACKSON MDWS RD	SIE	27 C4		JOE SMITH RD	INY	51 D4		K ST	BEN	153 A4		KIDDER CK RD S	SIS	3 D5
INDUSTRIAL PKWY	ALA	45 E2		JACKSON RCH RD	HUM	9 E5		JOHANSEN RD	STA	47 D2		K ST	MDO	162 B3		KIDDER CK RD S	SIS	11 D1
INDSTRL FARM RD	KER	78 C2		JACKSON VLY RD	AMA	40 D3		JOHN ST	RCO	100 B3		KADOTA AV	MCO	48 D5		KID LAKES	PLA	35 C1
INGHRAM RD	TEH	24 D2		JACK TONE RD	SJCO	40 B4		JOHN ST	SAL	171 C4		KAGEL CANYON RD	LACO	Q B1		KIDWELL RD	SOL	39 B1
INGLEWOOD AV	LACO	S B1		JACOBS	FRCO	58 B4		JOHN DALY BLVD	SMCO	45 B2		KAISER	SJCO	40 B5		KIEFER BLVD	SAC	39 E1
INGLEWOOD BLVD	LA	188 A4		JACOBS RD	SJCO	40 A5		J F KENNEDY DR	RCO	99 C3		KAISER RD	RCO	102 C4		KIEFER BLVD	SAC	40 B1
INGOMAR GRADE	MCO	55 D1		JACOBS WY	RCO	99 B4		J F KENNEDY DR	SF	141 B4		KAISER RD	STA	47 C4		KIERNAN AV	STA	47 B1
INGOMAR RD	MCO	47 D5		JACOBY CREEK RD	HUM	10 A5		JOHN FOX RD	STA	47 E2		KALIN RD	IMP	109 A4		KIETZKE LN	RENO	130 E3
INGOMAR RD	MCO	55 D1		JACQUELINE	SIS	4 C2		JOHN GIBSON BL	LA	191 A4		KAMM AV	FRCO	56 E5		KIFER RD	SCLR	150 D1
INGRAHAM ST	SD	212 B1		JADE AV	SIS	4 C2		JOHN LADD CHROM	SIS	3 B3		KAMM AV	FRCO	57 C5		KIFER RD	SVL	150 A1
INGRAHAM ST	SDCO	V A3		JAHANT	SJCO	40 A3		JOHN MUIR PKWY	CC	38 D5		KAMM AV	TUL	57 C5		KILAGA SPGS RD	PLA	34 B3
INGRAM LN	STA	33 B1		JAHANT RD	SJCO	40 A3		JOHNNY MDW RD	MNO	43 E5		KAMM AV	IMP	109 C5		KILAGA SPG RD N	PLA	34 B3
INGRAM CREEK RD	STA	33 B1		JAIL RD	AVLN	105 B5		JOHNNY MDW RD	MNO	50 E1		KANDRA RD	SIS	5 D2		KILBURN RD	NAP	133 A4
INK GRADE	NAPA	32 B5		JAKE RD	RCO	100 A5		JOHNNY MDW RD	MNO	51 A1		KANE RD	HUM	10 A3		KILE RD	SJCO	39 E3
INK GRADE	NAPA	38 B1		JALAMA RD	SB	86 B4		JOHNS DR	TUL	68 D3		KANE RD	SBD	91 E2		KILER CANYON RD	SLO	75 E1
INLAND DR	SJCO	40 A5		JAMACHA BLVD	SDCO	V D4		JOHNS RD	KER	79 C3		KANSAS AV	KIN	67 D2		KILER CANYON RD	SLO	76 A1
INLAND FRWY	SD	214 A3		JAMACHA RD	SDCO	V D4		JOHN SCHOOL RD	COL	33 A3		KANSAS AV	STA	47 C2		KILGORE RD	SUT	33 A2
INLAND FRWY	SD	216 C1		JAMACHA RD	SDCO	111 D1		JOHN SCHOOL RD	YOL	33 A3		KANSAS AV	TEH	18 E5		KILKARE RD	ALA	46 B2
INLAND FRWY	SDCO	V C5		JAMAICA BLVD	MOH	96 B4		JOHN SMITH RD	SBT	55 A3		KAPAPA RD	SBD	80 E1		KILLGORE HLS RD	SIS	4 A4
INLAND FRWY	SDCO	106 C5		JAMBOREE BLVD	IRV	198 E4		JOHNSON AV	MCO	47 D4		KAPRANOS RD	LAK	23 C5		KILROY	KER	79 D3
INLAND FRWY	SDCO	111 D2		JAMBOREE BLVD	IRV	200 C1		JOHNSON AV	SDCO	V D3		KARCHNER RD	PLA	34 A3		KILROY RD	MCO	47 D3
INLAND CTR DR	SBDO	207 B4		JAMBOREE BLVD	ORA	T C5		JOHNSON AV	SDCO	106 B3		KAREN AV	RCO	100 C3		KIMBALL LN	YUB	33 D1
INSKIP RD	TEH	19 A4		JAMBOREE RD	IRV	198 E4		JOHNSON AV	SNLO	172 A5		KARLO RD	LAS	21 C4		KIMBALL RD	TEH	18 B5
INTAKE BLVD	RCO	103 D5		JAMBOREE RD	NB	200 A4		JOHNSON AV	SLO	76 B3		KARNAK RD	SUT	33 C4		KIMBERLINA RD	KER	78 B2
INTERLAKE RD	SLO	65 D5		JAMBOREE RD	ORA	98 C5		JOHNSON CT	KER	79 C4		KASSON RD	SJCO	47 E2		KIMBERLY CT	KER	79 C5
INTERNATIONL AV	FRCO	57 D2		JAMES RD	FRCO	56 E4		JOHNSON DR	TUL	58 B4		KATELLA AV	ANA	193 C4		KIMBERLY DR	KER	79 C5
INTERNATIONL AV	IMP	109 B3		JAMES RD	IMP	109 B5		JOHNSON RD	HUM	10 B3		KATELLA AV	OR	194 B4		KIMBERLY RD	SHA	18 D3
INVESTOR AV	RCO	102 C4		JAMES RD	KER	78 D2		JOHNSON RD	HUM	15 E2		KATELLA AV	ORA	98 B5		KIMTU CT	HUM	16 B3
INWOOD RD	SHA	19 A3		JAMES LICK FRWY	SF	142 E1		JOHNSON RD	KER	78 C3		KATELLA AV	ORA	T D2		KINCAID RD	SCL	46 B4
INYO IN	INY	51 D3		JAMES LICK FRWY	SFCO	45 C2		JOHNSON RD	LACO	21 B3		KATHERINE RD	VEN	97 A1		KINE AV	RCO	99 C3
INYO ST	DN	1 D4		JAMES LICK SKWY	SF	142 D1		JOHNSON RD	LACO	89 D4		KAUFENBERG RD	LAS	14 A4		KINEVAN RD	SB	87 B4
INYOKERN RD	KER	80 D1		JAMES LICK SKWY	SF	143 D5		JOHNSON RD	MCO	55 E1		KAUFFMAN AV	TEH	18 E5		KING AV	KIN	67 C2
IONA AV	KIN	67 D2		JAMESON AV	FRCO	57 B5		JOHNSON RD N	MCO	55 D1		KAUFMAN RD	STA	47 D4		KING RD	COL	32 C2
IONE RD	SAC	40 C2		JAMESON AV	FRCO	57 B4		JOHNSON ST	RCO	108 B1		KAUT RD	TRI	10 E5		KING RD	IMP	112 C3
IONE BUENA VIS	AMA	40 D3		JAMESON RD	COL	32 E1		JOHNSON ST	SB	87 E3		KAVANAUGH RD	IMP	112 C3		KING RD	KER	67 C5
IONE MICHIGAN BR	AMA	40 C2		JAMESON RD	KER	79 D4		JOHNSON CYN RD	INY	72 A3		KEARNEY AV	FRCO	57 A3		KING RD	PLA	34 B4
IOWA AV	RCO	99 B2		JAMISON CK RD	SCR	53 D1		JOHNSON CYN RD	MON	55 A5		KEARNEY BLVD	FRE	165 B4		KING RD	SJ	152 D1
IOWA AV	STA	47 C3		JANE RD	SBD	92 D4		JOHNSON RCH RD	PLU	20 B3		KEARNY BLVD	SF	143 C2		KING RD	SCL	46 B4
IOWA CITY RD	YUB	33 D1		JANES RD	HUM	10 A5		JOHNSON SCH RD	LAS	21 B3		KEARNY VILLA RD	SD	213 E1		KING RD	SOL	39 C2
IOWA HILL	PLA	34 D2		JANESVLLE GRADE	LAS	21 B4		JOHNSTON AV	KER	80 D1		KEARNY VILLA RD	SDCO	V B3		KING RD	TEH	18 D5
IRIS AV	RCO	99 B3		JANICE AV	KER	79 E1		JOHNSTON AV	RCO	99 D4		KEARNY VILLA RD	SDCO	106 D5		KING RD	TRI	12 A4
IRIS CT	KER	79 C5		JANICE AV	KER	80 A1		JOHNSVILLE RD	SIE	26 D3		KEATON	MCO	47 D4		KING ST	BKD	166 C1
IRIS DR	SAL	171 C2		JANICE RD	SIS	4 C2		JOHNSVLLE MCCREA	PLU	26 D3		KECKS RD	KER	77 D1		KING ST	SBT	65 C1
IRIS LN	SDCO	106 D3		JANICE ST	KER	80 A4		JOHN WEST RD	MAD	49 D4		KEEFER RD	BUT	25 D4		KING CITY RD	SJCO	40 A4
IRIS RD	KER	80 A1		JANSS RD	VEN	96 D1		JOINES RD	YUB	33 D1		KEEGAN RD	COL	32 E2		KINGDON	SJCO	40 A4
IRIS RD	LAS	14 A3		JAPATUL LN	SDCO	107 B5		JOINT HWY 14	LAS	21 A3		KEELE RD	RCO	110 C1		KING RANCH RD	BUT	25 E5
IRIS WY	CAL	41 B2		JAPATUL LN	SDCO	112 B1		JOINT HWY 14	LAS	21 A3		KEIM BLVD	RCO	110 C1		KING RIDGE RD	SON	37 A1
IRIS CANYON RD	MONT	167 E5		JAPATUL RD	SBD	91 D1		JOINT RD	TEH	18 B5		KEITH RD	YUB	33 D1		KINGS AV	FRCO	66 D3
IRIS CANYON RD	MONT	168 E1		JAPATUL RD	SBD	91 D3		JOJOBA RD	RCO	107 A1		KELBAKER RD	SBD	83 C5		KINGS RD	SBD	90 E1
IRISH HILL RD	AMA	40 D2		JAPATUL RD	SDCO	107 B5		JOJOBA RD E	RCO	102 C1		KELBAKER RD	SBD	84 A5		KINGS RD	TUO	48 E1
IRISH TOWN PNE-				JAPATUL RD	SDCO	112 B1		JOLON PLEYTO	MON	65 B3		KELBAKER RD	SBD	93 C2		KINGS RD	YUB	33 D1
-GRV WIELAND RD	AMA	41 A2		JAPATUL VLY RD	SDCO	107 C5		JONATA PARK RD	SB	86 D3		KELBAKER RD	SBD	94 A3		KINGSBURY RD	TRI	17 D2
IRMULCO RD	MEN	22 E5		JAPATUL VLY RD	SDCO	112 C1		JONATHAN ST	SBD	91 B3		KELLEMS LN	SIS	3 D5		KINGS CANYON RD	PLCA	52 A3
IRONAGE RD	SBD	101 E1		JAQUIMA DR	CAL	41 A4		JONES AV	COL	32 E3		KELLEMS LN	SIS	11 D1		KINGS HILL	PLA	34 D2
IRONE AV	KER	89 C1		JARDINE RD	SLO	76 B1		JONES LN	MOD	1 D3		KELLER RD	RCO	99 C5		KINGSLEY ST	MTCL	203 A4
IRON MTN RD	SBD	91 C1		JARED LN	SB	86 B4		JONES RD	LAS	14 A5		KELLEY RD	SBD	101 D1		KINGS MTN RD	SMCO	45 C4
IRON MTN RD	SHA	18 B1		J ARTHUR YNGR FY	SMCO	45 D1		JONES RD	SJCO	47 D1		KELLOGG DR	ORA	T E1		KINGS PEAK RD	HUM	15 E3
IRON MTN PUMPNG	SBD	102 E1		J ARTHUR YNGR FY	FCTY	145 C1		JONES ST	FRCO	56 B3		KELLOGG SRRA BL	RCO	100 B3		KINGSTON RD	SBD	83 E2
IRONWOOD AV	RCO	99 C2		J ARTHUR YNGR FY	SM	145 D1		JONES ST	SF	143 A2		KELLY	SJCO	40 D5		KINNEY RD	DN	1 D1
IRONWOOD CT	KER	79 C5		JARVIS AV	ALA	45 E4		JONES ST	SMA	173 C1		KELLY RD	HUM	16 A1		KIOWA BLVD	MOH	96 B4
IRVINE AV	CM	199 C4		JARVIS RD	ALP	36 C4		JONES BAR RD	NEV	34 C1		KELLY RD	NAPA	38 D1		KIOWA AV	RCO	102 C4
IRVINE AV	ORA	199 E1		JASMINE RD	SBD	92 B3		JONES RANCH RD	SB	92 A3		KELLY ST	YUB	26 B5		KIOWA RD	SBD	91 C4
IRVINE AV	NB	199 C4		JASPER LN	YUB	33 E2		JONES VALLEY RD	SIE	27 C4		KELLY CREEK RD	SIS	11 D2		KIP ST	DN	1 E1
IRVINE BLVD	ORA	98 C4		JASPER RD	IMP	112 B4		JORDAN RD	HUM	16 A5		KELSEY CREEK RD	LAK	31 D1		KIRBY RD	MCO	48 C4
IRVINE BLVD	ORA	T E3		JASPER RD	TUO	48 B1		JORDAN RD	MCO	47 E4		KELSO AV	KER	79 E1		KIRBY ST	CAL	40 E4
IRVINE RD	IMP	109 C4		JASPER SEARS BR	MCO	55 C1						KELSO RD	ALA	46 D1		KIRKVILLE RD	SUT	33 C3
IRVINE CENTR DR	ORA	98 C4		JASPER SEARS RD	MCO	55 C1										KIRSCHENMANN RD	SBD	87 D1
IRVINE CENTR DR	ORA	T E3		JAVA AV	KIN	67 C2										KIT CARSON	AMA	35 C4
IRVINE LODGE RD	MEN	22 E4		JAVA DR	SVL	148 A5										KIT CARSON CPGD	ALP	36 B4
IRWIN RD	SBD	81 B5		JAVIS AV	KER	80 C1										KLAMATH BCH RD	DN	1 E5
IRWIN RD	SBD	82 A5		JAVIS AV	FRCO	67 C4												
IRWIN RD	SBD	208 B1		JAWBONE CYN RD	KER	79 E2												
IRWIN RD	TEH	24 C2		JAWBONE CYN RD	KER	80 B3												
IRWINDALE AV	LACO	R C5		JAY DEE LN	RCO	100 C5												
ISABELLA BLVD	KER	80 B4		JAYMAR RD	HUM	16 B3												
ISABELA-WLKR PS	KER	79 D1		JAYNE AV	FRCO	66 D3												
ISABEL A-WLKR PS	KER	80 B1		JAYNE AV	FRCO	67 C4												
ISHI PISHI RD	HUM	10 D2																	
ISLAND RD	SHA	13 D3																	

STREET	CO.	PAGE & GRID
KLAMATH BCH RD	DN	9 E1
KLAMATH BCH RD	DN	10 A1
KLAMATH MILL RD	DN	2 A5
KLAMATH MILL RD	DN	10 A1
KLAMATHON RD	SIS	4 B3
KLAMATH RIV RD	SIS	3 D3
KLASSETTE ST	KER	80 A4
KLAU MINE RD	SLO	75 D1
KLIPSTEIN ST	KER	78 A5
KLIPSTEIN CY RD	KER	78 A5
KLOKE RD	IMP	112 B4
KLONDIKE RD	SBD	93 C3
KLONDKE MINE RD	TRI	17 A3
KNEELAND RD	HUM	16 B1
KNIEBES RD	MCO	47 D5
KNIGHTON RD	SHA	18 C3
KNIGHTS RD	SUT	33 C3
KNIGHTSEN AV	CC	39 C5
KNOB HILL RD	MEN	31 B2
KNOB PK LKOT RD	SHA	17 D3
KNOTT AV	ORA	98 B3
KNOTT AV	ORA	T B2
KNOW	PLA	33 E5
KNOWLES RD	MAD	49 B5
KNOWLES RD	MCO	56 C1
KNOX RD	STA	47 E1
KNOXVL DVLHD RD	NAPA	32 C4
KOALA RD	SBD	91 A3
KOCH RD	KER	78 B2
KOENIGSTEIN RD	VEN	88 C4
KOESTER RD	KER	79 D3
KONOCTI RD	LAK	31 D3
KOPTA RD	TEH	24 E2
KOSTER RD	SJCO	47 A2
KOSTER ST	EUR	121 B1
KOWOLOWSKI RD	MOD	6 A2
KRAEMER BLVD	ORA	T D1
KRAFFT RD	MCO	48 D4
KRAFT RD	KER	78 E5
KRAMAR RD	IMP	111 E3
KRAMER BLVD	ORA	98 C3
KRAMER RD	LAS	14 B3
KRAMER RD	SBD	91 A1
KRATZMEYER RD	KER	78 C2
KREHE RD	SUT	33 C1
KROSENS RD	YUB	25 E5
KRUSE RD	COL	32 D1
KT RD	SBT	54 E3
KT RD	SBT	55 A3
KUBLER RD	IMP	111 E4
KUCK RD	SIS	4 B4
KUENZLI ST	RENO	130 D2
KUMBERG RD	IMP	112 C4
KUNA AV	SBD	92 E5
KURT RD	KER	77 E1
KUTZ RD	IMP	108 E5
KYLE AV	KER	70 A5
KYTE AV	KER	78 C2
L		
L ST	DVS	136 D3
L ST	DN	1 D4
L ST	MDO	162 B3
L ST	SCTO	137 B3
L ST	SDCO	V C5
L ST	SDCO	111 D2
LA BARR MDWS RD	NEV	34 C2
LABP & L RD	SBD	91 A4
LA BREA AV	LA	181 C4
LA BREA AV	LA	184 C3
LA BREA AV	LACO	97 D2
LA BREA AV	LACO	Q B5
LA BREA CK RD	SB	77 A5
LA BRISA DR	SBD	100 E1
LA BRISTA DR	SBD	100 D1
LA BRUCHERIE RD	IMP	112 A3
LA CADENA DR	CLTN	207 A4
LA CADENA DR	SBD	90 E3
LA CADENA DR	SBD	99 B2
LACEY BLVD	KIN	67 C1
LA CIENEGA BLVD	BH	183 E2
LA CIENEGA BLVD	CUL	183 E5
LA CIENEGA BLVD	ING	188 E4
LA CIENEGA BLVD	ING	189 E2
LA CIENEGA BLVD	LA	183 E4
LA CIENEGA BLVD	LACO	97 D2
LA CIENEGA BLVD	LACO	Q B5
LA CIENEGA BLVD	LACO	183 E2
LA CIENEGA BLVD	LACO	188 E1
LA CIENEGA BLVD	LACO	189 E2
LAC JAC	FRCO	58 A4
LACK RD	IMP	109 A4
LA COLINA	TUL	68 E3
LA COLINA LN	RCO	107 C1
LA CONTENTA RD	SBD	100 E2
LA COSTA AV	SDCO	106 C3
LA CRESCENTA AV	LACO	R D2
LA CRESTA DR	SDCO	107 A5
LA CRESTA RD	SDCO	V E3
LA CUARTA ST	LACO	R B5
LADD RD	STA	47 C2
LADDER RIDGE RD	LAK	31 D2
LADINO AV	MCO	48 B4
LA ENTRADA AV	LACO	R B5
LAFAYETTE RD	SIE	26 D5
LAFAYETTE ST	SCLR	151 B1
LAFAYETTE ST	S	160 D5
LA GLORIA RD	SBT	55 B5
LAGOMARSINO AV	MON	65 B2
LAGOON DR	KER	78 A2
LA GRANADA	SDCO	106 C4
LA GRANDE RD	COL	32 C2
LA GRANGE RD	MCO	48 C2
LA GRANGE RD	STA	48 C2
LA GRANGE RD	TUO	48 C1
LA GRANGE DM RD	STA	48 C2
LAGUE RD	YUB	26 A5
LAGUNA AV	FRCO	67 B1
LAGUNA FRWY	ORA	98 D4
LAGUNA FRWY	ORA	T E4
LAGUNA RD	SON	37 D2
LAGUNA RD	VEN	96 C1
LAGUNA CYN RD	LAG	201 B2
LAGUNA CYN RD	ORA	98 D5
LAGUNA CYN RD	ORA	T E5
LAGUNA CREEK TR	SOL	38 E3
LAGUNA MTN RD	SDCO	107 D5
LAGUNA SECA DR	SBD	91 D4
LAGUNA SECA RD	MCO	55 D3
LA HABRA BLVD	ORA	R C5
LA HABRA BLVD	ORA	T B1
LA HONDA RD	SMCO	45 C4
LAIRD RD	PLA	34 B4
LAIRD RD	STA	47 C3
LAIRO RED ROCK	SIS	5 B3
LA JOLLA AV	SDCO	106 C5
LA JOLLA BLVD	SD	105 B3
LA JOLLA BLVD	SDCO	V A3
LA JOLLA BLVD	SDCO	106 C5
LA JOLLA AMAGO	SDCO	107 A2
LA JOLLA MSA DR	SD	105 C5
LA JOLLA-SCNC DR	SD	211 B2

STREET	CO.	PAGE & GRID
LA JOLLA- -SCENIC DR S	SD	105 C4
LA JOLLA- -SCENIC DR S	SD	211 A4
LA JOLLA SHR DR	SD	211 A2
LA JOLLA VLG RD	SDCO	V B3
LAKE AV	FRCO	56 E3
LAKE AV	FRCO	57 A3
LAKE AV	KER	79 C2
LAKE AV	LACO	98 A1
LAKE AV	LACO	R E3
LAKE AV	PAS	190 D4
LAKE AV	SCR	54 C2
LAKE BLVD	SHA	18 C2
LAKE DR	SBD	91 C5
LAKE RD	FRCO	50 B5
LAKE RD	KER	80 C3
LAKE RD	MCO	48 C4
LAKE RD	STA	47 E2
LAKE RD	STA	48 A2
LAKE RD N	INY	51 B5
LAKE RD S	INY	51 C5
LAKE RD S	KER	78 B4
LAKE RD S	KER	78 C4
LAKE ST	MAD	57 A2
LAKE ST	RCO	99 B4
LK ALMANOR W DR	PLU	20 B4
LK ALMANR RD E	PLU	20 C4
LK ALPINE RD E	ALP	42 A1
LK ALPINE RD W	ALP	42 A2
LAKE ANNIE RD	MOD	7 D3
LK BRITTON LOOP	SHA	13 D4
LK BRITTON RAMP	SHA	13 D4
LAKE CALIF DR	TEH	18 D3
LAKE CANYON RD	LACO	89 B3
LAKE CANYON RD	LACO	89 C3
LAKE CITY RD	NEV	26 C5
LK CITY DUMP RD	MOD	7 D5
LAKE CREST RD	LAS	21 B4
LAKE DAVIS RD	PLU	27 B2
LAKE EARL DR	DN	1 D4
LAKE FOREST DR	ORA	98 D4
LAKE FRANCES RD	YUB	26 B5
LAKE HERMAN RD	SOL	38 D4
LAKE HERMAN RD	SOL	153 C1
LK JENNINGS PK	SDCO	107 A5
LAKELAND RD	LACO	R A5
LAKELAND RD	LACO	T A1
LAKE LEAVITT RD	LAS	21 B3
LAKE MARY RD	ML	164 A4
LAKE MARY RD	MNO	50 D2
LAKE MATHEWS DR	RCO	99 B3
LAKE MCCUMBER	SHA	19 B2
LAKE MEAD DR	CLK	74 E3
LAKE MORENA DR	SDCO	112 D1
LAKE MURRAY BL	SDCO	V C3
LAKE MURRAY BL	SDCO	106 D5
LAKEPORT BLVD	LAK	31 D3
LAKE POWAY RD	SDCO	106 D4
LAKERIDGE RD	SHA	19 A3
LAKE SHORE AV	O	158 B3
LAKESHORE BLVD	LAK	31 D3
LAKESHORE DR	KLAM	5 B1
LAKESHORE DR	LAK	32 A3
LAKESHORE DR	SHA	12 C5
LAKE SHORE DR	SIS	4 C5
LAKESHORE RD	MOD	7 B4
LAKESIDE DR	O	158 A3
LAKE SIDE LN	SIS	4 C2
LAKE STATION RD	KER	78 B4
LAKE TAHOE BLVD	SLT	129 A4
LAKEVIEW	KIN	67 C2
LAKEVIEW	PLA	34 A3
LAKEVIEW AV	ORA	T E2
LAKEVIEW AV	RCO	99 D3
LAKEVIEW DR	AMA	40 D3
LAKEVIEW DR	LAK	31 D2
LAKE VIEW DR	LAS	21 B4
LAKE VIEW DR	SLO	75 D1
LAKEVIEW RD	MPA	49 B3
LAKEVIEW RD	SCR	54 C2
LAKEVIEW RD	SDCO	V E3
LAKEVIEW RD	SDCO	107 A5
LAKE VIEW RD	SIS	4 C3
LAKEVIEW RD	SON	38 B3
LAKEVIEW CEM RD	SIS	5 A3
LK WILDWOOD DR	NEV	34 B1
LAKEWOOD BLVD	LACO	98 A3
LAKEWOOD BLVD	LACO	S E2
LAKEWOOD DR	MEN	23 A5
LAKIN DAM RD	SIS	13 A2
LA LOMA AV	B	156 B2
LA LOMA AV	MDO	162 C3
LA LOMA AV	VEN	88 C5
LA LOMA RD	LACO	R D3
LA LOMA RD	PAS	190 A5
LAMB BLVD	CLK	74 E2
LAMB CANYON RD	RCO	99 E3
LAMBERT LN	LAS	21 C4
LAMBERT RD	LACO	R B5
LAMBERT RD	ORA	R C5
LAMBERT RD	ORA	T C1
LAMBERT RD	SAC	39 E3
LAMBERT BRDG RD	SON	31 D5
LAMBIE RD	SOL	39 B3
LAMBUTH RD	STA	47 D1
LAMERT LN	GLE	24 D5
LA MESA BLVD	SDCO	V D4
LA MESA RD	SBD	90 E4
LA MIRADA AV	LACO	R B5
LA MIRADA AV	LACO	T B1
LA MIRADA BLVD	LACO	98 B3
LAMMERS RD	SJCO	46 E2
LAMPLEY RD	STA	48 A2
LAMPSON AV	GGR	195 A1
LAMPSON AV	ORA	T B2
LANCASTER BLVD	KER	90 B1
LANCASTER BLVD	LACO	90 A2
LANCASTER RD	LACO	88 E2
LANCASTER RD	LACO	89 A2
LANCASTER RD	STA	47 E1
LANCASTER RD	STA	48 A1
LANCHA PLANA- -BUENA VISTA RD	AMA	40 D3
LANDACRE RD	TRI	17 B2
LANDAU BLVD	RCO	100 D3
LANDECENA DR	TRI	17 D1
LANDER AV	MCO	47 D5
LANDER AV	STA	47 E3
LANDERGEN RD	HUM	15 E4
LANDES RD	TEH	18 C4
LANDESS RD	SCL	46 B4
LANDIS GULCH	TRI	17 C3
LANDRAM AV	MCO	48 B4
LANES RD	FRCO	57 C2
LANES VALLEY RD	TEH	19 A3
LANFAIR RD	SBD	84 D3
LANFAIR RD	SBD	94 E1
LANGDON RD	MCO	55 D2
LANGLL VLY RD E	KLAM	5 E1

STREET	CO.	PAGE & GRID
LANGLL VLY RD E	KLAM	6 A1
LANGLL VLY RD W	KLAM	5 E1
LANGLL VLY RD W	KLAM	6 A1
LANGWORTH RD	STA	47 D2
LANINI RD	MON	54 E5
LANINI RD	MON	55 A5
LANKERSHIM BLVD	LA	179 A5
LANKERSHIM BLVD	LACO	97 D1
LANKERSHIM BLVD	LACO	Q B2
LANNAGAN RD	TRI	11 B5
LANNAGAN RD	TRI	17 B1
LANPHERE RD	HUM	9 E5
LANSING AV	KIN	67 C2
LA PALMA AV	ANA	193 D1
LA PALMA AV	ANA	194 A1
LA PALMA AV	KER	80 A5
LA PALMA AV	ORA	98 A3
LA PALMA AV	ORA	T B2
LA PALOMA	AVLN	105 A4
LA PALOMA DR	TUL	68 E3
LA PALOMA RD	MCO	48 C4
LA PANZA AV	SB	87 E2
LA PAZ RD	ORA	98 D5
LA PORTE RD	BUT	25 D5
LA PORTE RD	BUT	26 B4
LA PORTE RD	YUB	26 A5
LA POSTA RD	SDCO	112 D1
LA PUENTE RD	LACO	U D4
LARCHMONT BLVD	LA	184 E1
LARGO GRANDE	RCO	107 B1
LARGO VISTA RD	LACO	90 D4
LARKELLEN AV	LACO	R C4
LARKIN RD	BUT	25 C4
LARKIN RD	SUT	33 C1
LARKIN VALLEY	SCR	54 B2
LARKMEAD LN	NAPA	29 B2
LARKSPUR DR	MLBR	144 B5
LARREA AV	SBD	101 B1
LARRY FLAT	MOD	7 D3
LARSEN RD	IMP	109 A5
LARSON LN	MNO	42 E1
LARSON RD	RCO	107 C1
LA RUE RD	YOL	136 B3
LA SALLE CANYON	SB	86 B3
LAS AMIGAS RD	NAPA	38 C3
LAS ANIMAS RD	SCL	46 C5
LAS FLORES AV	KER	80 C1
LA SIERRA AV	RCO	99 A3
LAS LOMAS AV	AVLN	105 A5
LAS PALMAS AV	STA	47 C3
LAS PASOS	VEN	96 C1
LASPINA DR	TUL	68 B2
LAS PLUMAS AV	BUT	25 D4
LS PULGAS CY RD	SDCO	106 A2
LAS ROCAS	RCO	100 D4
LASSELLE ST	RCO	99 C3
LASSEN AV	BUT	25 B3
LASSEN AV	FRCO	67 A1
LASSEN AV	FRCO	57 A3
LASSEN LN	SIS	12 C2
LASSEN RD	TEH	25 A2
LASSEN ST	LAS	8 B4
LASSEN ST	NAP	133 A1
LASSEN TRAIL	TEH	19 D4
LASSEN CREEK RD	MOD	7 C4
LASSEN PARK HWY	SHA	19 D2
LASSICS LKOT RD	TRI	16 E4
LAST CHANCE CYN	KER	80 C2
LAST CHANCE MNE	NEV	26 E5
LAST CHANCE MNE	NEV	35 A1
LAS TUNAS DR	LACO	R A3
LAS VARAS RD	SB	87 A4
LAS VEGAS BLVD	CLK	74 D3
LAS VEGAS BL S	CLK	209 C4
LAS VEGAS BL S	CLK	210 B5
LAS VEGAS BL S	LV	209 C4
LAS VIRGENES RD	LACO	97 A1
LATHAM RD	SUT	33 B3
LATHROP RD	MAN	161 A1
LATHROP RD	SJCO	47 A1
LATHROP RD	SJCO	161 D1
LATIGO CYN RD	LACO	97 A2
LA TIJERA BLVD	LA	188 C5
LA TIJERA BLVD	LACO	Q B5
LATKA LN	TEH	19 B4
LATROBE RD	AMA	40 D1
LATROBE RD	ED	40 C1
LATROBE RD	SAC	40 B1
LA TUNA CYN RD	LACO	97 D1
LA TUNA CYN RD	LACO	Q B2
LAUFFER RD	HUM	22 D1
LAUGHLIN RD	STA	47 E2
LAURA DR	LAS	27 E1
LAUREL AV	KIN	67 B2
LAUREL AV	ML	164 C4
LAUREL AV	MLBR	144 C5
LAUREL AV	SUT	33 D3
LAUREL DR E	MON	171 E2
LAUREL DR E	SAL	171 E2
LAUREL DR W	SAL	171 A2
LAUREL DR W	MON	171 A2
LAUREL LN	YUB	33 D1
LAUREL ST	NAP	133 A4
LAUREL ST	SD	215 D2
LAUREL ST	SDCO	V B4
LAUREL ST	SC	169 C3
LAUREL WY	TEH	18 C4
LAUREL CYN BLVD	LACO	97 D1
LAUREL CYN BLVD	LACO	Q A1
LAUREL DELL RD	LAK	31 C2
LAURELES GRADE	MON	54 C5
LAUREL GLEN RD	SCR	54 A1
LAUREL GROVE AV	MAR	139 B4
LAUREL GROVE AV	ROSS	139 A4
LAURELLEN RD	YUB	33 D2
LAURENT ST	SC	169 B3
LAURJOE RD	SBD	91 E3
LAUSTEN RD	COL	32 D1
LAUX RD	COL	33 A1
LAVA BED RD	BUT	25 B3
LAVA BDS NAT MN	MOD	6 A4
LAVA BDS MED LK	SIS	5 C5
LAVAL RD	KER	78 E5
LAVER CROSSING	LAS	21 E5
LAVERNE AV	MAR	140 A3
LA VETA AV	OR	196 B1
LAVEZZOLA RD	SIE	26 D4
LAVIC RD	SBD	92 E2
LA VISTA AV	VEN	88 C5
LAWNCREST RD	SHA	18 C2
LAWRENCE	AMA	41 A1
LAWRENCE EXPWY	SCLR	150 C4
LAWRENCE EXPWY	SJ	150 C4
LAWRENCE EXPWY	SVL	150 C4
LAWRENCE RD	AMA	40 E1
LAWSON LN	HUM	15 E2
LAXAQUE RD	MOD	8 D1
LAYTNVL DOS RIO	MEN	22 E3
LAZARO CARDENAS	BAJA	112 B4
LAZARUS LN	RCO	100 A5
L B CROW RD	STA	47 C4

STREET	CO.	PAGE & GRID
LEACH RD	YUB	33 D3
LEAR AV	SBD	101 B1
LEARY RD	SAC	39 D3
LEASTALK AV	SBD	84 C3
LEATHER RD	IMP	110 D5
LEAVENWORTH ST	SF	143 B2
LEAVESLEY RD	SCL	54 D1
LEAVITT RD	LAS	21 B3
LEE RD	MCO	48 A3
LEE RD	PLU	26 D1
LEE RD	SHA	13 E4
LEE RD	SUT	33 D4
LEEDS	MCO	48 C4
LEEGE AV	SB	86 B3
LEEK RD	STA	47 D2
LEE SCHOOL RD	SAC	40 B2
LEESVILLE RD	COL	32 C2
LEESVL-LODGA RD	COL	32 B1
LEFF RD	RCO	107 B1
LEFFINGWELL RD	LACO	R B5
LEFFINGWELL RD	LACO	T B1
LEGION AV	MCO	47 E4
LEGION AV	MCO	48 A4
LEGION PARK DR	MDO	162 D5
LE GRAND RD	MCO	48 D5
LEGRAY RD	KER	78 E5
LEIGHTON, H RD	SHA	18 C2
LEILA LN	SBD	101 E1
LEIMERT BLVD	LACO	Q B4
LEININGER RD	TEH	25 A1
LEISER RD	SUT	33 C4
LEISURE TOWN RD	SOL	39 A2
LELITER RD	KER	70 C5
LEMON AV	SDCO	V D4
LEMON AV	SDCO	111 E1
LEMON AV	SJCO	47 D1
LEMON AV	STA	47 B3
LEMON RD	SBD	91 C4
LEMON ST	ORA	T C1
LEMON ST	VAL	134 D5
LEMON CANYON RD	SIE	27 C4
LEMOS RD	SIS	4 A2
LENAHAN RD	COL	32 D1
LENARD RD	LAS	14 C3
LENINGER RD	BUT	25 A2
LENTELL RD	HUM	15 E1
LENWOOD RD	SBD	91 D1
LEO RD	RCO	107 A1
LEON AV	MCO	56 B2
LEON RD	RCO	99 D4
LEONA AV	LACO	89 D3
LEONARD AV	FRCO	57 D4
LEONARD AV	KER	78 A2
LEONARD RD	MPA	49 C3
LEONI RD	ED	41 B1
LEOTA ST	MCO	55 D1
LEPRECHAUN LN	RCO	107 B1
LERDO HWY	KER	77 D2
LERDO HWY	KER	78 A2
LEROY AV	SJCO	47 B1
LESSING ST	SBD	91 A3
LETTS VALLEY RD	COL	31 E1
LEVEE RD	FRCO	56 E4
LEVEE RD	IMP	112 D5
LEVEE RD	YOL	39 C2
LEVERONI RD	SON	38 B3
LEVERONI RD	SON	132 B5
LEVIATHAN LKOUT	ALP	36 D5
LEVIATHAN RD	ALP	36 D5
LEWELLING BLVD	ALA	146 B1
LEWIS RD	MON	54 C2
LEWIS RD	SHA	13 E4
LEWIS RD	SOL	39 B3
LEWIS RD	STA	47 C4
LEWIS RD	VEN	96 C1
LEWIS RD	YUB	33 E3
LEWIS CREEK RD	MON	65 D2
LEWIS RIDGE RD	BUT	26 B4
LEWISTON AV	FRCO	67 C1
LEWISTON RD	SHA	18 A1
LEWISTON RD	TRI	17 D1
LEWISTON TURNPK	TRI	17 E1
LEXINGTON AV	MCO	56 A2
LEXINGTON AV	SDCO	V E3
LEXINGTON AV	SDCO	106 E5
LEXINGTON ST	SCLR	151 B3
LEXINGTN HLL RD	PLU	26 C3
LIBERAL AV	TEH	24 D2
LIBERTY AV	MCO	48 A4
LIBERTY RD	SJCO	40 B3
LIBERTY RD W	BUT	25 B5
LIBERTY ISLD RD	SOL	39 C3
LIBRAMIENTO SUR	BAJA	111 D3
LIBRAMNT ORIENT	BAJA	111 D2
LICHEN WY	RCO	107 B1
LICHENS RD	SIS	4 B4
LIEBERT RD	IMP	111 E3
LIGGET AV	COL	32 E3
LIGHTHILL RD	SIS	3 D5
LIGHTHOUSE AV	MONT	167 D2
LIGHTHOUSE AV	MON	53 E2
LIGHTHOUSE AV	PAC	167 B2
LIGHTHOUSE RD	HUM	15 D4
LIGHTHOUSE RD	MEN	30 C3
LILI VALLEY WY	CAL	41 C2
LILLEY MTN DR	MAD	49 C5
LILY GAP RD	CAL	41 C2
LIM RD	LAS	14 C3
LIME CREEK RD	CAL	40 E3
LIMEDYKE LKOUT	TRI	16 E2
LIMEKILN RD	MON	54 D5
LIME KILN RD	NEV	34 C2
LIMEKILN RD	SBT	54 E4
LIMEKILN RD	SBT	55 A4
LIME KILN RD	TUO	41 C5
LIME SADDLE RD	BUT	25 C3
LIMONITE AV	RCO	99 A2
LINCOLN	LACO	97 C2
LINCOLN	MCO	48 B5
LINCOLN AV	ANA	193 B2
LINCOLN AV	ANA	194 B2
LINCOLN AV	FRCO	56 D4
LINCOLN AV	FRCO	57 A4
LINCOLN AV	FRCO	58 A4
LINCOLN AV	KIN	67 C2
LINCOLN AV	LACO	R E2
LINCOLN AV	LACO	190 B1
LINCOLN AV	OR	194 E2
LINCOLN AV	ORA	98 B3
LINCOLN AV	ORA	T B2
LINCOLN AV	PAS	190 B1
LINCOLN AV	RCO	98 E3
LINCOLN AV	SAL	171 C4
LINCOLN AV	SD	214 A5
LINCOLN AV	SDCO	106 D3
LINCOLN AV	SR	139 D3
LINCOLN AV	SA	196 C3
LINCOLN AV	SCL	46 B4
LINCOLN AV	YUB	33 E1
LINCOLN AV W	NAP	133 A3
LINCOLN BLVD	BUT	25 D5

STREET	CO.	PAGE & GRID
LINCOLN BLVD	LA	187 A1
LINCOLN BLVD	LA	189 A1
LINCOLN BLVD	LACO	Q A4
LINCOLN BLVD	LACO	187 D3
LINCOLN BLVD	MCO	47 E4
LINCOLN BLVD	MCO	48 A4
LINCOLN BLVD	SF	141 B2
LINCOLN BLVD	SMON	187 A1
LINCOLN RD	SBD	91 E4
LINCOLN RD	SUT	33 C2
LINCOLN RD	SUT	125 A5
LINCOLN RD	YUBA	125 A5
LINCOLN ST	NAPA	29 A1
LINCOLN ST	RCO	101 B5
LINCOLN ST	SC	169 D3
LINCOLN ST	S	160 C4
LINCOLN ST N	KER	77 E4
LINCOLN ST N	KER	78 A4
LINCOLN WY	AUB	126 D2
LINCOLN WY	SF	141 C4
LINCOLN WY	SFCO	45 B1
LINCOLN WY E	AUB	126 D2
LINCOLN WY E	PLA	126 D2
LINDA DR	SIS	4 B2
LINDA ROSA AV	SD	105 C5
LINDA VISTA AV	LACO	98 A1
LINDA VISTA AV	LACO	R D3
LINDA VISTA AV	NAP	133 A2
LINDA VISTA AV	PAS	190 A3
LINDA VISTA AV	TUL	68 D3
LINDA VISTA DR	SB	87 A3
LINDA VISTA RD	SBD	91 D1
LINDA VISTA RD	SD	213 B4
LINDA VISTA RD	SDCO	V B3
LINDA VISTA RD	SDCO	111 C1
LINDBERGH BLVD	KER	80 B4
LINDBLOOM RD	MCO	55 D3
LINDEN AV	MCO	56 A1
LINDEN AV	SBD	99 B2
LINDEN AV	SSF	144 B1
LINDENBERGER RD	RCO	99 D4
LINDERO CYN RD	LACO	96 E1
LINDLEY AV	LA	178 E4
LINDLEY AV	LACO	97 C1
LINDLEY RD	HUM	15 E4
LINDSAY RD	IMP	109 A3
LINDSAY RD	KER	78 C4
LINDSEY AV	GLE	24 E3
LINE RD	YOL	39 D2
LINEA DEL CIELO	SDCO	106 C4
LINGARD RD	MCO	48 C5
LINN RD	SJCO	40 C4
LINNE RD	SJCO	46 E2
LINNE RD	SLO	76 B1
LINSON AV	SBD	91 A3
LINWOOD AV	STA	47 C3
LINWOOD RD	MCO	47 E3
LINWOOD RD	MCO	48 A3
LISBON ST	MCO	48 A5
LISBON ST	SDCO	V C4
LISCOMB HILL RD	HUM	10 A5
LIST AV	TUL	68 C1
LITT RD	STA	47 D2
LITTLE AV	BUT	33 C1
LITTLE RD	LPAZ	104 A2
LITTLE BEAR RD	RCO	102 C4
LITL BLACK ROCK	TRI	17 C4
LTL BRWNS CK RD	TRI	11 D5
LTL BRWNS CK RD	TRI	17 D1
LITTLE GIANT ML	TEH	19 B4
LITTL GRASS VLY	PLU	26 C3
LITTL HONKR BAY	SOL	39 B3
LITTLE JOHN	SJCO	40 C5
LITTLE JOHN RD	CAL	41 A5
LITTLE LAKE RD	INY	70 C4
LITTLE LAKE RD	MEN	30 C1
LITL MORONGO DR	SBD	100 D1
LITL PANOCHE RD	FRCO	55 D4
LITL PANOCHE RD	SBT	55 D4
LITTLE RIVER	MEN	30 B1
LTL SLATE CK RD	SHA	12 B4
LTL SYCAMOR CYN	LACO	96 D2
LITL TUJUNGA RD	LACO	89 D5
LITTLE VLY RD	LAS	14 A4
LITTLE VLY RD	MEN	22 C4
LITTLE VLY DUMP	LAS	14 B5
LITL VIRGNIA LK	MNO	43 B4
LITTLE WALKR RD	MNO	42 E3
LITTLE WALKR RD	MNO	43 A3
LIVELY RD	BUT	25 B5
LIVE OAK	FRCO	58 B3
LIVE OAK AV	LACO	98 B1
LIVE OAK AV	SBD	99 A2
LIVE OAK AV	SCL	54 C1
LIVEOAK DR	BUT	25 B3
LIVE OAK DR	SBD	99 D1
LIVE OAK RD	ORA	98 E4
LIVE OAK RD	SBT	55 B4
LIVE OAK RD	SJCO	40 A4
LIVEOAK RD	SLO	76 A1
LIVE OAK RD	TEH	18 C5
LIVE OAK CYN RD	SBD	99 D2
LIVERMORE RD	NAPA	32 A5
LIVNGSTN CRESSY	MCO	47 E4
LIVNGSTN CRESSY	MCO	48 A4
LLAGAS RD	SCL	54 C1
LLANO RD	SON	37 E2
LLOYD LN	SHA	18 C3
LOBATA RD	YUB	33 E1
LOCAN AV	FRCO	57 D3
LOCH LOMOND RD	LAK	31 E4
LOCKHART RD	SBD	81 B4
LOCKWOOD RD	STA	47 D3
LOCKWOOD CEM RD	MON	65 C4
LOCKWD JOLON RD	MON	65 C4
LOCKWD SAN ARDO	MON	65 C4
LOCKWD SN LUCAS	MON	65 C3
LOCKWOOD VLY RD	VEN	88 C2
LOCO BILL RD	KER	79 D3
LOCUST AV	RCO	99 C2
LOCUST AV	SBD	81 A5
LOCUST AV	SBD	91 E4
LOCUST AV	STA	47 C3
LOCUST RD	SHA	18 D3
LOCUST TREE RD	SJCO	40 B4
LODGE RD	FRCO	58 A1
LODI LN	NAPA	29 B2
LODI RD	COL	33 A3
LOFGREN RD	BUT	25 B4
LOGAN AV	SD	216 E5
LOGAN LN	MEN	23 B2
LOG CABIN MINE	MNO	43 C5
LOGGING CAMP RD	MNO	50 E1
LOG HOUSE RD	SIS	4 E2
LOKERN RD	KER	77 D3
LOKOYA RD	NAPA	38 B2
LOLETA AV	TEH	24 D2
LOLETA RD	HUM	15 D2
LOMA AV	MCO	56 B1
LOMA ALTA DR	LACO	98 A1
LOMA ALTA DR	LACO	R E2

STREETS

Thomas Bros. Maps — COPYRIGHT © 1987 BY

STREETS

STREET	CO.	PAGE	GRID
MAST AV	KER	78	B1
MASTEN RD	TEH	18	B5
MASTERS AV	FRCO	56	D4
MASTERSONS RD	SIS	11	E2
MATHER ST	O	158	B1
MATHER FIELD RD	SAC	40	A1
MATHESON RD	SHA	18	B2
MATHEWS RD	LAS	14	B4
MATHEWS RD	SJCO	40	A5
MATHEWS RD	SJCO	47	A1
MATHEWS RD	SIS	5	A2
MATHILDA AV	SCL	45	E4
MATHILDA AV	SVL	148	D5
MATILIJA RD	VEN	88	A4
MATLOCK LP	TEH	18	C4
MATTERHORN DR	KER	79	C5
MATTHEWS LN	YUB	33	D1
MATTOLE RD	HUM	15	C3
MATTOLE RD	HUM	16	E4
MAUI RD	SBD	92	C1
MAURICO AV	RCO	99	C4
MAWSON RD	SUT	33	A2
MAXSON RD	FRCO	58	B2
MAXWELL LN	SOL	39	C2
MAXWELL RD	AMA	40	C2
MAXWELL CYN RD	NAPA	38	C1
MAXWLL SITES RD	COL	32	C1
MAY	CC	38	C5
MAYARADA	SBD	101	E1
MAYARO LODGE RD	BUT	25	E2
MAYBECK	SJCO	40	A5
MAYBERT RD	NEV	26	E5
MAYER AV	KER	78	B2
MAYER RD	YUB	33	D2
MAYFIELD RD	RCO	102	A4
MAYHEW AV	TEH	24	D2
MAYNARD RD	SHA	18	D2
MAY SCHOOL RD	ALA	46	C2
MAYS CANYON RD	SON	37	C2
MAYTEN RD	SIS	4	C5
MAZE BLVD	STA	47	C2
MAZOURKA CANYON	INY	60	A3
MCADAMS CK RD	SIS	3	D5
MCADAMS INDN CK	SIS	3	D4
MCARTHUR RD	SHA	13	C3
MCARTHUR RD	SUT	33	B2
MCAULIFFE RD	SHA	18	A3
MCAUSLAND RD	COL	24	E5
MCBEAN PKWY	LACO	89	B4
MCCABE RD	IMP	112	A3
MCCABE RD	MCO	47	B5
MCCABE RD	MCO	55	B1
MCCAHILL LN	HUM	15	E2
MCCAIN BLVD	COR	215	B5
MCCAIN VLY RD	SDCO	111	A4
MCCALL AV	FRCO	57	D3
MCCALL BLVD	RCO	99	C4
MCCANN RD	HUM	16	B4
MCCART RD	KER	68	A5
MCCARTHY RES RD	CAL	41	B2
MCCARTY RD	RCO	98	E3
MCCARTY RD	SBD	98	E3
MCCARTY RD	TEH	24	B2
MCCATER RD	MCO	48	E5
MCCAY	MPA	48	E3
MCCLAIN LN	RCO	107	B1
MCCLATCHY RD	SUT	33	B2
MCCLELLAN RD	CPTO	149	B5
MCCLELLAN RD	LAS	14	C3
MCCLELLAND LN	LAS	21	C3
MCCLELLN MTN RD	HUM	16	C3
MCCLINTOCK RD	STA	47	C4
MCCLOSKEY RD	SBT	54	E3
MCCLOSKEY RD	SBT	55	A3
MCCLOSKEY RD	SOL	39	C3
MCCLOUD AV	SIS	12	C2
MCCLOUD DUMP RD	SIS	12	E2
MCCLURE AV	TEH	24	D1
MCCLURE RD	STA	47	D2
MCCLURE SUB RD	MEN	31	B2
MCCOMBS RD	KER	77	E1
MCCOMBS RD	KER	78	B1
MCCONAHUE GL RD	SIS	11	E1
MCCONNELL RD	IMP	109	B5
MCCORMACK RD	SOL	39	B3
MCCOURTNEY RD	NEV	34	B2
MCCOURTNEY RD	NEV	127	A5
MCCOURTNEY RD	PLA	34	A3
MCCOY AV	KER	77	E1
MCCOY RD	LAS	20	C3
MCCOY RD	LAS	20	C3
MCCOY RD	MON	54	E5
MCCOY RD	MON	55	A5
MCCOY RD	TEH	18	C4
MCCRACKEN RD	STA	47	B3
MCCREERY RCH RD	SBT	55	C3
MCCRORY RD	SOL	39	A3
MCCULLACH RD	MCO	47	D4
MCCULLOCK BLVD	MOH	96	B4
MCCULLY RD	MOD	7	D5
MCCUNE RD	SOL	39	A2
MCDANIEL RD	IMP	112	D5
MCDERMOTT RD	COL	32	D1
MCDERMOTT RD	RCO	99	E4
MCDOEL DIST	SIS	4	E4
MCDOEL DORRS RD	SIS	5	A3
MCDONALD	SJCO	39	D5
MCDONALD AV	STA	47	C2
MCDONALD RD	IMP	109	A3
MCEWEN RD	CC	38	D4
MCEWEN RD	STA	47	E2
MCFADDEN	MON	54	C4
MCFADDEN AV	SA	195	A5
MCFADDEN AV	SA	196	C5
MCFARLND-WDY RD	KER	78	C1
MCGARY RD	SOL	38	D4
MCGEE AV	STA	47	D2
MCGEE CREEK RD	MNO	51	A3
MCGOWAN	YUB	33	D2
MCGRATH RD	SUT	33	B2
MCHENRY AV	MDO	162	B3
MCHENRY AV	SJCO	47	C2
MCHENRY RD	MCO	48	C5
MCINTIRE RD	SJCO	40	C3
MCINTOSH RD	HUM	10	D4
MCKEAN RD	SCL	46	C5
MCKEE RD	MCO	48	C4
MCKEE RD	SJ	152	E2
MCKEE RD	SCL	46	B4
MCKEE ST	MCO	48	D5
MCKEEN RD	SIS	11	D2
MCKELL RD	LAK	32	A5
MCKENZIE AV	FRE	165	D3
MCKENZIE RD	SAC	40	A3
MCKERNIE ST	RCO	99	E4
MCKIBBEN RD	KER	78	A1
MCKIM RD	IMP	109	B5
MCKINLEY AV	FRE	165	B2
MCKINLEY AV	FRCO	57	A3
MCKINLEY AV	SJCO	47	A1
MCKINLEY ST	RCO	99	A3

STREET	CO.	PAGE	GRID
MCKINLEYVLLE AV	HUM	9	E4
MCKINNEY CK RD	SIS	3	D4
MCKNNEY RUBICN-			
-SPRING RD	PLA	35	D2
MCLAIN RD	YUB	26	B4
MCLAUGHLIN AV	LA	187	E1
MCMASTER RD	MCO	48	C5
MCMILLAN CYN RD	SLO	76	C1
MCMULLIN	SJCO	47	A2
MCMULLIN GRADE	FRCO	57	A4
MCMURRY MDWS RD	INY	59	D1
MCNAMARA RD	MCO	48	C5
MCNEILL LN	SOL	39	B1
MCNELLA LN	PLU	27	C3
MCNERNEY RD	IMP	109	A3
MCRAE RD	BUT	25	B4
MCRAE RD	TUO	41	C5
MCSWAIN RD	MER	170	A3
MCSWAIN RD	MCO	170	A3
MEACHAM RD	KER	78	B3
MEAD RD	IMP	109	B4
MEADE AV	SD	214	B5
MEADOW DR	AMA	41	B2
MEADOW DR	MCO	48	A4
MEADOW RD	TRI	17	D1
MEADOW GLEN RD	CAL	41	C2
MEADOW LAKE RD	NEV	26	E5
MEADOW LAKE RD	NEV	27	B4
MEADOW LAKE RD	SIE	27	B5
MEADOW RIDGE RD	MAD	49	D5
MEADOWS DR	VAL	134	A1
MEADOWS RD	IMP	112	B4
MEADOWSWEET DR	CRTM	140	C1
MEADOW VLY RD	YUB	26	A5
MEADOW VIEW DR	SHA	18	C3
MEADOWVIEW RD	SAC	39	E2
MEADOW VISTA RD	PLA	34	C3
MEALEY RD	IMP	108	E5
MEAMBER CK RD	SIS	3	C4
MEARS RIDGE RD	SHA	12	C3
MECCA DALE RD	RCO	101	E3
MECHAM RD	SON	37	E3
MEDFORD AV	KIN	67	C2
MEDFORD RD	FRCO	57	E1
MEDICINE LK HWY	MOD	5	E5
MEDICINE LK HWY	SIS	5	D5
MEDICINE LK RD	SIS	5	C5
MEDICINE LK RD	SIS	13	B2
MEDLIN RD	STA	47	C4
MEEKS RD	SBD	92	D5
MEHRING RD	IMP	110	D5
MEHRTEN DR	TUL	68	D1
MEIER RD	STA	47	E2
MEIER RD	STA	48	A2
MEIGS RD	STB	174	A5
MEIKLE RD	STA	47	E2
MEIKLE RD	STA	48	A2
MEISS RD	SAC	40	B2
MEISS LAKE-			
-SAMS NECK RD	SIS	4	E3
MEISS LAKE-			
-SAMS NECK RD	SIS	5	A3
MELCHER RD	KER	78	B1
MELLA DR	AMA	41	A2
MELLO AV	SJCO	47	C1
MELLOR RD	STA	48	A2
MELODY CT	HUM	10	A5
MELOLANO RD	IMP	109	B5
MELON ST	RCO	102	C4
MELONES CT	TUO	41	B5
MELROSE AV	LA	181	B5
MELROSE AV	LA	182	C5
MELROSE AV	LACO	Q	B3
MELROSE AV	LACO	183	D1
MELROSE DR	SDCO	106	C3
MEMORY LN	SA	195	E2
MEMORY LN	SA	196	A2
MENALTO AV	MP	147	C1
MENDENHALL RD	TEH	18	C5
MENDIBOURE RD	LAS	8	B4
MENDIBURN	KER	79	D5
MENDIBURN RD	KER	80	B4
MENDOCINO AV	FRCO	57	E2
MENDOCINO AV	STR	131	C1
MENDOCINO PASS	MEN	23	B2
MENIFEE RD	RCO	99	C4
MENLO AV	RCO	99	E4
MERCED AV	FRCO	66	D3
MERCED AV	KER	78	A2
MERCED AV	LACO	R	C4
MERCED AV	MCO	47	E4
MERCEDES AV	MCO	48	B4
MERCED FALLS RD	MPA	48	D3
MERCED FALLS RD	TUO	48	D2
MERIDIAN AV	SCL	151	E5
MERIDIAN BLVD	ML	164	C3
MERIDIAN RD	BUT	25	A3
MERIDIAN RD	SBD	91	E2
MERIDIAN RD	SCL	46	B5
MERIDIAN RD	SOL	39	B3
MERIDIAN RD	SUT	33	A2
MERIDIAN ST	SJ	151	E5
MERLE AV	STA	47	D2
MERRIAM RD	STA	47	E3
MERRIAM RD	YUB	26	B5
MERRILL AV	FRCO	56	B2
MERRILL AV	SBD	98	D2
MERRILL RD	TEH	24	E2
MERRILL RD S	KLAM	5	C2
MERRILL ST	SBD	99	A2
MERRILL FLAT RD	LAS	20	D2
MERRILLVILLE RD	LAS	20	E2
MERRIMAC CTF RD	BUT	25	E3
MERRITT	LAK	31	D3
MERRITT DR	TUL	57	E5
MERRITT DR	TUL	58	A5
MERRITT LN	PLA	34	A3
MERVEL AV	MCO	55	E2
MESA DR	RCO	103	C5
MESA DR	RCO	110	C1
MESA DR	SBD	100	E1
MESA DR	SDCO	106	B3
MESA RD	MAR	37	E5
MESA RD	SBD	92	E5
MESA TK TR W	SDCO	107	C5
MESA COLLEGE DR	SD	213	D1
MESA COLLEGE DR	SDCO	V	B3
MESA GRANDE RD	SDCO	107	B3
MESQUITE RD	INY	61	B2
MESQUITE CYN RD	KER	80	C2
MESQUITE SPG RD	SBD	101	B1
MESQUITE VLY RD	INY	73	C3
MESSICK	SJCO	40	C4
MESSICK RD	SUT	33	D3
MESSILLA VLY RD	BUT	25	D3
MESSING RD	CAL	40	D4
MESTMAKER ST	KER	68	D5
METCALF RD	NEV	34	B2
METCALFE RD	SCL	46	C5
METROPOLE AV	AVLN	105	B5
METROPOLITAN RD	HUM	15	E2

STREET	CO.	PAGE	GRID
METTER RD	SUT	33	C1
METTLER AV	KER	68	B5
METTLER AV	KER	78	B2
METTLER RD	SJCO	40	A4
METTLER RD	STA	47	D1
METZ RD	MON	65	B1
METZGER RD	SHA	13	D3
MEXICAN LAKE RD	SBT	66	B1
MEYER RD	LACO	R	B5
MEYER RD	LACO	T	B1
MEYERS LN	SUT	33	B1
MEYERS GRADE RD	SON	37	B1
MICA RD	RCO	107	C1
MICHAEL RD	MCO	48	B5
MICHEL RD	CAL	41	B3
MICHELSON DR	IRV	198	C4
MICHELTORENA ST	STB	174	B3
MICHIGAN BAR RD	SAC	40	C2
MICHILLINDA BL	LACO	R	A3
MICHOACAN AVD	BAJA	112	B4
MICKE GROVE RD	SJCO	40	B4
MIDDLE AV	SCL	54	D1
MIDDLE RD	BLMT	145	C4
MIDDLE RD	MAR	37	D3
MIDDLE RD	SJCO	46	E1
MIDDLE TER	AVLN	105	B5
MIDDLE BAR RD	AMA	40	E3
MIDDLE BAR RD	AMA	41	A3
MIDDLE CREEK RD	SHA	18	B2
MIDDLE CREEK RD	SIS	3	C3
MIDDLE CK RCH	SIS	3	C3
MIDDLEFIELD RD	MP	147	A1
MIDDLEFIELD RD	PA	147	E3
MIDDLEFLD RD E	MVW	148	B4
MIDDLE FORK RD	MON	66	B4
MDDL FK GASQUET	DN	2	A3
MID FK HUMBG RD	SIS	3	E4
MIDDLE HARBR RD	O	157	C3
MIDDL HONCUT RD	BUT	25	D5
MIDDLE RIDGE RD	MEN	30	B2
MIDDLETON DR	DN	1	D3
MIDDLETON RD	SUT	33	B2
MIDDLETON RD	TRI	11	E3
MIDDLETOWN RD	PLCV	138	B2
MIDDLETWN PK DR	SHA	18	B2
MDL TWO ROCK RD	SON	37	E3
MDL TWO ROCK RD	SON	38	A3
MIDLAND AV	SDCO	106	D4
MIDLAND RD	RCO	103	B2
MIDLAND TR	KER	80	C2
MIDOIL RD	KER	77	E4
MIDWAY	BUT	25	B4
MIDWAY DR	SD	213	A5
MIDWAY DR	SDCO	V	B4
MIDWAY RD	KER	77	E4
MIDWAY RD	SBD	101	D1
MIDWAY RD	SOL	39	B2
MIDWAY WELLS	INY	61	D3
MIKISHA BLVD	SBD	92	D5
MILAN RD	KER	77	E2
MILE END	MON	64	E1
MILE END	MON	65	A1
MILES RD	MCO	48	C5
MILFORD RD	SBDO	81	A1
MILFORD CEM RD	LAS	21	C5
MILFORD GRADE	LAS	21	C5
MILGEO RD	SJCO	47	C2
MIL-GOR RD	SBD	101	E1
MILHAM AV	KIN	67	B3
MILITAR	BAJA	112	B4
MILITARY E	BEN	153	C4
MILITARY W	BEN	153	B4
MILITARY W	SOL	38	D4
MILITARY RD	SIS	13	A2
MILITARY PASS	SIS	12	D1
MILITARY PASS	SIS	13	A2
MILL AV	KER	78	B1
MILL RD	BUT	26	B4
MILL RD	MNO	52	C3
MILL RD	SLO	76	B1
MILL RD	TEH	19	C4
MILL RD	YUB	26	B4
MILL ST	GV	127	B4
MILL ST	NEV	34	C1
MILL ST	RENO	130	C3
MILL ST	SBD	99	C2
MILL ST	SBDO	207	C3
MILL ST	U	123	C3
MILLARD CYN RD	RCO	100	B2
MILLBRAE AV	MLBR	144	D5
MILLBRAE AV	SMCO	45	B3
MILLBROOK AV	FRCO	57	C2
MILL CANYON RD	MNO	42	E2
MILL CREEK RD	HUM	10	C3
MILL CREEK RD	MEN	31	B2
MILL CREEK RD	SBD	99	E1
MILL CREEK RD	SIS	3	C5
MILL CREEK RD	SIS	3	E4
MILL CREEK RD	SON	31	C5
MILL CREEK RD	SON	37	D1
MILL CK PWR HS	MNO	43	B4
MILLER	MAR	45	B1
MILLER AV	CPTO	150	A5
MILLER AV	FRCO	56	B2
MILLER AV	MV	140	A3
MILLER AV	MDO	162	D3
MILLER AV	VAL	134	E4
MILLER RD	COL	33	A3
MILLER RD	IMP	112	C3
MILLER RD	MCO	48	D4
MILLER RD	TRI	23	A1
MILLER RD	YOL	39	C2
MILLER ST	SMA	173	C3
MILLER RANCH RD	SIE	26	D4
MILLERTON RD	FRCO	57	D2
MILLERTON RD	MAD	57	D1
MILLIKEN AV	SBD	98	E2
MIL POTRERO HWY	KER	88	B1
MILLS AV	CLA	203	A4
MILLS AV	LACO	R	B5
MILLS AV	MTCL	203	A4
MILLS RD	MCO	47	C5
MILLS RD	SOL	39	C2
MILLS RD	SUT	33	B2
MILLS ORCHDS RD	COL	32	C1
MILLS PARK RD	SIE	27	A3
MILLUX AV	FRCO	56	B2
MILLUX RD	KER	78	C4
MILLVL PLAIN RD	SHA	18	D3
MILLWOOD DR	TUL	58	C5
MILLWOOD RD	FRCO	58	C3
MILNES RD	STA	47	D2
MILPAS DR	SBD	91	D4
MILPAS ST	STB	174	D3
MILPITAS RD	MON	64	E3
MILPITAS RD	MON	65	B3
MILPITAS WSH RD	IMP	110	B2
MILSAP BAR RD	BUT	25	E3
MILSAP BAR RD	BUT	26	A3
MILSTEAD RD	MEN	22	D1
MILTON RD	CAL	40	E5

STREET	CO.	PAGE	GRID
MILTON RD	NAPA	38	C3
MILTON RD	SJCO	40	C5
MILTON RD	STA	40	E5
MINA RD	MEN	23	A1
MINE RD	VEN	89	A5
MINER AV	S	160	D4
MINER RD	CC	45	D1
MINERAL RD	IMP	108	E1
MINERAL RD	SHA	19	C3
MINERAL KING AV	TUL	68	A1
MINERAL KING RD	TUL	59	B5
MINERAL SCHOOL	SHA	19	A1
MINERET RD	ML	164	C2
MINERS CREEK RD	SIS	11	D2
MINES RD	ALA	46	D3
MINES RD	SCL	46	D3
MING AV	KER	78	C3
MINI DR	VAL	134	C1
MINNEOLA RD	SBD	92	B1
MINNESOTA ST	SDCO	106	C2
MINNEWAWA AV	FRCO	57	D2
MINNEWAWA AV	FRCO	57	D5
MINNIEAR RD	STA	47	B3
MINNIETTA RD	INY	71	B2
MINT RD	MCO	56	B1
MINTURN RD	MCO	48	D5
MIRABEL RD	SON	37	D2
MIRAMAR RD	SDCO	V	B3
MIRAMAR RD	SDCO	106	D5
MIRAMAR WY	SDCO	V	B3
MIRAMAR WY	SDCO	106	D5
MIRA MESA BLVD	SDCO	V	B2
MIRA MESA BLVD	SDCO	106	C5
MIRASOL AV	KER	77	E3
MIRASOL AV	KER	78	A3
MISSION AV	MCO	48	C5
MISSION AV	SD	214	A5
MISSION AV	SDCO	106	B3
MISSION AV	SR	139	C3
MISSION BLVD	ALA	45	E2
MISSION BLVD	ALA	146	C1
MISSION BLVD	H	146	D2
MISSION BLVD	MTCL	203	A5
MISSION BLVD	ONT	203	D5
MISSION BLVD	ONT	204	B5
MISSION BLVD	POM	203	A5
MISSION BLVD	RCO	99	A2
MISSION BLVD	SBD	98	D2
MISSION BLVD	SBD	203	A5
MISSION BLVD	SD	212	A1
MISSION BLVD	SDCO	V	A3
MISSION BLVD	SDCO	106	C5
MISSION DR	LACO	R	A3
MISSION FRWY	SDCO	V	B4
MISSION RD	LA	186	D2
MISSION RD	LACO	98	A2
MISSION RD	LACO	R	E3
MISSION RD	MON	65	B3
MISSION RD	SDCO	106	C2
MISSION RD	SMCO	45	B2
MISSION ST	SF	142	C5
MISSION ST	SF	143	C5
MISSION ST	STB	174	A3
MISSION ST	SC	169	A4
MISSION TR	RCO	99	B5
MISSION BAY DR	SD	212	D1
MISSN BAY DR W	SD	212	B4
MISSION CTR RD	SD	213	E3
MISSION CK RD	RCO	100	C2
MISSION GORG RD	SDCO	V	C3
MISSION GRGE RD	SDCO	106	E5
MISSION LKS BL	RCO	100	C2
MISSN OLIVE RD	BUT	25	E5
MISSION RDGE RD	STB	174	D2
MISSION VLY FWY	SD	213	C5
MISSION VLY FWY	SD	214	A4
MISSION VLGE DR	SD	214	C1
MISSION VLGE DR	SDCO	V	C3
MISSION VLGE DR	SDCO	106	D5
MISSOURI AV	STA	47	E2
MISTLETOE DR	VEN	88	C4
MITCHELL RD	HUM	10	C3
MITCHELL RD	HUM	15	E1
MITCHELL RD	LAS	8	A5
MITCHELL RD	LAS	14	E5
MITCHELL RD	STA	47	D4
MITCHLLS CMP RD	IMP	110	C2
MIX CANYON RD	SOL	38	E2
MOANING CAVE RD	CAL	41	B4
MOBLEY	SJCO	40	C5
MOBLEY	SJCO	47	C1
MOCAL RD	KER	77	E4
MOCAL RD	KER	78	D4
MOCKINGBIRD CYN	RCO	99	B3
MODJESKA CYN RD	ORA	98	E4
MODOC AV	FRCO	57	A3
MODOC COUNTY RD	MOD	5	D3
MOFFAT BLVD	MAN	161	C4
MOFFAT BLVD	SJCO	161	C4
MOFFAT RANCH RD	INY	60	A4
MOFFATT RD	MCO	47	D5
MOFFET BLVD	MVW	148	A4
MOFFETT DR	TUL	68	D1
MOFFETT RD	STA	47	D3
MOFFETT CK RD E	SIS	3	E5
MOFFETT CK RD W	SIS	3	E5
MOHAVE RD	LPAZ	103	E3
MOHAVE ROSE DR	LACO	89	D3
MOHAVE VLY HWY	MOH	85	D5
MOHLER RD	SJCO	47	B2
MOJAVE AV	KER	89	C1
MOJAVE DR	SBD	91	B3
MOJAVE RD	SBD	91	B4
MOJAVE RD	SBD	101	C1
MOJAVE-RANDSBRG	KER	80	C4
MOJVE TRPICO RD	KER	79	E5
MOJVE TRPICO RD	KER	80	A5
MOJVE TRPICO RD	KER	89	E1
MOKELUMNE HILL-			
-CMP SECO TP RD	CAL	41	C3
MOLERA RD	MON	54	B3
MOLINO AV	MV	140	A3
MOLLER AV	TEH	24	E2
MONARCH MINE RD	SIE	26	E4
MONARCH MINE RD	SIE	27	A4
MONO DR E	MONO	43	C4
MONO WY	TUO	163	D4
MONROE	MCO	55	D1
MONROE AV	FRCO	57	B5
MONROE AV	FRCO	57	B3
MONROE AV	TEH	18	D5
MONROE ST	RCO	101	A4
MONROE ST	SCLR	150	C1
MONSON	FRCO	58	B4
MONTGUE AGER RD	SIS	4	B4
MONTAGUE GRNADA	SIS	4	B4
MONTANA AV	LA	180	A3
MONTANA AV	LACO	97	C2
MONTANA AV	SHA	18	C2
MONTANA ST	PAS	190	A1
MONTARA RD	SBD	91	E1

STREET	CO.	PAGE	GRID
MONTE RD	IMP	109	A4
MONTEBELLO BLVD	LACO	R	E4
MONTEBELLO BLVD	LACO	R	A4
MONTE BELLO RD	SCL	45	D4
MONTE BLOYD RD	MEN	30	D2
MONTECITO RD	SDCO	107	A4
MONTECITO RD	SLO	75	E2
MONTECITO ST	STB	174	D3
MONTE DIABLO AV	S	160	A4
MONTEREY AV	FRCO	56	D4
MONTEREY AV	FRCO	66	D2
MONTEREY AV	MDO	162	D4
MONTEREY AV	RCO	100	E4
MONTEREY BLVD	SFCO	45	B2
MONTEREY HWY	SCL	54	D1
MONTEREY RD	LACO	R	D3
MONTEREY RD	SLO	76	A1
MONTEREY RD	SLO	76	A2
MONTEREY RD	SCL	46	B4
MONTEREY ST	SAL	171	C4
MONTEREY ST	SNLO	172	C3
MONTEREY PSS RD	LACO	R	E4
MONTE VERDE AV	CAR	168	B3
MONTE VISTA AV	MCO	48	A3
MONTE VISTA AV	SBD	80	E1
MONTE VISTA AV	SBD	98	D1
MONTE VISTA AV	STA	47	C3
MONTE VISTA AV	STA	48	A3
MONTE VISTA DR	SDCO	106	C3
MONTE VISTA RD	SHA	18	B3
MONTEZUMA RD	SDCO	V	C3
MONTEZUMA RD	SDCO	111	D1
MONTEZUMA HL RD	SOL	39	B4
MONTFORD AV	MV	140	A3
MONTGOMERY AV	BUT	25	A3
MONTGOMERY DR	STR	131	D3
MONTGOMERY RD	IMP	109	B3
MONTGOMERY RD	TRI	11	B5
MONTGOMERY ST	SF	143	C2
MONTGOMERY ST	MCO	48	C3
MONTGOMRY CK RD	TRI	11	D5
MONTGMRY RCH RD	SHA	18	B2
MONTICELLO RD	NAPA	133	E1
MONTPELIER RD	STA	47	E3
MONTPELIER RD	STA	48	A3
MONUMENT RD	HUM	15	E3
MOODY RD	MEN	22	B2
MOODY ST	ORA	T	B2
MOON BEND RD	COL	32	A2
MOON BEND RD	COL	33	A2
MOONEY BLVD	TUL	68	B2
MOONEY RD	LAS	20	C2
MOONEY RD	LAS	20	C3
MOONEY FLAT RD	NEV	34	A1
MOONRIDGE RD	SBD	100	A1
MOONSHINE RD	YUB	26	B5
MOONWIND ST	KER	80	D1
MOORE RD	LAS	21	E4
MOORE RD	PLA	33	E4
MOORE RD	PLA	34	A4
MOORE RD	SUT	33	B2
MOOREHEAD RD	STA	47	C5
MOORES FLAT RD	NEV	26	D5
MOORPARK FRWY	VEN	88	E5
MOORPARK RD	VEN	96	D1
MOORPARK ST	LACO	Q	A3
MOORVILL RDG RD	BUT	26	B4
MOOSE CAMP RD	SHA	13	B5
MORADA LN	SJCO	40	B4
MORAGA AV	ALA	45	D1
MORAGA AV	MCO	55	D1
MORAGA AV	O	158	E1
MORAGA AV	P	158	D1
MORAGA AV	SD	211	E5
MORAGA RD	CC	45	E1
MORAN AV	MCO	48	A4
MORAN RD	CAL	41	C3
MORAN RD	STA	47	C4
MORAN RD	TEH	24	D1
MORCOURT AV	KER	80	C1
MOREHEAD RD	DN	1	D3
MOREHEAD RD	SUT	33	B2
MORELLO AV	CC	154	E3
MORELLO AV	M	154	E4
MORENA BLVD	SD	211	C4
MORENA BLVD	SD	212	E1
MORENA BLVD	SD	213	A4
MORENA BLVD W	SD	213	A4
MORENA RES DR	SDCO	112	D1
MORENO AV	SDCO	V	E2
MORENO AV	SDCO	106	E5
MORENO BLVD	SDCO	V	B3
MORENO BLVD	SDCO	111	C1
MORENO RD	STB	174	C2
MORENO ST	MTCL	203	C3
MORENO BEACH DR	RCO	99	C2
MORGAN RD	CAL	41	B5
MORGAN RD	HUM	15	D2
MORGAN RD	LAS	21	C1
MORGAN RD	SBD	101	D1
MORGAN RD	STA	47	D3
MORGAN WY	LPAZ	104	A5
MORGAN CYN RD	FRCO	57	E2
MORGAN TERRITRY	CC	39	B5
MORGAN TERRITRY	CC	46	B1
MORGAN VLY RD	LAK	32	B4
MORLEY AV	MCO	48	D5
MORMON ST	LA	191	C3
MORMN EMGRNT TR	ED	35	C5
MORNING DR	KER	78	E3
MORNING STAR RD	ALP	36	C5
MORNING STR CTO	SBD	84	B3
MORNING STAR MN	SBD	84	B3
MORONGO RD	RCO	100	A3
MORONGO RD	SBD	101	B1
MORONI RD	SUT	33	B2
MORRETTI CYN RD	SLO	76	B4
MORRILL RD	STA	47	D2
MORRIS AV W	MDO	162	A3
MORRIS RD	COL	33	A2
MORRIS RD	KER	78	A3
MORRIS RD	STA	47	C4
MORRIS MINE RD	MNO	51	C2
MORRISON RD	STA	48	A1
MORRISN BRYN RD	TEH	24	B2
MORRISON CYN RD	ALA	46	A3
MORRIS RANCH RD	RCO	100	C5
MORRO RD	KER	91	C3
MORSE RD	SJCO	40	B4
MORSE RD	YOL	39	D3
MORTON AV	TUL	68	D3
MORTON BL S	MDO	162	C4
MOSAIC CANYON	INY	61	D4
MOSELEY RD	DN	1	D3
MOSHER	MPA	49	A3
MOSQUITO RD	ED	34	E4
MOSQUITO RDG RD	PLA	34	E3
MOSS OLD MLL RD	TRI	10	E5
MOTHER DR	ED	34	D5
MOTHER LODE TR	MAD	49	C4
MOTOR AV	LA	183	B3

233
MOTOR AV
STREET INDEX
OLD LAMBERT RD

STREET	CO.	PAGE & GRID
MOTOR AV	LACO	Q A4
MOTT AIRPORT RD	SIS	12 D2
MOULTAN LOOP	TEH	19 A3
MOULTON PKWY	ORA	98 C4
MOULTON PKWY	ORA	T E3
MOUND SPGS RD	SBD	100 C1
MT ACADIA BLVD	SD	213 B2
MT ADA RD	AVLN	105 B5
MOUNTAIN AV	LACO	R B3
MOUNTAIN AV	RCO	100 A4
MOUNTAIN AV	SBD	98 D1
MOUNTAIN AV	UPL	203 E2
MOUNTAIN BLVD	O	156 E5
MOUNTAIN DR	STB	174 B2
MOUNTAIN RD	SBD	90 D4
MOUNTAIN RD S	VEN	88 C5
MOUNTAIN ST	LACO	Q C2
MTN CLIMBER WY	KER	79 C5
MTN HOME CK RD	SBD	99 E1
MTN HOME RCH RD	SON	38 A1
MTN HOUSE RD	ALA	46 D1
MTN HOUSE RD	MEN	31 C4
MTN HOUSE RD	SIE	26 D4
MTN LEMON RD S	VEN	88 C5
MTN MEADOW RD	SHA	19 C2
MTN QUAIL LN	MOD	7 B5
MOUNTAIN RCH RD	CAL	41 B3
MTN SCHOOL RD	SHA	13 B5
MTN SPRINGS RD	SBD	94 E1
MTN SPRINGS RD	SLO	76 A1
MOUNTAIN VW AV	FRCO	56 C5
MOUNTAIN VW AV	FRCO	57 D5
MOUNTAIN VW AV	SBD	99 C2
MOUNTAIN VW AV	RCO	99 E2
MOUNTAIN VW RD	HUM	16 B1
MOUNTAIN VW RD	KER	78 E3
MOUNTAIN VW RD	KER	79 A3
MOUNTAIN VW RD	MEN	30 E3
MOUNTAIN VW RD	RCO	100 D3
MOUNTAIN VW RD	SBD	92 B1
MOUNTAIN VW RD	SBD	91 C1
MOUNTAIN VW RD	STB	174 A4
MOUNTAIN VW RD	SCR	54 A1
MOUNTAIN VW RD	SHA	13 C5
MOUNTAIN VW RD	STA	47 D3
MOUNTAIN VW ST	BARS	208 A2
MTN VW-ALVSO RD	MVW	148 A5
MTN VIEW RCH RD	SON	31 C5
MT AUKUM RD	ED	40 E1
MT AUKUM RD	ED	41 A1
MT BALDY LKOUT	SIS	2 D3
MT BULLION CTFF	MPA	49 A3
MT EATON RD	TUO	41 D5
MT EDEN RD	SCL	45 E5
MT EMMA RD	LACO	90 A4
MT GAINES	MPA	48 E3
MT GLEASON AV	LACO	Q C2
MT HAMILTON RD	SCL	46 C4
MT HERMON RD	SCR	53 E1
MT HOUGH CRYSTL	PLU	26 D1
MT HOLLYWOOD DR	LA	182 A2
MT HOUSE RD	YUB	26 C5
MT MADONNA RD	SCL	54 C2
MT OLIVE RD	NEV	34 C2
MT OPHIR RD	MPA	49 A3
MT PIERCE LKOUT	HUM	15 E3
MT PINOS RD	KER	88 D2
MT PINOS RD	VEN	88 A1
MT PINOS RD	VEN	88 C2
MT REBA RD	ALP	42 A1
MT SHASTA DR	SIS	12 E2
MT VEEDER RD	NAPA	29 C4
MT VEEDER RD	NAPA	38 B2
MT VERNON AV	CLTN	207 B4
MT VERNON AV	KER	78 D3
MT VERNON AV	RCO	99 B2
MT VERNON AV	SBD	91 D1
MT VERNON AV	SBD	99 B2
MT VERNON AV	SBDO	207 B2
MT VERNON RD	PLA	34 B3
MT WHITNEY	FRCO	57 C5
MT WHITNEY AV	FRCO	66 D1
MT WHITNEY ST	KER	70 C5
MT WILSON	LACO	98 A1
MT WILSON RD	LACO	R A2
MT ZION RD	AMA	41 A2
MOVIE RD	INY	60 A4
MOWRY AV	ALA	46 A3
M T FREITAS PKY	SR	139 A1
MUCK VALLEY RD	LAS	14 B4
MUDD RD	IMP	109 A5
MUD LAKE RD	ALP	36 C4
MUD LAKE RD	MOD	6 A5
MUD LAKE RD	MOD	14 A1
MUELLER	SJCO	40 A5
MUELLER	SJCO	47 A1
MUIR AV	BUT	25 A3
MUIRLANDS DR	SD	105 C4
MUIRLANDS DR W	SD	105 B3
MUIR MILL RD	MEN	22 E5
MUIR MILL RD	MEN	23 A5
MUIR MILL RD	MEN	30 E1
MUIR MILL RD	MEN	31 A1
MUIR WOODS RD	MAR	45 A1
MULBERRY AV	MCO	48 B4
MULBERRY AV	RCO	99 A2
MULBERRY DR	LACO	R B5
MULBERRY ST	C	124 D5
MULE BRIDGE RD	SIS	11 C2
MULE CANYON RD	SBD	92 A1
MULE CREEK RD	TRI	11 D5
MULE DEER LN	MOD	7 B5
MULE TOWN RD	SHA	18 B2
MULHOLLAND DR	LA	177 A5
MULHOLLAND DR	LA	181 A2
MULHOLLAND DR	LACO	97 C1
MULHOLLAND DR	LACO	Q A3
MULHOLLAND HWY	LACO	97 A1
MULLER LN	DGL	36 B3
MULLER RD	KER	78 C5
MULLER RD	KER	79 A3
MULLOY RD	SIS	4 C3
MUMMA RD	COL	33 A3
MUMY RD	INY	51 C4
MUNCY RD	STA	47 C3
MUNJAR RD	BUT	25 A2
MUNRAS AV	MONT	167 D5
MUNRAS AV	MON	53 E4
MUNSEY RD	KER	80 C3
MUNRAS AV	MONT	168 D1
MUNZER RD	KER	78 B3
MURCHISON DR	MLBR	144 D5
MURIEL DR	BARS	208 C2
MURPHY LN	SCL	54 D1
MURPHY LN	SHA	19 A1
MURPHY RD	IMP	112 A3
MURPHY RD	MON	54 C2
MURPHY RD	NEV	26 C5
MURPHY RD	SBT	55 B3
MURPHY RD	SCR	54 C2
MURPHY RD	SJCO	47 C1
MURPHY RD	STA	47 C2
MURPHY RD	TUO	41 C5
MURPHYS GRD RD	CAL	41 B4
MURRAY RD	HUM	9 E4
MURRAY RD	HUM	10 A4
MURRAY RD	SJCO	40 C5
MURRAY RD	SUT	33 C3
MURRAY CK RD E	CAL	41 B3
MURRAY CK RD W	CAL	41 A3
MURRAY RIDGE RD	SD	214 A2
MURRIETA HT SPG	RCO	99 C5
MURRIETTA RD	RCO	99 C3
MUSCAT AV	FRCO	57 B4
MUSCAT AV	FRCO	57 D4
MUSCOTT ST	SBDO	207 A2
MUSTANG RD	RCO	100 A5
MUSTANG SPGS RD	SLO	76 A1
MUTAU FLAT RD	VEN	88 C2
MYER AV	TUL	68 C2
MYERS LN	COL	32 E2
MYERS RD	COL	32 D2
MYERS RD	SIS	4 E3
MYERS RD	SIS	5 A3
MYERS ST	BUT	25 D4
MYFORD RD	ORA	T E3
MYKLE OAKS RD	MPA	49 A3
MYRA AV	LA	182 C5
MYRTLE AV	DN	1 E5
MYRTLE AV	EUR	121 E1
MYRTLE AV	HUM	9 E5
MYRTLE AV	HUM	15 E1
MYRTLE AV	LACO	R B3
MYRTLEWOOD DR	MAD	57 C2
N		
NABORLY RD	SBD	101 D1
NACIMNTO-FER RD	MON	64 E3
NACIMNTO-FER RD	MON	65 A3
NACIMIENTO LAKE	MON	65 E4
NACMIENTO LK DR	SLO	75 E1
NACMIENTO LK DR	SLO	76 A1
NACIONAL ST	SAL	171 A3
NADEAU RD	INY	71 B1
NADER RD	PLA	34 A3
NAGEL CANYON RD	KER	79 D3
NAGLEE AV	SJ	151 D4
NANTES AV	MCO	55 E1
NAPA AV	FRCO	56 E5
NAPA RD	SBD	92 E5
NAPA RD	SON	38 B3
NAPA RD	SON	132 D3
NAPA ST E	SNMA	132 E4
NAPA ST E	SON	38 B3
NAPA ST W	SNMA	132 C4
NARANJO BLVD	TUL	58 D5
NARANJO BLVD	TUL	68 D1
NARBONNE AV	LACO	S C2
NARRAGANSETT AV	SDCO	V A4
NARRAGANSETT AV	SDCO	111 C1
NASHUA RD	MON	54 C3
NASON RD	MON	64 C1
NASON ST	RCO	99 C3
NATIONAL AV	SD	216 A4
NATIONAL AV	SDCO	V C4
NATIONAL AV	SDCO	111 D1
NATIONAL BLVD	CUL	183 D5
NATIONAL BLVD	LA	180 E5
NATIONAL BLVD	LA	183 C4
NATIONAL BLVD	LACO	Q A4
NATL TRAILS HWY	SBD	91 B2
NATL TRAILS HWY	SBD	92 A1
NATL TRAILS HWY	SBD	93 A2
NATL TRAILS HWY	SBD	94 A3
NATIVIDAD RD	MON	54 D4
NATOMAS RD	SUT	33 D4
NATURAL BRDG RD	INY	72 B1
NAUMAN RD	VEN	96 B1
NAUTILUS ST	SD	105 B3
NAUTILUS ST	SD	211 A4
NAVAJO DR	SAL	171 C1
NAVAJO RD	RCO	99 C4
NAVAJO RD	SBD	91 C3
NAVAJO RD	SDCO	V C3
NAVAJO RD	SDCO	111 D1
NAVARO ST	SDCO	V A4
NAVARRO RDG RD	MEN	30 C2
NAVELENCIA AV	FRCO	58 A4
NAVY DR	SJCO	40 A5
NEAL SPRING RD	SLO	76 B1
NEBO ST	SBD	92 A1
NEBRASKA AV	FRCO	57 B4
NEBRASKA AV	FRCO	57 C4
NEBRASKA AV	TUL	58 A4
NEBRASKA ST	VAL	134 C3
NECKLE RD	IMP	112 A3
NECTAR RD	RCO	107 B1
NEEDHAM RD	STA	47 B3
NEEDHAM ST	MDO	162 A3
NEEDLE PEAK RD	SLT	129 D4
NEELEY	SJCO	40 A4
NEENACH RD	LACO	89 E2
NEES AV	FRCO	56 C3
NEGRO CREEK DR	TUL	58 C4
NEGRO HOLE RD	SIS	5 C4
NEIGHBORS BLVD	RCO	103 D5
NEIGHBORS BLVD	RCO	110 D1
NEILSON RD	CAL	40 E3
NELANDER	MCO	47 E4
NELSON	SJCO	47 C1
NELSON AV	BUT	25 C4
NELSON DR	TUL	69 B2
NELSON RD	BUT	25 B4
NELSON RD	TRI	17 C2
NELSON BAR RD	BUT	25 D3
NELSON CREEK RD	SHA	13 B4
NELSON PIT RD	IMP	112 C3
NELSON RES RD	LAS	8 B3
NELSONS CROSSNG	BUT	26 A3
NELSN SHPPEE RD	BUT	25 B4
NEROLY RD	CC	39 C5
NEES AV	FRCO	57 C3
NESTLE AV	LA	178 D5
NETHERLANDS RD	YOL	39 D2
NETHERTON RD	MCO	47 C5
NEUGERBAUER	SJCO	39 E5
NEUMARKEL RD	KER	79 A3
NEURALIA RD	KER	80 B4
NEVA AV	TEH	24 D2
NEVADA AV	KIN	67 D2
NEVADA AV	KIN	67 C2
NEVADA ST	AUB	126 B3
NEVADA ST	NEVC	128 C4
NEVADA ST	NEV	128 D2
NEVADA CITY HWY	GV	127 D2
NEVADA CITY HWY	NEV	127 D2
NEVADA CITY HWY	NEV	128 A5
NEVIS AV	KER	78 C1
NEW AV	LACO	R A4
NEW AV	LACO	R A4
NEW AV	SCL	54 D1
NEWARK BLVD	ALA	45 E3
NEWBERRY RD	SBD	92 C1
NEW BIG OAK FLT	MPA	49 C1
NEW BIG OAK FLT	MPA	63 B4
NEWCASTLE	PLA	34 B4
NEWCASTLE RD	SJCO	40 B5
NEW CEMETERY RD	LAS	14 B3
NEW CHESTR DUMP	PLU	20 B4
NW CHG QRTZ MTN	AMA	40 E2
NEWCOMB AV	FRCO	56 C4
NEWCOMB ST	TUL	68 D3
NEW DOCK ST	LA	191 C2
NEW DOCK ST	LACO	S C2
NEWHALL AV	LACO	89 B4
NEWHALL RD	MCO	48 B5
NEWHALL RD	SUT	33 B2
NEWHALL ST	SJ	151 D3
NEW HOPE RD	SAC	39 E3
NEW HOPE RD	SAC	40 A3
NEWHOPE ST	FTNV	197 B2
NEWHOPE ST	GGR	195 A3
NEWHOPE ST	ORA	T C3
NEWHOPE ST	SA	195 A3
NEW IDRIA RD	SBT	55 E5
NEW IDRIA RD	SBT	56 A4
NEWLAND ST	ORA	T B3
NEWMARK AV	FRCO	57 E4
NEW PLEYTO RD	MON	65 D4
NEW PEORIA FLAT	TUO	41 B5
NEWPORT AV	GLE	24 D3
NEWPORT AV	ORA	98 C4
NEWPORT AV	ORA	T E2
NEWPORT BLVD	CM	199 C2
NEWPORT BLVD	NB	199 A4
NEWPORT BLVD	ORA	98 C4
NEWPORT BLVD	ORA	T E2
NEWPORT RD	MCO	48 A3
NEWPORT RD	RCO	99 C4
NEWPORT RD	RCO	99 D4
NEWPORT-CM FRWY	CM	197 E5
NEWPORT-CM FRWY	CM	198 B3
NEWPORT-CM FRWY	OR	194 E4
NEWPORT-CM FRWY	OR	196 E3
NEWPORT-CM FRWY	ORA	98 C4
NEWPORT-CM FRWY	ORA	T C4
NEWPORT-CM FRWY	ORA	196 E3
NEWPORT-CM FRWY	SA	196 E4
NEWPORT-CM FRWY	TUS	196 E4
NEWRIVER RD	TRI	11 A4
NEW ROME RD	NEV	34 C1
NEWSOM RD	MCO	47 C5
NEWSOM RD	MCO	55 C1
NEWTON AV	KIN	67 C3
NEWTOWN RD	ED	34 E5
NEWVILLE RD	GLE	24 B3
NEWVILLE RD	TEH	24 A2
NEW YORK DR	LACO	R E2
NEW YORK DR	LACO	R A2
NEW YRK FLAT RD	YUB	26 A4
NEW YRK HOUS RD	YUB	26 A5
NEW YORK MTN RD	SBD	84 C4
NEW YORK RCH RD	AMA	40 E2
NEW YORK RCH RD	AMA	41 A2
NICASIO VLY RD	MAR	37 E4
NICE LUCERNE	LAK	31 D2
NICHOLAS RD	MAD	57 E2
NICHOLLS RD	NEV	34 B2
NICHOLS RD	IMP	112 A3
NICHOLS RD	RCO	99 B4
NICHOLS CYN RD	LA	181 A3
NICHOLS MILL RD	SIE	27 B4
NICKEL RD	MCO	48 A5
NICOLAS RD	RCO	99 D5
NICOLAUS	PLA	33 E4
NIDER RD	IMP	109 B3
NIDERER RD	SLO	75 E1
NIDERER RD	SLO	76 A1
NIELSON	SJCO	40 C5
NIELSON AV	FRE	165 A3
NIELSEN AV	FRCO	57 A3
NIELSON RD	CAL	41 A3
NIESTRATH RD	SON	37 B1
NILAND AV	IMP	109 B3
NILAND MRINA RD	IMP	109 A2
NILE AV	SJCO	47 B1
NILE RD	SJCO	47 B1
NILES AV	KIN	67 D3
NILES ST	BKD	166 E2
NILES ST	KER	78 E3
NILES CANYON RD	ALA	46 A3
NILL AV	KER	78 C1
NIMITZ BLVD	SD	212 C5
NIMITZ BLVD	SDCO	V B4
NIMITZ BLVD	SDCO	111 C1
NIMITZ FRWY	ALA	45 D2
NIMITZ FRWY	ALA	146 C4
NIMITZ FRWY	H	146 C4
NIMITZ FRWY	O	157 D1
NIMITZ FRWY	O	158 B4
NIMITZ FRWY	O	159 C1
NIMITZ FRWY	SJ	152 A1
NINE RD	CAL	41 C4
NINE MILE CYN	INY	70 B4
NINTH ST	C	124 C5
NIPOMO ST	SNLO	172 C3
NIPTON RD	SBD	84 C2
NIPTON DESRT RD	SBD	84 C2
NIPTON MOORE RD	SBD	84 C2
NISQUALLY RD	SBD	91 B4
NISSEN RD	HUM	15 D2
NM 1	TUL	68 E5
NM 14	TUL	68 E4
NM 18	TUL	69 C4
NM 23	TUL	69 B4
NM 24	TUL	69 B4
NM 45	TUL	69 C4
NM 50	TUL	69 B4
NM 88	TUL	69 C4
NM 93	TUL	69 C4
NM 112	TUL	69 C3
NM 117	TUL	70 A3
NM 121	TUL	69 B3
NM 127	TUL	69 B3
NM 133	TUL	70 A3
NM 163	TUL	69 B3
NM 175	TUL	70 A3
NM 231	TUL	69 B2
NM 232	TUL	69 A2
NM 276	TUL	69 A1
NOBLE RD	YUB	33 D2
NOFFSINGER RD	IMP	109 B3
NOGALES ST	LACO	U D4
NOLAN RD	IMP	109 B4
NOLINA CIR	RCO	100 D4
NO NINE	MPA	48 E3
NONPAREIL AV	COL	32 E3
NOPEL AV	BUT	25 C2
NORD AV	BUT	124 A4
NORD AV	KER	78 C3
NORD HWY	BUT	25 A3
NORDAHL RD	IMP	110 D5
NORD GIANELLA	BUT	25 A3
NORDOFF ST	LACO	97 C1
NORFOLK ST	SM	145 A1
NORHAM PL	SBD	101 A1
NORIEGA RD	KER	78 C3
NORIEGA ST	SF	141 C5
NORMA ST S	KER	80 E1
NORMAL ST	SD	214 A5
NORMAL ST	SDCO	V B4
NORMAL ST	SDCO	111 D1
NORMAN	SUT	33 B2
NORMAN AV	KER	80 B5
NORMAN RD	COL	24 E5
NORMANDIE AV	LA	182 B5
NORMANDIE AV	LA	185 B5
NORMANDIE AV	LACO	Q C5
NORMANDIE AV	LACO	S C2
NORMAN HILLS RD	RCO	107 C1
NORRBOM RD	SON	132 D3
NORRBOM RD	SON	38 B3
NORRIS RD	KER	78 C2
NORRIS CYN RD	CC	46 A2
NORRISH RD	IMP	109 C5
NORTH AV	FRCO	56 C4
NORTH AV	FRCO	57 B4
NORTH AV	KIN	57 D5
NORTH AV	MCO	47 E3
NORTH AV	MCO	48 A3
NORTH AV	ORA	T C2
NORTH AV	SDCO	106 D3
NORTH AV	STA	47 C2
NORTH HWY	INY	61 E4
NORTH HWY	INY	62 A5
NORTH HWY	INY	72 B1
NORTH RD	STA	47 B2
NORTH ST	MAN	161 C3
NORTH ARM	PLU	20 D5
N BNK CHETKO RD	CUR	1 D2
NORTH BUSCH RD	MEN	23 B5
NORTH BUSCH RD	MEN	31 B1
NORTHCREST DR	DN	1 D4
NORTHRLY BR GRN	SLO	75 D2
NORTH FORK RD	HUM	15 D4
NORTH FORK RD	MAD	49 D5
NORTH FORK RD	SBT	66 A2
NORTH FORK RD	TUO	41 E4
N FK MAD RIV RD	TRI	17 B5
NORTHGATE BLVD	SAC	33 E5
NORTH GATE RD	CC	39 A5
NORTH GATE RD	SOL	39 A3
NORTH LIVERMORE	ALA	46 C2
NORTH RIDGE RD	SBD	100 C2
NORTHRUP RD	MCO	47 D4
NORTHRUP RD	MOD	8 A1
NORTHRUP RD	MOD	14 E1
NORTH SHORE	PLA	35 E1
NORTH SHORE DR	SBD	92 A5
NORTH SHORE RD	SIS	12 C2
NORTHSIDE DR	MPA	63 B2
NORTH SIDE RD	SBD	91 E3
NORTH STAR TR	SBD	100 C2
NORTH VALLEY RD	PLU	20 D5
NORTHWOODS BLVD	NEV	27 D5
NORTHWOODS BLVD	NEV	35 D1
NORTON RD	KER	80 B3
NORTON RD	SBT	55 E4
NORTON RD	SOL	39 C3
NORTONVILLE	CC	39 B5
NORVEL RD	LAS	20 C3
NORWALK BLVD	LACO	98 A3
NORWALK BLVD	LACO	R A5
NORWALK BLVD	LACO	T A1
NORWGIAN RCH RD	TRI	11 E4
NORWOOD AV	SR	139 A4
NOTRE DAME AV	BLMT	145 B5
NOVATO BLVD	MAR	38 A4
NOYES VALLEY RD	SIS	11 E2
NTU RD	SB	86 B1
NUESTRO RD	SUT	33 C2
NUEVO RD	RCO	99 C3
NUNES LN	SHA	19 C2
NUNNIEMAKER RD	HUM	16 C4
NURSE SLOUGH LN	SOL	39 A3
NYON RD	SBD	100 B1
O		
O ST	FRE	165 D3
OAHU RD	SBD	92 C1
OAK AV	DVS	136 C3
OAK AV	LAKE	7 B1
OAK AV	MCO	48 B4
OAK AV	SUT	33 D3
OAK AV	TRI	17 B2
OAK DR	SDCO	112 D1
OAK RD	MPA	49 B3
OAK ST	BKD	166 A4
OAK ST	MCO	47 E4
OAK ST	MCO	48 A4
OAK ST	SF	141 E4
OAK ST	SF	142 A4
OAK ST	SHA	18 B3
OAK ST	S	160 B4
OAK ST	U	123 C2
OAK WY	BUT	25 A3
OAK CREEK RD	KER	79 D5
OAK CREEK RD N	INY	59 E3
OAK CREEK RD S	INY	59 E3
OAKDALE RD	MCO	48 A3
OAKDALE RD	MCO	48 B3
OAKDALE RD	STA	47 D2
OAKDALE CYN RD	LACO	89 A2
OAKDL WTRFRD HY	STA	47 E2
OAK FLAT RD	SLO	75 E1
OAK FLAT RD	SLO	76 A1
OAK FLAT RD	STA	47 B4
OAK GLEN AV	SCL	54 C1
OAK GLEN RD	RCO	100 A4
OAK GLEN RD	SBD	99 E2
OAK GROVE	CC	38 E5
OAK GROVE	MPA	49 B4
OAK GRV SCHOOL	MPA	49 B4
OAK HILL RD	ED	34 E5
OAK HILL RD	SBD	91 A4
OAK KNOLL AV	LACO	R E3
OAK KNOLL AV	NAPA	29 E5
OAK KNOLL AV	NAPA	38 C2
OAK KNL RNG STA	SIS	3 D3
OAKLAND AV	FRCO	67 A1
OAKLAND AV	O	158 B2
OAKLAND AV	P	158 C1
OAKLAND RD	SJ	152 B1
OAKLAND CP RD	PLU	26 D1
OAKLEA RD	STA	47 B3
OAKLEY LN	YUB	33 E3
OAK MEADOW RD	NEV	34 B2
OAKMONT TR	SHA	18 C1
OAKMORE ST	TUL	68 B2
OAK RANCH RD	SIE	26 D4
OAK RIDGE RD	TRI	17 A2
OAK RUN RD	SHA	18 D2
OAK RUN RD	SHA	19 A1
OAK RUN TO FERN	SHA	19 A1
OAK SPG RNCH RD	SBD	90 E4
OAK SPRINGS RD	SBD	91 D4
OAKS AV	ONT	203 D5
OAKS RANCHO RD	KER	79 B4
OAK TREE RD	NEV	26 B5
OAK VALLEY DR	SIS	4 A4
OAK VALLEY RD	YUB	26 C4
OAK VIEW CT	KER	79 B4
OAKVILLE CROSS	NAPA	29 D3
OAKVLLE CRSS RD	NAPA	38 C2
OAKVILLE GRADE	NAPA	29 C4
OAKVILLE GRADE	NAPA	38 B2
OAKWAY	BUT	25 D2
OAKWOOD	SJCO	40 C5
OAKWOOD	SJCO	47 C1
OASIS RD	MON	65 C3
OASIS RD	INY	52 C3
OASIS RD	RCO	102 C4
OASIS RD	SBD	90 D4
OASIS RD	SHA	18 C2
OAT GAP RD	MEN	23 C5
OAT HILL RD	LAK	32 B5
OAT HILL RD N	NAPA	32 B5
OATMAN RD	MOH	85 D5
OATMN TOPOCK HY	MOH	95 E1
OBANION RD	SUT	33 C3
OBERLIN RD	SIS	4 A4
OBRIEN RD	JOS	2 C2
OBSIDAN DOME RD	MNO	50 D1
O'BYRNES FERRY	TUO	41 B5
OCCIDENTAL RD	SON	37 D2
OCEAN AV	CAR	53 D5
OCEAN AV	CAR	168 B3
OCEAN AV	SFCO	45 B2
OCEAN AV	SB	86 B3
OCEAN BLVD	LB	191 E2
OCEAN BLVD	LB	192 B3
OCEAN BLVD	LACO	98 A4
OCEAN BLVD	LACO	S D2
OCEAN DR	DN	1 D3
OCEAN DR	HUM	9 E4
OCEAN DR	MEN	22 C4
OCEANAIRE DR	SNLO	172 A4
OCEAN BEACH FWY	SD	212 C5
OCEAN PARK BLVD	LA	180 C5
OCEAN PARK BLVD	LACO	Q A4
OCEAN PARK BLVD	SMON	180 C5
OCEAN PARK BLVD	SMON	187 A1
OCEAN PARK RD	SB	86 A2
OCEANSIDE BLVD	SDCO	106 B3
OCEAN VIEW AV	INY	51 B3
OCEAN VIEW BLVD	LACO	R D2
OCEAN VIEW BLVD	PAC	167 A1
OCEAN VIEW BLVD	SD	216 B4
OCEAN VIEW BLVD	SDCO	V C4
OCEAN VIEW BLVD	SDCO	111 D1
OCEANVIEW DR	CUR	1 D2
OCEAN VIEW DR	DN	1 D3
OCONNOR WY	SLO	76 A3
OCOTILLO WY	SBD	91 C4
ODD FELLW PK RD	HUM	16 A3
ODOM LN	MEN	22 C5
O'FARRELL ST	SF	143 A5
OFFAL RD	MNO	42 E1
OFFIELD LOOKOUT	SIS	10 E1
OFFUTT RD	KER	78 B1
OGBURN CEM RD	SHA	19 A2
OGIER RD	IMP	112 C3
OGILBY RD	IMP	110 B4
OGULIN CANYON	LAK	32 A3
OHARA AV	CC	39 C5
OHIO AV	FRCO	56 C3
OHIO AV	LA	180 B4
OHM RD	COL	32 E2
OHM RD	TEH	18 D5
OIL CANYON RD	FRCO	66 D2
OIL CITY RD	FRCO	66 D2
OILER CT	KER	79 C3
OILFIELDS RD	KER	78 D2
OIL PLANT RD	MNO	43 C5
OIL WELL RD	HUM	15 E2
OJAI DR	SHA	18 C3
OJAI FRWY	VEN	88 A5
OJAI FRWY	VENT	175 A2
OJAI FRWY	VEN	175 A2
OJAI ST	VEN	88 B4
O'KEEFE ST	MP	147 B1
O'KEEFE ST E	SMCO	147 C1
OKEEFFE RD	SIS	5 D2
OKLAHOMA AV	TEH	18 D5
OKLAHOMA SCH RD	SIS	5 B3
OLANCHA DRWN RD	INY	70 E1
OLD HWY	COL	32 D1
OLD HWY	LAS	21 D5
OLD HWY	MPA	49 A4
OLD HWY	PLU	26 D1
OLD 99 HWY	SIS	12 B1
OLD HWY 138	LACO	89 D2
OLD AIRLINE HWY	SBT	55 B4
OLD ALLRED RD	MPA	49 B3
OLD ALTURAS HWY	MOD	5 E2
OLD ALTURAS HWY	MOD	6 A2
OLD ALTURAS RD	SHA	18 D2
OLD ARCATA RD	HUM	9 E5
OLD ARCATA RD	HUM	10 A5
OLD AUBURN RD	SAC	34 A5
OLD BANNG IDYWD	RCO	100 A3
OLD BAYSHRE HWY	SJ	152 A1
OLD BREA CYN RD	LACO	U D4
OLD CAMP TWO RD	SIS	13 C2
OLD CASTLE RD	SDCO	106 D2
OLD CEMETERY RD	LAS	14 B3
OLD CHAMPS FLAT	LAS	20 B1
OLD CHISHOLM DR	SBD	101 B1
OLD COAST HWY	SB	86 D3
OLD COPPER CITY	SBD	81 D3
OLD CORNING RD	TEH	24 D2
OLD CLTRV-YOSM	MPA	49 C1
OLD CLTRVL-YOSM	MPA	63 A4
OLD CUTOFF RD	LAS	21 B4
OLD DAVIS RD	SOL	39 C1
OLD DON PDRO RD	TUO	48 C1
OLD DRYTN PLYMT	AMA	40 D2
OLD EEL RIV RD	LAK	23 C5
OLD EEL ROCK	HUM	16 C4
OLD EL MIRAGE	SBD	90 D3
OLD ELSINORE RD	RCO	99 C3
OLDENBERG RD	SBD	91 D3
OLD FRIANT RD	FRCO	57 C2
OLD GASQUET TLL	DN	2 B3
OLD GULCH RD	CAL	41 B4
OLD HRLD PLM RD	LACO	90 A3
OLD HAUN RD	PLU	20 C4
OLD HERNANDZ RD	SBT	55 C5
OLD HONEY RUN	BUT	25 C3
OLD HIGHWAY 99	SIS	12 B1
OLD HWY RD	LAS	14 A4
OLD HWY RD	PLU	26 C1
OLD HWY RT 29	LAS	21 C5
OLD HWY S FORK	DN	2 A3
OLD KANE SPG RD	SDCO	108 A3
OLD KNOX RD	YUB	26 B4
OLD LAMBERT RD	AMA	40 C2

STREETS

STREET	CO.	PAGE & GRID
OLD LANDMARK DR	SBD	91 D1
OLD LEESVL GRAD	COL	32 C2
OLD LOMA RD	BUT	25 C1
OLD LONG VLY RD	LAK	32 A3
OLD MAIL RT	LAS	8 C5
OLD MAMMOTH RD	ML	164 A5
OLD MAMMOTH RD	MNO	50 D2
OLD MATTOLE RD	HUM	15 D4
OLD MIDLAND RD	KLAM	5 B1
OLD MILL RD	DN	1 D4
OLD MINE RD	SBD	101 A1
OLD MINE TR	RCO	100 B5
OLD MIRAMAR RD	SDCO	V B3
OLD MIRAMAR RD	SDCO	106 C5
OLD MORGN HL RD	TRI	17 B2
OLD MORRO RD	SLO	76 A2
OLD NATL TR HWY	SBD	94 D2
OLD OAK FLAT RD	MPA	49 C1
OLD PARKER RD	SBD	103 E2
OLD PIEDMONT RD	SCL	46 B4
OLD PLYMTH SAC-		
-VIA FIN RCH RD	AMA	40 D2
OLD PONY EXPRSS	ALP	36 B4
OLD RAILROAD GR	SHA	12 B4
OLD RANCH RD	KER	79 C5
OLD REDWOOD HWY	SON	37 D1
OLD RENO RD	NEV	27 D5
OLD RIDGE RD	LACO	89 A2
OLD RIVER RD	KER	78 C3
OLD RIVER RD	KER	78 C4
OLD RIVR SCHOOL	LACO	R E5
OLD SN FRANCSCO	SVL	150 A1
OLD SCHOOL RD	SHA	13 D3
OLD SCH HOUS RD	TRI	22 E1
OLD SEIAD HWY	SIS	3 B3
OLD SEIAD CK RD	SIS	3 B3
OLD SHASTA RIV	SIS	4 A3
OLD SHERWIN GRD	INY	51 B3
OLD SHERWOOD RD	MEN	22 E4
OLD SKYLINE	KIN	67 A3
OLD SONOMA RD	NAP	133 B4
OLD SONOMA RD	NAPA	38 C3
OLD SONOMA RD	NAPA	133 A5
OLD SPANISH TR	INY	72 E4
OLD SPANISH TR	INY	73 B4
OLD STAGE RD	MEN	30 D4
OLD STAGE RD	MON	54 D3
OLD STAGE RD	SIS	12 C2
OLD STAGE RD N	SIS	12 C1
OLD STAGEROAD	MEN	30 D4
OLD STATE HWY	HUM	9 E2
OLD STATE HWY	HUM	10 A2
OLD STATE HWY	INY	72 E3
OLD STATE HWY	INY	73 A3
OLD STATE HWY	KIN	67 B4
OLD STATE HWY	LAK	31 C2
OLD STATE HWY	MNO	43 C5
OLD STATE HWY	MNO	50 D2
OLD STATE HWY	SIS	4 E3
OLD STATE HWY	SIS	5 A4
OLD STEWRTS PT-		
-SKAGGS SPGS RD	SON	31 B5
OLD STOCKTON RD	AMA	40 D3
OLD STOCKTON-		
-IONE HWY	AMA	40 D2
OLD STRWBRRY RD	TUO	41 E3
OLD STRWBRRY RD	TUO	42 A3
OLD SUTTER CK-		
-AMADOR CITY HY	AMA	40 E2
OLD STTR HLL RD	AMA	40 E2
OLD TELEGRPH RD	VEN	88 E4
OLD TELEGRPH RD	VEN	89 A4
OLD THREE CK RD	HUM	10 C5
OLD TIM BELL RD	STA	47 E2
OLD TOLL	MPA	49 A3
OLD TOLL RD	INY	71 A1
OLD TOLL RD	LAS	14 A3
OLD TOLL RD	MEN	31 C3
OLD TOLL RD	YUB	26 B5
OLD TOPANGA CYN	LACO	97 B2
OLD TRUCKEE RD	SIE	27 C4
OLD WESTSIDE RD	SIS	4 B5
OLD WILBUR RD	COL	32 C2
OLD WITR SPG RD	LAK	31 C2
OLD WOMAN SPGS	SBD	100 D1
OLD WOMN SPG RD	SBD	92 A4
OLD YERMO CTOFF	SBD	91 E1
OLD YOSEMITE RD	MPA	49 A1
OLD 44 DR	SHA	18 C2
OLD 99 HWY	SIS	4 A4
OLEANDER	SJCO	47 B2
OLEANDER AV	BKD	166 C4
OLEANDER AV	RCO	99 B3
OLEMA ST	SBD	80 E1
OLINDA RD	SHA	18 C3
OLIVAS LN	SOL	39 A2
OLIVE AV	BUR	179 C5
OLIVE AV	COR	215 B5
OLIVE AV	FRE	165 B2
OLIVE AV	FRCO	57 A3
OLIVE AV	FRCO	57 C3
OLIVE AV	GLE	24 D3
OLIVE AV	MCO	48 A4
OLIVE AV	MCO	48 C4
OLIVE AV	RCO	99 B5
OLIVE AV	RCO	99 D4
OLIVE AV	SDCO	106 C3
OLIVE AV	SJCO	47 B2
OLIVE AV	STA	47 E1
OLIVE AV	STA	47 B3
OLIVE AV	STA	48 A1
OLIVE AV	TEH	24 D1
OLIVE AV	TUL	68 D3
OLIVE AV W	MER	170 B2
OLIVE DR	KER	78 D2
OLIVE DR E	DVS	136 D3
OLIVE HWY	BUT	25 D4
OLIVE LN	GLE	25 A4
OLIVE RD	TEH	24 D2
OLIVE RD	VEN	88 B5
OLIVE ST	AVLN	105 A4
OLIVE ST	LA	185 E4
OLIVE ST	LACO	R A3
OLIVE ST	MAR	38 B4
OLIVE ST	RCO	99 B4
OLIVE ST	SDCO	107 A4
OLIVE ST	SHA	18 B3
OLIVEHURST	YUB	33 D2
OLIVE LAKE BLVD	RCO	103 D5
OLIVENHAIN RD	SDCO	106 C4
OLIVE ORCHRD RD	CAL	40 D4
OLIVER RD	SBT	55 D4
OLIVERA DR	TUL	58 C5
OLIVE SCHOOL LN	SOL	39 A2
OLIVET RD	SON	37 D2
OLIVEWOOD AV	TEH	24 D2
OLNEY PARK DR	SHA	18 B2
OLSEN RD	MCO	48 B3
OLSEN RD	VEN	88 D5
OLSEN CREEK RD	TRI	16 E2
OLSON RD	LAS	8 B4

STREET	CO.	PAGE & GRID
OLYMPIC	LAK	32 A3
OLYMPIC BLVD	BH	183 B2
OLYMPIC BLVD	LA	183 B2
OLYMPIC BLVD	LA	184 B2
OLYMPIC BLVD	LA	185 B3
OLYMPIC BLVD	LA	186 B4
OLYMPIC BLVD	LA	180 C4
OLYMPIC BLVD	LACO	97 D2
OLYMPIC BLVD	LACO	Q B4
OLYMPIC BLVD	SMON	180 A5
OLYMPIC RD	MAD	57 B1
OLYMPIC RD	SBD	100 E1
OMAHA AV	KIN	67 B3
OMAHA AV	KIN	67 E3
OMEGA RD	NEV	26 E5
OMO RANCH RD	ED	40 E1
OMO RANCH RD	ED	41 B1
ONEAL RD	BUT	25 C4
ONEAL RD	MAD	57 D1
ONE HOLE SPG RD	SBD	92 C5
ONION VALLEY RD	ED	35 B4
ONION VALLEY RD	INY	59 E3
ONSTOTT RD	SUT	33 C2
ONTARIO AV	RCO	98 E3
ONYX AV	SIS	4 C5
OPAL RD	MCO	48 D4
OPAL WY	SHA	18 C1
OPAL FERRY RD	KER	88 D1
OPAL MTN RD	SBD	81 C4
OPENSHAW RD	BUT	25 C4
OPEN SHAW RD	PLU	20 D5
OPHIR RD	BUT	25 D5
OPHIR RD	INY	71 A2
ORANGE AV	BUT	25 E5
ORANGE AV	EC	217 D3
ORANGE AV	FRCO	57 C4
ORANGE AV	FRCO	57 D4
ORANGE AV	KIN	67 A3
ORANGE AV	KIN	67 D3
ORANGE AV	LACO	Q C2
ORANGE AV	LACO	R B4
ORANGE AV	LACO	S D2
ORANGE AV	ORA	T B2
ORANGE AV	RCO	99 C3
ORANGE AV	SD	214 C5
ORANGE AV	SDCO	V B4
ORANGE AV	SDCO	111 C1
ORANGE AV	SDCO	111 D2
ORANGE AV	SJCO	47 D1
ORANGE AV	SON	132 A4
ORANGE AV	STA	47 C3
ORANGE AV W	SSF	144 A1
ORANGE FRWY	ANA	194 A4
ORANGE FRWY	OR	196 A1
ORANGE FRWY	OR	196 A1
ORANGE FRWY	ORA	98 C3
ORANGE FRWY	ORA	T D1
ORANGE FRWY	ORA	194 A4
ORANGE RD	SDCO	107 A3
ORANGE ST	KER	78 B2
ORANGE ST	RCO	99 B2
ORANGE ST	SBD	99 C2
ORANGE BLOSM RD	STA	48 A1
ORANGEBURG AV E	MDO	162 D2
ORANGEBURG AV W	MDO	162 B2
ORANGE GROVE AV	LACO	98 C2
ORANGE GROVE AV	LACO	R A3
ORANGE GROVE AV	LACO	U E4
ORANGE GROVE BL	LACO	R E3
ORANGE GROVE BL	PAS	190 C3
ORANGE-OLIVE RD	OR	194 C3
ORANGE-OLIVE RD	ORA	98 C3
ORANGE-OLIVE RD	ORA	T D2
ORANGE PARK AV	ORA	T E2
ORANGE SHOW RD	CLTN	207 C5
ORANGE SHOW RD	SBDO	207 C5
ORANGETHORPE AV	ORA	98 B3
ORANGETHORPE AV	ORA	98 C3
ORANGETHORPE AV	ORA	T B1
ORANGEWOOD AV	ORA	T B2
ORANGEWOOD RD	TEH	24 D1
ORCHARD AV	H	146 E4
ORCHARD AV	SLO	76 C5
ORCHARD AV	TEH	24 D2
ORCHARD DR	FRCO	58 D4
ORCHARD DR	MCO	48 C5
ORCHARD RD	IMP	112 C3
ORCHARD RD	MCO	47 C5
ORCHARD RD	SJCO	40 B4
ORCHARD RD	STA	47 B2
ORCHARD ST	RCO	99 E2
ORCHARD WY	MCO	56 C1
ORCHARD PARK AV	MCO	48 B4
ORCHARD SPGS RD	NEV	34 D2
ORCUTT RD	SLO	76 B4
ORCUTT RD	SLO	172 D4
ORCUTT RD	SNLO	172 D4
ORCUTT RD	VEN	88 C4
ORCUTT-GAREY RD	SB	86 C1
ORD ST	SB	86 B2
ORD FERRY RD	BUT	25 A4
ORD MOUNTAIN RD	SBD	91 E2
ORD RANCH RD	BUT	25 C5
ORDWAY RD	SIS	12 C1
OREGON DR	MDO	162 D4
OREGON CREEK RD	SIE	26 D4
OREGON GULCH RD	BUT	25 D4
OREGON HILL RD	YUB	26 B5
OREGON MTN RD	DN	2 C3
OREGON-PAGE MLL	PA	147 D3
OREGON-PAGE MLL	SCL	45 E4
ORESTIMBA RD	STA	47 C4
ORINDA DR	SM	145 C4
ORLEANS AV	FRCO	55 E3
ORMONDE RD	SLO	76 B4
ORMSBY AV	FRCO	56 C2
ORNBAUN RD	MEN	30 E3
ORO FINO RD	SIS	3 D5
OROVILLE BANGOR	BUT	25 D4
OROVLL CHICO HY	BUT	25 B3
OROVLL DAM BL E	BUT	25 D4
OROVLLE GRIDLEY	BUT	25 C5
OROVILLE QUINCY	BUT	25 E3
OROVILLE QUINCY	BUT	25 D4
OROVILLE QUINCY	BUT	26 A3
ORR RD	SAC	40 A3
ORR & DAY RD	LACO	R E5
ORR & DAY RD	LACO	R A5
ORR & DAY RD	LACO	T A1
ORR CREEK LN	PLA	34 B3
ORRIS RD	RCO	102 A4
ORRLAND AV	TUL	68 B3
ORR MTN LOOKOUT	SIS	5 A4
ORR SPRINGS RD	MEN	30 E1
ORR SPRINGS RD	MEN	31 A1
ORSI RD	STA	47 E1
ORTEGA HWY	ORA	98 E5
ORTEGA HWY	SCL	202 E1
ORTIGALITA RD	MCO	55 D2
OSAGE RD	SOL	39 B2
OSBORN RD	SIS	5 D2

STREET	CO.	PAGE & GRID
OSBORN RD	TEH	24 B2
OSBORNE AV	RCO	102 C4
OSBORNE RD	SBD	91 D2
OSBORNE ST	LACO	97 C1
OSBORNE ST	LACO	Q A2
OSBORNE PARK RD	IMP	109 D4
OSDICK RD	SBD	80 E3
OSO PKWY	ORA	98 D5
OSO FLACO LK RD	SLO	76 B5
OSOS ST	SNLO	172 C2
OSPITAL RD	CAL	40 D4
OSTROM RD	YUB	33 E2
OSWALD RD	SUT	33 B2
OSWELL ST	KER	78 D3
OTAY LAKES RD	SDCO	V D4
OTAY LAKES RD	SDCO	111 E2
OTAY MESA RD	SDCO	V D5
OTAY MESA RD	SDCO	111 E2
OTAY VALLEY RD	SDCO	V D5
OTAY VALLEY RD	SDCO	111 E2
OTIS DR	A	159 A2
OTIS ST	LACO	R D5
OTOE RD	SBD	91 C3
OUR HOUS DAM RD	SIE	26 C5
OUTINGDALE	ED	40 E1
OUTINGDALE	ED	41 A1
OUTLAW MINE RD	RCO	102 A2
OUTPOST DR	LA	181 C3
OVERLAND AV	CUL	188 C1
OVERLAND AV	LA	183 B5
OVERLAND AV	LACO	Q A4
OVERLAND AV	MCO	55 D1
OVERLAND DR	SHA	18 C3
OWENS	SJCO	47 D1
OWENS AV	CLK	74 E2
OWENS RD	INY	51 D4
OWENS RD	SIS	5 A2
OWENS GORGE RD	MNO	51 B2
OWENS RIVER RD	MNO	50 E1
OWENS RV RCH RD	MNO	50 E1
OWENYO LONE PNE	INY	60 B4
OWL HOLE SPG RD	SBD	82 B1
OXALIS AV	FRCO	56 B2
OXBOW PL	SB	86 E3
OXFORD AV	FRCO	56 A2
OXFORD RD	SOL	39 D3
OXFORD ST	B	156 A2
OXNARD BLVD	OXN	176 C1
P		
P ST	BKD	166 D5
P ST	FRE	165 E3
P ST	KER	166 D5
P ST	SCTO	137 A3
P ST	SBD	91 D1
PACHECO BLVD	CC	38 E5
PACHECO BLVD	CC	154 C2
PACHECO BLVD	M	154 C2
PACHECO RD	KER	78 D3
PACHECO PASS HY	SCL	54 E2
PACHECO PASS RD	SCL	54 D2
PACIFIC AV	DN	1 D4
PACIFIC AV	LB	192 D3
PACIFIC AV	LA	187 A2
PACIFIC AV	LA	191 A4
PACIFIC AV	LACO	97 D4
PACIFIC AV	LACO	R C4
PACIFIC AV	LACO	S D2
PACIFIC AV	LACO	S C3
PACIFIC AV	PAC	167 C2
PACIFIC AV	SC	169 D3
PACIFIC AV	S	160 B1
PACIFIC AV	SUT	33 D3
PACIFIC AV	SUT	33 D4
PACIFIC AV	TUL	68 B2
PACIFIC BLVD	LACO	97 E2
PACIFIC BLVD	LACO	R D4
PACIFIC BLVD	SM	145 B4
PACIFIC HWY	SD	213 A5
PACIFIC HWY	SD	215 C2
PACIFIC ST	MONT	167 E4
PACIFIC ST	SBD	99 C1
PACIFIC BCH DR	SD	212 A2
PACIFIC BCH DR	SDCO	V A3
PACIFIC CST HWY	LB	192 D1
PACIFIC CST HWY	LA	192 D1
PACIFIC CST HWY	LACO	97 B2
PACIFIC CST HWY	LACO	97 D3
PACIFIC CST HWY	LACO	S B1
PACIFIC CST HWY	LACO	T A2
PACIFIC CST HWY	ORA	T A2
PACIFIC CST HWY	VEN	96 C2
PACIFC GRV-CRML	MONT	167 B4
PACIFC GRV-CRML	MON	53 D3
PACIFC GRV-CRML	MON	167 B4
PACIFC GRV-CRML	PAC	167 B4
PACIFIC HTS RD	BUT	25 C5
PACIFIC LUMBER	HUM	16 A1
PACIFIC MINE RD	SIE	26 C3
PACIFIC VIEW DR	MEN	30 C3
PACIFIC VIEW RD	VEN	96 C2
PACKER RD	COL	32 E1
PACKER LAKE RD	SIE	26 E3
PACKER LAKE RD	SIE	27 A3
PAC MINE RD	SIE	26 D3
PADUA AV	CLA	203 C1
PADUA AV	LACO	98 D1
PADUA AV	UPL	203 C1
PAGE AV	FRCO	67 B1
PAGE RD	STA	47 B2
PAGE MILL RD	PA	147 C5
PAGE MILL RD	SCL	45 D4
PA HA LN	INY	51 D4
PAIGE AV	TUL	68 B2
PAIGE BAR RD	SHA	18 B2
PAINE RD	AMA	40 D2
PAINT RD	CAL	41 B4
PAINTED CAVE	SB	87 C4
PAINTED GORG RD	IMP	111 C3
PAINTER AV	LACO	98 B2
PAINTER AV	LACO	R B5
PAJARO ST	SAL	171 C4
PALA RD	DN	1 D3
PALA RD	RCO	106 D1
PALA TEMECLA RD	SDCO	106 D1
PALAZZO RD	MCO	47 E5
PALAZZO RD	MCO	48 A5
PALAZZO RD	MCO	55 E1
PALERMO RD	BUT	25 D5
PALRMO HONCT HY	BUT.	25 D5
PALISADE AV	SBD	91 E3
PALISADES AV	RED	122 E1
PALISADES DR	LACO	97 C2
PALLETT CK RD	LACO	90 C4
PALM AV	AUB	126 C3
PALM AV	COR	215 C5
PALM AV	FRE	165 C2
PALM AV	FRCO	57 C3
PALM AV	KER	78 B1
PALM AV	KER	78 C3
PALM AV	LACO	R A5
PALM AV	MCO	48 A4

STREET	CO.	PAGE & GRID
PALM AV	RCO	99 B2
PALM AV	RCO	99 E4
PALM AV	SBD	99 B1
PALM AV	SDCO	V D4
PALM AV	SDCO	V C5
PALM AV	SDCO	111 D2
PALM AV	SDCO	111 E1
PALM AV	SCL	54 C1
PALM AV	SHA	18 B3
PALM DR	RIV	206 E1
PALM DR	RCO	100 D3
PALM DR	SDCO	106 C4
PALM ST	BKD	166 B4
PALM CANYON DR	PMSP	206 B5
PALM CANYON DR	RCO	100 D4
PALM CANYON DR	SDCO	107 E2
PALM CYN DR E	PMSP	206 C5
PALM CYN DR N	PMSP	206 A1
PALMDALE BLVD	LACO	90 B3
PALMDALE RD	SBD	90 E4
PALMDALE RD	SBD	91 A3
PALMER AV	FRCO	66 C2
PALMER RD	SB	86 C2
PALMER CREEK RD	HUM	15 E2
PALMETTO AV	BUT	124 C3
PALMETTO AV	ONT	203 E5
PALMETTO AV	ONT	204 A5
PALMETTO AV	C	124 C3
PALMETTO ST	SBD	80 E5
PALMETTO ST	SBD	81 A5
PALMETTO WY	LAS	20 D2
PALMS TO PINES	RCO	100 E4
PALO COLORDO RD	MON	64 B1
PALOMA RD	CAL	40 E3
PALOMAR AV	SDCO	V C5
PALOMAR AV	SDCO	111 D2
PALOMAR AV	SD	105 B4
PALOMAR ST	RCO	99 C5
PALOMAR APRT RD	SDCO	106 B3
PALOMAR DIV TK	RCO	106 D1
PALOMARES RD	ALA	46 A2
PALOMAS AV	KER	77 E3
PALOMAS AV	KER	78 A3
PALOMINO RD	SDCO	106 C2
PALOMINO WY	HUM	22 C1
PALO PRIETA CHO	SLO	76 D1
PALOS VERDES BL	LACO	S B2
PALOS VRDS DR E	LACO	97 D4
PALOS VRDS DR E	LACO	S B3
PALOS VRDS DR N	LACO	97 D3
PALOS VRDS DR N	LACO	S B2
PALOS VRDS DR S	LACO	97 D4
PALOS VRDS DR W	LACO	97 D4
PALOS VRDS DR W	LACO	S B2
PALO VERDE AV	LACO	S E2
PALO VERDE BLVD	MOH	96 B4
PALO VERDE RD	IMP	110 C1
PALO VERDE RD	SBD	100 C2
PALO VERDE ST	MTCL	203 C3
PAMELA ST	KER	79 C2
PAMO RD	SDCO	107 A3
PAMPA RD	KER	79 A3
PANAMA LN	KER	78 B3
PANAMA LN	KER	79 A3
PANAMA RD	KER	78 D3
PANAMA RD	KER	79 A3
PANAMINT VLY RD	INY	71 B1
PANCHO RD	RCO	107 A1
PANCHORICO RD	MON	65 E3
PANGBORN LN	INY	60 B4
PANOCHE RD	FRCO	56 D3
PANOCHE RD	SBT	55 B4
PANOCHE RD	SBT	56 A4
PANORAMA DR	KER	78 E2
PANORAMA PT RD	SHA	18 D3
PANORAMIC HWY	MAR	38 A5
PANORAMIC HWY	MAR	45 A1
PANTHER CK RD	TEH	19 C3
PANTHER GAP RD	HUM	16 A4
PAPPAS RD	KER	80 C3
PARADISE AV	MDO	162 A4
PARADISE AV	STA	47 C3
PARADISE DR	CRTM	140 D1
PARADISE DR	MAR	45 B1
PARADISE DR	RCO	100 C5
PARADISE RD	CLK	74 D2
PARADISE RD	CLK	209 C4
PARADISE RD	CLK	210 E3
PARADISE RD	COL	24 E5
PARADISE RD	LV	209 C4
PARADISE RD	SJCO	46 E1
PARADISE RD	SJCO	47 A1
PARADISE RD	SB	87 B3
PARADISE RD	STA	47 C2
PARADISE SPG RD	SBD	81 E4
PARADISE SPG RD	SBD	82 B5
PARADISE VLY RD	SDCO	V C4
PARADISE VLY RD	SDCO	111 D1
PARAISO SPGS RD	MON	64 E1
PARAISO SPGS RD	MON	65 A1
PARAMOUNT BLVD	LACO	98 A3
PARAMOUNT BLVD	LACO	R E4
PARAMOUNT BLVD	LACO	R A4
PARAMOUNT BLVD	LACO	S E1
PARDEE DAM RD	CAL	40 D3
PARDOES	AMA	41 D1
PARIS AV	KIN	67 D3
PARIS VALLEY RD	MON	65 D3
PARK AV	BUT	25 B3
PARK AV	C	124 C5
PARK AV	LAG	201 C2
PARK AV	O	157 D1
PARK AV	SJ	151 D3
PARK AV	SJ	152 B4
PARK AV	SCLR	151 C3
PARK AV	TRI	17 D2
PARK AV W	NAP	133 A3
PARK BLVD	ALA	45 D1
PARK BLVD	O	158 D3
PARK BLVD	SD	214 A5
PARK BLVD	SD	215 E3
PARK BLVD	SD	216 A1
PARK BLVD	SDCO	V B4
PARK BLVD N	SA	196 B2
PARK BLVD N	SA	196 B2
PARK DR S	CC	156 D1
PARK RD	BEN	153 D4
PARK RD	IMP	109 B4
PARK RD	SBT	55 A3
PARK RD E	COL	24 B5
PARK ST	HUM	9 E5
PARK ST	S	160 B4
PARK ST	TUL	68 B3
PARK WY	LAK	31 D2
PARK CREEK RD	ED	35 B4
PARKER RD	SBD	101 E1
PARKER RD	STA	47 D2
PARKER CREEK RD	MOD	7 B2
PARKER CREEK RD	MOD	8 B1
PARKER CK RD W	MOD	8 B1
PARKER DAM RD	SBD	104 B1

STREET	CO.	PAGE & GRID
PARKER LAKE RD	MNO	43 C5
PARKER LAKE RD	MNO	50 C1
PARKER-POSTN RD	LPAZ	103 E4
PARKFIELD GRADE	FRCO	66 C3
PARKFLD CEM RD	MON	66 C4
PARKFLD-COALNGA	FRCO	66 C4
PARK HILL RD	SLO	76 B3
PARKMAN RD	IMP	110 D5
PARK MARINA DR	RED	122 D1
PARK MOABI	SBD	95 E2
PARKMONT DR	LACO	89 D3
PK PRESIDIO BL	SF	141 C3
PARKS RD	SUT	33 C3
PARKSIDE DR	RCO	101 D5
PARKVIEW LN	KER	79 C5
PARKVILLE RD	SHA	18 D3
PARKWAY DR	DN	1 D4
PARKWAY DR	TEH	18 D4
PARLIER AV	FRCO	56 E4
PARLIER AV	FRCO	57 D4
PARLIER AV	FRCO	58 B4
PARNASSUS BLVD	SF	141 D5
PARR	CC	38 C5
PARROTTS FERRY	TUO	41 C4
PARSONS RD	FRCO	66 C2
PASADENA AV	LA	186 D1
PASADENA FRWY	LA	186 B2
PASADENA FRWY	LACO	97 E2
PASADENA FRWY	LACO	R D4
PASCOE RD	KER	69 B5
PASEO AV	SUT	33 C1
PASEO DEL MAR	LACO	97 D4
PASEO DEL MAR	LACO	S B3
PASKENTA RD	TEH	18 D5
PASKENTA RD	TEH	24 C1
PASKENTA CEM RD	TEH	24 B2
PASO ST	KER	78 A5
PASO NOGAL	CC	38 E5
PASO ROBLES BL	SLO	76 A1
PASO ROBLES HWY	KER	77 A1
PASQUALE RD	NEV	34 C1
PASS RD	SUT	33 A2
PASSONS BLVD	LACO	R E5
PASSONS BLVD	LACO	R A5
PAST TIME LN	RCO	100 A5
PATHFINDER RD	LACO	U D5
PAT MPHY MEM DR	DN	1 E5
PAT MPHY MEM DR	DN	2 A5
PATRICIA AV	SIS	4 C2
PATRICIA LN	CAL	41 C3
PATRICIA LN	MNO	42 E1
PATRICIA LN	MNO	43 A1
PATRICK RD	LPAZ	104 A2
PATRICK WY	SBD	100 E1
PATRICKS CK RD	DN	2 B3
PATRICKS PT	HUM	9 E3
PATTERSON AV	SB	87 B4
PATTERSON LN	MOD	8 D1
PATTERSON RD	HUM	10 D4
PATTERSON RD	KER	89 B1
PATTERSON RD	STA	47 D2
PATTERSON RD	VEN	96 B1
PATTERSON CK RD	SIS	3 C5
PATTERSON CK RD	SIS	11 D1
PATTRSN MILL RD	MOD	8 E3
PATTRSN PASS RD	ALA	46 C2
PATTRSN PASS RD	SJCO	46 D2
PATTERSN RCH RD	TRI	17 A1
PATTERSN SAWMLL	LAS	8 D3
PATTISON RD	CAL	40 D3
PATTON	MCO	55 E1
PATTON MILLS RD	TEH	24 A2
PATTYMOCUS-		
PATWIN RD	SBD	90 E3
PAUBA RD	RCO	106 D1
PAUI RD	RCO	107 B1
PAULARINO AV	CM	197 E4
PAULINE AV	STA	47 C2
RAUL NEGRA RD	MCO	55 E3
PAXTON RD	SBDO	100 E1
PAXTON ST	LACO	Q A1
PAYEN RD	SAC	40 C1
PAYMASTER MN RD	SBD	83 C4
PAYNE AV	CC	39 C5
PAYNE RD	IMP	108 E5
PAYNE RD	SUT	33 B2
PAYNE WY	KER	79 D3
PAYNES CK LOOP	TEH	19 A4
PAYNES CREEK RD	TEH	19 A4
PAYNES CREEK RD	TEH	18 D4
PEABODY RD	SOL	39 A3
PEACEFUL GLEN	SOL	39 A2
PEACH AV	FRCO	57 D2
PEACH AV	FRCO	57 D5
PEACH AV	GLE	24 E4
PEACH AV	MCO	47 E4
PEACH AV	MCO	48 A4
PEACH TREE RD	MON	65 E2
PEACH TREE RD	MON	66 A2
PEACHY CYN RD	SLO	75 E1
PEACHY CYN RD	SLO	76 A1
PEAK RD	TRI	16 E5
PEAR AV	GLE	25 A4
PEAR AV	STA	47 C4
PEARBLOSSOM HWY	LACO	90 A4
PEARL RD	SJCO	40 B3
PEARL ST	SDCO	V A3
PEARL ST	SDCO	106 C5
PEARL ST	SD	105 B3
PEAR MAIN ST	SBD	91 B3
PEARSON RD	BUT	25 C3
PEARSON RD	INY	70 C5
PEASE RD	SUT	33 C2
PEAVINE RDG RD	ED	35 B4
PEBBLE BEACH DR	DN	1 D4
PEBBLY BEACH RD	AVLN	105 B5
PECHO VALLEY RD	SLO	75 E3
PECK RD	LACO	98 B1
PECK RD	LACO	R B4
PEDERSON	FRCO	58 A3
PEDLEY RD	RCO	99 A2
PEDRICK RD	SOL	39 B2
PEDRICK RD	SOL	39 B1
PEDRO RANCH RD	MNO	51 C1
PEDROS RD	STA	47 D3
PEGASUS DR	KER	78 D2
PEGASUS ST	KER	79 B4
PELGER RD	SUT	33 B3
PELICAN RD	STA	47 B2
PELLERIN RD	STA	47 E2
PELLET RD	IMP	108 E4
PELLISER RD	KER	79 B4
PELTIER RD	SJCO	39 E3
PELTIER RD	SJCO	40 A3
PENCIL RD	MOD	7 B5
PENDLETON RD	SBD	92 A1
PENDOLA RD	YUB	26 B4
PENDOLA EXT	YUB	26 C4
PENDOLA GARDEN	MPA	49 A3
PENFIELD AV	LA	178 A4
PENINSULA DR	HUM	15 E5

STREETS

STREET	CO.	PAGE & GRID	
PENINSULA DR	PLU	20	B4
PENMAN SPGS RD	SLO	76	B1
PENNINGTON RD	BUT	25	B5
PENNINGTON RD	SUT	33	B1
PENNSYLVANIA AV	FRFD	135	B3
PENNSYLVANIA AV	LACO	Q	C2
PENNSYLVANIA AV	RIV	205	E3
PENNSYLVANIA AV	RCO	99	E3
PENNSYLVANIA AV	SOL	135	B4
PENNSYLV GCH RD	CAL	41	C4
PENON LOOKOUT	MPA	48	D1
PENOYAR GRAS LK	SIS	4	E5
PENOYAR TENNANT	SIS	5	A5
PENROSE ST	LACO	Q	B2
PENTLAND RD	KER	78	B5
PENTZ RD	BUT	25	C3
PENTZ MAGALIA	BUT	25	D3
PEORIA RD	YUB	34	A1
PEPPER AV	SBD	99	B2
PEPPER DR	KER	78	E3
PEPPER RD	SON	37	E3
PEPPER RD	SON	38	A3
PEPPER ST	MCO	47	E4
PEPPER ST	MCO	48	A4
PEPPER ST	SBD	80	E5
PEPPER ST	SBD	81	A5
PERALTA BLVD	ALA	46	A3
PERALTA ST	O	157	C2
PERCH ST	KER	79	C4
PERCY AV	YUBA	125	D3
PERCY RD	KER	79	D1
PEREZ RD	IMP	112	D5
PERI RD	MON	65	D4
PERIMETER RD	NEV	34	B2
PERINI RD	LAK	32	A4
PERKINS AV	KER	78	B1
PERKINS RD	CLO	33	A3
PERKINS RD	SB	87	C1
PERKINS ST	U	123	B3
PERRAL RD	KER	77	D2
PERRIN AV	FRCO	57	D2
PERRIN RD	SJCO	47	B2
PERRIS BLVD	RCO	99	C3
PERRY RD	COL	32	D1
PERRY RD	RCO	99	B4
PERRY CREEK RD	ED	41	A1
PERSHING AV	S	160	A1
PERSHING AV	SJCO	40	A5
PERSHING DR	LA	187	D5
PERSHING DR	LACO	Q	A5
PERSHING DR	SD	216	A3
PERSHING DR	SDCO	V	B4
PESCADERO CK RD	SMCO	45	C5
PETALUMA AV	SON	132	B4
PETALUMA HLL RD	STR	131	D4
PETALUMA HLL RD	SON	38	A2
PETALUMA HLL RD	SON	131	D4
PETE MILLER RD	STA	47	C5
PETERSBOURGH S	CAL	40	E3
PETERSBURG RD	SIS	11	B3
PETERSON DR	NAPA	29	B2
PETERSON LN	LAK	31	D3
PETERSON RD	COL	32	C1
PETERSON RD	FRCO	58	B1
PETERSON RD	IMP	109	B3
PETERSON RD	KER	68	C5
PETERSON RD	KER	77	E1
PETERSON RD	KER	78	B1
PETERSON RD	LPAZ	104	A3
PETERSON RD	LACO	89	D4
PETERSON RDG RD	YUB	26	B5
PETRIFIED FORST	NAPA	38	A1
PETRIFIED FORST	SON	38	A1
PETRO RD	INY	72	C2
PETROGLYPH RD	MNO	51	D3
PETRLEUM CLB RD	KER	78	A4
PETTINGER RD	CAL	40	D4
PETTYJOHN RD	TEH	17	E5
PEW RD	SBD	85	C5
PEZZI RD	SJCO	40	B4
PFE RD	PLA	33	E5
PFITZER RD	MCO	47	D5
PHEASANT CT	KER	79	B4
PHEASANT DR	MOD	7	B5
PHEASANT LN	SIS	4	B4
PHELAN RD	HUM	15	D1
PHELAN RD	SBD	91	A4
PHELPS AV	FRCO	66	D2
PHILADELPHIA ST	LACO	98	E2
PHILADELPHIA ST	SBD	98	E2
PHILBRIC RD	SB	86	C1
PHILBROOK RD	BUT	25	D1
PHILDOW RD	LAS	20	E3
PHILIP	PLA	33	E4
PHILIPS RD	MCO	55	E1
PHILLIPE LN	SIS	4	A4
PHILLIPS	LAK	32	A3
PHILLIPS DR	SBD	82	A5
PHILLIPS RD	KER	78	C1
PHILLIPS RD	KER	78	D4
PHILLIPS RD	KER	80	B4
PHILLIPS RD	SHA	19	A1
PHILLIPS RD	SOL	39	B1
PHILLIPSVLLE RD	HUM	16	C4
PHILO GRNWD RD	MEN	30	C2
PHOENIX LAKE RD	TUO	41	D5
PHYLLIS RD	TEH	18	C4
PICACHO RD	IMP	110	D5
PICADOR BLVD	SDCO	V	C5
PICADOR BLVD	SDCO	111	D2
PICARD RD	SIS	4	E2
PICARD RD	SIS	5	A2
PICRD SAMS NECK	SIS	4	E2
PICARDY DR	S	160	B4
PICAYUNE RD	MAD	49	D5
PICKENS RD	LAS	21	D5
PICKERING AV	LACO	R	B5
PICKETT RD	IMP	109	B4
PICO BLVD	LA	180	D4
PICO BLVD	LA	183	B3
PICO BLVD	LA	184	C3
PICO BLVD	LA	185	A3
PICO BLVD	LACO	Q	A4
PICO BLVD	SMON	180	B5
PICO BLVD	SMON	187	A1
PICO CANYON RD	LACO	89	B4
PIEDMONT AV	B	156	B3
PIEDMONT AV	O	158	B1
PIEDRA RD	FRCO	58	A3
PIEDRA AZUL	MCO	55	D3
PIEDRAS DR	RCO	99	B3
PIER AV	LACO	S	B1
PIERCE LN	SOL	38	E4
PIERCE RD	SCL	45	E5
PIERCE RD	SUT	33	C3
PIERCE ST	BKD	166	A2
PIERCE ST	RCO	99	A3
PIERCE ST	RCO	101	B4
PIERCE CK MTRWY	PLU	20	E4
PIERCE POINT RD	MAR	37	D4
PIERI RD	KER	78	B4

STREET	CO.	PAGE & GRID	
PIERLE RD	IMP	108	E5
PIERSON BLVD	RCO	100	C2
PIGEON PASS RD	RCO	99	C2
PIGEON POINT RD	HUM	15	E1
PIGEON SPG RD	KER	79	C5
PIKE RD	STA	47	D3
PIKE CITY RD	SIE	26	C5
PIKE CITY RD	YUB	26	C5
PILAR RD	SIS	4	D5
PILE ST	SDCO	107	A4
PILGRIM CK RD	SIS	12	E2
PILITAS HUERHRO	SLO	76	C2
PILOT SPRING RD	MNO	43	D5
PILOT SPRING RD	MNO	50	E1
PIMLICO DR	RCO	100	C5
PINAL ST	SB	86	D1
PINE AV	BUT	25	B3
PINE AV	LB	192	D3
PINE AV	MEN	31	C1
PINE AV	PAC	167	C2
PINE AV	SBD	98	D2
PINE AV	TRI	17	B2
PINE DR	HUM	16	B4
PINE DR	LAS	20	E2
PINE DR	MPA	48	E1
PINE ST	C	124	C4
PINE ST	MONT	167	D2
PINE ST	MON	53	E2
PINE ST	NAP	133	B4
PINE ST	RED	122	B1
PINE ST	RCO	100	C4
PINE ST	SDCO	107	A4
PINE ST	SF	142	A3
PINE ST	SF	143	A4
PINE ST	SHA	18	C3
PINE ST	U	123	C2
PINE CANYON RD	MON	65	B3
PINE CANYON RD	SB	76	E5
PINE COVE TR	KER	79	D2
PINE CREEK BLVD	MOD	8	B1
PINE CREEK RD	INY	51	B4
PINE CREEK RD	HUM	10	C3
PINE CREEK RD	SIS	2	E3
PINE FLAT	SON	31	E5
PINE FLAT RD	SBD	91	E5
PINE FLAT RD	SCR	53	D1
PINE GROVE	VEN	88	C4
PINE GROVE RD	KLAM	5	C1
PINE GRV TABEAU	AMA	41	A2
PINE GRV VOLCNO	AMA	41	A2
PINE GULCH RD	AMA	40	E2
PINE HILLS RD	SDCO	107	C4
PINEHURST RD	CC	45	D1
PINE MTN DR	TUO	48	E1
PINE MTN RD	KER	78	E1
PINE MTN RD	KER	79	A1
PINE MTN RD	MEN	31	D4
PINE NUT RD	MNO	42	E1
PINE RIDGE	FRCO	58	C3
PINE RIDGE RD	HUM	10	C3
PINE RIDGE RD	MEN	31	A2
PNES TO PLMS HY	RCO	100	B4
PINE TREE CY RD	KER	80	A4
PINE VALLEY RD	MON	65	D3
PINEVISTA CIR	RCO	100	A3
PINEWOOD LN	FRCO	58	B1
PINEY CK LOOP	MON	64	D2
PINKSTON CYN RD	BUT	25	D3
PINNACLE RD	SBD	81	A1
PINOLI RIDGE RD	NEV	26	E4
PINOLI RIDGE RD	NEV	27	A4
PINON CANYON RD	KER	79	C4
PINON VILLGE RD	TUL	70	A3
PINTO DR	CAL	41	B4
PINTO RD	RCO	101	E4
PINTO BASIN RD	RCO	101	D4
PINTO MTN RD	SBD	101	C1
PIONEER AV	STA	47	D1
PIONEER BLVD	LACO	98	A3
PIONEER BLVD	LACO	T	A1
PIONEER DR	KER	78	E3
PIONEER RD	DN	2	B3
PIONEER RD	MCO	55	D1
PIONEER RD	STA	47	D3
PIONEER TR	SLT	129	C4
PIONEER CK RD	AMA	41	B2
PIONEERTOWN RD	SBD	100	D1
PIONEER TR RD	ED	36	A4
PIPE CREEK RD	RCO	100	C5
PIPE LINE AV	SBD	98	D2
PIPES RD	SBD	100	C1
PIPES CANYON RD	SBD	100	D1
PIPI RD	ED	41	C1
PIRCEN RD	LAS	14	B3
PIRU CANYON RD	LACO	89	A4
PIRU CANYON RD	VEN	88	E4
PISGAH CRATR RD	SBD	92	E2
PISTACHIO RD	KER	77	B1
PIT RD	MNO	51	A2
PIT #1 PWRHS RD	SHA	13	D4
PITTMAN HILL RD	FRCO	58	A2
PITT RIV CYN RD	LAS	14	A4
PITT SCHOOL RD	SOL	39	B2
PITTVILLE RD	LAS	20	A1
PITTVILLE RD	SHA	13	E4
PITTVILLE BENCH	LAS	14	A4
PITTZER RD	IMP	112	B3
PIUMA RD	LACO	97	A2
PIUTE MTN RD	KER	79	D2
PIUTE PINES RD	KER	79	D3
PLACENTIA AV	CM	199	A3
PLACENTIA AV	NB	199	A3
PLACENTIA AV	ORA	T	C4
PLACER AV	FRCO	56	E4
PLACER CT	KER	79	D2
PLACER RD	SHA	18	B3
PLACER RD	SUT	33	E3
PLACER ST	RED	122	A2
PLACER ST	SHA	18	B2
PLACER ST	TRI	17	D1
PLACER HILLS RD	PLA	34	C3
PLACERITA CYN	LACO	89	C5
PLACERVILLE DR	PLCV	138	A3
PLACERVILLE RD	SAC	34	B5
PLAINS RD	CC	39	C5
PLAINSBURG RD	MCO	48	D5
PLANO ST	TUL	68	D3
PLANTATION ST	RCO	102	C4
PLANT FIVE RD	INY	51	C4
PLANZ RD	KER	78	D3
PLASKETT RDG RD	MON	64	E2
PLATEAU CIR	SHA	18	B2
PLATEAU PINE RD	SHA	19	B3
PLATFORM RD	MAR	37	E4
PLATINA RD	SHA	18	A3
PLATINA RD	SHA	17	E3
PLATINA RD	SHA	17	D3
PLATINA SCH RD	SHA	17	D4
PLAYA AZUL	AVLN	105	B4
PLAZA ST	SDCO	106	C4
PLEASANT	CC	38	E5

STREET	CO.	PAGE & GRID	
PLEASANT AV	SON	37	E1
PLEASANT RD	SLO	66	B5
PLEASANT GROVE	PLA	33	D4
PLEASANT GROVE	SUT	33	E4
PLEASANT GRV LN	BUT	25	E5
PLEASANT HILL	SON	37	D2
PLEASNT HL RD E	M	154	C4
PLEASANT OAK DR	TUL	68	E3
PLEASANTN SUNOL	ALA	46	B2
PLEASANT PT RD	HUM	15	E2
PLEASNTS VLY RD	SOL	38	E2
PLEASNTS VLY RD	SOL	39	A2
PLEASANT VLY AV	O	156	B5
PLEASANT VLY RD	ALP	36	B5
PLEASANT VLY RD	ED	34	E5
PLEASANT VLY RD	NEV	34	B1
PLEASANT VLY RD	STA	47	D1
PLEASANT VLY RD	VEN	96	B1
PLEASNT VLY DAM	INY	51	C3
PLESANTE RD	MON	54	C3
PLEYTO CEM RD	MON	65	C4
PLINCO MINE RD	PLU	21	C5
PLUMAS AV	FRCO	57	A3
PLUMAS ST	RENO	130	B4
PLUMAS ARBGA RD	YUB	33	D3
PLUMB LN E	RENO	130	D5
PLUMB LN W	RENO	130	C5
PLUMBAGO RD	SIE	26	D5
PLUM CREEK RD	TEH	19	A4
PLUMMER LKOT RD	TRI	17	B3
PLUM VALLEY RD	MOD	7	C4
PLUNKETT RD	HUM	10	A5
PLYMIRE RD	TEH	18	C5
PLYMOUTH AV	KIN	67	A3
PLYMOUTH RD	SBD	80	E5
PLYMTH SHNDOAH	AMA	40	B1
POCK LN	SJCO	40	B5
POCKET RD	SAC	39	D2
POE RD	IMP	108	E3
POE POWERHOUSE	BUT	25	E3
POINSETTIA LN	SDCO	106	B3
PT LAKEVIEW RD	LAK	32	A3
POINT LOMA AV	SDCO	V	A4
POINT LOMA AV	SDCO	111	C1
POINT LOMA BLVD	SDCO	V	B4
POINT LOMA BL W	SD	212	B5
PT OF TIMBER RD	CC	39	D5
PT PLEASANT RD	SAC	39	E3
POINT RANCH RD	MNO	43	B3
PT REYES RD	MAR	37	E4
PT REYES PETLMA	MAR	37	E4
POINT SAL RD	SB	86	A1
POKER BAR RD	TRI	17	D1
POKER FLAT RD	SIE	26	D3
POLE LINE RD	LAS	20	A1
POLE LINE RD	MCO	55	E2
POLELINE RD	SBD	93	A5
POLE LINE RD	SHA	13	E5
POLETA RD	INY	51	D4
POLETA LAWS RD	INY	51	D4
POLI ST	VENT	175	E2
POLK AV	FRCO	57	B3
POLK AV	FRCO	67	B1
POLK AV	FRCO	57	B5
POLK ST	LACO	Q	A1
POLK ST	RCO	101	B5
POLLACK FLAT	SIS	5	A5
POLSON RD	NAPA	38	D3
POMEGRANATE AV	STA	47	C3
POMELO AV	STA	47	C3
POMERADO RD	SDCO	V	C2
POMERADO RD	SDCO	106	D5
POMEROY AV	SCLR	150	C3
POMEROY LS BERS	SLO	76	C5
POMONA AV	COR	215	C5
POMONA AV	CM	199	B3
POMONA AV	TEH	24	D1
POMONA BLVD	LACO	R	E4
POMONA FRWY	LACO	98	A2
POMONA FRWY	LACO	R	C4
POMONA ST	CC	38	D4
POND RD	KER	68	A5
PONDER WY	SHA	18	B3
PONDEROSA BLVD	LAS	21	B4
PONDEROSA RD	CAL	41	C4
PONDEROSA WY	AMA	41	B3
PONDEROSA WY	BUT	25	C2
PONDEROSA WY	BUT	25	D2
PONDEROSA WY	BUT	25	D3
PONDEROSA WY	BUT	26	A4
PONDEROSA WY	CAL	41	B3
PONDEROSA WY	MPA	49	B3
PONDEROSA WY	PLA	34	D3
PONDEROSA WY	SHA	19	B2
PONDEROSA WY	TEH	19	B3
PONDOSA WY	SIS	13	C3
PONY RD	SBD	92	C4
PONY WY	CAL	41	A4
PONY EXPRESS TR	ED	35	A4
POOLE AV	KER	80	C1
POOLE LN	SIE	27	D3
POOLE RD	HUM	15	D2
POOLE RD	MCO	48	D5
POOL STATION RD	CAL	41	A3
POONKINNEY RD	MEN	23	A3
POOP OUT HL RD	SBD	100	A1
POOR BOY CK RD	ALP	36	C5
POORE RD	IMP	109	C4
POPE ST	NAPA	29	C2
POPE CANYON RD	NAPA	38	C1
POPE VALLEY RD	NAPA	29	C1
POPE VALLEY RD	NAPA	32	B5
POPE VALLEY RD	NAPA	38	B1
POPLAR AV	KER	78	B2
POPLAR AV	MLBR	144	D5
POPPET FLAT RD	RCO	100	A3
POPPY BLVD	KER	80	B4
PORTAL RD W	MNO	43	C5
PORTER	FRCO	58	A4
PORTER AV	RCO	99	C3
PORTER RD	SOL	39	B2
PORTER CREEK RD	SON	37	E1
PORTER CREEK RD	SON	38	A1
PORTERVILLE HWY	KER	68	D5
PORTERVILLE HWY	KER	78	D1
PORTERVILLE WY	KER	78	C1
PORT KENYON RD	HUM	15	D2
PORTOLA AV	RCO	100	E4
PORTOLA BLVD	ALA	46	C2
PORTOLA DR	SFCO	45	B2
PORTOLA RD	SLO	76	A2
PORTOLA RD	SMCO	45	D4
PORTOLA STAT PK	SMCO	45	D5
PORTOLA MCLEARS	PLU	27	B3
PORTUGUESE BEND	SUT	33	C4
PORTUGUESE CYN	MON	66	B4
PORT WINE RIDGE	PLU	26	C3
PORT WINE RIDGE	SIE	26	C4
PORTY ST	KER	78	D4
POSO AV	KER	77	E1
POSO AV	KER	78	A1

STREET	CO.	PAGE & GRID	
POSO FLAT RD	KER	79	A1
POST AV	TEH	24	E2
POST RD	RCO	99	B4
POST ST	SF	142	B3
POST ST	SF	143	A4
POST MTN RD	TRI	17	B3
POTRERO AV	SF	142	D4
POTRERO RD E	VEN	96	D1
POTRERO RD W	VEN	96	C1
POTRERO GRDE BL	LACO	R	A4
POTRERO GRDE DR	LACO	R	E4
POTTER RD	MON	54	D4
POTTEROFF RD	CAL	41	B3
POUND RD	IMP	109	A3
POUNDSTONE RD	COL	33	B3
POURROY RD	RCO	99	D5
POVERTY RD	SAC	39	D3
POVERTY HILL RD	SIE	26	C4
POWAY RD	SDCO	106	D4
POWDER HILL RD	SIS	5	C5
POWDER HILL RD	SIS	13	C1
POWELL AV	SON	37	D1
POWELL RD	SBD	92	D5
POWELL RD	SUT	33	B1
POWELL RD	VEN	88	E4
POWELLTOWN RD	BUT	25	D2
POWER RD	TRI	17	C1
POWER HOUSE RD	FRCO	57	E1
POWER HOUSE RD	MEN	23	B5
POWERHOUSE RD	TRI	11	E5
POWERHOUSE RD S	TEH	19	B3
POWER HSE HL RD	BUT	25	C5
POWER INN RD	SAC	40	A1
POWER LINE RD	MNO	52	C3
POWER LINE RD	RCO	106	E1
POWER LINE RD	SAC	33	D5
POWER LINE RD	SBD	83	A3
POWER LINE RD	SBD	91	C3
POWER LINE RD	SHA	18	B2
POWER LINE RD	SUT	33	D4
POWERS AV	MAN	161	D3
POZOS RD	RCO	99	C3
PRADO RD	SNLO	172	B5
PRAHSER RD	SJCO	40	C5
PRAIRE WY	MEN	22	C5
PRAIRE WY	MEN	30	B1
PRAIRIE AV	LACO	S	B1
PRAIRIE AV	SBD	91	C1
PRAIRIE DR	LAS	8	A5
PRAIRIE CK RD	TRI	17	A1
PRAIRIE FLOWER	STA	47	D4
PRAIRIE FLWR RD	STA	47	D3
PRATT RD	TUL	68	B1
PRATT RANCH RD	MEN	31	C3
PRATVLL BTT RES	PLU	20	B5
PREFUMO CYN RD	SLO	75	E4
PREFUMO CYN RD	SLO	76	A4
PRELL RD	SB	86	C1
PRESCOTT AV	MONT	167	C3
PRESCOTT RD	MON	53	D3
PRESCOTT AV	PAC	167	C3
PRESCOTT RD	SJCO	47	B1
PRESIDIO AV	SF	142	A2
PRESIDIO BLVD	SFCO	45	B1
PRESSLEY RD	SON	38	A2
PRESTON	MPA	49	A5
PRESTON RD	BUT	25	C4
PRESTON RD	IMP	111	E4
PRESTON RD	MCO	47	C4
PREVITALI RD	AMA	41	A2
PRICE CREEK RD	HUM	15	E3
PRICE CK CAMPBL	TRI	17	B1
PRICE CK SCH RD	HUM	15	E2
PRICE CANYON RD	SLO	76	B4
PRIEST COLTRVLL	MPA	48	D1
PRIEST COLTRVLL	TUO	48	E1
PRIEST VLY RD	MON	66	A2
PRIM RD	IMP	109	B5
PRIMROSE MN RD	SIE	26	E4
PRINCE AV	FRCO	56	A2
PRINCE RD	MCO	47	C4
PRINCESS PAT MN	SBD	90	E2
PRINCETON	FRCO	58	A3
PRINCETON RD	MCO	48	B5
PROGRESS RD	SUT	33	B2
PROSPECT AV	KER	78	A1
PROSPECT AV	ORA	T	E2
PROSPECT AV	SDCO	V	D3
PROSPECT BLVD	PAS	190	A3
PROSPECT PL	SD	105	B2
PROSPECT RD	SCL	45	E4
PROSPECT ST	SDCO	V	A3
PROSPECT ST	SDCO	106	C5
PROSPECT ST	SD	105	B3
PROSPERITY AV	TUL	68	A2
PROSSER DAM RD	NEV	27	D5
PROUTY RD	SJCO	40	B3
PROVIDENCE RCH	SBD	84	B4
PRUNE AV	STA	47	C3
PRUNERIDGE AV	CPTO	150	A4
PRUNERIDGE AV	SJ	151	A4
PRUNERIDGE AV	SCLR	150	C4
PRUNERIDGE AV	SCL	151	A4
PUDDING CK RD	MEN	22	C5
PRUSSIAN HLL RD	CAL	41	B3
PUEBLO AV	KIN	67	C3
PUEBLO AV	NAP	133	B2
PUENTE AV	LACO	98	B2
PUENTE AV	LACO	R	B4
PULGA RD	BUT	25	D2
PULLMAN RD	IMP	111	E4
PUMICE MILL RD	MNO	51	D3
PUMICE MINE RD	MNO	50	D1
PUMICE MINE RD	MNO	51	C1
PUMP RD	MCO	55	E2
PUMP RD	STA	47	C4
PUMPHOUSE RD	COL	32	D2
PUMPHOUSE RD	SIS	4	B5
PUMPHOUSE RD	YOL	39	D2
PUNKIN CTR RD	LAS	14	B4
PURDON RD	NEV	26	C5
PURDY AV	KER	80	A5
PURISIMA RD	SB	86	B3
PURISIMA CK RD	SMCO	45	C4
PURITAN MINE RD	LACO	89	E4
PUTAH LN	LAK	32	A4
PUTAH CREEK RD	SOL	39	A1
PUTNAM RD	COL	25	A5
PUTNAM WY	COL	32	E3
PYLE RD	CAL	41	B5
PYLE RD	LAK	31	D2
PYRAMID HILLS	KIN	67	A5
PYRITE RD	RCO	99	A2
Q			
QUAIL AV	KIN	67	B3
QUAIL DR	RCO	100	B5
QUAIL HILL RD	HUM	16	A2
QUAIL ST	KER	80	C1
QUAIL WY	RCO	100	A5
QUAIL HILL RD	CAL	41	A5
QUAIL HOLLOW RD	SCR	P	A5

STREET	CO.	PAGE & GRID	
QUAIL SPGS RD	SBD	101	A1
QUAIL SPGS SPUR	SBD	101	A2
QUAKER ST	HUM	9	E5
QUAKR HL CRS RD	NEV	34	D1
QUALITY RD	KER	68	C5
QUARRY RD	HUM	9	E4
QUARRY RD	MAD	49	B5
QUARRY RD	PA	147	A3
QUARRY RD	SDCO	V	D4
QUARRY RD	SDCO	111	E1
QUARRY RD S	HUM	10	A5
QUARTZ AV	SIS	4	C4
QUARTZ ST	BUT	25	D2
QUARTZ ST	SBD	84	C3
QUARTZ ST	TUO	41	C5
QUARTZ HILL RD	SHA	18	C2
QUARTZ MT LKOUT	SIS	3	D5
QUARTZ MTN RD	MAD	49	D5
QUARTZ VLY DR	SIS	3	C5
QUARTZ VLY RD	SIS	3	C5
QUARTZ VLY RD E	SIS	3	C5
QUATAL CYN RD	KER	87	E2
QUATAL CYN RD	SB	87	E2
QUATAL CYN RD	VEN	88	A1
QUEBEC AV	KIN	67	E3
QUEBEC AV	KIN	67	A3
QUEEN OF SHEBA	INY	72	A3
QUEENS AV	YUBA	125	A1
QUEENS WY	LB	192	D4
QUESTHAVEN RD	SDCO	106	C3
QUICK RD	IMP	112	C5
QUIEN SABE RD	SBT	55	B3
QUIEN SABE RCH	SBT	55	B3
QUIMBY RD	SCL	46	C4
QUINCY RD	SIE	26	D3
QUINCY RD	STA	47	E3
QUINCY JCT RD	PLU	26	D1
QUINCY LA PORTE	PLU	26	D2
QUINCY LA PORTE	PLU	26	C4
QUINLEY AV	MCO	48	B5
QUINN RD	HUM	15	D1
QUINN RD	KER	68	D5
QUISENBERRY RD	STA	47	C3
QUITO RD	SCL	46	A5
R			
R ST	FRE	165	E3
R ST	MER	170	B4
RABBIT BRUSH LN	SIS	4	B4
RABBIT RANCH RD	MNO	51	C2
RABBIT SPGS RD	SBD	91	E4
RABBIT SPGS RD	SBD	92	A4
RABER ST	KER	80	A5
RACE ST	SJ	151	E4
RACE TRACK RD	SAC	39	D3
RACE TRACK RD	TUO	163	A3
RACETRACK VLY	INY	61	A2
RACINE AV	KIN	67	E3
RACQUET CLUB DR	SR	139	B3
RADIO LN	RED	122	C5
RADIO STATN RD	SOL	39	B2
RAGAN MEADWS RD	TRI	17	A3
RAG DUMP RD	BUT	25	D2
RAGLIN RIDGE RD	TEH	23	E1
RAGLIN RIDGE RD	TEH	24	A1
RAGSDALE RD	RCO	102	B4
RAHILLY RD	MCO	48	B5
RAIL CANYON RD	COL	24	B5
RAIL CANYON RD	GLE	24	B5
RAIL CREEK RD	SIS	12	A2
RAILROAD AV	DN	1	D4
RAILROAD AV	HUM	16	D4
RAILROAD AV	RED	122	B3
RAILROAD AV	SMA	173	B2
RAILROAD AV	SOL	135	E3
RAILROAD AV	SUT	33	C2
RAILROAD AV	VAL	134	A4
RAILROAD ST	SBD	84	C3
RAILROAD CYN RD	RCO	99	C4
RAILRD FLAT RD	CAL	41	B3
RAINBOW	FRCO	57	E3
RAINBOW BASN RD	SBD	81	D5
RAINBOW CYN RD	SBD	93	B4
RAINBOW GLEN RD	SDCO	106	C1
RAINBOW LAKE RD	SHA	18	A3
RAINES RD	STA	47	B3
RAIN TREE LN	BUT	25	A2
RAJNUS RD	KLAM	5	E2
RALPH RD	IMP	109	A5
RALSTON AV	BLMT	145	C5
RALSTON AV	SMCO	45	C3
RAMAL RD	SON	38	C3
RAMBLA PACIFICO	LACO	97	B2
RAMELI GREIG RD	PLU	27	D2
RAMIREZ RD	YUB	33	D1
RAMON RD	PMSP	206	C4
RAMON RD	RCO	100	D3
RAMON RD	RCO	100	E3
RAMONA AV	LACO	U	E3
RAMONA AV	MTCL	203	B5
RAMONA AV	SBDO	203	B5
RAMONA AV	SBD	91	C3
RAMONA AV	SBD	98	D2
RAMONA BLVD	LACO	R	B3
RAMONA BLVD	RCO	99	E3
RAMONA EXPWY	RCO	99	C3
RAMONA EXPWY	RCO	99	D3
RAMONA FRWY	SDCO	V	D3
RAMONA FRWY	SDCO	106	E5
RAMOS RD	MCO	55	D1
RAMP RD	MNO	43	B3
RAMSEY RD	RCO	107	B1
RAMSEY RD	SOL	38	E3
RAMSEY MINE RD	LPAZ	104	D4
RAMS HILL DR	SDCO	107	E3
RAMSHORN RD	TRI	12	A3
RAMS HORN GRADE	AMA	41	A2
RAMSHN MUMBO CK	TRI	12	B3
RANCH RD	HUM	15	E2
RANCH RD	MCO	48	C5
RANCH RD	MNO	52	C3
RANCH RD	SBD	92	E5
RANCHERIA RD	KER	69	C5
RANCHERIA RD	KER	78	E2
RANCHERIA RD	KER	79	A2
RANCHERIA RD	MEN	30	C3
RANCHERIA CK RD	SIS	4	A3
RANCHERIAS RD	SBD	91	C3
RANCHERIA-SAWML	KER	79	B1
RANCHERO	SBD	91	B4
RANCHITA CYN RD	MON	66	C5
RANCHITA CYN RD	SLO	66	B5
RANCHITO RD	MPA	48	D2
RANCHLAND DR	SHA	18	B2
RANCH LAND RD	SDCO	106	E4
RANCHO AV	SBD	99	B2
RANCHO DR	KER	78	E4
RANCHO DR	KER	79	A4
RANCHO DR	SBD	91	A3
RANCHO RD	KER	78	E5
RANCHO RD	KER	79	A5
RANCHO RD	LV	209	A2

STREETS

STREET	CO.	PAGE & GRID
RANCHO RD	SB	76 C5
RANCHO RD	SB	86 B1
RANCHO RD	SHA	18 C2
RNCHO ALISAL RD	SB	86 E3
RCHO BAUTSTA RD	RCO	100 B5
RO BERNARDO RD	SDCO	106 D4
RANCHO CALIF RD	RCO	99 D5
RANCHO CALIF RD	RCO	106 C1
RANCHO CANADA	SDCO	107 A5
RNCHO CONEJO BL	VEN	96 D1
RO SANTA FE RD	SDCO	106 C3
RANCHO VIEJO RD	SJC	202 E1
RANDALL AV	SBD	99 A2
RANDALL RD	KER	77 E4
RANDOLPH RD	MCO	47 E4
RANDOLPH RD	SAC	40 A2
RANDSBURG RD	SBD	81 C2
RANDSBRG CUTOFF	KER	80 A4
RANDSBRG CUTOFF	SBD	80 E3
RANDSBG INYOKRN	KER	80 D1
RANDSBG WASH RD	SBD	80 E1
RANDSBG WASH RD	SBD	81 A1
RANGE RD	MCO	48 B5
RANGER STA RD	INY	51 B3
RANGER STA RD	INY	60 A4
RANGER STA RD	TRI	17 B1
RANNELS BLVD	RCO	103 C5
RANNELS BLVD	RCO	110 C1
RASOR RD	SBD	83 A4
RATTLESNAKE RD	NEV	34 C2
RATTLESNAKE RD	TRI	17 B3
RATTLSNK BTT RD	MOD	14 E1
RATTLSNK CYN RD	SBD	92 C5
RATTLSNAK CK RD	SIS	3 D5
RAWHIDE RD	TUO	41 C5
RAWSON RD	TEH	18 D5
RAY	SJCO	40 A3
RAY	SJCO	40 A4
RAY RD	SB	86 B1
RAYHOUSE RD	YOL	32 C4
RAYMOND AV	ORA	T C1
RAYMOND RD	ALA	46 C2
RAYMOND RD	MAD	49 C5
RAYMOND RD	MAD	57 B1
RAYNOR RANCH	MCO	48 E5
READING RD	TEH	18 D5
REAL RD	BKD	166 A4
REAL RD	KER	166 A5
REALTY RD	SJCO	40 B4
REATA RD	INY	51 D4
RECALDE RD	SBT	55 E4
RECHE RD	SBD	92 D5
RECHE RD	SDCO	106 C2
RECHE CANYON RD	RCO	99 C2
RECLAMATION RD	LAK	31 D2
RECLAMATION RD	SUT	33 C3
RECTOR RD	NEV	34 C1
RED BANK RD	TEH	18 B5
RED BANK RD	TEH	24 C1
RED BOX RD	LACO	R A2
RED CAP RD	HUM	10 D2
RED CLOUD MN RD	RCO	102 B4
REDDING AV	KIN	67 D3
REDDING CYN RD	INY	51 E4
REDDING CK RD	TRI	17 D2
REDDINGTON AV	COL	32 E3
RED DOG RD	NEV	34 D1
RED GRADE RD	TRI	17 D1
RED HEAD CYN RD	MON	65 D3
RED HILL AV	CM	198 A4
RED HILL AV	IRV	198 D3
RED HILL AV	ORA	T D3
RED HILL BLVD	ORA	98 C4
REDHILL RD	CAL	41 B4
RED HILL RD	IMP	109 A3
RED HILL RD	INY	51 C4
RED HILL RD	TRI	17 C1
REDHILL RD	TUO	48 C1
REDINGER LK RD	MAD	49 E5
REDINGER LK RD	MAD	50 A5
REDLANDS BLVD	RCO	99 C2
REDLANDS BLVD	SBDO	207 D5
REDLANDS BLVD	SBD	99 C2
REDLANDS FRWY	RCO	99 D2
REDLANDS FRWY	SBD	99 D2
REDLANDS ST	SBD	99 D2
REDMEYER RD	MEN	31 B2
REDMOND RD	HUM	9 E5
RED MOUNTAIN RD	KER	80 E3
RED MOUNTAIN RD	MCO	55 B1
RED MOUNTAIN RD	RCO	100 A5
RED MOUNTAIN RD	SBD	80 E3
RED MOUNTAIN RD	SHA	13 C3
RED MOUNTAIN RD	TRI	17 B4
RED MTN LKOUT	GLE	24 A3
RED MTN MOTORWY	TRI	17 B4
RED MTN TK TR	RCO	106 C1
RED OAK CYN RD	SIE	26 C2
REDONDO AV	LACO	98 A4
REDONDO AV	LACO	S E2
REDONDO BLVD	LA	184 B4
REDONDO BCH BL	LACO	S B1
REDPARK RD	HUM	9 A1
RED ROCK RD	LAS	8 D4
RED ROCK RD	LAS	27 E2
RED ROCK RD	SIS	5 A3
REDROCK-INYOKRN	KER	80 C1
REDROCK-INYOKRN	KER	80 C2
REDROCK-RANDSBG	KER	80 B3
RED ROVER MN RD	LACO	89 E4
RED SHANK LN	RCO	100 A5
REDSTONE AV	KER	79 C3
RED TOP RD	SOL	38 D3
RED TOP MTN RD	MAD	57 C1
RED VISTA RD	ALP	36 A5
REDWING RD	SBD	91 D3
REDWOOD BLVD	KER	80 B4
REDWOOD DR	HUM	16 C5
REDWOOD DR	TUL	69 B2
REDWOOD HWY	CRTM	140 C2
REDWOOD HWY	DN	1 E3
REDWOOD HWY	DN	2 A5
REDWOOD HWY	DN	9 E3
REDWOOD HWY	HUM	15 E3
REDWOOD HWY	HUM	16 A3
REDWOOD HWY	HUM	16 B4
REDWOOD HWY	MAR	38 A4
REDWOOD HWY	MAR	140 C2
REDWOOD HWY	MEN	22 D2
REDWOOD HWY	SR	139 D2
REDWOOD HWY	STR	131 C2
REDWOOD HWY	SON	31 C4
REDWOOD HWY	SON	37 E2
REDWOOD HWY	SON	38 A3
REDWOOD RD	ALA	47 E1
REDWOOD RD	NAPA	29 D5
REDWOOD RD	NAPA	38 C2
REDWOOD RD	STA	47 D3
REDWOOD ST	VAL	134 B3
REDWD HOUSE RD	HUM	16 B3
REDWOOD RETREAT	SCL	54 C1

STREET	CO.	PAGE & GRID
REED	FRCO	58 A4
REED AV	KER	80 A5
REED AV	SVL	150 B1
REED RD	KER	68 C5
REED RD	SUT	33 C2
REEDER RD	KLAM	5 C1
REED MTN RD	HUM	22 C1
REED ORCHARD RD	TEH	25 A1
REEDS CREEK RD	TEH	18 B5
REEDS TURNPIKE	CAL	41 A5
REED VALLEY RD	RCO	100 A5
REESE AV	COL	33 A1
REESE RD	BUT	25 A2
REEVES RD	VEN	88 B4
REEVES CYN RD	MEN	31 A1
REFUGIO RD	SB	86 E3
REGENTS RD	SD	211 D2
REGENTS RD	SDCO	V B3
REGENTS RD	SDCO	106 C5
REGLI LN	HUM	15 E2
REICHART RCH RD	MNO	51 C1
REID AV	TUL	68 D3
REID RD	KER	79 E2
REID RD	KER	80 A2
REILLY RD	MCO	48 C5
REINA RD	KER	78 C2
REINO RD	VEN	96 D1
REIS AV	VAL	134 E5
RELIEF HILL RD	NEV	26 D5
RELIEZ RD	CC	38 E5
RELIZ CANYON RD	MON	65 A2
REMANN AV	SHA	19 E1
REMBACH WY	KER	79 C1
RENFRO RD	KER	78 C3
RENO AV	TEH	24 D1
RENWICK AV	SB	86 B3
REQUA RD	DN	1 E5
REQUA RD	DN	2 A5
RESEDA BLVD	LA	178 D3
RESEDA BLVD	LACO	97 C1
RESERVATION RD	COL	32 E1
RESERVATION RD	MON	54 B4
RESERVATION RD	TUL	68 E3
RESERVE RD	KER	77 D3
RESERVOIR RD	BUT	25 D5
RESERVOIR RD	ED	34 D3
RESERVOIR RD	SOL	38 D4
RESERVOIR RD	STA	48 A2
RESERVOIR ST	LACO	98 D2
RETRAC WY	NEV	34 B2
RETSON RD	BUT	25 D2
REVIS RD	MAD	49 C5
REWARD RD	KER	77 D3
REYES ADOBE RD	LACO	96 E1
REYNARD WY	SD	215 D2
REYNOLDS AV	MCO	56 B2
REYNOLDS HWY	MEN	23 A5
REYNOLDS RD	SHA	13 E4
REYNLDS FRRY RD	TUO	41 B5
RHELM	CC	38 C5
RHONDA RD	SHA	18 C3
RIALTO AV	SBD	99 B1
RIALTO AV	SBDO	207 C2
RIATA RD	LAK	32 A4
RIATA WY	CAL	41 A4
RICE AV	SBD	101 A1
RICE AV	VEN	96 E1
RICE RD	FRCO	57 C2
RICE RD	MCO	48 B5
RICE RD	STA	47 E2
RICE RD	VEN	88 A4
RICE CANYON RD	LAS	21 B3
RICE CANYON RD	LAS	21 B3
RICE CREEK RD	LAK	23 D5
RICE CREEK RD	LAK	31 D1
RICES CROSNG RD	NEV	34 B1
RICES CROSNG RD	YUB	26 A5
RICES TEX HL RD	YUB	26 A5
RICETON HWY	BUT	25 C5
RICH LN	RCO	106 E1
RICH RD	KER	68 C5
RICHARD RD	SIS	4 D5
RICHARD ST	KER	70 A5
RICHARDS AV	BUT	33 C1
RICHARDS BLVD	DVS	136 D3
RICHARDSON AV	SF	142 A1
RICHARDSON RD	SBD	91 A3
RICHARDSON RD	SIS	4 E3
RICHARDSON RD	SIS	5 A2
RICHARDSON SPGS	BUT	25 B2
RICH BAR RD	PLU	26 B1
RICHEY RD	CLO	33 A3
RICHFIELD RD	TEH	24 D1
RICH GULCH RD	PLU	26 B1
RICHLAND RD	SUT	125 B5
RICHMOND RD	LAS	21 A3
RICHMOND ST	SD	215 E1
RICHVALE HWY	BUT	25 B4
RIDER ST	RCO	99 B3
RIDGE DR	SHA	18 B2
RIDGE RD	AMA	40 E2
RIDGE RD	CAL	41 B2
RIDGE RD	NEV	34 C1
RIDGE RD	NEV	127 A2
RIDGE RD	NEV	128 A4
RIDGE RD	SIE	26 C5
RIDGE RD	SIS	3 E4
RIDGE RD	TEH	18 C5
RIDGECREST BLVD	KER	80 D1
RIDGE ROUTE RD	ED	34 E4
RIDGEWAY DR	ED	35 B4
RIDGEWAY HWY	MEN	23 B5
RIDGEWOOD	MEN	23 A5
RIDGEWOOD DR	HUM	15 E1
RIDGEWOOD RD	SHA	18 C2
RIEBLI RD	SON	37 E1
RIEBLI RD	SON	38 A1
RIEFF RD	LAK	32 B4
RIEGO RD	SUT	33 D5
RIGGIN AV	TUL	68 A1
RIGGINS RD	SUT	33 C4
RIGGS RD	LAK	31 D3
RIGGS RD	SBD	83 B2
RIKER ST	SAL	171 B5
RILEY RD	BUT	25 B5
RILEY RD	SB	86 E3
RILEY RD	SAC	40 A2
RIM O T WRLD HY	SBD	91 C5
RIM O T WRLD HY	SBD	99 D1
RIMPAU BLVD	LA	184 C3
RIMROCK RD	BARS	208 D4
RIM ROCK RD	RCO	107 C1
RIMROCK RD	SBD	91 D1
RIMROCK RD	SBD	100 C1
RIM ROCK CANYON	RCO	107 C1
RINCON AV	SDCO	106 D3
RINCON AV	SON	38 A2
RINCON RD	SBD	91 C4
RINCNADA LS PIL	SLO	76 C3
RIO RD	CAR	168 C5
RIO RD	MON	168 C4

STREET	CO.	PAGE & GRID
RIO BLANCO	SJCO	40 A4
RIO BONITO RD E	BUT	25 C5
RIO BONITO RD W	BUT	25 C5
RIO DEL SOL RD	RCO	100 E3
RIOLINDA AV	FRCO	57 B4
RIO LINDA BLVD	SAC	33 E5
RIO OSO RD	SUT	33 D3
RIORDON RD	COL	32 D1
RIOSA RD	PLA	33 E3
RIOSA RD	PLA	34 A3
RIO VISTA AV	FRCO	58 A4
RIO VISTA AV W	TEH	18 D4
RIO VISTA RD	SUIS	135 C4
RIO VISTA ST	ORA	T D2
RIPONE RD	STA	47 C2
RIPPON RD N	SJCO	47 C1
RIPPON RD W	SJCO	47 B2
RISING HILL RD	SIS	4 C5
RITCHEY ST	SA	198 E1
RITTER RD	COL	13 D3
RITTS MILL RD	SHA	19 B2
RIVER AV	BUT	33 C1
RIVER BLVD	KER	78 D3
RIVER RD	BUT	25 A3
RIVER RD	BUT	25 A3
RIVER RD	COL	33 A1
RIVER RD	HUM	15 D3
RIVER RD	HUM	16 D5
RIVER RD	MAD	49 C5
RIVER RD	MAD	57 B1
RIVER RD	MCO	47 D4
RIVER RD	MON	54 D4
RIVER RD	RCO	98 E3
RIVER RD	RCO	99 C4
RIVER RD	SBD	85 C5
RIVER RD	SBD	95 D1
RIVER RD	SJCO	47 C1
RIVER RD	SLO	66 A5
RIVER RD	SLO	76 A1
RIVER RD	SLO	76 C3
RIVER RD	SON	37 D2
RIVER RD	STA	47 B3
RIVER RD	STA	47 D1
RIVER RD	STA	162 D5
RIVER RD	TEH	24 D1
RIVER RD S	YOL	39 D2
RIVER ST	SC	169 C1
RIVER ST	SCR	169 C1
RIVER ST	SON	31 C4
RIVER BENCH RD	LAS	20 E3
RIVERBEND AV	FRCO	57 E3
RIVERCREST DR	HUM	16 B5
RIVEREDGE RD	SDCO	106 C1
RIVERFORD RD	SDCO	V D3
RIVERFORD RD	SDCO	106 E5
RIVER GRADE RD	LACO	R B3
RIV JCT FRMS RD	SJCO	47 B2
RIVER RANCH RD	SHA	18 C3
RIVER ROCK RD	TRI	17 D1
RIVERSIDE	WSH	130 B3
RIVERSIDE AV	MCO	47 D4
RIVERSIDE AV	RCO	103 C5
RIVERSIDE AV	SBD	99 B1
RIVERSIDE AV	SHA	18 C3
RIVERSIDE AV	TEH	18 D5
RIVERSIDE BLVD	SCTO	137 B4
RIVERSIDE BLVD	SAC	39 D1
RIVERSIDE DR	LA	179 B5
RIVERSIDE DR	LA	182 D3
RIVERSIDE DR	LACO	Q C3
RIVERSIDE DR	LACO	Q A3
RIVERSIDE DR	RED	122 A1
RIVERSIDE DR	RCO	99 B4
RIVERSIDE DR	SBD	98 D2
RIVERSIDE DR	SDCO	V D3
RIVERSIDE DR	SDCO	106 E5
RIVERSIDE DR	SHA	18 C2
RIVERSIDE DR	SON	132 B3
RIVERSIDE DR	STA	47 D2
RIVERSIDE FRWY	ANA	194 C1
RIVERSIDE FRWY	ORA	98 C3
RIVERSIDE FRWY	ORA	T E1
RIVERSIDE FRWY	RCO	99 A3
RIVERSIDE RD	HUM	10 A5
RIVERSIDE RD	INY	51 D4
RIVERSIDE RD	SBD	92 C1
RIVERSIDE ST	KER	78 A2
RIVERSIDE PK RD	HUM	16 A3
RIVER SPRINGS	MNO	44 B5
RIVERVIEW DR	SHA	12 C5
RIVER VIEW RD	SBD	91 C1
RIVERVIEW RD	TRI	17 B2
RIVER WAY DR	TUL	68 B1
RIVIERA	RED	122 A5
RIVIERA DR	SD	212 B2
RIVIERA DR	SDCO	V A3
RIVIERA DR	SHA	18 C2
RIVIERA RD	SUT	33 C1
ROAD 1	LAS	20 B1
ROAD 1	MAD	56 B1
ROAD 4	LAS	20 B1
ROAD 4	MAD	56 C1
ROAD 5	MAD	56 C1
ROAD 5 1/2	MAD	56 C2
ROAD 6	MAD	56 C1
ROAD 7	MAD	56 C1
ROAD 8	MAD	56 C1
ROAD 8 1/2	MAD	56 C3
ROAD 9	LAS	20 B1
ROAD 9	MAD	56 C1
ROAD 10	MAD	56 D1
ROAD 10 1/2	MAD	56 D2
ROAD 11	MAD	56 D1
ROAD 12	MAD	56 D1
ROAD 12	TUL	57 E5
ROAD 13	MAD	56 D1
ROAD 14	MAD	56 D1
ROAD 14 1/2	MAD	56 D1
ROAD 15	MAD	56 D1
ROAD 15 1/2	MAD	56 D1
ROAD 16	MAD	56 D2
ROAD 16	TUL	57 E5
ROAD 16 1/2	MAD	56 D2
ROAD 17	MAD	56 D2
ROAD 18	MAD	56 E1
ROAD 18 1/2	MAD	56 E1
ROAD 19	MAD	56 E1
ROAD 19 1/2	MAD	56 E2
ROAD 20	MAD	56 E2
ROAD 20 1/2	MAD	56 E2
ROAD 21	MAD	56 E2
ROAD 21 1/2	MAD	56 E2
ROAD 22	MAD	48 E5
ROAD 22 1/2	MAD	48 E5
ROAD 23	MAD	48 E5
ROAD 23 1/2	MAD	56 E1
ROAD 24	MAD	56 E1
ROAD 24	TUL	57 E5
ROAD 24	TUL	67 E2
ROAD 24 1/2	MAD	56 E2
ROAD 24 1/2	MAD	57 A2

STREET	CO.	PAGE & GRID
ROAD 25	LAS	20 B1
ROAD 25	MAD	57 A2
ROAD 26	MAD	57 A2
ROAD 26 1/2	MAD	57 A2
ROAD 27	MAD	57 A1
ROAD 28	MAD	57 A2
ROAD 28	TUL	57 E5
ROAD 28	TUL	67 E2
ROAD 28 1/2	MAD	57 A2
ROAD 29	MAD	49 B5
ROAD 29 1/2	MAD	57 B2
ROAD 30	MAD	57 B2
ROAD 30 1/2	MAD	57 B2
ROAD 31	MAD	57 B3
ROAD 31 1/2	MAD	57 B2
ROAD 32	MAD	57 B2
ROAD 32	TUL	57 E5
ROAD 33	MAD	57 B2
ROAD 33 1/2	MAD	57 B2
ROAD 34	MAD	57 B3
ROAD 34	TUL	67 E4
ROAD 34	TUL	68 A4
ROAD 34 1/2	MAD	57 B2
ROAD 35	MAD	57 B2
ROAD 36	MAD	57 B2
ROAD 36	TUL	57 E5
ROAD 37	MAD	57 B2
ROAD 37 1/2	MAD	57 C2
ROAD 38	MAD	57 C2
ROAD 38	TUL	67 E4
ROAD 39	MAD	57 C2
ROAD 39 1/2	MAD	57 C2
ROAD 40	MAD	57 C2
ROAD 40	TUL	57 E5
ROAD 40 1/2	MAD	57 C2
ROAD 42	TUL	57 E4
ROAD 44	TUL	57 E5
ROAD 46	TUL	68 A4
ROAD 48	TUL	57 E4
ROAD 48	TUL	68 A4
ROAD 50	TUL	68 A4
ROAD 52	TUL	58 A4
ROAD 52	TUL	68 A1
ROAD 56	TUL	58 A5
ROAD 56	TUL	68 A1
ROAD 60	TUL	58 A5
ROAD 60	TUL	68 A1
ROAD 64	TUL	58 A4
ROAD 64	TUL	68 A1
ROAD 68	TUL	58 A5
ROAD 68	TUL	68 A1
ROAD 72	TUL	58 A4
ROAD 74	TUL	58 A5
ROAD 76	TUL	58 A5
ROAD 76	TUL	68 A1
ROAD 78	TUL	58 A4
ROAD 80	TUL	58 A5
ROAD 80	TUL	68 A2
ROAD 84	TUL	58 A5
ROAD 84	TUL	68 A1
ROAD 88	TUL	58 A5
ROAD 88	TUL	68 A3
ROAD 92	TUL	68 A2
ROAD 96	TUL	58 A4
ROAD 100	TUL	58 B5
ROAD 100	TUL	68 B1
ROAD 104	TUL	58 B5
ROAD 108	TUL	68 B1
ROAD 109	TUL	58 B4
ROAD 110	MEN	31 B3
ROAD 112	TUL	58 B5
ROAD 114	TUL	58 B4
ROAD 116	TUL	58 B5
ROAD 120	TUL	58 B5
ROAD 124	TUL	58 B4
ROAD 124	TUL	68 B2
ROAD 128	TUL	58 B4
ROAD 128	TUL	68 B3
ROAD 132	TUL	58 B4
ROAD 132	TUL	68 B1
ROAD 136	TUL	58 B4
ROAD 136	TUL	68 B3
ROAD 138	TUL	68 B1
ROAD 140	TUL	58 B4
ROAD 140	TUL	68 B1
ROAD 143	TUL	58 B4
ROAD 144	TUL	58 B5
ROAD 148	TUL	58 B5
ROAD 148	TUL	68 B1
ROAD 152	TUL	58 B4
ROAD 152	TUL	68 B1
ROAD 156	TUL	58 B5
ROAD 156	TUL	68 B1
ROAD 158	TUL	68 B1
ROAD 164	TUL	68 C1
ROAD 166	TUL	68 C1
ROAD 168	TUL	68 C1
ROAD 172	TUL	68 C2
ROAD 176	TUL	68 C3
ROAD 180	TUL	58 C5
ROAD 180	TUL	68 C1
ROAD 182	TUL	58 C5
ROAD 182	TUL	68 C1
ROAD 184	TUL	58 C5
ROAD 188	TUL	68 C3
ROAD 190	TUL	68 C1
ROAD 192	TUL	68 C1
ROAD 194	TUL	58 C5
ROAD 196	TUL	58 C5
ROAD 196	TUL	68 C1
ROAD 197	TUL	58 C5
ROAD 200	TUL	58 C5
ROAD 200	TUL	68 C1
ROAD 202	TUL	68 C3
ROAD 204	MAD	57 C2
ROAD 204	TUL	58 C5
ROAD 205	MAD	57 C2
ROAD 206	TUL	58 C5
ROAD 208	TUL	58 C5
ROAD 208	TUL	68 C1
ROAD 209	MAD	57 C1
ROAD 210	TUL	68 C1
ROAD 212	TUL	58 C5
ROAD 212	TUL	68 D1
ROAD 216	MAD	57 D1
ROAD 216	TUL	68 C2
ROAD 220	TUL	58 D5
ROAD 220	TUL	68 D1
ROAD 222	TUL	68 D1
ROAD 224	TUL	68 D4
ROAD 228	TUL	68 D1
ROAD 232	TUL	68 D2
ROAD 235	MAD	50 A5
ROAD 236	TUL	68 D1
ROAD 240	TUL	68 D4
ROAD 244	TUL	68 D1
ROAD 248	TUL	68 D1
ROAD 252	TUL	68 D2
ROAD 256	TUL	68 D3
ROAD 260	TUL	68 D2
ROAD 264	TUL	68 D3

STREET	CO.	PAGE & GRID
ROAD 266	TUL	68 D4
ROAD 268	TUL	68 D3
ROAD 272	TUL	68 D4
ROAD 276	TUL	68 D2
ROAD 296	TUL	68 E3
ROAD 320	TUL	68 E3
ROAD 406	MAD	57 C1
ROAD 434	MAD	49 D4
ROAD 601	MAD	49 D4
ROAD 602	MAD	57 B1
ROAD 612	MAD	49 C5
ROAD 810	MAD	49 C4
ROAD 812	MAD	49 C4
ROAN RD	CAL	41 B4
ROBB RD	RCO	99 B4
ROBBEN RD	SOL	39 B3
ROBBEN RD	SOL	39 B2
ROBBINS RD	SUT	33 B3
ROBBINS RNCH RD	NEV	26 D5
ROBBY RD	KER	79 B4
ROBERTA AV	LAKE	7 C1
ROBRTNO RIGHETI	SLO	76 B4
ROBERTS LN	KER	78 D2
ROBERTS RD	SJCO	40 A5
ROBERTS RD	SJCO	47 A1
ROBERTS RD	SON	38 A3
ROBERTS FRRY RD	STA	48 B2
ROBERTSON BLVD	BH	183 D2
ROBERTSON BLVD	CUL	183 D5
ROBERTSON BLVD	LA	183 D4
ROBERTSON BLVD	LACO	Q B4
ROBERTSON BLVD	LACO	183 D2
ROBERTSON BLVD	MAD	56 D1
ROBERTS RES RD	MOD	14 B3
ROBINSON	SJCO	47 C1
ROBIN AV	MCO	47 E4
ROBIN AV	MCO	48 A4
ROBINHOOD DR	S	160 A1
ROBINSON RD	IMP	109 A5
ROBINSON RD	MCO	48 C3
ROBINSON RD	SOL	39 B3
ROBINSON CYN RD	MON	54 B5
ROBINSON CK RD	MEN	31 A2
ROBINSN MILL RD	BUT	25 E5
ROBNSN RCHRIA W	LAK	31 D2
ROBLAR AV	SB	86 E3
ROBLAR RD	SON	37 D3
ROBLEY POINT RD	BUT	25 D2
ROBS RD	MOD	8 B3
ROCA LN	SBD	90 E2
ROCK CANYON RD	LAS	14 A3
ROCK CANYON RD	RCO	107 C1
ROCK CREEK DR	BUT	25 B2
ROCK CREEK RD	CAL	40 E4
ROCK CREEK RD	CAL	41 A4
ROCK CREEK RD	ED	34 E4
ROCK CREEK RD	INY	51 A3
ROCK CREEK RD	MNO	51 A3
ROCK CREEK RD	NEV	34 C1
ROCK CREEK RD	SHA	18 B2
ROCK CREEK RD	SHA	19 B3
ROCK CK GRBG PT	MNO	51 B3
ROCKERFELLER RD	BUT	25 E3
ROCKHAVEN	SBD	101 A2
ROCKING CHR RD	SBD	101 A2
ROE RD	BUT	25 C3
ROCKLIN	PLA	34 B4
ROCK PILE RD	KER	79 A4
ROCKPILE RD	SON	31 B4
ROCKRIDGE RD	RCO	100 A5
ROCK RIVER RD	STA	48 B1
ROCK RIVER RD	TUO	48 B1
ROCK SPRINGS RD	SBD	91 C4
ROCKVILLE	SOL	38 D3
ROCKWOOD RD	IMP	112 A4
ROCKY CT	KER	79 D5
ROCKY LN	KER	79 D3
ROCKY RD	RCO	99 B5
ROCKY BAR RD	ED	41 A1
ROCKY BLUFF RD	RCO	99 B4
ROCKY CANYON RD	SLO	76 B2
ROCKYDALE RD	JOS	2 C1
ROCKY PT CMPGRD	PLU	20 B5
RODDEN RD	STA	47 E1
RODEO AV	TEH	24 D1
RODEO BLVD	LACO	Q B4
RODEO RD	LA	184 A5
RODEO RD	SBD	91 C2
RODEO GULCH RD	SCR	54 A2
RODUNER RD	MCO	48 B5
ROEDING RD	STA	47 D3
ROEN RD	STA	48 A2
ROGERS RD	KER	80 B3
ROGERS RD	STA	47 B3
ROGERS CREEK RD	SIS	10 E1
ROHNERVILLE RD	HUM	15 E2
ROLAND DR	SIS	4 C5
ROLINDA AV	FRCO	57 B5
ROLLING HLLS RD	LACO	S B2
ROLLINS RD	MLBR	144 E5
ROLLINS LAKE RD	PLA	34 D2
ROMEL ST	CAL	41 A4
ROMERO	MCO	55 C1
ROMERO RD	MCO	47 C5
ROMERO CYN RD	SB	87 D4
ROMERS DAIRY RD	MEN	31 B2
ROMIE LN E	SAL	171 C5
RONNIE AV	KER	79 B5
ROOP RD	SCL	54 D1
ROOSEVELT RD	MCO	48 C5
ROOST AV	KER	79 B4
ROOT AV	KER	78 B1
ROOT RD	RCO	99 E5
ROOT RD	STA	47 D2
ROSA RD	MCO	47 D4
ROSAMOND BLVD	KER	89 D1
ROSAMOND BLVD	KER	90 B1
ROSAMND HLLS RD	RCO	107 C1
ROSAMUND BLVD	KER	80 C5
ROSARITA DR	SAL	171 D2
ROSCOE BLVD	LACO	97 C1
ROSCOE RD	HUM	15 E4
ROSCOE RD	STA	47 E2
ROSE AV	FRCO	56 E4
ROSE AV	FRCO	57 C4
ROSE AV	LA	187 A2
ROSE AV	MCO	47 E4
ROSE AV	MCO	48 B4
ROSE AV	MDO	162 E2
ROSE AV	VEN	88 B5
ROSE AV	VEN	96 B1
ROSE DR	ORA	T D1
ROSE RD	KER	79 E2
ROSE RD	KER	80 A2
ROSE RD	SIS	5 D2
ROSE RD	TRI	17 B1
ROSE RD	YOL	39 D2
ROSE ST	SDCO	106 D3
ROSEBURG AV	MDO	162 B2
ROSECRANS	LACO	97 D3
ROSECRANS AV	ELS	189 B5

STREETS

STREET	CO.	PAGE & GRID
ROSECRANS AV	MB	189 B5
ROSECRANS AV	ORA	98 B3
ROSECRANS AV	ORA	T C1
ROSECRANS BLVD	SDCO	111 C1
ROSECRANS ST	SDCO	V B4
ROSE GARDEN RD	MCO	47 C5
ROSEDALE HWY	KER	78 C3
ROSE HILLS RD	LACO	R B4
ROSE LAWN AV	MCO	47 E3
ROSELAWN AV	MDO	162 A5
ROSE LAWN AV	STA	47 E3
ROSELLE AV	STA	47 D2
ROSE MARIE LN	S	160 A2
ROSEMARY RD	SB	86 C1
ROSEMEAD BLVD	LACO	98 A2
ROSEMEAD BLVD	LACO	R C5
ROSE MINE RD	SBD	92 B5
ROSEMORE AV	STA	47 C2
ROSER RD	TEH	24 C2
ROSES RD	LACO	R A3
ROSE VALLEY RD	VEN	88 B3
ROSEWOOD AV	VEN	96 C1
ROSEWOOD BLVD	KER	80 B5
ROSINA AV	MDO	162 D3
ROSITA ST	LA	178 B5
ROSS AV	EC	217 A4
ROSS RD	IMP	111 E3
ROSS RD	IMP	112 D5
ROSSI ST	SAL	171 C3
ROSSMORE AV	LA	184 D2
ROSSMORE AV	LACO	Q B4
ROSY RIDGE RD	RCO	107 B1
ROUGH&READY RD	NEV	34 B1
ROULTS RD	MNO	51 B3
ROUND HOUSE RD	MAD	49 D4
ROUND MTN LKOUT	SIS	13 D1
ROUND MTN RD	KER	78 D2
ROUND MTN RD	MNO	51 B2
ROUND ROBIN DR	RCO	100 B4
ROUND VALLEY RD	SBD	100 B1
ROUND VALLEY RD	TEH	23 D2
ROUND VLY RD N	INY	51 B4
ROUND VLY RD S	INY	51 C4
RND VLY TUNGSTN	INY	51 C4
ROUNDY RD	TRI	11 D5
ROUNDY RD	TRI	17 D1
ROUSE AV	STA	162 A5
ROUSE RD	RCO	99 C4
RT OLYMPC TORCH	LAS	20 D2
ROUTE 4 FRWY	CC	154 D3
ROUTE 4 FRWY	M	154 D3
ROUTE 47 FRWY	LB	191 E2
ROUTE 47 FRWY	LB	192 A2
ROUTE 47 FRWY	LA	191 E2
ROUTE 47 FRWY	LA	192 A2
ROUTE 47 FRWY	LACO	97 E4
ROUTE 47 FRWY	LACO	S C2
ROUTE 52 FRWY	SD	211 E3
ROUTE 94 FRWY	SD	216 C3
ROUTE 101 FRWY	STB	173 D5
ROUTE 101 FRWY	SB	86 D4
ROUTE 101 FRWY	SB	87 D4
ROUTE 101 FRWY	SMA	173 C1
ROWDY CREEK RD	DN	1 E3
ROWENA AV	LA	182 D3
ROWLEE RD	KER	77 E2
ROWLEE RD	KER	78 A2
ROWLES RD	TEH	24 E2
ROXBURY DR	SIS	3 C4
ROXBURY RD	MCO	56 B1
ROXFORD ST	LACO	89 C5
ROXFORD ST	LACO	Q A1
ROYAL AV	VEN	88 E5
ROYAL AV	VEN	89 A5
ROYAL OAKS DR	LACO	R B3
ROY JONES RD	SIS	4 B3
ROYO RNCHERO DR	SUT	33 C2
RUBIDOUX BLVD	RCO	99 B2
RUBLE RD	STA	47 C3
RUCKER AV	SCL	54 D1
RUDD RD	KER	78 C3
RUDDICK	MEN	31 B2
RUDNICK RD	KER	80 C4
RUDOLPH DR	KER	79 C4
RUDOLPH RD	INY	51 D3
RUEGGER RD	IMP	109 A3
RUFF LN	GLE	24 E5
RUFFIN RD	SDCO	V C3
RUFFIN RD	SDCO	106 D5
RUGGED TRAIL RD	RCO	107 C1
RUMBLE RD	STA	47 C2
RUNGE RD	SOL	39 C2
RUSH ST	RCO	107 C1
RUSH CREEK DR	TRI	11 D5
RUSH CREEK RD	MNO	43 C5
RUSH CREEK RD	TRI	17 D1
RUSH CK SHORTCT	TRI	17 D1
RUSH CK CAMP RD	TRI	11 D5
RUSHNG HILL LKT	TUO	48 B1
RUSS LN	HUM	15 D2
RUSSEL AV	KER	79 A4
RUSSELL AV	FRCO	56 A3
RUSSELL BLVD	DVS	136 B3
RUSSELL BLVD	YOL	38 E1
RUSSELL BLVD	YOL	39 A1
RUSSELL RD	CAL	41 A3
RUSSELL RD	SAC	39 D3
RUSSELL RD	STA	47 B2
RUSSELL RD	TEH	18 C3
RUTH AV	BLMT	145 C4
RUTH DUMP RD	TRI	17 A4
RUTHERFORD	NAPA	29 D3
RUTHERFORD RD	IMP	109 A4
RUTH HILL RD	FRCO	58 C3
RUTH HILL RD	FRCO	58 B3
RUTH ZENIA RD	TRI	16 E4
RYAN AV	KER	80 A4
RYAN RD	LAS	21 B3
RYAN RD	SLO	76 C2
RYAN CREEK RD	MEN	23 A5
RYE CANYON RD	LACO	89 B4
RYE GRASS SWALE	MOD	8 A1
RYE GRASS SWALE	MOD	14 E1
RYER RD E	SOL	39 D3
S		
S ST	EUR	121 E2
SABINANA RD	YUB	33 E1
SABODAN ST	KER	78 D5
SACHREITER RD	COL	33 A2
SACRAMENTO AV	BUT	25 A3
SACRAMENTO AV	C	124 A4
SACRAMENTO AV	FRCO	56 D4
SACRAMENTO AV	SUT	33 D3
SACRAMENTO BLVD	SCTO	137 E5
SACRAMENTO DR	SHA	18 C2
SACRAMNTO FWY N	SCTO	137 D1
SACRAMENTO ST	AUB	126 C4
SACRAMENTO ST	PLA	34 D1
SACRAMENTO ST	PLCV	138 C3
SACRAMENTO ST	VAL	134 B2
SACRMNTO VLY RD	SUT	33 C3
SACRMNTO VLY BL	SUT	33 C4
SADDLE CT	KER	79 C5
SADDLEBACK RD	SIE	26 D4
SADDLEHORN RD	SBD	84 C3
SADDLE PEAK RD	LACO	97 B2
SADDLE TRAIL RD	SHA	18 B3
SADDLE VIEW CT	SHA	13 E4
SAGE AV	SBD	100 D1
SAGE RD	HUM	15 D2
SAGE RD	RCO	99 E4
SAGEBRUSH LN	SIS	4 E3
SAGE CANYON RD	KER	80 B1
SAGE FLATS DR	INY	70 B2
SAGE HEN RD	MNO	51 A2
SAGE HEN RD	NEV	27 D5
SAGE HEN MDW RD	MNO	43 E5
SAGE HEN MDWS	MNO	50 E1
SAGE HEN MDWS	MNO	51 A1
SAGEHORN RD	MOD	7 D3
SAGELAND CT	KER	79 B4
SAGE VALLEY RD	LAS	21 D5
SAGINAW AV	FRCO	57 E4
SAHARA AV	LV	209 A4
SAHARA AV E	CLK	74 D2
SAHARA AV W	CLK	74 C2
ST CATHERINE WY	AVLN	105 B4
ST FRANCIS AV	STA	47 C2
ST GEORGE ST	LA	182 D3
ST HELENA HWY	NAPA	29 D4
ST HELENA RD	SON	38 A1
ST JAMES ST	SJ	152 C3
ST JOHN RD	TRI	16 E2
ST JOHN LOOP RD	TRI	16 E2
ST LOUIS AV	KER	80 A4
ST LOUIS RD	HUM	10 A5
ST LOUIS RD	HUM	9 E5
ST LOUIS RD	PLU	26 C3
ST MARYS AV	TEH	18 D5
ST MARYS RD	CC	45 E1
SALE LN	TEH	18 D5
SALEM AV	KIN	67 E3
SALEM RD	SOL	39 B3
SALINAS RD	MON	54 C2
SALINAS ST	STB	174 E3
SALINE VLY ALT	INY	70 E1
SALINE VLY RD	INY	60 C3
SALINE VLY RD	INY	60 D5
SALMON CREEK RD	HUM	16 B4
SALMON FALLS RD	ED	34 C5
SALMON LAKE RD	SIE	26 E3
SALMON LAKE RD	SIE	27 A3
SALMON RIVER RD	SIS	10 E2
SALMON RIVER RD	SIS	11 A2
SALT RD N	SHA	12 C4
SALT CREEK RD	MCO	55 D2
SALT CREEK RD	SHA	12 D5
SALTDALE RD	KER	80 C3
SALTON DR	IMP	108 C2
SALTON RD	SBD	80 E5
SALTON RD	SBD	81 A5
SALTON BAY DR	IMP	108 C2
SALTON VIEW RD	RCO	101 B3
SALT POOL RD	INY	72 A1
SALT SPG VLY RD	CAL	40 E4
SALT SPG VLY RD	CAL	41 A4
SALTUS RD	SBD	93 E3
SALTUS RD	SBD	94 A3
SALVADORI RD	SIS	4 B5
SAM ALLEY RIDGE	LAK	31 D2
SAMEL DR	SBD	100 D2
SAMPLE RD	FRCO	57 E2
SAMPSON ST	SD	216 B5
SAMSON AV	TEH	18 D5
SAMSON AV	TEH	24 D2
SAN ANDREAS RD	SCR	54 B2
SAN ANDREAS RD	SBD	100 E2
SAN ANDREAS ST	STB	174 A3
SN ANTONE CP RD	CAL	41 B4
SAN ANTONIO AV	CAR	53 D5
SAN ANTONIO AV	ONT	204 A3
SAN ANTONIO AV	SBD	98 D1
SAN ANTONIO AV	UPL	204 A3
SN ANTONIO AV N	CAR	168 B4
SAN ANTONIO DR	LACO	S D2
SAN ANTONIO DR	LACO	T A1
SAN ANTONIO RD	MON	65 D5
SAN ANTONIO RD	SB	86 B2
SAN ANTONIO RD	SCL	45 E4
SAN ANTONIO ST	SJ	152 E3
SAN ANTONIO VLY	SCL	46 D4
SAN BENACIO RD	MON	54 C4
SAN BENITO AV	FRCO	56 D4
SAN BENITO AV	TEH	18 D5
SN BERNARDNO AV	FRCO	56 C3
SN BERNARDNO AV	SBD	98 D2
SN BERNARDNO FY	CLA	203 A3
SN BERNARDNO FY	LA	186 D3
SN BERNARDNO FY	LACO	98 B2
SN BERNARDNO FY	LACO	R B4
SN BERNARDNO FY	MTCL	203 A3
SN BERNARDNO FY	ONT	203 A3
SN BERNARDNO FY	ONT	204 B3
SN BERNARDNO FY	SBD	98 E2
SN BERNARDNO FY	UPL	204 B3
SN BERNARDNO RD	LACO	R C3
SN BERNARDNO RD	SBD	80 E1
SN BERNARDNO RD	UPL	204 C2
SN BERNARDNO ST	MTCL	203 B3
SN BERNARDNO ST	POM	203 C3
SN BERNARDNO CK	SLO	75 E3
SN BERNARDNO CK	SLO	76 A3
SANBORN RD	SUT	33 C2
SANBORN RD S	SAL	171 E5
SAN BRUNO AV	SBR	144 B3
SAN BRUNO AV	SMCO	45 B2
SAN CARLOS AV	SMCO	45 D3
SAN CARLOS RD	MCO	55 D2
SAN CARLOS ST	CAR	168 B4
SAN CARLOS ST	SJ	151 D5
SAN CARLOS ST	SJ	152 C4
SAN CARLOS ST	SCL	151 D5
SANCHES RD	MCO	47 C4
SANCHEZ RD	MON	54 E5
SAND CANYON AV	ORA	98 C4
SAND CANYON AV	ORA	T E4
SAND CANYON RD	INY	51 C4
SAND CANYON RD	KER	70 C5
SAND CANYON RD	KER	79 D4
SAND CANYON RD	LACO	89 C4
SAND CANYON RD	SBD	99 D2
SAND CREEK RD	COL	32 D3
SAND CREEK RD	FRCO	58 B4
SAND CREEK RD	TUL	58 B4
SAND CREST DR	IMP	108 C2
SANDERS RD	STA	47 C3
SANDERS RD	SUT	33 C2
SANDERSON AV	RCO	99 E4
SAND FLAT RD	SIS	12 D2
SAND FLAT CTOFF	MNO	50 E1
SAND HILL RD	SMCO	45 D4
SANDIA CREEK DR	SDCO	106 C1
SAN DIEGO AV	FRCO	56 C4
SAN DIEGO AV	SD	213 B5
SAN DIEGO FRWY	CUL	188 A1
SAN DIEGO FRWY	HAW	189 E3
SAN DIEGO FRWY	ING	188 D4
SAN DIEGO FRWY	IRV	198 E5
SAN DIEGO FRWY	LA	180 C2
SAN DIEGO FRWY	LA	188 D4
SAN DIEGO FRWY	LACO	97 C2
SAN DIEGO FRWY	LACO	S B1
SAN DIEGO FRWY	LACO	180 C2
SAN DIEGO FRWY	LACO	189 E3
SAN DIEGO FRWY	ORA	98 D4
SAN DIEGO FRWY	ORA	197 A3
SAN DIEGO FRWY	ORA	198 A4
SAN DIEGO FRWY	ORA	202 C4
SAN DIEGO FRWY	ORA	T B3
SAN DIEGO FRWY	SD	211 D1
SAN DIEGO FRWY	SD	212 E3
SAN DIEGO FRWY	SD	215 D3
SAN DIEGO FRWY	SD	216 A3
SAN DIEGO FRWY	SDCO	V B3
SAN DIEGO FRWY	SDCO	106 B3
SAN DIEGO FRWY	SDCO	111 D2
SAN DIEGO FRWY	SJC	202 C4
SAN DIEGO ST	KER	78 B2
SN DIEGO MSN RD	SD	214 D2
SAN DIMAS AV	LACO	U E3
SN DIMAS CYN RD	LACO	U E3
SANDMOUND BLVD	CC	39 D5
SAN DOMINGO RD	CAL	41 B4
SAND RIDGE RD	ED	34 E5
SAND RIDGE RD	ED	40 E1
SANDRINI RD	KER	78 D4
SANDROCK RD	SD	214 B1
SANDROCK RD	SDCO	V B3
SANDROCK RD	SDCO	106 D5
SAND SLOUGH RD	MCO	47 E5
SAND SLOUGH RD	MCO	48 A5
SANDY AV	KER	80 C1
SANDY DR	RCO	107 C1
SANDY RD	MON	66 B4
SANDY ST	KER	80 C1
SANDY HILLS RD	RCO	107 C1
SANDY MUSH RD	MCO	48 B5
SANDY PRAIRIE	HUM	15 E2
SAN FELIPE RD	SBT	54 E2
SAN FELIPE RD	SBT	55 A2
SAN FELIPE RD	SDCO	107 C2
SAN FELIPE RD	SCL	46 C4
SAN FERNANDO BL	BUR	179 C1
SAN FERNANDO BL	LA	179 C1
SAN FERNANDO RD	BUR	179 E2
SAN FERNANDO RD	GLEN	182 D1
SAN FERNANDO RD	LA	186 D1
SAN FERNANDO RD	LACO	89 B5
SAN FERNANDO RD	LACO	89 C5
SAN FERNANDO RD	LACO	97 E1
SAN FERNANDO RD	LACO	Q A1
SANFORD RD	SON	37 D2
SANFORD RCH RD	MEN	31 B2
SN FRANCSQT CYN	LACO	89 B4
SAN GABRIEL BL	LACO	98 A2
SAN GABRIEL BL	LACO	R A3
SAN GABRIEL FWY	LACO	98 A3
SAN GABRIEL FWY	LACO	S E1
SAN GABRIEL RD	LACO	R C3
SAN GABRIEL CYN	LACO	98 C1
SAN GABRIEL CYN	LACO	R C2
SN GABRL RV FWY	LACO	T A2
SN GABRL RV PKY	LACO	R A4
SAN GORGONIO AV	RCO	100 A3
SN GUILLERMO RD	VEN	88 B2
SANHEDRIN RD	GLE	24 A4
SAN IGNACIO RD	RCO	99 E5
SANITARIUM RD	NAPA	29 C2
SAN JACINTO RD	RCO	99 C4
SAN JACINTO ST	SBD	100 C2
SAN JACINTO RDG	RCO	100 A4
SAN JOAQUIN AV	FRCO	66 D3
SAN JOAQUIN AV	LAK	32 A3
SAN JOAQUIN RD	ORA	T E3
SAN JOAQUIN ST	S	160 D3
SN JQUIN HLS RD	NB	200 A4
SAN JOSE BLVD	MAR	38 A4
SAN JOSE RD	CLO	32 E2
SN JOSE AVNALES	SLO	76 D3
SN JOSE L PANZA	SLO	76 C3
SN JOSE-STA MAR	SLO	76 B3
SN JS ST MAR LK	SLO	76 C3
SN JS ST MAR MT	SLO	76 D3
SAN JUAN AV	SAC	34 A5
SAN JUAN HWY	SBT	54 D2
SAN JUAN RD	MCO	56 B1
SAN JUAN RD	MON	54 C2
SAN JUAN CYN RD	SBT	54 D3
SAN JUSTO RD	SBT	54 D3
SANKEY RD	SUT	33 D4
SAN LUCAS RD	MON	65 C3
SAN LUIS DR	SNLO	172 D3
SAN LUIS BAY DR	SLO	76 A4
SAN LUISITO CK	SLO	75 E3
SAN LUISITO CK	SLO	76 A3
SAN MARCOS RD	SLO	76 A1
SAN MARCOS RD	SB	87 B4
SN MARCOS PS RD	SB	87 B3
SAN MARTIN AV	SCL	54 D1
SN MARTNZ CHQT	LACO	89 A4
SN MARTNZ GD CN	LACO	89 A4
SAN MATEO AV	FRCO	56 D5
SAN MATEO AV	SBR	144 B1
SAN MATEO AV	SSF	144 B1
SAN MATEO RD	SDCO	105 E1
SAN MATEO ST	SBD	99 C2
SAN MIGUEL	CC	45 E1
SAN MIGUEL AV	SAL	171 C5
SAN MIGUEL DR	NB	200 C5
SN MGUEL CYN RD	MON	54 C3
SN MIGUELITO RD	SB	86 B3
SAN PABLO AV	ALA	45 D1
SAN PABLO AV	CC	38 C5
SAN PABLO AV	ELC	155 E4
SAN PABLO AV	O	157 E2
SAN PABLO AV	R	155 D2
SAN PABLO AV	SP	155 B1
SN PABLO DAM RD	CC	38 C5
SN PABLO DAM RD	SP	155 C1
SAN PASQUAL RD	SDCO	106 D3
SAN PASQUAL RD	SB	86 B3
SAN PASQUAL VLY	SDCO	106 E3
SAN PEDRO AV	SBD	84 C3
SAN PEDRO RD N	MAR	38 B5
SAN PEDRO RD N	MAR	139 C2
SAN PEDRO RD N	SR	139 C2
SAN PEDRO ST	LA	185 E5
SAN PEDRO ST	LA	186 A4
SAN PEDRO ST	LACO	S C1
SAN RAFAEL AV	PAS	190 A4
SAN RAFAEL DR	RCO	100 C3
SN RAMON VLY BL	CC	46 A2
SANS BAKER RD	FRCO	58 C3
SN SIMEON CK RD	SLO	75 C1
SANTA ANA AV	CM	199 C3
SANTA ANA AV	NB	199 C3
SANTA ANA AV	ORA	T C4
SANTA ANA AV	ORA	199 E1
SANTA ANA AV	SBD	99 A2
SANTA ANA BLVD	SA	196 A4
SANTA ANA FRWY	ANA	193 D4
SANTA ANA FRWY	LA	186 D3
SANTA ANA FRWY	LACO	98 A2
SANTA ANA FRWY	LACO	T B1
SANTA ANA FRWY	ORA	98 A2
SANTA ANA FRWY	ORA	T B1
SANTA ANA FRWY	SA	196 B2
SANTA ANA RD	VEN	88 A5
SANTA ANA ST	ANA	193 B2
STA ANA CYN RD	ORA	98 C3
STA ANA CYN RD	ORA	T E2
STA ANA VLY RD	SBT	55 A3
SANTA ANITA AV	LACO	98 B2
SANTA ANITA AV	LACO	R B2
SANTA ANITA AV	LACO	R A4
SANTA ANITA RD	SBT	55 B3
STA BARBARA ST	SDCO	111 C1
STA BARBARA ST	STB	174 B2
STA BARBARA CYN	SB	87 D1
STA BARBARA ST	SDCO	V A3
SANTA CLARA	A	159 A1
SANTA CLARA AV	O	158 B2
SANTA CLARA AV	SA	195 E2
SANTA CLARA AV	SA	196 A2
SANTA CLARA AV	VEN	88 B5
SANTA CLARA ST	SJ	152 C3
SANTA CLARA ST	SCL	46 B4
SANTA CLARA ST	VAL	134 B4
SANTA CLARA WY	SM	145 C3
STA CRZ GUN CLB	MCO	55 E2
STA CRZ GUN CLB	MCO	56 A2
SANTA FE	MCO	48 C4
SANTA FE AV	KIN	67 E3
SANTA FE AV	LB	192 B2
SANTA FE AV	LA	186 C5
SANTA FE AV	LACO	R D4
SANTA FE AV	LACO	S D2
SANTA FE AV	MCO	48 D5
SANTA FE AV	SBD	81 B5
SANTA FE AV	SDCO	106 C2
SANTA FE AV	SJCO	47 D1
SANTA FE AV	STA	47 D2
SANTA FE BLVD	MAD	57 B2
SANTA FE DR	MCO	48 A3
SANTA FE DR	SDCO	106 C4
SANTA FE GRADE	FRCO	56 C3
SANTA FE GRADE	MCO	47 D4
SANTA FE RD	SBD	92 B4
SANTA FE ST	SBD	92 A1
SANTA FE WY	KER	78 B2
STA FE FIRE RD	SBD	91 A5
STA FE SPGS RD	LACO	R A5
SANTA INEZ AV	SMCO	45 C3
SANTA ISABEL	CM	199 D1
SANTA LUCIA	SBR	144 B4
SANTA LUCIA AV	CAR	168 B4
SANTA LUCIA AV	MCO	55 D1
SANTA LUCIA RD	SLO	76 A2
SANTA MARIA WY	SB	86 C1
STA MAR MESA RD	SB	86 C1
SANTA MONICA BL	BH	183 A2
SANTA MONICA BL	LA	180 C3
SANTA MONICA BL	LA	181 C5
SANTA MONICA BL	LA	182 A5
SANTA MONICA BL	LA	183 A2
SANTA MONICA BL	LACO	97 D2
SANTA MONICA BL	LACO	181 C5
SANTA MONICA BL	LACO	183 A2
SANTA MONICA BL	SMON	180 C3
SANTA MONICA FY	LA	184 A4
SANTA MONICA FY	LA	185 A4
SANTA MONICA FY	LA	186 A4
SANTA MONICA FY	LACO	97 C2
SANTA MONICA FY	LACO	Q A4
SANTA MONICA FY	SMON	180 B5
SANTA PAULA FWY	VEN	88 B5
SANTA PAULA ST	VEN	88 C5
STA RITA GRADE	MCO	56 B1
SANTA RITA RD	ALA	46 B2
STA RITA OLD CK	SLO	75 E2
SANTA ROSA AV	MDO	162 D4
SANTA ROSA AV	SON	37 E2
SANTA ROSA AV	STR	131 D4
SANTA ROSA RD	INY	60 D5
SANTA ROSA RD	RCO	99 B4
SANTA ROSA RD	SBD	91 D4
SANTA ROSA RD	SB	86 C3
SANTA ROSA RD	VEN	88 D5
SANTA ROSA ST	SNLO	172 C2
STA ROSA CK RD	SLO	75 C2
STA ROSA MTN TK	RCO	100 D5
SANTA TERESA BL	SCL	46 B5
SANTA TERESA BL	SCL	54 D2
SANTA YSABEL RD	SLO	75 E3
SANTIAGO BLVD	OR	194 E2
SANTIAGO BLVD	ORA	98 C3
SANTIAGO BLVD	ORA	T E2
SANTIAGO CYN RD	ORA	98 D3
SANTIAGO CYN RD	ORA	T E2
SAN TIMOTEO CYN	SBD	99 D2
SAN TIMOTEO CYN	RCO	99 D2
SAN TOMAS EXPWY	SJ	150 E5
SAN TOMAS EXPWY	SCLR	150 E2
SAN TOMAS EXPWY	SCLR	151 A1
SAN TOMAS EXPWY	SCL	46 A5
SANTOS AV	SJCO	47 C1
SANTOS RD	SB	86 D3
SANTOS ST	SB	86 B1
SAN VICENTE BL	LA	180 A3
SAN VICENTE BL	LA	183 E2
SAN VICENTE BL	LA	184 B3
SAN VICENTE BL	LACO	97 C2
SAN VICENTE BL	LACO	Q B4
SAN VICENTE RD	MON	55 A5
SAN VICENTE RD	MON	65 A1
SAN VICENTE RD	SDCO	107 A4
SAN VINCENTE AV	SAL	171 B4
SAPAQUE RD	MON	65 C5
SARATOGA AV	KER	80 E1
SARATOGA AV	SJ	150 E5
SARATOGA AV	SCLR	150 E5
SARATOGA AV	SCLR	151 A4
SARATOGA AV	SCL	45 E5
SARTGA-LS GATOS	SCL	45 E5
SARATOGA SPGS	LAK	31 C2
SARATOGA SPG RD	SBD	72 D5
SARATOGA SPG RD	SBD	82 D1
SARATOGA-SVL RD	SCL	45 E5
SARATOGA-SVL RD	SVL	149 D2
SARBO RD	MCO	55 D1
SARDINE LAKE RD	SIE	27 A4
SARGENT RD	SJCO	40 A4
SARGENTS RD	MON	65 E4
SARGENTS RD	MON	66 A4
SARIDA AV	KER	79 C4
SARINA RD	DN	1 D3
SARON FRUIT COL	TEH	18 D4
SASIA RD	KER	79 B4
SATICOY AV	VEN	88 B5
SATICOY ST	LA	177 A1
SATICOY ST	LA	178 C1
SAUGUS VNTRA RD	LACO	89 A4
SAVANA	MCO	48 D5
SAVIERS RD	OXN	176 C5
SAWMILL	INY	51 C4
SAW MILL RD	ALP	36 B5
SAWMILL RD	BUT	25 C3
SAWMILL RD	KER	69 C5
SAWMILL RD	KER	79 C1
SAWMILL RD	MNO	50 E2
SAW MILL CREEK	SBT	66 B1
SAWMILL CRSSOVR	MNO	51 B1
SAWMILL CUTOFF	MNO	50 D2
SAWMILL FLAT RD	TUO	41 C4
SAWMILL MDWS RD	MNO	51 B1
SAWTELLE AV	SUT	33 C3
SAWTELLE BLVD	CUL	188 A1
SAWTELLE BLVD	LA	180 C3
SAWTELLE BLVD	LA	188 B2
SAWTOOTH PEAK	KER	80 C1
SAWYER AV	STA	47 D1
SAWYERS BAR RD	SIS	11 C1
SAYLOR RD	STA	47 E3
SAYRE ST	LACO	Q A1
SCALA LN	SIS	4 B4
SCALES RD	YUB	26 C4
SCANDIA RD	SOL	39 A3
SCARFACE RD	SIS	3 E5
SCARFACE RD	SIS	4 A5
SCARLT BUGLE RD	RCO	100 C5
SCARONI AV	KER	78 B2
SCENIC DR	STA	47 D2
SCENIC DR	MDO	162 D3
SCENIC RD	CAR	168 B4
SCHAAD RD	COL	32 D2
SCHADD RD	CAL	41 C2
SCHAEFER AV	SBD	98 E2
SCHAEFFER RD	SB	87 D1
SCHAFER AV	TEH	18 E5
SCHAGLE RD	SUT	33 C3
SCHALLOCK RD	KER	78 C5
SCHARTZ RD	IMP	109 B4
SCHATZ RD	KER	79 C4
SCHEAFER	MPA	49 B3
SCHEIBER RD	SUT	33 D3
SCHELL RD	IMP	112 C3
SCHILLING	MPA	48 E2
SCHILLING AV	FRCO	67 B1
SCHLAG RD	SUT	33 C2
SCHLEISMAN RD	RCO	98 E2
SCHMIDT DR	RCO	107 A1
SCHMIDT RD	MCO	47 C5
SCHOBER LN	INY	51 D4
SCHOOL RD	IMP	112 D5
SCHOOL RD	MNO	50 E2
SCHOOL RD	MNO	51 A2
SCHOOL ST	HUM	15 E2
SCHOOL ST	MEN	30 C3
SCHOOL ST	U	123 C2
SCHOOLER RD	SBD	101 D1
SCHOOL HOUSE RD	LAS	8 C5
SCHOOL HOUSE RD	MPA	49 A4
SCHLHOUSE HL RD	SIS	4 D3
SCHOTT RD	BUT	25 C2
SCHOTT RD	LAS	14 B3
SCHROEDER AV	SUT	33 C1
SCHROEDER MINE	SIS	3 E4
SCHUETTE RD	LAK	31 C2
SCHULMEYER RD	SIS	4 A4
SCHULTE RD	SJCO	46 E2
SCHULTZ RD	KER	80 D5
SCHUSTER RD	KER	68 B5
SCIARONE RD	ED	35 B5
SCOFIELD AV	KER	78 A1
SCOTT AV	LACO	R B5
SCOTT BLVD	SCLR	151 A2
SCOTT RD	CAL	41 C3
SCOTT RD	LAS	27 E2
SCOTT RD	MPA	49 C3
SCOTT RD	RCO	99 C4
SCOTT RD	SAC	40 C1
SCOTT RD	SIS	5 D2
SCOTT BAR RD	SIS	3 D4
SCOTT CREEK RD	ALA	46 B3
SCOTT DAM RD	LAK	23 C5
SCOTT FORBES RD	YUB	34 A1
SCOTT LUMBER RD	SHA	19 C1
SCOTT MTN RD	SIS	11 E2
SCOTT RIVER RD	SIS	3 B4
SCOTTS CREEK RD	LAK	31 C3
SCOTTS FLAT RD	NEV	34 D1
SCOTTS VLY RD	LAK	31 C2
SCOTTS VLY RD	SCR	54 A1
SCOTT VALLEY RD	SIS	3 D5
SCOTT VALLEY RD	SIS	11 D1
SCOTT VLY AIRPT	SIS	3 D5
SCOUT RD	BUT	19 D5
SCOUT ST	SHA	18 B3
SCOVELL AV	RCO	99 E4
SCRANTON AV	TUL	68 D3
SEAL BEACH BLVD	ORA	98 A4
SEAL BEACH BLVD	ORA	T A3
SEARLES STA RD	KER	80 E2
SEARLES STA RD	SBD	80 E2
SEARLES STA CTO	SBD	80 E2
SEARS RD	LAS	21 B4
SEARS POINT RD	SOL	38 C4
SEARS POINT RD	SOL	134 B2
SEARS POINT RD	VAL	134 B2
SEASIDE AV	LA	191 D3
SEASIDE BLVD	LACO	S C3
SEATTLE AV	KIN	67 D3
SEA VIEW DR	IMP	108 C2
SEAVIEW RD	SON	37 A1
SEAVW QUARRY RD	SON	37 B1
SEAWARD AV	VENT	175 D3
SEBASTIAN RD	KER	78 E5
SEBASTIAN RD	KER	79 A5
SEBASTOPOL AV	STR	131 C4
SEBASTOPOL FRWY	STR	131 B4
SEBASTOPOL FRWY	SON	131 B4
SEBASTOPOL RD	SON	131 B4
SECO ST	PAS	190 A3
SECOND ST	C	124 B5
SECRETARIAT RD	KER	79 B4
SECRET SPGS RD	SIS	4 E3
SECTION OLD RED	PLU	19 E3
SEE CANYON RD	SLO	75 E4
SEE CANYON RD	SLO	76 A4
SEE VEE LN	INY	51 D4
SEIAD CREEK	SIS	3 B3
SEIAD OAKS RD	SIS	3 B3
SEIDNER	SJCO	47 D1
SEIGLER CYN RD	LAK	32 A4
SEIGLER SPGS RD	LAK	31 E4

STREETS

STREET	CO.	PAGE & GRID	
SELLERS AV	CC	39	C5
SELMADOLPH ST	SBD	91	E3
SELVA RD	ORA	202	A4
SEMINARY AV	ALA	45	D1
SEMINARY AV	O	159	E1
SEMINARY DR	MAR	140	C4
SEMINARY DR	MV	140	C4
SENATOR WASH RD	IMP	110	E5
SENECA RD	PLU	20	B5
SENECA RD	SBD	91	B4
SENECA RD	SBD	91	B4
SENILIS AV	SBD	100	C2
SENTER RD	SJ	152	E5
SENTER RD	SCL	46	B4
SEPULVEDA BLVD	CUL	188	A1
SEPULVEDA BLVD	ELS	189	C3
SEPULVEDA BLVD	LA	180	A5
SEPULVEDA BLVD	LA	183	A5
SEPULVEDA BLVD	LA	188	C4
SEPULVEDA BLVD	LA	189	C3
SEPULVEDA BLVD	LACO	97	C1
SEPULVEDA BLVD	LACO	Q	A2
SEPULVEDA BLVD	LACO	S	B2
SEPULVEDA BLVD	LACO	180	B2
SEPULVEDA BLVD	MB	189	C3
SEQUOIA BLVD	KER	80	B4
SEQUOIA RD	FRCO	58	D3
SEQUOIA RD	HUM	16	C4
SERENADE DR	SBD	80	E1
SERENE DR	SHA	18	B2
SEREND DR	VAL	134	C2
SERFAS CLUB DR	RCO	98	E3
SERPA LN	SIS	3	D5
SERPA LN	SOL	39	B2
SERRANO RD	VEN	96	C2
SERVICE RD	SIE	26	C4
SERVICE RD	STA	47	C3
SESPE RD	VEN	88	B3
SESPE RIVER RD	VEN	88	B3
SEVEN MILE LN	BUT	25	A4
SEVEN MI SLOUGH	HUM	15	D2
SEVEN OAK RD	SBD	100	A1
SEVERE RD	IMP	110	C4
SEWARD DR	HUM	16	C4
SEXTON	SJCO	47	C1
SEYMOUR RD	SUT	33	B4
SEYMOUR CK RD	VEN	88	C2
SHABELL LN	INY	59	E3
SHACKELFORD RD	STA	47	B2
SHADOW CYN RD	SLO	75	E2
SHADOW MTN RD	SBD	83	D2
SHADOW MTN RD	SBD	90	E2
SHADOW MTN RD	SBD	91	A2
SHADOW MTN RD	SBD	101	D1
SHADY LN	SR	139	A4
SHADY DELL RD	SIS	5	A3
SHAFFER RD	MCO	48	B3
SHAFFER ST	OR	194	D3
SHAFTER AV	KER	78	B2
SHAFTER ST	KER	78	C4
SHAIN AV	FRCO	56	B2
SHAIN RD	FRCO	56	B2
SHAKELEY LN	AMA	40	D2
SHAKE RIDGE RD	AMA	40	E2
SHAKE RIDGE RD	AMA	41	A2
SHALE RD	KER	77	E4
SHAMROCK RD	SIS	4	A4
SHANDON CEM RD	SLO	76	D1
SHANDON-SN JUAN	SLO	76	D1
SHANK RD	IMP	109	A5
SHANNON DR	SBD	101	D1
SHANNONDALE RD	LACO	89	E4
SHANNON VLY RD	LACO	89	E4
SHARON RD	MCO	55	E2
SHARON RD	YOL	136	A1
SHARPE RD	SON	38	A1
SHARP PARK RD	SMCO	45	B2
SHASTA AV	FRCO	56	E3
SHASTA AV	FRCO	56	E3
SHASTA BLVD	TEH	18	E5
SHASTA BLVD	TEH	24	E1
SHASTA WY	VAL	134	D4
SHASTA WY	C	124	B4
SHASTA WY	KLAM	5	C1
SHASTA CO RD	MOD	13	B3
SHA DAM ACCS RD	SHA	18	B1
SHA SPG MCCLOUD	SIS	12	D2
SHASTA VIEW DR	MOD	14	E1
SHASTA VIEW DR	SHA	18	C2
SHASTA VISTA RD	SIS	4	C5
SHATTUCK AV	B	156	A4
SHATTUCK AV	O	156	A4
SHAVES AV	SBD	91	C1
SHAW AV	FRCO	57	A3
SHAWMUT RD	TUO	41	C5
SHAWMUT RD	TUO	48	C1
SHAW PIT RD	MOD	14	B2
SHAWS FLAT RD	SNRA	163	A2
SHAWS FLAT RD	TUO	163	A2
SHAWS FLAT RD	TUO	41	C5
SHAWS FT JMSTWN	TUO	41	C5
SHAY CREEK RD	ALP	36	B5
SHEE CAMP RD	MNO	51	B2
SHEEP CREEK RD	SBD	90	B4
SHEEP CK SPG RD	SBD	82	E1
SHEEP CK TK TR	SBD	90	B4
SHEEP MTN RD	SIS	5	A3
SHEEP RANCH RD	CAL	41	B3
SHEEPY CREEK RD	SIS	5	B2
SHEEPY ISLND RD	SIS	5	B2
SHEFFIELD ST	SJ	33	C3
SHEKELL	VEN	88	D5
SHELBY ST	KER	78	B5
SHELDON RD	SAC	39	E2
SHELDON ST	LACO	98	B2
SHELL AV	MCO	56	A1
SHELL BLVD	CC	38	E5
SHELL BLVD	FCTY	145	A1
SHELL RD	FRCO	66	C2
SHELL RD	TUO	41	C5
SHELL CANYON RD	IMP	111	C5
SHELLCO RD	KER	67	C5
SHELL GULCH RD	SIS	11	D1
SHELL NO 2	YUB	33	D1
SHELLEY	SJCO	40	B4
SHELLEY RD	SIS	4	A4
SHELTER COVE RD	HUM	22	A1
SHELTER ISLD DR	SDCO	V	B4
SHELTON RD	SBD	101	D1
SHELTON RD	SJCO	40	C1
SHELTN BUTTE RD	HUM	10	D2
SHENANDOAH SCHL	AMA	40	E1
SHEPHERD AV	FRCO	57	C2
SHEPHERD RD	MOD	14	B3
SHEPPARD RD	VEN	88	C5
SHERIDAN	FRCO	58	A4
SHERIDAN RD	ALA	46	B3
SHERIDAN RD	SLO	76	B5
SHERMAN RD	SBD	100	C2
SHERMAN WY	LA	177	B1
SHERMAN WY	LA	178	C1
SHERMAN WY	LACO	97	C1
SHERWIN CK RD	MNO	50	E2
SHERWOOD AV	KER	77	E1
SHERWOOD AV	KER	78	B1
SHERWOOD AV	MDO	162	B1
SHERWOOD BLVD	TEH	24	E1
SHERWOOD DR	SAL	171	C3
SHERWOOD DR	MEN	22	E4
SHERWD RNCHERIA	MEN	22	E4
SHETLAND CT	CAL	41	B5
SHETLAND CT	FRCO	56	A3
SHIELDS AV	FRCO	57	A3
SHIELDS AV	SHA	17	C3
SHIELDS RD	STA	47	C4
SHIELLS RD	STA	47	C4
SHILOH RD	SOL	39	B4
SHILOH RD	SON	37	E1
SHIMMINS RDG RD	MEN	22	E4
SHIMMINS RDG RD	MEN	23	A4
SHINGLE RD S	ED	40	C1
SHINGLETWN DUMP	SHA	19	B3
SHINGLETOWN RDG	SHA	19	A3
SHINN RANCH RD	LAS	21	D2
SHIPPEE RD	BUT	25	C4
SHIPPEE RD	MCO	48	B5
SHIRK RD	TUL	68	A1
SHIRLAND	PLA	34	C4
SHIRLEY RD	CAL	41	A5
SHIRLEY MDWS RD	KER	79	C1
SHIRT TAIL CYN	PLA	34	C4
SHIVELY RD	HUM	16	A3
SHOEMAKE AV	STA	47	B2
SHOEMAKER AV	LACO	T	A1
SHOEMAKER RD	HUM	10	C4
SHOEMAKER RD	SIS	4	C4
SHOP RD	MNO	42	E1
SHOP ST	INY	70	B2
SHORE RD	SBT	54	E2
SHORELINE DR	LB	192	D3
SHORELINE DR	STB	174	C5
SHORELINE HWY	MAR	37	D4
SHORELINE HWY	MEN	22	C3
SHORELINE HWY	MEN	30	C4
SHORELINE HWY	MEN	140	B4
SHORELINE HWY	MAR	140	B4
SHORT AV	KER	91	C3
SHORT AV	KER	78	A5
SHORT CREEK RD	MEN	23	B2
SHORTYS WELL RD	INY	72	A2
SHOSHONE VLY RD	SBD	93	B5
SHOSHONI LOOP	SHA	13	C4
SHOUP AV	LA	177	B3
SHOUP RD	SHA	18	A3
SHOWER PASS RD	HUM	16	B2
SHRODE LN	LAS	21	C4
SHULTZ RD	MCO	56	C1
SHUMWAY RCH RD	RCO	100	D5
SHUTE MTN RD	BUT	25	B3
SHUTT ST	DN	1	D3
SHY ST	MCO	47	C5
SHY ST	MCO	55	C1
SICARD FLAT RD	YUB	34	A1
SIDDING RD	KER	78	B3
SIDEWINDER RD	IMP	110	C3
SIDEWINDER RD	RCO	102	C3
SIDEWINDER RD	SBD	91	D2
SIDNEY GULCH RD	TRI	17	D1
SIEGLER SPGS RD	LAK	32	A4
SIERRA AV	FRCO	57	C3
SIERRA AV	NAP	133	A1
SIERRA AV	SBD	99	A2
SIERRA DR	MPA	48	E3
SIERRA DR	MDO	162	B4
SIERRA HWY	KER	80	A5
SIERRA HWY	KER	90	A1
SIERRA HWY	LACO	89	C4
SIERRA PKWY	CAL	41	D3
SIERRA RD	LAS	20	E3
SIERRA RD	SBD	46	B4
SIERRA RD	STA	47	E1
SIERRA ST	RENO	130	B1
SIERRA WY	KER	69	D5
SIERRA WY	KER	79	D1
SIERRA WY	SBDO	207	D3
SIERRA WY	SBD	99	C1
SIERRA WY	TUL	58	A5
SIERRA CTR DR	SHA	13	E4
SRA COLLEGE BL	PLA	34	B5
SIERRA DEL SOL	RCO	100	B3
SIERRA MADRE AV	LACO	98	C1
SIERRA MADRE AV	LACO	R	A3
SIERRA MADRE BL	LACO	R	A3
SIERRA MADRE BL	LACO	R	A3
SIERRA VISTA AV	TEH	24	D1
SIERRA VISTA ST	KER	80	C1
SIERRA VLY RD	PLU	27	C3
SIEVERS RD	SOL	39	B2
SIGNAL RD	IMP	111	B4
SIGNAL BUTTE RD	LAS	20	E1
SIGNAL RIDGE RD	MEN	30	D3
SIKES RD	SOL	39	C2
SILAXO AV	FRCO	56	C2
SILLS RD	COL	32	D3
SILSBEE RD	IMP	112	A3
SILVA RD	MPA	49	B3
SILVA RD	SIS	4	C3
SILVERA CT	BUT	25	C5
SILVERADO TR	NAP	133	E4
SILVERADO TR	NAPA	29	A1
SILVERADO TR	NAPA	38	C2
SILVER BAR RD	MPA	49	B4
SILVER BRDG RD	SHA	18	D2
SILVER CYN RD	INY	51	E4
SILVRADO CYN RD	ORA	98	E4
SILVER CREEK RD	MOH	85	D4
SILVER CREEK RD	SCL	46	B4
SILVER CK CMPGD	ALP	42	C1
SILVER HILL RD	ALP	36	C5
SILVER KING RD	SHA	18	B2
SILVER LAKE BL	LA	182	C4
SILVER LAKE BL	LA	185	D1
SILVER LAKE BL	LACO	Q	C4
SILVER LAKE RD	LAS	20	B3
SILVER BAR RD	MPA	49	B4
SILVER PUFF DR	KER	89	E3
SILVER QUEEN RD	KER	80	E5
SILVER QUEEN RD	KER	80	A5
SILVR RAPIDS RD	CAL	40	D4
SILVR STRAND BL	VEN	O	B5
SILVR STRAND BL	SDCO	111	B1
SILVERTHORN RD	SHA	18	D1
SLVR TIP CPGRD	ALP	42	A2
SILVER VLY RD	SBD	92	B1
SILVEYVILLE RD	SOL	39	B2
SIMAS RD	SB	86	B1
SIMI VALLEY- SN FERN VLY FY	LA	89	B3
SIMI VALLEY- SN FERN VLY FY	VEN	88	E5
SIMMERHORN RD	SAC	40	A3
SIMMLER RD	SLO	77	A2
SIMMLR BITTRWTR	SLO	76	E1
SIMMLR BITTRWTR	SLO	77	A1
SIMMLR SN DIEGO	SLO	77	B3
SIMMLR SN DIEGO	SLO	77	C4
SIMMLER SODA LK	LAK	23	C4
SIMMONS RD	SHA	18	B2
SIMMONS RD	SHA	31	D3
SIMMONS RD	STA	47	E1
SIMPSON LN	MEN	22	E4
SIMPSON LN	YUB	33	D2
SIMPSON RD	RCO	99	D4
SIMPSON RD	TEH	24	C1
SIMPSN DATNI RD	YUB	33	D2
SIMS RD	TUO	41	C5
SIMS RD	TUO	48	C1
SIMS CREEK RD	TRI	17	C3
SIMS LOOKOUT RD	SHA	12	C4
SINCLAIR FRWY	ALA	46	B3
SINCLAIR FRWY	SJ	151	A3
SINCLAIR FRWY	SCL	46	B3
SINCLAIR RD	IMP	109	A3
SINEX AV	PAC	167	C2
SINGLE SPRINGS	SIS	4	C3
SINGLETON RD	RCO	99	D2
SINGLE TREE	SBD	100	B5
SINGLETREE DR	CAL	41	A5
SINGLEY RD	HUM	15	E2
SINNARD AV	SUT	33	C1
SINTON RD	SB	86	B1
SIR FRNCS DRAKE	MAR	37	E4
SIR FRNCS DRAKE	MAR	38	A4
SIR F DRAKE BL	ROSS	139	A4
SIR F DRAKE BL	SANS	139	A4
SISK RD	STA	47	C2
SISKIYOU AV	FRCO	57	A3
SISKIYOU AV	FRCO	67	A2
SITES-LODOGA RD	COL	24	D5
SITES-LODOGA RD	COL	32	B1
SIX MILE RD	SJ	151	B4
SKAGGS ISL RD	SOL	38	C4
SKAGGS SPGS RD	SON	31	C5
SKIDOO RD	INY	71	D1
SKI HILL RD	MOD	7	D1
SKI RUN BLVD	SLT	129	C3
SKITTONE RD	STA	47	D2
SKULL FLAT RD	CAL	41	C4
SKUNK RANCH RD	CAL	41	C4
SKYLINE BLVD	ALA	45	D1
SKYLINE BLVD	KIN	67	A3
SKYLINE BLVD	SMCO	45	C3
SKYLINE DR	KER	79	B4
SKYLINE DR	MONT	167	C4
SKYLINE DR	MON	53	D4
SKYLINE DR	SDCO	V	C4
SKYLINE DR	SDCO	111	D1
SKYLINE MOTORWY	PLU	20	D4
SKYLINE RD	KER	77	E3
SKYLINE RD	KIN	67	A3
SKYLINE RD	SON	31	A5
SKY LINE RD	VAL	134	E3
SKYLINE FRST DR	MONT	167	C5
SKYLINE FRST DR	MONT	168	D4
SKYLINE FRST DR	MON	53	D4
SKYLINE RCH RD	SBD	100	C5
SKY RANCH RD	MON	54	C5
SKY VALLEY RD	RCO	100	E3
SKY VALLEY RD	SOL	38	D4
SKY VIEW DR	IMP	108	C2
SKYVIEW RD	MAD	57	C2
SKYWAY	BUT	25	C2
SKYWAY DR	SB	86	B2
SKYWAY RD	BUT	19	D5
SKYWAY RD	BUT	25	D1
SLACKS CYN RD	MON	66	B3
SLASH X RCH RD	SBD	91	C2
SLATE RD	YUB	26	A4
SLATE CREEK RD	SHA	12	A4
SLATE CREEK RD	TRI	11	D5
SLATE GULCH	MPA	48	E3
SLATE MTN RD	TRI	11	A4
SLATE MTN LO RD	SHA	12	A4
SLATER AV	ORA	T	B3
SLATER RD	HUM	16	B2
SLATER RANGE	INY	71	B2
SLATER BUTTE LO	SIS	2	E3
SLAUGHTERHOUSE	MPA	49	B3
SLAUSON AV	CUL	188	D1
SLAUSON AV	LACO	97	D2
SLAUSON AV	LACO		D3
SLAUSON AV	LACO	R	D3
SLAUSON AV	LACO	188	D3
SLAYTON RD	IMP	109	C5
SLIGER MINE RD	ED	34	D3
SLOAT BLVD	SFCO	45	B2
SLOAT RD	PLU	26	E2
SLOUGH RD	SIS	3	B1
SLOUGH RD	SIS	4	B1
SLOUGHHOUSE RD	SAC	40	B1
SLOVER AV	SBD	99	A2
SLUG GULCH RD	ED	41	A1
SLUSSER RD	SON	37	D2
SLY PARK RD	ED	35	A5
SMALLEY RD	FRCO	56	E3
SMARTS RANCH RD	SBD	92	B5
SMARTVILLE RD	YUB	34	A1
SMITH	YUB	33	E1
SMITH AV	FRCO	57	E4
SMITH AV	KER	78	B1
SMITH AV	KER	70	A5
SMITH GRADE	SCR	53	D1
SMITH RD	MON	66	B3
SMITH RD	SBD	80	E1
SMITH MTN RD	MON	66	B3
SMITH PK LKOUT	TUO	48	E1
SMITH PK LKOUT	TUO	49	A1
SMITHNECK RD	SIE	27	D4
SMITHSON RD	SBD	90	B2
SMITH STA RD	MPA	48	E1
SMITH STA RD	MPA	49	A1
SMITH STA RD	TUO	48	E1
SMITH STA RD	TUO	49	A1
SMOKE CK RCH RD	LAS	21	D3
SMOKE TREE RD	SBD	90	E4
SNAVELY RD	DN	1	E2
SNEATH LN	SMCO	45	B2
SNEATH LN	SBR	144	A4
SNELL ST	SNRA	163	A3
SNELLING HWY	MER	170	A1
SNELL VALLEY RD	NAPA	32	B5
SNOW RD	KER	78	C2
SNOW RD	KER	78	C2
SNOW ST	KER	79	E1
SNOW CAMP RD	HUM	16	D5
SNOWDN HOVEY GL	SLO	85	C4
SNOW'S RD	ED	35	A5
SNOWSHOE SPGS	ALP	36	B4
SNOW TENT RD	NEV	26	E4
SNYDER RD	IMP	109	C5
SNYDER RD	MCO	47	C5
SOAP CREEK RD	RCO	99	E3
SOBOBA ST	RCO	3	E5
SOBOBA ST	RCO	100	A4
SOBRANTE AV	CC	38	C5
SODA BAY RD	LAK	31	D3
SODA CANYON RD	NAPA	38	C3
SODA CREEK RD	SHA	12	C3
SODA LAKE RD	KER	78	A5
SODA LAKE RD	KER	87	E1
SODA LAKE CK RD	SLO	77	B3
SODA LK SN DIEG	SLO	77	B3
SODA LK SN DIEG	SLO	77	D4
SODA ROCK LN W	SON	31	D5
SODA SPRINGS RD	BUT	19	D5
SODA SPRINGS RD	SON	30	D5
SOETH RD	GLE	32	A1
SOLANO AV	NAP	133	A2
SOLANO AV	VAL	134	C5
SOLDIER MTN DR	SHA	13	D3
SOLDIER MTN RD	SHA	13	D3
SOLEDAD AV	SD	105	C3
SOLEDAD DR	MONT	167	D4
SOLEDAD DR	MON	53	D4
SOLEDAD DR	MON	53	E4
SOLEDAD FRWY	SDCO	V	B3
SOLEDAD FRWY	SDCO	106	C5
SOLEDAD CYN RD	LACO	89	E4
SOLEDAD MTN RD	SD	105	D4
SOLEDAD MTN RD	SD	211	B6
SOLOMAN RD	SB	86	B1
SOMAVIA RD	MON	54	B3
SOMEO ST	SB	86	B1
SOMERSVILLE RD	CC	39	B5
SONOMA AV	FRCO	56	D4
SONOMA AV	FRCO	66	D1
SONOMA AV	STR	131	E3
SONOMA BLVD	VAL	134	C4
SONOMA HWY	SNMA	132	C3
SONORA	SJCO	40	D5
SONORA	STA	41	A5
SONORA RD	STA	47	D5
SONORA RD	STA	48	A1
SONORA ELEM SCH	TUO	163	D4
SOPHIE ST	RCO	99	C4
SOQUEL AV	SC	169	C1
SOQUEL DR	SCR	54	A2
SOQUEL-SAN JOSE	SCR	54	A2
SORENSON RD	HUM	16	B3
SORENSON RD	RCO	100	B1
SORREL WY	CAL	41	A4
SORRENTO VLY	SDCO	106	C4
SOSCOL AV	NAP	133	D3
SOSCOL RD	NAPA	38	C3
SOTO ST	LA	186	D5
SOTO ST	LACO	R	D4
SOULE LN	SIS	4	C4
SOULSBYVILLE RD	TUO	41	D5
SOUTH AV	FRCO	56	E4
SOUTH AV	MCO	47	B4
SOUTH AV	MCO	47	A4
SOUTH AV	TEH	24	A4
SOUTH DR	SF	141	E4
SOUTH RD	DN	1	E4
SOUTH RD	MNO	51	C1
SOUTH ST	BLMT	145	C2
SOUTH ST	ANA	193	B5
SOUTH ST	ANA	194	A2
SOUTH ST	GLE	24	A2
SOUTH ST	LACO	98	A2
SOUTH ST	LACO	S	D1
SOUTH ST	LACO	T	A1
SOUTH ST	ORA	T	C2
SOUTH ST	RED	202	B2
SOUTH ST	SBD	90	A4
SOUTH ST	SNLO	172	B4
SOUTH ST	SHA	18	D4
SOUTH ST	COL	24	C5
SOUTHAM RD	COL	24	C5
SOUTHAMPTON RD	BEN	153	A3
S BNK CHETKO RD	CUR	1	C1
SOUTH BAY FRWY	SDCO	V	C4
SOUTH BAY FRWY	SDCO	111	D1
SOUTHBAY FRWY	SVL	148	C4
SOUTHERN AV	SIS	12	A1
S EMBARCADRO FY	SF	142	E4
S EMBARCADRO FY	SFCO	45	C2
SOUTH FORK DR	TUL	58	E1
SOUTH FORK DR	TUL	68	E1
SOUTH FORK RD	DN	1	E4
SOUTH FORK RD	SHA	18	B3
SOUTH FORK RD	TRI	10	D5
SOUTH FORK RD	TRI	16	E2
SOUTH FORK RD	TUO	41	E2
S FK LOOKOUT RD	SHA	18	B2
S FK MAD RIV RD	TRI	17	B3
S FORK MTN RD	TRI	16	E3
S FORK SALMON R	SIS	11	B3
SOUTH GRADE RD	SDCO	107	A2
SOUTH GRADE RD	MPA	49	B4
SOUTHSIDE DR	SBT	54	B3
SOUTHSIDE RD	SBT	55	A3
SOUTH VLY FRWY	SCL	54	C1
SOUTHWORTH RD	CAL	40	D4
SOUZA RD	TRI	17	A4
SOWLES RD	SJCO	40	B3
SPA RD	IMP	108	C2
SPACER DR	TUL	68	B2
SPALDING RD	LAS	20	B2
SPANGLE GOLD RD	MAD	49	C5
SPANGLER RD	KER	100	A4
SPANISH DAGGER	RCO	100	C5
SPANISH DRY DGN	ED	34	D3
SPANISH RCH RD	PLU	26	B1
SPANISH RCH BTT	PLU	25	A2
SPANISH RCH BUT	PLU	26	A2
SPANISH VALLEY	NAPA	32	C5
SPARKS RD	MCO	48	A1
SPARKS RANCH RD	SOL	39	B1
SPEAR AV	HUM	10	A5
SPECIMAN SPG RD	MAD	49	A1
SPENCE RD	MON	54	D4
SPENCER LN	SON	38	A1
SPENCER LN	SON	38	A1
SPENCER RD	COL	24	E5
SPENCER RD	STA	47	A2
SPENCEVILLE RD	NEV	34	A1
SPENCEVILLE RD	YUB	33	E1
SPERRY AV	STA	47	A4
SPERRY RD	STA	47	A4
SPGNOLI MINE RD	AMA	41	A2
SPILLWAY RD	MNO	51	B2
SPINELLI RD	MAD	49	C5
SPINK RD	CAL	41	B2
SPLICER RD	COL	33	A4
SPOONER RD	LAS	8	A4
SPOONER RD	LAS	14	E4
SPORTS ARENA BL	SD	212	C1
SPORTS ARENA BL	SD	213	A5
SPRECKELS BLVD	MON	54	C4
SPRING RD	VAL	134	C4
SPRING ST	LACO	S	E2
SPRING ST	NAPA	29	C3
SPRING ST N	LA	186	B2
SPRING TR	LAK	31	D2
SPRING BRNCH RD	TEH	18	D3
SPRING BRNCH RD	TEH	19	A3
SPRING CREEK RD	SHA	18	D3
SPRINGDALE ST	ORA	T	B3
SPRINGFIELD AV	FRCO	56	E4
SPRINGFIELD AV	FRCO	57	B4
SPRING GAP RD	TUO	41	E3
SPRING GAP RD	TUO	42	A3
SPRING GARDEN	PLA	34	D3
SPRING GULCH RD	LAS	14	B4
SPRING GULCH RD	SHA	18	C3
SPRING HILL RD	LAS	14	E4
SPRING HILL RD	SON	37	E3
SPRING HILL RD	SON	38	A3
SPRING LAKE RD	KLAM	5	B1
SPRING MDWS RD	SIS	12	E3
SPRING MTN RD	NAPA	29	A2
SPRING MTN RD	NAPA	38	B1
SPRINGS RD	SOL	38	D4
SPRING VLY LTRL	COL	32	C2
SPRING VLY RD	MEN	31	B1
SPRING VLY RD	YUB	33	E1
SPRINGVILLE AV	TUL	68	D3
SPRINGVILLE MILO	TUL	69	A2
SPROUL CREEK RD	HUM	22	B1
SPRUCE AV	SSF	144	B1
SPRUCE RD	TUL	68	C3
SPRUCE RD EXT	LAK	32	A4
SPRUCE ST	B	156	A1
SPRUCE CAMP RD	MCO	55	E4
SPRUCE GROVE RD	LAK	32	B4
SPUNKY CYN RD	LACO	89	C3
SQUIRREL CK RD	PLU	26	D2
STADIUM WY	LACO	Q	C4
STADIUM WY	SD	214	B3
STADIUM WY	SDCO	V	B3
STADIUM WY	SDCO	111	D1
STAFFORD RD	HUM	16	A3
STAG RD	AVLN	105	B4
STAGE RD	BUT	25	C2
STAGE RD	LAS	3	D5
STAGE RD	SMCO	45	C5
STAGE RD	TEH	24	C1
STAGE COACH LN	HUM	16	B2
STAGECOACH RD	SB	87	B3
STAGECOACH CYN	NAPA	32	C5
STAGHORN RD	RCO	107	C1
STAHL RD	IMP	109	B4
STALLARD RD	IMP	110	C2
STALLION VLY RD	CAL	41	B4
STAMPEDE DAM RD	SIE	27	E5
STAMPFLI LN RD	PLU	20	D5
STANDARD RD	TUO	41	D5
STANDARD MNE RD	TUO	20	D5
STANDIFORD AV	STA	47	B4
STANDISH PIT RD	LAS	21	B3
STANDLEY ST	U	123	B3
STANISLAUS AV	FRCO	56	E3
STANISLAUS RD W	STA	47	D3
STANLEY	SJCO	40	C5
STANLEY AV	VEN	88	A5
STANLEY BLVD	ALA	46	B2
STANLEY RD	CAL	41	B4
STANLEY RD	IMP	109	B5
STANLEY RD	RCO	100	A5
STANWOOD DR	STB	174	E3
STANYAN ST	SF	141	E3
STAPP RD	HUM	16	A3
STAR AV	STA	47	E2
STARBRIGHT MINE	SBD	82	A4
STARDUST RD	CLK	210	A1
STARK	SJCO	40	A5
STARK	SJCO	47	A1
STARK RD	STA	47	B3
STARKEY RD	SLO	76	D1
STARLING ST	LACO	90	C4
STARLITE DR	INY	51	E4
STARR RD	SON	37	D2
STATE LN	IMP	109	C5
STATE RD	SBD	100	B1
STATE ST	LACO	R	D5
STATE ST	MTCL	203	B5
STATE ST	ONT	203	B5
STATE ST	POM	203	B5
STATE ST	RCO	99	E4
STATE ST	SB	87	C4
STATE ST	SD	215	B4
STATE ST N	U	123	B3
STATE ST S	MEN	31	B1
STATE ST S	U	123	B3
STATE COLLGE BL	ORA	T	C3
STATE COLLGE BL	ORA	98	C2
STATE COL BL N	ANA	193	E5
STATE COL BL N	OR	193	E5
STATE COL PKWY	SBD	99	B1
STATE FRSTRY RD	SON	31	A3
STATE LINE RD	MOD	5	E2
STATE LINE RD	MNO	52	C3
STATE LINE RD	INY	72	D1
STATE LINE RD	SIS	5	D1
STATEN ISLND RD	SJCO	39	D4
STATE RANCH RD	SUT	33	A1
STATION RD	KER	78	A3
STATRVILLE RD	SIE	27	A5
STATE RD	STA	47	C3
STEARNS RD	LACO	S	E2
STEARNS ST	VEN	89	A5
STEELE AV	LACO		E3
STEELE LN	SON	37	E2
STEELE LN W	STR	131	B2
STEEL BRIDGE RD	TRI	17	D1
STEELHEAD CIR	TRI	17	D1
STEELHEAD RD	HUM	16	D5
STEELE CYN RD	NAPA	38	D2
STEEL SWAMP RD	MOD	6	C3

239
STEFFAN ST

STREET INDEX

TRACY BLVD

STREET	CO.	PAGE & GRID	
STEFFAN ST	VAL	134	E5
STEIDLMAYER RD	CLU	33	A2
STEINEGUL	SJCO	47	D1
STEINER RD	AMA	40	E1
STEINER RD	SUT	33	B3
STEINER FLAT RD	TRI	17	C1
STELLAR RD	SBD	92	A4
STELLING RD N	CPTO	149	C4
STELLING RD S	CPTO	149	D5
STENT CUTOFF	TUO	41	C5
STEPHENS MNE RD	SBD	80	E2
STEPHENS MNE RD	SBD	81	A2
STEPHENSON BLVD	RCO	110	C1
STEPHENSON BLVD	RCO	110	C1
STEPHENS RIDGE	BUT	25	E3
STERCHI LN	SIS	4	C4
STERLING AV	SBD	99	C2
STERLING RD	INY	70	C4
STERLING LAKE	NEV	27	B5
STETSON AV	RCO	99	E4
STEVEN ST	KER	78	B5
STEVENS RD	IMP	111	E3
STEVENS CK BLVD	CPTO	149	C5
STEVENS CK BLVD	CPTO	150	A5
STEVENS CK BLVD	SCLR	150	A5
STEVENS CK BLVD	SCL	46	A4
STEVENS CK FRWY	MVW	148	A4
STEVENS CK RD	SCL	45	E5
STEVENSN BDG RD	SOL	39	B1
STEVENS PASS RD	SIS	5	A5
STEVENS PASS RD	SIS	13	B1
STEWART	MOD	14	D1
STEWART AV	BUT	124	A5
STEWART LN	INY	51	E5
STEWART LN	SOL	39	C4
STEWART RD	HUM	16	C4
STEWART RD	INY	51	D4
STEWART RD	SJCO	47	A1
STEWART RD	SUT	33	D2
STEWART RD	TEH	18	C5
STEWART ST	SB	86	C1
STEWARTS POINT--SKAGGS SPGS RD	SON	30	E5
STEWARTS POINT--SKAGGS SPGS RD	SON	31	A5
STEWART RCH RD	HUM	16	D4
STEWART SPGS RD	SIS	12	B1
STICE RD	TEH	18	D4
STILLWELL AV	MONT	167	D3
STILLWELL AV	MON	53	E3
STILSON CYN RD	BUT	25	B3
STIMPSON RD	BUT	25	D5
STIMPSON RD	BUT	33	D1
STINE RD	BKD	166	A5
STINE RD	KER	78	D3
STINGY LN	SHA	18	C3
STOCKDALE HWY	KER	78	A3
STOCKDALE RD	SLO	76	A1
STOCKER ST	LACO	Q	B4
STOCKTON AV	MCO	48	B4
STOCKTON AV	SJ	151	E3
STOCKTON BLVD	SCTO	137	E4
STOCKTON BLVD	SAC	39	E1
STOCKTON RD	VEN	88	D5
STOCKTON ST	SF	143	C2
STOCKTON ST	SNRA	163	A5
STOCKWLL MNE RD	INY	71	B4
STODDARD RD	STA	47	C2
STODDARD RD	STA	47	E2
STODDARD MTN RD	SBD	91	C2
STODDARD WELLS	SBD	91	D2
STOEKEL RD	SHA	18	B3
STONE AV	STA	47	C2
STONE RD	LAS	20	E1
STONE RD	MCO	55	D1
STONEBORO RD	MEN	30	C3
STONE CANYON RD	MON	66	B3
STONE COAL RD	MOD	14	B2
STONEHEDGE DR	YUB	25	E5
STONEHILL DR	ORA	202	B3
STONE HOUSE RD	SAC	40	C1
STONEHURST AV	LACO	Q	B2
STONERIDGE DR	ALA	46	A2
STONE VALLEY RD	CC	46	A1
STONEWLL CYN RD	MON	65	A1
STONEY CREEK RD	LAS	21	D2
STONY CREEK RD	AMA	40	D3
STONYFD-LDGA RD	COL	24	B5
STONY POINT RD	STR	131	A3
STONY POINT RD	SON	38	A3
STONY POINT RD	SON	37	E2
STONY POINT RD	SON	37	E3
STONY POINT RD	SON	131	A4
STOREY	FRCO	56	C2
STORRIE RD	PLU	25	E2
STORY RD	SJ	152	E4
STORY RD	SCL	46	B4
STORY RD	STA	47	E3
STOVALL RD	COL	32	D2
STOVEPIPE WELLS	INY	61	D4
STOVER RD	HUM	10	B4
STOW	SJCO	40	C5
STOW	SJCO	47	C1
STOWELL RD	STB	173	B4
STOWELL RD	SB	86	B1
STOWELL RD	SMA	173	B4
STRADLEY AV	KER	68	B5
STRAND, THE	LAS	20	E1
STRATTON LN	SOL	39	B4
STRAWBERRY DR	MAR	140	D3
STRAWBERRY LN	SHA	18	C3
STRAWBERRY RD	MON	54	C3
STREETER AV	RCO	99	B2
ST OF GL LNTERN	ORA	202	A4
STREET 200	MAD	57	D1
STREET 225	MAD	50	A5
STREET 600	MAD	49	B1
STREET 600	MAD	49	C4
STREET 603	MAD	57	B1
STREIBY RD	IMP	109	B4
STRINGTOWN RD	BUT	25	E4
STRIPLIN RD	SUT	33	D4
STROUD AV	FRCO	57	C5
STRUCKMAN RD	CAL	41	B3
STUBBLEFIELD RD	KER	78	A5
STUBBLEFIELD RD	KER	87	E1
STUBBY SPRGS TR	RCO	101	A2
STUDEBAKER RD	LACO	98	A3
STUDEBAKER RD	LACO	S	E1
STUDEBAKER RD	LACO	S	E2
STUDEBAKER RD	LACO	T	A1
STUHR RD	STA	47	C4
STUKEY ST	DN	1	D3
STUMPFIELD MTN	MPA	49	C3
STUMPTOWN RD	HUM	9	E4
STUNT RD	LACO	97	B2
STURGIS RD	VEN	96	B1
STURM RD	HUM	16	C3
SUBACO RD	SUT	33	B3
SUBSTATION RD	MNO	50	E2
SUCCESS DR	TUL	68	D3
SUCCESS VLY DR	TUL	68	E3
SUCKER RUN RD	BUT	26	A4
SUCKOW RD	KER	80	D5
SUDDEN RD	SB	86	B3
SUE AV	KER	89	C1
SUE ST	KER	80	B5
SUEY RD	SMA	173	E3
SUEY CREEK RD	SLO	76	D5
SUGAR CREEK RD	SIS	11	D2
SUGARLOAF RD	FRCO	58	A1
SUGAR LOAF RD	INY	51	D5
SUGRLF LKSHR RD	SHA	12	B5
SUGRLOAF LKT RD	SHA	12	B5
SUGARLOAF TK TR	SBD	99	E1
SUGAR PINE	PLA	34	E2
SUGAR PINE PL	BUT	25	C2
SUGAR PINE RD	TUO	41	E4
SUGAR PINE SPG	LAS	14	A3
SUISUN VLY RD	SOL	38	E3
SULFUR RD	INY	52	D5
SULKEY CT	CAL	41	A5
SULLENGER RD	SUT	33	B2
SULLIVAN RD	KER	78	A2
SULLIVAN RD	MPA	49	B3
SULLIVAN RD	STA	47	C5
SULLIVAN ST	ORA	T	C3
SULLIVAN ST	SA	195	D5
SULPHUR BANK DR	LAK	32	A3
SULPHUR MTN RD	VEN	88	B4
SULPHR MTN RD E	VEN	88	B4
SULPHUR SPGS RD	MON	65	B3
SULTANA DR	MCO	48	A4
SULTZE AV	KER	78	B5
SUMMERHILL DR	TUO	42	A3
SUMMER HOMES RD	ML	164	C2
SUMMERS LN	KLAM	5	C1
SUMMERS RD	LAS	21	E5
SUMMERSET RD	SBD	91	C1
SUMMIT AV	GLE	24	D3
SUMMIT AV	SBD	99	A1
SUMMIT RD	BUT	25	D5
SUMMIT RD	KER	79	C4
SUMMIT RD	SCR	54	B1
SUMMIT CREEK RD	TRI	17	C2
SUMMIT LAKE DR	NAPA	38	B1
SUMMIT LEVEL RD	CAL	41	C3
SUMMITROSE ST	LACO	Q	C2
SUMMIT TRUCK TR	SBD	91	B5
SUMMY	SUT	33	B2
SUMNER AV	AVLN	105	B5
SUMNER AV	FRCO	56	E4
SUMNER AV	FRCO	58	B4
SUMNER AV	RCO	98	E2
SUMNER ST	BKD	166	E3
SUNBURST AV	SBD	100	E1
SUNEVER RD	SBD	101	A1
SUNFAIR RD	SBD	101	A1
SUNFLOWER AV	CM	197	D3
SUNFLOWER AV	CM	198	A3
SUNFLOWER AV	LACO	U	D3
SUNFLOWR SPG RD	SBD	94	D2
SUNFLR SPGS SPR	SBD	94	E3
SUNKIST ST	ANA	194	A2
SUNKIST ST	ORA	T	D2
SUNKIST TR	LPAZ	104	C4
SUNLAND BLVD	LACO	97	D1
SUNLAND BLVD	LACO	Q	B2
SUNLAND DR	INY	51	D4
SUNNY LN	AVLN	105	B5
SUNNY ACRES AV	MCO	47	E3
SUNNY ACRES AV	MCO	48	A3
SUNNYBRAE BLVD	SM	145	A2
SUNNY BRAE LN	HUM	10	A5
SUNNY HILL RD	SHA	18	A3
SUNNYSIDE AV	FRCO	57	D3
SUNNYSIDE AV	FRCO	57	D4
SUNNYSIDE AV	MAD	57	A1
SUNNYSIDE AV	MV	140	A2
SUNNYSIDE RD	LAS	21	B4
SUNNYSLOPE	FRCO	58	B2
SUNNYSLOPE RD	SBD	90	E4
SUNNYVALE AV	CPTO	149	D1
SUNNYVALE AV	SVL	148	E5
SUNNY VISTA RD	SBD	100	E1
SUNRISE	SBD	101	B1
SUNRISE AV	MDO	162	C1
SUNRISE BLVD	SAC	34	A5
SUNRISE BLVD	SJCO	40	B2
SUNRISE HWY	SDCO	107	D4
SUNRISE HWY	SDCO	107	D5
SUNRISE WY	PMSP	206	C5
SUNRISE WY	RCO	100	D3
SUNRISE SPGS RD	SBD	93	A5
SUNSET	SAC	34	B5
SUNSET AV	FRFD	135	D3
SUNSET AV	KER	79	E5
SUNSET AV	LACO	R	B4
SUNSET AV	MAD	57	A2
SUNSET AV	MCO	55	D1
SUNSET AV	RCO	99	E3
SUNSET AV	SOL	135	D3
SUNSET BLVD	BH	183	A1
SUNSET BLVD	KER	79	A4
SUNSET BLVD	LA	181	B4
SUNSET BLVD	LA	182	A4
SUNSET BLVD	LA	185	D1
SUNSET BLVD	LA	186	A1
SUNSET BLVD	LACO	97	C2
SUNSET BLVD	LACO	Q	B3
SUNSET BLVD	SD	213	B5
SUNSET BLVD	SDCO	V	B4
SUNSET BLVD	SF	141	A5
SUNSET BLVD	SFCO	45	B2
SUNSET BLVD	LA	180	C1
SUNSET BLVD W	PLA	33	E4
SUNSET BLVD W	PLA	34	A4
SUNSET DR	IMP	108	C2
SUNSET DR	INY	60	B4
SUNSET DR	MCO	47	E4
SUNSET DR	MCO	48	A4
SUNSET DR	MONT	53	C2
SUNSET DR	PAC	167	B2
SUNSET DR	SDCO	106	C3
SUNSET PKWY	MAR	38	A4
SUNSET RD	CC	39	C5
SUNSET RD	CLK	74	D3
SUNSET RD	GLE	24	D3
SUNSET RD	SBD	100	E1
SUNSET ST	FRCO	66	D2
SUNSET CYN DR	LACO	Q	C2
SUNSET CLIFS BL	SD	212	B5
SUNSET CLIFS BL	SDCO	V	A4
SUNSET CLIFS BL	SDCO	111	C1
SUNSET CRSNG RD	LACO	U	E4
SUNSET LAKE RD	ALP	42	B1
SUNSHINE MNE RD	KER	80	E3
SUPERIOR AV	CM	199	A3
SUPERIOR AV	NB	199	A3
SUPERIOR RD	KER	78	B3
SURPRISE CYN RD	INY	71	C3
SURPRISE SPG RD	SBD	100	E1
SURPRISE VLY RD	LAS	8	E3
SURPRISE VLY RD	MOD	7	E3
SURPRISE VLY RD	MOD	8	E3
SUSAN HILLS DR	LAS	20	E3
SUSANVILLE RD	LAS	14	B3
SUSQUEHANNA RD	SIS	4	D3
SUTLIFF RD	SJCO	47	D1
SUTTENFIELD RD	SJCO	40	B3
SUTTER AV	FRCO	56	E4
SUTTER AV	FRCO	66	E3
SUTTER AV	MDO	162	A5
SUTTER LN	AMA	40	D2
SUTTER RD	HUM	9	E4
SUTTER RD	HUM	10	A4
SUTTER RD	YOL	39	D3
SUTTER ST	AMA	40	E2
SUTTER ST	SF	142	B3
SUTTER ST	SF	143	C4
SUTTER CK IONE--BACK CUTOFF RD	AMA	40	D2
SUTTR CK VOLCNO	AMA	40	E2
SUTTR CK VOLCNO	AMA	41	A2
SUTTER ISLND RD	SAC	39	D3
SUTTERVILLE RD	SAC	39	D1
SWAN RD	MCO	48	B4
SWAN RD	SOL	39	C2
SWAN MTN RD	PLU	20	B3
SWANSEA RD	LPAZ	104	D3
SWANSON AV	FRCO	57	B5
SWANSON AV	FRCO	57	C5
SWANSON RD	STA	47	E3
SWANTON RD	SCR	53	D1
SWARTHOT CYN RD	SBD	91	A5
SWASEY DR	SHA	18	B2
SWEDE CREEK RD	SHA	18	D2
SWEDE CREEK RD	TRI	11	A5
SWEDES FLAT RD	BUT	25	E5
SWEENEY RD	ED	35	B5
SWEENEY RD	SB	86	C3
SWEENEY RD	SOL	39	A2
SWEENEY PASS RD	SDCO	108	A5
SWEENY RD	MCO	55	C2
SWEET RD	IMP	109	A5
SWEETEN LN	SBD	91	D1
SWEETLAND RD	NEV	26	B5
SWEETSER RD	KER	89	E1
SWEETWATER RD	SDCO	V	C4
SWEETWATER RD	SDCO	111	E1
SWEETWATER RD	SDCO	111	D2
SWEETWTR SPG BL	SDCO	V	D4
SWEETWTR SPG RD	SON	37	D1
SWEITZER LN	SBD	92	D5
SWENSEN RD	MCO	47	D4
SWETZER RD	SUT	33	E3
SWIFT AV	MCO	56	A2
SWIFT RD	SBD	80	E5
SWIFT ST	SC	169	A4
SWIFT CREEK	TRI	11	E4
SWIGART RD	SIS	4	B4
SWISS RANCH RD	CAL	41	B3
SX RD	MOD	14	E1
SYCAMORE AV	FRCO	57	A4
SYCAMORE AV	MDO	162	B2
SYCAMORE AV	SDCO	106	C3
SYCAMORE DR	LACO	88	E5
SYCAMORE LN	DVS	136	B3
SYCAMORE RD	KER	78	E4
SYCAMORE RD	KER	79	A4
SYCAMORE RD	SDCO	V	C5
SYCAMORE RD	SDCO	111	D2
SYCAMORE RD	VEN	88	D4
SYCAMORE ST	ANA	193	B2
SYCAMORE ST	MCO	47	E3
SYCAMORE ST	MCO	48	A3
SYCAMORE CYN RD	SB	87	C4
SYCAMORE CYN RD	STB	174	E3
SYCAMORE CUTOFF	CLU	33	A2
SYCAMRE FLAT RD	MON	65	A2
SYCAMORE SL RD	COL	33	A2
SYCAMORE VLY RD	CC	46	A1
SYDNOR AV	KER	80	D1
SYKES RD	INY	70	B3
SYLVAN AV	STA	47	D2
SYLVESTER RD	MCO	55	D1
SYMMES RD	INY	59	E3
T			
T ST	BKD	166	D4
T ST	STA	47	C4
TABL MTN OVRCRS	BUT	25	C4
TABLE BLUFF RD	HUM	15	D1
TABLE MTN BL	BUT	25	C4
TABLE MTN RD	FRCO	57	D2
TABLE MTN RD	RCO	100	C5
TABLE MTN TK TR	RCO	107	C1
TABLEROCK RD	SIS	4	C4
TABOOSE CK RD	INY	59	E1
TABOR AV	FRFD	135	B2
TABOR AV	SOL	39	A3
TABOR AV E	FRFD	135	C2
TAECKER RD	IMP	109	B4
TAFT AV	OR	194	C3
TAFT AV	ORA	98	C3
TAFT AV	ORA	T	D2
TAFT HWY	KER	78	C3
TAFT ST	TEH	24	E1
TAGE RD	SBD	101	D1
TAGLIO RD	MCO	47	D5
TAHOE ST	MCO	48	B4
TAHQTZ-MCCLM WY	PMSP	206	A4
TALBERT AV	FTNV	197	A3
TALBERT AV	ORA	98	B4
TALBERT AV	ORA	T	B3
TALBERT LN	SOL	39	B4
TALBOT ST	SDCO	V	A4
TALC CITY RD	INY	70	D1
TALMAGE RD	U	123	D4
TAMALPAIS AV	MAR	38	B5
TAMALPAIS DR	CRTM	140	B1
TAMARACK AV	SDCO	106	B3
TAMARACK RD	SHA	13	C5
TAMARACK RD	SHA	19	C1
TAMARACK RD	TEH	19	C4
TAMARACK LK RD	TRI	12	B3
TAMARACK PK RD	SHA	13	C5
TAMPA AV	LA	178	B3
TAMPA AV	LACO	97	B1
TANABE RD	YUB	33	D1
TANATEA ST	RCO	107	C1
TANK FARM RD	KER	78	A4
TANK FARM RD	SLO	76	B4
TANK FARM RD	SLO	172	C5
TANK FARM RD	SNLO	172	C5
TANNERY GLCH RD	TRI	11	D5
TAPADERO ST	CAL	41	A4
TAPIA LN	SBD	90	E2
TAPLIN RD	NAPA	29	C3
TAPO RD	VEN	89	A5
TAPO CANYON RD	VEN	89	A5
TARA AV	KER	69	B5
TAR CANYON RD	KIN	66	E4
TARKE RD	SUT	33	B2
TARPON DR	SIS	4	B3
TASSAJARA RD	MON	64	D2
TATE CREEK RD	SIS	13	A2
TAVERN RD	SDCO	107	B5
TAVERNETTI RD	MON	54	E5
TAVERNETTI RD	MON	55	A5
TAVERNOR RD	SAC	40	B2
TAYLOR AV	KER	78	B1
TAYLOR BLVD	MLBR	144	C5
TAYLOR BLVD	CC	38	E5
TAYLOR LN	SIS	5	B4
TAYLOR RD	CC	39	C4
TAYLOR RD	STA	47	C3
TAYLOR ST	SF	143	B2
TAYLOR ST	SJ	152	B2
TAYLORSVL TRANS	PLU	20	D5
TEAFORD SDLE RD	MAD	49	E4
TEAGUE AV	FRCO	57	D2
TEAGUE AV	MON	65	B2
TEAL DR	MOD	7	A5
TEALE RD	KER	78	D4
TEALE RD	KER	79	A4
TEAPOT	TUL	68	C3
TECHNR RBSN RD	SIS	5	A4
TECOLOTE RD	SDCO	V	B3
TECOLOTE RD	SDCO	111	C1
TECOPA HOT SPGS	INY	73	A4
TED ELDER RD	SHA	13	D3
TED KIPF RD	IMP	109	C3
TED KIPF RD	IMP	110	A4
TEDOC RD	TEH	17	D4
TEFFT ST	SLO	76	C5
TEGAN RD	SAC	39	E2
TEGNER RD	MCO	47	D4
TEHACHAPI BLVD	KER	79	D4
TEHACHP-WLW SPG	KER	79	D5
TEHAMA AV	KIN	67	A4
TEHAMA AV	TEH	24	D1
TEHAMA ST	GLE	24	D4
TEHAMA & VNA RD	TEH	24	E1
TEJON RD	LACO	90	C4
TELEGRAPH AV	B	156	B3
TELEGRAPH AV	O	156	B3
TELEGRAPH RD	CAL	40	E5
TELEGRAPH RD	CAL	41	A5
TELEGRAPH RD	LACO	89	A4
TELEGRAPH RD	LACO	98	A2
TELEGRAPH RD	LACO	R	B4
TELEGRAPH RD	MPA	49	B3
TELEGRAPH RD	VEN	88	E4
TELEGRPH CYN RD	SDCO	V	D5
TELEGRPH CYN RD	SDCO	111	D2
TELEGRAPH CK RD	HUM	22	A1
TELEGRAPH MN RD	SBD	83	D3
TELEPHONE RD	SB	86	C1
TELEPHONE RD	VEN	88	B5
TELESCOPE PK RD	RD	10	C4
TELL BLVD	DN	1	D3
TEMESCAL CYN RD	RCO	99	A3
TEMPERANCE AV	FRCO	57	D2
TEMPERANCE AV	FRCO	57	D5
TEMPLE AV	LACO	R	B4
TEMPLE AV	LACO	S	E2
TEMPLE ST	LA	185	C1
TEMPLE ST	LA	186	B2
TEMPLE CITY BL	LACO	R	A3
TEMPLE CREEK	SJCO	40	C5
TEMPLE CREEK	SJCO	47	C1
TEMPLE HILLS DR	LAG	201	D2
TEMPLETON RD	SLO	76	A2
TENAJA RD	RCO	99	B5
TENAJA TRUCK TR	RCO	99	B5
TENAYA DR	STA	162	D4
TENMILE RD	MEN	30	D4
TENMILE CUTF RD	MEN	30	D4
TENNANT AV	SCL	54	D1
TENNANT RD	SIS	4	E5
TENNANT RD	SIS	5	A5
TENNANT LAVA BD	MOD	5	E4
TENNANT LAVA BD	SIS	5	B5
TENNANT MT HRBN	SIS	5	A4
TENNESSEE ST	SBD	99	C2
TENNESSEE ST	VAL	134	C4
TENNESSEE ST E	FRFD	135	C3
TENNYSON RD	ALA	45	E2
TEPUSQUET RD	SB	86	D1
TEQUEPIS CYN RD	SB	87	A3
TERCEIRA RD	MCO	55	E2
TERMINAL RD	AVLN	105	B5
TERMINOUS RD	SAC	39	D4
TERMO GRASSHPPR	LAS	8	A5
TERMO GRASSHPPR	LAS	14	E5
TERRA BELLA ST	LACO	Q	A2
TERRACE	FRCO	58	A3
TERRACE RD	RCO	100	D4
TERRY MILL RD	SHA	13	A5
TERWER RIFFL RD	DN	10	A1
TERWILLIGER RD	RCO	107	C1
TESLA RD	ALA	46	C2
TESORO RD	SBD	90	E3
TEST STATION	MNO	43	C5
TEXAS AV	KER	79	E5
TEXAS AV	KER	80	A5
TEXAS RD	STA	47	C2
TEXAS ST	FRFD	135	A3
TEXAS ST	SD	216	B1
TEXAS ST	SDCO	V	B4
TEXAS ST	SDCO	111	D1
TEXAS ST N	SOL	38	E3
TEXAS ST N	FRFD	135	C3
TEXAS HILL	MPA	48	E2
TEXAS HILL RD	YUB	26	A5
TEXAS SPGS RD	SHA	18	B2
THATCHER RD	SHA	19	C2
THATCHER MLL RD	SHA	19	C2
THATCHER RDG RD	BUT	25	D1
THE BRADSHAW TR	RCO	102	A5
THEDA ST	RCO	99	C4
THE INDIAN RD	MOD	8	B3
THEODORE ST	RCO	99	D3
THEODORIC RD	SBD	84	C4
THING RD	SDCO	112	C2
THIRD ST	C	124	B5
THISSELL RD	SOL	39	B2
THOMAS	SON	31	E5
THOMAS	SON	37	E1
THOMAS RD	HUM	16	B5
THOMAS RD	KER	90	C1
THOMAS RD	MCO	55	C2
THOMAS RD	SBT	55	A3
THOMAS RD	SHA	18	B3
THOMAS RD	SHA	19	A1
THOMAS ST	KER	80	A4
THOME RD	YUB	33	D1
THOMES AV	TEH	24	D1
THOMPSON AV	FRCO	57	D3
THOMPSON AV	FRCO	57	D5
THOMPSON BLVD	VENT	175	B2
THOMPSON RD	IMP	109	A5
THOMPSON RD	LAS	14	B4
THOMPSON RD	MNO	43	B4
THOMPSON RD	SBD	81	C5
THOMPSON RD	SLO	76	C5
THOMPSON RD	SUT	33	C3
THOMPSON CYN AV	KER	79	C2
THOMPSON CYN RD	MON	65	B2
THOMSEN RD	SOL	39	C2
THORNBERRY RD	MAD	49	D4
THORNBURG ST	SMA	173	B3
THORNE AV	FRE	165	B4
THORNTON AV	ALA	45	E3
THORNTON AV	ALA	46	A3
THORNTON RD	MCO	48	B4
THORNTON RD	SJCO	40	A4
THOUSND OAKS BL	LACO	96	E1
THOUSND OAKS BL	VEN	96	D1
THOUSND PLMS RD	RCO	100	E3
THOUSAND SPGS	SHA	13	D3
THREE CHOP RD	MEN	22	D5
THREE FLAGS HWY	KER	80	D1
THREE PINES CYN	KER	80	B1
THREE SLASHS RD	IMP	110	C2
THRIFT RD	MCO	48	C5
THRUSH DR	SIS	4	B3
THUNDER	SDCO	106	B3
THUNDERBIRD BL	KER	80	C4
THUNDERBIRD RD	SBD	91	C3
THUNDER CYN RD	SLO	75	D2
TIBURON BLVD	MAR	140	E3
TICE VALLEY BL	CC	45	E1
TICINO ST	SB	86	B1
TIEDEMAN RD	STA	47	B2
TIERNEY RD	HUM	16	B3
TIERRA BUENA RD	SUT	33	C2
TIERRA DEL SOL	SDCO	112	E2
TIERRA RJADA RD	VEN	88	E5
TIERRA SANTA BL	SDCO	V	C3
TIERRA SANTA BL	SDCO	106	D5
TIFFANY RCH RD	SLO	76	B4
TIGER CREEK RD	SIS	11	D2
TILTON DR	LACO	89	E3
TIM BELL RD	STA	48	A2
TIMBER COVE RD	SON	37	A1
TIMBER CRATER	SHA	13	D3
TIMBUCTOO RD	YUB	34	A1
TIMM RD	SOL	39	A2
TIMMONS AV	KER	68	B5
TIMMONS RD	SIS	4	B5
TIM MULLEN RD	HUM	16	B1
TIMS RD	SB	86	E2
TIN BARN RD	SON	31	A5
TIN BARN RD	SON	37	A1
TINDALL RCH RD	MEN	31	B2
TINNEMAHA RD	INY	59	E1
TIOGA PASS RD	MPA	42	E5
TIOGA PASS RD	MPA	43	A5
TIOGA PASS RD	MPA	50	A1
TIOGA PASS RD	MPA	63	D3
TIOGA PASS RD	MNO	43	A5
TIOGA PASS RD	TUO	42	E5
TIOGA PASS RD	TUO	50	A1
TIOGA PASS RD	TUO	63	A4
TIONESTA RD	MOD	5	E5
TIONESTA RD	MOD	6	A4
TIONESTA RD	SIS	5	D5
TIPPECANOE ST	SBD	99	C2
TIPTOP RD	MPA	49	C3
TISDALE	SUT	33	B3
TITLOW HILL RD	HUM	10	C5
TITSWORTH RD	IMP	109	C4
TIZON RD	RCO	107	B1
TOBACCO	SJCO	40	C5
TOBIN DR	VAL	134	B1
TODAYANA WY	PLA	34	D2
TODCO RD	KER	69	B5
TODD RD	SON	37	E2
TODD EYMANN RD	FRCO	58	D3
TODD VALLEY	PLA	34	D3
TOEWS AV	MCO	48	D4
TOFT DR	RCO	99	A4
TOKAY COLONY RD	SJCO	40	C4
TOLAND LN	SOL	39	C4
TOLAND RD	VEN	88	C4
TOLAND PARK RD	VEN	88	C4
TOLL GATE WY	BUT	25	C2
TOLL HOUSE RD	FRCO	57	D2
TOLL HOUSE RD	FRCO	58	A2
TOMALES RD	SON	37	E3
TOMALES PETALMA	MAR	37	D3
TOM GREEN MN RD	SHA	18	A1
TOMKI RD	MEN	23	B5
TOMPKNS HILL RD	HUM	15	E2
TOM SHAW RD	HUM	16	B2
TOM WELLS RD	LPAZ	104	A5
TONNER CYN RD	ORA	U	D5
TONZI RD	AMA	40	D2
TOOBY DR	FRFD	135	A3
TOOME CAMP	TEH	24	A2
TOOMES RD	STA	47	C2
TOPA LN	VEN	88	C4
TOPANGA CYN BL	LA	177	B3
TOPANGA CYN BL	LACO	97	B1
TOPAZ LN	MNO	42	E1
TOPAZ RD	SBD	91	B3
TOPEKA DR	LA	178	C4
TOPO RD	MON	65	B1
TOPO VALLEY RD	SBT	65	C1
TOPOCK DAVIS DM	MOH	95	E1
TOPPEN DORFF LN	HUM	15	D2
TORO CANYON RD	SB	87	D4
TORO CREEK RD	SLO	75	E2
TORO CREEK RD	SLO	76	A2
TORRANCE BLVD	LACO	97	D3
TORRANCE BLVD	LACO	S	B2
TORREY PINES RD	SD	105	B3
TORREY PINES RD	SD	211	B2
TORREY PINES RD	SDCO	V	A3
TORREY PINES RD	SDCO	106	C5
TORREY RD N	VEN	88	E4
TORREY RD S	VEN	88	E4
TOTH RD	HUM	22	A1
TOTTEN RD	SHA	13	E4
TOVEY AV	LACO	90	A3
TOWER RD	MCO	48	C4
TOWER RD	SLO	76	B1
TOWER LINE RD	KER	79	A4
TOWNE AV	LACO	U	E3
TOWNSEND RD	IMP	109	C5
TOWNSEND RD	SIS	4	C4
TOWNSEND ST	SBD	91	D1
TOWNSHIP AV	VEN	88	E5
TOWNSHIP AV	VEN	89	A5
TOWNSHIP RD	KLAM	5	B2
TOWNSHIP RD	YUB	34	A1
TOWNSHIP RD N	SUT	33	C2
TOWNSHIP RD S	SUT	33	C3
TOZER ST	MAD	57	A2
TRABUCO RD	ORA	98	D4
TRABUCO RD	ORA	T	E3
TRACTOR AV	FRCO	66	D2
TRACY AV	KER	78	A2
TRACY BLVD	SBD	100	D1

STREETS

STREET INDEX

STREET	CO.	PAGE & GRID
TRACY BLVD	SJCO	39 E5
TRACY BLVD	SJCO	46 E1
TRAGEDY SPGS RD	AMA	35 E5
TRAIL CANYON RD	INY	72 A1
TRAILS END LN	RCO	107 C1
TRAILS END RD	SIS	4 C5
TRAILS END CAMP	SBD	96 B5
TRAMPA CYN RD	MON	64 C1
TRAMWAY RD	TEH	19 C4
TRANCAS ST	NAP	133 C2
TRANCAS ST	NAPA	133 D2
TRASK AV	GGR	195 B2
TRASK AV	ORA	T B2
TRAUTWEIN RD	RCO	99 B3
TRAVIS BL	FRFD	135 B3
TRAYNHAM RD	COL	33 A3
TREAT BLVD	CC	38 E5
TREAT BLVD	CC	39 A5
TREDWAY	SJCO	40 A4
TREFOIL LN	SHA	18 D3
TREMONT RD	SOL	39 C1
TREMONT ST	AVLN	105 B5
TRENTHAM RD	IMP	109 B5
TRES CERITOS AV	RCO	99 D4
TRESTLE GLEN	MAR	45 B1
TRESTLE GLEN RD	O	158 C3
TRETHEWAY RD	SJCO	40 B4
TRIANGLE RD	MPA	49 B3
TRIANGLE RCH RD	MOD	6 D4
TRIANGLE RCH RD	STA	47 D2
TRIMMER SPGS RD	FRCO	58 A3
TRIMMER SPGS RD	INY	58 C2
TRINDADE RD	MCO	48 B4
TRNIDAD SCNC DR	HUM	9 E4
TRINITY	TEH	18 D5
TRINITY AV	FRCO	56 E3
TRINITY AV	FRCO	57 A4
TRINITY RD	SON	38 B2
TRINITY ST	FRE	165 C4
TRINITY ALPS RD	TRI	11 D5
TRINITY DAM BL	TRI	11 D5
TRINITY DAM BL	TRI	17 E1
TRINITY MTN RD	SHA	12 A5
TRINITY PINE DR	TRI	17 B3
TRIPP FLATS RD	RIV	100 B5
TRIUNFO CYN RD	LACO	96 E1
TRONA RD	SBD	80 E2
TRONA RD	SBD	81 A1
TRONA AIRPRT RD	INY	71 B4
TRONA WLDRSE RD	INY	71 B4
TROPICANA AV	CLK	74 D3
TROPICANA AV	CLK	210 C4
TROWER	MPA	49 A3
TROWER AV	NAP	133 A1
TROY RD	SBD	92 C2
TRUCKEE AV	TEH	24 D1
TRUCKE ARPRT RD	NEV	27 D5
TRUCKE-TAHO ARP	NEV	35 E1
TRUESDALE RD	SLO	76 D1
TRUEX RD	BUT	25 D3
TRUMAN RD	KER	89 D1
TRUMAN MDWS RD	MNO	44 C5
TRUMBULL RD	LAS	21 D2
TRUXTUN AV	BKD	166 B3
TRUXTUN AV	KER	78 D3
TSCHIRKY RD	SIS	5 D2
TUBBS RD	SOL	39 A2
TUCACOTA HLS RD	RCO	99 E5
TUCKER RD	KER	79 C4
TUCKER RD	LAS	21 D5
TUCKER CYN RD	SLO	76 D1
TUCSON AV	KIN	67 D4
TUDOR RD	SUT	33 C3
TUGG WY	CAL	41 A5
TUJUNGA AV	LACO	Q B3
TUJUNGA CYN BL	LACO	Q C1
TUJUNGA CYN RD	LACO	Q B1
TULARE AV	KER	77 E2
TULARE AV	FRCO	57 C3
TULARE AV	TUL	68 B1
TULARE ST	FRE	165 D4
TULAROSA RD	SB	86 C3
TULE LN	CC	39 C5
TULE LN	GLE	24 E4
TULE RD	COL	33 A3
TULE RD	YOL	39 D2
TULE CYN TK TR	RCO	107 C1
TULE CREEK RD	TRI	17 B2
TULEDAD RD	LAS	8 D5
TULE PEAK RD	RCO	107 B1
TULE SPRING RD	INY	72 A2
TULE SPGS TK TR	SDCO	107 B4
TULIP AV	STA	47 C4
TULLOCH RD	MCO	48 B1
TULLOCH RD	TUO	41 B5
TULLY RD	MDO	162 A2
TULLY RD	SJCO	40 C4
TULLY RD	SCL	46 B4
TULLY RD	STA	47 C2
TULLY CREEK RD	HUM	10 C3
TUMBLEWEED RD	LACO	90 C4
TUNA CANYON RD	LACO	97 B2
TUNGSTEN RD	MNO	51 D3
TUNGSTEN CTY RD	INY	51 C4
TUNITAS CK RD	SMCO	45 C4
TUNNEL RD	B	156 C4
TUOLUMNE AV	FRCO	56 D4
TUOLUMNE BLVD	MDO	162 A4
TUOLUMNE DR	MLBR	144 B5
TUOLUMNE RD	STA	47 C3
TUOLUMNE ST	VAL	134 D2
TUPMAN RD	KER	78 B3
TURK ST	SF	142 A3
TURK ST	SF	143 B5
TURKEY AV	BUT	25 D5
TURKEY FLAT RD	MON	66 D4
TURKEY HILL RD	KLAM	5 E2
TURLOCK AV	SCL	54 D1
TURLOCK RD	MCO	48 B3
TURNBULL CYN RD	LACO	98 B2
TURNBULL CYN RD	LACO	R B5
TURNELL RD	TEH	18 C4
TURNER AV	BUT	33 C1
TURNER AV	MCO	47 D4
TURNER AV	SBD	98 E2
TURNER DR	TUL	68 B2
TURNER RD	AMA	40 E2
TURNER RD	MCO	47 D4
TURNER RD	SJCO	39 E4
TURNER RD	SJCO	40 A4
TURNER RD	STA	47 D3
TURNER ISLND RD	MCO	56 A1
TURQUOISE ST	SD	105 C5
TURQUOISE ST	SD	211 A5
TURQUOISE ST	SDCO	V A3
TURQUOISE ST	SDCO	106 C5
TURRI RD	SLO	75 E3
TURRI RD	SLO	76 A3
TURTLE MTN RD	SBD	95 C4
TURTLE VLY RD	SBD	91 C2
TUSCAN SPGS RD	TEH	18 D4
TUSSING RCH RD	SBD	91 C4
TUSTIN AV	CM	199 C3
TUSTIN AV	NB	199 C3
TUSTIN AV	OR	194 E3
TUSTIN AV	OR	196 E2
TUSTIN AV	ORA	98 C4
TUSTIN AV	ORA	196 E4
TUSTIN AV	ORA	199 C3
TUSTIN AV	SA	196 E4
TUSTIN AV	ORA	T D2
TU SU LN	INY	51 D4
TUTTLECREEK RD	INY	60 A4
TUTTLETOWN RD	TUO	41 C5
TUXEDO AV N	S	160 C3
TUXFORD ST	LACO	Q B2
TWEEDY BLVD	LACO	R D5
TWENTIETH ST	C	124 E5
TWENTY-EIGHT MI	STA	47 E1
TWNTY MULE TEAM	INY	72 A1
TWNTY MULE TEAM	KER	80 C4
TWNTYNINE PALMS	SBD	100 E1
TWNTYNINE PALMS	SBD	101 D1
TWENTY-SIX MILE	STA	47 D1
TWIN RD S	MNO	43 A3
TWIN CITIES RD	SAC	39 E3
TWIN CITIES RD	SAC	40 A3
TWIN LAKES RD	MNO	43 B3
TWIN LAKES RD	TRI	12 B3
TWIN LKS CMPST	ALP	35 E5
TWIN OAKES RD	KER	79 D3
TWIN OAKS VLY	SDCO	106 C3
TWIN PEAKS RD	SDCO	106 D4
TWIN PINES RD	RCO	100 A3
TWIN VALLEY RD	LAK	31 E2
TWIN VIEW BLVD	SHA	18 C2
TWISSELMAN RD	KER	67 B5
TWIST RD	TUO	41 C5
TWIST RD	TUO	48 C1
TWITCHLL ISL RD	SAC	39 C4
TWO MILE RD	COL	32 D1
TWO MILE RD	SBD	101 B1
TYLER AV	LACO	R B4
TYLER RD	AMA	40 E1
TYLER RD	TEH	18 D5
TYLER ST	MONT	167 E3
TYLER ST	RCO	99 A3
TYLER ST	RCO	101 B4
TYLER ST	SAL	171 B2
TYLER ST	SDCO	V D4
TYLER ST	SDCO	111 D1
TYLER FOOT CRSG	NEV	26 B5
TYLER GULCH RD	SIS	3 D4
TYLER ISLAND RD	SAC	39 D4
U		
U ST	FRE	165 E3
UBEHEBE RD	INY	60 E4
UGO ST	MCO	48 A4
UKIAH RD	MEN	31 B2
UKIAH BOONVILLE	MEN	30 E3
UKIAH BOONVILLE	MEN	31 A3
UKONOM LKOUT RD	SIS	2 E5
ULLREY AV	SJCO	47 C1
ULRIC ST	SD	213 D3
ULRIC ST	SDCO	V B3
ULRIC ST	SDCO	111 C1
UNDERPASS RD	MEN	22 E4
UNDERSTOCK DR	BUT	25 C2
UNDERWOOD LN	INY	51 D4
UNDERWOOD RD	MON	54 C5
UNDERWD MTN RD	TRI	16 E1
UNDINE RD	SJCO	46 E1
UNION AV	BKD	166 E3
UNION AV	KER	166 E5
UNION AV	FRFD	135 C4
UNION AV	SB	86 C1
UNION AV	SCL	46 B5
UNION AV	SOL	38 E3
UNION RD	KER	78 B4
UNION RD	MAN	161 A3
UNION RD	SBT	54 E3
UNION RD	SJCO	47 B1
UNION RD	SLO	76 B1
UNION ST	EUR	121 C2
UNION ST	HUM	15 E1
UNION CITY BLVD	ALA	45 E3
UNION HILL RD	TRI	17 D2
UNION RIDGE RD	ED	34 E5
UNION SCHOOL RD	SHA	18 C1
UNION SUGAR AV	SB	86 B3
UNITED ST	KER	80 A5
UNIVERSITY AV	KER	78 E2
UNIVERSITY AV	PA	147 B2
UNIVERSITY AV	RIV	205 B2
UNIVERSITY AV	RCO	99 B2
UNIVERSITY AV	SAL	171 A4
UNIVERSITY AV	SD	214 D5
UNIVERSITY AV	SD	215 D1
UNIVERSITY AV	SD	216 D1
UNIVERSITY AV	SDCO	V B4
UNIVERSITY AV	SDCO	111 D1
UNIVERSITY DR	IRV	200 C2
UNIVERSITY DR	ORA	98 C4
UNIVERSITY DR	ORA	T D4
UPAS ST	SD	216 A1
UPHAM RD	BUT	25 E5
UPHILL RD	SBD	101 A1
UPJOHN RD W	KER	80 D1
UPLAND RD	VEN	88 C5
UPPER TER	AVLN	105 B5
UPPER BEAR RIV	HUM	15 D3
UPPR COUGR FIRE	SIS	4 D5
UPPR COUGR FIRE	SIS	12 D1
UPPER DIVISN CK	INY	59 E2
UPPER DORRAY RD	CAL	41 A2
UPPER FALL RD	SIS	13 A2
UPPER LK CTY RD	MOD	7 D5
UPR MAD RIV RD	TRI	17 A4
UPPER PALRMO RD	BUT	25 D5
UPPER SHOTGN RD	SHA	12 C4
UPPER S FORK RD	TRI	16 E2
UPPR SUMMRS MDW	MNO	43 B3
UPPER TOBY RCH	HUM	16 C5
UPPER WILLOW CK	SIS	4 C3
UPTON RD	AMA	40 E1
USAL RD	MEN	22 B2
USFS CAMP RD	TRI	17 A1
USONA RD	MPA	49 C4
USTICK RD	STA	47 C3
UTAH AV	SSF	144 C1
UTAH DR	INY	70 E1
UTAH ST	FRFD	135 B3
UTAH TR	SBD	101 C1
UTAH MINE RD	BUT	25 D2
UTICA AV	KIN	67 D4
UTICA PWRHSE RD	CAL	41 C4
UVAS RD	SCL	54 C1
UXMAL	BAJA	112 B4
V		
V ST	MER	170 A4
VADNEY AV	TEH	24 E2
VAIL	SJCO	39 E3
VAIL RD	IMP	109 A3
VAIRA RANCH RD	AMA	40 D2
VALDOR RD	TRI	17 C1
VALENCIA AV	LACO	89 B4
VALENCIA AV	ORA	98 C3
VALENCIA AV	ORA	T D1
VALENCIA BLVD	TUL	58 C5
VALENCIA BLVD	TUL	68 C1
VALENCIA RD	SCR	54 B2
VALENSIN RD	SAC	40 A3
VALENTINE AV	FRCO	57 C4
VALENTINE AV	FRCO	67 C1
VALERIA AV	FRCO	56 B2
VALERIO ST	STB	174 B3
VALK RD	STA	47 E2
VALLECITO ST	SHA	18 C1
VALLECITOS RD	ALA	46 B2
VALLE VISTA AV	VAL	134 C3
VALLE VISTA RD	SBD	101 B1
VALLEY AV	ALA	46 B2
VALLEY BLVD	LACO	97 E2
VALLEY BLVD	LACO	98 B2
VALLEY BLVD	LACO	R B4
VALLEY BLVD	SBD	99 A2
VALLEY PKWY	SDCO	106 D3
VALLEY RD	ED	34 C5
VALLEY RD	KER	80 C3
VALLEY RD	MEN	23 A5
VALLEY RD	PLA	34 A3
VALLEY RD	SAC	34 C5
VALLEY RD E	SB	87 D4
VALLEY RD W	MOD	8 B3
VALLEY CTR RD	SBD	92 B1
VALLEY CTR RD	SDCO	106 E3
VALLEY CIR BL	LACO	97 B1
VALLEY CTOFF RD	LAS	14 B3
VALLEY FORD RD	SON	37 D3
VLY FRD/FRNKLN- -MARSH RD	MAR	37 D3
VLY FRD/FRNKLN- -SCHOOL RD	MAR	37 D3
VALLEY HOME RD	STA	47 D1
VALLEY SAGE RD	LACO	89 D4
VALLEY VIEW DR	CAL	41 C3
VALLEY VIEW DR	SBD	102 C1
VALLEY VIEW RD	JKSN	3 E1
VALLEY VIEW RD	SBD	91 C1
VALLEY VIEW ST	ORA	98 B3
VALLEY VIEW ST	ORA	T B2
VALLEY VW LKOUT	TEH	24 A2
VALLEY VISTA BL	LA	178 E5
VALLEY WELLS RD	INY	71 B4
VALLEY WELLS RD	SBD	81 C5
VALLEY WEST RD	KER	78 A4
VALLOMBROSA AV	BUT	25 B3
VALLOMBROSA AV	BUT	124 D4
VALLOMBROSA AV	C	124 D4
VALOS RD	KER	78 E5
VALPARAISO AV	SCL	45 D4
VALPICO RD	SJCO	46 E2
VALPREDO AV	KER	78 D5
VAL VERDE	PLA	34 B4
VALYERMO	LACO	90 C4
VAN ALDEN AV	LA	178 C4
VAN ALLEN	SJCO	40 C5
VAN ALLEN	SJCO	47 C1
VAN ARSDALE RD	MEN	23 B5
VAN BRMMR LKOUT	SIS	5 B4
VAN BUREN BLVD	RCO	99 A2
VAN BUREN ST	MONT	167 E4
VAN BUREN ST	RCO	101 A4
VANCE AV	HUM	15 D5
VAN CLIFF	MCO	47 E5
VANDEGRIFT BLVD	SDCO	106 B2
VANDEGRIFT RD	SDCO	106 B2
VANDEN RD	SOL	39 A3
VANDENBERG RD	SB	86 B2
VANDER LINDN RD	IMP	112 C3
VANDER POEL RD	IMP	112 A3
VANDER VEER RD	RCO	101 C5
VAN DOLLEN RD	SLO	66 B5
VAN DUSEN CYN	SBD	92 A5
VAN DUZEN RD	TRI	16 E4
VAN DUZEN RD E	TRI	16 E3
VAN GORDN CK RD	SLO	75 C1
VAN LOON CUTOFF	MNO	51 D2
VAN NESS AV	FRE	165 D3
VAN NESS AV	FRCO	57 C3
VAN NESS AV	LACO	Q C5
VAN NESS AV	SF	143 A4
VAN NESS AV	SFCO	45 C1
VAN NESS AV S	SF	142 C4
VAN NESS RD	TRI	12 A5
VAN NUYS BLVD	LACO	89 C5
VAN NUYS BLVD	LACO	97 C1
VAN NUYS BLVD	LACO	Q A1
VANOWEN ST	BUR	179 B2
VANOWEN ST	LA	177 A2
VANOWEN ST	LA	178 B2
VANOWEN ST	LA	179 B2
VAN SICKLE RD	SOL	39 A4
VARGAS RD	ALA	46 B3
VARNER RD	RCO	100 D3
VARNI RD	SCR	54 B2
VASCO RD	ALA	46 C2
VASCO RD	CC	46 C1
VASQUEZ CYN RD	LACO	89 C4
VASQUEZ CK RD	SBT	55 D4
VASSAR AV	MCO	48 C5
VASSAR ST	RENO	130 C4
VAUGHN AV	MCO	48 B4
VAUGHN RD	RCO	108 E1
VAUGHN RD	SOL	39 B2
VAWTER RD	COL	32 E3
VAWTER RANCH RD	RCO	99 E5
VEDDER RD	SHA	13 C5
VEE BEE ST	RCO	100 E3
VENCILL RD	IMP	112 C3
VENDEL RD	IMP	108 E4
VENICE BLVD	LA	183 C5
VENICE BLVD	LA	184 C3
VENICE BLVD	LA	185 C3
VENICE BLVD	LA	187 C2
VENICE BLVD	LA	188 A1
VENICE BLVD	LACO	97 C2
VENICE BLVD	LACO	Q A5
VENTURA AV	FRCO	57 D3
VENTURA AV	MAD	56 D1
VENTURA AV	VEN	88 A5
VENTURA AV	VENT	175 B2
VENTURA BLVD	LA	177 D4
VENTURA BLVD	LA	178 A4
VENTURA BLVD	LACO	97 C1
VENTURA FRWY	BUR	179 C5
VENTURA FRWY	LA	177 C4
VENTURA FRWY	LA	178 B4
VENTURA FRWY	LA	179 C5
VENTURA FRWY	LACO	97 A1
VENTURA FRWY	VENT	175 C2
VENTURA FRWY	VEN	88 A5
VENTURA FRWY	VEN	96 C1
VENTURA RD	MCO	48 B5
VENTURA RD	OXN	176 A4
VENTURA RD	VEN	96 B1
VENTURA ST	FRE	165 D5
VENTURA ST	VEN	88 D4
VENTURE VLY RD	SDCO	107 D3
VENZKE RD	SHA	18 D3
VERA AV	KER	80 D1
VERANO AV	SON	132 C3
VERBENA AV	C	124 E2
VERBENA AV	SBD	91 B3
VERBENA DR	RCO	100 D2
VERDE AV	MCO	47 D4
VERDEMNT RCH RD	SBD	99 B1
VERDE SCHOOL RD	IMP	112 C3
VERDI PEAK RD	SIE	27 E4
VERDUGO AV	BUR	179 B4
VERDUGO AV	LACO	Q B3
VERDUGO BLVD	LACO	R D2
VERDUGO LN	KER	78 C2
VERDUGO RD	LACO	R D3
VERMICULITE MN	SBD	100 E2
VERMONT AV	ANA	193 C3
VERMONT AV	LA	182 B5
VERMONT AV	LA	185 C5
VERMONT AV	LACO	97 D3
VERMONT AV	LACO	S C2
VERMONT CYN RD	LA	182 B2
VERNON AV	LACO	97 D2
VERNON AV	LACO	Q C4
VERNON AV	LACO	R C3
VERNON RD	SUT	33 D4
VERSAILLES AV	A	159 A2
VESTA ST	SDCO	111 D1
VESTA ST	SDCO	V C4
VESTAL RD	TEH	18 A4
VETERAN AV	LACO	Q A4
VETERANS HALL	TRI	10 E5
VIA CAPRI	SD	211 A3
VIA DE LA VALLE	SDCO	106 C4
VIA DEL REY	MONT	167 D4
VIA DEL REY	MON	53 E3
VIADUCT BLVD	SBDO	207 B2
VIA GAYUBA	MONT	167 D4
VIA PARAISO	MONT	167 D4
VIA RANCHO PKWY	SDCO	106 D4
VIA SECO ST	SBD	92 A3
VIA VERDE	LACO	U D4
VICHY SPGS RD	MEN	31 B2
VICKREY LN	SOL	38 E2
VICTOR AV	SHA	18 C2
VICTOR RD	SJCO	40 B4
VICTOR ST	KER	80 D1
VICTORIA AV	RCO	99 A3
VICTORIA AV	RIV	205 C4
VICTORIA CT	KER	79 C4
VICTORIA DR	SDCO	107 B5
VICTORIA DR	SHA	18 B2
VICTORIA ST	LACO	97 E3
VICTORIA ST	LACO	S C1
VICTORIA ST	ORA	T C4
VICTORIA ST	SM	199 A2
VICTORIA ST	STB	174 B4
VICTORY AV	STA	47 D1
VICTORY BLVD	BUR	179 B2
VICTORY BLVD	LA	177 C2
VICTORY BLVD	LA	178 B3
VICTORY BLVD	LA	179 B2
VICTORY BLVD	LACO	97 D1
VICTORY BLVD	LACO	Q A2
VICTORY HWY	CC	39 C5
VICTORY PL	BUR	179 D2
VICTORY PL	LACO	Q C2
VICTORY RD	SJCO	47 D1
VIEJAS GRADE	SDCO	107 B5
VIERRA RD	YUB	26 A5
VIEUDELOU AV	AVLN	104 B4
VIEW DR	TUL	58 B4
VIEW LAND RD	LAS	21 D3
VILAS RD	BUT	25 C2
VILLA AV	EC	217 C1
VILLA AV	SR	139 D3
VILLA RD	IMP	109 B5
VILLA ST	SAL	171 B3
VILLA CREEK RD	SLO	75 D2
VILLAGE DR	AMA	40 D3
VILLAGE RD	SDCO	V B3
VILLAGE RD	SDCO	106 C5
VLLA L JOLLA DR	SD	211 C1
VLLA MANUCHA RD	STA	47 C4
VILLA PARK RD	ORA	T E2
VINA RD	TEH	24 E2
VINCENT AV	LACO	R C3
VINCENT RD	MCO	47 E3
VINCENT RD	MCO	48 A3
VINCENT RD	STA	47 E3
VINCENT RD	STA	48 A3
VINE AV	MCO	48 B4
VINE AV	SJCO	47 D1
VINE ST	LA	181 D5
VINE ST	LACO	Q D3
VINE ST	SDCO	V E3
VINE ST	SDCO	107 A5
VINE ST	SJ	152 B4
VINE WY	KER	79 C1
VINE HILL RD	SCR	54 A1
VINELAND AV	FRCO	57 A4
VINELAND AV	LACO	97 D1
VINELAND AV	LACO	Q B3
VINELAND RD	KER	78 E4
VINEWOOD AV	MCO	47 E4
VINEWOOD AV	MCO	48 A4
VINEYARD AV	ALA	46 B2
VINEYARD AV	OXN	176 D1
VINEYARD AV	SBD	98 E2
VINEYARD AV	VEN	176 D1
VINEYARD DR	SLO	75 E1
VINEYARD DR	SLO	76 A1
VINEYARD RD	PLA	34 A5
VINEYARD RD	SJCO	40 A2
VINEYARD RD	STA	47 B3
VINEYARD RD	YUB	34 A2
VINEYARD WY	MCO	56 B1
VINEYARD CYN RD	MON	66 B4
VINNUM RD	HUM	16 B4
VINTON GULCH RD	BUT	25 D3
VINTON LOYALTON	PLU	27 D3
VIOLA AV	TEH	24 D2
VIOLA MINERAL	TEH	19 C3
VIRGIL AV	LACO	Q E4
VIRGINIA	SBD	92 D5
VIRGINIA AV	KIN	67 E4
VIRGINIA AV	MDO	162 B3
VIRGINIA RD	LACO	R E3
VIRGINIA RD	STA	47 E2
VIRGINIA RD	STA	48 A2
VIRGINIA RD	YUB	33 E1
VIRGINIA ST	RCO	99 D3
VIRGINIA ST N	RENO	130 B2
VIRGINIA ST S	RENO	130 B3
VIRGINIA LK RD	MNO	43 B4
VIRGINIATOWN RD	PLA	34 B3
VISALIA RD	FRCO	58 D4
VISALIA RD	TUL	68 C1
VISTA AV	MCO	48 D5
VISTA AV	RCO	98 E3
VISTA AV	SBD	98 D1
VISTA LN	LAS	21 B4
VISTA RD	SBD	91 B2
VISTA WY	SDCO	106 B3
VISTA CHINO	PMSP	206 A2
VISTA CHINO	RCO	100 D3
VISTA DEL MAR	LACO	97 C2
VISTA DL MAR BL	ELS	189 A4
VISTA DL MAR BL	LACO	Q A5
VISTA DEL VALLE	LA	182 B1
VISTA DE ORO	RCO	100 E3
VISTA ENCINA AV	MDO	162 D3
VISTA GRANDE DR	KER	79 D1
VISTA MINE RD	IMP	110 A4
VIVIAN RD	STA	47 C3
VLASNIK RD	KER	77 E2
VOGEL RD	IMP	111 E3
VOGEL RD	KER	79 D5
VOLCANO CIR	BUT	25 B3
VOLCANO PIONEER	AMA	41 A2
VOLCANOVILLE RD	ED	34 E3
VOLLEY RD	PLA	34 C3
VOLTA RD	MCO	55 D1
VOLTAIRE ST	SDCO	V A4
VOLTAIRE ST	SDCO	111 C1
VON GLAHN	SJCO	47 C1
VOORHESS RD	MCO	48 D5
VORDEN RD	SAC	39 D3
VOTAW RD	AMA	40 E1
VULCAN MINE RD	SBD	84 A5
VULCAN MINE RD	SBD	94 A1
W		
WAALEW RD	SBD	91 C3
W A BARR RD	SIS	12 C2
WABASH AV	SBD	99 D2
WABASH BLVD	SD	214 C5
WABASH BLVD	SD	216 C5
WABASH BLVD	SDCO	111 D1
WABASH BLVD	SDCO	V C4
WACHTEL WY	SAC	34 B5
WACKERMAN RD	TEH	24 C2
WADDELL ST	TUL	68 C2
WADDINGTON RD	HUM	15 E2
WADE AV	MCO	48 E5
WADLEIGH RD	COL	32 D1
WAGNER	SJCO	47 C1
WAGNER AV	ANA	194 A3
WAGNER AV	COL	32 E3
WAGON RD	BUT	25 C2
WAGON WHEEL	SBD	101 A1
WAGSTAFF RD	BUT	25 C3
WAHL RD	IMP	112 A3
WAINWRIGHT	MCO	47 D4
WAKEFIELD	FRCO	58 A4
WALCH AV	TEH	24 E2
WALDO RD	YUB	34 A2
WALERGA	PLA	33 E5
WALGROVE AV	LA	187 C1
WALKER DR	SHA	13 D4
WALKER PL	MNO	51 C1
WALKER RD	DN	1 E3
WALKER RD	IMP	108 E3
WALKER RD	LAS	14 C3
WALKER RD	MEN	23 A5
WALKER RD	MEN	31 A1
WALKER RD	NAPA	32 B5
WALKER RD	SBD	92 C5
WALKER RD	SIS	3 C3
WALKER RD	SON	37 E3
WALKER ST	GLE	24 D3
WALKER ST	ORA	T B2
WALKER WY	IMP	110 B5
WALKER BASIN RD	KER	79 C3
WALKER CREEK RD	INY	70 B2
WALKER CREEK RD	SIS	3 B3
WALKER LNDNG RD	SAC	39 D3
WALKER MINE RD	PLU	26 E1
WALKER MINE RD	SHA	18 B1
WALKER PLAINS	BUT	25 E2
WALKUP RD	COL	32 B1
WALL RD	SJCO	40 C4
WALLACE AV	VAL	134 D4
WALLACE RD	KER	78 C1
WALLACE RD	SON	37 E2
WALLACE RD	SON	38 A2
WALLACE CK RD	SON	37 D1
WALLEN RD	TEH	18 D4
WALLER ST	SF	141 E4
WALLER ST	SF	142 A4
WALLIS RD	STA	48 A3
WALLY HILL RD	CAL	41 B4
WALMORT RD	SAC	40 A2
WALNUT AV	CC	38 E5
WALNUT AV	FRE	165 C5
WALNUT AV	FRCO	57 C4
WALNUT AV	LACO	Q C2
WALNUT AV	MCO	48 A4
WALNUT AV	ORA	T E3
WALNUT AV	STA	47 C3
WALNUT AV	STA	47 D1
WALNUT AV	TUL	68 B1
WALNUT AV	U	123 B3
WALNUT AV	YUB	33 D2
WALNUT BLVD	CC	39 C5
WALNUT BLVD	CC	46 C1
WALNUT DR	COL	32 D2
WALNUT DR	HUM	15 E1
WALNUT DR	NAPA	29 D4
WALNUT DR	SJCO	40 C4
WALNUT LN	GLE	25 A4
WALNUT RD	TEH	24 D2
WALNUT ST	ANA	193 B4
WALNUT ST	C	124 A5
WALNUT ST	ORA	T C1
WALNUT ST	PAS	190 B3
WALNUT ST	TEH	18 C5
WALNUT ST	VAL	134 C1
WALNUT GROVE AV	LACO	R A4
WALNUT GROVE RD	SJCO	39 E3
WALSER RD	KER	79 C2
WALTERS RD	LAS	14 C3
WALTERS RD	SOL	39 A3
WALTERS CAMP RD	IMP	110 C2
WALTERS MINE RD	BUT	26 B3
WALTON AV	SUT	33 C2
WALTON AV	SUT	125 A5
WALTZ RD	PLA	33 E3
WAMBLE RD	STA	47 E1
WAMBLE RD	STA	48 A1
WANGENHEIM RD	STA	47 C4
WARD AV	STA	47 B4
WARD RD	HUM	10 B5
WARD RD	LACO	89 E4
WARD RD	MCO	55 E1
WARD CREEK RD	PLU	26 E1
WARD LAKE RD	LAS	21 B3

STREETS

STREET	CO.	PAGE	GRID
WARDLOW RD	LACO	98	A3
WARDLOW RD	LACO	S	E2
WARDLOW RD	LACO	T	A2
WARDROBE AV	MCO	48	B4
WARDS FERRY RD	TUO	41	D5
WARDS FERRY RD	TUO	48	D1
WARE RD	COL	32	E2
WARE RD	IMP	112	B4
WARING RD	SDCO	V	C3
WARING RD	SDCO	111	D1
WARING RD	STA	47	E3
WARM SPGS BLVD	ALA	46	B3
WARM SPRINGS RD	INY	51	D4
WARM SPRINGS RD	SON	38	B2
WARNER AV	FTNV	197	D2
WARNER AV	ORA	98	B4
WARNER AV	ORA	T	C3
WARNER AV	ORA	T	E3
WARNER AV	SA	197	D2
WARNER AV	SA	198	A1
WARNER AV	TUS	198	D2
WARNER RD S	LAS	8	C3
WARNER RD W	MOD	8	C1
WARNER ST	C	124	A3
WARNERVILLE RD	STA	47	E2
WARNERVILLE RD	STA	48	A2
WARREGARD RD	CAL	41	B3
WARREN AV	RCO	99	D4
WARREN AV	TEH	18	C4
WARREN FRWY	ALA	45	D1
WARREN FRWY	O	156	E5
WARREN RD	CAL	40	D4
WARREN RD	RCO	99	D5
WARREN RD	RCO	99	D4
WARREN VISTA AV	SBD	100	E1
WASCO WY	KER	78	A3
WASCO POND RD	KER	68	B5
WASHBURN WY	KLAM	5	B1
WASHINGTON AV	RCO	99	C5
WASHINGTON AV	SBD	99	B2
WASHINGTON AV	SDCO	V	D3
WASHINGTON AV	SDCO	106	E5
WASHINGTON AV	SA	195	D3
WASHINGTON AV	SA	196	A3
WASHINGTON BLVD	CUL	183	D5
WASHINGTON BLVD	CUL	187	C3
WASHINGTON BLVD	CUL	188	A2
WASHINGTON BLVD	DN	1	D4
WASHINGTON BLVD	LA	183	D5
WASHINGTON BLVD	LA	184	D4
WASHINGTON BLVD	LA	185	B4
WASHINGTON BLVD	LA	186	C5
WASHINGTON BLVD	LA	187	A3
WASHINGTON BLVD	LACO	97	E2
WASHINGTON BLVD	LACO	98	A2
WASHINGTON BLVD	LACO	R	E3
WASHINGTON BLVD	LACO	R	A5
WASHINGTON BLVD	MCO	47	E4
WASHINGTON BLVD	MCO	48	A4
WASHINGTON BLVD	PAS	190	A2
WASHINGTON PL	CUL	188	A2
WASHINGTON PL	LA	188	A2
WASHINGTON PL	SD	213	C5
WASHINGTON RD	MCO	56	B1
WASHINGTON RD	NEV	26	D5
WASHINGTON RD	SBD	92	A3
WASHINGTON RD	STA	47	D3
WASHINGTON ST	SB	87	C1
WASHINGTON ST	FRCO	66	D3
WASHINGTON ST	LA	187	B3
WASHINGTON ST	MONT	167	E4
WASHINGTON ST	RCO	99	B3
WASHINGTON ST	RCO	100	E4
WASHINGTON ST	RIV	99	D5
WASHINGTON ST	SD	213	D5
WASHINGTON ST	SD	215	C1
WASHINGTON ST	SDCO	V	B4
WASHINGTON ST	SDCO	111	C1
WASHINGTON ST	SCLR	151	C3
WASHINGTON ST	SNRA	163	B2
WASHINGTON ST	S	160	A5
WASHINGTON ST	TUO	163	B2
WASHINGTON ST E	SON	38	A3
WASHOE	FRCO	56	C4
WASHOE AV	FRCO	56	C3
WASIOJA RD	SB	77	C5
WASIOJA RD	SB	87	B1
WATER ST	AMA	40	E2
WATER ST	SC	169	D2
WATER ST	SCR	54	A2
WATER CANYON RD	KER	80	B3
WATER CANYON RD	KER	79	C5
WATERFRONT RD	CC	154	E1
WATERLOO LN	DGL	36	C3
WATERLOO RD	SJCO	40	B5
WATERMAN AV	SBD	99	C2
WATERMAN AV	SBD	207	E3
WATERMAN AV	SBDO	207	E3
WATERMAN BLVD	FRFD	135	A2
WATERMAN RD	AMA	40	D2
WATERMAN RD	SAC	40	A2
WATERS RD	VEN	88	D5
WATERS END RD	SLO	76	C4
WATERTOWN RD	CAL	40	E3
WATER TROUGH RD	SON	37	D2
WATKINS DR	RCO	99	B2
WATKINS RD	TEH	24	D2
WATKINS TR	KER	79	C5
WATKINSON RD	SJCO	40	B3
WATSON RD	MEN	31	B2
WATSONVILLE RD	SCL	54	D1
WATT AV	SAC	34	A5
WATT AV	SAC	40	A1
WATT LN	BUT	25	C5
WATTENBURG RD	MEN	23	A3
WATTRSN TROUGHS	MNO	51	B2
WATTS AV	SUT	33	D3
WATTS DR	KER	79	C3
WATTS VALLEY RD	FRCO	57	E3
WATTS VALLEY RD	FRCO	58	A3
WAUCOBA SALINE	INY	60	C2
WAUKEENA RD	YOL	39	D2
WAVERLY	SBD	91	D1
WAVERLY	SJCO	40	D5
WAY RD	MCO	55	E1
WAYBUR RD	SUT	33	C3
WEAVER CREEK E	TRI	17	D1
WEAVER CT	KER	79	D3
WEAVER RD	IMP	109	A4
WEAVER HILLS DR	RCO	107	A1
WEAVERVLL SCOTT	TRI	12	A2
WEAVERVLL SCOTT	TRI	11	D5
WEAVERVLL SCOTT	TRI	11	E3
WEBB RD	IMP	109	C5
WEBB RD	SHA	18	D3
WEBB RD	SUT	33	C4
WEBER AV	FRE	165	A2
WEBER AV	S	160	C4
WEBER RD	SOL	39	B2
WEBSTER AV	RCO	99	C3
WEBSTER RD	SBD	91	E1
WEBSTER ST	A	157	E5
WEBSTER ST	ALA	45	D1
WEBSTER ST	FRFD	135	B4
WEBSTER ST	O	158	A3
WEDEL AV	KER	77	E1
WEED RD	IMP	112	A4
WEEDPATCH HWY	KER	78	E3
WEEDS POINT RD	YUB	26	C4
WEEMASOUL RD	TEH	18	A5
WEGIS RD	KER	78	C3
WEIMAR CROSS RD	PLA	34	C3
WEINERT RD	IMP	109	A5
WEIR AV	MCO	47	E4
WEIR CANYON RD	ORA	98	D3
WEISS RD	SUT	33	B2
WEISER RD	KER	77	C1
WEITCHER RD	MOD	14	E1
WELCH CT	CAL	41	B5
WELCOME AV	KER	80	D1
WELDON	FRCO	58	A3
WELLBARN AV	FRCO	57	E1
WELLOCK RD	TRI	17	D1
WELLS AV	RENO	130	C3
WELLS AV N	RENO	130	C2
WELLS DR	LA	178	C4
WELLS LN	SJCO	40	B4
WELLS RD	COL	32	D1
WELLS RD	MAD	49	C5
WELLS RD	RCO	103	D4
WELLS RD	VEN	88	B5
WELLSFORD RD	STA	47	D2
WELLSONA RD	SLO	76	A1
WELTY RD	STA	47	A3
WENDEL RD	LAS	21	D3
WENGLER HILL RD	SHA	19	A2
WENTE ST	ALA	46	C2
WENTWORTH ST	LACO	89	D5
WENTWORTH ST	LACO	Q	B1
WENTWTH SPGS RD	ED	34	E3
WENTWTH SPGS RD	ED	35	B3
WERICK RD	RCO	99	A3
WESCOTT RD	COL	33	A2
WEST AV	FRE	165	A1
WEST AV	FRCO	57	C4
WEST AV	FRCO	67	C1
WEST AV	RCO	110	C1
WEST DR	RCO	100	D2
WEST LN	S	160	E2
WEST LN	SJCO	40	A5
WEST LN	MCO	48	B4
WEST LN	SJCO	160	D1
WEST RD	COL	33	A3
WEST RD	LACO	R	B5
WEST RD	MEN	31	B1
WEST RD	STA	47	C4
WEST ST	ANA	193	B4
WEST ST	EUR	121	E1
WEST ST	O	157	E2
WEST ST	ORA	T	C2
WEST ST	TUL	68	A2
WESTBROOK LN	DN	1	E3
WESTCLIFF DR	NB	199	C4
WEST COAST RD	HUM	16	C5
W END OREGN MTN	TRI	17	C1
WESTERN AV	KER	78	A2
WESTERN AV	LA	182	A4
WESTERN AV	LA	185	A5
WESTERN AV	LACO	97	D3
WESTERN AV	LACO	Q	C5
WESTERN AV	LACO	Q	C3
WESTERN AV	LACO	S	C3
WESTERN AV	ORA	T	B2
WESTERN CYN RD	LA	182	A3
WESTERN HILL RD	RCO	100	B5
WESTERN MINE	LAK	32	A5
WESTRN MINERALS	KER	78	A5
WESTFALL	MPA	49	C3
WESTFALL W	MPA	49	A4
WESTGATE AV	HUM	9	E3
WESTGATE DR	HUM	15	E1
WESTGATE DR	NAPA	38	D2
WESTHAVEN DR	HUM	9	E4
WESTLAKE BLVD	VEN	96	E1
WEST LAWN AV	FRCO	57	B4
WEST LAWN AV	FRCO	57	B5
WESTMINSTER AV	GGR	195	B3
WESTMINSTER AV	ORA	98	A4
WESTMINSTER AV	ORA	T	A2
WESTMINSTER AV	SA	195	B3
WESTMORELAND RD	IMP	108	E5
WESTON RD	TEH	24	B2
WESTOVER DR	TEH	18	D5
WESTOVER DR	TEH	24	D1
WEST PORTAL RD	MNO	50	D1
WESTRIDGE RD	TRI	17	B3
WESTSIDE BLVD	MCO	47	E4
WESTSIDE BLVD	MCO	48	A4
WESTSIDE FRWY	FRCO	56	B4
WESTSIDE FRWY	FRCO	66	E2
WEST SIDE FRWY	KER	77	D1
WEST SIDE FRWY	KER	78	D4
WESTSIDE FRWY	KIN	67	B4
WESTSIDE FRWY	MCO	55	D1
WESTSIDE FRWY	STA	47	B3
WEST SIDE HWY	INY	72	A1
WEST SIDE HWY	KER	67	B5
WEST SIDE HWY	KER	78	A4
WESTSIDE RD	IMP	111	E3
WEST SIDE RD	JOS	2	C1
WEST SIDE RD	LAS	8	A5
WESTSIDE RD	MOD	7	B3
WESTSIDE RD	MOD	8	A3
WESTSIDE RD	SHA	18	B1
WESTSIDE RD	SIE	27	C3
WESTSIDE RD	SIE	27	B3
WESTSIDE RD	SON	37	D1
WSIDE POTTR VLY	MEN	31	B1
WESTWOOD BLVD	LA	183	A4
WESTWOOD BLVD	LACO	Q	C4
WESTWOOD ST	TUL	68	D3
WET MEADOW RD	MNO	50	E1
WETMORE RD	ALA	46	C2
WEYER RD	STA	47	E2
WEYMOUTH BLUFF	HUM	15	E2
WHEALAN RD	MCO	48	D5
WHEATLAND RD	SUT	33	E3
WHEDBEE DR	SOL	38	E3
WHEELER RD	IMP	108	E5
WHEELER RD	SBD	91	C2
WHEELER CYN RD	VEN	88	B5
WHEELER NURSERY	SHA	12	E5
WHEELER RDG RD	KER	78	E5
WHEEL GULCH RD	TRI	17	B1
WHEELOCK RD	BUT	25	C3
WHISKEY CK RD	COL	32	E3
WHISKEY CK RD	SHA	18	B2
WHSKEY SLIDE RD	CAL	41	B3
WHISLER RD	KER	78	B1
WHITAKER BLF RD	MAR	37	D3
WHITE AV	LACO	U	C2
WHITE DR	BUT	25	B4
WHITE LN	KER	78	D3
WHITE LN	NAPA	29	C3
WHITE LN	SJCO	40	B5
WHITE RD	COL	33	A3
WHITE RD	MCO	47	D3
WHITE RD	MON	66	C4
WHITE RD	SBD	91	A4
WHITE RD	SCL	46	B4
WHITE COTTGE RD	NAPA	29	C2
WHITE COTTGE RD	NAPA	38	B1
WHITE CRANE RD	MCO	47	E4
WHITE CRANE RD	MCO	48	A4
WHITEHORSE RD	MOD	13	E2
WHITEHORSE RD	MOD	14	A2
WHITEHURST RD	SCL	54	C2
WHITE MTN RD	INY	51	E4
WHITE MTN RD	INY	60	D4
WHITE MTN RD	INY	60	D5
WHITE OAK DR	SHA	18	C3
WHITE PINE LN	SB	86	E2
WHITE PINE LN	SB	87	A2
WHITEPINE ST	SIS	4	B3
WHITE RIVER RD	KER	69	A5
WHITE ROCK RD	ED	40	C1
WHITE ROCK RD	MPA	49	A4
WHITE ROCK RD	MPA	48	E5
WHITE ROCK RD	MCO	48	E5
WHITE ROCK RD	SAC	40	A1
WHITE ROCK RD	SHA	17	C3
WHTE ROCK LK RD	NEV	27	B5
WHITES BRDGE AV	FRCO	56	D3
WHITES BRDGE AV	FRCO	57	C3
WHITES GULCH RD	SIS	11	C2
WHITES MILL RD	KER	69	B5
WHITES MILL RD	KER	79	B1
WHITEWTR CYN RD	RCO	100	C2
WHITE WOLF RD	TUO	42	D5
WHITE WOLF RD	TUO	63	C3
WHITLEY AV	KIN	67	D3
WHITLOCK RD	IMP	109	C5
WHITLOCK RD	MPA	49	A3
WHITLOCK RD E	MPA	49	B3
WHITLOW RD	HUM	16	C4
WHITMORE AV	STA	47	D2
WHITMORE RD	SHA	18	E2
WHITMORE RD	SHA	19	A2
WHITMRE TUBS RD	MNO	50	E2
WHITMRE TUBS RD	MNO	51	A2
WHITNEY AV	VAL	134	D1
WHITNY PORTL RD	INY	60	A4
WHITSETT AV	LACO	Q	A3
WHITTIER AV	RCO	99	E4
WHITTIER BLVD	LA	186	D4
WHITTIER BLVD	LACO	98	A2
WHITTIER BLVD	LACO	R	E4
WHITTIER BLVD	LACO	R	B5
WHITTIER BLVD	ORA	R	B5
WHITTLE AV E	AVLN	105	B5
WHITTLE RD	CAL	41	B4
WHITWELL WY	RCO	107	C1
WHITWORTH RD	MCO	47	C5
WHITWORTH RD	MCO	55	C1
WIASMUL RD	RCO	107	B1
WIBLE RD	KER	166	B5
WIBLE RD	KER	78	D4
WICKENDEN WAY	MOD	8	A1
WICKMAN RD	BUT	25	B5
WICKS ST	SB	86	C1
WIDGEON RD	YOL	39	D3
WIDOW SPGS DR	SIS	12	E2
WIDOW VALLEY RD	MOD	13	E3
WIDOW VALLEY RD	MOD	14	A3
WIGHT WY	LAK	31	D3
WILBUR	CC	39	B5
WILBUR AV	LA	178	C3
WILBUR RD	BUT	25	C4
WILBUR SPRGS RD	COL	32	B3
WILCOX RD	SHA	19	D1
WILCOX RD	TEH	18	D4
WILCOX RANCH RD	TUO	41	C5
WILD RD	SBD	91	B2
WILDASS RD	SBT	66	B1
WILDCAT RD	MCO	55	E2
WILDCAT RD	SHA	18	E3
WILDCAT RD	SHA	19	A3
WILDCAT RD	TEH	19	A3
WILD CAT TR	RCO	100	A5
WILDCAT CK RD	SIS	11	D2
WILDCAT CYN RD	CC	45	D1
WILDCAT CYN RD	SDCO	107	A5
WILD DUCK RD	MCO	55	E2
WILDER RD	HUM	16	A2
WILDER RD	TEH	18	D5
WLDRNSS LDGE RD	MEN	22	D3
WILDER RIDGE RD	HUM	16	A4
WILDHORSE RD	SBD	92	B1
WILDHORSE CY RD	MON	65	C2
WILDMAN RD	KER	78	E4
WILD PLUM RD	SIE	27	A4
WILDROSE RD	INY	61	C5
WILD WASH RD	SBD	91	C2
WILDWOOD AV	SLT	129	D3
WILDWOOD RD	COL	32	E3
WILDWOOD RD	KER	78	A2
WILDWOOD RD	SJCO	47	C1
WILDWOOD RD	TRI	17	C2
WILDWOOD CYN RD	SBD	99	E2
WILEY WELLS RD	RCO	103	B5
WILFRED CYN RD	MNO	51	B2
WILHOLT RD	SJCO	40	A5
WILKIE AV	SUT	33	D3
WILKINS AV	STA	47	D1
WILKINS RD	IMP	109	B2
WILKINS RD	IMP	112	D5
WILKINSON RD	IMP	109	A3
WILLARD RD	TEH	18	C5
WILLARD CK RD	LAS	20	E3
WILLIAM RD	BUT	25	C3
WILLIAM ST	SJ	152	C4
WILLIAMS	SJCO	47	C1
WILLIAMS AV	MCO	47	D4
WILLIAMS RD	IMP	109	B4
WILLIAMS RD	KER	79	E2
WILLIAMS RD	KER	80	D4
WILLIAMS RD	LAS	8	B4
WILLIAMS RD	MON	54	D4
WILLIAMS RD	SHA	13	E4
WILLIAMS CK RD	HUM	15	D2
WILLIAMSON RD	KER	79	D4
WILLIAMSON RD	RCO	107	A1
WILLIAMSON RD	TUO	41	B5
WILLIAM TELL TR	KER	79	C5
WILLIAMS VLY RD	PLU	20	C5
WILLIAMS WLL RD	SBD	81	E5
WILLIS RD	MCO	56	B1
WILLISTON RD	SUT	33	C1
WILLMOTT RD	MCO	55	D1
WILLMS RD	STA	48	A1
WILLOUGHBY RD	IMP	112	A4
WILLOW AV	CRTM	140	B1
WILLOW AV	FRCO	57	D2
WILLOW AV	GLE	24	E5
WILLOW AV	KER	89	C1
WILLOW DR	KER	78	A2
WILLOW DR	MAD	57	B1
WILLOW RD	MP	147	A2
WILLOW RD	SBD	91	C4
WILLOW RD	SDCO	V	E3
WILLOW RD	SDCO	107	A5
WILLOW RD	SLO	76	B5
WILLOW RD	SMCO	45	D3
WILLOW ST	LACO	97	E3
WILLOW ST	LACO	S	D2
WILLOW ST	SJ	152	C5
WILLOW WY	LAS	20	E2
WILLOW CREEK RD	AMA	40	D2
WILLOW CREEK RD	INY	52	D4
WILLOW CREEK RD	SBT	55	C5
WILLOW CREEK RD	SLO	75	E1
WILLOW CREEK RD	SLO	76	A1
WILLOW CREEK RD	SIS	4	C3
WILLOW CREEK RD	YUB	26	B5
WLLW CK RED RCK	SIS	5	B3
WILLOW GLEN DR	SDCO	V	E4
WILLOW GLEN DR	SDCO	111	E1
WILLOW GLEN RD	YUB	26	A5
WILLOW PASS RD	CC	39	A5
WILLOW POINT RD	YOL	39	D2
WILLOW RCH RD S	MOD	7	C3
WILLOWS RD	SDCO	107	B5
WILLOW SPGS EXT	SIS	13	A2
WILLOW SPGS RD	KER	79	D5
WILLOW SPGS RD	KER	89	D1
WILLOW SPGS RD	KER	90	A1
WILLOW SPGS RD	LAS	14	A5
WILLOW SPGS RD	LACO	89	C3
WILLOW SPGS RD	SCL	54	C1
WILLOW VLY RD	NEV	34	C1
WILL S GREEN RD	COL	32	E2
WILMINGTON AV	LACO	97	E3
WILMINGTON AV	LACO	S	D2
WILMINGTON BLVD	LA	191	B1
WILMINGTON BLVD	LACO	S	C2
WILSHIRE AV	SBD	101	C1
WILSHIRE BLVD	BH	183	B2
WILSHIRE BLVD	LA	180	D2
WILSHIRE BLVD	LA	183	B2
WILSHIRE BLVD	LA	185	A2
WILSHIRE BLVD	LACO	97	D2
WILSHIRE BLVD	LACO	Q	B4
WILSHIRE BLVD	LACO	180	D2
WILSHIRE BLVD	SMON	180	A4
WILSHIRE RD	SBD	92	A4
WILSON AV	COL	32	E3
WILSON AV	MAR	38	A4
WILSON AV	VAL	134	A3
WILSON DR	LA	181	A2
WILSON DR	TUL	68	E3
WILSON RD	IMP	112	D5
WILSON RD	KER	78	D3
WILSON RD	MCO	55	D1
WILSON RD	SUT	33	D3
WILSON ST	KER	79	C3
WILSON ST	RIV	100	A3
WILSON ST	TEH	24	E1
WILSON WY	PLA	34	B3
WILSON WY	SJCO	40	B5
WILSON WY	S	160	E4
WILSON BEND RD	COL	33	B3
WILSON CREEK RD	DN	1	E5
WILSON HILL RD	MAR	37	E4
WILSON HILL RD	SHA	19	A3
WILSON LAKE RD	TEH	19	D4
WILSON LANDING	BUT	25	A2
WILSON RANCH RD	SBD	90	E4
WILSON SPGS RD	LAS	14	A5
WILSON VLY RD	RCO	107	A1
WILTON PL	LA	181	E5
WILTON PL	LA	182	A5
WILTON PL	LA	184	E3
WILTON PL	LA	185	A3
WILTON RD	SAC	40	A2
WIMER RD	SJCO	40	D4
WINCHESTER BLVD	SCL	46	A5
WINCHESTER RD	RCO	99	D4
WINCHUCK RD	CUR	1	D2
WINDING WY	SR	139	B4
WINDING WY	SHA	18	D2
WINDING WY	SIS	12	E2
WINDLASS DR	RCO	101	C5
WINDSONG WY	RCO	107	B1
WINDSOR AV	LACO	R	B2
WINDSOR RD	SON	37	D1
WINDSOR RIV RD	SON	37	D1
WINE CREEK RD	SON	31	D5
WINE CREEK RD	SON	37	D1
WINEMAN RD	SLO	76	E5
WINEVILLE AV	SBD	99	A2
WINGATE RD	INY	71	C3
WINGFIELD RD	LAS	21	A3
WING LEVEE RD	SJCO	46	E1
WINNETKA AV	LA	178	A3
WINNETKA AV	LACO	97	B1
WINSHIP RD	SOL	39	C2
WINSHIP RD	YUBA	125	D4
WINSLOW RD	IMP	109	A2
WINSOME WY	SHA	18	B2
WINTER GRDNS BL	SDCO	V	E2
WINTER GRDNS BL	SDCO	106	E5
WINTERGREEN RD	SBD	90	E4
WINTERS RD	SBD	100	E1
WINTERS RD	SOL	39	A1
WINTRS GULCH RD	SIS	4	A5
WINTON AV W	ALA	45	E2
WINTON AV W	H	146	C4
WINTON RD	CAL	41	B2
WINTON WY	MCO	48	B4
WINTOON WY	SIS	12	E2
WIRT RD	IMP	109	B3
WISCONSIN AV	COL	32	E3
WISCONSIN AV	TEH	24	E2
WISE RD	PLA	33	E3
WISE RD	PLA	34	A3
WISHON AV	FRE	165	C2
WISHON DR	TUL	69	B2
WISTOS LN	LAS	21	B3
WITHERS AV	CC	38	E5
WITHROW RD	SHA	19	A2
WITTER SPG E RD	LAK	31	C2
WIXOM RD	IMP	111	E3
WOHLFORD RD	SDCO	106	E3
WOLF RD	NEV	34	C2
WOLF CREEK RD	ALP	36	C5
WOLF CREEK RD	NEV	34	C2
WOLFE RD	CPTO	150	A4
WOLFE RD	SCL	45	E4
WOLFE RD	SCL	46	A4
WOLFE RD	SVL	150	A3
WOLFE RD	VEN	96	C1
WOLFE GRADE	MAR	139	C5
WOLFSEN	MCO	47	E5
WOLFSEN	MCO	55	E1
WOLFSKILL	SOL	39	A1
WONDER AV	KER	80	A4
WONDERLAND BLVD	SHA	18	C1
WONDERLAND DR	RCO	100	A3
WONDER STUMP RD	DN	1	E3
WONDERVIEW RD	RCO	100	A3
WOO RD	MCO	55	E2
WOOD RD	RCO	99	B3
WOOD RD	SUT	33	B2
WOOD RD	VEN	96	C1
WOOD ST	GLE	24	D4
WOODBINE RD	RCO	100	C5
WOODBRIDGE RD	SJCO	39	E4
WOODBRIDGE RD	SJCO	40	B4
WOODBURY RD	LACO	R	B2
WOODBURY RD	PAS	190	A1
WOOD CANYON RD	INY	71	D1
WOODCUTTERS WY	SHA	19	B3
WOODEN VLY RD	NAPA	38	D2
WOODFORD-TEH RD	KER	79	C4
WOODHILL DR	SHA	13	A5
WOODHOUSE MINE	CAL	41	B2
WOODLAND AV	MCO	48	C4
WOODLAND AV	SR	139	E5
WOODLAND AV	STA	47	C2
WOODLAND AV	TEH	24	D1
WOODLAND DR	MPA	49	C3
WOODLAND WY	SHA	19	B3
WOODLF TUNNL RD	BUT	26	B4
WOODLEY RD	SDCO	106	C4
WOOLEY RD E	VEN	96	B1
WOODMAN AV	LACO	97	C1
WOODMAN AV	LACO	Q	C2
WOOD RANCH RD	LAS	21	B2
WOODRIDGE RD	SHA	19	B3
WOODROW AV	SC	169	C5
WOODRUFF AV	LACO	S	E2
WOODRUFF AV	LACO	T	A2
WOODRUFF LN	YUB	33	D1
WOODSBRO RD	SJCO	40	A5
WOODSIDE AV	SDCO	V	E2
WOODSIDE AV	SDCO	106	E5
WOODSIDE RD	SMCO	45	D3
WOODS LAKE RD	ALP	36	A5
WOODSON AV	TEH	24	D2
WOODSON RD	SJCO	40	A3
WOOD VALLEY RD	SDCO	106	E3
WOODVIEW LN	MPA	49	B4
WOODWARD AV	SJCO	47	A1
WOODY RD	KER	78	D1
WOODY ST	KER	78	E1
WOODY-GRANIT RD	KER	68	E5
WOODY-GRANIT RD	KER	69	A5
WOODY-GRANIT RD	KER	78	E1
WOODY-GRANIT RD	KER	79	A1
WOOKEY RD	BUT	25	A2
WOOLEY RD	OXN	176	A4
WOOLLOMES AV	KER	68	A5
WOOLNER AV	FRFD	135	A4
WORDEN AV	MCO	48	C5
WORDEN RD	CAL	41	B3
WORK RD	KER	90	B1
WORKMAN ST	LACO	Q	C1
WORKMAN MILL RD	LACO	98	A2
WORKMAN MILL RD	LACO	R	B4
WORMWOOD RD	IMP	111	E4
WORSLEY RD	RCO	100	C2
WORTH AV	TUL	68	D3
WORTH RD	SUT	33	D4
WORTHINGTON RD	IMP	108	E5
WORTHINGTON RD	MCO	47	C5
WORTHINGTON ST	KER	79	E1
WRAGG CANYON RD	NAPA	38	D2
WRAN RD	LAS	21	C4
WREN RD	STA	47	E2
WRIGHT AV	SVL	149	B3
WRIGHT AV	TUL	68	B3
WRIGHT RD	IMP	109	C5
WRIGHT RD	SIS	5	D3
WRIGHTS LAKE RD	ED	35	D4
WRIGLEY RD	HUM	15	E1
WRIGLEY TER RD	AVLN	105	B5
WUNPOST RD	MCO	65	E4
WYANDOTTE AV	BUT	25	D4
WYNDTT MNRS RCH	BUT	25	D4
WYE RD	INY	51	D4
WYER RD	COL	32	E3
WYLIE DR	MDO	162	E2
WYLIE ST	SB	87	D1
WYMAN CREEK RD	INY	52	A3
WYNCOOP RD	SUT	33	B2
WYNDAM LN	RED	122	C4
WYNDHAVEN DR	TEH	18	D4
WYO AV	GLE	24	E3
WYSE RD	LACO	89	D4
X			
XIMENO AV	LACO	S	E3
Y			
YAJOME ST	NAP	133	C2
YANKEE HILL RD	TUO	41	C4
YAQUI GULCH RD	MPA	49	B3
YAQUI PASS RD	SDCO	107	E3
YARD RD	TEH	18	D4
YELLOW BUTTE RD	SIS	4	D5
YELLW JACKET RD	MNO	51	C1
YELLW JACKET RD	TEH	19	C4
YERBA BLVD	KER	80	B4
YERBA BUENA RD	VEN	96	D2
YERMO RD	SBD	82	C5
YERMO RD	SBD	92	A1
YERMO CUTOFF	SBD	81	E5
YERMO CUTOFF	SBD	82	A5
YGNACIO VLY RD	CC	45	E1
YGNACIO VLY RD	CC	39	A5
YMCA RD	FRCO	58	D3
YOAKIM BRDG RD	SON	31	C5
YOCUM RD	IMP	109	B3
YOKE ST	SHA	18	C3
YOLANDA AV	KER	89	C2
YOLANO RD	SOL	39	C2
YOLO AV	FRCO	56	E4
YOLO ST	STA	47	C4
YOLO CO LINE RD	COL	32	E3
YOLO CO LINE RD	COL	33	A3
YORBA LN	SBD	90	E3
YORBA LINDA BL	ORA	98	C3
YORBA LINDA BL	ORA	T	D1
YORK AV	KIN	67	A5
YORK BLVD	LACO	97	E1
YORK BLVD	LACO	R	A3
YORK RD	IMP	110	D5
YORK RD	SIS	4	C3
YORK ST	NAP	133	C3
YOSEMITE AV	MAN	161	A4
YOSEMITE AV	MCO	48	C4
YOSEMITE AV	SJCO	47	B1
YOSEMITE BLVD	MDO	162	D4
YOSEMITE BLVD	STA	47	D2
YOSEMITE BLVD	STA	48	B2
YOSEMITE RD	TUO	41	D5
YOSEMTE OAKS RD	MPA	49	B3

STREETS

STREET INDEX

STREET	CO.	PAGE & GRID
YSMTE SPGS PKWY	MAD	49 C5
YOU BET RD	NEV	34 D2
YOUD RD	MCO	48 B3
YOUNG AV	COL	32 E3
YOUNG RD	COL	24 E5
YOUNG RD	IMP	109 B3
YOUNG RD	STA	47 C3
YOUNG ST	RCO	99 E4
YOUNG LOVE AV	SC	169 B4
YOUNGS HILL RD	YUB	26 C4
YOUNGSTOWN RD	MCO	47 E4
YOUNT ST	NAPA	29 D4
YOUNTVLLE CROSS	NAPA	29 D4
YOUNTVLL CRS RD	NAPA	38 C2
YOWELL RD	MOD	14 B3
YREKA AGER RD	SIS	4 B4
YREKA MONO	SIS	4 A4
YREKA WALKER RD	SIS	3 D3
YREKA WALKER RD	SIS	4 A4
YTURRIARTE RD	SBT	55 D4
YUBA AV	FRCO	56 E3
YUBA NEVADA RD	YUB	26 B5
YUBA PASS RD	SIE	27 B4
YUCAIPA BLVD	SBD	99 D2
YUCCA RD	RCO	107 C1
YUCCA RD	SBD	90 E3
YUCCA TR	SBD	100 E1
YUCCA LOMA RD	SBD	91 C4
YUCCA MESA RD	SBD	100 E1
Z		
ZABALA RD	MON	54 D4
ZABRISKIE PT RD	INY	72 A1
ZACA STATION RD	SB	86 E2
ZACHARIAS RD	STA	47 B3
ZACHARY AV	KER	78 C1
ZANES RD	HUM	15 E1
ZAPPONE RD	IMP	110 A4
ZAYANTE RD	SCR	54 A1
ZEDIKER AV	FRCO	57 E3
ZEDIKER AV	FRCO	57 E4
ZEERING RD	STA	47 C3
ZEIGLER PT RD	HUM	10 D5
ZELDA LN	SBD	101 E1
ZENIA RD	MEN	23 A2
ZENIA BLUFF RD	HUM	16 D5
ZENIA LK MTN RD	TRI	17 A5
ZENIA LK MTN RD	TRI	23 A1
ZENO RD	LAK	31 D2
ZERKER RD	KER	78 C2
ZERMATT DR	KER	79 C5
ZINC HILL RD	INY	70 E1
ZINC MINE RD	SBD	84 A3
ZINFANDEL DR	SAC	40 A1
ZINFANDEL LN	NAPA	29 C3
ZINK RD	BUT	25 E3
ZITZMAN RD	SIS	3 C5
ZLABEK RD	SIS	5 D2
ZOGG MINE RD	SHA	18 B2
ZOO DR	LACO	Q C3
ZULU QUEN MN RD	RCO	102 A2
ZUMWALT	SJCO	47 C1
ZUMWALT AV	TUL	68 A2
ZUMWALT RD	COL	32 D2
ZZYZX RD	SBD	83 B4
NUMERIC STREETS		
1ST AV	BARS	208 B1
1ST AV	BUT	25 B3
1ST AV	GLE	24 E3
1ST AV	IMP	112 D5
1ST AV	LPAZ	104 B2
1ST AV	LACO	R B5
1ST AV	LACO	T B1
1ST AV	MCO	47 E4
1ST AV	PLU	20 A4
1ST AV	SBD	208 C1
1ST AV	SD	215 D4
1ST AV	SDCO	V B4
1ST AV	SDCO	V C5
1ST AV	SDCO	111 D2
1ST ST	ALA	46 C2
1ST ST	BEN	153 B4
1ST ST	DN	1 D3
1ST ST	DVS	136 D3
1ST ST	FRCO	57 C3
1ST ST	LA	186 A2
1ST ST	LACO	Q C4
1ST ST	NAP	133 C4
1ST ST	ORA	98 B4
1ST ST	ORA	T D3
1ST ST	RCO	98 E3
1ST ST	SF	143 D4
1ST ST	SJ	151 E1
1ST ST	SJ	152 B3
1ST ST	SA	195 A4
1ST ST	SA	196 A4
1ST ST	SCL	46 A4
1ST ST	SCL	54 D2
1ST ST	SHA	18 C3
1 1/2 AV	KIN	68 A1
2ND AV	COL	33 B3
2ND AV	GLE	24 E3
2ND AV	KIN	68 A1
2ND AV	LPAZ	104 B1
2ND AV	MCO	47 D4
2ND AV	RCO	103 D4
2ND AV S	MCO	48 A4
2ND ST	FRFD	135 A3
2ND ST	KER	68 B5
2ND ST	LA	186 A2
2ND ST	LACO	S E2
2ND ST	MER	170 A5
2ND ST	SDCO	V D3
2ND ST	SDCO	106 B3
2ND ST	SDCO	106 E5
2ND ST	SR	139 C4
2ND ST E	BEN	153 C4
2ND ST E	RENO	130 B3
2ND ST E	SOL	38 D4
2ND ST W	RENO	130 A3
2 1/2 AV	KIN	67 E2
3RD AV	FCTY	145 C1
3RD AV	GLE	24 E3
3RD AV	LPAZ	104 B1
3RD AV	MCO	47 D4
3RD AV	NAPA	38 D3
3RD AV	RCO	103 D4
3RD AV	SBD	99 B1
3RD AV	SDCO	V C5
3RD AV	SDCO	111 D2
3RD AV	SMCO	45 C3
3RD AV	TEH	18 E5
3RD AV	TEH	24 E1
3RD ST	BH	183 C1
3RD ST	CC	38 C5
3RD ST	COR	215 B5
3RD ST	DVS	136 D3
3RD ST	EUR	121 C1
3RD ST	LB	192 D3
3RD ST	LA	183 C1
3RD ST	LA	184 B1
3RD ST	LA	185 A1
3RD ST	LA	186 A3
3RD ST	LACO	Q B4
3RD ST	NAP	133 C4
3RD ST	RIV	205 C2
3RD ST	SBDO	207 D2
3RD ST	SBD	99 C1
3RD ST	SF	143 D4
3RD ST	SR	139 C1
3RD ST	SHA	18 C3
3RD ST	TEH	24 D2
3RD ST	YOL	137 A2
4TH AV	CAR	168 C3
4TH AV	GLE	24 E3
4TH AV	KIN	67 E1
4TH AV	MCO	47 D4
4TH AV	MON	168 C3
4TH AV	RCO	103 D4
4TH AV	SD	215 D3
4TH AV	SDCO	V C5
4TH AV	SDCO	111 D2
4TH ST	BKD	166 C4
4TH ST	COR	215 C5
4TH ST	EC	217 D4
4TH ST	EUR	121 C1
4TH ST	KER	166 C4
4TH ST	LA	186 A3
4TH ST	MAR	38 B5
4TH ST	MOD	8 B1
4TH ST	ONT	203 D3
4TH ST	ONT	204 B3
4TH ST	RCO	99 C4
4TH ST	SBD	99 D2
4TH ST	SDCO	V B4
4TH ST	SDCO	111 C1
4TH ST	SJ	152 B2
4TH ST	SR	139 B3
4TH ST	SA	196 B4
4TH ST	SCL	54 E3
4TH ST	SHA	18 D3
4TH ST	STR	131 D3
4TH ST E	RENO	130 B2
4TH ST W	RENO	130 A2
5TH AV	CAR	168 B3
5TH AV	GLE	24 E3
5TH AV	GLE	24 E3
5TH AV	KIN	67 E1
5TH AV	LPAZ	104 A2
5TH AV	LACO	R B3
5TH AV	SBD	92 D5
5TH AV	SBD	99 D2
5TH AV	SDCO	106 D3
5TH AV	SR	139 B3
5TH AV E	SIS	4 B4
5TH ST	DVS	136 C3
5TH ST	EUR	121 C1
5TH ST	HUM	9 E5
5TH ST	LA	186 A3
5TH ST	RCO	99 A3
5TH ST	SCTO	137 A3
5TH ST	SBD	99 C1
5TH ST	SBD	207 C2
5TH ST	SBDO	207 C2
5TH ST	SF	143 C5
5TH ST	SA	195 C4
5TH ST	TEH	24 E1
5TH ST	VAL	134 D5
5TH ST	VEN	96 B1
5TH ST E	BEN	153 C5
5TH ST E	OXN	176 D4
5TH ST E	VEN	176 D4
5TH ST W	LACO	90 A2
5 1/2 AV	KIN	67 E2
6TH AV	CAR	168 B3
6TH AV	GLE	24 E3
6TH AV	KIN	67 E1
6TH AV	MCO	47 E4
6TH AV	RCO	103 D4
6TH AV	SD	215 E3
6TH AV	SDCO	V B4
6TH ST	GLE	24 D3
6TH ST	LB	192 D3
6TH ST	LA	184 C2
6TH ST	LA	185 C2
6TH ST	LA	186 A3
6TH ST	ONT	203 D3
6TH ST	RCO	99 A3
6TH ST	YUB	33 E2
6 1/2 AV	KIN	67 E2
7TH	CC	38 C5
7TH AV	CAR	168 B3
7TH AV	KIN	67 E1
7TH AV	LPAZ	104 A2
7TH AV	LACO	R B4
7TH AV	SF	141 D4
7TH AV	SFCO	45 B2
7TH AV	SCR	54 A2
7TH AV	YUB	33 D2
7TH ST	EUR	121 C1
7TH ST	IMP	109 A4
7TH ST	KER	78 B1
7TH ST	LB	192 D3
7TH ST	LA	185 C2
7TH ST	LA	186 A3
7TH ST	LACO	97 C2
7TH ST	LACO	98 A4
7TH ST	LACO	S E2
7TH ST	LACO	T A2
7TH ST	O	157 C3
7TH ST	O	158 A4
7TH ST	RIV	205 B2
7TH ST	RCO	99 B2
7TH ST	RCO	99 E4
7TH ST	SBD	91 B4
7TH ST	SBD	99 B2
7TH ST	SBD	99 D2
7TH ST	SJ	152 B3
7TH ST	SLO	75 E3
7TH ST	STA	47 E3
7TH ST	UPL	203 E3
7TH ST N	MDO	162 B4
7TH ST S	MDO	162 B4
7TH ST S	STA	162 B4
7TH ST W	BEN	153 B4
7TH STANDARD RD	KER	77 C2
7 1/2 AV	KIN	57 E5
8TH AV	CAR	53 D5
8TH AV	CAR	168 B3
8TH AV	KIN	67 D1
8TH AV	RCO	103 D4
8TH AV	SD	215 E3
8TH ST	BKD	166 C4
8TH ST	BUT	25 C5
8TH ST	EC	217 C3
8TH ST	IMP	112 A3
8TH ST	LA	185 A2
8TH ST	LA	186 A3
8TH ST	O	157 C3
8TH ST	RCO	99 E3
8TH ST	SBD	98 E2
8TH ST	SDCO	V C4
8TH ST	SDCO	106 B3
8TH ST	SDCO	111 D1
8TH ST	SJCO	40 B5
8TH ST	UPL	203 E2
8TH ST E	DVS	136 C3
8TH ST W	DVS	136 B3
8 1/2 AV	KIN	57 D5
9TH AV	KER	68 C5
9TH AV	KIN	67 D1
9TH AV	LPAZ	104 A2
9TH AV	SD	215 E4
9TH AV	SDCO	106 D3
9TH ST	GGR	195 A2
9TH ST	LB	192 C2
9TH ST	LA	185 A3
9TH ST	LA	186 A4
9TH ST	LA	191 A4
9TH ST	LACO	S C3
9TH ST	MDO	162 B3
9TH ST	SBD	203 E2
9TH ST	SBDO	207 C1
9TH ST	SF	143 B5
9TH ST	UPL	203 E2
9TH ST	UPL	204 B2
9TH ST	YUMA	112 C5
9TH ST S	MDO	162 B4
9TH ST S	STA	162 B4
9 1/2 AV	KIN	67 D1
10 MI HOUSE TR	BUT	25 C2
10TH	CC	38 C5
10TH AV	KIN	67 D1
10TH AV	RCO	103 D5
10TH ST	LB	192 D2
10TH ST	MDO	162 B4
10TH ST	RCO	99 D3
10TH ST	SF	142 D4
10TH ST	SJ	152 B2
10TH ST	UPL	203 E2
10TH ST	YUB	33 D2
10TH ST	YUMA	112 C5
10TH ST E	LACO	90 A3
10TH ST W	BEN	153 A3
10TH ST W	LACO	89 E3
10 1/2 AV	KIN	67 D2
11TH AV	KIN	67 D1
11TH AV	LPAZ	104 A2
11TH AV	RCO	103 D5
11TH AV	SBD	91 E1
11TH AV	SD	215 E4
11TH AV	SDCO	V B4
11TH ST	LAK	31 D3
11TH ST	MDO	162 B3
11TH ST	SBD	91 B4
11TH ST	SJCO	47 A2
11TH ST	YUMA	112 C5
12TH AV	KIN	67 D1
12TH AV	LPAZ	104 A2
12TH AV	SD	215 E4
12TH AV	SDCO	V B4
12TH ST	BUT	25 C4
12TH ST	HUM	15 E2
12TH ST	MOD	8 A1
12TH ST	O	157 C2
12TH ST	SCTO	137 C3
12TH ST	YUB	33 D2
12TH ST E	O	159 C1
12TH ST N	SCTO	137 C2
12 3/4 AV	KIN	67 D1
13TH AV	ALA	45 D1
13TH AV	CAR	168 B4
13TH AV	KIN	67 D1
13TH AV	LPAZ	104 A2
13TH AV	O	158 C4
13TH ST	CC	38 C5
13TH ST	SJ	152 B2
13 1/4 AV	KIN	67 D1
14 MILE HOUSE	BUT	25 C2
14TH AV	KIN	67 D1
14TH AV	LPAZ	104 A2
14TH AV	O	158 C4
14TH AV	RCO	100 D3
14TH AV	RCO	103 D5
14TH AV E	O	158 D5
14TH ST	ALA	146 B1
14TH ST	CC	39 B5
14TH ST	EUR	121 B2
14TH ST	MDO	162 B3
14TH ST	O	157 C2
14TH ST	RIV	99 E2
14TH ST	RIV	205 C3
14TH ST	RCO	99 B2
14TH ST	SBD	99 D2
14TH ST E	ALA	45 E2
14TH ST E	DVS	136 C2
14TH ST E	O	159 D1
14TH ST W	DVS	136 C2
14 1/2 AV	KIN	67 D2
15TH AV	KIN	67 D1
15TH AV	RCO	103 C5
15TH AV	SDCO	106 D3
15TH ST	KER	80 A5
15TH ST	MDO	162 B3
15TH ST	SCTO	137 B4
15 1/2 AV	KIN	67 C1
16TH AV	KIN	67 C1
16TH AV	RCO	100 D3
16TH AV	RCO	103 D5
16TH ST	MER	170 B3
16TH ST	SCTO	137 C4
16TH ST	SBD	98 D1
16TH ST	SBD	99 D2
16TH ST	SD	215 E4
16TH ST	SD	216 A4
16TH ST	SDCO	V B4
17 MILE DR	MON	53 B3
17 MILE DR	MON	167 A3
17 MILE DR	PAC	167 B2
17TH AV	KIN	67 C1
17TH AV	SCR	54 A2
17TH ST	CM	199 B3
17TH ST	MDO	162 C3
17TH ST	ORA	98 C4
17TH ST	ORA	98 C4
17TH ST	ORA	T D3
17TH ST	ORA	T B3
17TH ST	ORA	T C4
17TH ST	SF	141 E5
17TH ST	SF	142 A5
17TH ST	SJ	152 C2
17TH ST	SA	195 D3
17TH ST	SA	196 A3
18TH AV	KIN	67 C1
18TH AV	RCO	100 D3
18TH AV	RCO	103 D5
18TH ST	BKD	166 B3
18TH ST	LAK	32 A3
18TH ST	SDCO	V C4
18TH ST	SDCO	111 D2
18 3/4 AV	KIN	67 C1
19TH AV	KIN	67 C3
19TH AV	SFCO	45 B2
19TH ST	BKD	166 B3
19TH ST	CM	199 A2
19TH ST	KER	80 A5
19TH ST	ORA	T C4
19TH ST	SBD	98 D1
20TH AV	KIN	67 C1
20TH AV	RCO	100 D3
20TH AV	RCO	103 C5
20TH ST	KER	80 B5
20TH ST	KIN	80 A5
20TH ST E	LACO	90 A3
20TH ST W	KER	89 E1
20 1/2 AV	KIN	67 C2
21ST AV	KIN	67 C3
21ST ST	BKD	166 B3
21ST ST	MER	170 D3
21ST ST	SCTO	137 C4
21ST ST	SJ	152 C2
21 1/2 AV	KIN	67 C1
22ND AV	KIN	67 C1
22ND AV	RCO	100 E3
22ND AV	RCO	103 C5
22ND ST	RCO	100 A3
22ND ST	YUB	33 D2
22 1/2 AV	KIN	67 C1
23RD AV	KIN	67 C1
23RD AV	O	158 C4
23RD ST	BKD	166 C3
23RD ST	CC	38 C5
23RD ST	R	155 B3
23RD ST	SP	155 B3
23RD ST	SMON	187 B1
23 1/2 AV	KIN	67 B1
24TH AV	KIN	67 B1
24TH AV	RCO	100 E3
24TH AV	RCO	103 C5
24TH ST	BKD	166 C2
24TH ST	KER	78 D3
24TH ST	SAC	39 E1
24TH ST	SBD	98 D1
24TH ST	SDCO	V C4
24TH ST	SDCO	111 D2
24TH ST	SJ	152 D2
24 1/2 AV	KIN	67 B1
25TH AV	KIN	67 B1
25TH AV	KIN	67 B4
25TH AV	RCO	103 C5
25TH AV	SF	141 B3
25TH AV	SM	145 A3
25TH ST	LACO	S C3
25TH ST	SD	216 A4
25TH ST	SDCO	V B4
25TH ST E	LACO	90 A3
25TH ST W	KER	89 E1
26TH AV	RCO	101 A3
26TH AV	RCO	103 C5
26TH ST	SD	216 B5
26 1/4 AV	KIN	67 B1
27TH AV	KIN	67 B1
27TH ST	SDCO	V C5
27TH ST	SDCO	111 D2
28TH AV	KIN	67 B2
28TH AV	RCO	101 A3
28TH AV	RCO	110 D1
28TH AV	SM	145 A3
28TH ST	SD	216 B4
28TH ST	SDCO	V B4
28TH ST	SDCO	111 D1
29TH ST	SCTO	137 D4
30TH AV	KIN	67 B3
30TH AV	RCO	100 D3
30TH AV	RCO	110 C1
30TH ST	BKD	166 D2
30TH ST	KER	80 B5
30TH ST	SD	214 B5
30TH ST	SD	216 B4
30TH ST	SDCO	V C4
30TH ST	SDCO	111 D1
30TH ST	SDCO	111 D2
30TH ST E	LACO	90 A3
30TH ST W	KER	89 E1
30TH ST W	LACO	89 E2
31ST AV	SM	145 A4
32ND AV	RCO	101 A3
32ND AV	RCO	110 C1
32ND ST	KER	80 B5
32ND ST	LAK	32 A3
32ND ST	SD	216 C4
32ND ST	SDCO	V C4
32ND ST	SDCO	111 D1
34TH AV	RCO	100 D3
34TH AV	RCO	110 C1
34TH ST	BKD	166 C2
35TH AV	O	158 E5
35TH AV	RCO	110 C1
36TH AV	KIN	67 A4
36TH AV	RCO	100 D4
36TH AV	RCO	110 D1
36TH ST	LAK	32 A3
37TH ST	KER	80 B5
38TH AV	RCO	101 A4
38TH AV	RCO	110 D1
38TH ST	SD	216 D5
39TH AV	SM	145 C3
40TH AV	RCO	101 A4
40TH AV	SF	141 A3
40TH AV	SM	145 B4
40TH ST	SBD	99 B1
40TH ST	SD	214 D5
40TH ST	SDCO	V C4
40TH ST E	LACO	90 A3
40TH ST W	KER	89 E1
40TH ST W	LACO	89 E2
41ST AV	SCR	54 A2
41ST ST	LACO	Q C4
42ND AV	RCO	101 A4
42ND AV	SM	145 B4
43RD ST	SD	214 E5
43RD ST	SD	216 E1
44TH AV	RCO	100 E4
47TH AV	RCO	101 A4
47TH AV	SAC	39 E1
47TH ST E	LACO	90 A3
48TH AV	RCO	101 A4
50TH AV	RCO	101 A4
50TH ST E	LACO	90 A3
50TH ST W	KER	89 E1
50TH ST W	LACO	89 E2
51ST ST	LACO	Q C4
52ND AV	RCO	101 A4
54TH AV	RCO	101 A4
54TH ST	RCO	99 A2
54TH ST	SDCO	V C4
54TH ST	SDCO	111 D1
55TH ST E	LACO	90 B3
57TH ST E	LACO	90 B3
58TH AV	RCO	101 A5
60TH AV	RCO	101 A5
60TH ST	SDCO	V C4
60TH ST E	LACO	90 B2
60TH ST W	KER	89 E2
60TH ST W	LACO	89 E2
62ND AV	RCO	101 B5
64TH AV	RCO	101 B5
65TH EXPWY	SAC	39 E1
65TH ST E	LACO	90 B2
65TH ST W	LACO	89 E2
66TH AV	RCO	101 B5
67TH ST	RCO	101 A5
68TH AV	RCO	101 B5
68TH AV	TEH	18 E5
70TH AV	RCO	101 B5
70TH ST	SDCO	V C4
70TH ST	SDCO	111 D1
70TH ST E	LACO	90 B3
70TH ST W	LACO	89 E2
72ND AV	RCO	101 B5
74TH AV	RCO	101 B5
76TH AV	RCO	101 B5
76TH ST E	LACO	90 B3
78TH AV	RCO	108 B1
80TH AV	RCO	107 C1
80TH AV	RCO	108 B1
80TH ST E	LACO	90 B3
80TH ST W	KER	89 D2
80TH ST W	LACO	89 D3
81ST AV	RCO	108 B1
82ND AV	RCO	108 B1
84TH AV	RCO	108 B1
85TH ST W	LACO	89 D3
87TH ST E	LACO	90 B4
87TH ST W	LACO	89 D3
90TH ST E	LACO	90 B3
90TH ST W	KER	89 D2
90TH ST W	LACO	89 D3
92ND ST	LACO	Q C5
92ND ST W	LACO	89 D3
95TH ST W	LACO	89 D3
96TH ST E	LACO	90 B4
97TH ST W	LACO	89 D3
98TH AV	ALA	45 D2
98TH AV	O	159 D4
98TH ST W	LACO	89 D3
99-97 CUTOFF	SIS	4 B4
100TH ST E	LACO	90 B2
100TH ST W	KER	89 D2
103RD ST	LACO	Q C5
105TH ST E	LACO	90 B3
106TH ST E	LACO	90 B4
110TH ST E	LACO	90 B3
110TH ST W	KER	79 D5
110TH ST W	LACO	89 D2
115TH ST W	KER	79 D5
120TH ST E	LACO	90 B2
120TH ST W	LACO	89 D2
121ST ST E	LACO	90 B4
130TH ST E	LACO	90 C2
130TH ST W	LACO	89 D2
131ST ST E	LACO	90 C4
135TH ST	LACO	S C1
137TH ST E	LACO	90 C2
140TH ST E	LACO	90 C2
140TH ST W	KER	89 D1
145TH ST	KER	89 D1
145TH ST E	LACO	90 C3
146TH ST	KER	89 D1
147TH ST	KER	89 C1
149TH ST	KER	89 C1
150TH ST E	LACO	90 C3
152ND ST W	KER	89 C1
155TH ST	KER	89 C1
157TH ST W	KER	89 C1
160TH ST W	LACO	89 C2
164TH ST	LACO	S B1
165TH ST E	LACO	90 C3
170TH ST E	LACO	90 C3
170TH ST W	KER	89 C2
170TH ST W	LACO	89 C2
175TH ST E	LACO	90 C3
176TH ST	KER	89 C1
177TH ST	KER	89 C1
180TH ST E	LACO	90 C3
180TH ST W	LACO	89 C2
182ND ST	LACO	S C1
185TH ST E	LACO	90 C3
185TH ST W	KER	89 C2
190TH ST	LACO	97 D3
190TH ST	LACO	S B1
190TH ST E	LACO	90 C2
190TH ST W	LACO	89 C2
195TH ST	LACO	S E1
195TH ST	LACO	T A1
195TH ST E	LACO	90 C2
195TH ST W	KER	89 C2
200TH ST E	LACO	90 D2
200TH ST E	LACO	90 C3
204TH ST E	LACO	90 D4
210TH ST	KER	89 C1
210TH ST E	LACO	90 D3
215TH ST W	KER	89 C2
220TH ST	LACO	S C2
220TH ST E	LACO	90 D3
223RD ST	LACO	S C2
223RD ST E	LACO	90 D4
225TH ST E	LACO	90 D2
228TH ST	LACO	S C2
230TH ST E	LACO	90 D3
230TH ST W	KER	89 B2
233RD ST E	LACO	90 D4
235TH ST W	KER	89 B2
235TH ST W	LACO	89 B2
240TH ST E	LACO	90 D3
295TH ST W	KER	89 B2
300TH ST W	KER	89 B2
8001	MAD	50 A5
8003	MAD	50 A4
8004	MAD	50 A4
8005	MAD	50 A4
8006	MAD	50 A4
8007	MAD	50 A4
8008	MAD	50 A5
8009	MAD	50 A4
8009	MAD	50 A5
8013	MAD	50 B4
8014	MAD	50 B4
8015	MAD	50 B4
8016	MAD	50 A4
8020	MAD	50 A4
8021	MAD	49 E4
8023	MAD	50 B3
8024	MAD	50 A3
8026	MAD	50 B3
8027	MAD	50 B3
8029	MAD	50 A4
8041	MAD	49 E4
8042	MAD	49 D3
8046	MAD	49 D3
8063	MAD	57 C1
8066	MAD	57 D1
8067	MAD	57 E1
8080	MAD	57 D1
8081	MAD	49 D5
8082	MAD	49 D5

STREETS

HIGHWAY INDEX

ROUTE NO.	CO.	PAGE & GRID
FEDERAL		
6	ESM	44 E4
6	MIN	44 D5
6	MNO	51 C1
50	CRSN	36 B2
50	DGL	36 B2
50	ED	35 B4
50	ED	36 A3
50	LYON	36 D1
50	SAC	40 A1
60	LPAZ	104 D4
93	CLK	74 E2
93	MOH	85 E1
95	CLK	74 D2
95	LPAZ	103 E5
95	MIN	44 A1
95	NYE	62 B2
95	RCO	103 E2
95	SBD	85 B4
95	SBD	95 B1
95	SBD	103 D1
95	YUMA	112 E5
97	KLAM	5 B1
97	SIS	4 D5
97	SIS	5 A3
97	SIS	12 C1
101	CUR	1 C1
101	DN	10 A1
101	HUM	9 E3
101	HUM	10 A2
101	HUM	15 D2
101	HUM	16 B4
101	HUM	22 C1
101	LACO	97 B1
101	LACO	Q D3
101	MAR	38 B5
101	MAR	45 B1
101	MAR	L B2
101	MEN	22 C2
101	MEN	31 A1
101	MON	54 C3
101	MON	55 A5
101	MON	65 B2
101	SB	86 C1
101	SB	87 A4
101	SBT	54 D3
101	SCL	46 A4
101	SFCO	45 B1
101	SFCO	L B4
101	SLO	76 A1
101	SMCO	45 C2
101	SMCO	L C5
101	SMCO	N C1
101	SCL	54 D1
101	SCL	P C3
101	SON	32 D5
101	SON	37 E1
101	SON	33 A3
101	VEN	88 A5
101	VEN	96 D1
197	DN	1 E3
199	DN	1 E3
199	DN	2 C3
395	CRSN	36 C2
395	DGL	36 C3
395	INY	51 C3
395	INY	59 E1
395	INY	60 A3
395	INY	70 B1
395	KER	70 C5
395	KER	80 D1
395	LAKE	7 C1
395	LAS	8 B3
395	LAS	21 B3
395	LAS	27 E1
395	MOD	7 C3
395	MOD	8 B2
395	MNO	42 E2
395	MNO	43 A2
395	MNO	50 D1
395	SBD	80 E3
395	SBD	91 A2
395	WSH	28 A3
INTERSTATE		
5	COL	32 D1

ROUTE NO.	CO.	PAGE & GRID
5	COL	33 A3
5	FRCO	55 E3
5	FRCO	56 B4
5	FRCO	66 D1
5	GLE	24 D3
5	JKSN	4 A1
5	KER	77 E2
5	KER	78 B3
5	KER	88 D1
5	KIN	67 C4
5	LACO	88 E2
5	LACO	89 A3
5	LACO	97 E1
5	LACO	98 B3
5	LACO	Q D2
5	LACO	R C5
5	MCO	47 C5
5	MCO	55 E2
5	ORA	98 B3
5	ORA	105 E1
5	ORA	T E3
5	ORA	U A5
5	SAC	39 E2
5	SDCO	106 A2
5	SDCO	111 D2
5	SDCO	V A2
5	SJCO	39 E4
5	SJCO	40 A4
5	SJCO	47 A2
5	SHA	12 C3
5	SHA	18 C2
5	SIS	4 B3
5	SIS	12 D2
5	STA	47 A3
5	TEH	18 D4
5	TEH	24 D1
5	YOL	33 A4
8	IMP	111 B4
8	SDCO	107 A5
8	SDCO	111 C1
8	SDCO	112 D1
8	SDCO	V B3
8	YUMA	112 D5
10	LPAZ	103 E5
10	LACO	97 D2
10	LACO	98 A2
10	LACO	Q D4
10	LACO	U B2
10	RCO	99 E3
10	RCO	100 A3
10	RCO	101 A4
10	RCO	102 D4
10	RCO	103 B5
10	SBD	99 A1
10	SBD	U E2
15	CLK	74 E1
15	RCO	99 B4
15	SBD	82 C5
15	SBD	83 D3
15	SBD	84 A2
15	SBD	91 D2
15	SBD	92 B1
15	SDCO	106 D3
15	SDCO	V C1
15	SBD	99 A1
40	SBD	92 A1
40	SBD	93 D2
40	SBD	94 D2
40	SBD	95 C1
80	ALA	L C4
80	CC	38 C5
80	CC	L C3
80	NEV	27 C6
80	NEV	35 D1
80	PLA	34 D2
80	PLA	35 A1
80	SAC	33 E5
80	SAC	34 A5
80	SAC	39 E1
80	SFCO	45 C1
80	SFCO	L C4
80	SOL	38 E3
80	SOL	39 A2
80	WSH	28 A4
80	YOL	39 D1
105	LACO	Q D5
105	LACO	S B1
110	LACO	97 D3
110	LACO	Q E5

ROUTE NO.	CO.	PAGE & GRID
110	LACO	S C1
205	SJCO	46 D2
210	LACO	89 E5
210	LACO	97 E1
210	LACO	98 B1
210	LACO	Q C1
210	LACO	R A2
210	LACO	U A2
215	SBD	99 B1
238	ALA	45 E2
238	ALA	L E5
280	SCL	45 E4
280	SCL	N E3
280	SCL	P A3
280	SFCO	45 B2
280	SFCO	L C5
280	SMCO	45 B2
280	SMCO	N C2
380	SMCO	45 C2
380	SMCO	N C1
405	LACO	97 C1
405	LACO	Q B3
405	LACO	S C2
405	ORA	98 B4
405	ORA	T A2
480	SFCO	45 C1
505	SOL	39 A2
505	YOL	33 A4
505	YOL	39 A1
580	ALA	45 A1
580	ALA	46 A2
580	ALA	L D4
580	ALA	M A5
580	CC	L C3
580	MAR	38 B5
580	SJCO	46 D2
605	LACO	98 B2
605	LACO	R D4
605	LACO	S E2
605	LACO	T A2
680	ALA	46 B2
680	ALA	P B1
680	CC	38 E5
680	CC	46 A1
680	CC	L E4
680	CC	M A3
680	SCL	46 B4
680	SCL	P B2
680	SOL	38 E4
680	SOL	L E2
780	SOL	38 D4
780	SOL	L E2
805	SDCO	106 C5
805	SDCO	111 D2
805	SDCO	V B1
880	ALA	P B2
980	ALA	45 D1
980	ALA	L D4
STATE		
1	HUM	15 D3
1	LACO	96 D2
1	LACO	97 B2
1	LACO	Q C4
1	LACO	S B2
1	MAR	37 E4
1	MAR	45 A1
1	MAR	L B4
1	MEN	22 C2
1	MEN	30 C3
1	MON	54 B3
1	MON	64 B2
1	MON	65 A4
1	ORA	98 C5
1	ORA	105 D1
1	ORA	T B3
1	SFCO	45 B1
1	SFCO	L B4
1	SLO	65 A5
1	SLO	75 B1
1	SLO	76 A4
1	SMCO	45 B2
1	SMCO	L B5
1	SMCO	N B1
1	SB	86 B2
1	SCR	53 C1
1	SCR	54 B2
1	SCR	N D5

ROUTE NO.	CO.	PAGE & GRID
1	SON	30 D5
1	SON	37 B1
1	VEN	96 C1
2	LACO	90 C4
2	LACO	97 E1
2	LACO	Q C4
2	LACO	R A1
2	SBD	90 E5
3	SIS	3 D5
3	SIS	4 A4
3	SIS	11 D1
3	SIS	12 A2
3	TRI	11 E4
3	TRI	12 A3
3	TRI	17 B2
4	ALP	36 C5
4	ALP	42 B1
4	CAL	41 D2
4	CC	38 D5
4	CC	39 C5
4	CC	L E3
4	CC	M B3
4	SJCO	39 E5
4	SJCO	40 B5
4	STA	40 E5
9	SCL	45 E5
9	SCL	N E4
9	SCL	P A4
9	SCR	53 D1
9	SCR	N E4
9	SCR	P A5
12	CAL	40 D4
12	CAL	41 A3
12	NAPA	38 C3
12	NAPA	L C1
12	SAC	39 C4
12	SAC	M E2
12	SJCO	39 E4
12	SJCO	40 A1
12	SOL	38 E3
12	SOL	39 A3
12	SOL	M B1
12	SON	37 E2
12	SON	38 A2
13	ALA	45 D1
13	ALA	L D4
14	KER	80 C1
14	KER	89 E1
14	LACO	89 E2
15	SDCO	V C3
16	COL	32 C3
16	SAC	39 E1
16	SAC	40 A1
16	YOL	32 D4
17	SCR	54 A1
17	SCR	P B5
18	LACO	90 D4
18	SBD	91 A4
18	SBD	92 A4
18	SBD	99 C1
19	LACO	98 A3
19	LACO	R C3
19	LACO	S E1
20	COL	32 E2
20	COL	33 A2
20	LAK	31 E3
20	LAK	32 A3
20	MEN	22 D5
20	MEN	31 C2
20	NEV	34 C1
20	SUT	33 C2
20	YUB	33 E1
22	ORA	98 B4
22	ORA	T A3
23	LACO	96 E2
23	VEN	88 D5
23	VEN	96 E1
24	ALA	L D4
24	CC	38 E5
24	CC	45 E1
24	CC	L E4
24	CC	M A3
25	MON	65 D2
25	SBT	55 A3
25	SBT	65 D1
26	CAL	41 B2
26	SJCO	40 D4
27	LACO	97 B1
27	LACO	Q A2

ROUTE NO.	CO.	PAGE & GRID
28	CRSN	36 B2
28	PLA	35 E1
28	WSH	36 A1
29	LAK	31 D2
29	LAK	32 A4
29	NAPA	38 B1
29	NAPA	L D1
29	SOL	38 D4
30	LACO	98 D1
30	LACO	U C2
30	SBD	98 E1
30	SBD	99 B1
30	SBD	U E1
31	RCO	98 E2
31	RCO	U E4
32	BUT	25 A3
32	GLE	24 D3
32	TEH	19 E4
33	FRCO	56 B2
33	FRCO	66 D2
33	KER	67 B5
33	KER	77 B1
33	KER	78 A5
33	KIN	67 A4
33	MCO	47 C5
33	MCO	55 C1
33	SJCO	47 A2
33	SLO	87 E1
33	SB	87 E1
33	STA	47 B3
33	VEN	88 A2
34	VEN	88 C5
34	VEN	96 C1
35	LACO	T A1
35	SFCO	45 B2
35	SFCO	L B5
35	SMCO	45 C3
35	SMCO	L B5
35	SMCO	N B1
35	SCL	46 A5
36	HUM	15 E2
36	HUM	16 C3
36	LAS	20 E3
36	LAS	21 A3
36	PLU	20 A4
36	SHA	17 E4
36	TEH	17 E4
36	TEH	18 C4
36	TEH	19 C4
36	TRI	16 E3
36	TRI	17 A3
37	MAR	L B2
37	SOL	38 D4
37	SOL	L C2
37	SON	38 C4
38	SBD	91 E5
38	SBD	92 A5
38	SBD	99 E1
38	SBD	100 B1
39	KLAM	5 C1
39	LACO	98 C1
39	LACO	R E3
39	LACO	U A2
39	ORA	98 B4
39	ORA	R D5
39	ORA	T C1
41	FRCO	57 C3
41	KIN	67 C2
41	MAD	49 D4
41	MAD	57 C2
41	MPA	63 C5
41	SLO	66 D5
41	SLO	76 A2
42	LACO	97 E2
42	LACO	Q C5
42	LACO	R B5
43	FRCO	57 D5
43	KER	68 B5
43	KER	78 B2
43	KIN	67 E2
43	TUL	68 A3
44	LAS	20 A2
44	SHA	18 C2
44	SHA	19 C2
45	COL	32 E1
45	COL	33 A2
45	GLE	24 E3
45	YOL	33 C4
46	JOS	2 D1

ROUTE NO.	CO.	PAGE & GRID
46	KER	77 A1
46	KER	78 B1
46	SLO	66 D5
46	SLO	75 E2
46	SLO	76 B1
47	LACO	191 C3
48	LACO	89 A2
49	AMA	40 D1
49	CAL	41 A3
49	ED	34 D4
49	MAD	49 D4
49	MPA	48 E2
49	MPA	49 A3
49	NEV	34 C1
49	PLA	34 C3
49	PLU	27 D3
49	SIE	26 C4
49	SIE	27 C4
49	TUO	41 C5
49	TUO	48 D1
49	YUBA	26 C4
50	ED	34 C5
50	SAC	39 E1
50	SAC	40 A1
52	SDCO	106 C5
52	SDCO	V B2
53	LAK	32 A3
54	SDCO	111 E1
54	SDCO	V D4
55	ORA	98 C4
55	ORA	T D3
56	SDCO	106 D4
57	LACO	98 C2
57	LACO	U B3
57	ORA	98 C3
57	ORA	T D1
58	KER	77 E3
58	KER	78 B3
58	KER	80 A4
58	SBD	91 C1
58	SLO	76 B3
58	SLO	77 A3
59	MCO	48 C4
60	LACO	98 B2
60	LACO	R D4
60	RCO	99 B2
60	SBD	98 D2
60	SBD	U E3
61	ALA	45 D2
61	ALA	L D5
62	RCO	100 C2
62	RCO	102 E2
62	SBD	101 A1
62	SBD	102 A2
62	SBD	103 B2
63	FRCO	58 B4
63	TUL	58 B5
63	TUL	68 B2
65	KER	68 D6
65	KER	78 D2
65	PLA	34 A3
65	TUL	68 C2
65	YUB	33 D3
66	JKSN	4 A1
66	KLAM	4 D1
66	SBD	98 E1
66	SBD	99 B1
66	SBD	U D2
67	SDCO	106 E4
67	SDCO	107 A4
67	SDCO	V E2
68	MOH	85 D4
68	MON	54 B4
70	BUT	25 D3
70	KLAM	5 D1
70	LAS	27 E2
70	PLU	26 A1
70	SUT	33 D4
70	YUB	33 D1
71	LACO	98 D2
71	LACO	U C3
71	RCO	98 D2
71	SBD	98 D2
71	SBD	U C3
72	LPAZ	104 B2
72	LACO	97 E2
72	LACO	98 A2
72	LACO	R B4
73	ORA	98 C4

ROUTE NO.	CO.	PAGE & GRID
73	ORA	T D4
74	ORA	98 E5
74	ORA	99 A5
74	RCO	99 C4
74	RCO	100 A4
75	SDCO	111 C1
75	SDCO	V B4
76	SDCO	106 D2
76	SDCO	107 B2
77	ALA	L D5
77	ALA	45 D1
77	ALA	159 C1
78	IMP	108 C3
78	IMP	109 A4
78	IMP	110 C2
78	RCO	103 D5
78	RCO	110 C1
78	SDCO	106 C3
78	SDCO	107 C3
78	SDCO	108 A3
79	RCO	99 E3
79	RCO	106 D1
79	SDCO	107 B1
80	SFCO	L C5
82	SCL	46 A4
82	SCL	P A3
82	SMCO	45 C2
82	SMCO	N B1
83	SBD	98 D2
83	SBD	U D3
84	ALA	45 E3
84	ALA	46 B3
84	ALA	M C5
84	SMCO	45 D4
84	SMCO	N D3
84	YOL	39 D1
85	SCL	45 E4
85	SCL	P A3
86	IMP	108 C2
86	IMP	109 A4
86	RCO	101 B4
86	RCO	108 B1
87	SCL	46 B4
87	SCL	P B3
88	ALP	36 C4
88	AMA	35 D5
88	AMA	41 A2
88	DGL	36 C3
88	SJCO	40 C3
89	ALP	36 B4
89	ED	35 E3
89	ED	36 A4
89	MNO	36 D5
89	NEV	27 D5
89	PLA	35 D1
89	PLU	20 A4
89	PLU	26 C1
89	SHA	13 C3
89	SHA	19 E1
89	SIE	27 C4
89	SIS	12 E2
89	SIS	13 B3
89	TEH	19 D3
90	LACO	Q D4
90	ORA	98 C3
90	ORA	T E1
91	LACO	97 E3
91	LACO	S C1
91	ORA	98 C3
91	ORA	T C2
91	RCO	99 A3
91	RCO	U D5
92	ALA	45 D3
92	ALA	N E1
92	SMCO	45 D3
92	SMCO	N C2
94	SDCO	111 E1
94	SDCO	112 D2
94	SDCO	V D3
95	LPAZ	104 B2
95	MOH	85 D5
95	MOH	95 D1
95	MOH	96 B3
96	HUM	10 C3
96	SIS	2 E4
96	SIS	3 C3
96	SIS	10 E1
98	IMP	111 C3
98	IMP	112 C4

HIGHWAY INDEX

ROUTE NO.	CO.	PAGE & GRID
99	BUT	25 B3
99	FRCO	57 B3
99	JKSN	3 E1
99	KER	68 B5
99	KER	78 C2
99	MAD	56 D1
99	MAD	57 B2
99	MCO	48 B4
99	MCO	56 D1
99	SAC	39 E2
99	SAC	40 A2
99	SJCO	40 B4
99	SJCO	47 B1
99	STA	47 D3
99	SUT	33 C3
99	TEH	18 D5
99	TUL	57 E5
100	CRSN	36 C2
103	LACO	97 E4
103	LACO	S D2
104	SAC	40 C2
107	LACO	97 D3
107	LACO	S B2
108	MNO	42 E2
108	STA	47 D2
108	TUO	41 D4
108	TUO	42 B2
110	LACO	97 E2
110	LACO	R B3
111	IMP	108 D1
111	IMP	109 B3
111	IMP	112 B3
111	RCO	100 C3
111	RCO	101 A4
111	RCO	108 D1
112	ALA	45 D2
112	ALA	L E5
113	SOL	39 B2
113	SOL	M C1
113	SUT	33 C3
113	YOL	33 C5
114	SMCO	N D2
115	IMP	109 B3
115	IMP	112 C3
116	SON	37 D2
116	SON	38 A3
116	SON	L A1
117	SDCO	111 E2
117	SDCO	V D5
118	LACO	89 B5
118	LACO	Q C1
118	VEN	88 C5
118	VEN	89 A5
119	KER	78 B3
120	MNO	43 C5
120	MNO	51 B1
120	SJCO	47 B1
120	STA	48 A1
120	TUO	41 C5
120	TUO	48 C1
120	TUO	49 B1
121	NAPA	38 D2
121	NAPA	L C1
121	SON	38 B3
121	SON	L B1
123	ALA	L D4
124	AMA	40 D2
125	SDCO	106 E4
125	SDCO	V D2
126	LACO	89 A4
126	VEN	88 D4
126	VEN	89 A4
127	INY	72 D2
127	SBD	72 E5
127	SBD	83 B2
128	MEN	30 C2
128	MEN	31 B4
128	NAPA	38 B2
128	SON	31 D5
128	SON	38 A1
128	YOL	39 A1
129	SCR	54 D2
130	SCL	46 C4
130	SCL	P C3
131	MAR	38 B5
131	MAR	45 B1
131	MAR	L B4
132	MPA	48 D2
132	SJCO	47 A2

ROUTE NO.	CO.	PAGE & GRID
132	STA	47 B2
132	STA	48 B2
133	ORA	98 D5
133	ORA	T E4
134	LACO	97 D1
134	LACO	Q E3
134	LACO	R A3
135	SB	86 C1
136	INY	60 B4
137	TUL	68 B2
138	LACO	88 E2
138	LACO	89 A2
138	LACO	90 A3
138	SBD	91 A5
139	LAS	14 C3
139	LAS	20 E1
139	LAS	21 A3
139	MOD	5 E3
139	MOD	6 A4
139	MOD	14 D1
139	SIS	5 E3
140	KLAM	5 C1
140	LAKE	7 A1
140	MCO	47 D4
140	MCO	48 A4
140	MPA	48 E4
140	MPA	49 C2
142	ORA	T E1
142	ORA	U B4
142	SBD	98 D2
144	SB	87 C4
145	FRCO	57 A4
145	FRCO	66 E1
145	MAD	57 B2
146	CLK	74 E3
146	MON	55 B5
146	SBT	55 C5
147	PLU	20 C4
149	BUT	25 C4
150	SB	87 E4
150	VEN	88 B4
151	SHA	18 C1
152	MAD	56 C1
152	MCO	55 E1
152	MCO	56 B1
152	SCL	54 D2
152	SCR	54 C2
154	SB	87 A3
155	KER	68 B5
155	KER	69 B5
155	KER	79 C1
156	CLK	72 E1
156	CLK	74 A1
156	MON	54 C3
156	SBT	54 E2
156	SBT	55 A2
157	CLK	73 E2
157	CLK	74 A2
158	CLK	73 E1
158	CLK	74 A1
160	CLK	73 E3
160	CLK	74 B3
160	NYE	73 C2
160	SAC	39 E1
160	SAC	M D2
161	CLK	74 C5
161	SIS	5 B2
162	BUT	25 B5
162	GLE	24 B4
162	GLE	25 B5
162	MEN	22 E4
162	MEN	23 A3
163	CLK	85 C4
163	SDCO	106 D5
163	SDCO	V B3
164	CLK	84 E2
164	LACO	98 A1
165	MCO	47 E5
165	MCO	55 E2
166	KER	77 A4
166	KER	78 B5
166	SB	86 B1
166	SLO	76 D5
167	MNO	43 E4
168	FRCO	50 B5
168	FRCO	57 E2
168	FRCO	58 A1
168	INY	51 E5
168	INY	52 C3

ROUTE NO.	CO.	PAGE & GRID
168	MNO	52 C3
169	DN	1 E5
169	DN	2 A5
169	DN	10 A1
169	HUM	10 C3
170	LACO	97 D1
170	LACO	Q C2
172	TEH	19 D4
173	SBD	91 C5
174	NEV	34 D2
175	LAK	31 E3
175	LAK	32 A5
175	MEN	31 C3
176	SB	86 C1
177	RCO	102 D2
178	INY	72 D3
178	INY	73 A3
178	KERN	69 E5
178	KER	70 A5
178	KER	78 E2
178	KER	79 A2
178	KER	80 B1
178	SBD	81 A1
180	FRCO	56 E3
180	FRCO	57 C3
180	FRCO	58 B3
180	FRCO	59 A3
182	MNO	43 C2
183	MON	54 C3
184	KER	78 E3
185	ALA	45 D1
185	ALA	L D5
188	SDCO	112 C2
189	SBD	91 C5
190	INY	61 D4
190	INY	70 C1
190	INY	72 C1
190	TUL	68 B3
190	TUL	69 A3
191	BUT	25 C3
192	SB	87 C4
193	ED	34 E4
193	PLA	34 B3
195	RCO	101 B5
198	FRCO	66 E2
198	KIN	67 C2
198	MON	65 D2
198	MON	66 A2
198	TUL	58 E5
198	TUL	59 A5
198	TUL	68 B1
200	HUM	9 E5
200	HUM	10 A5
201	TUL	58 B5
202	KER	79 C4
203	MNO	50 D2
204	KER	78 D3
206	DGL	36 B3
206	SBD	99 B1
207	DGL	36 B3
208	DGL	36 E4
208	MEN	22 B2
209	SDCO	111 C1
209	SDCO	V A4
213	LACO	S C3
213	LACO	97 D3
215	RCO	99 C3
216	TUL	68 C1
217	SB	87 B4
218	MON	54 B4
219	STA	47 C2
220	SOL	39 D3
221	NAPA	L D1
221	NAPA	38 D3
223	KER	78 D4
223	KER	79 A4
224	SB	87 E4
225	SB	87 C4
227	SLO	76 B4
229	SLO	76 B2
232	VEN	88 B5
233	MAD	56 D1
236	SCR	53 D1
236	SCR	N D4
237	SCL	46 B4
237	SCL	P A3
238	ALA	46 A2
238	ALA	P A1
243	RCO	100 A3

ROUTE NO.	CO.	PAGE & GRID
245	TUL	58 C4
245	TUL	68 C1
246	SB	86 C3
247	SBD	91 E2
247	SBD	92 B4
247	SBD	100 D1
249	FRCO	58 D4
250	ORA	98 C3
253	MEN	31 A3
254	HUM	16 B4
255	HUM	9 E5
255	HUM	10 A5
259	SBD	99 B1
262	ALA	46 A3
262	ALA	P B2
263	SIS	4 A4
264	ESM	52 A1
265	ESM	52 E1
266	ESM	52 E3
266	MNO	52 C3
267	ESM	61 C1
267	PLA	35 E1
267	PLA	36 A1
269	FRCO	67 A1
270	MNO	43 B3
271	MEN	22 C1
273	SHA	18 C2
274	SDCO	106 C5
274	SDCO	V B2
281	LAK	31 E3
282	SDCO	111 C1
282	SDCO	V B4
284	PLU	27 D2
299	HUM	10 B4
299	LAS	14 A3
299	MOD	7 C5
299	MOD	8 B1
299	MOD	14 D1
299	SHA	13 B5
299	SHA	18 B2
299	TRI	10 D5
299	TRI	16 E1
299	TRI	17 D1
330	SBD	99 C1
338	LYON	43 B1
341	LYON	36 D1
341	WSH	28 C5
359	MIN	44 B2
360	MIN	44 E3
371	RCO	100 B5
372	NYE	73 B2
373	NYE	62 D5
374	NYE	62 A3
380	SMCO	N B1
428	WSH	36 C1
429	WSH	36 B1
430	WSH	28 B4
431	WSH	28 B5
431	WSH	36 B1
445	WSH	28 D1
446	WSH	28 E2
447	WSH	28 E2
480	SFCO	L C4
512	CRSN	36 C2
513	CRSN	36 C2
604	CLK	74 E2
666	WSH	28 B4
710	LACO	97 E2
710	LACO	R B5
710	LACO	S D2
880	ALA	45 E2
880	SCL	46 B4
COUNTY		
1	LPAZ	103 E3
1	LPAZ	104 A1
3	LPAZ	104 B2
10	LPAZ	104 A2
14	LPAZ	103 E2
14	LPAZ	104 A2
17	LPAZ	103 E2
17	LPAZ	104 A2
21	LPAZ	103 E3
21	LPAZ	104 A3
25	LPAZ	103 E3
29	LPAZ	103 E3
30	LPAZ	103 E3
30	LPAZ	104 A3

ROUTE NO.	CO.	PAGE & GRID
34	LPAZ	103 E3
38	LPAZ	103 E3
44	LPAZ	103 E3
44	LPAZ	104 A3
50	LPAZ	103 E4
56	LPAZ	103 E4
A 1	LAS	20 D2
A 2	LAS	14 C3
A 3	LAS	21 B4
A 5	TEH	18 C3
A 6	TEH	18 E4
A 6	TEH	19 B3
A 7	TEH	18 D5
A 8	TEH	18 D5
A 9	TEH	24 D2
A10	SIS	12 C2
A11	TEH	24 D1
A12	SIS	4 B5
A13	PLU	20 B4
A14	PLU	27 A3
A15	PLU	27 B2
A16	SHA	17 E3
A16	SHA	18 A3
A16	SHA	122 A2
A17	SHA	18 D3
A17	SHA	19 A3
A18	SHA	18 C2
A19	SHA	13 D3
A21	LAS	20 C2
A22	PLU	20 D5
A23	PLU	27 C2
A23	SIE	27 C3
A24	PLU	27 D3
A25	LAS	21 D5
A26	LAS	21 D5
A27	LAS	21 B3
B 2	BUT	25 D4
D 1	DN	1 E3
D 2	DN	1 D4
D 3	DN	1 D3
D 5	DN	1 D2
E 1	ALP	36 C5
E 4	YOL	32 E4
E 4	YOL	33 A4
E 6	YOL	39 B1
E 6	YOL	136 A2
E 7	SOL	39 B1
E 7	YOL	33 B5
E 8	YOL	33 C4
E 8	YOL	39 C1
E 8	YOL	136 E1
E 9	YOL	39 D2
E10	YOL	33 B4
E11	YOL	33 D3
E13	SAC	39 D3
E16	AMA	40 E1
E16	ED	35 B4
G 1	SBT	54 E3
G 2	SCL	46 A4
G 2	SCL	P A3
G 2	SCLR	150 C2
G 3	PA	147 D3
G 3	SCL	45 D4
G 3	SCL	147 B6
G 3	SCL	N E3
G 4	SCL	46 A4
G 4	SCL	P B3
G 4	SCLR	150 E1
G 4	SCLR	151 A1
G 5	PA	147 C6
G 5	SCL	45 E4
G 5	SCL	147 A5
G 5	SCL	149 A3
G 5	SCL	N E3
G 6	MVW	148 C5
G 6	SCL	45 E4
G 6	SCL	46 A4
G 6	SCL	148 C5
G 6	SCLR	151 B1
G 6	SVL	148 C5
G 7	SCL	54 D2
G 8	SCL	46 B5
G 8	SCL	54 C1
G 8	SCL	P B4
G 9	SCL	54 D2
G10	SCL	46 B5
G10	SCL	P B4
G11	MON	54 C3
G12	MON	54 C3

ROUTE NO.	CO.	PAGE & GRID
G13	MON	65 C2
G13	SBT	65 C1
G14	MON	65 B3
G15	MON	65 B1
G16	MON	54 B5
G16	MON	64 C1
G16	MON	65 B1
G16	MON	168 E4
G17	MON	54 C4
G17	MON	65 A1
G18	MON	65 D4
G19	MON	65 E5
G20	MON	54 C5
J 1	FRCO	55 E3
J 1	FRCO	56 A3
J 1	SBT	55 B4
J 2	ALA	46 C2
J 2	ALA	M D5
J 2	ALA	P D1
J 2	SJCO	46 E1
J 3	S	160 E2
J 3	SJCO	47 B2
J 3	SJCO	160 E2
J 4	CC	46 D1
J 4	SJCO	46 E2
J 4	SJCO	47 A2
J 5	SJCO	40 B4
J 5	SJCO	47 C1
J 6	SJCO	40 C5
J 6	SJCO	47 D1
J 7	MCO	47 E3
J 7	MCO	48 A3
J 7	SJCO	40 B5
J 7	SJCO	47 C1
J 7	STA	47 D2
J 8	SCTO	137 D5
J 9	SJCO	47 C1
J 9	STA	47 D1
J 9	STA	48 A3
J11	SAC	39 D3
J11	SJCO	39 D3
J12	SJCO	40 C3
J13	SJCO	46 E1
J14	STA	40 E5
J14	STA	47 E1
J15	TUL	68 B2
J16	MPA	48 E3
J16	MCO	48 B3
J16	STA	47 D3
J17	MCO	48 A3
J17	STA	47 C3
J18	STA	47 C4
J19	FRCO	58 B4
J19	TUL	58 A5
J20	MPA	48 E2
J20	TUO	48 E1
J21	TUL	58 D5
J22	TUL	68 B4
J23	TUL	58 C5
J23	TUL	68 C2
J24	TUL	68 B4
J25	TUL	68 A1
J27	TUL	68 C2
J28	TUL	68 C2
J29	TUL	68 D2
J30	TUL	68 B1
J32	TUL	68 A1
J34	TUL	68 A1
J38	TUL	57 E5
J38	TUL	58 B5
J40	TUL	58 A5
J41	TUL	70 B4
J42	TUL	68 E3
J42	TUL	69 A3
J44	TUL	68 C5
J59	MCO	48 C2
J59	TUO	48 C1
N 1	LACO	97 B2
N 2	LACO	89 A2
N 3	LACO	89 E5
N 3	LACO	90 A4
N 5	LACO	90 A2
N 6	LACO	90 C4
N 7	LACO	S B3
N 8	LACO	98 C2
N 8	LACO	R D5
N 8	LACO	U A3
N 8	LACO	T B1
N 9	LACO	96 E2

ROUTE NO.	CO.	PAGE & GRID
N 9	LACO	97 A2
R 2	RCO	102 B4
R 3	RCO	99 E5
R 3	RCO	100 A5
R 3	RCO	106 E1
R 3	RCO	107 A1
S 1	SDCO	107 D4
S 1	SDCO	112 D1
S 2	IMP	111 B3
S 2	SDCO	107 C3
S 2	SDCO	108 A4
S 2	SDCO	111 B3
S 3	SDCO	107 E3
S 4	SDCO	106 D4
S 4	SDCO	V C1
S 5	SDCO	106 D4
S 6	SDCO	106 E2
S 6	SDCO	107 A2
S 7	SDCO	107 A2
S 8	SDCO	106 C4
S 9	SDCO	106 C4
S10	SDCO	106 C3
S11	SDCO	106 C3
S12	SDCO	106 D3
S13	SDCO	106 C1
S14	SDCO	106 C3
S15	SDCO	106 C2
S16	RCO	106 D1
S16	SDCO	106 D1
S17	SDCO	V E3
S17	SDCO	111 E1
S17	SDCO	112 A1
S18	ORCO	98 D4
S19	ORCO	98 E4
S20	SB	86 B2
S21	SDCO	V A1
S21	SDCO	106 C5
S22	IMP	108 C2
S22	SDCO	107 E2
S22	SDCO	108 B2
S24	IMP	112 D5
S24	IMP	110 D5
S26	IMP	109 A4
S27	IMP	109 A5
S28	IMP	109 A5
S28	IMP	112 C3
S29	IMP	108 E5
S29	IMP	111 E3
S30	IMP	109 A3
S30	IMP	112 A3
S31	IMP	109 B4
S31	IMP	112 B3
S32	IMP	109 C4
S32	IMP	112 C3
S33	IMP	109 C4
S33	IMP	112 C4
S34	IMP	110 B4
S80	IMP	108 C5
S80	IMP	109 A5
S80	IMP	111 D3
S80	IMP	112 A3

POINTS OF INTEREST INDEX

NAME & ADDRESS	PAGE & GRID		NAME & ADDRESS	PAGE & GRID	
AIRPORTS			TRUCKEE AIRPORT, 4 miles E of Truckee	35	E1
			TULELAKE MUNI AIRPORT, N of Hw 139 near Newell	5	E3
ALTURAS MUNICIPAL AIRPORT, 1 mi W of Alturas	8	A1	UKIAH AIRPORT, State St	123	D5
AMADOR COUNTY AIRPORT, near Amador	40	D2	VENTURA COUNTY AIRPORT, Oxnard	176	A4
ANTIOCH AIRPORT, Lone Tree Wy, Antioch	M	C3	YUBA COUNTY AIRPORT, Olivehurst	33	D2
ARCATA AIRPORT, off Hwy 101 at Airport Rd	10	A4	YUCCA VALLEY AIRPORT, Hwys 62 & 247, Yucca Valley	100	D1
AUBURN AIRPORT, 4 mi N of Auburn	34	C3	**AMUSEMENT PARKS**		
BAKERSFIELD AIRPARK, Watts Dr & Union Av	78	D3			
BARSTOW-DAGGETT, Nat'l Trails Hwy, Barstow	92	B1	DISNEYLAND, Harbor Blvd, Anaheim	193	B4
BENTON AIRPORT, Gold St, Redding	122	A3	Amusement park-7 theme sections, rides, shops.		
BISHOP AIRPORT, 2 mi E of Bishop	51	D4	KNOTTS BERRY FARM, 8039 Beach Bl, Buena Park	T	B2
BRACKETT FIELD, McKinley Av, La Verne	U	C2	Ride 'Corkscrew' & 'Log Ride'; shops, rstrnts.		
BUCHANAN FIELD AIRPORT, John Glenn Dr, Concord	M	A3	MARINE WORLD AFRICA, 1000 Fairgrounds, Vallejo	134	E1
BURBANK-GLENDALE-PASADENA, 2627 N Hollywood Wy	179	B1	Land & sea animal shows; natural setting		
CALAVERAS CO AIRPORT, Hwy 49 S of San Andreas	41	A4	MARRIOTT'S GREAT AMERICA, 1 Great America Pkwy	P	B3
CANNON INTERNATIONAL AIRPORT, 2 of Reno	28	C4	Family amusement park, American history theme.		
CARSON CITY, Carson City, Nevada	36	C1	RAGING WATERS, 111 Via Verde, San Dimas	P	C3
CATALINA AIR & SEA TERMINAL, Harbor Blvd	191	B3	Pools, slides, picnic area.		
CHICO MUNICIPAL AIRPORT, 5 mi NW of Chico	25	B2	RAGING WATERS, off Capitol Expwy, San Jose	U	B2
CHINO AIRPORT, Hwy 83, Chino	U	D3	Pools, slides, picnic area.		
COLUSA COUNTY AIRPORT, 3 mi S of Colusa	33	A2	SAN DIEGO WILD ANIMAL PARK, 5 mi W of Escondido	106	D3
DELANO MUNICIPAL AIRPORT, Hwy 99, Delano	68	B5	Tour through preserve for endangered species.		
DOUGLAS COUNTY AIRPORT, Minden, Nevada	36	C3	SEA WORLD, 1720 S Shores Rd, Mission Bay Park	212	C4
FANTASY HAVEN AIRPORT, 2 mi SE of Tehachapi	79	D4	Marine life amusement pk, shows; Japanese Vlg.		
FRESNO AIR TERMINAL, 5175 E Clinton Av	57	D3	SIX FLAGS MAGIC MOUNTAIN, I-5 at Valencia Av	89	B4
FRESNO-CHANDLER DOWNTOWN AIRPORT, Amador & Thorne	165	B4	Family amusement park; thrill rides and shops.		
IMPERIAL COUNTY AIRPORT, Hwy 86 at Main, Imperial	109	A5	SPLASHDOWN WATERSLIDE, 200 Dempsey, Milpitas	P	C2
INYOKERN COUNTY AIRPORT, Hwy 395, Inyokern	80	D1	Water flumes; picnic area.		
JOHN MCNAMARA FIELD, nr Crescent City	1	C4	UNIVERSAL STUDIOS & AMPHITHEATER, Univ City Plaza	181	B1
JOHN WAYNE AIRPORT, MacArthur Blvd	198	B5	Features tours of movie and TV sets; shows.		
KERN VALLEY AIRPORT, Sierra Wy N of Lake Isabella	69	D5	WET 'N WILD, 2600 Las Vegas Blvd, Las Vegas	209	C4
LAKEVIEW MUNICIPAL AIRPORT, near jct of 140 & 395	7	B1	Wave pool, flumes, water roller coaster.		
LAMPSON AIRPORT, SW of Clear Lake off Hwy 175	31	D3	WILD RIVERS, Irvine Center Drive, Orange Co.	98	C5
LIVERMORE AIRPORT, Stanley Blvd, Livermore	M	C5	Water slides and activities.		
LONE PINE AIRPORT, 1 mile south of Lone Pine	60	B4	WINDSOR WATERWORKS, 8225 Conde, Windsor	37	E1
LONG BEACH MUNICIPAL, 4100 Donald Douglas Dr	S	E2	Pool, flumes, picnic area.		
LOS ANGELES INTERNATIONAL, 1 World Wy	189	C2	**BEACHES**		
MADERA AIRPORT, Hwy 99 & Av 17	57	A2			
MARIPOSA YOSEMITE AIRPORT, near Mariposa	49	A3	ARROYO BURRO BEACH COUNTY PARK, 2981 Cliff Dr	87	C4
McCARRAN INTERNATIONAL, 5 miles S of Las Vegas	210	C5	Swimming, picnicking, surf fishing.		
MEADOWS FIELD, Skyway & Airport Drs	78	D2	ASILOMAR STATE BEACH, Sunset Dr, Pacific Grove	167	A1
MENDOCINO COUNTY AIRPORT, Hwy 1 S of Little River	30	B1	Conference facilities in a beautiful setting.		
MERCED MUNICIPAL AIRPORT, 2 mi SW of Merced	170	A5	ATASCADERO STATE BEACH, Jct Hwy 1 and Hwy 41	75	D3
MONTEREY PENINSULA AIRPORT, off Hwy 68	54	B1	Swimming, fishing and camping.		
NORTH LAS VEGAS AIR TERMINAL, 3.5 miles NW of L V	74	D2	AVILA STATE BEACH, Front St	76	A4
OAKDALE AIRPORT, 8191 Laughlin Rd, Oakdale	47	E1	Fishing, fire rings, swimming.		
OAKLAND INTERNATIONAL, Doolittle & Airport Wy	159	B4	BAKER BEACH, NW shore Presidio, San Francisco	141	B2
OCOTILLO WELLS AIRPORT, HWY 78, Ocotillo	108	B3	Fishing, hiking nearby, no swimming.		
ONTARIO INTERNATIONAL AIRPORT, 2 mi E of Ontario	204	E5	BEAN HOLLOW STATE BEACH, S of Half Moon Bay	N	B4
OROVILLE AIRPORT, 3 mi SW of Oroville	25	C4	Fishing and camping on the beach.		
PALMDALE AIRPORT, Sierra Hwy	90	A3	BOLSA CHICA STATE BEACH, N of Huntington Beach	T	A3
PALM SPRINGS MUNICIPAL, 2 mi E of Palm Springs	206	E3	Sandy beach, body surfing, picnicking.		
PEARCE AIRPORT, 2 mi N of Lower Lake	32	A3	BOOMER BEACH, Coast Blvd, La Jolla	105	B2
PLACERVILLE AIRPORT, S of Hwy 50 near Smithflat	34	E5	Scenic beach, swimming and fishing.		
REDDING MUNICIPAL AIRPORT, 7 miles SE of Redding	18	C2	CABRILLO BEACH, E of Pacific Av, San Pedro	S	C3
SACRAMENTO CO METRO ARPRT, 12 mi NW of Sacramento	33	D5	Public boat ramp, surf fishing, barbeque pits.		
SACRAMENTO EXECUTIVE AIRPORT, 6151 Freeport Blvd	39	D1	CAPISTRANO BEACH, San Juan Capistrano	202	D5
SALINAS MUNICIPAL AIRPORT, off Hwy 101	54	D4	Sandy beach, body surfing, picnicking.		
SAN DIEGO INTERNATIONAL AIRPORT, Lindbergh Field	215	B2	CAPITOLA CITY BEACH, 30th Av, Capitola	54	A2
SAN FRANCISCO INTL, Airport Wy off Bayshore Fwy	144	D3	Swimming and fishing.		
SAN JOSE INTERNATIONAL AIRPORT, 1661 Airport Blvd	151	C1	CARDIFF STATE BEACH, Cardiff	106	B4
SANTA BARBARA AIRPORT, James Fowler Rd	87	B4	Fine beach for fishing or swimming.		
SANTA MARIA PUBLIC AIRPORT, Skyway Dr, Sta Maria	86	B1	CARLSBAD STATE BEACH, 3 mi S of Carlsbad Bl	106	A3
SANTA MONICA MUNICIPAL AIRPORT	187	C1	Fish, swim, surf, camp, store, concessions.		
SHAFTER-KERN COUNTY AIRFIELD, Lerdo Hwy	78	B2	CARMEL RIVER STATE BEACH, Scenic Rd	168	B4
SISKIYOU COUNTY AIRPORT, Montague	4	C4	Skin diving, fishing, bird watching sites.		
STOCKTON METRO AIRPORT, 5000 S Airport Wy	40	B5	CARPINTERIA STATE BEACH, Linden Av	87	D4
SUSANVILLE AIRPORT, 5 mi SE of Susanville	21	B3	Camping, picnicking, fishing pier, boat ramp.		
SUTTER COUNTY AIRPORT, off Samuel Dr	125	E4	CASA BEACH, Coast Blvd, La Jolla	105	A3
TAFT-KERN AIRPORT, West Side Hwy, Taft	78	A4	Swimming and fishing.		
TAHOE AIRPORT, Pioneer Trail Rd	36	A3			
TEHACHAPI-KERN CO AIRPORT, Green & J Sts	79	D4			

POINTS

NAME & ADDRESS	PAGE & GRID		NAME & ADDRESS	PAGE & GRID	
CASPER HEADLANDS STATE RESERVE, Hwy 1 near Casper Scenic environment with good fishing.	22	A5	NATURAL BRIDGES STATE BEACH, W Cliff Dr Natural sandstone formation; picnics, fishing.	53	E2
CASPER STATE BEACH, off Hwy 1 near Casper Scenic area for picnicking and fishing.	22	B5	NEW BRIGHTON STATE BEACH, off Hwy 1 Sandy beach, tide pools.	54	A2
CAYUCOS STATE BEACH, on Ocean Front Rd Fishing pier, barbeque & picnic facilities.	75	D2	NEWPORT DUNES AQUATIC PARK, off Pacific Coast Hwy Swimming and other aquatic recreation.	199	D4
CORAL BEACH, Hwy 1 W of Malibu Beach Fishing, swimming and picnicking.	97	A2	OCEANSIDE CITY BEACH, The Strand & Pacific Popular resort; 4 mi beach, swim, skin dive.	106	A3
CORONA DEL MAR STATE BEACH, Corona Del Mar Sandy beach, tidepools, body surfng, picnckng.	T	D5	PELICAN STATE BEACH, 21 miles N of Crescent City Fishing; no swimming.	1	D2
DOCKWEILER STATE BEACH, Venice Swimming, picnicking, fishing.	187	A4	PESCADERO STATE BEACH, Hwy 1 S of Half Moon Bay Good beach for fishing.	N	B4
DOHENY STATE BEACH, Puerto & Del Obispo Sts Surfing, camping, fire rings & picnic areas.	202	B4	PISMO STATE BEACH, off Hwy 101, Pismo Beach Camping & hiking among sandy beaches & dunes.	76	B5
EAST BEACH, E Cabrillo Blvd, Santa Barbara BBQ & picnic facilities, volleyball courts.	174	E4	POINT DUME STATE BEACH, Hwy 1 Good beach for picnicking, hiking or fishing.	96	E2
EL CAPITAN STATE BEACH, Avenida del Capitan Surfing, hiking, camping, boat rentals.	87	A4	POINT REYES NATIONAL SEASHORE, near Olema Sandy beach, tide pools; picnic, camp, hike.	37	D5
EL DORADO BEACH, off Hwy 50, South Lake Tahoe On the south shore of lovely Lake Tahoe.	129	A3	POINT SAL STATE BEACH, Sal Point Rd Many varieties of marine life.	86	A1
EMMA WOOD STATE BEACH, Hwy 101 & Hwy 33 Camping, fishing and swimming.	88	A5	POMPONIO STATE BEACH, Hwy 1 S of Half Moon Bay Lovely beach for picnicking and fishing.	N	B3
GARRAPATA STATE BEACH, Hwy 1, Carmel Good fishing and hiking trails.	54	A5	PORT HUENEME BEACH, off Hueneme Rd Fishing pier, playground, bike paths.	96	B1
GAZO CREEK ANGLING ACCESS, Gazo Creek Rd Beach access for fishing.	N	C4	REDONDO STATE BEACH, Redondo Beach Adjacent to King Harbor Marina; swim, fish.	S	A2
GOLETA BEACH COUNTY PARK, 5990 Sandspit Rd Fishing pier, swimming, boat hoist.	87	B4	REFUGIO STATE BEACH, Refugio Rd Tidepools; camping, fishing.	86	E4
GRAYWHALE COVE STATE BEACH, N of Half Moon Bay Good beach for fishing.	N	A1	ROBERT H MEYER MEM STATE BEACH, Hwy 1 W of Malibu Swimming. picnicking facilities, fishing.	96	E2
HALF MOON BAY STATE BEACH, near Half Moon Bay Camp on bluffs above beaches, hike, picnic.	N	B2	ROBERT W. CROWN MEMORIAL STATE BEACH, Alameda Day use only; youth programs offered.	L	D5
HERMOSA BEACH, btwn Redondo & Manhattan Beaches Public fishing pier, swimming, surfing.	S	A1	ROYAL PALMS STATE BEACH, Paseo dl Mar, Ls Angeles Good beach to swim, picnic, or fish.	S	C3
HUNTINGTON BEACH STATE PARK, Huntington Beach Sandy beach, good surfing, picnicking.	T	B4	SALINAS RIVER STATE BEACH, Potrero Rd Wide sandy beach & dunes; clamming & fishing.	54	B3
ISLA VISTA COUNTY BEACH PARK, Camino Del Sur Sandy beach, tidepools.	87	B4	SAN BUENAVENTURA STATE BEACH, Harbor Bl, Ventura Good swimming, beach equipment rentals.	175	C3
J D PHELAN BEACH, El Camino del Mar, Sn Francisco Swimming cove protected from the wind.	141	A2	SAN CLEMENTE STATE BEACH, San Clemente Surfing, camping; BBQ & picnic facilities.	105	D1
LAS TUNAS STATE BEACH, near Jct Hwy 1 & Hwy 27 Swimming in the surf, fishing, and picnicking.	Q	A4	SAN ELIJO STATE BEACH, Cardiff Good beach for camping, fishing and swimming.	106	B4
LEADBETTER BEACH, Shoreline Dr, Santa Barbara Very wide, sandy beach; picnic facilities.	174	C5	SAN GREGORIO STATE BCH, Hwy 1 S of Half Moon Bay Good fishing beach; picnicking.	N	B3
LEO CARRILLO STATE BEACH, S of Hwy 101 Good surfing, diving and swimming.	96	D2	SAN ONOFRE STATE BEACH, San Onofre Surf fishing, clamming; surfing & camping.	105	E2
LEUCADIA STATE BEACH, Leucadia Scenic beach for fishing and swimming.	106	B4	SAN SIMEON STATE BEACH, Hwy 1 Camping, hiking; dunes to explore.	75	B1
LITTLE RIVER STATE BEACH, South of Trinidad Beautiful beaches, delta, nature trails.	9	E4	SANTA CRUZ BEACH, Beach St Swimming, surfing, surf fishing.	169	D4
MALIBU LAGOON STATE BEACH, near Malibu Site of famous surfrider beach, swimming.	97	B2	SANTA MONICA STATE BEACH, Palisades Beach Rd Most popular beach in the Los Angeles area.	Q	B4
MANCHESTER STATE BEACH, near Point Arena Beaches, sand dunes, Point Arena Lighthouse.	30	B3	SEACLIFF STATE BEACH, 5 mi S of Hwy 1 Swimming; marine museum - open in summer.	54	B2
MANHATTAN STATE BEACH, Manhattan Beach Public fishing pier, swimming, surfing.	S	A1	SILVER STRAND STATE BEACH, Hwy 75, S of Coronado Beautiful beach to swim, picnic, or fish.	V	B4
MANRESA STATE BEACH, off San Andreas Rd Sandy beach, tide pools.	54	B2	SONOMA COAST STATE BEACH, N of Bodega Bay Camp, hike, picnic; scenic beaches.	37	B2
MARINA STATE BEACH, 10 mi N of Monterey Good fishing area.	54	B4	SOUTH CARLSBAD STATE BEACH, S of Carlsbad Camping, fishing and swimming.	106	B3
MARINE STREET BEACH, La Jolla Fishing, swimming and sunbathing.	105	A3	STILLWATER COVE, Hwy 1 S of Walsh Landing Good swimming and fishing.	37	A1
MCGRATH STATE BEACH, S of Santa Clara River Hiking, camping, fishing.	96	A1	SUNSET STATE BEACH, W of Watsonville Scenic bluffs; camp, fish, clam dig, picnic.	54	B2
MONTARA STATE BEACH, N of Half Moon Bay Fishing beach.	N	A2	THORNTON STATE BEACH, off Hwy 35 E of Daly City Good fishing; hiking trails.	L	B5
MONTEREY STATE BEACH, Park Av Sandy beach, fishing, swimming in summer.	54	B4	TOPANGA STATE BEACH, Topanga Canyon Blvd Swimming in the surf, picnicking.	Q	A4
MOONLIGHT STATE BEACH, Encinitas Sandy beach for swimming and fishing.	106	B4	TORREY PINES STATE BEACH, S of Del Mar Scenic beach for hiking, swimming, exploring.	V	A1
MORRO STRAND STATE BEACH, end of Yerba Buena Rd Sand dunes, streams; camping permitted.	75	D2	TRINIDAD STATE BEACH, off Hwy 101, Trinidad Beaches, bluffs, nature trails, picnicking.	9	E4
MOSS LANDING STATE BEACH, off Hwy 1 Fishing and equestrian trails.	54	B3	TWIN LAKES STATE BEACH, Santa Cruz Swimming, fire pits; day use only-no camping.	54	A2

POINTS OF INTEREST INDEX

NAME & ADDRESS	PAGE & GRID		NAME & ADDRESS	PAGE & GRID	
PISMO DUNES STATE VEHICULAR REC AREA, Pismo Beach Off-road, 4-wheel drive trails; camp & picnic.	76	B5	CAL STATE COLLEGE, BAKERSFIELD, 4001 Stockdale Hy Small, new campus; good student-profssr ratio.	78	C3
PISMO STATE BEACH, off Hwy 101, Pismo Beach Camping & hiking along sandy beaches & dunes.	76	B5	CALIF STATE COLLEGE, SN BERNRDNO, 5000 St College On a 3-3 system: 3 quarters, 3 classes.	99	B1
PLUMAS EUREKA STATE PARK, Hwy A14 at Johnsville Camping, scenic creeks, trails, lakes & mtns.	26	E2	CALIF STATE COLLEGE, STANISLAUS, Turlock Small, intimate campus in San Joaquin Valley.	47	D3
POINT MUGU STATE PARK, Hwy 1 Camp near the ocean; fishing, swimming.	96	C2	CALIF STATE POLYTECH UNIV, POMONA, 3801 W Temple Outstanding programs in architecture.	U	B2
PORTOLA STATE PARK, W of Hwy 35 Camping, recreational facilities.	N	D4	CAIFORNIA STATE UNIVERSITY, CHICO, W 1st St Offers a variety of quality academic programs.	124	B4
PRAIRIE CREEK REDWOODS STATE PARK, N of Orick Camping, fishing, picnic areas, hiking.	10	A1	CALIF STATE UNIV, DOMINGUEZ HLLS, 1000 E Victoria Noted as a leader in innovative programs.	S	D1
PROVIDENCE MTNS STATE REC AREA, Essex Rd Camping facilities in scenic surroundings.	94	B1	CALIF STATE UNIV, FRESNO, Shaw & Cedar Av Noted for agriculture, business, engineering.	57	C3
RED ROCK CANYON STATE PARK, Hwy 14 at Ricardo Camping, picnicking, hiking and exhibits.	80	B3	CALIF STATE UNIV, FULLERTON, Fullerton Good academic opportunities in many subjects.	T	D1
REFUGIO STATE BEACH, Refugio Rd Tidepools; camping and fishing.	86	E4	CALIF STATE UNIV, HAYWARD, Hayward Strong programs in sciences & liberal arts.	M	A5
RICHARDSON GROVE STATE PARK, S of Garberville Scenic camping area; fish, swim, hike.	22	B1	CALIF STATE UNIV, LONG BEACH, 1250 Bellflower Bl One of largest universities in CSUC system.	T	A2
RUSSIAN GULCH STATE PARK, S of Fort Bragg Camp, hike to waterfall, rocky headlands.	30	A1	CALIF STATE UNIV, LOS ANGELES, 5151 State Coll Dr Wide spectrum of programs with an urban focus.	R	B4
SADDLEBACK BUTTE STATE PARK, E of Lancaster Camping, picnicking, and hiking trails.	90	C3	CALIF STATE UNIV, NORTHRIDGE, 18111 Nordhoff St A broad range of educational opportunities.	Q	A2
SALTON SEA STATE RECREATION AREA, off Hwy 111 Good area to camp, boat, waterski, or hike.	108	E2	CALIF STATE UNIV, SACRAMENTO, 6000 J St Situated halfway between S F & the Sierras.	39	E1
SALT POINT STATE PARK, N of Fort Ross off Hwy 1 Camping, beaches, underwater preserve, trails.	37	A1	CAL TECH-CALIF INSTITUTE OF TECH, 1201 E Calif Bl Largest private technical college in Calif.	190	D4
SAMUEL P. TAYLOR STATE PARK, off Hwy 1 near Olema Camping, fishing, winter sports, riding.	37	E4	CLAREMONT COLLEGES, College Av & Foothill Blvd Distinguished group of six schools & colleges.	203	A1
SAN CLEMENTE STATE BEACH, San Clemente Surfing, camping; barbeque, picnic facilities.	105	D1	CLAREMONT GRADUATE SCHOOL, Claremont Colleges Studies in educatn, business, history, Englsh.	203	A1
SAN ELIJO STATE BEACH, Cardiff Camping & picnicking on the beach; swimming.	106	B4	CLAREMONT McKENNA COLLEGE, Claremont Colleges Studies in political science & economics.	203	B2
SAN LUIS RES STATE REC AREA, 16 mi W of Los Banos Lovely area to camp, waterski, fish & hike.	55	C1	HARVEY MUDD COLLEGE, Claremont Colleges Studies in sciences, engineering, mathematics.	203	A1
SAN ONOFRE STATE BEACH, San Onofre Surf fishing, clamming, surfing and camping.	105	E2	HUMBOLDT STATE UNIV, Arcata Beautiful campus in a redwood forest.	10	A5
SAN SIMEON STATE BEACH, Hwy 1, Morro Bay Camping and hiking; sand dunes to explore.	75	B1	LOYOLA-MARYMOUNT UNIVERSITY, Los Angeles Fine academic Catholic university.	188	A4
SILVERWOOD LAKE STATE RECREATION AREA, Hwy 138 Camping, swimming, boating and fishing.	91	B5	PEPPERDINE UNIVERSITY, 8035 S Vermont Av Features two campuses: Malibu & Los Angeles.	Q	D5
SINKYONE WILDERNESS ST PK, Humboldt & Mendocno Co Tent camping, picnicking, hiking and fishing.	22	A1	PITZER COLLEGE, Scott Hall, Claremont Colleges Studies in liberal arts and humanities.	203	B1
SONOMA COAST STATE BEACH, N of Bodega Bay Camp, hike, picnic; scenic beaches.	37	B2	POMONA COLLEGE, Sumner Hall, Claremont Colleges Studies in history, social & natural sciences.	203	B2
SOUTH CARLSBAD STATE BEACH, S of Carlsbad Scenic beach for camping, fishing or swimming.	106	B3	ST MARYS COLLEGE, St Marys Rd, Moraga Studies in liberal arts & economics.	L	E4
STANDISH HICKEY STATE REC AREA, 1 mi N of Leggett Camping, fishing, hiking trails, swimming.	22	C2	SAN DIEGO STATE UNIV, 5300 Campanile Dr Largest in the CSUC system.	V	C3
STOVEPIPE WELLS CAMPGROUND, Death Valley Natl Mon 200 campsites (RV & tents) in the valley.	61	C4	SAN FRANCISCO STATE UNIV, 1600 Holloway Av Many interdisciplinary programs.	L	A5
SUGARLOAF RIDGE STATE PARK, Adobe Canyon Rd Camping, fishing and riding.	38	A2	SAN JOSE STATE UNIVERSITY, 125 S 7th St Campus of 27,000 students in Santa Clara Vly.	152	C4
SUNSET CAMPGROUND, Furnace Creek Ranch, Death Vly Campsites near the heart of Death Valley.	62	A5	SCRIPPS COLLEGE, Balch Hall, Claremont Colleges Studies in social sci, literature, fine arts.	203	B1
SUNSET STATE BEACH, W of Watsonville Scenic beach to camp, fish, dig for clams.	54	B2	SCRIPPS INST OF OCEANOGRAPHY, San Diego Branch of UCSD, oceanographic research.	211	A1
TAHOE STATE RECREATION AREA, N of Tahoe City Camp, swim, fish, boat, picnic.	35	E2	SCRIPPS INST SUBMERGED LAND AREA, San Diego Part of Scripps Institute of Oceanography.	211	A1
TEXAS SPRINGS CAMPGROUND, Furnace Creek Ranch RV and tent campsites in scenic Death Valley.	62	A5	SONOMA STATE UNIV, 1801 E Cotati Av Offers programs in sciences and liberal arts.	38	A3
TURLOCK LAKE STATE REC AREA, SW of La Grande Waterski, fish, boat, hike and camp.	48	B2	STANFORD UNIVERSITY, Junipero Serra Blvd Distinguished univ; beautifl church on campus.	147	A3
WESTPORT UNION LANDING STATE BCH, N of Westport Camping and fishing.	22	B3	UNIV OF CALIF, BERKELEY, 2200 University Av Oldest & largest of the Univ Of Cal campuses.	156	B2
WOODSON BRIDGE STATE RERC AREA, SE of Corning Camping, fishing, swimming, nature trail.	24	D2	UNIV OF CALIF, DAVIS, Russell Bl & La Rue Studies in law, medicine, agricultre, science.	136	B3

🎓 COLLEGES & UNIVERSITIES

NAME & ADDRESS	PAGE & GRID		NAME & ADDRESS	PAGE & GRID	
			UNIV OF CALIF, IRVINE, Campus Dr Good programs in sciences & medicin.	200	D2
CAL POLYTECH STATE UNIV, SAN LUIS OBISPO Noted for studies in agriculture & business.	172	C1	UNIV OF CALIF, LOS ANGELES, 405 Hilgard Av Outstanding liberal arts & medical schools.	180	C1
			UNIV OF CALIF, RIVERSIDE, 900 University Av Desert campus lies at base of foothills.	205	E3

POINTS OF INTEREST INDEX

NAME & ADDRESS	PAGE & GRID	NAME & ADDRESS	PAGE & GRID

UNIV OF CALIF, SAN DIEGO, La Jolla Village Dr
  Specializes in physicl & naturl sci, medicine.
	V A2	PORT HUENEME HARBOR, end of Hueneme Rd
		  Dominated by US Naval installation.
			96 B1

UNIV OF CALIF, SAN FRANCISCO, 3rd & Parnassus Avs
  Small campus, tours available.
	141 E5	PORT OF SACRAMENTO, off Lake Washington
		  Furthest inland port of Sac deep-watr channel.
			39 D1

UNIV OF CALIF, SANTA BARBARA, Ward Memorial Bl
  Beautiful campus beside the ocean.
	87 A4	PORT OF STOCKTON, off Hwy 5 in Stockton
		  Busy inland agricultural seaport.
			160 A5

UNIV OF CALIF, SANTA CRUZ, Hill St
  Overlooks bay, excellent marine research dept.
	169 A2	RICHMOND INNER HARBOR, Richmond
		  Commercial port in San Francisco Bay.
			155 B5

UNIVERSITY OF NEVADA, LAS VEGAS, Flamingo Rd
  Noted for music & theater; concert hall.
	210 E3	SAN DIEGO BAY, W of I-5
		  Busy deepwater port, home of USN 11th Fleet.
			V C4

UNIVERSITY OF NEVADA, RENO, N Virginia & 9th Sts
  Beautiful site overlooking Truckee Meadows.
	130 B1	SAN FRANCISCO HARBOR, Fisherman's Wharf
		  Major commercial port; 1st in W Coast shippng.
			L B4

UNIVERSITY OF THE PACIFIC, Stadium Dr, Stockton
  Noted for Liberal Arts & Sciences.
	160 B2	SANTA CRUZ HARBOR
		  Small commercial harbor in Monterey Bay.
			169 E4

UNIVERSITY OF SAN DIEGO, Alcala Park Fine academic programs, small campus.	213 B4	**HISTORICAL SITES**	

UNIVERSITY OF SAN FRANCISCO, 2130 Fulton St
  Fine academic programs on a small campus
	141 E3	ALPINE COUNTY HIST COMPLEX, Hwy 89, Markleeville
		  Historic museum and restored buildings.
			36 C5

UNIVERSITY OF SANTA CLARA, The Alameda
  Mission Santa Clara is on this campus.
	151 C3	ANDERSON MARSH STATE HIST PARK, near Clear Lake
		  Buildings from Anderson Ranch & Indian site.
			32 A3

UNIV OF SOUTHERN CALIF, 3551 University Av, L A
  Largest private university in California.
	185 C5	ANGELS HOTEL, Angels Camp
		  Hotel in Twain's 'The Jumpng Frog of Calv Co'.
			41 B4

GOLF COURSES		ARROYO DE CANTUA, off Hwy 5 Headqrtrs of notorious bandit Jquin Murieta.	66 D1

ALMADEN GOLF & COUNTRY CLUB, San Jose
  Konica San Jose Classic, LPGA.
	P B4	ASTRONOMICAL OBSERVATORY, off Shake Ridge Rd
		  1st observ in Cal - discvrd Great Comet 1861.
			41 A2

BERMUDA DUNES COUNTRY CLUB, 42360 Adams St
  Bob Hope Desert Classic, PGA.
	101 A4	AVERY HOTEL, Moran Rd, Avery
		  Wooden hotel built in 1853.
			41 C3

CYPRESS POINT COUNTRY CLUB, 17 Mile Dr
  AT&T Pebble Beach National Pro-Am, PGA.
	53 A4	BALCLUTHA, Fishermans Wharf, Aquatic Park
		  Square-rigged Cape Horn ship; tour at Pier 43.
			143 B1

DESERT INN & COUNTRY CLUB, Las Vegas
  Panasonic Las Vegas Invitational.
	210 C1	BALE GRIST MILL ST HISTORIC PARK, on Hwy 29
		  Restored mill was built in 1846.
			38 B1

ELDORADO COUNTRY CLUB, Indian Wells
  Bob Hope Chrysler Classic.
	100 E4	BANNING PARK, 401 E M St, Wilmington
		  House built in 1850s by Gen Phineas Banning.
			S C2

FAIRBANKS RANCH COUNTRY CLUB, San Diego
  Kyocera Inamori Classic.
	106 C4	BARNSDALL PARK, 4800 Hollywood Bl
		  Site of Frank Lloyd Wright's Hollyhock House.
			182 B4

INDIAN WELLS COUNTRY CLUB, 4600 Club Dr, Riversde
  Bob Hope Classic, PGA.
	100 E4	BENICIA CAPITOL STATE HISTORIC PARK, H & 1st Sts
		  Capitol of California in 1853.
			153 B4

LA COSTA COUNTRY CLUB, Carlsbad
  MONY Tournament of Champions, PGA.
	106 C3	BIDWELL MANSION ST HIST PK, 525 Esplanade, Chico
		  Restored Victorian home of Chico founder.
			124 B4

LA QUINTA COUNTRY CLUB, Eisenhower Dr & 50th Av
  Bob Hope Classic, PGA.
	101 A4	BODIE STATE HISTORICAL PARK, Bodie, off Hwy 395
		  Gold boom town, now a restored ghost town.
			43 C3

MESA VERDE COUNTRY CLUB, Costa Mesa
  Uniden Invitational, LPGA.
	197 A4	BOK KAI TEMPLE (CHINESE JOSS HOUSE), Marysville
		  Only temple in USA for worship of River God.
			33 D2

MISSION HILLS COUNTRY CLUB, Rancho Mirage
  Nabisco Dinah Shore Invitational, LPGA.
	100 D4	BORAX MUSEUM, Furnace Creek Ranch, Death Valley
		  Memorabilia from the old borax mine.
			62 A5

OAKMONT COUNTRY CLUB, Glendale
  GNA Classic.
	Q E2	BOWERS MANSION, Washoe Valley
		  Granite home built 1864 wth rewards of mining.
			36 B1

PEBBLE BEACH GOLF LINKS, off 2nd Av
  AT&T Pebble Beach National Pro-Am, PGA.
	168 B3	BRAND PARK, San Fernando Bl, Los Angeles
		  Picturesque atmosphere of early Cal missions.
			Q D2

RIVIERA COUNTRY CLUB, Pacific Palisades
  Los Angeles Open, PGA.
	Q B4	BRIDGEPORT COVERED BRIDGE, Bridgeport
		  Longest single-span wood-covered bridge in US.
			34 B1

SPYGLASS HILL G C, Spyglass Hill & Stevenson
  AT&T Pebble Beach National Pro-Am, PGA.
	53 B4	BURBANK MEMORIAL GARDENS, Santa Rosa Av
		  A living memorial dedicated to the naturalist.
			131 D4

TAMARISK C C, 70240 F Sinatra Dr, Rancho Mirage
  Bob Hope Desert Classic, PGA.
	100 D4	CALICO GHOST TOWN, 10.5 miles NE of Barstow
		  Restored mining town - tour of mine & museum.
			92 A1

TORREY PINES GOLF COURSE, La Jolla
  Shearson Lehman Bros-Andy Williams Open, PGA.
	V A1	CALIFORNIA STANDARD OIL WELL, McKittrick Field
		  Discovery well started new oil field in 1899.
			77 E3

HARBORS		CAMP CURTIS, 1 mi N of Arcata Estab for the protection of white settlers.	9 E5

ALAMEDA HARBOR, Embarcadero & 9th Av
  Major shipping center of northern California.
	158 B4	CAMP SALVATION, Calexico
		  Refugee ctr for emigrants in search of gold.
			112 B4

BODEGA BAY HARBOR, Hwy 1 at Bodega Bay
  Small but busy harbor; parks nr harbor & bay.
	37 C3	CAMRON STANFORD HOUSE, 14418 Lakeside Dr
		  Built in 1876 it serves as the Oakland Museum.
			158 A3

INNER HARBOR, between Oakland & Alameda
  Busy commercial section of SF Bay.
	157 D4	THE CASTLE, 70 S B St, Virginia City
		  Built 1868 - restored; antique furnishings.
			36 D1

LONG BEACH HARBOR, Ocean Blvd
  Shares largest man-made harbr with Ls Angeles.
	192 A5	CATALINA ISLAND MUSEUM, Casino Building
		  Features displays on the island's history.
			97 B4

LOS ANGELES HARBOR, Seaside Av
  Busy commercial port of state's largest city.
	191 C5	CHARCOAL KILNS, near Wildrose, Death Vly Natl Mon
		  Large old kilns used during the mining days.
			71 D2

		CHILDREN'S PARK, S Morton Bl, Modesto Childrens playground wth old train & airplane.	162 C4

POINTS OF INTEREST INDEX

HHHHHHHHHHHHHHHHHHHHHHHHHHHHHHHHHHHHHHHHHHHHHHHHHHHHHHHHHHHHHHHHH

H HOTELS
HHHHHHHHHHHHHHHHHHHHHHHHHHHHHHHHHHHHHHHHHHHHHHHHHHHHHHHHHHHHHHHHH

* Indicates information obtained from AAA.

POINTS

POINTS OF INTEREST INDEX

NAME & ADDRESS	PAGE & GRID		NAME & ADDRESS	PAGE & GRID	

*AIRPORTER INN, 18700 MacArthur Blvd
  Across from John Wayne Airport.
	198	C5	*CARRIAGE HOUSE INN, Junipero Av nr 8th Av, Carml
			  13 units; fireplaces, bay windows; early Amer.
				168	C3

*ALADDIN, 3667 Las Vegas Bl, Las Vegas
  Casino, restaurants, entertainment, shops.
	210	B2	CASTAWAYS, 3320 Las Vegas Bl, Las Vegas
			  Casino, garden temple.
				210	B2

ALEXIS PARK RESORT, 375 E Harmon Av, Las Vegas
  500 rooms; pools, putting green, tennis.
	210	D3	*CENTURY PLAZA HOTEL, 2025 Avenue of the Stars
			  Near Shubert Theater & ABC Entertainment Ctr.
				183	A2

*AMBASSADOR HOTEL, 3400 Wilshire Blvd
  Classic hotel; spacious landscaped grounds.
	185	B2	*CIRCUS-CIRCUS, 2880 Las Vegas Blvd
			  Casino, entertainment, game room, circus acts.
				209	B5

AMFAC HOTEL, 8601 Lincoln Blvd, Los Angeles
  750 rooms; pool, entertainment, diningroom.
	188	A5	*CIRCUS-CIRCUS, 500 N Sierra St, Reno
			  Hotel, casino, restaurant, entertainment.
				130	B2

ANAHEIM HILTON & TOWERS, 777 N Convention Wy
  1600 units; pool, sauna, and whirlpool.
	193	C5	*CLAREMONT RESORT, Ashby & Domingo Avs, Oakland
			  Lovely hotel & tennis club with vw of S F Bay.
				156	C3

*ANAHEIM MARRIOTT HOTEL, 100 W Convention Wy
  750 units;pool, whirlpool, balconies & patios.
	193	C5	CLARION HOTEL, 401 Millbrae Av, Millbrae
			  223 rooms; dining room & coffee shop, pool.
				144	E5

ARROWHEAD HILTON, in Lake Arrowhead Village
  175 rooms; pool, whirlpool, boat dock.
	91	C5	*CLIFT HOUSE, 495 Geary St, San Francisco
			  380 units; newly renovated rooms, restaurant.
				143	C3

BAKERSFIELD HILTON INN, Rosedale Hwy, Bakersfield
  197 units; pool, whirlpool, disco.
	166	A2	COLONIAL INN, 910 Prospect St, La Jolla
			  75 rooms; swimming pool, dining room.
				105	B2

*BALLY'S, 3645 Las Vegas Blvd, Las Vegas
  Casino, restaurants, entertainment.
	210	B2	CONCORD HILTON, 1970 Diamond Blvd, Concord
			  340 rooms; pool & whirlpool, restaurant.
				38	E5

*BALLYS HOTEL - RENO, 2500 E 2nd St, Reno
  Casino, restaurants, theatres, shows, shops.
	28	C4	*CONESTOGA INN, 1240 S Walnut St, Anaheim
			  254 units; pool, whirlpool, restaurant.
				193	B4

*BARBARY COAST HOTEL, 3595 Las Vegas Blvd S
  Casino, restaurant, entertainment.
	210	B2	*COTO DE CAZA, 14 mi E of I-5 via El Toro Rd
			  100 rooms; pools & saunas, fishing, tennis.
				98	E5

BARNEY'S, Hwy 50 in South Lake Tahoe
  Casino, shows and restaurant.
	129	E1	*DEL WEBB'S HIGH SIERRA, 255 N Sierra St
			  Casino, restaurant, entertainment, shops.
				129	E1

*BEST WESTERN CAMERON PARK INN, on US Hwy 50
  61 rooms; pool. Restaurant adjacent.
	34	C5	*DESERT INN, 3145 Las Vegas Bl, Las Vegas
			  Casino, restaurant, entertainment.
				209	B5

*BEST WESTERN CAVALIER INN, 3.5 mi S of Sn Simeon
  66 rooms; oceanfront, pool, restaurant.
	75	C1	*DISNEYLAND HOTEL, 1150 W Cerritos Av
			  Served by Disneyland Monorail.
				193	B4

*BEST WESTERN DANISH INN LODGE, 1455 Mission Dr
  81 rooms; pool, garage, dining room.
	86	E3	DOUBLETREE HOTEL, 1000 The City Dr, Orange
			  460 rooms; tennis, pool, whirlpool.
				195	E1

*BEST WESTERN FLAGWAVER, 937 North H St, Lompoc
  50 rooms; pool, coffeeshop.
	86	B3	DREAM INN, 175 West Cliff Dr, Santa Cruz
			  163 rooms; entertainment, pool, whirlpool.
				169	D4

*BEST WESTERN LAWRENCE WELK VILLAGE INN, Escndido
  90 rooms; pool, golf, tennis, entertainment.
	106	D3	*DUNES, 3650 Las Vegas Bl, Las Vegas
			  Casino, restaurants, entertainment, shops.
				210	B2

*BEST WESTERN PONDEROSA MOTOR INN, H St near 11th
  98 units; pool & sauna, 3 blocks from capitol.
	137	C2	*EL DORADO HOTEL & CASINO, 4th & Virginia, Reno
			  Gambling, restaurant and entertainment.
				130	B2

*BEST WESTERN ROYAL LAS VEGAS, 99 Convention Ctr
  237 units; pool, restaurant and casino.
	209	D5	EL RANCHO HOTEL, on the Strip, Las Vegas
			  Newly renovated; casino, shows & restaurant.
				209	C5

*BEST WESTERN ROYAL SCOT, 1680 Oceanside Blvd
  80 rooms; pool & sauna, movies, dining room.
	106	B3	EMBASSY SUITE, 7762 Beach Blvd, Buena Park
			  203 rooms; whirlpool & pool, dining.
				T	B4

*BEST WESTERN STATION HOUSE INN, S Lake Tahoe
  100 rooms; near beach, casinos and skiing.
	36	A3	EMBASSY SUITES, 1211 Garvey, Covina
			  264 rooms; restaurant, attractive grounds.
				98	C2

BEST WESTERN BONANZA INN, 1001 Clark Av, Yuba Cty
  125 rooms; convention center, restaurant.
	125	C2	EMBASSY SUITES, 8425 Firestone Blvd, Downey
			  220 rooms; sauna, whirlpool & swimming pool.
				R	B5

*BEVERLY GARLAND MOTOR LODGE, 1780 Tribute, Sacto
  210 rooms; pool & whirlpool, playground.
	39	E1	EMBASSY SUITES, 1440 Imperial Av, El Segundo
			  351 rooms; near Los Angeles Internatl Airport.
				189	C2

BEVERLY HERITAGE, 3350 Av of the Arts, Costa Mesa
  238 rooms; near the Performing Arts Center.
	193	A3	EMBASSY SUITES, off Dyer Rd, Santa Ana
			  280 rooms; swimming pool, dining room.
				198	C2

*BEVERLY HILLS HOTEL, 9641 Sunset Blvd
  Excellent accomodations on beautiful grounds.
	183	A1	EMERALD HOTEL, 1717 S West St, Anaheim
			  508 rooms; pool, close to Disneyland.
				193	B4

*BEVERLY HILTON HOTEL, 9876 Wilshire Blvd
  Large hotel offers exceptional facilities.
	183	A2	*ENCINA LODGE, 2220 Bath St, Santa Barbara
			  122 units; lovely grounds, pool, sauna.
				174	A3

*BEVERLY WILSHIRE HOTEL, 9500 Wilshire Blvd
  Long established with excellent accomodations.
	183	C2	*FAIRMONT HOTEL & TOWER, Calif & Mason Sts
			  Offers excellent view of city; rooftop garden.
				143	C3

*BILTMORE HOTEL, 515 S Olive St, Los Angeles
  Lovely long established hotel of the 1920's.
	186	A3	*FLAMINGO HILTON, 3555 Las Vegas Bl, Las Vegas
			  Casino, restaurant, entertainment, shops.
				210	B2

BINION'S HORSESHOE HOTEL, 128 Fremont
  Casino, pool, cafe.
	209	C2	*FOREST INN, Park Av, South Lake Tahoe
			  125 units; lovely grounds, 2 pools, saunas.
				129	E2

*BREAKERS MOTEL, Morro Bay Bl & Market, Morro Bay
  25 rooms; ocean view, pool, restaurant.
	75	E3	FOUR QUEENS, 202 E Fremont St, Las Vegas
			  Casino, restaurant, entertainment.
				209	C1

BURBANK AIRPORT HILTON, 2500 Hollywood Wy,Burbank
  277 rooms; pool, sauna, whirlpool.
	17	B2	*FOUR SEASONS APARTMENT HOTEL, San Jacinto Dr
			  11 units; pool, whirlpool, bicycles, kitchens.
				100	C3

*CAESAR'S PALACE, 3570 Las Vegas Bl, Las Vegas
  Casino, restaurants, entertainment, shops.
	210	B2	FOUR SEASONS HOTEL, Newport Ctr Dr, Newport Bch
			  319 rooms; tennis, pool, 3 dining rooms.
				200	A4

*CAESAR'S, 1 blk N of US 50, Stateline, Nevada
  Cafe, convention facilities, golf, hlth club.
	129	E1	FREMONT HOTEL, 200 Fremont St, Las Vegas
			  Casino, restaurant, game room.
				209	C2

*CALIFORNIA CLUB, 1st & Ogden, Las Vegas
  325 units; dining room & coffee shop, casino.
	209	C2	FRESNO HILTON, Van Ness Av, Fresno
			  200 units; pool, dining room.
				165	D4

*CANYON HOTEL RACQUET & GOLF RESORT, S Palm Cyn
  460 rooms; golf, tennis, health spa, 3 pools.
	100	C4	*FRONTIER HOTEL, 3120 Las Vegas Bl, Las Vegas
			  Casino, restaurants, music hall, shops.
				209	B5

CARLTON OAKS LODGE & COUNTRY CLUB, Santee
  59 rooms; pool, sauna, tennis.
	V	D2	*FURNACE CREEK INN, off Hwy 190 in Death Valley
			  Tennis, golf, lawn games; airport transport.
				62	A5

Thomas Bros Maps

COPYRIGHT, © 1987 BY

N →

POINTS

NAME & ADDRESS	PAGE & GRID	NAME & ADDRESS	PAGE & GRID
MURPHY'S HOTEL, off Hwy 4 in Murphys Historical monument still in full operation.	41 C4	*SANDS, 3355 Las Vegas Bl, Las Vegas Casino, restaurants, star entertainment.	210 B2
*NAPA VALLEY LODGE BEST WESTERN, Yountville 55 rooms; lovely view, pool & whirlpool.	38 C2	*SANDS HOTEL & CASINO, RENO, Arlington & 3rd Gambling, cafe, shops.	130 A2
NEWARK HILTON, 39900 Balentine, Newark 318 rooms; pool, sauna, whirlpool, dining.	P A2	SAN FRAN AIRPORT MARRIOTT, Bayshore Hy, Burlingame 689 rooms; dining, health club, pool.	N C1
NEW OTANI HOTEL, Los Angeles St, Los Angeles 448 rooms; beautiful garden, pool & sauna.	186 A4	*SAN LUIS BAY INN, Avila Beach 76 rooms; ocean view, golf, swim, dining room.	76 A4
NEWPORT BCH MARRIOTT, Newport Ctr Dr, Newport Bch 400 rooms; 2 pools, tennis, dining.	200 A4	*SANTA BARBARA INN, 435 Milpas St S 71 units; across from the beach, pool.	174 D3
OAKLAND AIRPORT HILTON, Hegenberger Rd, Oakland 367 rooms; pool, restaurant, entertainment.	159 D4	*SANTA CLARA MARRIOTT, Great America Parkway 502 rooms; near Great America Theme Park.	P B3
ONTARIO AIRPORT HILTON, 700 'G' St, Ontario 319 rooms; dining, whirlpool & swimming pool.	U E2	*THE SHASTA INN, 2180 Hilltop Dr, Redding 148 rooms; pool & whirlpool, restaurant.	18 C2
PACIFICA HOTEL, 6161 Centinela Av, Culver City 368 rooms; swimming pool, restaurant.	188 C3	SHENANDOAH HOTEL, 120 E Flamingo Rd, Las Vegas Casino, shows and restaurant.	210 B3
*PACIFIC PLAZA, 501 Post St, San Francisco 140 units; restaurant, pay valet garage.	143 C3	SHERATON-ANAHEIM, 1015 W Ball Rd, Anaheim 500 rooms; entertainment, dining, pool.	193 B3
PALA MESA RESORT, Jct I-15 & Hwy 76, Fallbrook 135 rooms; pool, whirlpool, golf, tennis.	106 C2	*SHERATON AT FISHERMAN'S WHARF, 2500 Mason St, SF 525 units; pool, restaurant and coffee shop.	143 B1
PALM SPRINGS HILTON RIVIERA, Palm Springs 467 rooms; 2 pools, wading pool, tennis.	206 B2	*SHERATON HOTEL, 45 John Glenn Dr, Concord 168 rooms; pool, dining room, entertainment.	M A3
*PALM SPRINGS SPA HOTEL, Indian Av N & Tahquitz-M 230 units; pool, 2 hot minerl pools, steam rm.	206 B3	SHERATON HOTEL, Industry Hills Pkwy, Industry 298 rooms; golf, tennis, 2 swimming pools.	R E4
PASADENA HILTON, 150 Los Robles Av, Pasadena 253 rooms; entertainment, dining room, pool.	190 C4	SHERATON INN, 1177 Airport Blvd, Burlingame 316 rooms; dining room & coffee shop; pools.	45 C3
*PEPPER TREE MOTOR INN, 3850 State St, Sta Barbra 150 rooms; patios, 2 pools & sauna, restaurnt.	87 C4	*SHERATON NEWPORT BEACH, 4545 MacArthur Blvd Beautiful facilities, entertainment.	198 B5
*PICADILLY INN AIRPORT, 5115 E McKinley, Fresno 185 rooms; pool, whirlpool, restaurant.	57 D3	*SHERATON PLAZA, 6101 W Century Blvd Beautiful facilities, easy access to LAX.	189 C1
*PICADILLY INN-SHAW, 2305 W Shaw Av, Fresno 203 rooms; pool, airport trans, restaurant.	57 C3	*SHERATON PLAZA-PALM SPRINGS, 400 E Tahquitz-McC 263 units; pool, saunas, whirlpools, diningrm.	206 B4
PINE INN, Ocean Av, Carmel 49 rooms; Victorian decor, beautiful view.	168 B3	SHERATON PREMIERE, off Lankershim, Universal City 450 rooms; exercise room, pool & whirlpool.	181 A1
PLEASANTON HILTON, Johnson Dr, Pleasanton 298 rooms; racquetball, tennis, swimming pool.	M B5	*SHERATON SANTA BARBARA HOTEL, 1111 E Cabrillo 150 rooms; ocean view, pool, dining room.	87 D4
*QUAIL LODGE, 8205 Valley Greens Dr, Carmel Vly 100 rooms; scenic grounds, golf, tennis.	54 B5	*SHERATON SUNNYVALE INN, 1100 N Mathilda Av 174 rooms; pool, restaurant, cocktail lounge.	148 D4
QUALITY INN, 616 Convention Wy, Anaheim 281 rooms; pool, dining & entertainment.	193 C5	SHERATON SUNRISE, Point East Dr, Rancho Cordova 265 rooms; dining room, swimming pool.	40 B1
QUALITY ROYALE, 1433 Camino del Rio, San Diego 265 rooms; pool, sauna, putting green.	214 A4	SHERATON UNIVERSAL, off Lankershim, Universal City 475 rooms; entertainment, pool & sauna.	181 A1
*QUEEN MARY, Pier J, Long Beach British liner now serves as hotel & restrnt.	192 E4	SHERATON VALLEY INN, 5101 California Av, Bakrsfld 200 rooms; pool and restaurant.	78 C3
*QUEENSWAY BAY HILTON, 700 Queenswy Dr, Long Bch Located on the waterfront next to Queen Mary.	192 D4	*SHORE CLIFF LODGE, 2555 Price St, Pismo Beach 99 rooms; ocean view, heated pool, restaurant.	76 B4
RAMADA INN, 1331 Katella Av, Anaheim 240 rooms; pool, jacuzzi, restaurant & lounge.	193 E4	*SILVERADO COUNTRY CLUB RESORT, 1600 Atlas Peak 260 rooms; 7 pools, golf, tennis, bicycles.	38 D3
*RAMADA INN, 114 E Highway 246, Buellton 98 rooms; pool, convention & conference facil.	86 D3	*SMUGGLERS INN, 3737 N Blackstone Av, Fresno 210 rooms; beautiful landscape, pool, restrnt.	57 C3
*RANCHO BERNARDO INN, 17550 Bernardo Oaks Dr 151 rooms; 2 pools, golf, bicycling, tennis.	106 D4	*SOUTH COAST PLAZA HOTEL, 666 Anton Bl, Costa Msa 400 units; pool, putting green, tennis.	198 A3
RED LION INN, Camino del Rio Ct, Bakersfield 262 units; pool, whirlpool.	166 A2	*STANFORD COURT, 905 California St, Nob Hill Gracious 1900s decor in Old Stanford House.	143 C3
*RED LION MOTOR INN, 1830 Hilltop Dr, Redding 194 rooms; pool, putting green, dining room.	18 C2	STARDUST HOTEL, 3000 Las Vegas Blvd S Casino, restaurant, entertainment, pool.	209 B5
*RED LION MOTOR INN, 2001 Point West Wy, Sacto 448 rooms; pools, airport trans, dining room.	39 E1	*STOCKTON HILTON, 2323 Grand Canal 202 rooms; 3 pools, dining room & coffee shop.	40 A5
*REGISTRY HOTEL, 18800 MacArthur Blvd Across from John Wayne Airport.	198 C5	STOUFFER CONCOURSE, 5400 Century Bl, Los Angeles 750 rooms; restaurant, swimming pool.	189 E1
*RENO HILTON, 255 N Sierra Lovely hotel with pool, casino & restaurants.	130 B3	SUNDANCE HOTEL & CASINO, 3rd & Fremont, Las Vegas 650 units; restaurant, buffet and casino.	209 C2
*RIO BRAVO RESORT, 11200 Lake Ming Rd, Rio Bravo 112 rooms; tennis, golf, pools, airstrip.	78 E2	*SUNNYVALE HILTON INN, 1250 Lakeside Dr 299 rooms; pool, restaurant, airport trans.	P A3
RITZ CARLTON, 33533 Shoreline Dr, Laguna Niguel 393 rooms; golf, tennis, pools, ocean view.	105 D1	THE CHATEAU, 4195 Solano Av, Napa 115 rooms; Country-French atmosphere, pool.	38 C2
*RIVIERA, 2901 Las Vegas Bl, Las Vegas Casino, restaurants, entertainment, shops.	209 C5	*TICKLE PINK MOTOR INN, 155 Highland Dr, Carmel 29 rooms; beautiful view and lovely location.	54 A5
*SACRAMENTO INN, 1401 Arden Wy 387 rooms; pools, putting green, dining room.	39 E1	TORRANCE MARRIOTT, 3635 Fashion Wy, Torrance 487 rooms; 2 pools, sauna, whirlpool.	S B2
*SAHARA (DEL WEBB'S), 2535 Las Vegas Bl, Ls Vegas Casino, restaurants, entertainment, shops.	209 C4	TOWN & COUNTRY, Hotel Circle, San Diego 1000 rooms; 4 pools, sauna & whirlpool.	213 D4
*SAN DIEGO HILTON, 1775 E Mission Bay Dr 356 units; pool, beach, rental boats & bikes.	212 E3	*THE TREE HOUSE BEST WESTERN, off I-5, Mt Shasta 69 rooms; indoor pool, bicycles, dining room.	12 C2

NAME & ADDRESS	PAGE & GRID		NAME & ADDRESS	PAGE & GRID	
*TROPICANA, 3801 Las Vegas Bl, Las Vegas Casino, cafe, entertainment, theater, shops.	210	B4	AHJUMAWI LAVA SPRINGS STATE PARK, Island Rd Accessible by boat only.	13	E3
*UNION PLAZA HOTEL, 1 Main St, Las Vegas Casino, restaurant, entertainment.	209	C1	ALAMEDA PARK, Micheltorea & Anacapa Sts Displays 280 species of plants and shrubs.	174	C3
*UNIVERSITY HILTON, 3540 E Figueroa St, LA 241 units; next to USC campus; pool.	185	C5	AMERICAN RIVER PARKWAY, from Nimbus Dam 23 mi long greenbelt along banks of Sacto Riv.	137	B1
*VACATION VILLAGE, Mission Bay Pk, San Diego 449 bungalows, rooms & suites; 5 pools.	212	B3	ANCIENT BRISTLECONE PINE FOREST, White Mountn Rd 4600 yr old pine forest, nature trails.	52	A3
WAWONA HOTEL, S entrance to Yosemite Valley A grand mountain resort built in the 1800's.	49	D3	ANDREW MOLERA STATE PARK, W of Hwy 1, Big Sur 50 campsites, sandy beach, hiking, meadows.	64	B2
*WEST BEACH MOTOR LODGE, Cabrillo Bl & Bath St 45 units; across from yacht harbor & beach.	174	C4	ANGELES NATIONAL FOREST, N of Los Angeles In rugged mtns of LA, hiking & winter sports.	Q	D1
*THE WESTGATE, 2nd Av at C St, San Diego 223 units; elegant decor, restaurant.	215	D3	ANGEL ISLAND STATE PARK, E San Francisco Bay Isl pk has hiking, bike rentl, picnc, day use.	L	B4
*WESTIN BONAVENTURE, 6th & Flower, Los Angeles Rooftop restaurnt & revolvng cocktl lounge.	186	A3	ANNADEL STATE PARK, Channel Dr Riding & hiking.	38	A2
*WESTIN ST FRANCIS, Union Square, San Francisco Fashionable shops, skyline view from elevator.	143	C3	ANTELOPE VALLEY CAL POPPY RESERVE, W of Lancaster Scenic area for picnicking.	89	D2
*WESTWOOD MARQUIS, Hilgard Av near Wilshire Bl,LA 250 elegant suites; pool, sauna, whirlpool.	180	D2	ANZA BORREGO DESERT STATE PARK, San Diego County Beautiful wildflowers in spring; camp, hike.	108	A4

MISSIONS

			ARMSTRONG REDWOODS STATE RESERVE, E of Fort Ross Giant redwoods, picnicking, hiking trails.	37	C1
MSN BASILICA SAN DIEGO DE ALCALA, 10818 SD Msn Rd 1769, 1st missn estblshd along El Camino Real.	214	E3	AUSTIN CREEK STATE RECREATION AREA, E of Ft Ross Camp, horseback ride, meadows, vllys, forests.	37	C1
MISSION LA PURIMISA CONCEPCION, 15 mi W of US 101 1787, 11th missn, rebuilt by original methods.	86	B2	AZALEA STATE RESERVE, off Hwy 101, Arcata Beautiful azaleas bloom late May - early June.	10	A4
MISSION NUESTRA SENORA DE LA SOLEDAD, off US 101 1791, 13th missn, stood in ruins for 100 yrs.	65	A1	BENBOW LAKE STATE REC AREA, 2 mi S of Garberville Horse trails, fish, hike, swim, picnic.	22	B1
MISSION SAN ANTONIO DE PADUA, off U S 101 1771, 3rd msn, one of largest restored missns.	65	B3	BENICIA STATE RECREATION AREA, W of Benicia Good fishing; picnicking facilities.	L	D2
MISSION SAN ANTONIO DE PALA, off Hwy 76 Built in 1816 to help the Sn Luis Rey Mission.	106	E2	BIG BASIN REDWOODS STATE PARK, on Hwy 236 First state park to preserve redwoods.	N	D4
MISSION SAN BUENAVENTURA, Main & Figueroa Sts 1782, 9th missn, last founded by Father Serra.	175	B2	BOGGS MOUNTAIN STATE FOREST, N of Hwy 175 Picnicking; hiking trails.	32	A4
MISSION SAN CARLOS BORROMEO, Lasuen Dr, Carmel 1770, 2nd missn, burial place of Father Serra.	168	B4	BONELLI REGIONAL COUNTY PARK, Park Rd, San Dimas Picnicking facilities and hiking trails.	U	B2
MSN SAN FERNANDO REY DE ESPANA, 15151 SF Msn Bl 1797, 17th msn, destroyed by '71 quake; rstrd.	Q	C1	BORDER FIELD STATE PARK, 15 mi S of San Diego Good area to picnic, fish, swim, or hike.	V	B5
MISSION SAN FRANCISCO DE ASIS, Dolores & 16th Sts 1776, 6th missn, chapel unchanged for 175 yrs.	142	C4	BOTHE-NAPA VALLEY STATE PARK, on Hwy 29 Hiking, picnic & camping areas, swimming pool.	38	A1
MISSION SAN FRANCISCO SOLANO, Spain & 1st Sts 1823, 21st missn, northernmost & last of msns.	132	D3	BROOKSIDE PARK, Rosemont Av, Pasadena Site of Rosebowl; swimming, hiking, golfing.	190	A3
MISSION SAN GABRIEL ARCANGEL, 1120 Old Mill Rd 1771, 4th missn, at crossroads in early Calif.	R	C3	BUCKSKIN MOUNTAIN STATE PARK, Hwy 95, Arizona Scenic area to hike and picnic.	104	C1
MISSION SAN JOSE, 43300 Mission Blvd 1777, 14th missn, noted for outstanding music.	P	B2	BURTON CREEK STATE PARK, E of Tahoe State Park Camping and picnicking.	35	E1
MISSION SAN JUAN BAUTISTA, off US 101 1797, 15th msn, near othr buildngs of msn era.	54	D3	BUTANO STATE PARK, E of Hwy 1 at Gazos Creek Rd Camping, recreational facilities.	N	C4
MISSION SAN JUAN CAPISTRANO, off I-5 at Ortega 1776, 7th mission, swallows return annually.	202	E1	CALAVERAS BIG TREES STATE PARK, E of Arnold 2 giant Redwood groves - self-guided tours.	41	D3
MISSION SAN LUIS OBISPO, Chorro & Monterey Sts 1772, 5th mission, 1st misn to use tile tools.	172	C3	CANDLESTICK POINT RECREATION AREA, US 101 Scenic hiking trails; picnicking & fishing.	L	C5
MISSION SAN LUIS REY DE FRANCIA, on Hwy 76 1798, 18th missn, most successful of all msns.	106	B3	CASTLE CRAG STATE PARK, S of Dunsmuir Pinnacles, crags, cliffs, green pines, rec.	12	D3
MISSION SAN MIGUEL ARCANGEL, 801 Mission St 1797, 16th missn, last msn secularized - 1834.	66	A5	CASTLE ROCK STATE PARK, near Jct Hwy 9 and Hwy 35 Nature & hiking trails; picnicking & camping.	N	E4
MISSION SAN RAFAEL ARCANGEL, A St & 5th Av 1817, 20th missn, founded to aid sick Indians.	139	D3	CASWELL MEMORIAL STATE PARK, Hwy 99 S of Manteca Camp, fish, swim, hike, picnic.	47	B2
MISSION SANTA BARBARA, Laguna & Los Olivos Sts 1786, 10th missn, famed as most beautiful msn.	174	B2	CHABOT REGIONAL PARK, Lake Chabot 5000 acre park; fish, picnic, moto-X, boat.	L	E5
MISSION SANTA CLARA DE ASIS, Grant & Franklin St 1777, 8th missn, bell dated 1798 still clangs.	151	B2	CHANNEL ISLANDS NATIONAL PARK, off Santa Barbara Consists of 5 islands, 20 to 60 mi offshore.	87	C5
MISSION SANTA CRUZ, School & Emmet Sts 1791, 12th msn, destroyed, replica built 1931.	169	D2	CHINA CAMP STATE PARK, N of San Rafael Recreational facilities and camping.	L	B3
MISSION SANTA INES, 1760 Mission Dr 1804, 19th mission, favorite mission of many.	86	E3	CHINO HILLS STATE PARK, off Hwy 71, Orange Co Hiking trails, picnic areas.	U	C4

PARKS, STATE & FEDERAL, & NATIONAL FORESTS

			CLEAR LAKE STATE PARK, near Lakeport Camp, boat, wtrski, hike, fish, swim, picnic.	31	D3
			CLEVELAND NATL FOREST, San Diego & Orange Co's Hiking, boating, riding, fishing, camping.	107	B4
			COL. ALLENWORTH STATE HIST PARK, 20 mi N of Wasco Historical exhibits; picnicking facilities.	68	B4
ADM WILLIAM STANDLEY STATE REC AREA, Laytonville Beautiful scenery; no camping facilities.	22	C3	CRYSTAL COVE STATE PARK, N of Laguna Beach 3 miles of beaches for swimming & picnicking.	T	D5

POINTS

POINTS OF INTEREST INDEX

NAME & ADDRESS	PAGE & GRID	NAME & ADDRESS	PAGE & GRID
CUYAMACA RANCHO STATE PARK, on Hwy 79, Julian In old Indian territory; camp, hike; horses.	107 C4	LAKES EARL & TOLOWA, 8 miles N of Crescent City Fishing; primitive camping sites.	1 D3
DAYTON STATE PARK, Hwy 50 near Dayton Hiking and picnicking facilities.	36 D1	LAKE TAHOE NEVADA STATE PARK, E Lake Tahoe Boating, swimming, fishing, hiking, picnickng.	36 B1
DEL NORTE COAST REDWOODS ST PK, S of Crescent Cty Dense forests, giant redwoods, good camping.	1 E4	LASSEN NATIONAL FOREST, S of Hwy 299 Dense foliage throughout this lake rec area.	13 D5
DEVIL'S POSTPILE NATL MONUMNT, Mammoth Lakes Area Spectacular mass of hexagonal basalt columns.	50 C2	LASSEN PEAK, Lassen Volcanic National Park. Only active volcano in Cal, last erupted 1921.	19 D3
D. L. BLISS STATE PARK, North of Emerald Bay Dense forest, trails, camping, beach area.	35 E3	LASSEN VOLCANIC NATIONAL PARK, S of Hwy 44 Volcanoes, lava flows, hot springs, lakes.	19 E2
DONNER MEMORIAL STATE PARK, 2 mi W of Truckee Rec at Donner Lake, Donner Prty memorial, mus.	35 D1	LOS OSOS OAKS STATE RESERVE, Los Osos Valley Rd Hiking trails through beautiful scenery.	75 E3
EL DORADO NATIONAL FOREST, north of Hwy 88 Rugged mtns, dense foliage, scattered lakes.	36 A4	LOS PADRES NATIONAL FOREST, near Santa Barbara Camping, riding, fishing, hiking, hunting.	76 D4
EMERALD BAY STATE PARK, Emerald Bay Scenic; camping, swimming, picnicking.	35 E3	MAILLIARD REDWOODS STATE RES, NW of Cloverdale Scenic area for picnicking.	31 A4
FOREST OF NISENE MARKS, 4 mi N of Aptos Picnicking, hiking trails, and camping.	P B5	MALAKOFF DIGGINS STATE HIST PK, NE of Nevada City Colorful slopes exposed by hydraulic mining.	26 D5
FREMONT FORD STATE REC AREA, 5 mi E of Gustine Good area for fishing.	47 D4	MALIBU CREEK STATE PARK, Malibu Canyon Rd Picnicking, fishing, hiking trails.	97 A2
FREMONT NATIONAL FOREST, SE Oregon Good fishing, camping & rock climbing.	7 D2	MARSHALL GOLD DISCOVERY STATE HIST PARK, Hwy 49 Marshall's discov in 1848 started 'Gold Rush'.	34 D4
FREMONT PEAK STATE PARK, S of San Juan Bautista Picnicking, hiking trails and camping.	54 D3	McARTHUR-BURNEY FALLS MEM STATE PK, NE of Burney Well developed, scenic park.	13 C4
GAVIOTA STATE PARK, Gaviota Beach Rd Camping, fishing, boat launch, picnic areas.	86 D4	McCONNELL STATE RECREATION AREA, 5 mi SE of Delhi Picnicking, fishing, swimming and camping.	48 A3
GEORGE HATFIELD STATE REC AREA, 28 mi W of Merced Picnicking, fishing, hiking and camping.	47 D4	MENDOCINO HEADLANDS STATE PARK, S of Fort Bragg Rocky bluffs, hiking, wave carved tunnels.	30 A1
GOLDEN GATE PARK, between Lincoln Wy & Fulton St Vast city park, walk, equestrn trails, skate.	141 B4	MENDOCINO NATIONAL FOREST, E of Hwy 101 Scenic wilderness, horseback riding, hiking.	24 A4
GRIZZLY CREEK REDWOODS STATE PARK, E of Fortuna Scenic; camp, fish, nature trails, creeks.	16 B3	MODOC NATIONAL FOREST, south of Cal-Oregon border Good fishing and hunting; volcanic features.	13 E1
GROVER HOT SPRINGS STATE PARK, W of Markleeville Camping, swim at hot springs, fish in creeks.	36 B5	MONTANA DE ORO STATE PARK, Pecho Valley Rd Barbeque, camping, riding & hiking.	75 E3
HERRY A MERLO STATE RECREATION AREA, N of Eureka Boating and fishing.	9 E3	MONTGOMERY WOODS STATE RESERVE, Orr Springs Nature trails, picnicking.	31 A2
HENDY WOODS STATE PARK, near Philo on Hwy 128 Picnic, camp, fish, hike and swim.	30 D3	MORRO BAY STATE PARK, on Morro Bay Camping, fishing, clam digging, boating.	75 D3
HENRY COE STATE PARK, 14 mi NE of Morgan Hill Picturesque; camp & picnic grnds, day use fee.	P E4	MOUNTAIN HOME TRACT STATE FOREST, N of Hwy 90 Beautiful streams, mountains, forests.	69 B2
HENRY COWELL REDWOODS STATE PK, 5 mi N on Hwy 9 Equestrn trails, hiking, fishing, picnic grds.	N E5	MT DIABLO STATE PARK, Diablo Rd Hiking trails, campsites on peak.	M B4
HOLLISTER HILLS VEHICULAR REC AREA, S of Hollistr Motorcycle trails; hiking, camping, picnickng.	54 E3	MT SAN JACINTO STATE PARK, Hwy 111 near Palm Spgs Hiking, picnicking, some camping.	100 B3
HUMBOLDT REDWOODS STATE PARK, Redwood Hwy Tallest redwoods, camp, fish, picnic, hike.	16 A4	MT TAMALPAIS STATE PARK, 6 mi N Hwy 1, Marin Co Hiking, equestrian trails, camping.	L A3
HUNGRY VALLEY STATE VEHICULAR REC AREA, Gorman Camping, off-road trails.	88 E2	MUIRWOODS NATL MONUMENT, Mt Tamalpais State Park Named for naturalist John Muir; day hikes.	L A4
INYO NATIONAL FOREST, near Calif-Nevada border Winter sports, boat facilities, camping.	51 D3	NEVADA STATE PARK, N of Carson City, Nevada Rec at Washoe Lake-camp, boat, nature trails.	36 C1
JACKSON STATE FOREST, Hwy 20 near Dunlap Scenic area for hiking and picnicking.	30 C1	NOJOQUI FALLS COUNTY PARK, S of Solvang Picnic facilities with a view of the falls.	86 E3
JOAQUIN MILLER PARK, Skyline Bl Named for 'Poet of the Sierras'.	L D4	OCOTILLO WELLS STATE VEHICULAR REC AREA, Hwy 78 Trails for off-road vehicle use; camping.	108 B3
JOSHUA TREE NATIONAL MONUMENT, S of Hwy 62 Camp, hike, climb rocks in desert environment.	101 A2	PALOMAR MOUNTAIN STATE PARK, Birch Hill Rd Sierra-like country, many camps, picnic sites.	107 A2
J SMITH REDWOODS STATE PARK, NE of Crescent City Giant redwoods, camping, Smith River fishing.	1 E4	PARK MOABI, off I-40 Boat rentals & ramp, camping, fishing.	95 D2
JUG HANDE STATE RESERVOIR, near Noyo Self-guided nature trails; picnicking.	22 C5	PATRICKS POINT STATE PARK, N of Trinidad Camping, hiking, biking, picnicking.	9 D3
JULIA PFEIFFER BURNS STATE PARK, E & W of Hwy 1 Picnic areas, hike to view McWay Waterfall.	64 C2	PAUL M. DIMMICK WAYSIDE CAMPGROUND, W of Navarro Primitive campground with swimming & fishing.	30 C2
KING RANGE NATL CONSERVATION AREA, Cape Mendocino Camp, picnic, hike, backpack, scenic shores.	15 E5	PETRIFIED FOREST, on Petrified Forest Hwy Ancient redwoods preserved in volcanic ash.	38 A1
KINGS BEACH STATE REC AREA, NE of Tahoe City Picnicking, swimmming, fishing & boating.	36 A1	PFEIFFER BIG SUR STATE PARK, E of Hwy 1, Big Sur 215+ dev sites - hiking, store, swim , fish.	64 B2
KINGS CANYON NATIONAL PARK, Hwy 180 Trails, backpacking, horses, camping, fishing.	59 B2	PINNACLES NATIONAL MONUMENT, on Hwy 146 Remnant of volcanic mtn; hike & explore caves.	55 B5
KLAMATH NATIONAL FOREST, Siskiyou County Camping, boating, fishing, riding.	3 D3	PIO PICO STATE HIST PARK, Whittier Blvd, Whittier Second adobe home of last Mexican governor.	R D4
KRUSE RHODODENDRON STATE RESERVE, N of Ft Ross Colorful rhododendrons bloom April thru June.	37 A1	PISMO DUNES STATE VEHICULAR REC AREA, Pismo Beach Sand dunes, off-road trails; swim, camp, fish.	76 B5
LAKE HAVASU STATE PARK, S of Interstate 40 Resorts, camping, boat rentals, hunting.	96 B4	PLACERITA CYN STATE PARK, Hwy 14 N of Sn Fernando Scenic area for picnicking and hiking.	89 C5

POINTS OF INTEREST INDEX

NAME & ADDRESS	PAGE & GRID	NAME & ADDRESS	PAGE & GRID
PLUMAS EUREKA STATE PARK, Hwy A14 at Johnsville Scenic creeks, mountains, lakes and trails.	26 E2	TAHOE NATIONAL FOREST, W of Lake Tahoe Good fishing, camping, snow skiing, scenic.	26 E3
PLUMAS NATIONAL FOREST, south of Hwy 36 Waterfall, lakes, grassy valleys, woodlands.	20 B5	TAHOE STATE RECREATION AREA, N of Tahoe City Good camping, boating, beach, nature trails.	35 E2
POINT LOBOS STATE RESERVE, W of Hwy 1 Spectacular view of coast; swim in China Cove.	54 A5	TECOLOTE CYN NATURAL PK, Linda Vista Rd, Sn Diego Large natural park in the city of San Diego.	213 B2
POINT MUGU STATE PARK, Hwy 1 Scenic campsite; fish, swim, picnic, hike.	96 C2	TOIYABE NATIONAL FOREST, E Sierra Nev into Nevada Camp, fish, hunt; forest, grass, sagebrush.	73 D1
PORTOLA STATE PARK, W of Hwy 35 Camping, recreational facilities.	N D4	TOMALES BAY STATE PARK, Tomales Bay Hike to scenic beaches; rocky, wave-cut coves.	37 D4
PRAIRIE CREEK REDWOODS STATE PARK, N of Orick Good camping, scenic trails thru lush forest.	10 A1	TOPANGA STATE PARK, Hwy 27, in Santa Monica Mtns Picnicking, hiking, horseback riding.	Q A4
PROVIDENCE MTNS STATE REC AREA, Essex Rd Scenic area for camping; exhibits.	94 B1	TORREY PINES STATE RESERVE, S of Del Mar Beautiful hiking area; nature trail, exhibits.	V A1
RANCHO SIERRA VISTA, Ventura County Native American Cultural Center.	96 C1	TRINITY NATIONAL FOREST, along Hwy 299 Good hunting and fishing; rivers & lakes.	17 B3
RED ROCK CANYON STATE PARK, Hwy 14 at Ricardo Picnicking, hiking trails, camping facilities.	80 B3	TULE ELK RESERVE STATE PARK, Tupman Rd Several acres grazed by native valley elk.	78 B3
REDWOOD NATIONAL PARK, Crescent City, Orick Giant redwoods, picturesque coast & rivers.	2 A4	VAN DAMME STATE PARK, south of Fort Bragg Camp near beach, hiking trails, Pygmy Forest.	30 C1
RICHARDSON GROVE STATE PARK, south of Garberville Scenic, camp, fish, swim, hiking trails.	22 B1	W. IDE STATE HISTORIC PARK, 2 mi NE of Red Bluff Home of the California Pioneer. Picnic & swim.	18 D4
ROBERT LOUIS STEVENSON STATE PK, off Hwy 29 Scenic area for picnicking and hiking.	32 A5	WILL ROGERS STATE HISTORIC PARK, Sunset Bl Will Roger's home locatd within 186 acre park.	Q B4
ROEDING PARK, north of Belmont Av Picnic areas, boat rides, children's zoo.	165 B2	WOODSON BRIDGE STATE REC AREA, SE of Corning Camping, fishing, swimming, nature trail.	24 D2
ROGUE RIVER NATIONAL FOREST, South Central Oregon Fishing & white-water rafting on Rogue River.	3 C2	YOSEMITE NATIONAL PARK, off Hwy 120 Beautiful wtrflls, lakes, cyns, streams, mtns.	49 D1
RUSSIAN GULCH STATE PARK, S of Fort Bragg Rocky headlands, camping, hike to waterfall.	30 A1	POINTS OF INTEREST	
SADDLEBACK BUTTE STATE PARK, E of Lancaster Scenic area for picnicking, hiking & camping.	90 C3	A B C STUDIOS, 2020 Avenue of the Stars Tour sets & watch filming of TV programs.	182 C4
SALTON SEA STATE RECREATION AREA, off Hwy 111 Camp, hike, picnic, boat, waterski.	108 E2	ACADEMY OF SCIENCES, Golden Gate Park Renowned science museum incl Morrsn Planetarm.	141 D4
SALT POINT STATE PARK, N of Fort Ross off Hwy 1 Underwater presrve, beachs, tidepools, trails.	37 A1	AEROSPACE HISTORY CENTER, Balboa Park, San Diego Aeronautical displays of the past and present.	215 E2
SAMUEL P TAYLOR STATE PARK, off Hwy 1 Camping, fishing, riding, winter sports.	37 E4	ALCATRAZ ISLAND, San Francisco Bay Former maximum security prison; 1/2 day tours.	L B4
SAN BRUNO MOUNTAIN STATE PARK, S of Daly City Enjoy a picnic amid the beautiful scenery.	L B5	AMADOR COUNTY MUSEUM, 225 Church St, Jackson Working models of old gold mines.	40 E2
SAN FRANCISCO BAY WILDLIFE REFUGE, south S F Bay Preservation of nature at its best.	N E2	AMERICAN FOREST PRODUCTION MILL, North Fork Tours of the lumber mill are conducted daily.	49 E5
SAN FRANCISCO FISH & GAME REFUGE, off Hwy 280 Lovely area for hiking and picnicking.	N B1	AMERICAN VICTORIAN MUSEUM, 325 Spring St Collection of Victorian artifacts.	128 B2
SAN GABRIEL WILDERNESS AREA, off Hwy 2 Preserve of natural & rugged mountain country.	R E1	AMTRAK STATION, Kettner & D St, San Diego Train station with access to zoo & othr sites.	215 C3
SAN ONOFRE STATE PARK, off I-5, San Onofre Scenic area for hiking and picnicking.	105 E1	ANAHEIM CONVENTION CENTER, Katella & Harbor Concerts, sports events, shows.	193 B5
SEQUOIA NATIONAL PARK, Hwy 198 With Kings Canyon, museum, logging, rec area.	59 B5	ANAHEIM STADIUM, 2000 State College Bl, Anaheim Home of Angels baseball & Rams football teams.	194 A5
SEQUOIA NATIONAL FOREST, Hwy 198 Fishing, camping, boating, winter sports.	69 D2	ANGEL'S CAMP MUSEUM, Main St, Angels Camp History museum; also known for Frog Jumping.	41 B4
SHASTA NATIONAL FOREST, off I-5 Large lakes, steep mountains, rec facilities.	13 D2	ANO NUEVO STATE RESERVE, off Hwy 1, San Mateo Co. Reserve for seals, sea lions & elephant seals.	N C5
SHASTA STATE HISTORIC PARK, 6 miles W of Redding Restored buildings were blt in Gold Rush days.	18 B2	ANTELOPE VALLEY INDIAN MUSEUM, 15701 E Avenue 'M' Exhibits of Indian artifacts.	90 C3
SIERRA NATIONAL FOREST, S of Yosemite Natl Park Grand sequoias; wtrsports at lakes, hunting.	49 C3	ARCO PLAZA, 505 S Flower St, Los Angeles Subterranean shopping center.	186 A3
SINKYONE WILDERNESS ST PK, Humboldt & Mendocno Co Tent camping, picnicking, hiking & fishing.	22 A1	ARTIST'S DRIVE, Death Valley National Monument Rainbow-colored canyon of geological interest.	72 A1
SISKIYOU NATIONAL FOREST, SW Oregon Rugged mtns, winding creeks, old mining towns.	1 E2	ASIAN ART MUSEUM, near Japanese Tea Garden, GGP Outstanding Oriental collection; jade display.	141 C4
SIX RIVERS NATIONAL FOREST, NW corner of CA Many rivers, good fishing, forest-coverd mtns.	10 D3	ATMOSPHERIUM & PLANETARIUM, University of Nevada Space & star programs shown on dome ceilings.	130 A1
SMITHE REDWOODS STATE RESERVE, E of Hwy 101 Trails to waterfall, Eel River, picnicking.	22 C2	AVENUE OF THE GIANTS, N of Garberville Scenic route thru groves of majestic redwoods.	16 C4
STANDISH HICKEY STATE REC AREA, 1 mi N of Leggett Picnicking, hiking, biking, camping.	22 C2	BADWATER, in Death Valley, south of Hwy 190 Lowest pt in N America, 282' below sea level.	72 A1
STANISLAUS NATIONAL FOREST, SE of Hwy 4 Deep, stream-cut canyons, meadows, evergreens.	41 D4	BALBOA PARK, off Hwy 163 in San Diego Large central park; gardens, zoo, museums.	216 A2
SUGARLOAF RIDGE STATE PARK, Adobe Canyon Rd Fishing, riding & camping.	38 B2	BALBOA PAVILION, Balboa Bl, Newport Beach Beautiful landmark of Newport Bay; cruises.	199 D5
SUGAR PINE POINT STATE PARK, north of Meeks Bay Grove of sugar pines; camp, cross-country ski.	35 E2		

POINTS OF INTEREST INDEX

NAME & ADDRESS	PAGE & GRID	NAME & ADDRESS	PAGE & GRID
FISHERMAN'S WHARF, off Foam St, Monterey Art gallery, shopping & theater.	167 E3	HUNTINGTON LIBRARY, 1151 Oxford Rd Includes an art gallery & botanical gardens.	R C3
FISHERMAN'S WHARF, ft of Taylor at Jefferson, S F Open air markets, restaurants, vw fshng fleet.	143 B1	HURD CANDLE FACTORY, 3020 St Helena Hwy North Distinctive hand-made candles.	38 B1
FLEET SPACE THEATER & SCIENCE CENTER, Balboa Park Exquisite celestial displays and films.	216 A2	INDIAN CULTURAL CENTER, Yosemite Village Indian history in the area, displays, relics.	63 D1
FOREST LAWN MEMORIAL PARK, 1712 S Glendale Av Large collection of stained glass & statuary.	179 D5	IRVINE BOWL PARK, off Laguna Canyon Rd Natural amphitheater-Pageant of the Masters.	201 B2
THE FORUM, Manchester & Prairie Sts Popular center for sports & entertainment.	Q D5	JACK LONDON SQUARE, foot of Broadway Site of the 1st & Last Chance Saloon.	157 E4
FRESNO CONVENTION CENTER, Tulare & M Sts Various shows, conventions, exhib & displays.	165 E4	JACKSON SQUARE, Jackson & Montgomery Sts Former 'Barbary Coast'; now shopping plaza.	143 D2
FRESNO METROPOLITAN MUSEUM, Van Ness Av, Fresno Natural and historical exhibits.	165 D3	JAPAN CENTER, Post & Geary Sts, Japantown Hub of growing Japantown; traditional culture.	143 A3
FRONTIER MUSEUM, Rancho California Rd, Temecula Collection of artifacts of early settlers.	99 C5	JAPANESE TEA GARDEN, Golden Gate Park Creatd 1894; oriental landscape, cherry trees.	141 C4
FROST AMPHITHEATER, Stanford University Outdoor theater which seats 9,500.	147 A3	KELLY GRIGGS MUSEUM, 311 Washington, Red Bluff Restored Victorian home; furnshd wth antiques.	18 D5
FURNACE CREEK VISITOR CENTER, Death Valley Ranger talks, museum, information & gift shop.	62 A5	KINGS RIVER, Kings Canyon National Park Middle fork runs thru natl pk; exclnt fishing.	59 B2
GAMBLE HOUSE, 4 Westmoreland Pl, Pasadena Great architectural work, originl furnishings.	190 B3	KNIGHT MARITIME MUSEUM, 550 Calle Principal Exhibits feature history of whaling industry.	167 E4
GENERAL GRANT GROVE, Redwd Mtn Kings Cyn Nat'l Pk Seasonal festivities, horse & foot trails.	58 E4	LA BREA TAR PITS, 5801 Wilshire Bl, Los Angeles Displys of prehistoric animals found in pits.	184 B2
GHIRARDELLI SQUARE, N Point, Beach & Larkin Sts Shops, outdoor cafes by old chocolate factory.	143 A1	LAGUNA BEACH MUSEUM OF ART, 307 Cliff Dr Features continually changing collections.	201 A3
GIANT FOREST, Sequoia National Forest One of largest & finest Sequoia groves.	59 A4	LA JOLLA CAVES, 1325 Coast Blvd, La Jolla Formed by wave action; curio shop.	105 C2
GLACIER POINT, S of Curry Village 3200' abve the vly, vw vly & snow-covrd peaks.	63 D2	LA JOLLA MUSEUM CONTEMPORARY ART, 700 Prospect St Collection of architecture, photos & films.	107 B5
GOLDEN CANYON, S of Hwy 190, Death Valley Hike through dramatically colored, scenic cyn.	62 A5	LAKE COUNTY DIAMONDS, 875 Lakeport Blvd, Lakeport Largest open-pick diamond field.	32 A4
GOLDEN GATE BRIDGE, on Hwy 101 Famous bridge offers spectacular view.	141 C1	LAKE SHASTA CAVERNS, Shasta Caverns Rd E of I-5 Colorful rock formatns; boat tours available.	18 C1
GOLD RUSH SCENIC HWY 49, Mariposa to Vinton Historic 300 mi drive through the Mother Lode.	27 D3	LA MESA DEPOT/PACIFIC RR MUSEUM, 4695 Railroad Av Memorabilia of the Pacific SW Railroad.	V D3
GOLDEN GATE PROMENADE, along SF Bay shoreline Walkway along marina green.	141 D1	LAS VEGAS CONVENTION CENTER Conventions & exhibits, banquets.	209 D5
GRAND CANYON OF THE TUOLUMNE, N of White Wolf Trails to deep-cut canyons, waterfalls, mdws.	42 C5	LAVA BEDS NATIONAL MONUMENT, 30 mi S of Tulelake Cooled lava forming cones, canyons & caves.	5 D4
GRAND CENTRAL MARKET, Hill & 4th Sts Food bazaar specializing in foods of Mexico.	186 A3	LEGION OF HONOR MUSEUM, Lincoln Park Modeled after French Legn; fine art, graphics.	141 A3
GREAT PETALUMA MILL, 6 Petaluma Bl N Shops & restaurants in restored grain mill.	L A1	LEONIS ADOBE & PLUMMER HOUSE, Calabasas Restored pioneer homes.	97 B1
GRIFFITH OBSERVATORY, 2800 Observatory Rd Features displys, planetarium, laserium shows.	182 B3	LICK OBSERVATORY, Mt Hamilton 120" reflecting telescope.	P D3
GRIFFITH PARK, Los Feliz Bl & Riverside Dr One of nation's largest municipal parks.	182 B2	LITTLE TOKYO, Central Av & 2nd St, Los Angeles Teahouses, sushi bars, shops & hotels.	186 B3
HALL OF FLOWERS, Golden Gate Park Suberb seasonal flower displays.	141 C4	LODGE POLE, Sequoia National Forest Visitors center has geologic displays in park.	59 B4
HANCOCK PARK, 5801 Wilshire Bl, Los Angeles La Brea Tar Pits, LA County Museum of Art.	184 A2	LOG CABIN MUSEUM, 980 Star Lake Av at Hwy 50 Displays the history of the Lake Tahoe area.	129 A4
HAPPY ISLES NATURE CENTER, Yosemite Valley Mus, ranger explains vly featres & Indn caves.	63 D2	LOMBARD STREET, between Hyde & Leavenworth Sts 'Worlds Crookedest Street'; picturesque.	143 B2
HARRAH'S AUTO COLLECTION, Glendale Rd, Sparks Grand collection of automobiles.	28 C4	LONG BEACH CATALINA CRUISES, Golden Shore Boats depart daily for 22 mile trip to island.	192 D4
HASTINGS BUILDING, 2nd & J Sts Museum featuring the history of Sacramento.	137 A2	LONG BEACH CONVENTION CENTER, Shoreline Dr Hosts many shows and concerts.	192 E3
HAVASU NATIONAL WILDLIFE REFUGE, Lake Havasu Good fishing, many beaches along river.	96 A3	LONDON BRIDGE, at Lake Havasu Moved from the Thames River to Lake Havasu.	96 A4
HAYWARD AREA HISTORICAL SOCIETY MUS, 22701 Main California & local historical exhibits.	146 E2	LOS ANGELES STATE & COUNTY ARBORETUM, Arcadia Beautiful gardens featuring numerous plants.	R C3
HEARST SAN SIMEON STATE HIST MONUMENT, off Hwy 1 Tours of fabulous estate of William R Hearst.	75 B1	LOS ANGELES COLISEUM, Exposition Pk, Los Angeles Major sports events; UCLA vs USC football.	Q E4
HERSHEY CHOCOLATE CO, 1400 S Yosemite, Oakdale Visitors center, tours of chocolate factory.	47 E1	LOS ANGELES CONVENTION CENTER, 1201 S Figueroa A variety of large exhibits and shows.	185 D3
HOLLYWOOD BOULEVARD, Los Angeles Possibly the best known street in L A.	181 D4	LOS ANGELES CO MUSEUM OF ART, 5905 Wilshire Blvd Large collection of impressionist paintings.	184 A2
HOLLYWOOD PARK RACE TRACK, 1050 Prairie St Features thoroughbred & harness racing.	Q D5	LOS ANGELES COUNTY MUSEUMS, Exposition Park Natural history, science & many more exhibits.	Q E4
HOLLYWOOD WAX MUSEUM, 6767 Hollywood Bl Life-sized figures of many famous moviestars.	181 C4	LOS ANGELES ZOO, 5333 Zoo Dr 15 acre park features more than 2000 animals.	182 B1
HONEY LAKE, SE of Susanville Sierra Ordnance Depot - military facility.	21 C4	LOWER KLAMATH NATIONAL WILDLIFE REFUGE, Tulelake Great stopping point for migrating waterfowl.	5 C3

NAME & ADDRESS	PAGE & GRID	NAME & ADDRESS	PAGE & GRID
MARCH FIELD MUSEUM, March Air Force Base Exhibits of aircraft & memorabilia.	99 C3	OAKLAND MUSEUM, 1000 Oak St at 10th St Unusual environmtl mus follows Calif history.	158 A3
MARIPOSA GROVE, Southern Yosemite Natl Pk Giant Sequoias; Grizzly Giant is oldest here.	49 D3	OAKWOOD LAKE RESORT, off I-5 S of Manteca Water theme park with camping facilities.	47 A1
MARITIME MUSEUM STAR OF INDIA, 1306 N Harbor Dr Restored windjammer - oldest iron ship afloat.	215 C3	OAKLAND WORLD TRADE CENTER, Embarcadero Busy trade center near Inner Harbor at SF Bay.	157 E4
McHENRY MUSEUM, 1402 I St, Modesto Historical displays, photos & models.	162 B3	OAKLAND ZOO, Knowland Dr & 98th Av Picinic area, amusmt pk, aerail trm, baby zoo.	L E5
MENDOCINO COAST BOTANICAL GARDENS, S of Ft Bragg Gardens open daily; admission charged.	22 B5	OIL MUSEUM, Hwy 33, Taft History of oil industry & processing methods.	78 A5
MENDOCINO COUNTY MUSEUM, 400 E Commrcial, Willts Indian, pioneer, art & logging exhibits.	23 A5	OLD EAGLE THEATER, J & Front Sts First theater in California, opened in 1849.	137 B2
MERCED COUNTY FAIRGROUNDS, nr Jct of Hwy 99 & 59 Hosts Merced County Fair in mid-July.	170 D4	OLD FAITHFUL GEYSER OF CALIFORNIA, on Tubbs Rd Eruptions occur every 50 minutes.	38 A1
MERCER CAVERNS, 1 mi N of Murphys Colorful limestone formations found in 1885.	41 B4	OLD GOVERNOR'S MANSION, 16th & H Sts, Sacramento Victorian gothic mansion built in 1877; tours.	137 C3
MINING MUSEUM, Univ of Nevada, Reno History of mining, equipment & minerals.	130 B1	OLD TOWN ART GUILD, G & 2nd Sts, Eureka Galleries, gift shops, art supplies.	121 C1
MOANING CAVE, 5150 Moaning Cave Rd Limestone formations, Indian relics & bones.	41 B4	ORANGE EMPIRE RAILWAY MUSEUM, Perris An extensive collection of early trains.	99 B4
MODOC COUNTY MUSEUM, 600 S Main St, Alturas Displays of Indian objects & old firearms.	7 B5	OREGON CAVES NATIONAL MONUMENT, off Hwy 46 Spectacular formations of mineral deposits.	2 E2
MODOC NATIONAL WILDLIFE REFUGE, south of Alturas Popular nesting area for a variety of birds.	8 B1	PACIFIC SW RAILWAY MUSEUM, Highway 94, Campo Exhibits of the Pacific SW Railway.	112 D2
MOJAVE RIVER VLY MUSEUM, 270 Virginia Wy, Barstow Mining, railroad & Indian artifacts displayed.	208 B3	PAGE MUSEUM, 5801 Wilshire Blvd Exhibits of prehistoric animals from tar pits.	184 B2
MONO HOT SPRINGS, northeast of Lakeshore Hot and cold currents, beach, near campsites.	50 D4	PAINTED GORGE, off Hwy 195, N of Salton Sea Bluffs of colorfully layered rock.	101 C5
MONTEREY BAY AQUARIUM, Cannery Row, Monterey Unique aquarium with 'hands on' exhibits.	167 E2	PALM SPRINGS AERIAL TRAMWAY, Tramway Dr Spectacular view of desert floor below.	100 C3
MORETON BAY FIG TREE, Chapala & Montecito Largest fig tree of its kind in the nation.	174 D4	PALOMAR OBSERVATORY, Hwy 56, Mt Palomar Operated by Cal Tech; tours; 200" telescope.	107 A2
MORMON TEMPLE, 10777 Santa Monica Bl One of the largest Mormon temples in the US.	180 D3	PAULEY PAVILION, U C L A Campus Features many sports events.	180 C1
MORRISON PLANETARIUM, in Golden Gate Park Interesting celestial films and displays.	141 D4	PELTON WHEEL MINING MUSEUM, Allison Ranch Rd Pelton waterwheel, old mining tools.	127 B4
MORRO BAY AQUARIUM, 595 Embarcadero More than 300 fish & marine animal displays.	75 D3	PIER 39, northern waterfront, San Francisco Recreates old SF street scene; shops, rstrnts.	143 C1
MT SHASTA, off Hwy 5 N of Dunsmuir Mighty 14,162 ft mtn covered by 5 glaciers.	12 D1	PIONEER MUSEUM & HAGGIN GALLERIES, Stockton Historical displays, paintings & art objects.	160 B4
MT SHASTA FISH HATCHERY, 1 mi W of Mt Shasta Trout produced to stock Northern Cal streams.	12 C2	PLACER COUNTY MUSEUM, 1273 High St, Auburn Displays of early mining equipment.	126 C4
MT WHITNEY, Whitney Portal Rd At 14,495' it is highest mtn in contiguous US.	59 E4	PLACER COUNTY VISITORS INFORMATION CTR, Newcastle Historical & informational displays 24 hours.	34 B4
MOUNT WILSON OBSERVATORY, Mt Wilson Rd Famous for huge Hooker telescope & camera.	R C2	PT ARENA LIGHTHOUSE & MUS, off Hwy 101, Pt Arena Daily tours; maritime artifacts.	30 B3
MOVIELAND OF THE AIR, John Wayne Airport Large collectn of authentic antique airplanes.	198 A5	POINT HUENEME, end of Hueneme Rd Marks entrance to Port Hueneme Harbor.	96 B1
MOVIELAND WAX MUSEUM, 7711 Beach Bl, Buena Park Wax displays of celebrities & movie scenes.	T B2	POINT LOMA, 10 miles W on Catalina Bl Site Cabrillo Nat Monmt, lighthse, scenic vw.	V A4
MUD BATHS, in Calistoga Attracts visitors year around.	38 A1	POINT PINOS LIGHTHOUSE, Monterey Harbor Oldest lighthouse still in use on West Coast.	167 A1
MUSIC CONCOURSE, Golden Gate Park Free opn air concrts givn alng tree lined wlk.	141 D4	PONDEROSA RANCH, Tahoe Blvd, Incline Village Westrn town amusmnt pk, 'Bonanza' TV shw site.	36 B1
MUSEUM OF MINING, Johnsville Historical museum of mining in California.	26 E3	PORTS O'CALL VILLAGE, on Harbor Blvd, San Pedro Nautical shopping village with harbor tours.	191 B4
NATIONAL MARITIME MUSEUM, foot of Polk Street Displays nautical models, figureheads, photos.	143 A1	QUEEN MARY, Pier J, Long Beach Tours, restaurants & hotel on famous liner.	192 E4
NATURAL BRIDGE, Death Valley National Monument Colorful hike to natural arch in Black Mtns.	72 B1	RACETRACK, Death Valley National Monument Clay playa, rocks tilt during high winds.	60 E3
NBC STUDIOS, 3000 W Alameda Av, Burbank A look at behind-the-scenes TV production.	179 D5	RAMONA BOWL & MUSEUM, 2 mi SE of Hemet Home of the annual Ramona Pageant.	99 E4
NEVADA STATE CAPITOL, N Carson St, Carson City Built 1871, silver dome caps large stone bldg.	36 B2	RANCHO SANTA ANA BOTANIC GARDENS, Foothill Blvd Exclusively native plants of California.	203 A1
NEVADA ST MUS, N Carson at Robinson, Carson City Mining, pioneer, R R objects & exhibits.	36 B2	REDDING MUSEUM & ART CENTER, 1911 Rio, Redding Interesting Indian relics & art coll displayd.	18 B2
NOB HILL, at Calif, Sacramento, Jones & Tyler Sts Symbolic of elegant living; cable car access.	143 C3	RICHMOND ART CENTER, Barrett Av, Richmond Displays of painting & other art objects.	155 B3
NORTON SIMON MUSEUM, 411 W Colorado Blvd Outstanding collection of art & sculpture.	190 B4	RIM OF THE WORLD HIGHWAY Scenic route leads to mountain resort areas.	99 E1
OAKDALE MUSEUM, 1st & F Sts, Oakdale Features local and natural history artifacts.	47 E2	RIVERSIDE INTERNATIONAL RACEWAY, on Hwy 60 Features many varieties of auto racing.	99 B3
OAKLAND-ALAMEDA COUNTY COLISEUM, Nimitz Fy, Av 66 2 bldg sprts complex, indr arena, outdr stadm.	159 D2	ROARING CAMP/BIG TREES NARROW GAUGE RAILRD,Felton Restored 1880's steam locomotives featured.	P A5

POINTS OF INTEREST INDEX

NAME & ADDRESS	PAGE & GRID	NAME & ADDRESS	PAGE & GRID
ROBERT RIPLEY MEMORIAL MUSEUM, in Juilliard Park Museum is in the Church of One Tree.	131 D4	SOLAR ONE, National Trails Hwy, Daggett Nation's first solar electric power plant.	92 A1
ROSE BOWL, in Brookside Park Famous stadium of New Year's Football game.	190 A3	SOLVANG, Hwy 246 Authentic Danish village.	86 E3
ROSICRUCIAN EGYPTIAN MUS & PLANETARIUM, San Jose Largest Egyptian collection on the West Coast.	151 D4	SPORTS ARENA, Exposition Park, Los Angeles Sports events for college & profesnl athletes.	185 C5
ROY ROGERS MUSEUM, I-15, Victorville Memorabilia of Roy Rogers and Dale Evans.	91 B3	SPRUCE GOOSE, Queens Wy, Long Beach Harbor Features Howard Hughes' airplane made of wood.	192 E4
SACRAMENTO SCIENCE CTR & JR MUSEUM, 3615 Auburn Nature trails and animals to touch.	33 D5	STATE CAPITOL, Capitol Mall, Sacramento Daily guided tours through capitol building.	137 B3
SACRAMENTO NATIONAL WILDLIFE REFUGE, S of Willows Nesting area for migratory waterfowl.	24 D5	STATE INDIAN MUSEUM, 2618 K St, Sacramento Features various California Indian cultures.	137 D3
SALTON SEA NATIONAL WILDLIFE REFUGE, E of Hwy 111 Scenic view of nesting birds at Salton Sea.	109 A3	STEARNS WHARF, lower State St The main pier extends beyond State Street.	174 E4
SAN BERNARDINO COUNTY MUSEUM, Redlands Artifacts and history of the early settlers.	99 C2	STEINHART AQUARIUM, Golden Gate Park In Acadmy of Sci; features circular fish tank.	141 D4
SAN BERNARDINO NATIONAL FOREST, Hwy 18 Camping, picnicking; year-round sports.	U D1	STRYBING ARBORETUM, South Dr, Golden Gate Park More than 5000 plant species displayed.	141 C4
SAND DUNES, E of Stovepipe Wells, Death Valley Shifting sand creates scenic area for a walk.	62 D4	TECOPA HOT SPRINGS, west of Hwy 127 Old Indian healing pl, baths open to public.	72 E4
SAN DIEGO-LA JOLLA UNDERWATER PK, Torrey Pines Rd Protected marinie life area open to public vw.	V A1	TELEGRAPH HILL, at Lombard & Kearny Sts Park, Coit Tower at top with view; tours.	143 C2
SAN DIEGO MUSEUM OF ART, Balboa Park, San Diego Contains American and European art.	216 A2	TELEVISION CITY - CBS, 7800 Beverly Blvd Actual site of many telecasts.	184 A1
SAN DIEGO STADIUM, Inland Fwy (805) at Friars Rd Home of the Padres and the Chargers.	214 C3	TITUS CANYON, E of Hwy 374, Death Valley Natl Mon Colorful, exciting drive thru a narrow canyon.	62 D3
SAN DIEGO WILD ANIMAL PARK, 5 mi W Esconddo CA 78 Tour through preserve for endangered species.	106 D3	TREES OF MYSTERY, 16 miles S of Crescent City Unusual&handcarved redwood trees; Indian Mus.	1 E5
SAN DIEGO ZOO, Balboa Park, San Diego One of the largest and lovliest in the world.	215 E1	TRONA PINNACLES, S of Trona near Pinnacle Tall pinnacles formed by algae of a sea.	81 B1
SAN FRANCISCO ART INSTITUTE, 800 Chestnut, SF Three galleries; tours available.	143 B2	TUCKER WILDLIFE SANCTUARY, 28322 Modjeska Canyon Features a variety of hummingbirds.	98 D4
SAN FRANCISCO-OAKLAND BAY BRIDGE, I-80 Main link to East Bay.	L C4	TULARE COUNTY MUSEUM, 27000 S Mooney, Mooney Grve Restored buildings; Indian & Pioneer artifcts.	68 B2
SAN LUIS OBISPO CO HIST MUSEUM, 696 Monterey Displays of early Californian & Indian relics.	172 C3	TULE LAKE NATL WILDLIFE REFUGE, S of Tulelake Great stopping point for migrating waterfowl.	5 D3
SAN ONOFRE VISITOR'S CENTER, off I-5 Nuclear power generating plant with displays.	105 E1	TUOLUMNE COUNTY MUSEUM, 158 W Bradford, Sonora Located in the old jail; gold rush objects.	163 B3
SANTA ANITA PARK, 285 W Huntington Dr One of the nation's famous horseracing tracks.	R D3	TUOLUMNE MEADOWS, Tioga Pass Rd Camp, fish, backpack, mtn climb, horses.	43 A5
SANTA BARBARA CO COURTHOUSE, downtown Sta Barbara One of the most beautiful buildings in West.	174 C3	20TH CENTURY FOX STUDIO, Pico Blvd One of the oldest studios in Hollywood.	183 B3
SANTA BARBARA MUSEUM OF ART, State & Anapamu Sts Orientl & American art glasswares, sculptres.	174 B3	UBEHEBE CRATER, Death Valley National Monument Crater created by volcanic steam explosion.	61 A2
SANTA CRUZ BOARDWALK, near Municipal Pier Shopping, restaurants, outdoor shows, rides.	169 D4	UNDERSEA WORLD, Hwy 101 S of Crescent City View sea plants & animals, scuba diving show.	1 D4
SANTA CRUZ MUNICIPAL PIER, off West Cliff Dr Shops and arcades over the ocean.	169 E5	UNION SQUARE, Geary, Powell, Post & Stockton Sts Fashionable shopping center; park, fountain.	143 C3
SAUSALITO FERRY TERMINAL, Anchor St Commuter service to San Francisco.	L B4	UNION STATION, 800 N Alameda St, Los Angeles One of the landmarks of Los Angeles.	186 C2
SCOTIA LUMBER MILL, Main St, Scotia Tour mill, debarking, sawing, shipping logs.	16 A3	VICTORIAN TOUR HOUSE, 401 Pine St, Nevada City Privately owned restored home-tours by appt.	128 C2
SCOTTY'S CASTLE, Death Valley National Monument Tour unique mansion built by Death Vly Scotty.	61 B1	VIKINGSHOLM, at Emerald Bay Large Scandanavian castle with furnishings.	35 E3
SCRIPPS AQUARIUM MUSEUM, 8602 La Jolla Shores Sea exhibits & tidepools.	211 A1	VISITOR CENTER YOSEMITE VILLAGE, Yosemite Lodge Displays, photos of Yosemite, films.	63 C1
SEAL ROCKS, Golden Gate National Recreation Area View of seal and bird habitats.	L A5	WASSAMA ROUND HOUSE STATE HIST, 55 mi N of Fresno Picturesque picnic area.	49 C4
SESPE WILDLIFE AREA, E of I-5 off Hwy 126 Established to preserve near-extinct condors.	88 C4	WAYFARER'S CHAPEL, 5755 Palos Verde Dr Striking glass church sits atop hill by sea.	S B3
SEVENTEEN MILE DRIVE, Monterey Peninsula Magnificent drive between Carmel & Monterey.	53 A5	WHISKEYTOWN-SHASTA-TRINITY REC, NW of Redding Camp, backpack, picnic, boat, water sports.	18 A1
SHASTA DAM & POWER PLANT, 15 miles NW of Redding 2nd largest dam in US; exclnt vw of Mt Shasta.	18 B1	WHITNEY PORTAL, W from Lone Pine Starting point for Mt Whitney trail.	59 E4
SIERRA BUTTES, N of Sierra City Giant rugged granite outcrops, scenic.	27 A4	WILLIAM S HART PARK, Newhall Av at Sn Fernando Rd Tour the silent screen actor's beautiful home.	89 B5
SIERRA NEVADA MUSEUM OF ART, 549 Court St, Reno Collections of art from all over the world.	130 A3	WINCHESTER MYSTERY HOUSE, Winchester Bl, San Jose Fascinating house and museum.	151 B5
SIERRA MONO MUSEUM, St 274 & St 225, North Fork Artifacts of Native Indian Tribes.	49 E5	WOODMINSTER AMPHITHEATER, S of Orinda Centerpiece of pk, sumr concerts, light opera.	L E4
SILVERADO MUSEUM, 1490 Library Ln Memorabilia of Robert Louis Stevenson.	38 B1	WRIGLEY MEMORIAL & BOTANICAL GARDN, Avalon Cyn Rd Beautiful cactus, flowers & trees at monument.	97 A5
SISKIYOU COUNTY MUSEUM, 910 S Main St, Yreka Indn objects, displays of old & new indstry.	4 A4	YOSEMITE FALLS, Yosemite National Park Two beautiful waterfalls fall over 2,400 feet.	63 D1

NAME & ADDRESS	PAGE & GRID	NAME & ADDRESS	PAGE & GRID
YOSEMITE MTN SUGAR PINE RR, Hwy 41 N of Sugr Pine 4 miles trip on a steam-powered railroad.	49 D3	CONVICT LAKE, 37 miles north of Bishop 90+ dev sites - boat, fish, backpack, horses.	50 E2
YOSEMITE VALLEY, Mariposa County Picturesque, campng, domes, wtrflls, meadow.	63 A1	COYOTE RESERVOIR, N of Gilroy 70+ dev sites - boat, waterski, fish, hike.	P E5
ZABRISKIE POINT, off Hwy 190 in Death Valley Overlooks Death Vly from badland of Black Mtn.	62 B5	CUYAMACA RESERVOIR, off Hwy 79 south of Julian Camping, fishing, duck hunting; no swimming.	107 C4
ZALUD HOUSE MUSEUM, 393 N Hocket, Porterville 1891 home with period furniture.	68 D3	DANA POINT MARINA, S of Del Obispo St Shopping, restaurants, boating facilities.	202 B5
RECREATION LAKES, RIVERS & MARINAS		DON PEDRO RESERVOIR, W of Coulterville 500+ dev sites - hseboat, watrski, fish, hike.	48 C2
		DORRIS RESERVOIR, east of Alturas Good fishing & swimming; day use only.	8 B1
ALPINE LAKE, 51 mi NE of Angels Camp 100+ dev sites - boat, backpack, fish, swim.	42 A1	DOWNTOWN LONG BEACH MARINA, off Shoreline Dr Shopping, restaurants, boating facilities.	192 E4
ANTELOPE LAKE, 45 miles NE of Quincy 200+ dev sites - boat, waterski, fish, hike.	21 A4	EAGLE LAKE, 20 mi N of Susanville 300+ dev sites - boat, waterski, fish, hike.	20 E2
AQUATIC PARK, foot of Polk St, San Francisco Curved fishing pier creates cold swim lagoon.	143 A1	EASTMAN LAKE PARK & RECREATION AREA, N of Madera Scenic area for picnicking and water sports.	49 A5
BALBOA MARINA, 2751 W Pacific Coast Hwy One of the largest marinas on the west coast.	199 B4	EL CAPITAN RESERVOIR, El Monte Rd E CA 67 N I-8 Fish, boat, camp at nearby Lk Jennings Co Pk.	107 A5
BARNHILL MARINA, Inner Harbor, Alameda Pleasure boat marina in the Inner Harbor.	157 E4	ELLERY LAKE, 10 miles west of Lee Vining 10+ dev sites - boat, fish, rock climb, hike.	43 B5
BASS LAKE, E of Oakhurst 220+ dev sites - boat, waterski, fish, hike.	49 E4	FALLEN LEAF LAKE, southwest of South Lake Tahoe 200+ dev sites - boat, fish, swim, horses.	35 E3
BENICIA MARINA, end of E 3rd St Pleasure boat marina south of Benicia Point.	153 B5	FOLSOM LAKE STATE REC AREA, 1 mile N of Folsom Dev camps - boat, fish, waterski, horses.	34 B5
BERKELEY AQUATIC PARK, Foot of Bancroft Av Saltwatr lake, watr sports, model boat racing.	L C4	FRANKS TRACT STATE RECREATION AREA, S of Rio Vista Accessible by boat; swimming and fishing.	M E3
BERKELEY MARINA, foot of University Av Base for poplr sport fshng fleet, fshng pier.	L C4	FRENCHMAN RES STATE REC AREA, 35 mi N of Chilcoot 140+ dev sites - boat, waterski, fish, hike.	27 D1
BIG BEAR LAKE, off Hwy 18 Resort area has many winter & summer sports.	91 E5	FRENCH MEADOWS RESERVOIR, NE of Michigan Bluff 100+ dev sites - boat, fish, swim, hike.	35 C2
BIG SAGE RESERVOIR, NW of Alturas Boating, fishing, no camping facilities.	7 A5	GOLDEN GATE NATL REC AREA, San Francisco & Marin Gardens, historic sites, rec facilities.	141 A2
BLACK BUTTE LAKE, 9 miles west of Orland 90+ dev sites - boat, waterski, fish, hike.	24 B3	GOLDEN GATE YACHT CLUB, off Marina Bl, SF Private yacht club at SF yacht harbor.	142 A1
BLUE LAKE, 42 mi SE of Alturas 40+ dev sites - boat, waterski, fish, hike.	8 C3	HELL HOLE RESERVOIR, NE of Michigan Bluff 50+ dev sites - boat, waterski, fish, hike.	35 C2
BOCA RESERVOIR, NE of Truckee 90+ dev sites - boat, waterski, fish, hike.	27 E5	HENSLEY LAKE PARK & REC AREA, 17 mi N of Madera Camping, picnincking, waterskiing & swimming.	49 B5
BOWMAN LAKE, 40 mi NE of Nevada City Primitive sites-fish, backpack, swim, picnic.	27 A5	HOGAN RESERVOIR, 3 mi W of San Andreas Dev & undev sites - boat, fish, hike, swim.	40 E4
BRANNAN ISLAND STATE REC AREA, S of Rio Vista Boating & fishing; swim, picnic; visitor ctr.	M D2	HUNTINGTON HARBOUR, Huntington Beach Waterfront homes & marina facilities.	T A3
BRIDGEPORT RESERVOIR, just north of Bridgeport 60+ dev sites - boat, fish, swim, backpack.	43 B3	HUNTINGTON LAKE, north of Camp Sierra 300+ dev sites - boat, waterski, fish, horses.	50 B5
BUCKS LAKE, southwest of Quincy 70+ dev sites - boat, waterski, fish, hike.	26 B2	ICE HOUSE RESERVOIR, 12 mi N of Riverton 80+ dev sites - boat, fish, swim, hike.	35 C4
BULLARDS BAR RESERVOIR, E of Camptonville 90+ dev sites - boat, watrski, fish, picnic.	26 B5	INDIAN CREEK RESERVOIR, east of Markleeville 20+ dev sites - boat, fish, backpack, picnic.	36 C4
BUTTE LAKE, Lassen Volcanic National Park 90+ dev sites - sail, fish, swim, backpack.	20 A2	IRON GATE RESERVOIR & LAKE COPCO, NE of Henley Camp, picnic, fish, swim, raft, hike, hunt.	4 C2
BUTT VALLEY RESERVOIR, off Prattville Butt Res Rd Sailing; recreational facilities.	20 B5	JACK LONDON MARINA, Embarcadero, Oakland Pleasure boat marina in the Inner Harbor.	157 D4
CAMANCHE RESERVOIR, W OF San Andreas 1150+ dev sites - boat, fish, hike, swim.	40 C3	JACKSON MEADOW RESERVOIR, SE of Sierra City 120+ dev sites - boat, waterski, fish, hike.	27 B4
CAMP FAR WEST RESERVOIR, 29 mi NW of Auburn 30+ dev sites - boat, waterski, fish, swim.	34 A2	JENKINSON LAKE, 18 mi E of Placerville 290+ dev sites - hseboat, fish, swim, hike.	35 B4
CAPLES LAKE, near Kirkwood on Hwy 88 30+ dev sites - boat, fish, hike, horses.	36 A5	JUNE LAKE LOOP, 18 miles north of Mammoth Lakes 280+ dev sites - boat, fish, backpack, horses.	50 C1
CASTAIC LAKE STATE RECREATION AREA, N of Castaic Boating, picnicking and swimming.	89 B4	JUNIPER LAKE, Lassen Volcanic National Park Sail, swim, backpack, hike, picnic, horses.	20 A3
CATALINA YACHT HARBOR, Avalon Bay, Catalina Islnd Yacht moorings, glass bottom boat tours.	97 B4	LAKE ALMANOR, southwest of Susanville 170+ dev sites - boat, waterski, fish, hike.	20 B4
CHANNEL ISLANDS HARBOR, Oxnard Small marina, Channel Islands Museum.	96 A1	LAKE AMADOR, 7 mi S of Ione Dev camps - boat, fish, waterslide, hike.	40 D3
CHERRY LAKE, 31 mi E of Tuolumne 40+ dev sites - boat, waterski, fish, horses.	42 B4	LAKE ARROWHEAD, Hwy 173 Charming resort area; fishing, winter sports.	91 C5
CLEAR LAKE, near Lakeport 140+ dev sites - boat, waterski, fish, hike.	31 D2	LAKE BERRYESSA, on Hwy 128, Napa County Camping, fishing, waterskiing, resorts.	32 D5
COLORADO RIVER, on the California-Arizona border Camp, hike along the river; boat, swim.	110 C3	LAKE BRITTON, 13 mi N of Burney 120+ dev sites - boat, waterski, fish, horses.	13 C4
COLUSA-SACRAMENTO RIVER STATE REC AREA, Colusa Undev camps, boat, fish, picnic, waterski.	33 A1	LAKE CACHUMA RECREATION AREA, 11 mi S of Solvang Fishing, boating, camping; no swimming.	87 A3

POINTS OF INTEREST INDEX

NAME & ADDRESS	PAGE & GRID	NAME & ADDRESS	PAGE & GRID
LAKE CASITAS RECREATION AREA, 11311 Santa Ana Rd Fishing, boating, camping.	88 A4	MAMMOTH POOL RESERVOIR, east of Bass Lake 60+ dev sites - boat, waterski, fish, hike.	50 B4
LAKE CROWLEY, 35 miles north of Bishop Dev campsites - boat, waterski, fish, picnic.	51 A2	MANZANITA LAKE, Lassen Volcanic National Park 170+ dev sites - sail, fish, hike, horses.	19 D2
LAKE DAVIS, north of Portola 110+ dev sites - boat, fish, hike, picnic.	27 A2	MARINA DEL REY, Via Marina Berths more than 10,000 yachts.	187 C4
LAKE DEL VALLE STATE REC AREA, off Hwy 84 Boating and recreation facilities.	P D1	MARTINEZ YACHT HARBOR, Martinez Small pleasure craft marina.	154 B1
LAKE ELSINORE STATE RECREATION AREA, Lk Elsinore Scenic area to swim, fish, camp and boat.	99 B4	MARTIS CREEK RESERVOIR, SE of Truckee 20+ dev sites - sail, fish, swim, hike.	35 E1
LAKE HENSHAW, off CA 76, Santa Ysabel 400+ dev sites - fish, boat, hike.	107 B2	MEDICINE LAKE, 48 miles NE of McCloud 70+ dev sites - boat, waterski, fish, horses.	5 D5
LAKE HODGES, off S6 on Lake Dr, Escondido Owned by SD City for day use only; fish, boat.	106 D4	MILLERTON LAKE REC AREA, 22 miles East of Madera 130+ dev sites - boat, waterski, fish, horses.	57 D1
LAKE ISABELLA, 48 mi NE of Bakersfield One of the most complete rec lakes in Calif.	79 D1	MISSION BAY, Mission Bay Park, W of I-5 Separate courses for diverse water sports.	212 D2
LAKE JENNINGS, Jennings Pk Rd N off I-8 RV & tent camping; boat, limited fishing.	107 A5	MONO LAKE TUFA STATE RESERVE, Hy 395 Lee Vining Interesting salt formatns surround saltwtr lk.	43 D4
LAKE KAWEAH, 17 mi E of Visalia via Hwy 198 Campsites, boating, fishing, swimming.	68 D1	MONTEREY MARINA, Ocean View Blvd Small craft harbor near Fisherman's Wharf.	167 E3
LAKE McCLOUD, 12 mi S of McCloud Undev campsites - boat, fish, picnic, hike.	12 E3	MORENA LAKE, Oak Dr & Buckman Spgs Rd, W of I-8 Campsites, fishing, boating, hiking, horses.	112 D1
LAKE McCLURE, S of Coulterville 550+ dev sites - housebt, fish, swim, picnic.	48 D2	NOYO HARBOR, south of Fort Bragg Small, scenic eastern-like fishing village.	22 B5
LAKE MEAD NATL RECREATION AREA, Hwy 93 & Lakeshre One of largest artificial lakes in the world.	85 C1	OCEANSIDE HARBOR, 1540 Harbor Dr N Deep sea & sport fishing; pier fishng; sailng.	106 A3
LAKE MENDOCINO, N of Ukiah 300+ dev sites - boat, waterski, fish, hike.	31 B2	OTAY RESERVOIR, Wueste Rd, E Chula Vista S D City 1k, co campgrd; fish, boat, no swim.	V E4
LAKE MERRITT, downtown Oakland Large natural salt water lake.	158 B3	PARDEE RESERVOIR, 3.5 mi E of Buena Vista 180+ dev sites & pool - boat, fish, bicycle.	40 D3
LAKE MOHAVE, E of Searchlight, Nevada Boat, fish, swim, camp, beaches, marinas.	85 C2	PICACHO STATE RECREATION AREA, W of Picacho Fish, boat, camp, picnic or hike.	110 C4
LAKE NACIMIENTO, 40 mi NW of Paso Robles 350+ dev sites - waterski, boat, swim, hike.	65 D5	PINE FLAT RESERVOIR REC AREA, 20 mi N of Fresno Dev camps - houseboat, waterski, fish, hike.	58 B2
LAKE OROVILLE STATE REC AREA, NE of Oroville 200+ dev sites - boat, waterski, fish, horses.	25 D4	PROSSER CREEK RESERVOIR, N of Truckee Dev & undev sites - boat, fish, swim, picnic.	27 D5
LAKE PERRIS STATE REC AREA, off Ramona Expressway Bike trails, boat rentals, camping.	99 C3	PYRAMID LAKE RECREATION AREA, off I-5 25+ dev sites-boat, waterski, fish, swim.	88 E3
LAKE PILLSBURY, near Scott Dam 100+ dev sites - boat, waterski, fish, hike.	23 D5	RICHMOND MARINA BAY, 1340 Marina Wy S, Richmond Large boat marina on San Francisco Bay.	155 B5
LAKE SABRINA, 18 mi SW of Bishop Dev sites - boat, fish, backpack, picnic.	51 B5	ROCK CREEK LAKE, SW of Toms Place 220+ dev sites - boat, fish, backpack, picnic.	51 B3
LAKE SAN ANTONIO RECREATION AREA, W of Bradley 650+ dev sites-boat, fish, swim, hike, horses.	65 D4	ROLLINS RESERVOIR, N of Colfax 240+ dev sites - boat, waterski, fish, hike.	34 D2
LAKE SHASTA, off I-5 north of Redding 400+ sites - houseboating, fishing, wtrskiing.	18 C1	RUTH LAKE, N of Ruth 60+ dev sites - boat, waterski, fish, horses.	16 E4
LAKE SHASTINA, 7 mi N of Weed 70+ dev sites - boat, waterski, fish, hike.	4 C5	SADDLEBAG LAKE, 12.5 miles north of Lee Vining 20+ dev sites - boat, fish, mtn climb, hike.	43 B5
LAKE SISKIYOU, 3 mi W of Mt Shasta 280+ dev sites - boat, fish, windsurf.	12 C2	ST FRANCIS YACHT CLUB, off Marina B1, Sn Frncsco Long established yacht club in the Bay Area.	142 A1
LAKE SPAULDING, N of Emigrant Gap 20+ dev sites - boat, waterski, hike, fish.	35 B1	SALTON SEA STATE RECREATION AREA, off Hwy 111 Boat, waterski, hike, camp, picnic.	108 E2
LAKE SUCCESS, 20 mi E of Tipton via Hwy 190 100+ dev sites - boat, fish, swim, hike.	68 D3	SALT SPRINGS RESERVOIR, 20.5 mi SE of Hams Sta 20+ dev sites - boat, fish, swim, hike.	41 D1
LAKE TAHOE, California-Nevada border Dev camps, boat, wtrski, fish, swim, horses.	35 E2	SAN FRANCISCO BAY Boat tours of the bay, harbor and Alcatraz.	L C5
LAKE TURLOCK STATE REC AREA, SW of La Grange 60+ dev sites - boat, waterski, fish, hike.	48 B2	SAN LUIS RES STATE REC AREA, 16 mi W of Los Banos 70+ dev sites - boat, waterski, fish, hike.	55 C1
LAKE VALLEY RESERVOIR, E of Emigrant Gap Camp, boat, fish, swim, hike, picnic.	35 B1	SANTA BARBARA YACHT HARBOR, W Cabrillo B1 Boat rentals, hoist & ramp, sport fishing.	174 D4
LEWISTON LAKE, 35 mi NW of Redding 90+ dev sites - sail, canoe, fish, hunt.	17 E1	SANTA MARGARITA LAKE, 19 mi from San Luis Obispo 80+ dev sites - boat, fish, swim, hike, picnc.	76 C3
LITTLE GRASS VALLEY RESERVOIR, W of Gibsonville 240+ dev sites - boat, waterski, fish, hike.	26 C3	SAN VICENTE RESERVOIR, Moreno Av, off CA 67 S D City lake, day use; boat, fish, no swim.	V E1
LONG BEACH MARINA & MARINE STADIUM, Long Beach One of the largest marinas on the west coast.	S D3	SCOTTS FLAT RESERVOIR, E of Nevada City 180+ dev sites - boat, waterski, goldpn, fish.	34 D1
LOON LAKE, NW of Emerald Bay 50+ dev sites - boat, fish, hike, picnic.	35 D3	SHAVER LAKE, south of Camp Sierra 60+ dev sites - boat, waterski, fish, hike.	58 B1
LOPEZ LAKE, 23 mi N of Santa Maria 300+ sites - boat, waterski, fish, picnic.	76 C4	SILVER LAKE, 50 mi NE of Jackson 90+ dev sites - boat, fish, horseback ride.	35 E5
LOWER NEWPORT BAY, Newport Beach Leads to vast estuary in Upper Newport Bay.	199 C5	SILVERWOOD LAKE STATE RECREATION AREA, Hwy 138 Swimming, fishing, boating, camping.	91 B5
LUNDY LAKE, 12 miles north of Lee Vining 30+ dev sites - boat, fish, picnic, backpack.	43 B4	SOUTH LAKE, 22 mi SW of Bishop Dev sites - boat, fish, backpack, picnic.	51 C5

POINTS OF INTEREST INDEX

POINTS OF INTEREST INDEX

NAME & ADDRESS	PAGE & GRID		NAME & ADDRESS	PAGE & GRID	
GOLD MINE WINERY, Parrotts Ferry Rd, Columbia Open daily for tasting & sales; picnic area.	41	C4	MILANO WINERY, 14594 S Hwy 101, Hopland Tasting room, retail sales; tours by appt.	31	B3
GRAND CRU, 1 Vintage Ln, Glen Ellen Open daily for tasting; tours by appointment.	38	B2	MIRASSOU VINEYARDS, 3000 Aborn Rd, San Jose Tasting room and tours available.	P	C4
GRGICH HILLS CELLAR, Hwy 29 north of Rutherford Informal tours and sales daily.	29	C3	MONDAVI WINERY, 7801 St Helena Hwy, Oakville Tasting & tours; musical events & art exhibit.	29	C3
GUENOC WINERY, 21000 Butts Cyn Rd, Middletown Wine tasting, tours & retail sales; picnics.	32	B6	MONTALI WINERY, 600 Addison St, Berkeley Tasting room and sales; picnic area.	45	C1
GUILD WINERIES, N of Lodi Guided tours and tasting room open.	40	B4	MONTEREY VINEYARDS, 800 S Alta St, Gonzales Tours and tasting available.	54	E5
GUIMARRA VINEYARDS, Edison Hwy, Edison Tasting room open Tuesday through Saturday.	78	E3	MONTEVINA WINERY, Shenandoah Rd, Plymouth Visitors welcome daily; tasting room & sales.	40	E1
GUNDLACH-BUNDSCHU, 3775 Thornberry Rd, Sonoma Open daily for tasting and tours.	L	B1	MONTICELLO CELLARS, 4242 Big Ranch Rd, Napa Tasting room and retail sales.	29	E5
HACIENDA, 1000 Vineyard Ln, Sonoma Open daily for tasting; tours by appointment.	L	C1	MONT ST JOHN CELLARS, 5400 Old Sonoma Rd, Napa Wine tasting & sales; picnic facilities.	38	C3
HANNS KORNELL CHAMPAGNE CELLARS, Larkmead Ln Guided tours and tasting daily.	29	B2	MT PALOMAR, 33820 Rancho California Rd, Temecula Guided tours, tasting, sales & deli; picnic.	86	D5
HAYWOOD WINERY, 18701 Gehricke Rd, Sonoma Open daily for tasting & retail sales.	38	C3	NAPA CELLARS, 7481 St Helena Hwy Informal tours and tasting daily.	29	D4
HECKER PASS WINERY, 4605 Hecker Pass Hwy, Gilroy Wine tasting & retail sales; tours by appt.	54	C2	NAPA CREEK WINERY, Silverado Tr, St Helena Retail sales.	29	C3
HEITZ CELLARS, 436 St Helena Hwy Tours by appointment only.	29	C3	NAVARRO WINERY, 5801 Hwy 128, Philo Tasting room open daily; tours by appointment.	30	D2
HOP KILN WINERY, 6050 Westside Rd, Healdsburg Historic landmk; tasting & sales; picnic area.	37	D2	NERVO WINERY, 19550 Geyserville Av, Geyserville Open daily for tasting; no tours.	31	D5
HUSCH VINEYARDS, 4900 Hwy 128, Philo Winery tours, tasting room open daily.	30	D2	NEVADA CITY CELLARS, 321 Spring St, Nevada City Tours and tasting daily; picnic area.	128	B2
INGLENOOK VINEYARD, 1991 St Helena Hwy S, Ruthrfd Wine tasting, museum & gift shop; tours.	29	C3	NOVITIATE WINERY, S of Los Gatos Guided tours and tasting room.	P	B4
ITALIAN SWISS COLONY, River Rd, Asti Tours and tasting available daily.	31	D4	OAKRIDGE VINEYARDS, Hwy 12, Lodi Guided tours and wine tasting room.	40	B4
JEKEL VINEYARD, 40155 Walnut Av, Greenfield Guided tours, sales & wine tasting; picnic.	65	A1	OBESTER WINERY, 12341 San Mateo, Half Moon Bay Tasting room and retail sales; picnic area.	N	C2
J. LOHR, 1000 Lenzen, San Jose Tasting, sales & guided tours.	151	E4	OLSON VINEYARDS, 3560 Road B, Redwood Valley Wine tasting room & retail sales; picnic area.	31	B1
JOHNSON'S ALEXANDER VLY, 8333 Hwy 128, Healdsburg Open daily for tasting and tours.	31	D5	OZEKI SAN BENITO, 249 Hillcrest Rd, Hollister Tasting room, Pier 39, San Francisco.	55	A3
J ROCHIOLI VINEYARDS, 6192 Westside Rd, Healdsbrg Daily tasting and sales; picnic area.	37	C1	PARDUCCI WINE CELLARS, 501 Parducci Rd, Ukiah Tasting room, tours hourly.	31	A2
KENWOOD, 9592 Sonoma Hwy, Kenwood Open daily for tasting; tours by appointment.	38	B2	PASTORI, 23189 Geyserville Av, Cloverdale Open daily for tasting; no tours.	31	D5
KIRIGIN CELLARS, 11550 Watsonville Rd, Gilroy Tasting room open daily; tours by appointment.	P	D5	PAT PAULSEN VINEYARDS, 25510 River Rd, Cloverdale Open daily; picnic area and tasting room.	31	C4
KONOCTI CELLARS, Hwy 29 at Thomas Dr, Kelseyville Tasting room, group tours by appointment.	31	D3	PAUL MASSON, 13159 Saratoga Av, Saratoga Self-guided tour, tasting.	P	A4
KORBELL CHAMPAGNE CELLARS, 13260 Old River Rd Champagne tasting room; tours.	37	C1	PEDRIZZETTI WINERY, 1845 San Pedro Av, Morgan Hll Tasting room on Hwy 101, Morgan Hill.	P	D4
LAMBERT BRIDGE, 4085 W Dry Creek, Healdsburg Daily tasting & sales; picnic area.	31	C5	PEDRONCELLI, 1220 Canyon Rd, Geyserville Open all week for tasting; tours by appointmt.	31	C5
LA MONT WINERY, Bear Mtn Wine Rd, Di Giorgio Tasting room and sales Monday through Friday.	79	A3	PEJU PROVINCE WINERY, 8466 St Helena Hy, Rutherfd Tasting room and retail sales.	29	C3
LANDMARK VINEYARDS, 9150 Los Amigos Rd, Windsor Open Sat & Sun, or by appointment; tours.	37	E1	PESENTI WINERY, 2900 Vineyard Dr, Templeton Informal winery tours; wine tasting & sales.	76	B1
LIVERMORE VLY CELLARS, 1508 Wetmore Rd, Livermore Winery tours daily; wine tasting and sales.	P	C1	JOSEPH PHELPS VINEYARDS, 200 Taplin Rd, St Helena Guided tours by appointment; sales Mon-Sat.	29	D3
LOS VINEROS WINERY, Hanson Wy, Santa Maria Tours and tasting room.	173	A3	PINE RIDGE WINERY, 5901 Silverado Trail, Napa Wine tasting & picnic area; tours by appt.	29	E4
LOUIS M MARTINI, 254 St Helena Hwy Guided tours and wine tasting room open daily.	29	C3	PIPER SONOMA CELLARS, 11455 Old Redwood Hwy Guided tours and tasting room.	37	D1
LOWER LAKE WINERY, Hwy 29, Lower Lake Tours and tasting available.	32	A4	RANCHO SISQUOC WINERY, Foxen Cyn Rd SE of Sisquoc Tours and sales; tasting room.	86	D1
MADRONA VINEYARDS, Gatlin Rd, Camino Open daily for tasting & sales; picnic area.	35	A4	R & J COOK WINERY, Netherlands Rd, Clarksburg Tasting & sales daily; picnic area.	39	D2
MARKHAM WINERY, Hwy 29 at Deer Park Rd Guided tours by appointment.	29	B2	RAPAZZINI WINERY, 4350 Monterey Hwy, Gilroy Tours and wine tasting daily.	54	D2
MARK WEST VINEYARD, 7000 Healdsburg Rd, Healdsbrg Wine tasting and retail sales.	37	D2	RAYMOND VINEYARD & CELLAR, 849 Zinfandel Ln Tours by appointment only.	29	C3
MARTIN BROS. WINERY, Hwy 46, Paso Robles Tasting room and sales; picnic area.	76	B1	ROBERT PEPI WINERY, 7585 St Helena Hwy, Oakville Winery tours and tasting by appointment.	29	D4
MASTANTUONO, Hwy 46, Paso Robles Tasting room and gift shop; picnic area.	76	A1	ROBERT STEMMLER, 3805 Lambert Bridge Rd, Healdsbg Wine tasting and retail sales; picnicking.	31	D5
McDOWELL VLY VINEYARDS, 3811 SR 175, Hopland Tasting room, retail sales; tours by appt.	31	C3	RODNEY STRONG, 11455 Old Redwood Hwy, Healdsburg Tasting & sales; concerts & cultural events.	37	D1

POINTS OF INTEREST INDEX

NAME & ADDRESS	PAGE & GRID		NAME & ADDRESS	PAGE & GRID	
ROSS-KELLER WINERY, 900 McMurray Rd, Buellton Tours and tasting daily.	86	D3	VALLEY OF THE MOON, Madrone Rd, Glen Ellen Tasting room, retail sales; no tours.	38	B2
ROSS-KELLER, 985 Orchard Av, Nipomo Tasting room and sales daily; picnic area.	76	C5	VEGA VINEYARDS, 9495 Santa Rosa Rd, Buellton Tours and tasting available.	86	D3
ROUND HILL CELLARS, Lodi Ln, St Helena Tours by appointment; retail sales.	29	B2	VENTANA VINEYARDS, Los Coches Rd W of Greenfield New Monterey district winery.	65	B1
RUSTRIDGE VINEYARD & WINERY, St Helena Open daily for tasting & sales; picnic area.	29	E2	VICHON WINERY, 1595 Coombsville Rd, Napa Tours by appt; wine tasting & retail sales.	29	C4
RUTHERFORD HILL WINERY, End of Rutherford Hill Rd Tours daily; tasting 2nd Saturday each month.	29	D3	VILLA MT EDEN, Oakville Cross Rd, Oakville Tours weekdays by appointment.	29	D3
RUTHERFORD VINTNERS, 1673 St Helena Hwy S Tasting room; group tours by appointment.	29	C3	V SATTUI WINERY, White Ln at Hwy 29 S, St Helena Tasting room, tours, gift shop; founded 1885.	29	C3
ST FRANCIS WINERY, 8450 Sonoma Hwy, Kenwood Tasting & sales daily; tours by appointment.	38	B2	WEIBEL CHAMPAGNE, Stanford Av, Mission San Jose Champagne tasting room.	P	B2
SAN ANTONIO WINERY, 737 Lamar St, Los Angeles Tours, wine tasting, restaurant; picnic area.	186	D2	WEIBEL VINEYARDS, 7051 N State St, Redwood Valley Tasting room and gift shop; no tours.	31	B1
SANFORD WINERY, 7250 Santa Rosa Rd, Buellton Tours, tasting & sales Monday-Saturday;picnic.	86	D3	WENTE BROS, 5555 Tesla Rd, Livermore 4th generation winery; excellent tour/tasting.	P	D1
SAN MARTIN WINERY, 13000 Depot Av, San Martin Tasting room open year around.	P	D5	WENTE BROS SPARKLING WINE CELLARS, Livermore Hourly tours available; restaurant.	P	D1
SAN PASQUAL, 13455 San Pasqual Rd, San Diego Wine tasting & retail sales; tours by appt.	106	E3	WHITEHALL LANE WINERY, St Helena Hwy S Retail sales.	29	C3
SANTA BARBARA, 202 Anacapa St, Santa Barbara Tasting room open.	86	C2	WINTERS WINERY, 15 Main St, Winters Wine tasting and retail sales daily.	39	A1
SANTA YNEZ VALLEY, 365 N Refugio Rd, Santa Ynez Tours and tasting on Saturday; M-F by appoint.	86	E3	WOODBURY WINERY, 32 Woodland Av, San Rafael By appointment only.	139	E4
SANTINO WINERY, Steiner Rd, Plymouth Informal tours and tasting room.	40	E1	YANKEE HILL WINERY, Yankee Hill Rd, Columbia Wine tasting; tours by appointment.	41	C4
SEBASTIANI VINEYARDS & WINERY, 389 4th St E 1st vineyard in Sonoma Vly; tours and tasting.	132	E4	YORK MOUNTAIN WINERY, Hwy 46, Templeton Tasting room; tours by appointment only.	75	E2
SEQUOIA GROVE, 8338 St Helena Hwy, Napa Winery tours by appointment; tasting & sales.	29	D3	ZACA MESA WINERY, Foxen Cyn Rd, Los Olivos Tour provides a good overview of winemaking.	86	E2
SIERRA WINERY, 1925 N Mooney Blvd, Tulare Tasting and sales daily; picnic area.	68	B2			
SIMI VALLEY WINERY, 16275 Healdsburg Av, Healdsbg Wine tasting, guided tours.	31	D5			
SODA ROCK, 8015 Hwy 128, Healdsburg Wine tasting; historic stone winery building.	31	D5			
SOUVERAIN, Independence Ln & Hwy 101, Geyserville Open daily for tasting and tours; restaurant.	31	D5			
SPRING MOUNTAIN VINEYARDS, 2805 Spring Mtn Rd Tours by appointment only.	29	B3			
STEARNS WHARF VINTNERS, Santa Barbara Retail sales.	174	D4			
STEPHEN ZELLERBACH, 14350 Chalk Hill Rd, Healdsbg Picnic, tasting, retail sales; tours by appt.	32	B5			
STERLING VINEYARDS, 1111 Dunaweal Ln, Calistoga Tasting & tours; aerial tramway to hlltp wnry.	29	A2			
STEVENOT WINERY, San Domingo Rd near Murphys Tasting room and retail sales.	41	B4			
STONEGATE WINERY, 1183 Dunaweal Ln, Calistoga Tours by appointment; retail sales most days.	29	A2			
STRINGER'S ORCHARDS, 3/4 mile S of New Pine Creek Daily tours and tasting; gift shop.	7	D2			
SUMMER HILL VINEYDS, 3920 Hecker Pass Hwy, Gilroy Wine tasting & retail sales; picnic area.	54	D2			
SUSINE CELLARS, 301 Spring St, Suisun Tasting and sales available Tuesday-Saturday.	135	C4			
SUTTER HOME, 227 St Helena Hwy S, St Helena Tasting room and gift shop.	29	C3			
THOMAS VINEYARD, 8916 Foothill Blvd, Cucamonga Wine tasting & sales; picnic; historic landmk.	U	E2			
THOMAS KRUSE WINERY, 4390 Hecker Pass Hwy, Gilroy Retail sales & wine tasting; picnic area.	54	C2			
TOPOLOS AT RUSSIAN RIVER, 5700 Gravenstein Hwy Tasting room; tours by appointment.	37	D2			
TOYON WINERY, 9643 Highway 128, Healdsburg Wine tasting & retail sales by appointment.	31	D5			
TREFETHEN VINEYARDS, Oak Knoll Av, Napa Tours, tasting and retail sales by appointmnt.	29	E5			
TRENTADUE, 19170 Redwood Hwy, Geyserville Open all week for tasting.	31	D5			
TURNER WINERY, 3750 Woodbridge Rd, Woodbridge Guided tours and a tasting room.	40	A4			